SOC

Society and Culture

Society and Culture

PRENTICE-HALL, INC.

Englewood Cliffs, N.J.

FRANCIS E. MERRILL

Professor of Sociology

Dartmouth College

AN INTRODUCTION TO SOCIOLOGY *Third Edition*

PRENTICE-HALL INTERNATIONAL, INC., *London*
PRENTICE-HALL OF AUSTRALIA, PTY., LTD., *Sydney*
PRENTICE-HALL OF CANADA, LTD., *Toronto*
PRENTICE-HALL OF INDIA PVT., LTD., *New Delhi*
PRENTICE-HALL OF JAPAN, INC., *Tokyo*

Prentice-Hall Sociology Series
Herbert Blumer, Editor

SOCIETY AND CULTURE: An Introduction to Sociology, Third Edition

Francis E. Merrill

Designed by John J. Dunleavy

C - 8 1 9 6 4

To the Memory of my Mother and Father

Preface

This is the third edition of this book. The author thus has an obligation to certain old, as well as new, readers. This obligation involves both a statement of the changes in the new edition and a statement of its basic conceptual scheme. The present edition of *Society and Culture* follows the same theoretical approach as the preceding one. The concept of society is basic and the other major concepts follow therefrom. The central theme is social interaction, which means that people engage in meaningful and reciprocal activity. Social interaction arises when two or more persons "take each other into account" and react accordingly. Each is aware of the other, makes an appraisal of him, and tries to respond appropriately. A society exists when several persons interact over an appreciable period of time.

Culture is the second major concept. Culture is the learned behavior that issues from past interaction and channels present interaction. In the course of his social development, each individual incorporates into his personality the culture he has acquired through social interaction. In this context, personality is the "subjective aspect of culture," and as such constitutes the third major concept of this book. The fourth is social structure, which refers to the ordered relationships that arise in a society and persist as human beings perform certain essential social functions. The fifth major concept is social change, wherein social structure is viewed as a dynamic system of related parts. Both logically and in "real life," structure and change follow from social interaction, which is the unifying theme of the book.

The second function of this preface is to indicate some of the changes that distinguish the present edition from its predecessor(s). Sociology is a dynamic field and is continually being enriched by theoretical analyses and empirical studies. A central task of a revised introductory text is, therefore, to present some of these new studies to the beginning student. In this sense, the over-all additions, deletions, and revisions are so extensive that they cannot even be summarized here. The new edition has, furthermore, been reduced in length without sacrificing any of the sociological material. Indeed, as indicated below, this material has been increased by the addition of three new chapters, plus a number of shorter sections within other chapters. This compression has been attained by omitting the chapters on methods and further curtailing the anthropological material in the previous edition. These latter fields are manifestly important in themselves. In the considered judgment of the author, however, they are relatively less central to introductory sociology than the subjects that take their place. The net result of these changes is a shorter and (I trust) more consistently *sociological* book.

This edition contains two entirely new chapters — Chapter 17 on Bureaucracy and Chapter 24 on Mass Society. These two aspects of society are increasing in scope and influence, and a knowledge of their operation is important to an understanding of the modern world. These trends toward a bureaucratic, mass society have, not surprisingly, given rise to a proliferation of the related sociological literature. Some, although by no means all, of this literature has been incorporated into the new chapters. Chapter 4 deals with Primary

Groups and is a revised and extended discussion of a subject hitherto treated more briefly. In recent years, the primary group has been "rediscovered" and its influence reaffirmed, not only in immediate individual relationships but also in such seemingly remote fields as bureaucratic behavior and mass society.

In addition to these major innovations, a number of other topics are considered at length for the first time. New sections of several pages each have been introduced into the various chapters and deal with such topics as: deviance from the group; the structural aspects of personality; inconsistencies in social status; culture and social character; culture and "human nature"; the nature of race prejudice; prejudice and social structure; the blue-collar worker; the functional aspects of the urban community; the patterns of social change; social change in underdeveloped countries; public opinion in a democracy; and social problems and social action. The variety of these substantive additions suggests the wide-ranging nature of the current research in sociology and related fields. In this connection, it is again apparent how much this book owes to the hundreds of scholars, past and present, whose work has been summarized, interpreted, and integrated into the present volume. These inadvertent collaborators have been appropriately indicated in the text and their indispensable help is once more gratefully acknowledged.

A final and pleasant obligation incumbent upon the author is to thank the two persons who have been most instrumental in the preparation of this book. In continuation of a personal and editorial relationship extending over several decades, Dr. Herbert Blumer, Editor of the Prentice-Hall Sociology Series, has again given me the benefit of his wise, tolerant, and enlightened advice. I express my thanks to him. Emily Archibald Merrill has once more been of immeasurable aid in typing the manuscript, reading the proofs, and preparing the indexes. Without her gracious assistance, extended above and beyond the call of conjugal duty, this book could never have been written.

F. E. M.

Contents

CULTURE AND PERSONALITY *Part Two*

SOCIAL STRUCTURE *Part Three*

Society and Culture

SOCIETY AND GROUP

INTERACTION *Part One*

1 The Study of Sociology

The Study of Society

The world is changing. We live in a society in which change is the rule, rather than the exception. Change is increasingly apparent in the family, the church, the state, and the school. Modern man is faced with decisions that are far more complex than those faced by his grandparents. He must decide what to do with the forces that science has placed at his disposal. He must make up his mind whether he wishes to perish in a third world war or participate in a workable society of nations. He must reconcile the interests of such competing institutions as the state and the corporation. He must learn that many of the old ways will no longer work in the brave new world of the nuclear age. He must learn, in short, to control the society he has created.

The primary task of past generations was to conquer the physical environment. They suffered from epidemic diseases that periodically destroyed a large part of the population. They had to build homes in the wilderness and protect them against a hostile nature. They lived in a world of scarcity imposed by their inability to utilize the resources of the physical world. The present generation has learned to control such natural limitations as cold, heat, fire, flood, epidemic, and famine. This control is not perfect and nature still occasionally gets out of hand. The great epidemics of the past, however, are now largely checked by preventive medicine. Engineering knowledge and technical materials are now available to provide most of the creature comforts. Recent generations have seen an unprecedented increase in both the intellectual and physical resources necessary to control the natural environment.

But not the social environment. The principal problems of our day arise from the inability of man to control the social forces he has set in motion: problems of government, economics, poverty, crime, population, and war, among others. Some of these problems are so acute that they must be solved if society is to continue. The rise of the national state has coincided with advances in science that make war increasingly suicidal; this has become the century of total war. Periodic crises in economic relationships are beyond the understanding of the man on the street and often of the specialists themselves. The family has in a few generations changed from an agricultural and multifunctional institution to a personal relationship lacking many of the traditional functions. These modifications in the basic social institutions bring about a pervasive sense of anxiety, as men see the web of secure relationships crumble before their eyes.

The contradictions and insecurities of modern society thus face the individual on every hand. Neither the institutions nor the forces disintegrating them were imposed from without. Man in a very real sense has made himself; he has created the customs, traditions, and institutions of his society in the same sense that he has built its skyscrapers and hydrogen bombs. The democratic state, the monogamous family, and the capitalistic system were not handed down by supernatural force. These and other aspects of society are the product of millennia of *social* evolution. They were constructed by man, acting generally without conscious plan or design.

Many of the customs of this world are so inconsistent that they create conflicts in the individual and the society. Man must therefore direct his most intelligent efforts at resolving these social inconsistencies, just as he has increased his control of the natural forces of his environment. The task of future generations will be to understand the social world, as past generations have learned to understand the physical world. In this process, man must apply the methods of science to society, even as he has previously applied them to his physical environment. In this way, he can add to his ordered knowledge about himself. And knowledge means power.

The Nature of Science

There are numerous definitions of science. One of the most famous was given many years ago by Karl Pearson, who defined science in terms of its function. "The classification of facts, the recognition of their sequence and relative significance," he said, "is the function of science." [1] His conception of a general methodology embracing every form of science was an important contribution to scientific thought.[2] This approach is not peculiar to any one science or group of sciences. The physical and biological sciences have no monopoly on the scientific method; the latter is applicable to social as well as to physical phenomena. "The unity of all science," continued Pearson, "consists alone in its method, not in its material. The man who classifies facts of any kind whatever, who sees their mutual relation and describes their sequences, is applying the scientific method and is a man of science." [3]

The continuity of science and the scientific method is evident in a definition given half a century after that of Pearson. "Science," says Barber, "is . . . the collection and ordering of facts in terms of a conceptual scheme, the scheme always being subject to reconstruction as its use or the use of technique results in new facts." [4] The emphasis here is upon the conceptual scheme by which the mutual relationships of the phenomena are made clear and meaningful. The man who collects and orders facts in terms of an emerging theoretical scheme is thus a scientist, no matter what the nature of his data. Science is, in Redfield's words, "one way of making order of experience." [5]

There are other ways of "making order of experience." Religion is one; philosophy is another; art is a third. Their methods are essentially different from those of science, however, for they stress other faculties and approaches. The religious way of making order of experience is based upon faith and emphasizes the relationship of the individual to the supernatural. Philosophy is an attempt to find order in experience through reason, rather than through the collection and organization of empirical facts. The artist seeks to give meaning to life by creating beauty out of his experience, thereby attaining an immortality that as an individual he is denied. Each of these ways is valid and necessary to a complete picture of the universe and the place of man in it. We are concerned here, however, with science.

Science may be considered under two different, although related, headings: either "pure" or "applied." "Pure" science "is primarily and immediately devoted to the development of conceptual schemes, such development including their extension, revision, and testing, an inherently endless process of establishing provisional 'truth.'" [6] "Applied" science is "devoted to making conceptual

---

[1] Karl Pearson, *The Grammar of Science* (London: Adam and Charles Black, 1900), p. 6.
[2] Helen M. Walker, "The Contributions of Karl Pearson," *Journal of the American Statistical Association*, 53:23-27 (March, 1958), p. 22.
[3] Pearson, *op. cit.*, p. 12.
[4] Bernard Barber, *Science and the Social Order* (Glencoe, Ill.: The Free Press, 1952), p. 20.
[5] Robert Redfield, "Social Science in Our Society," *Phylon*, 11:31-41 (First Quarter, 1950), p. 32.
[6] Barber, *op. cit.*, p. 95.

schemes instrumental to some other social purpose than that of the pursuit of conceptual schemes as ends-in-themselves." [7]

These two aspects of science overlap and often cannot be profitably separated. In theory, however, a distinction can be made. The "pure" scientist, as noted, is primarily concerned with making conceptual order out of experience, with no other motive than intellectual pleasure or the advancement of learning. The "applied" scientist is primarily interested in advancing some purpose, "practical" or otherwise, and not simply knowledge for its own sake. Sociology started largely as an "applied" social science and many early sociologists were concerned with such eminently practical problems as poverty, unemployment, crime, mental disease, and prostitution. In recent years, the emphasis has shifted somewhat to "pure" sociology, but the application of scientific knowledge in the applied field nevertheless remains fundamental to the discipline.[8]

The man on the street thinks of science largely in its application to the immediate problems of his life. Science to him means advancements in medicine, improvements in communication, and ameliorations in daily living. He often fails to realize that these desirable elements are dependent upon advances in pure conceptual organization, whereby new relationships are sought between phenomena without any consideration of their application. Someone has well said that there is nothing as practical as a good theory. The point is that the theory must come first and, once established, may lead to "practical" applications not even remotely anticipated by the original discoverer. The most striking example of the relationship between theory and practice is the development and application of the concepts of nuclear fission and fusion to the atomic and hydrogen bombs. The "pure" scientist has, perforce, become a very "practical" man.[9]

The present age has been termed the age of science. Advancements in the physical and biological sciences have been without precedent and have posed social problems whose complications defy ultimate solution. Modern society is generally favorable to science to an extent unique in history. A combination of circumstances is present that has never before existed, circumstances both technical and social, in the sense that they include both the technical knowledge and the social climate for the rapid development of science. This unique situation has been summarized as follows: "In the degree in which one finds *all* these things—the cultural values of rationality, utilitarianism, universalism, individualism, and melioristic progress; and the social structures of a highly specialized division of labor, an open-class system, and a non-authoritarian political system—in that degree science flourishes in a modern society." [10]

The development of science has not progressed without impediment. In recent years, this process has been impaired by the fear and suspicion marking the

---

[7] *Ibid.*

[8] Alvin W. Gouldner, "Theoretical Requirements of the Applied Social Sciences," *American Sociological Review,* 22:92-102 (February, 1957).

[9] Lewis Mumford, "Anticipations and Social Adjustments in Science," *Bulletin of the Atomic Scientists,* 10:34-36 (February, 1954).

[10] Barber, *op. cit.,* p. 73.

social climate of certain segments of society.[11] The tensions of the Cold War brought a pervasive sense of anxiety and insecurity to many persons. Suspicions and aggressions were widely generated by these fears and directed against intellectuals in general and scientists in particular. These attitudes have interfered with the free flow of information so necessary to the development of science. The national security program has quite rightly curtailed the dissemination of information on matters directly pertaining to the national defense. In many other fields of science only remotely related, if at all, to these "sensitive" areas, communication between scientists has also been interrupted. If science is to develop, free communication must exist between a comparatively small number of qualified persons. Without this free flow of communication, as one thoughtful observer puts it, "a science could not exist." [12]

The Sciences of Society

Man has thus learned to control many aspects of the physical and biological universe. This control was preceded by centuries of cumulative knowledge, to which generations of scientists have added. The social sciences are the newest of the sciences and sociology is among the newest of the social sciences. Information on many social relationships is still lacking. The physical sciences can accurately predict the effects of many processes. The biological sciences can predict in their field with considerable accuracy. The social sciences, however, are still unable to predict (let alone control) some of the most elementary human relationships because they lack the necessary information.

The social sciences study man and his relationships. They bring the general procedures of science to bear upon the complex and ongoing reality of society.[13] Different aspects of this reality appear as man makes a living, raises a family, develops his personality, and governs himself. Economics, sociology, psychology, and political science are among the social sciences that have arisen to study these relationships. Each has developed special subject matters, methods of investigation, and conceptual schemes. We are interested here in establishing the field and competence of the social sciences in general. We shall examine the science of sociology in our subsequent discussion.

Human life is complex. No single science has a monopoly on the study of human relationships. Any light on these relationships is welcome, no matter whence it may come, and the social sciences have much to learn from each other. The sociologist and the economist both study the stock exchange, since, as a meeting place for buyers and sellers of corporate securities, it plays an important part in the economic system. The stock exchange is also a social institution, with many of the characteristics of other institutions. When the

---

[11] Samuel A. Stouffer, *Communism, Conformity, and Civil Liberties* (New York: Doubleday & Company, 1955).

[12] Edward A. Shils, "Security and Science Sacrificed to Loyalty," *Bulletin of the Atomic Scientists,* 11:106-109 (April, 1955), p. 106.

[13] John Gillin (ed.), *For a Science of Social Man* (New York: The Macmillan Company, 1954).

sociologist and the economist cooperate in the study of institutions and associations, the resultant knowledge is more meaningful.

Sociology, anthropology, psychology, economics, and political science have the same general scientific task: to study the various aspects of human activities, collect facts about them, observe their sequences, and establish conceptual generalizations on the basis of these sequences.[14] The assumption underlying these sciences is that the different parts of a society are related in definite ways that can be known. These relationships are very complex because human beings interact on the basis of shared meanings and human awareness. These factors complicate the task of the social scientist, but they do not render it impossible.

The ultimate purpose of the social sciences is to enhance human welfare by giving man increasing knowledge of his environment. Such knowledge is still in its rudimentary stages, and the degree of control is correspondingly slight. But mere control is not enough. Science is a nonmoral (*not* immoral) instrument, but it may be used for immoral purposes by unscrupulous men. It is therefore conceivable that greater knowledge about society (for example, the manipulation of public opinion through mass communications) might be used by one group to the detriment of another or of society as a whole.[15] The basis for control is important. The fascist states used scientific resources to perfect the instruments of torture and destruction. Their control of the environment was directed toward increasing their power to kill and destroy. In a democratic state, science should ultimately be directed to the welfare of the group as a whole.

This functional role of the social sciences has been examined by the president of the Russell Sage Foundation. In a recent report, he stated that "scientists must assume responsibility for showing that their science can make positive contributions to the achievement of human goals." It is, he continued, "probably fair to say that in general the freedom and support a society will grant a scientific discipline is roughly proportionate to: (*a*) the perceived actual or potential contribution such a discipline can make in an area of practical action; and (*b*) the perceived importance of that area in the value system of the society." [16] Social science, like any other enterprise, must pay its way. It must demonstrate that it is both concerned with, and competent to further an understanding of, "the contemporary human predicament." [17]

The Science of Sociology

We have outlined some of the principal steps in the emergence of a science of society. We have indicated: (*a*) the increasing need for the study of society; (*b*)

---

[14] Cf. Mirra Komarovsky (ed.), *Common Frontiers of the Social Sciences* (Glencoe, Ill.: The Free Press, 1957).

[15] Arnold M. Rose, "The Social Responsibility of the Social Scientist," *Social Problems,* 1:85-90 (January, 1954).

[16] Russell Sage Foundation, *Annual Report: 1960-1961,* New York, 1961, p. 9.

[17] Alvin W. Gouldner, "Anti-Minotaur: The Myth of a Value-Free Society," *Social Problems,* 9:199-213 (Winter, 1962), p. 205.

the nature of science and the scientific method; and (c) the sciences of society that endeavor to explain this complex phenomenon. We shall now turn to our primary interest, one that will occupy us for the remainder of this book: the science of sociology. The other social sciences deal with specific aspects of human relationships; the field of sociology is human relationships as such. The sociologist is interested in the way human beings interact with other human beings, the customs that grow out of this interaction, the institutions that crystallize about human needs, the changes that occur in these institutions, and the possibility of directing some of these changes in the ultimate interest of human welfare.

This is admittedly a large order. The sociologist cannot study all of the possible combinations of social relationships, nor can he anticipate the behavior of a single individual. He deals rather with *typical* relationships and the way in which these relationships form, modify, and control behavior. As a scientist, he is interested in the general, the typical, and the recurrent, rather than the specific, the individual, and the unique. The sociologist isolates and analyzes the distinctive products of human interaction, whether the material products of the factory or the cultural products of the church, laboratory, or classroom. He also studies the manner in which social institutions evolve and play their part in society. He is concerned, finally, with the general course of social change and the trends apparent in this process.

Sociology is *the science of group interaction.* Sociology studies man as a social (group) animal. It deals with social groups and the products of their interaction. These groups produce customs and behavior patterns that are handed down from generation to generation by learning. Society is held together by these patterns. Continuous and integrated social life would be impossible without group patterns, and cooperative activity could not exist in their absence. The relationships between human beings in groups are determined by these elements; together they constitute the social heritage. Sociology seeks ordered knowledge of these relationships and the beliefs that sustain them. In the broadest sense, therefore, sociology is the study of group interaction and the products of that interaction.

Human beings form relatively permanent groups to meet certain social needs. At the core of these groups are common meanings and values. These clusters of values and the accompanying patterns of behavior are known as social institutions. The major institutions in our society are the family, the church, the school, the government, and the economic system. The individual is largely a product of his contacts with these institutions. They mold him and hand on the social heritage to him. Social institutions are found in all societies and provide a consistent basis for human action. The sociologist studies social institutions in general and his own in particular.[18]

The sociologist classifies forms of group interaction and formulates generalizations about them. These generalizations become the basis for prediction and,

---

[18] Arnold M. Rose, "The Comparative Study of Institutions," Chapter 1 in Arnold M. Rose (ed.), *The Institutions of Advanced Societies* (Minneapolis: University of Minnesota Press, 1958), p. 30.

at times, for control. In his role as scientist, the sociologist is continually formulating, investigating, and (if possible) solving problems. In the process of
problem-formulation, the following progressive stages appear: "First is the
originating question, a statement of what one wants to know. Second is the
rationale, stating why one wants to have the particular question answered. And
third are the specifying questions that point toward possible answers to the
originating question in terms that satisfy the rationale for having raised it."[19]

We know more about some of these problems than others. We know a good
deal about such matters as birth and death rates, but comparatively little about
such equally important matters as the formation of personality and the transmission of knowledge. We have indicated that the scientific method involves
the classification and ordering of facts and the working out of a conceptual
scheme to explain their sequences. The following typical stages are apparent:
(1) The facts are gathered. (2) The facts are classified. (3) Relationships between facts are established. (4) Generalizations are made on the basis of these
relationships. (5) Predictions are based upon the generalizations. The sociologist as scientist is therefore concerned with the discovery of new knowledge.
He is interested in enlarging the understanding of the processes of group interaction and the products of this interaction. Sociology seeks to become a full-
fledged science, for only by the methods of science can knowledge be *systematically* advanced.

The Scientific Difficulties of Sociology

Predictions in sociology are not as accurate as those in the natural sciences,
since there are differences in the nature of the subject matter between the natural and the social sciences. Although efforts have been made to introduce the
precise techniques of the physical and biological sciences into the social sciences,
these efforts may never be fully realized because of the differences in material.
Sociology is a science, but not an exact science in the same sense as physics or
chemistry. This is only one of a number of difficulties encountered in the scientific development of sociology. Some of them are being overcome; others may
never be fully overcome.

1. *The nature of the material.* The physical sciences study the forms of inor-
ganic matter in their physical relationships, and the biological sciences study
the forms of living matter in their organic relationships. Sociology, however,
studies human beings in their group relationships—groups, societies, cultures,
personalities, institutions, and associations. Human beings interact in terms of
meanings that are mutually understood; they are more than physical objects.
The sociologist, therefore, studies something of which he is an intimate part.
He is a member of many groups, participates in different institutions, and develops a personality partially derived from these relationships. Hence it is often

---

[19] Robert K. Merton, "Introduction: Notes on Problem-Finding in Sociology," in Robert K. Merton,
Leonard Broom, and Leonard S. Cottrell, Jr. (eds.), *Sociology Today* (New York: Basic Books, Inc., 1959),
p. xiii.

difficult for him to detach himself sufficiently from his subject matter to maintain his scientific objectivity. The natural scientist ordinarily has no such difficulty; he does not usually investigate the very relationships that form his personality.

2. *The complexity of the material.* Human relationships are highly complex. A social problem such as juvenile delinquency involves such varied factors as: the customs of the local neighborhood; the laws of the larger society; the physical structure of the community; the character of the child; the personalities of his brothers and sisters; his relationships to the school; the gangs with which he associates; his native intelligence; his emotional makeup; his physical capacities or infirmities; the public institutions for treatment or punishment to which he is exposed; and the trends in the business cycle. With so many variables coming into play, it is difficult to discover and isolate the actual motivating forces in delinquency. A related difficulty arises when we attempt to formulate generalizations concerning the prevention and treatment of juvenile delinquency. Similar complexity is apparent in other human relationships.

3. *The difficulty of controlled experiment.* Many hypotheses of the natural sciences can be verified by controlled experiment. All natural sciences, it is true, do not rely upon such methods—the astronomer, for example, cannot introduce the heavenly bodies into his laboratory to control their movements. But much of the material of the natural sciences is, nevertheless, subject to experiment. The sociologist is handicapped in this regard. Individuals, groups, institutions, and societies ordinarily make unwilling subjects for controlled experiment. The experimental study of group behavior in laboratory settings is currently developing, however, thus making possible the controlled study of certain forms of social interaction. [20] We shall examine this important development in Chapter 3. But for the most part the sociologist is still obliged to observe group behavior under "natural" conditions.[21]

4. *The presence of vested interests.* A vested interest is a person, group, or institution with a material or psychological stake in things as they are. The natural scientist deals with phenomena that are often too abstruse for the average man to understand. Since many societal phenomena are "real" and important to everyone—the family, the church, the economic system, and other forms of vital relationships—investigation of them is often resented by those who benefit from the present patterns. The sociologist may be regarded as "subversive" because he calls attention to maladjustments in social institutions.

The Role of Social Values

The sociologist operates in a world of social values that arise from the fact that man is a social animal. Man needs values as intangible justifications in order to be content with his lot—they are an important element in his existence. Since

---

[20] G. E. Swanson, "Some Problems of Laboratory Experiments with Small Populations," *American Sociological Review*, 16:349-358 (June, 1951).

[21] Robert F. Bales, *Interaction Process Analysis* (Cambridge, Mass.: Addison-Wesley Press, Inc., 1950).

social institutions exist for the purpose of realizing human values, the work of sociology is "a human activity carried on within and responsible to the moral values which govern human life, and it is of necessity governed by the norms to which those ultimate values give rise."[22] In our society, the basic values are grounded in democratic principles.

A value is a social judgment of what is important to individual and group welfare. As defined by Gillin, a value "can be thought of as a conception, culturally held, concerning what is regarded as desirable with respect to human beings and their behavior in relation to each other and with the non-human universe."[23] In this sense, a value may be related either to material or nonmaterial objects, and its ultimate locus may be either tangible or intangible. Many important value judgments relate to nonmaterial elements, since human beings often desire psychological satisfactions more fiercely than physical ones. Status may be more important than bread.

Social values exist at different levels, and value judgments may be attached to anything from a beefsteak to a philosophy of life. Values may be finite or "infinite"—that is, transcending all other considerations. Among the "infinite" psychological values are: (*a*) human life itself; (*b*) the creative achievements of human beings; (*c*) human cooperation for a better life; (*d*) the worshiping of a power higher than the individual; (*e*) the fullest possible development of moral character; and (*f*) the ultimate development of human abilities.[24] Science is one agency in the fulfillment of these infinite values.

Social values differ from one society to another and within the same society at different times.[25] Their existence, however, cannot be questioned. Every human being cherishes values in some form, even though he may not be aware of them. He absorbs them through the learning process from his earliest childhood. Attempts to disregard them in sociology lead to a distortion of social reality. Man is what he is precisely because he *has* values. They are the mainspring of the human relationships the sociologist observes. As one sociologist has stated, "The essential data for sociological research are values."[26] The sociologist disregards this fact at the risk of obscuring his subject.

The sociologist is thus obliged to act in a dual role: as a scientist and as a human being. As a scientist, he studies human behavior as objectively as he can, but at the same time he must play his various roles as a human being and guide his personal behavior by the very phenomena he is studying. This is a difficult, although not an impossible, task. The sociologist can act *as a scientist* in an objective study of the relationships between human beings. He gathers the pertinent facts, classifies them, formulates conceptual schemes, and tests these

---

[22] William L. Kolb, "The Impingement of Moral Values on Sociology," *Social Problems*, 2:66-70 (October, 1954), p. 68.

[23] John Gillin, "National and Regional Cultural Values in the United States," *Social Forces*, 34:107-113 (December, 1955).

[24] William R. Catton, Jr., "Exploring Techniques for Measuring Human Values," *American Sociological Review*, 19:49-55 (February, 1954), p. 53.

[25] Cf. Cora Du Bois, "The Dominant Value Profile of American Culture," *American Anthropologist*, 57:1232-1239 (December, 1955).

[26] Ernest W. Burgess, "Values and Sociological Research," *Social Problems*, 2:16-20 (July, 1954), p. 16.

schemes with the best available scientific techniques. If this objectivity is lacking or impaired, the sociologist fails in his role as a scientist. Unlike the philosopher, who deals with human values in terms of their ultimate qualities, the sociologist deals with values as data—as objects to be studied. He should reach his conclusions objectively.[27]

The statement is sometimes made that the sociologist destroys social values by studying the institutions that embody them. The values incorporated in the church and the family, for example, are allegedly threatened by the cold hand of the social scientist, in the mere process of subjecting these institutions to scientific investigation. In one sense, this statement is partially true, insofar as the sociologist is unable to view an institution such as the family as being established by supernatural means and nurtured by supernatural sanctions. In a more fundamental sense, however, the sociologist enhances social values. To him, the family is a human relationship that may be subjected to the rational processes of science, for the *ultimate* purpose of making it serve human needs more completely. In the final analysis, the family is a means to an end, not an end in itself.[28]

As a scientist, the sociologist owes his primary loyalty to the pursuit of truth. The value to which he is dedicated as a scientist is that of organized human reason. As a human being, he acts within the framework of social values that underlie his society. Science is only *one* of these values; the individual is also moved by economic, religious, political, familial, and status values. Taken in and of themselves, the end results of science are *instrumental*, not *final*. They are instruments for enhancing the basic values of society.

In our own society, these basic values are humanitarian, in the sense that they hold the purposes of organized group life to be the ultimate freedom, development, and general welfare of human beings. The findings of social science, for example, have been applied in expert testimony before the United States Supreme Court in the cases outlawing racial segregation in the public schools. The psychologist, sociologist, and psychiatrist presented the findings of their respective disciplines to the general conclusion that segregation injures the person against whom it is practiced. These results have come from the analysis of the relationship of segregation. The scientific data are thereby applied *in the interests* of the humanitarian values of our society.[29]

The relationship between sociology and values may be summarized as follows: (*a*) Sociology is a human activity carried on in a world motivated by social values. (*b*) *As a human being*, the sociologist is molded by these values and he must take them into account in his actions. (*c*) *As a scientist*, the sociologist is dedicated to the furtherance of scientific truth. (*d*) In his study of social institutions, he subjects the underlying social values to careful study. (*e*) In so doing, he may modify or rearrange these values, but he does not destroy them.

---

[27] Florian Znaniecki. "Should Sociologists Be Also Philosophers of Values?" *Sociology and Social Research*, 37:79-84 (November-December, 1952).

[28] Redfield, "Social Science in Our Society," *op. cit.*, p. 39.

[29] Kenneth B. Clark, "The Social Scientist as an Expert Witness in Civil Rights Litigation," *Social Problems*, 1:5-10 (June, 1953).

(*f*) The sociologist does not deny the importance of values *as such* in human relationships. (*g*) The knowledge derived from scientific study is instrumental, in that it may ultimately enhance the accepted social values. (*h*) In this way, the sociologist contributes to the "infinite" values that are the most important elements in a democratic society.[30]

The Educational Function of Sociology

We have considered some of the general aspects of sociology as a science. We have also reviewed the need for sociology as a source of knowledge of an environment that is becoming increasingly complex. As a man of science, one of the basic roles of the sociologist is to advance this knowledge by a combination of conceptual schemes and empirical data. An equally important role of the sociologist, however, is to transmit this knowledge to students at the college and university level. "Clearly this teaching function," comments Parsons, "has always been one of the principal responsibilities of the profession and still is. It is," he continues, "primarily a general education function, helping to orient the student to aspects of the world in which he lives." [31] We may indicate some of these general educational functions of sociology in the liberal arts curriculum.

1. *Introductory function.* The first and most obvious function is to introduce the student to the vocabulary, methods, and concepts of sociology. Many of the terms used in sociology are also used in ordinary discourse. In sociology, however, they have special meanings, a situation that often leads to some confusion. *Society, culture, group, custom, race,* and *institution* are among the commonly used words that take on new meanings or new shades of meaning for the sociologist. Other sociological terms represent a more specialized vocabulary, one that the student rarely encounters in any other context. *Folkways, mores, deviance, ethnocentrism,* and *ecology* are new words for the beginning student.[32] Advanced courses are based upon the conceptual scheme outlined in the beginning course and presuppose an elementary knowledge of this material. The pursuit of knowledge in sociology, like that in any other field, is a gradual and cumulative process.

2. *Informational function.* The introductory course in sociology also offers a great deal of specific information that is probably new to the average student. This information includes the following: the nature of the human group; the formation of personality; the role of culture in behavior; the meaning of racial differences; the forms and functions of the family, church, school, and state; the numbers and composition of population; the role of social stratification and its principal forms in our society; the nature of collective behavior, including crowds, masses, and publics; and the ways by which society changes and

---

[30] Kolb, "The Impingement of Moral Values on Sociology," *op. cit.*

[31] Talcott Parsons, "Some Problems Confronting Sociology as a Profession," *American Sociological Review,* 24:547-559 (August, 1959), p. 554.

[32] See N. S. Timasheff, "The Basic Concepts of Sociology," *American Journal of Sociology,* 58:176-186 (September, 1952). Also Emory S. Bogardus, "Selected Sociological Concepts for Beginning Students in Sociology," *Sociology and Social Research,* 44:200-208 (January-February, 1960).

grows. The student himself is involved in these and many other relationships, and he will ordinarily have more than a casual interest in them. When he has completed the elementary course in sociology, he will have acquired considerable factual information about his own life and that of other persons and groups.

3. *Cultural function.* This function of the introductory course refers to the understanding of the student's relationship to society and culture and their role in forming his own personality and that of others. The human being is born with certain genetic abilities and tendencies that are subsequently modified by the forces of his social and cultural environment. The institutions arising from and perpetuated by the relationships between socialized human beings are not immutably established. They are changing all the time to meet the demands of new forces. The family, the church, the school, and the state all undergo such modifications, some deliberate and others unplanned adaptations to changing conditions. The person who has learned the relationships between himself and the institutions of a dynamic society has taken an important step toward acquiring wisdom.[33]

4. *Tolerance function.* The student in the introductory course also acquires specific knowledge of his own and other societies. This knowledge should increase his tolerance of customs other than his own. The customs of his own society are correct for him; they are so deeply incorporated into his personality that he could not change them if he would. The customs of other societies are likewise correct for *them.* The evidence indicates strongly that education increases tolerance. A representative sampling of the American people indicated that those with more education were uniformly more tolerant than those with less.[34] The extreme national intolerance of the contemporary world of nations means that the threat of nuclear war, with its annihilating potentiality, is always present. Knowledge of the ways of life of other peoples helps to break down this suicidal attitude. The student of introductory sociology can learn much that will make him a better citizen of his own country and the world.

5. *Democratic function.* A further function of the introductory course in sociology should, in our view, be the encouragement of the ultimate values of democracy. Teachers and students are working within the framework of a democratic society. One of the essential features of this way of life is the opportunity it presents for the individual to make the most effective use of his capabilities. The *undemocratic* point of view is that each person belongs to a certain race, creed, class, caste, or other closed social group. This membership automatically denies him the opportunity to better himself in terms of his abilities. The student of sociology learns that membership in a minority group in no way defines individual ability. Given the native aptitudes, any person is potentially able to rise above his status at birth. A society that fails to utilize the abilities of *all* of its citizens is not completely democratic.

---

[33] Cf. Robin M. Williams, "Application of Research to Practice in Intergroup Relations," *American Sociological Review*, 18:78-83 (February, 1953).

[34] Stouffer, *op. cit.*, Chapter 4.

6. *Humanistic function.* The introductory course in sociology is an important part of the liberal arts curriculum. The subject matter of sociology is man in his human relationships, which is very close to that of the humanistic studies. The chief concern of the humanist and social scientist alike is (or should be) an increased knowledge, appreciation, and understanding of man as a human being. As aptly stated by Bierstedt, the humanistic position recognizes that "sociology, like the other arts, is one of the ornaments of the human mind, that its literature extending from Plato to our contemporaries is in a great and humane tradition. . . ." [35] The president of the Social Science Research Council further affirms the close relationship between the social and humanistic studies. "It is well," he remarks, "to remind ourselves that arguments of an 'either-or' nature about science and the humanities serve little constructive purpose since we so greatly need all that can be drawn from either source." [36] In the cooperative search for truth about human beings in society, both the social sciences and the humanities can make a unique contribution. [37]

7. *"Sociological imagination" function.* The educational function of the introductory course may, finally, be broadly viewed as the development of what Mills has called "the sociological imagination." This is a point of view, a state of mind, and a way of looking at the world and the place of the individual in it. The student who has acquired the sociological imagination will better understand both the institutions of his society and his own personality. Furthermore, "the sociological imagination enables us to grasp history and biography and the relations between the two within society." [38] Commenting upon the role of the social sciences in this educational enterprise, Pendleton Herring suggests that these disciplines involve "a way of looking at the world more than [they do] a neat set of scientific principles." [39] A single introductory course in sociology— or a dozen such courses—is obviously not enough to reach this goal of the sociological imagination. But such a course should begin to orient the student to the broad currents of contemporary society.

The Introduction to Sociology

The introduction to sociology in this book is divided into five general sections. The *first* section deals with the general nature of the society into which the individual is born. The interaction of human beings is the fundamental social reality. Social interaction brings about the formation of groups. This section is devoted to the study of the group, the forms it takes, the conditions under which it is formed, and the patterns of expectations that it evolves. Group ex-

---

[35] Robert Bierstedt, "Sociology and Humane Learning," *American Sociological Review*, 25:3-9 (February, 1960), p. 9.

[36] Pendleton Herring, *Annual Report of the President, 1960-61*, Social Science Research Council, New York, 1961, p. 17.

[37] Arthur M. Schlesinger, Jr., "The Humanist Looks at Empirical Social Research," *American Sociological Review*, 27: 768-771 (December, 1962).

[38] C. Wright Mills, *The Sociological Imagination* (New York: Oxford University Press, 1959), p. 6.

[39] Herring, *op. cit.*, p. 19.

pectations determine many, but not all, of the activities of the members of a society.

In the *second* section, we consider the products of social interaction. In the course of thousands of years of continuous interaction, each society has evolved a complex social heritage that is handed down from generation to generation through the learning process. The social heritage and the organized patterns of behavior of a society make up its culture. This second section deals with the relationships between society, culture, and the individual. In the sociological sense, personality is largely the product of these relationships. The genetic basis of personality is the combination of traits that the individual receives in the germ plasm. These elements represent potentialities, not the finished product. Personality may be studied in terms of the groups with which the individual is associated and the culture transmitted by these groups.

The *third* section takes up some of the constituent elements of the structure of society. Included in this category are such factors as: the number and composition of the people (population); the principal biological groups into which human beings are divided (race); and the principal forms of stratification that have arisen within different societies (class and caste). Population and race are basically determined by biological factors, but they have sociological significance because of the social definitions placed upon them. Social stratification in the form of class and caste is primarily a social product, born of social interaction and capable of modification in the same way. The structure of our own society is increasingly important as the implications of caste and class for behavior become more widely understood.

The *fourth* section comprises social institutions and their role in the community. Social institutions are the products of interaction over extended periods and are centered about recurrent group needs. The family, the church, the school, and the government are among the institutional forms that these group products take. The life of a community revolves about its major institutions, each of which performs a definite function or functions in the satisfaction of human wants. In this sense, the community is viewed as a constellation or related pattern of institutions. The modern community is then examined in terms of the general forms it assumes and the functions it performs. The section also includes a discussion of bureaucracy and the increasing tendency of many contemporary institutions to become bureaucratized.

The *fifth* section deals with collective behavior and social change. Collective behavior is the stuff of social change, whereby a new way of life emerges. Under the impetus of collective behavior, men may break many of the social patterns that formerly held them together in organized interaction. Some of these changes occur in an orderly manner and involve only slight social maladjustment. Others are marked by an abruptness that disorganizes individuals and institutions alike. Mass society is seen as a characteristically modern, dynamic system in which the mass media of communication play an increasingly important part. This section concludes with an analysis of social problems as an inescapable legacy of a rapidly changing society.

SELECTED BIBLIOGRAPHY

Barber, Bernard, *Science and the Social Order*. Glencoe, Ill.: The Free Press, 1952. This is a stimulating and thoughtful analysis of the nature of science and its role in the modern world. The author uses the conceptual tools of an emerging science (sociology) to analyze the functions of science as such.

Current Sociology (London: Basil Blackwell), published for UNESCO. This journal publishes periodic examinations and evaluations of contemporary research in the various fields of Sociology (e.g., Class, Caste, Social Mobility, Ideology, The Family). The reports are prepared by internationally known scholars and offer excellent summaries of the latest work being done in all parts of the world. Extensive annotated bibliographies are appended.

Gillin, John (ed.), *For a Science of Social Man*. New York: The Macmillan Company, 1954. In this ingeniously conceived symposium, the interrelationships among the social sciences are explored from the points of view of different specialists.

Gouldner, Alvin W., "Anti-Minotaur: The Myth of a Value-Free Society," *Social Problems*, 9:199-213 (Winter, 1962). The author here takes a strong stand in defense of the ultimate value of social science as contributing to an understanding of "the contemporary human predicament."

———, "Theoretical Requirements of the Applied Social Sciences," *American Sociological Review*, 22:92-102 (February, 1957). This article examines the relationships between theory and application and stresses the continuing importance of the latter. Applied sociology is pictured as neither marginal nor unimportant, but rather as emerging "from the deepest taproots" of the subject and as having the "most venerable tradition."

Merton, Robert K., *Social Theory and Social Structure*. Glencoe, Ill.: The Free Press, 1957 (revised and enlarged edition). In this collection of essays, a leading sociologist makes some significant contributions to theory and application in a wide range of sociological problems. Several of the essays have, through successive revisions, become sociological classics by virtue of their combination of keen insight and felicitous phrasing.

———, Leonard Broom, and Leonard S. Cottrell, Jr., (eds.), *Sociology Today*. New York: Basic Books, Inc., 1959. In this symposium, many of the leading figures in contemporary American sociology consider the important problems of understanding and research facing their respective specialities. This book is not so much a summary of existing knowledge as an attempt to formulate ways in which new knowledge may be gained.

Mills, C. Wright, *The Sociological Imagination*. New York: Oxford University Press, 1959. This is a provocative and hence controversial statement of the role of sociology in understanding the major problems of contemporary society. The author conceives of "the sociological imagination" as "a quality of mind that will help them [its possessors] to use information and to develop reason in order to achieve lucid summations of what is going on in the world and of what may be happening within themselves."

Park, Robert E., and Ernest W. Burgess, *Introduction to the Science of Sociology*. Chicago: University of Chicago Press, 1924. This is probably the most influential sociology textbook ever written in this country. Published four decades ago, it contains many insights and concepts that have subsequently been developed by other sociologists.

Parsons, Talcott, *et al.* (eds.), *Theories of Society*. Glencoe, Ill.: The Free Press, 1961, two volumes. These two massive volumes contain selections from the great precursors of contemporary sociological theory. Each group of selections is based upon a related set of concepts (e.g., "Differentiation and Variation in Social Structure"), and is prefaced by an extensive introduction by one of the editors. These volumes are indispensable to the student who seeks to understand the intellectual currents that led up to the study of sociology.

Williams, Robin M., Jr., "Continuity and Change in Sociological Study," *American Sociological Review,* 23:619-633 (December, 1958). This presidential address to the American Sociological Society surveys some of the broad trends in the discipline. The title suggests that *both* continuity and change are visible in this rapidly emerging field of scientific study.

Wirth, Louis, "Responsibility of Social Science," *Annals of the American Academy of Political and Social Science,* 249:143-151 (January, 1947). The responsibilities of social science in the modern world are greater than ever before. This article suggests some of the fields into which the trained intelligence of the social scientist may be directed.

2 *Social Interaction*

The Nature of Social Interaction

We begin with society in being—that is, with large numbers of persons engaged in social interaction. The central fact of society is social interaction, and the subsequent implications of the study of society grow out of this process. Social interaction is a continuous and reciprocal series of contacts between two or more socialized human beings.[1] These contacts may be physical, in the sense that each person does something physically to the other; more often they are symbolic, in the sense that each

---

[1] Alvin W. Gouldner, "The Norm of Reciprocity," *American Sociological Review*, 25:161-78 (June, 1960).

person exchanges symbolic meanings with the other, in the form of language or other significant gestures. A society exists when many persons interact regularly and continuously on the basis of expectations of behavior whose meanings have been previously established. The limits of a society are those of social interaction.[2]

Social interaction is "a twofold process of reaction to and influence upon the environment."[3] The environment in this case consists of other persons, and each person is a part of the environment of the others. In social interaction, each takes the other into account. This means that each person is aware of the other, makes a judgment or appraisal of him, and tries to discover what he is thinking or is about to do.[4] The essence of this process is its reciprocal character. Each takes the other into account in order to guide his own behavior, for only in this way can each individual act in a meaningful fashion. When we interact with other persons, we continually adjust our behavior to a changing relationship.[5]

This approach to social interaction has been explored by Strauss. "Face-to-face interaction," he remarks, "is a fluid, moving, 'running' process; during its course the participants take successive stances vis-a-vis each other. Sometimes they fence, sometimes they move in rhythmic psychological ballet, but always they move through successive phases of position."[6] When people encounter each other—whether for the first or the hundredth time—each makes a judgment of the other's identity, and this judgment sets the stage for the interaction. The child and his mother, the boy and his friend, and the soldier and his buddy have established each other's identity from long experience. People meeting for the first time, such as a salesman and his prospect, must make a rapid judgment about each other and continue from there.

Two persons in interaction thus take each other into account and respond to each other's behavior. The process is, however, more complicated than this, for each party to the interaction is also responding to *his own* behavior. The angry man responds to his own emotion as much as to the acts of the other. Each may shock himself by his words or actions and find it necessary to "apologize" to himself. The other may respond with an insulting word, which may cause him in his turn to feel guilty toward himself. We shall examine this situation in Chapter 8, in connection with our analysis of the social self. The point here is that interaction between the person and himself may be as important as that between himself and another.[7]

---

[2] Marion J. Levy, *The Structure of Society* (Princeton: Princeton University Press, 1952), p. 113.

[3] Franklin J. Shaw and Robert S. Ort, *Personal Adjustment in the American Culture* (New York: Harper & Brothers, 1953), p. 4.

[4] Herbert Blumer, "Psychological Import of the Human Group," Chapter 8 in Muzafer Sherif and M. O. Wilson (eds.), *Group Relations at the Crossroads* (New York: Harper & Brothers, 1953), p. 194.

[5] Cf. George C. Homans, *Social Behavior: Its Elementary Forms* (New York: Harcourt, Brace & World, Inc., 1961), p. 35.

[6] Anselm L. Strauss, *Mirrors and Masks: The Search for Identity* (Glencoe, Ill.: The Free Press, 1959), p. 55.

[7] *Ibid.*, p. 57.

In interaction, finally, more than two persons may take part in the drama. Each of the actors may interact with (take into account) a third person, unknown to his face-to-face companion. A son may act with reference to his mother and may (consciously or unconsciously) strive to please her, even though she may be dead. A doctor may be aware of his colleagues while interviewing a patient—or even while operating on him. A teacher may think of the superintendent while disciplining a child; the latter may think of his influential parents who will (he hopes) bring pressure upon the superintendent. In such situations, each person constantly interacts with others in his mind, even as he seems to be confining his attention to the person before him. Interaction is an involved process, conducted in a "thickly peopled and complexly imaged" setting.[8]

The Role of Communication

Social interaction is based upon communication. In a very real sense, it *is* communication. As John Dewey pointed out long ago, "Society not only continues to exist *by* transmission, *by* communication, but it may fairly be said to exist *in* transmission, *in* communication." [9] When two persons interact, they exchange meaningful gestures—whether words, smiles, signs, frowns, or yawns. They interpret these acts in the behavior of the other person and respond appropri-

[8] *Ibid.*, pp. 56-57.
[9] John Dewey, *Democracy and Education* (New York: The Macmillan Company, 1916), p. 5.

Social interaction is essentially a process whereby two or more human beings take each other into account.

ately themselves. In their interaction with others, they are constantly reading these signs and responding to them. As one responds, the other adjusts his behavior accordingly. This is a dynamic process, for the relationships change from moment to moment and each person must continually modify his own responses to those of the other.

Interaction may thus be said to occur between two persons "when, within a given time span, one of the personalities acts with reference to the second personality, and the second personality acts with reference to the first." [10] When two friends are talking, two boys are fighting, or two athletes are competing, each is acting with reference to the other and modifying his behavior accordingly. By its very nature, therefore, interaction is *social* rather than *personal*, because it needs at least two persons. In interaction there is a constant process of mutual adjustment to the actual or anticipated behavior of the other(s). "By interaction," then, "we refer to mutually adjustive behavior between two or more persons." [11]

When we think of social interaction, we are also thinking in group terms. "Social interaction," says Stogdill, "is an interpersonal rather than a personal characteristic of behavior. It takes place in a group situation." [12] Without an adjustment, neither the group nor society could exist. In most cases, we are not aware of this adjustment, but it is nevertheless going on at every moment. From the intimate group of mother and child to the largest group of the nation-state, the essence of the relationship is social interaction. The study of society (sociology) is in its essentials a study of social interaction.

In communication between human beings, each person is an "actor" as well as a "reactor." This means that each is constantly doing and saying things that stimulate other persons, as well as reacting to stimuli that originate with the others. The early notion that a man is a passive agent, reacting only to stimuli from outside, must therefore be discarded. In its place is the realization that each man is an "actor" in his own right, who is continually stimulating others by his behavior and at the same time is stimulating himself. When we are engaged in an argument, our words are stimuli to the other person. At the same time, our words stimulate us to further anger. In the continual process of interaction, we constantly respond to stimuli arising from our communication both with others and with ourselves. [13]

Each member of a society interacts with others through communication, and in so doing adjusts his behavior to their expectations. Communication is a continuous and ongoing process, and millions of meaningful exchanges take place every moment in any large society. All over the United States, people are continually interacting with others through the various media of communication.

[10] Robert M. Huntington, *Needs and Interaction: A Study of the Marital Relationship*, Ph.D. Thesis, Department of Social Relations, Harvard University, Cambridge, 1955, p. 29.

[11] Douglas Oliver, "An Ethnographer's Method for Formulating Descriptions of 'Social Structure,'" *American Anthropologist*, 60:801-826 (October, 1958), p. 901.

[12] Ralph M. Stogdill, *Individual Behavior and Group Achievement* (New York: Oxford University Press, 1959), p. 17.

[13] Sheldon Stryker, "Symbolic Interaction as an Approach to Family Research," *Marriage and Family Living*, 21:111-119 (May, 1959).

Communication is the most thoroughly *human* activity. When people are communicating, they are acting in their most intensely *human* capacity.

Communication is subject to many variations. Some persons are obviously more articulate than others and communicate verbally with greater skill and ease. Others are not so vocal and make their wishes and emotions known by frowns, sighs, or smiles. Communication also appears to vary between social classes, with the middle class tending to be more articulate than the lower class. Communication is a learned reaction, and the facilities for learning are ordinarily more advanced among members of the middle class than among those on a lower social level.[14]

The common interpretation of meaningful acts and the appropriate reaction by large numbers of persons make up the life of a society. This society may be small and intimate, as in the case of a primitive folk group. In this instance, a few hundred people may live completely self-sufficient lives in virtual isolation from other societies; communication here is entirely by word of mouth.[15] In a society such as our own, the unit is the large nation-state, and face-to-face communication is supplemented by such mass media as newspapers, radio, television, and the movies. In the mass media, communication occurs between persons who are physically separated and who react to each other's behavior indirectly.[16] All of this activity constitutes the social interaction that binds people together in a society. Interaction is thus the fundamental social reality.

The Symbolic Basis of Social Interaction

"The term 'symbolic interaction,'" says Blumer, "refers ... to the peculiar and distinctive character of interaction as it takes place between human beings. The peculiarity consists in the fact that human beings interpret or 'define' each other's actions instead of merely reacting to each other's actions." [17] Social interaction is essentially a symbolic process, conducted by human beings employing verbal and physical gestures having a special meaning. In this sense, a symbol is defined as "a stimulus that has a learned meaning and value for people" and the response to a symbol "is in terms of its meaning and value rather than in terms of its physical stimulation." [18] A symbol is something that *stands for* something else. It may be physical (a flag) or nonphysical (a word). The most obvious form of symbolic communication is language, in which each word is a symbol standing for something.

Human beings do not interact like billiard balls bouncing off each other; they interact in terms of significant symbols mutually understood by the partici-

---

[14] Leonard Schatzman and Anselm L. Strauss, "Social Class and Modes of Communication," *American Journal of Sociology*, 60:329-338 (January, 1955).

[15] Robert Redfield, "The Folk Society," *American Journal of Sociology*, 52:293-308 (January, 1947).

[16] Donald Horton and Anselm L. Strauss, "Interaction in Audience-Participation Shows," *American Journal of Sociology*, 62:579-587 (May, 1957).

[17] Herbert Blumer, "Society as Symbolic Interaction," Chapter 9 in Arnold M. Rose (ed.), *Human Behavior and Social Processes* (Boston: Houghton Mifflin Company, 1962), p. 180.

[18] Arnold M. Rose, "A Systematic Summary of Symbolic Interaction Theory," Chapter 1 in Arnold M. Rose (ed.), *op. cit.*, p. 5.

pants. Social interaction is conducted in a setting of expectations, rules, and norms learned at an early age by the individual, who then attempts to govern his behavior accordingly. Social interaction is thus characterized by "the presence of expressive acts on the part of one or more persons, the conscious or unconscious perception of such expressive actions by other persons, and the return observation that such expressive actions have been perceived by others." [19]

Social interaction is carried on by socialized individuals, each with a definite personality and a social self acquired through contact with other similarly developed individuals. In the process of socialization, the individual learns to "take the role of the other" and mentally put himself in the place of the one with whom he is reacting.[20] In this way, each weighs the impact of his words or gestures upon the other. In taking the role of the other, he also stimulates himself. Social interaction involves not only the interaction of one person with another person, but of each person with himself. In a fight between two boys, one hesitates before knocking a chip off the other's shoulder. By putting himself in the place of the other (taking his role), the potential aggressor decides what *he* would do under similar circumstances. In this way, he stimulates himself as well as his opponent. The self and the other are parts of the same process.

This element of self-interaction distinguishes human from animal interaction. Human beings can interact with themselves through symbols, as in the case of an American stimulating himself with such symbols as the flag, the nation, or the enemy. Animals can stimulate each other by direct sensory action—a herd of cattle stampeded by its own sounds—but they are not capable of stimulating either each other or themselves by symbolic means. Their interaction is accordingly on a different level from that of human beings. Animals enter into many relationships found in human societies, such as sex, mutual care, and dependency. The symbolic element, however, introduces refinements into the interaction of human beings (saying one thing and doing another) that are not found in animal societies.[21]

The process of taking the other into account has other implications for social interaction. The human being can *restrain* as well as stimulate himself by taking the role of the other. His insight into the thoughts and emotions of the other may inhibit his own impulses, inclinations, and feelings. The aggressive schoolboy may hesitate to knock the chip off the other's shoulder because of his fear of the reactions that might follow. By taking the role of the other, he may save himself considerable mental and physical discomfort. In any society, the individual must inhibit many of his impulses in the interests of group harmony. Socal interaction implies both stimulation and inhibition of behavior between members of a society.

The nature of social interaction means that it is, within limits, predictable.

---

[19] Jurgen Ruesch, "Synopsis of the Theory of Human Communication," *Psychiatry*, 16:215-143 (August, 1953), p. 242.

[20] George H. Mead, *Mind, Self, and Society* (Chicago: University of Chicago Press, 1934).

[21] John P. Scott, "Implications of Infra-Human Social Behavior for Problems of Human Relationships," Chapter 2 in Sherif and Wilson (eds.), *op. cit.*, pp. 33-73.

The element of predictability applies in two related senses. *First,* it means that each member of a society can tell what the other person is going to do in his ordinary social relationships. He predicts the behavior of the other on the basis of what he himself would do under similar circumstances. Without some such predictability, organized society could not exist because nobody would know what the other was about to do. In the *second* place, the predictability of social interaction means that it can be scientifically studied by persons who understand the system and are familiar with its methods of communication. The sociologist can study the interaction of his own society and of the constituent groups within it. If all human behavior were truly "individual" (unpredictable), a science of society would be manifestly impossible.

The generalizations of social science grow out of social interaction. Human behavior is the reality and, as such, is the main object of observation. The sociologist sees people talking to each other, laughing at each other, throwing balls at each other, locking each other up behind bars, applauding each other—and in many other ways exchanging meaningful gestures. From the behavior of human beings in interaction, the sociologist *abstracts* certain general ideas and conceptual schemes that he subjects to further verification in different ways. In this way, the science of sociology grows by the observation of human behavior in social interaction, as each takes the other(s) into account.[22]

Social interaction is a series of relationships whereby human beings act in terms of their awareness of each other. In summary, social interaction is "a moving process in which the participants note and gauge each other's actions, each organizing his action with regard to the other and, in so doing, inhibiting himself, encouraging himself, and guiding himself as he builds up his action." [23] Interaction occurs within a framework previously established by the society. We shall consider this framework in terms of folkways, mores, culture, status, and role. These social elements are produced by social interaction, although the production usually takes place in the past. In point of both time and logic, therefore, social interaction comes first. This is the first and basic reality of society.[24]

The Levels of Social Interaction

In the process of social interaction, the individual takes into account the forces of his social environment. In so doing, he influences both himself and the other elements of the environment. The man who responds with an angry word to a similar act of another is interacting in this double sense. He is angering himself and simultaneously angering the other. This reciprocal interaction is characteristically human. When a person looks at a sunset, on the other hand, he is exerting no appreciable influence upon the natural environment. We may further examine the social environment in terms of social interaction.

---

[22] A. Paul Hare, Edgar F. Borgatta, and Robert F. Bales, *Small Groups: Studies in Social Interaction* (New York: Alfred A. Knopf, Inc., 1955), p. vi.

[23] Blumer, *op. cit.,* p. 197.

[24] Robert F. Bales, *Interaction Process Analysis* (Cambridge, Mass.: Addison-Wesley Press, 1950).

1. Interaction between individuals. The most obvious form of social interaction occurs between individuals: a husband and wife are talking; a boy and his friend are playing; a mother is comforting her child. The units of interaction are individuals, who take each other's behavior into account, each thereby influencing both himself and the other. The first interaction for the infant usually involves his mother. She represents virtually his entire functioning social environment during his early weeks. She cares for his physical wants, gives him affection and protects him against hunger and pain. As he grows older, the interaction becomes less onesided, as he learns to take the role of his mother toward himself and thereby respond to her behavior in a meaningful way. In thus taking his mother into account, the child has perhaps his first truly social experience.

The world of the child enlarges as he comes in contact with others. He begins to interact with the other members of his family and then with persons outside the family group. As his world continues to expand, he interacts with members of the play group, his classmates in school, and his teachers. We cannot consider all of the levels of individual interaction here, but merely indicate that they occur. In all of these relationships, the person is part of the social environment of others who respond in much the same fashion as he to them. Each one influences and is influenced by the others and hence interacts with them.[25]

---

[25] Shaw and Ort, *op. cit.*, p. 29.

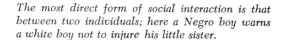

The most direct form of social interaction is that between two individuals; here a Negro boy warns a white boy not to injure his little sister.

2. *Interaction between individuals and groups.* Social interaction also occurs between individuals and groups. The group may be provisionally defined as two or more persons who interact with each other, either actively or potentially, over an appreciable period and are motivated by a common goal.[26] Interaction on the individual-group level occurs between an officer and a company, a preacher and a congregation, a coach and a team, and a teacher and a class. The officer influences the company and vice versa. The teacher lecturing to a class influences them as a group, and at the same time reacts to their attention and morale. When it interacts as a group, the class becomes more than a number of individuals. The whole becomes greater than the sum of its parts. The force binding individuals together in the group is the common goal.[27]

The interaction between the individual and the group may occur in another, and more subtle, fashion. We refer to the influence exerted upon the individual by the *expectations* of the group. When a group has interacted over an appreciable period, it develops certain expectations of behavior, or ways in which each member is *supposed* to behave. The boy who enters a new neighborhood learns the expectations of the local gang about rules of the game, fighting, and authority. In like manner, when the individual enters any new situation—whether neighborhood gang, high school clique, or group of army buddies—he must adjust to the prevailing group expectations. In this process, he exerts some influence upon the group, but most of the interaction is the other way. The social environment of group expectations is so pervasive that the individual ordinarily can do little to change it.[28]

3. *Interaction between individuals and culture.* The third level of social interaction occurs between the individual and culture. We shall consider the nature of culture in later chapters. In the present context, we need merely indicate that culture is the broad term used "to designate general habits, customs, and modes of thought, action, and interpersonal relationships that prevail in a society." [29] The culture refers to the general modes of interaction prevalent in a society. Interaction between individual and culture follows logically from that between individual and group, for the culture is similar to the common expectations of a group. Culture is ordinarily held by a much larger number of persons than a group, and the expectations of a society are more complex than those of a group. The culture of the society of the United States is clearly more complex in form and more basic in influence than the expectations of a neighborhood group.

The individual is not, however, a helpless and supine pawn in an all-embracing cultural interaction. Each person reacts to the expectations of a culture in his own way. Such individual reactions do not ordinarily differ appreciably, but the important consideration is the fact that they occur. The culture is presented by others, each with his unique interpretation, and much of this interac-

---

[26] Bales, *op. cit.*, p. 33.

[27] George C. Homans, *The Human Group* (New York: Harcourt, Brace and World, 1950).

[28] Shaw and Ort, *op. cit.*, pp. 26-30.

[29] *Ibid.*, p. 30.

tion also occurs between individuals. Culture is an important part of the environment with which the individual interacts. The goals, aspirations, standards, and values that he incorporates into his personality are parts of his culture. Interaction between individuals and culture is so varied and important that we have, in effect, devoted the first two sections of this book to it.

4. *Interaction between individuals and the mass media.* Interaction between individuals and culture also occurs through the mass media of communication, as well as through the face-to-face contacts of individuals. The culture is handed on by such agencies as the radio, television, the motion pictures, and the newspaper. This interaction is literally between the individual and culture, since the individual responds to the words he hears and the figures he sees. The heroine on the screen is not so much a real person as a symbol of such social values as beauty, wealth, power, prestige, and love. The mass media of communication are increasingly important as a source of interaction between the individual and culture. In an earlier society, the child learned his culture by interacting with his parents, siblings, friends, teachers, ministers, and associates. This form of interaction is still basic to the development of the personality, but the impersonal agencies are growing in importance.[30]

The mass media have also introduced a new *form* of interaction between the individual and culture. Although interaction between persons on a face-to-face basis means that each takes the other into account and reacts accordingly, interaction through the mass media partially eliminates this reciprocal relationship. The individual listening to the radio or viewing television cannot influence the speaker. The latter, in turn, cannot directly take into account the reactions of his millions of anonymous listeners. Neither party is able directly to observe the effect of his action upon the other, and the interaction becomes correspondingly impersonal. The relationships between cause and effect are obscured, as each side is unable to come to grips with the other.[31]

The impersonality of the mass media is, however, modified by an important factor. This is the intervention of people. Recent research in this dynamic field has indicated that people intervene between the mass media and large numbers of listeners. The process is briefly as follows. In every group and community, there are certain persons who listen to the radio, read the papers, study the mass magazines, and otherwise immerse themselves in the mass media to a greater extent than the others. These active listeners, viewers, and readers *then* communicate the information to those in their immediate environment—families, neighbors, friends, and fellow workmen.[32]

This process is known as the "two-step flow of communication," and it is an important factor in the interaction between individual and culture through the mass media. Interpersonal interaction plays a basic role in the exposure to the

---

[30] David Riesman, *et al.*, *The Lonely Crowd* (New Haven: Yale University Press, 1961), abridged edition with a new preface, Chapter 4.

[31] Jurgen Ruesch and Gregory Bateson, *Communication: The Social Matrix of Psychiatry* (New York: W. W. Norton & Company, 1951), p. 16.

[32] Elihu Katz and Paul F. Lazarsfeld, *Personal Influence: The Part Played by People in the Flow of Mass Communications* (Glencoe, Ill.: The Free Press, 1955), Chapter 1.

mass media. As they hand on the information from the media, the opinion leaders are themselves influenced by those with whom they interact. The opinion leader must always take the other(s) into account and adjust his reactions accordingly. He must transmit the information and opinions in a way that will be understandable to others. Like all social interaction, this is a mutual process of give-and-take, and the opinion leader often "takes" as much as he "gives." [33]

Social *interaction* is the general series of activities of two or more persons in meaningful contact. Social *process* refers to the recurrent forms that social interaction takes. Park and Burgess define social process as "the name for all changes which can be regarded as changes in the life of the group." [34] The social processes involve forms of social interaction that occur again and again in the group. The importance of social process has long been recognized by sociologists, but they have not agreed on the precise application of this concept. In the following discussion, we shall follow the analysis of Park and Burgess, whose insights have influenced much of the subsequent work in this field. They reckon four major social processes: competition, conflict, accommodation, and assimilation. To this number we shall add a fifth, cooperation.

Competition as a Social Process

Competition is defined by Park and Burgess as "the process through which the distributive and ecological order of society is created. Competition determines the distribution of population territorially and vocationally. The division of labor and all the vast organized interdependence of individuals and groups . . . characteristic of modern life are a product of competition." [35] This is the most impersonal of the social processes. The individual is often unaware that he is competing for scarce values. In other cases, he may be aware that he is competing, but may have no personal contact with his competitors. The farmer may not realize that he is in competition with millions of other farmers, in this country and abroad, in determining the world price of wheat.

Competition arises from the scarcity of goods, statuses, and services that are widely or universally desired. In the struggle for these scarce goals, competition is usually restrained by tradition, custom, or law. These limiting factors keep it within bounds, and unrestricted competition is seldom found in actual behavior. Even in economic enterprise, the members of the society are prevented from engaging in unlimited competition by a variety of social restraints. In a football game, each team is anxious to win, but at the same time each knows that it must remain within the rules. A victory gained by breaking the rules loses its savor. Competition, furthermore, is expected to take place between

---

[33] Elihu Katz, "The Two-Step Flow of Communication: An Up-to-Date Report on an Hypothesis," *Public Opinion Quarterly*, 21:61-78 (Spring, 1957). Also Elihu Katz, "Communication Research and the Image of Society: Convergence of Two Traditions," *American Journal of Sociology*, 65:435-440 (March, 1960).

[34] Robert E. Park and Ernest W. Burgess, *Introduction to the Science of Sociology* (Chicago: University of Chicago Press, 1924), p. 51.

[35] *Ibid.*, p. 508.

equals, and the group usually tries to maintain this equality. The antitrust laws are an attempt to maintain competition between economic associations and to prevent one unit from swallowing up the others.

Competition is an impersonal struggle for limited ends, operating in accordance with socially prescribed rules. The *goals* of competition are likewise socially defined. In our own society, the most obvious goal is money, defined as a means of attaining desired goods and services. Money also leads to a further socially desirable end, namely, prestige, often more important than any other consideration in motivating competition.[36] Other societies have other goals, both material and symbolic, for which their members compete. The symbols of success may vary from a yacht to a string of beads, from a fine house to a red ribbon in the buttonhole, from a million dollars to a framed piece of paper. The individual does not invent these symbols, nor does he seek them because of any innate drive for them. The symbols of success are social products and, as such, constitute goals that the individual learns to seek. Society both sets the standards and defines the goals of competition.[37]

Competitive goals are learned in the process of becoming a socialized human being. The tendency to engage in competitive behavior and the goals of this behavior are fostered by the society through the culture. In our own society, competition *as such* is considered important. Experimental evidence has indicated that "the rudiments of competition and cooperation appear among children during the first year of life, but these types of behavior are not apparent until about the third year, after which they undergo rapid development until about the sixth year, when they are observable in all or nearly all children." [38] In the home, in the school, and on the playground, the child learns the importance of competition early in life. He soon realizes that many important goals and prestige symbols can be gained only through successful competition.

Competition is an important factor in a dynamic society as both the cause and effect of social change. Competition occurs between groups as well as between individuals. Corporations, labor unions, business associations, and many other large social units engage in competition (as well as the other social processes) and thereby contribute to the dynamic quality of society.[39] Competition is a *cause* of social change in that it forces persons to adopt new forms of behavior to attain desired goals. These forms of behavior involve innovations useful in economic competition. Mass production enables the corporation to produce more efficiently and compete more effectively. Competition is an *effect* of social change because a changing society has more goals open to competition than a static society. Our own society is both competitive and dynamic. This combination of change and competition is not accidental.

---

[36] Nicholas J. Spykman, *The Social Theory of Georg Simmel* (Chicago: University of Chicago Press, 1925), p. 251.

[37] Mark A. May and Leonard W. Doob, *Competition and Cooperation* (New York: Social Science Research Council, 1937), p. 100.

[38] *Ibid.*, p. 27.

[39] Arnold M. Rose, "Voluntary Associations Under Conditions of Competition and Conflict," *Social Forces,* 34:159-163 (December, 1955).

Cooperation as a Social Process

Competition and cooperation may be distinguished in terms of means and ends. Both processes are forms of social interaction between two or more individuals, directed toward the same ends. The distinction arises from the means used to gain these ends. "In competition . . . the end sought can be achieved . . . by some and not by all of the individuals . . . ; whereas in cooperation it can be achieved by all or almost all of the individuals concerned." [40] Cooperation may thus be defined as a form of social interaction wherein two or more persons work together for a common end.

Competition and its accompanying values are so pervasive in our society that the importance of cooperation is often overlooked. Many persons assume that competition is the principal, if not the only, form of interaction and that human relationships have been and always will be primarily characterized by competition for scarce goals and prestige symbols. Such persons view any effort— from social security legislation to psychiatric aid—to regulate or mitigate the effects of competition as a misguided attempt to eliminate a form of social interaction that should be allowed free play in the interests of a healthy society. This attitude is incorrect in the face of human development. From earliest prehistory to the present, cooperation between group members has been more important than competition.[41]

This error in emphasis concerning the relative importance of competition and cooperation arose in the nineteenth century. It stemmed from a misapplication of the Darwinian hypothesis of the survival of the fittest, advanced to explain the *origins* of the various species, man among them. Darwin maintained that the competitive struggle was most severe between individuals of the same species. In applying this judgment to man, Darwin overemphasized the importance of competition and underemphasized that of cooperation *after the human species had fully developed.*

The role of cooperation or "mutual aid" in social development was emphasized many years later by Kropotkin, but his theory never received the sympathetic hearing of Darwin's. Kropotkin pointed out that the earliest social interaction was probably some form of the family. By its nature, this group depended upon cooperation in caring for the young, securing food, and combating a hostile environment.[42]

Cooperation takes a variety of forms and involves different groups, ranging in size and cohesion from the conjugal family to the United Nations. The important consideration, however, is the fact that persons and groups work together toward a common end, rather than separately toward personal or selfish ends. Cooperation, furthermore, involves a basic agreement on rules of procedure and forms of behavior. In addition, there is a toleration of differences

---

[40] May and Doob, *op. cit.,* p. 6.
[41] Francis Ashley Montagu, *On Being Human* (New York: Henry Schuman, 1950).
[42] P. Kropotkin, *Mutual Aid: A Factor in Evolution* (New York: Alfred A. Knopf, Inc., 1922).

that may be either open or tacit. Members of a family and members of the United Nations both agree on these matters and, indeed, on many others. In uniting for the pursuit of common ends, cooperation implies a spirit of live and let live.[43]

The emphasis upon some social processes and the minimization of others is a reflection of social values. The individual strives for certain ends, but both their nature and the means of attaining them are defined by the society. This general principle has been stated as follows: "Human beings by original nature strive for goals, but striving with others (cooperation) or against others (competition) are learned forms of behavior." [44] Learning occurs within a particular social setting and the individual gradually acquires the appropriate group expectations.

Differences in emphasis between societies in this respect are shown in a classic study of two primitive peoples, the Zuni of New Mexico and the Kwakiutl of the Northwest Coast of North America. The prevailing emphasis among the Zuni is on cooperation, whereas the Kwakiutl emphasize competition. The Zuni are a mild and inoffensive people, whose goals are centered about the performance of religious ceremonials. They have no desire to excel in competition, and the man who wins races too consistently is forbidden to run any more. The individual, furthermore, has no desire for personal power and avoids public office if possible. The group, not the individual, is the functioning unit, and the virtues of cooperation are highly praised.[45]

The Kwakiutl are an extremely individualistic people, in whom competition is excessively encouraged. Their basic goals center about individual achievement, whereby the person stands out from the group and causes his rivals to be ridiculed. The competition is largely for nonmaterial possessions, such as names, crests, myths, songs, and special privileges. Material property is chiefly used to gain social prestige by *giving it away*. A chief therefore shames his rival who cannot give away or destroy so many blankets, copper plates, or other forms of material wealth. Superiority of the individual and consequent inferiority of the rival are the prevailing motivations of behavior.[46]

Different societies thus emphasize some forms of social interaction and minimize others. The entire range of social processes is, however, found to some degree in every society. No society is completely cooperative or completely competitive, nor are conflict, accommodation, and assimilation ever found exclusive of one another. The degree of emphasis is the important consideration. Unlike the Zuni, our society encourages competition and discourages cooperation. This tendency applies not only to economic behavior, but also to education, sport, and the competitive search for affection. Some societies place a high pre-

---

[43] Irving L. Horowitz, "Consensus, Conflict, and Cooperation," *Social Forces*, 41:177-188 (December, 1962).

[44] May and Doob, *op. cit.*, p. 23.

[45] Ruth Benedict, *Patterns of Culture* (New York: Penguin Books, Inc., 1946), Chapter 4, "The Pueblos of New Mexico."

[46] *Ibid.*, Chapter 6, "The Northwest Coast of America."

mium upon the warlike virtues that find their expression in conflict, whereas others attempt to develop personalities that will be peaceful and passive.[47]

Conflict as a Social Process

Both competition and conflict are marked by an attempt of two or more persons to reach the same goals. In competition, the emphasis is primarily upon the acquisition of scarce values and only incidentally upon the fate of the competitors. In conflict the emphasis shifts to the opponents, who may attempt to handicap, injure, or even destroy each other. The impersonal competitive struggle between individuals, groups, organizations, and nations becomes personal and conscious, evoking deep emotions on both sides.[48] Conflict is thus distinguished from competition by the element of mutual *awareness*. In this sense, conflict may be defined as "a situation of competition in which the parties are *aware* of the incompatibility of potential future positions and in which each party wishes to occupy a position that is incompatible with the wishes of the other." [49]

The emotions of distrust, hatred, and fear are accentuated in conflict. Conflicting groups may lose sight of their goals and concentrate upon incapacitating their opponents. The opposing players in a football game, for example, may forget that their major goal is to win the game, and become so angry that they attempt to injure each other. The rules are disregarded and the interaction

[47] Margaret Mead, *Sex and Temperament in Three Primitive Societies* (New York: William Morrow & Company, 1935).

[48] Park and Burgess, *op. cit.*, p. 574.

[49] Kenneth E. Boulding, *Conflict and Defense* (New York: Harper & Row, 1962), p. 5.

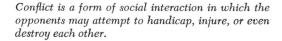

Conflict is a form of social interaction in which the opponents may attempt to handicap, injure, or even destroy each other.

becomes one of pure conflict. This behavior may be self-defeating if the offenders are ejected from the game and their respective teams penalized. In a competitive situation, the opponents must abide by the rules. When they fail to do so, the interaction moves toward conflict.

Organized society is based upon a complex pattern of reciprocal expectations intended to minimize conflict between members of the group. Efficient social functioning requires that conflict be controlled, for otherwise the stability, and sometimes the very existence, of the group is threatened. In conflict between members of the same society, each may try to eliminate his enemies in every possible way, up to and including murder. Such violence must obviously be controlled in the interest of the common welfare, and many of the formal and informal social codes have arisen for this purpose.[50]

Conflict also emphasizes the differences between people and minimizes their similarities. It obscures the similar ends that unite men in a common purpose.[51] When conflict is carried to extremes, these common goals are ignored, and the opponents are unable to see anything but the differences between them. Race conflict stresses certain comparatively superficial biological differences between human beings. It overlooks their basic similarities as members of the same species. Such conflict situations in this country obscure the many similarities of outlook, ideology, and way of life that have arisen from the participation of Negro and white in a common culture.

Conflicts between social classes, religious denominations, racial groups, and national states have marked a large part of human history. As the structure of society has changed, the social values have also changed, and men at different times have fought over such different values as religion, race, or national interest. In the period immediately following the Reformation, religious values were all-important, and conflict generated about these ends. More recently, economic and political values have become the basis for large-scale conflict. The current scene finds the world divided among great ideological systems, with groups of nations and entire peoples uniting into hostile groups.[52]

Forms of conflict are, like the other types of social interaction, products of the social setting. The members of all societies appear to have some degree of hostility (or at least suspicion) toward other groups. The sentiment that produces this potential hostility is known as *ethnocentrism*, a phenomenon that Sumner described as a point of view "in which one's own group is the center of everything, and all others are scaled and rated with reference to it."[53] The extent and intensity of this generalized feeling vary between individuals within the same society, as well as between different societies. Identification with social groups *as such* is common to all societies and is perhaps the most important characteristic of human beings. The nature of these group norms, the ends the

---

[50] Cf. Georg Simmel, *Conflict* and *The Web of Group-Affiliations* (Translated by Kurt H. Wolff and Reinhard Bendix) (Glencoe, Ill.: The Free Press, 1955), Chapter 1.

[51] Kingsley Davis, *Human Society* (New York: The Macmillan Company, 1949), p. 161.

[52] Arthur K. Davis, "Conflict Between Major Social Systems: The Soviet-American Case," *Social Forces,* 30:29-36 (October, 1951).

[53] William Graham Sumner, *Folkways* (Boston: Ginn and Company, 1906), p. 13.

groups seek, and the manner in which they seek them are all functions of the society and vary accordingly.[54]

Within the same society, conflict may vary according to such factors as frustration and insecurity. Frustration arises when the individual is blocked in his attempt to reach a goal. The goal may be the satisfaction of a biological drive such as hunger and sex, or a socially-induced goal such as the desire for money, power, prestige, or social status.[55] In a society where large numbers of people are unable to reach the goals held out to them, there is potential conflict. This conflict may be primarily within the individual or it may be between the individual and other persons. When people are unable to achieve their life goals, they often become hopeless, discouraged, and demoralized. The conflict here is primarily within their own personality.[56]

Conflict is not always dysfunctional for a given society.[57] Under some conditions, conflict may even increase the cohesion of the society in certain respects. In time of war, for example, the suicide rate declines. This relationship was stated long ago by Durkheim. "Great social disturbances and great popular wars," he said, "rouse collective sentiments, stimulate partisan spirit and patriotism, political and national faith . . . and . . . at least temporarily cause a stronger integration of society." [58] Obviously, this decline in the suicide rate does not compensate for the other losses suffered by a nation at war. The point is that group solidarity is increased when the group is threatened with conflict from *without*.[59]

Accommodation as a Social Process

Conflict is seldom continuous. Competition is a steady contest for similar goals, but conflict typically takes place by fits and starts. Conflicts between enemies do not occur continuously; industrial struggles have long periods of comparative quiet;[60] and wars are always followed by intervals of peace. These periods of armed neutrality, uneasy peace, or cold war are known as accommodation. Park and Burgess state this relationship as follows: "Accommodation is the natural issue of conflicts. In an accommodation, the antagonism of the hostile elements is, for the time being, regulated, and conflict disappears as overt action, although it remains latent as a potential force." [61]

---

[54] Robin M. Williams, Jr., *The Reduction of Intergroup Tensions* (New York: Social Science Research Council, 1947), p. 51.

[55] John Dollard, *et al., Frustration and Aggression* (New Haven: Yale University Press, 1939).

[56] Dorothy L. Meier and Wendell Bell, "*Anomie* and Differential Access to the Achievement of Life Goals," *American Sociological Review,* 24:189-202 (April, 1959).

[57] For an excellent discussion of this problem, see Lewis A. Coser, *The Functions of Social Conflict* (Glencoe, Ill.: The Free Press, 1956).

[58] Emile Durkheim, *Suicide* (translated by John A. Spaulding and George Simpson) (Glencoe, Ill.: The Free Press, 1951), p. 208.

[59] William R. Catton, Jr., "The Functions and Dysfunctions of Ethnocentrism: A Theory," *Social Problems,* 8:201-211 (Winter, 1960-1961).

[60] Clark Kerr, "Industrial Conflict and Its Mediation," *American Journal of Sociology,* 60:230-245 (November, 1954).

[61] Park and Burgess, *op. cit.,* p. 665.

Accommodation is an equilibrium of conflicting forces that may break out again into open violence. The tensions and hostilities that gave rise to the original conflict have not disappeared. They have merely been momentarily held in check by factors ranging from sheer exhaustion to elaborate systems of social organization. The traditional system of race relationships in the South is a form of accommodation. One race was to be in permanent dominance over the other. This dominance has been enforced by custom and (until recently) by law. This system was, in part at least, the result of the racial conflict of the reconstruction period that followed the freeing of the slaves.

This situation has been characterized as one of "subordination and super-ordination," meaning that one group remains more or less permanently in a position of superiority. This relationship is a reciprocal one. The subordinate group has both rights and duties in relation to the superordinate group, and vice versa. The slave influences the master as much as the master influences the slave. Both groups operate within a complex social system, made up of mutual expectations and obligations. Accommodation gives rise to and maintains the system of subordination and superordination.[62]

The whites in the South receive definite "gains" from the system, such as preference in jobs, higher social status, and the sexual exploitation of Negro women.[63] The whites are concerned with the attitudes of the Negroes and are anxious that the latter continue to accept their subordinate position with a minimum of organized resentment. One of the ways in which the whites have attempted to maintain this relationship is through what has been called "accommodating leadership." This phrase refers to Negro leaders who accept the caste system and persuade their people to do likewise. These leaders must have prestige among their own people, for otherwise they would be of no value in maintaining the accommodation.[64] In recent years, such leaders have become fewer and fewer.

Accommodation under other conditions may involve compromise, as the former opponents agree to sacrifice something in their common desire to gain a workable arrangement. Labor conflict often produces this form of accommodation, when workers and management eventually end a strike and attempt to work out a compromise by mutual concession. Neither side is able to gain fully the ends for which they were fighting, but at the same time each side gains something. The increased bargaining power of organized labor in recent decades has resulted in greater equality in labor struggles and a corresponding increase in accommodation.

The modern democratic state is a triumph of accommodation in internal relationships. The machinery of government provides peaceful solutions to individual differences that in an earlier day were the subject of conflict. The law is a medium for the peaceful settlement of differences that otherwise might be

---

[62] *Ibid.*, pp. 695-697.

[63] John Dollard, *Caste and Class in a Southern Town* (New Haven: Yale University Press, 1937).

[64] Gunnar Myrdal, *An American Dilemma*, Volume II (New York: Harper & Row, 1944), Chapter 34, "Accommodating Leadership."

settled by force. The democratic election is an accommodative device where, as Park and Burgess suggest, we "count noses when we do not break heads." [65] In all of these situations, hostilities remain, but the opposing groups have learned to live together in a mutually acceptable framework.

Accommodation is important in reducing the hostility among racial and religious groups. Responsible members of both minority and majority groups are aware of this latent hostility, and they devote much time and energy to the development of accommodative machinery. Accommodation in this difficult and explosive field is fostered by a variety of devices, among them: information, education, propaganda, legal pressure, public commendation, and research into the causes of intergroup hostility and the ways of mitigating it. There are literally hundreds of such organizations, local and national, that in one way or another are concerned with accommodation.

Assimilation as a Social Process

The classic definition of assimilation, like that of many of the other social processes, is given by Park and Burgess: ". . . a process of interpenetration and fusion in which persons and groups acquire the memories, sentiments, and attitudes of other persons or groups, and, by sharing their experience and history, are incorporated with them in a common cultural life." [66] Assimilation is a gradual process by which the individual comes to share the expectations of another group and slowly acquires a new set of definitions. This process of taking the life of another group into account cannot occur overnight.

---

[65] Park and Burgess, *op. cit.*, p. 575.
[66] *Ibid.*, *op. cit.*, p. 735.

Assimilation is a process whereby members of different cultures learn the patterns of a common culture; here a Dutch and an American boy exchange experiences.

The United States has been the scene of the most extensive assimilation in modern history. Millions of immigrants have come to this country and have gradually become identified with its values and expectations. Assimilation is virtually synonymous with Americanization; the way of life has been incorporated into the personalities of millions of new citizens. This identification, however, should not obscure the fact that assimilation is common to *all* societies where two or more cultures come together.[67]

The ability to communicate is the most important single requisite for successful assimilation. Communication is essential to all social interaction, but the form of communication varies between competition and assimilation. Many persons compete with each other who have never been in direct communication. Intimate social contact, however, is necessary for assimilation. A common language is the basis of this process, since language allows the stranger to participate symbolically in the life of the group and thus to acquire the meanings and goals basic to social existence. The first step in assimilation into a new society, therefore, is to learn the language.

Assimilation occurs more readily when the contacts are intimate, personal, and face-to-face. It functions more slowly when interaction is impersonal, casual, and indirect. Immigrant groups that are disdained by the larger society become assimilated only with painful slowness. Many early immigrant groups were able to participate in the other social processes, but not readily in assimilation. They got jobs, earned a living, competed with their fellows, and occasionally engaged in industrial conflict (strikes). But through no fault of their own, they were segregated in the large industrial cities and were long unable to experience the intimate relationships that alone can produce assimilation.[68]

There is no short cut to assimilation. In a literal sense, it is a part of life itself, as the individual slowly learns to participate in the expectations and experiences of another group. It can be hastened by learning the language, getting a job, reading the newspapers, joining a union, affiliating with a church, and going to school. But all these things take time. The person who has spent his formative years in one society has acquired the basic values of that society in a thousand subtle respects of which he himself is hardly aware. When he tries to become a member of another society, the adjustment is difficult. The longer he has lived in the society of his birth, the harder the assimilation. Complete adjustment to the new society is impossible to the adult because the patterns of the old are such an integral part of his personality. He has been "uprooted" from his traditional environment and finds the going hard in a new one.[69]

Social interaction is the central fact of society. It is a reciprocal process, whereby each individual takes into account the behavior and intentions of the other and is treated similarly in return; it is also a symbolic process that de-

---

[67] Clarence Glick, "The Relation Between Position and Status in the Assimilation of Chinese in Hawaii," *American Journal of Sociology*, 47:667-679 (March, 1942).

[68] Otis D. Duncan and Stanley Lieberson, "Ethnic Segregation and Assimilation," *American Journal of Sociology*, 64:364-374 (January, 1959).

[69] Oscar Handlin, *The Uprooted* (Boston: Little, Brown and Company, 1951).

pends upon language and other symbols. Among the principal forms of social interaction are competition, cooperation, conflict, accommodation, and assimilation. Although we have analyzed these forms separately, they seldom occur in such a clearly defined way. All the forms of interaction are operating in every functioning society, as individuals and groups take each other into account in different ways. Each society stresses certain forms and minimizes others, but all organized human groups exhibit these and other forms of social interaction.

SELECTED BIBLIOGRAPHY

Bales, Robert F., *Interaction Process Analysis*. Cambridge: Addison-Wesley Press, Inc., 1950. This monograph is an ingenious attempt to apply mathematical techniques to the study of interaction and, as such, is an important pioneer work in a rapidly emerging field.

Blumer, Herbert, "Psychological Import of the Human Group," in Muzafer Sherif and M. O. Wilson (eds.), *Group Relations at the Crossroads*. New York: Harper & Brothers, 1953, Chapter 8. The social-psychological implications of interaction are explored in this insightful essay, whose central theme is that interacting persons "take the other into account" and react accordingly.

———, "Society as Symbolic Interaction," Chapter 9 in Arnold M. Rose (ed.), *Human Behavior and Social Processes*. Boston: Houghton Mifflin Company, 1962. This essay further explores the interactionist theory of society, as viewed by one of its leading proponents. Human society is seen as acting (or interacting) people and social life as comprising their actions.

Goslin, David A., "Accuracy of Self Perception and Social Acceptance," *Sociometry*, 25:283-296 (September, 1962). This article makes a real contribution both to the theory of social interaction and the nature of the social self. The author states that "A set of mutual expectations about the way the social system is organized and the way the other individuals involved are going to behave forms the basis for effective social interaction . . ."

Homans, George C., *Social Behavior: Its Elementary Forms*. New York: Harcourt, Brace & World, Inc., 1961. A leading social theorist gets down to fundamentals in this discussion of social interaction, in which he reduces this basic human process to its most elemental forms.

Huntington, Robert M., "The Personality-Interaction Approach to Study of the Marital Relationship," *Marriage and Family Living*, 20:43-46 (February, 1958). This interesting article briefly explores the material set forth in a longer study — namely, the role of social interaction in the husband-wife relationship. Interaction is said to occur between two persons when each acts with reference to the other.

May, Mark A., and Leonard W. Doob, *Competition and Cooperation*. New York: Social Science Research Council, 1937. This monograph examines the literature on a number of primitive societies and offers a series of general propositions concerning the motivation, incidence, and effects of competition and cooperation. Some societies are characterized by an emphasis upon one process, other societies stress the other.

Oliver, Douglas, "An Ethnographer's Method for Formulating Descriptions of 'Social Structure'," *American Anthropologist*, 60:801-826 (October, 1958). In this important article, a leading ethnographer offers a theoretical analysis of social structure based upon social interaction. Starting from this basic fact, the author establishes a series of related concepts whereby the structure of any society, primitive or advanced, may be analyzed.

Park, Robert E., and Ernest W. Burgess, *Introduction to the Science of Sociology*. Chicago: University of Chicago Press, 1924. This book contains the classic analysis of social interaction in American sociological literature. As such, it has served as the conceptual basis for much of the subsequent development of the general interactional point of view.

Rose, Arnold M. (ed.), *Human Behavior and Social Processes*. Boston: Houghton Mifflin Company, 1962. This symposium is the best single source of information on the theory of symbolic interaction. The subjects treated by the various authors deal with a number of different problems, but they are held together by their common theoretical orientation. This book is indispensable to the student who seeks to understand both the rationale and the ramifications of symbolic interaction.

Simmel, Georg, *Conflict* and *The Web of Group-Affiliations*. Glencoe, Ill.: The Free Press, 1955 (translated by Kurt H. Wolff and Reinhard Bendix). This new translation of the writings of Simmel on conflict and other social processes makes available in English one of the subtlest analyses in the sociological literature.

Strauss, Anselm L., *Mirrors and Masks: The Search for Identity*. Glencoe, Ill.: The Free Press, 1959. This essay is an extremely subtle and intuitive analysis of such questions as social interaction, personal identity, and the social self. The general thesis is that each person derives his sense of identity through interaction with others and his anticipation of their judgments of himself.

3 *Group Interaction*

The Nature of the Group

Man is a group animal, and his social interaction occurs in a group setting. He comes into the world with the genetic potentialities for becoming a human being, and his personality is determined by the persons and groups with which he interacts. These potentialities would never be realized without the constant influence of social interaction. From birth to death, human behavior is modified by the most important process in human life—taking other people into account. In a very real sense, social interaction *is* human life, for it produces the very stuff of "human" qualities. Without intimate and continued interaction with others, conducted largely through groups, the biological infant would never become a human being. Interaction is indispensable to the development and preservation of those characteristics that distinguish man from the animals.[1]

A group may be defined as two or more persons who interact over an appreciable period and share a common purpose. The essence of the group is social interaction.[2] When people mutually and continuously adjust to one another in pursuit of a common goal, they constitute a group. The family, the play group, the group of adult friends, the fraternity, the factory group, the group of army buddies, the boys' gang, the bomber crew, the group assembled to solve a particular task, and many other human combinations interact over a definite time and thus constitute groups. A group, therefore, is an "interaction system." [3]

The word "system" does not imply that the group has a formal organization. It merely means that members of groups occupy different positions, each with its own rights, duties, privileges, and obligations. These positions (roles) take the form of a pattern (system) that can be systematically studied, since the various positions call forth similar behavior during the life of the group. The positions of husband and wife come readily to mind, as do the positions of leader and follower in the play group and those of two friends in the adult group.

These and other group positions have grown out of previous interaction between persons in the same relationships, and they carry with them a sense of obligation. Husband, wife, and children are all subject to the expectations connected with their positions. Some of these expectations are formally expressed in laws; others take the form of unwritten commands carrying strong moral overtones; and still others merely indicate desirable (but not necessarily obligatory) behavior.[4] We shall consider these expectations in Chapter 6. The essential point here is that prolonged interaction between persons gives rise to systems of group expectations.

Social groups have "structures," which are the forms taken by the interaction. In the family, husband and wife interact over an extended period in much the same way. In this interaction, each has his own forms (roles), which make up the group structure.[5] In much the same way, we can speak of the "structure" of the peer group of high school students, the Catholic Church, or the United States Army. The structure of these groups varies in complexity and in formality, but each structure represents ways in which the members interact over time. As stated by Oliver, "the structure of a group . . . is nothing more or less than a

---

[1] Harry Stack Sullivan, *The Interpersonal Theory of Psychiatry* (New York: W. W. Norton & Company, Inc., 1953), pp. 20-26.

[2] Ralph M. Stogdill, *Individual Behavior and Group Achievement* (New York: Oxford University Press, 1959), p. 17.

[3] *Ibid.*, p. 274. See also Michael S. Olmstead, *The Small Group* (New York: Random House, 1959), p. 21.

[4] Frederick L. Bates, "A Conceptual Analysis of Group Structure," *Social Forces*, 36:103-111 (December, 1957), p. 109.

[5] *Ibid.*, p. 104.

formulation . . . which summarizes the interaction among members of the group in terms of the dimensions of their interaction and the frequencies thereof." [6]

The tendency to interact in groups is perhaps the most important characteristic of human beings. Other animals share some of his gregarious tendencies, but man has developed his group life to a greater extent than any other species. In the broad sweep of human development, man has acted largely as a member of a group. Throughout most of his history, the principal group has been some form of the family. Church, state, school, and the rest of the groups have developed comparatively late. During most of his development, man lived with others in intimate and cooperative interaction in the family. As an isolated individual, acting by himself and with no permanent group ties, man would never have survived on earth.

The Origins of the Group

Contrary to the popular assumption, this tendency of men to come together in groups cannot be explained by an "instinct" of gregariousness or some such innate predisposition. This latter explanation has been discarded, along with the instinctive explanation of other forms of social behavior. The formation of groups seems rather to be a *learned reaction,* acquired during the early life experience of all human beings. It is not a set of specific behavior patterns transmitted in the germ plasm.[7] The group experience is universal in all societies, but this is the result of similar *experience,* not genetic inheritance. The primary group is found in all societies, a fact that constitutes the basis for the statement that human nature is the same the world over.[8]

We may examine more closely the nature of this universal human experience. Linton suggests that the tendency to form groups grows out of the early dependence of the infant upon other persons, plus his close association in a group relationship during the formative years of childhood. The infant is completely dependent upon others for food, warmth, affection, and, indeed, his very life during his early months and years. In this period, he develops a feeling of comfort and security in the presence of other persons—his parents and his brothers and sisters. This deep emotional sense of security with others, Linton believes, is the most important single factor in the tendency to form groups. No matter where they are reared, human beings have this feeling in their innermost beings. Throughout their lives, this need can be satisfied only through group participation.[9]

This early tendency is enforced during the several years when the child remains in the family group. No matter how simple the society or how generous

[6] Douglas Oliver, "An Ethnographer's Method for Formulating Descriptions of 'Social Structure,'" *American Anthropologist,* 60:801-826 (October, 1958), p. 810.

[7] Robert E. L. Faris, "Development of the Small-Group Research Movement," Chapter 7 in Muzafer Sherif and M. O. Wilson (eds.), *Group Relations at the Crossroads* (New York: Harper & Brothers, 1953), pp. 163-167.

[8] Charles Horton Cooley, *Social Organization* (New York: Charles Scribner's Sons, 1909), pp. 23-27.

[9] Ralph Linton, *The Tree of Culture* (New York: Alfred A. Knopf, Inc., 1955), p. 30.

the natural environment, the human being is not physically self-sufficient much before the age of twelve. In most societies, he remains in the family group until long after this age. In societies where there is no artificial limitation on births, children are born at intervals of from eighteen months to two years. This means that the child ordinarily lives for many years not only with his parents but also with brothers and sisters who are both older and younger than he is. This close and continuous association, Linton maintains, reinforces the feeling of infantile dependency that the individual first learns in the family group. The necessity for cooperation with and adjustment to other persons in groups is the product of these years from birth to adolescence.[10]

We may summarize our understanding of the group to this point. The group is a social unit composed of two or more people who are: (a) in interaction over a more or less continuous period; (b) mutually aware of each other as members; (c) able to communicate effectively with each other; and (d) established in a definite "interpersonal structure." In the course of its development, furthermore, the group: (a) establishes regular channels of communication; (b) works out different positions (roles) for its members; (c) agrees upon various group functions; and (d) sets certain goals for its activities. After further social interaction, as we shall see, the group evolves accepted standards of behavior (norms) for its members. These are characteristically group products. And, in evolving its own norms, the group produces something more than the sum of its individual parts. The new norms represent a "collective performance" that is, in certain respects, something new under the sun.[11]

The role of the group has long been intuitively grasped. More than half a century ago, Simmel indicated the nature of the group relationship. "As the person becomes affiliated with a social group," he said, "he surrenders himself to it." A combination of these feelings creates a group.[12] Membership in a group, furthermore, enables the individual to reach certain goals that he could not reach alone. This situation is evident in the case of marriage, but it is also true in the fulfillment of every other human desire. The mere fact of group membership, finally, seems to satisfy a strong need in most persons, no matter what the nature of the group. The proliferation of groups of all sizes and functions in the modern world indicates the human desire for group participation. From the family to the national state, man is a group animal.

The Study of the Group

The study of the group has both practical and theoretical implications. In the practical sense, we study families and bomber crews. In the theoretical sense,

---

[10] *Ibid.*

[11] The above is adapted from Donald W. Olmstead, "A Developmental Model of the Social Group," *The Sociological Quarterly*, 3:195-207 (July, 1962).

[12] Georg Simmel, *Conflict* and *The Web of Group-Affiliations* (translated by Kurt H. Wolff and Reinhard Bendix) (Glencoe, Ill.: The Free Press, 1955), p. 141.

A small group of old friends meets around the stove in a Vermont country store.

these studies lead to a greater understanding of social interaction. In the latter context, "The study of small groups is . . . a method for the study of social systems, of culture, and of personality. . . ." [13] A growing number of courses are being introduced at the college and university levels dealing with group interaction or, as it is sometimes called, group dynamics.[14] This study allows the social scientist to examine social systems in miniature and under controlled conditions, with the ultimate purpose of finding out more about social interaction.[15]

The study of the group likewise has significant implications for the broader social climate in which we live. There is an increasing emphasis upon social adjustment, the desire to be liked, and the importance of "teamwork" in contemporary society. The person who is successful in getting along with others has a skill that is valuable in selling, advertising, and management. Many studies of group interaction are concerned, directly or indirectly, with the nature of this ability and, by implication, with increasing it. There is some difference of

[13] A. Paul Hare, Edgar F. Borgatta, and Robert F. Bales, *Small Groups: Studies in Social Interaction* (New York: Alfred A. Knopf, Inc., 1955), p. v.

[14] Herbert Bonner, *Group Dynamics* (New York: The Ronald Press Company, 1959).

[15] Fred L. Strodtbeck, "The Case for the Study of Small Groups," *American Sociological Review*, 19:651-657 (December, 1954).

opinion among sociologists as to the ultimate desirability of such concentration.[16] There is no question, however, of the "practical" importance of group relationships.[17]

The unit in most of these studies is the *small* group, comprising from two to perhaps seven persons. In this more specialized sense, the group is defined as a number of persons "in interaction with each other in a single face-to-face meeting or a series of such meetings, in which each member receives some impression or perception of each other member distinct enough so that he can . . . give some reaction to each of the others as an individual person." [18]

A variety of small groups have been investigated. Among them are: "those formed for group discussion and group therapy, for counseling, planning, training programs, and experimental teaching procedures . . . policy-forming committees, boards and panels, diagnostic councils in clinical work, problem-solving groups in experimental social psychology and sociology, teams and work groups, family and household groups, children's play groups, adolescent gangs, adult cliques, social and recreational clubs, and small associations of a great many kinds. . . ." [19] The study of such groups deals with the basic process of social interaction. With the small group as the unit of investigation, it is possible to introduce quantitative and experimental methods into the study of social interaction.[20]

Certain problems arise in connection with the study of these and other groups. These problems are especially apparent when one compares the interaction in the "laboratory" group and that in the group found in "real" life. The first is composed of persons (usually students) brought together in a laboratory for the purpose of solving a particular problem or evoking a special group climate. The second comprises families, play groups, gangs, committees, and other groups that involve more permanent positions. The roles of husband, wife, and child, for example, are a basic part of the entire structure of a society. The roles of the members of a laboratory group are ordinarily not so firmly imbedded in the social structure; their positions evolve during the life of the group and dissolve when the group is ended.[21]

Such differences between the two types of groups are very real. Interaction between members of a family has overtones that could not possibly be shared by members of a laboratory group. Nonetheless, the latter's casual and "unstructured" interaction is widely found in contemporary society. Many persons *do* interact on a casual and temporary basis that closely approximates that of

---

[16] Lewis A. Coser, "The Functions of Small-Group Research," *Social Problems*, 3:1-6 (July, 1955).

[17] Francis E. Merrill, "The Self and the Other: An Emerging Field of Social Problems," *Social Problems*, 4:200-207 (January, 1957).

[18] Robert F. Bales, *Interaction Process Analysis* (Cambridge, Mass.: Addison-Wesley Press, Inc., 1950), p. 33.

[19] *Ibid.*, p. 1.

[20] G. E. Swanson, "Some Problems of Laboratory Experiments with Small Populations," *American Sociological Review*, 16:349-358 (June, 1951).

[21] Edgar F. Borgatta and Leonard S. Cottrell, Jr., "Directions for Research in Group Behavior," *American Journal of Sociology*, 63:42-48 (July, 1957). For a more extensive study of these relationships, see Edgar F. Borgatta, "Small Group Research," *Current Sociology*, 9:173-271, London, 1960.

the laboratory group. Attempts to study the interaction between a married couple, however, have encountered many of the above difficulties and have not been notably successful.[22] Husband and wife not only interact over a long time, but they also play roles and occupy statuses that carry complex social sanctions.

The basic unit of measurement in these group studies is the *meaningful act*. This term refers to any act of communication, whether consciously enunciated or not, that can be quantitatively determined. The unit of the *verbal* act is ordinarily a subject and predicate, although single words and even grunts are included. The unit of the *nonverbal* act is the simplest meaningful element of behavior for one or more group members. A frown, shrug, laugh, nod, fidget, and yawn are meaningful acts in this sense. We are dealing here with the fundamental elements of group interaction. The very existence of the group depends upon such communication.[23] Without it the group could not function.

"The whole group," suggests Stephan, ". . . is composed of individual systems in an active state, coupled to each other by the verbal and nonverbal communication processes." [24] Communication in this sense is the process of representing the essential elements in the mind of one group member to the mind of another. Each is aware that he is sharing something with the other. Group interaction is made up of meaningful gestures that the members direct at one another. In the scientific study of this interaction, the observer perceives and records "the sequences of surges of externally active communication between individual systems." [25] The observer can often, although not always, infer meaning from the external gestures of communication.

Groups interact on the basis of *symbolic meanings*. Human beings communicate by signs and sounds, the meanings of which are mutually agreed upon by the group members. A symbol, it will be remembered, is an entity standing for something else. This entity may be a physical object or a combination of verbal sounds. Much of the social, as distinguished from the animal, behavior of human beings depends upon the ability to communicate through symbols. Speech is the most complete form of symbolic behavior. Written language was a tremendous historical step in the development of social interaction, for it meant that man could preserve his ideas for the future, as well as communicate at a distance in his own time.[26]

Human beings employ symbols that they have learned as members of groups. Their communication is based upon symbolic understanding. A symbol thus represents a *shared* meaning among members of a group, whether family, clan, tribe, or nation. This shared meaning is the basis for common action, whereby the group acts in a more or less intelligible fashion. Symbolic communication is

---

[22] William F. Kenkel and Dean K. Hoffman, "Real and Conceived Roles in Family Decision Making," *Marriage and Family Living*, 18:311-316 (November, 1956).

[23] Robert F. Bales, *et al.*, "Channels of Communication in Small Groups," *American Sociological Review* 16:461-468 (August, 1951).

[24] Frederick F. Stephan, "The Relative Rate of Communication Between Members of Small Groups," *American Sociological Review*, 17:482-486 (August, 1952), p. 486.

[25] *Ibid.*

[26] Leslie A. White, "Culturological vs. Psychological Interpretations of Human Behavior," *American Sociological Review*, 12:686-698 (December, 1947).

the basis for social interaction, which is the central fact of society. Without a set of meaningful symbols, the group would cease to exist, for the members would be unable to act in common.[27]

The Formation of the Group

We have considered some of the characteristics of the group as a social entity. We shall next turn our attention to the *dynamics* of the group, by which we mean the forces that build up and break down this basic unit. Group dynamics deals with such factors as the formation of the group, the role of communication in group unity, the cohesiveness of the group, the deviations from it, and finally its disorganization. We shall see the group in dynamic terms, as a structure that is constantly coming together, maintaining an unstable equilibrium, and breaking down.

Some groups are more dynamic than others. Many groups formed in the laboratory are limited in life span by the time it takes to solve a problem or reach agreement on a single issue. Others are formed under different conditions. A conjugal family group is united by marriage and its life is based upon continuous participation in this relationship. Death, desertion, and divorce are the principal factors that disrupt this most intimate of small groups. During the lifetime of the marriage group, its functional (as distinguished from its legal) existence depends upon the interaction of husband and wife.

The group comes together because it satisfies (or appears to satisfy) some need or needs of its members. This need may be the comparatively uncomplicated one of simple sociability or the infinitely complex ones related to marriage. These motivations, furthermore, may or may not be completely conscious. The individual is often unaware that he has needs and, if so, what they are. The man who wishes to marry a certain girl may think that he is attracted solely by her beauty and vivacity. His unconscious needs for this person may be both more complicated and more exacting. He may, in fact, marry in order to satisfy a strong unconscious need to be mothered, admired, or dominated. The girl, in her turn, may have an equally strong need to mother, admire, or dominate someone. In this sense, their needs are complementary. Each gives the other what he or she wants and at the same time satisfies a need of his own.[28]

As we have indicated, the need to come together in groups is found in all societies, by virtue of the common experience of all men. The need for such interaction is not, however, completely uniform among all individuals, even those living in the same society. Some people are more "gregarious" than others. This difference reflects a different biological heritage and hence is an element of individual temperament. It also reflects a different social experience.

---

[27] Anselm L. Strauss, "Concepts, Communication, and Groups," Chapter 4 in Sherif and Wilson, *op. cit.,* pp. 110-113. See also Arnold M. Rose, "A Systematic Summary of Symbolic Interaction Theory," Chapter 1 in Arnold M. Rose (ed.), *Human Behavior and Social Processes* (Boston: Houghton Mifflin Company, 1962).

[28] Robert F. Winch, *Mate-Selection: A Study of Complementary Needs* (New York: Harper & Brothers, 1958).

Children who grow up in families with a high degree of "sociability" seem to have a similarly high degree of and need for sociability themselves.

In a study of rural families, it was found that "the social participation of individuals is closely associated with the participation of other members of the family and that participation is to a considerable degree a family characteristic." [29] Participation here refers to membership in, and active identification with, local organizations. In another study, a clear relationship was apparent between the group behavior of parents and children. In general, children were more cooperative if their parents understood them, liked them, maintained happy relations with them, and were confident in their treatment of them. [30]

The formation of the group has been analyzed in more general terms. The need for participation has been considered in relation to the following motivations for joining groups: (a) *Personal attraction.* Individuals join with others to form groups because they like the others and want to be with them. (b) *Group prestige.* Individuals join groups because it is an honor to belong to them and their personal status is enhanced by this participation. (c) *Task performance.* Individuals join groups because they wish to perform a task that is facilitated by group membership. They are consciously or unconsciously aware that they cannot solve a problem or reach a goal without the aid of other persons engaging in the common activity. [31]

These reasons for group participation are clearly interrelated. In many cases, they overlap. A student will join a fraternity because he likes the members and because he gains prestige. A man and a woman will marry because of romantic love and other emotional needs, plus a desire to perform such basic life-tasks as establishing a home and founding a family. Businessmen will form a partnership or a corporation to carry out certain goals involving both financial and prestige factors. The motivation for any human behavior is seldom simple. The motivation for participation in group interaction is no exception.

The Role of Communication

We have considered some of the factors that bring individuals together to form groups. The central factor keeping the group together after it is formed is communication. We have already discussed some of the general implications of communication, especially its symbolic quality. The present discussion deals with the *process* of communication, whereby meaningful gestures are exchanged between two or more persons in the setting of the group. The efficiency of the group depends upon the efficiency of communication.

In the experimental study of the group, each member is observed as an agent of communication. This means that he is an originator of sentences, words,

---

[29] W. A. Anderson, "The Family and Individual Social Participation," *American Sociological Review,* 8:420-424 (August, 1943), p. 424.

[30] C. T. Meyer, "The Assertive Behavior of Children as Related to Parent Behavior," *Journal of Home Economics,* 39:77-80 (1947), cited by Faris, *op. cit.,* pp. 166-167.

[31] Kurt W. Back, "Influence Through Social Communication," *Journal of Abnormal and Social Psychology,* 46:9-23 (January, 1951).

laughs, nods, interjections, admonitions, yawns, grunts, and other meaningful gestures. These gestures may be directed at other individuals or the group as a whole, but the first fact of interest is the comparative frequency with which each member makes them. Some members are more active than others, but the most active communicators may or may not be the leaders of the group. The most active originators *are* also the most active receivers. In the setting of the small group, social interaction is clearly seen as the process whereby two or more persons exchange meaningful acts.[32]

In an interesting essay, Homans explored the broader implications of this exchange principle, showing that social interactions may be viewed as "an exchange of goods, material goods but also non-material ones, such as the symbols of approval or prestige." [33] In this process, people who give much to others get much in return, and those who receive much from others are under a strong obligation to give equally. In this way, a rough equilibrium is worked out in the personal interaction of each individual, as the "cost and value of what he gives and of what he gets vary with the quantity of what he gives and gets." [34] Men and women who give much of themselves through love, cooperation, and friendship therefore receive more of these intangible but priceless commodities than persons who are more selfish and less prodigal of themselves. This principle is close to the Biblical admonition to cast one's bread upon the waters.

Group communication has also been explored in a study of adolescents in a New Jersey high school. The *level* of communication was defined in terms of the number of times the individual mentions, or is mentioned by, his friends in the group. The high communicator was the one mentioned most frequently by his friends and who likewise mentioned them. The low communicator had the opposite characteristics. Boys and girls who measured high were most apt to belong to clubs and student organizations and were the most popular members. The high communicators thus participated most completely in the world of the adolescent peer group. This world is characterized in terms of "the irresponsible desire to 'have a good time,' with the accent on humor, comedy, fads and crazes, popular music and 'teen-age stuff'; in terms of social activities in company with the opposite sex; in athletic prowess for boys and glamor for girls; and in the stereotype of the all-around 'swell guy'. . . ." [35]

The high communicators in the adolescent world are therefore the extroverts, the conformists, and the conventionally-minded boys and girls who enter whole-heartedly into the group activities. The high communicators are perfectly satisfied with their role in the group and the other members are equally satisfied with them. When asked to imagine an "ideal" social condition, the high communicators can think of no more satisfactory one than to be surrounded by

[32] Bales, *et al.*, "Channels of Communication in Small Groups," *op. cit.*

[33] George C. Homans, "Social Behavior as Exchange," *American Journal of Sociology*, 63:597-606 (May, 1958), p. 606.

[34] *Ibid.* See also George C. Homans, *Social Behavior: Its Elementary Forms* (New York: Harcourt, Brace & World, Inc., 1961).

[35] Matilda W. Riley and Samuel H. Flowerman, "Group Relations as a Variable in Communications Research," *American Sociological Review*, 16:174-180 (April, 1951), p. 175.

their present companions.[36] These young people cheerfully accept the "cult of mediocrity," want to be like everyone else, and have no desire to stand out from the group. They are the persons whom Riesman has called "other-directed," in the sense that their supreme ambition is to get along with the group and be "directed" by it. This goal is comparatively easy to attain, and most other-directed persons derive great emotional satisfaction from membership in and communication with the group.[37]

The low communicators present a very different picture. They comprise the isolated adolescents, who keep to themselves and rarely communicate. They are the ones who are shy, reclusive, withdrawn, and insecure. In addition to these deviants, however, the low communicators may also include some of the group leaders, boys and girls who are looked up to by their peers but who keep somewhat aloof from them. The low communicators also include some who are more adult than their fellows, who find adolescent group values childish, and who have no desire to conform to them. Many of the latter disdain to interact with their age group and prefer to be with persons older and more experienced than themselves. The degree of communication, therefore, does not necessarily mean leadership. The high communicator is often the mediocre, run-of-the-mill follower, not the leader and innovator.[38]

Communication has hitherto been viewed in terms of the *number* of meaningful acts directed by or to the various group members. We may next consider the *direction* of the communication—that is, to whom the meaningful acts are addressed in group interaction. When communication is examined in this context, in studies of small groups, certain relationships emerge: (a) The leader addresses more of his acts to the group as a whole than to specific members. (b) Persons of lower rank direct more of their meaningful acts to specific persons, notably the leader. (c) The leader receives more from the members than he gives to them *as individuals*, since his acts are more frequently addressed to the group than to its constituent members. The leader acts as a center for communications and a source of decisions. He receives the meaningful acts of the members, considers and synthesizes them, and comes forth with decisions. Significantly, the leader directs these decisions at the group.[39]

As the group continues to act over a period of time, communication ordinarily, although not always, becomes easier. Certain common developments make it easier for the members to share their reactions, such as: (a) the growth of a common language, or at least a common use of certain words and expressions; (b) the evolution of a common set of agreements on recurring situations, so that each meeting can build upon the previous ones; (c) the development of common physical arrangements, so that the same persons sit in the same places each time; (d) the organization of specialized facilities for gathering the facts and assessing the work accomplished; and (e) the emergence of specialized

---

[36] *Ibid.*, p. 176.

[37] David Riesman, *et al.*, *The Lonely Crowd* (New Haven: Yale University Press, 1961).

[38] Riley and Flowerman, *op. cit.*, pp. 176-177.

[39] Robert F. Bales and Fred L. Strodtbeck, "Phases in Group Problem Solving," *Journal of Abnormal and Social Psychology*, 46:485-495 (October, 1951).

roles, with one member acting as secretary, another gathering information, and another as leader.[40]

The evolutionary interaction within a continuing group produces a set of common experiences unique to the group. No other person or combination of persons has had precisely the same experience. Only the members of this particular group have the same common memories. These may include successes, misfortunes, jokes, and incidents during the life of the group. The members share the larger culture of the society, but they also share a subculture unique to the group. We shall see later how the pattern of memories constituting a culture is handed down from one person to another through the learning process. In the study of the small group, we can observe this process on a smaller scale.[41]

Communication does not always increase in efficiency with the life of the group. Some groups actually *decrease* in efficiency as they continue to function. Certain members are motivated by insecurity, anxiety, and jealousy, and they direct these emotions against the others. Other members may withdraw from the group and erect effective barriers to further communication. Still others become actively aggressive toward their colleagues, and communication becomes distorted. Behavior of this kind interferes with group functioning. The members are still communicating, but they are working at cross purposes.[42]

The group is, finally, a "communications network" in the process of mass communication. This means that the members of small groups receive the message from one of their fellows who has himself been influenced by the radio, television, or newspaper. He then passes the information on to them and they react accordingly. Social interaction between many persons and the mass media thus takes place at one step removed, as it were. In this indirect way, attitudes are formed, opinions are worked out, and people make up their minds about questions ranging from politics to movie-going and from fashion to international affairs.[43]

The Cohesiveness of the Group

Group cohesiveness is a function of the efficiency of communication. Cohesiveness may be defined as the "forces which are acting on the members to stay in a group . . . the attraction of membership in a group for its members." [44] Groups are effective only as long as they function as such. When they disintegrate because of lack of cohesiveness, they naturally cease to perform their functions. A family group, a high school clique, and a delinquent gang are important only as long as they continue to act toward their respective goals. Society con-

[40] Bales, *Interaction Process Analysis, op. cit.*, p. 138.

[41] George A. Theodorson, "Elements in the Progressive Development of Small Groups," *Social Forces*, 31:311-320 (May, 1953).

[42] Christoph Heinicke and Robert F. Bales, "Developmental Trends in the Structure of Small Groups," *Sociometry*, 16:7-38 (February, 1953).

[43] Elihu Katz and Paul F. Lazarsfeld, *Personal Influence: The Part Played by People in the Flow of Mass Communications* (Glencoe, Ill.: The Free Press, 1955), pp. 44-45.

[44] Back, *op. cit.*, p. 9. See also Peter M. Blau, "Structural Effects," *American Sociological Review*, 25:178-193 (April, 1960), pp. 185-188.

tinues to exist by the interaction of persons acting as members of groups. It is important to understand the factors that keep these groups together.[45]

In a study of adolescent cliques in a midwestern high school, Hollingshead investigated some of the factors that bring boys and girls together and keep them there. "The impact of clique controls on the adolescent," he says, "produces a sense of his personal importance in his relations with other members, as well as with persons outside the clique, for the clique has a powerful emotional influence on him which he tends to carry over into outside social relations, using it to bolster his own conception of himself." [46]

The cohesiveness of the clique depends upon the extent to which it satisfies the adolescent need to be favorably regarded by others, notably those of his own age. The adolescent in American society is especially in need of such emotional assurance, for his position in the society is ambiguous. In some ways he is an adult, in other ways a child.[47] Status derived from membership in a clique is highly valued, and the adolescent does his best to continue as a member in good standing.[48]

Cohesiveness is related to the reasons people enter groups and the extent to which this relationship lives up to their expectations. We have indicated that people enter groups for three general reasons or combinations of reasons— namely, personal attraction, group prestige, and task performance. As each of these factors increases, the cohesiveness of the group increases correspondingly. The striving for cohesiveness takes a different form, however, with different types of groups. If an individual enters a group primarily because of friendship, he will try to be as pleasant as possible to the members. If he is attracted to a group because of its prestige, he will carefully watch his behavior lest he do something that will deprive him of this benefit. If he is interested in a certain goal that can be reached only by group membership, he will carry out his tasks as efficiently as possible, with less concern for his personal relationships with other members.[49]

The degree of cohesiveness also makes for differences in group behavior. Strongly cohesive groups do not act the same as those that are not. In groups with high cohesiveness, members work harder to reach an agreement than in those with low cohesiveness. Highly cohesive groups make a greater effort to understand their members than do groups of low cohesiveness. The attitudes of other members are important in cohesive groups, whereas in noncohesive groups this factor does not greatly matter. Each member of a noncohesive group is concerned with his own reactions, needs, and problems. He seeks to satisfy his own needs, and they are not necessarily the same as those of the group. In the cohesive group, the members care about each other and the wel-

[45] Cf. Leon Festinger, *et al., Social Pressures in Informal Groups* (New York: Harper & Brothers, 1950).
[46] August B. Hollingshead, *Elmstown's Youth* (New York: John Wiley & Sons, Inc., 1949), p. 206.
[47] Raymond G. Kuhlen, *The Psychology of Adolescent Development* (New York: Harper & Brothers, 1952), Chapter 4.
[48] Cf. James S. Coleman, *The Adolescent Society* (Glencoe, Ill.: The Free Press, 1961), Chapter 1.
[49] Back, *op. cit.,* pp. 22-23.

fare of the group. In the noncohesive group, individual and selfish needs predominate.[50]

Communication is also a factor in group cohesiveness, insofar as communication involves changing opinions and bringing members into line with the group. The degree to which these changes are possible depends in turn upon the group motivation. When motivation is high and group members believe that uniformity of opinion is vital to success, it is comparatively easy to change divergent opinions. The opinions of the members are important to each other, especially as they pertain to the central purposes of the group. In highly cohesive groups, the members direct a large number of meaningful acts at the dissenter in an effort to bring him back to the group. In this way, the group strives toward uniformity through communication.[51]

Group cohesiveness has important implications for groups ranging in function from hospital units and submarine crews to the conjugal family. The reasons for forming the latter group are complex and may include personal attraction, prestige, and task performance at the same time. In prestige terms, many persons marry: (a) because of the greater prestige of marriage over the single state; (b) because of the prestige of marrying a particularly attractive or wealthy spouse; (c) because of social status, family background, or similar considerations. Persons who marry for prestige reasons may preserve their marriage by acting cautiously, retaining their status, and observing the proprieties, rather than by entering fully into marital interaction. Marriage in our society is a highly *personal* relationship, however, that implies complete and wholehearted participation by both parties.[52]

Group cohesiveness has other implications for the family. Society has insisted upon the permanence of the marital union until broken by death. The traditional definition of the efficiency of the marital group, therefore, has been largely based upon its permanence. Marriages considered successful have, in the past, been those that stayed together, no matter what the sentiments of the spouses or the nature of the interaction. The criteria of success at the present time, however, are not so simple. Marriage is supposed, among other things, to increase the happiness of the participants. When this happiness is not forthcoming, many persons believe that the group may be broken by divorce and a new group formed through remarriage. Cohesiveness as such, therefore, is no longer the only consideration in the success of the marital group.[53]

The Deviance from the Group

The members of the group do not always accept its standards. Members may depart from the practices that are the basis of group life. This process is known

---

[50] Heinicke and Bales, *op. cit.*

[51] Leon Festinger and John Thibaut, "Interpersonal Communications in Small Groups," *Journal of Abnormal and Social Psychology,* 46:92-99 (January, 1951).

[52] Fred L. Strodtbeck, "Husband-Wife Interaction Over Revealed Differences," *American Sociological Review,* 16:468-473 (August, 1951).

[53] William L. Kolb, "Sociologically Established Family Norms and Democratic Values," *Social Forces,* 26:451-456 (May, 1948).

as *deviance* and the individual concerned is called a *deviant*. In performing a deviant act, the actor violates the rights of another member of the group as these rights are defined by the group itself. In this sense, the basic characteristic of a deviant act is that "it is not consistent with the behavior which the victim has been led to expect from others on the basis of the social position he occupies." [54] The deviant fails to follow the rules and his action may even challenge their legitimacy. From the standpoint of the group, he is a threat to its authority.

Deviance is not something inevitably found in certain forms of behavior, but is rather a group definition of any behavior that appears to threaten its legitimacy. The group may be a play group, a criminal gang, or an entire society. The important consideration is that the group defines whether or not a given form of behavior is deviant. Deviance is a departure from *something*, and this something is the pattern of rules of the group. Deviance is, furthermore, a relative matter, and deviance from one group may be conformity to another. The member of a college fraternity who steals from his brothers is a deviant. The member of a criminal group who does *not* steal from members of the larger society is likewise a deviant. In short, "the critical variable in the study of deviance is the social *audience* rather than the individual *person*, since it is the audience which eventually decides whether or not any given action or actions will become a visible case of deviation." [55]

Deviance is related to group cohesiveness. In a sense, one is the reverse of the other. If a group is not cohesive, membership is not especially attractive and members do not care how much others deviate from the rules. In a cohesive group, the members identify with the group and are anxious for everybody else to do likewise. Hence they resent members who consistently engage in deviant acts. The cohesive group is less tolerant of those who deviate and efforts are constantly made to assure uniformity of behavior. [56] As stated in one study, "The degree of rejection is a direct function of how attractive belonging to the group is for its members and of the importance for the group of the issues on which the member does not conform." [57]

In its definition of deviance, the group follows an established sequence, whether the members are aware of it or not. *First*, the group interprets certain behavior as deviant (homosexuality, stealing). *Second*, it defines the person who engages in this behavior as deviant (homosexual, thief). *Third*, it treats the deviant in what is considered the appropriate fashion (ostracism, imprisonment). [58] There is, accordingly, a formal *confrontation* of the suspected deviant by a designated member of the community, who pronounces a *judgment* upon

---

[54] Richard A. Cloward and Lloyd E. Ohlin, *Delinquency and Opportunity* (Glencoe, Ill.: The Free Press, 1960), p. 2.

[55] Kai T. Erikson, "Notes on the Sociology of Deviance," *Social Problems*, 9:307-314 (Spring, 1962), p. 308.

[56] Stanley Schachter, "Deviation, Rejection, and Communication," *Journal of Abnormal and Social Psychology*, 46:190-270 (April, 1951).

[57] Festinger and Thibaut, *op. cit.*, p. 92.

[58] John I. Kitsuse, "Societal Reaction to Deviant Behavior: Problems of Theory and Method," *Social Problems*, 9:247-256 (Winter, 1962), p. 248.

the suspect, and consigns him to a particular *place* considered appropriate to his behavior. This process is known as assigning the deviant role, and in our society, for instance, the deviant may thus become an inmate of a mental hospital, a house of correction, or a maximum security prison. Once assigned, this deviant role is difficult to reverse. Once convicted as a felon (or a homosexual), the individual lives down his role only with the greatest difficulty.[59]

There are, of course, other and less drastic ways by which the group punishes the deviant. Among these are "expulsion or avoidance, restriction of relations to those of a less intimate character, ridicule, slight gestures of disapproval, and the imagined possibility of any of these." [60] In the Army, small groups of enlisted men place a high premium upon loyalty and conformity. The private who obviously seeks the approval of his superior officers incurs the enmity of his fellows, who feel that he is being disloyal to the group. A central function of this type of group is to maintain a united front against authority. Violation of this norm is interpreted as deviance.[61]

Deviance is usually regarded as dysfunctional to the group—that is, as interfering with its activities and perhaps threatening its very existence. Under certain conditions, however, deviance may perform functions that are important, if not vital, to successful group operation. Deviance is a "normal" aspect of group behavior and is not necessarily a sign of pathology.[62] Furthermore, the person who fails to live up to the standards of the group may in effect emphasize these standards to the other members. Deviant behavior, therefore, often "functions in enduring groups to help maintain group equilibrium."[63] In a group of boys who bowl, jump, swim, or run, there are always some who fall below group expectations. Rather than weakening the group standards, however, these deviants may strengthen the norms by making the leaders look good.

In the larger society, the individual often deviates from group norms because he is unable to reach certain culturally approved goals by legitimate means. The criminal who seeks such a goal (money) by illegitimate means (stealing) is an obvious example of the deviant in this sense.[64] The man who seeks sexual gratification with prostitutes likewise deviates from society's moral standards. In each instance, the person has rejected one of the norms of the society and to that extent threatened its stability. A society can continue only as long as most of its members follow the norms most of the time. The deviant, by definition, is in the minority.[65]

---

[59] Erikson, *op. cit.*, pp. 311-312.

[60] Faris, "Development of the Small-Group Research Movement," *op. cit.*, p. 175.

[61] Robert K. Merton and Alice S. Kitt, "Contributions to the Theory of Reference Group Behavior," in Robert K. Merton and Paul F. Lazarsfeld (eds.), *Continuities in Social Research* (Glencoe, Ill.: The Free Press, 1950), pp. 94-95.

[62] Albert K. Cohen, "The Study of Social Disorganization and Deviant Behavior," in Robert K. Merton, *et al.* (eds.), *Sociology Today* (New York: Basic Books, Inc., 1959), pp. 461-484.

[63] Robert A. Dentler and Kai T. Erikson, "The Functions of Deviance in Groups, *"Social Problems,* 7:98-107 (Fall, 1959), p. 100.

[64] Richard A. Cloward, "Illegitimate Means, Anomie, and Deviant Behavior," *American Sociological Review,* 24:164-176 (April, 1959), p. 164.

[65] Robert Dubin, "Deviant Behavior and Social Structure: Continuities in Social Theory," *American Sociological Review,* 24:147-164 (April, 1959), p. 163.

The average person thus tends to regard deviance as unfortunate, undesirable, and (often) evil. Conformity is sought at all costs. It must be remembered, however, that many of the great innovators of history were deviants, or at least nonconformists, inasmuch as they departed in substantial respects from group standards and practices. In religion, government, literature, art, and science, the man who refused to accept the prevalent beliefs often made a vital contribution, even though he sometimes paid for his pains with his life. The line between deviance and conformity is often an arbitrary one in practice. But without some such departures, by whatever name, social change would never occur. A backward society is backward precisely because of its stupefying conformity. The group is so "cohesive" and tradition-bound that new ideas rarely arise and are even more rarely put into practice.[66]

The Disorganization of the Group

Disorganization of the group means that the network of relationships joining the members together breaks down.[67] We have been primarily concerned hitherto with the forces that bring people together in groups and keep them there. Group disorganization is the reverse of this process and is characterized by a decline in the motivations that bring members together. In this process, at least three factors may be typically present: (a) The needs that the members thought would be satisfied in the group have diminished. (b) The needs are still there, but the members no longer believe that they can be satisfied in a particular group. (c) The needs continue to exist but many persons have ceased to believe that their needs can be satisfied in *any* group.

The disorganization of the group is a relative matter. In some societies, participation in a particular group may be less important than in other societies. In our own society, the original marital group is less cohesive than in many other societies. At the same time, the effective desire to participate in *some* marital group is greater in our society than in any comparable one. The proportion of persons over fifteen in this country who are married is greater than in any similar society. In addition, persons participate in play, neighborhood, political, economic, religious, and recreational groups. In a society with change as prevalent as it is, the wonder is not the disorganization but the stability of so many groups.

Experimental studies of group organization and disorganization involve, for the most part, groups formed in the laboratory and hence somewhat artificial. Social interaction among such groups differs in certain respects from groups formed "naturally" and spontaneously, such as a neighborhood gang, a group of army buddies, or a married pair. Many of these laboratory groups are easier to dissolve than those formed in answer to emotional needs. Experimental evi-

---

[66] Lewis A. Coser, "Some Functions of Deviant Behavior and Normative Flexibility," *American Journal of Sociology*, 68:172-181 (September, 1962).

[67] Mabel A. Elliott and Francis E. Merrill, *Social Disorganization* (New York: Harper & Row, 1961), Fourth Edition, Chapter 2.

dence of group *disorganization* is not so extensive as that concerning group formation, continuance, and cohesiveness.[68]

Social disorganization is group disorganization on a large scale. It is characterized by the weakening or breaking of large numbers of groups in a society. In his study of the group, Homans calls this process "social disintegration," but the two concepts are essentially similar. He defines social disintegration as a condition "marked by a decline in the number of activities in which the members of a group collaborate, by a decrease in the frequency of interaction between these members, and by a weakening of the control exercised by the group over the behavior of individuals." [69] Group functioning demands the active participation of the members. Without this participation, the group ceases to exist.

Group functioning is equally important for the welfare of its members. The individual needs the group as much as the group needs the individual. The person must remain in symbolic communication with several social groups or suffer an impaired personality. A normal personality is the product of social interaction in various groups. The family, the friendship group, the neighborhood group, and the business group all play their part in developing and maintaining personal health. Homans has stated the plight of the isolated individual as follows: "If his group is shattered around him, if he leaves a group in which he was a valued member, and if, above all, he finds no new group to which he can relate himself, he will, under stress, develop disorders of thought, feeling, and behavior." [70]

The disorganization of the group also has important implications for the larger society. The small group has always been the basic social unit, whether we are speaking of "primitive" or "civilized" societies. The most important group has been the family.[71] In addition to the family, the individual has depended upon other face-to-face groups for his social relationships. The customs, traditions, and other expectations have been those of the small group, and these standards have been the basic determinants of social existence. Contemporary society may be correspondingly weakened in the face of the declining importance of small group interaction. Continued failure to maintain the small group as a central unit may threaten the existence of the society.[72]

Social disorganization is an inescapable product of a dynamic society. Technological innovation, industrialization, and urbanization are among the forces making for social change, which brings social disorganization and social problems in its wake. As Burgess has said, "Social disorganization is always accompanied by problems of concern to the given society, to one of its constituent groups, or to the individuals immediately affected." [73] Persons who directly

---

[68] Cf. Neal Gross and William E. Martin, "On Group Cohesiveness," *American Journal of Sociology,* 57:546-564 (May, 1952).

[69] George C. Homans, *The Human Group* (New York: Harcourt, Brace and Company, 1950), p. 369.

[70] *Ibid.,* p. 457.

[71] Carle C. Zimmerman, *Family and Civilization* (New York: Harper & Brothers, 1947).

[72] Homans, *op. cit.,* Chapter 17.

[73] Ernest W. Burgess, "Social Problems and Social Processes," Chapter 20 in Arnold M. Rose (ed.), *Human Behavior and Social Processes* (Boston: Houghton Mifflin Company, 1962), p. 387.

experience the impact of social disorganization—whether as revolution, the growth of cities, or automation—are shaken and sometimes broken by the massive social forces which they can neither understand nor control. At the same time, Burgess continues, "social disorganization is a necessary prelude to social reorganization, which usually makes for the greater general welfare." [74]

[74] *Ibid.*

SELECTED BIBLIOGRAPHY

Bales, Robert F., *Interaction Process Analysis.* Cambridge: Addison-Wesley Press, Inc., 1950. The small group is here observed as a social system in action. This book is an important contribution to the theory and methodology of group study in the laboratory.

Borgatta, Edgar F., "Small Group Research," *Current Sociology,* 9:173-271, Published for UNESCO, London, 1960. This is a balanced statement of the current status of small-group research, together with an extensive annotated bibliography of the material in this expanding field.

————, and Leonard S. Cottrell, Jr., "Directions for Research in Group Behavior," *American Journal of Sociology,* 63:42-48 (July, 1957). This article examines some of the theoretical problems relating to the study of the group. Among the problems considered are the size of the group, the "laboratory" group versus the "real-life" group, and the changes that groups undergo.

Coser, Lewis A., "Some Functions of Deviant Behavior and Normative Flexibility," *American Journal of Sociology,* 68:172-181 (September, 1962). In this long and thoughtful essay, the author considers the different circumstances under which deviance is functional or dysfunctional to the group. He concludes that, on balance, the evidence is not universally on the side of conformity. Under certain conditions, indeed, deviance may be highly functional.

Erikson, Kai T., "Notes on the Sociology of Deviance," *Social Problems,* 9:307-314 (Spring, 1962). This article, like that of Coser (above), is concerned with the nature, functions, and dysfunctions of deviance as a departure from group norms. The author calls attention to the difficulty of *reversing* the deviant role (delinquent, criminal, insane person) once it has been conferred upon an individual by society.

Golembiewski, Robert T., *The Small Group.* Chicago: University of Chicago Press, 1962. This is a careful analysis of the history, methodology, and rationale of small group study. The author has been interested in the application of this form of research to relations within the business and factory organization.

Hare, A. Paul, Edgar F. Borgatta, and Robert F. Bales, *Small Groups: Studies in Social Interaction.* New York: Alfred A. Knopf, Inc., 1955. This is a collection of studies of group interaction, ranging in time from the early work of Simmel and Cooley to the later research in the laboratories of human relations. The book contains considerable connecting theory, as well as an annotated bibliography of some 584 titles in this burgeoning field.

Homans, George C., *The Human Group.* New York: Harcourt, Brace and Company, 1950. This is an outstanding contribution to the scientific study of the group. The author examines several empirical studies of the group in terms of his own framework of interaction. In this sense, the book is a model of theory and empirical analysis.

Olmstead, Donald W., "A Developmental Model of the Social Group," *The Sociological Quarterly*, 3:195-207 (July, 1962). This article is an important contribution to the theoretical analysis of the group. The author considers the group in terms of (*a*) its rudimentary attributes (e.g., "continuity of social interaction"), (*b*) its emergent attributes (e.g., "differential group functions"), and (*c*) its mature attributes (e.g., "standards for approved behavior" or norms).

Olmstead, Michael S., *The Small Group*. New York: Random House, Inc., 1959. In this volume, the author gives an extremely lucid, brief presentation of the current work in small groups. In addition to this exposition, the author makes an important contribution to the theory of small groups as forms of social interaction.

Strodtbeck, Fred L., "The Case for the Study of Small Groups," *American Sociological Review*, 19:651-657 (December, 1954). This article, whose title is self-explanatory, is the introduction to a special issue of the *Review* dealing with various aspects of the study of small groups, both in the laboratory and in the larger society.

Whyte, William F., *Street Corner Society*. Chicago: University of Chicago Press, 1955 (rev. ed.). This is perhaps the most important single study yet made of small groups in operation. The study was made in a large eastern city and it deals with several (more specifically with one) street-corner gangs in that environment. The empirical material is enriched by generalizations on the nature of social interaction in this "real-life" setting.

4 *Primary Groups*

The Nature of the Primary Group

Social interaction is the basic reality of society. A human society, indeed, "is a more or less discrete combination of interacting human . . . beings."[1] In the course of this interaction, groups are formed, each with its characteristic pattern of interaction by which the members regulate their behavior. In the preceding chapter, we analyzed the group as an interaction pattern, with particular reference to the work currently being done in the

[1] Douglas Oliver, "An Ethnographer's Method for Formulating Descriptions of 'Social Structure,'" *American Anthropologist*, 60:801-826 (October, 1958), p. 801.

laboratory on the small group. In the present chapter, we shall examine some of the forms assumed by the group in "real life"—that is, outside of the laboratory.

The primary group is the universal human relationship. In all societies, the individual comes in contact with this group earliest, and it exerts the most powerful influence over him. The nature of human life, with its long period of infantile dependence, means that the child spends his first days, weeks, months, and years in close contact with a few persons who feed him, clothe him, keep him warm, and give him some form of affection. Without a minimum of these physical and psychological ministrations, the child could not survive. He learns to associate these pleasant sensations with a few other persons in an intimate and face-to-face relationship—in short, with a primary group. It is in this sense that the primary group is universal and is a part of the social heritage of every human being. The individual does not have to be born with a rigid pattern of "gregarious" instincts to account for his tendency to enter such groups throughout his life. He could not avoid this tendency if he tried, for it is a crucial part of his learned behavior.[2]

In our society, the family, the childhood play group, the adolescent clique, the boys' gang, the group of army buddies, and the adult friendship group are examples of this primary relationship. In these and other primary groups, the interaction is marked by a spontaneity not found in more formal groups. The primary group offers a social setting in which the individual can "be himself." His fellow members are comparatively uncritical of his behavior, as long as he conforms to the standards of the group. In the long history of mankind, the primary group has been the fundamental form of social interaction.[3]

The classic analysis of the primary group was made many years ago by Charles Horton Cooley. He defined the primary group in terms of "intimate face-to-face association and cooperation" and indicated that this interaction is basic to human nature. The primary group, he continued, is the product of long and intimate interaction under informal conditions. We belong to primary groups because we happen to be born into a particular family in a particular neighborhood. We do not join them because we wish to better our economic condition or social status. The effect of social interaction on the primary group level is, in Cooley's words, "a certain fusion of individualities in a common whole, so that one's very self . . . is the common life and purpose of the group."[4]

This process of interaction gives rise to what Cooley called a "we" feeling, one that "involves the sort of sympathy and mutual identification for which 'we' is the natural expression."[5] The member is emotionally involved with the group as an entity and with the common symbols that emerge from group interaction. In the close and continuous contacts of the primary group, the infant, child, adolescent, and adult are socialized and humanized. The result of

[2] Ralph Linton, *The Tree of Culture* (New York: Alfred A. Knopf, Inc., 1955), pp. 30-31.
[3] Robert E. L. Faris, "Development of the Small-Group Research Movement," Chapter 7 in Muzafer Sherif and M. O. Wilson (eds.), *Group Relations at the Crossroads* (New York: Harper & Brothers, 1953), pp. 157-158.
[4] Charles Horton Cooley, *Social Organization* (New York: Charles Scribner's Sons, 1909), pp. 23-27.
[5] *Ibid.*

primary group interaction is a mature human being, with the attitudes, beliefs, prejudices, and values of his society. We shall examine the formation of personality in more detail in subsequent chapters. We are concerned here with indicating the central place of the primary group.

The nature of the primary group has been further explored by Ellsworth Faris. He suggested that some of the physical characteristics stressed by Cooley may be incidental, rather than central, to the primary group. Two persons in a buyer-seller relationship, for example, are face-to-face, but hardly constitute a primary group. The judge and the defendant in a courtroom are in physical proximity, but their relationship is anything but primary; whereas a family whose members are widely separated may constitute a continuing primary group through letters and common memories. Faris concludes: "The nature of the primary group . . . lies not in its parts but in its organization. It depends not upon its spatial contiguity but upon its functional interrelation. . . . The primary group cannot exist without memories; it cannot endure without purposes. . . . It is a changing organization of functional activities tending toward an end, influenced by its past and guided by its purposes and its future." [6]

The Interaction of the Primary Group

The primary group therefore owes its importance to the relationships between its members. The form of social interaction is the central consideration, rather than the number of persons in the group. Social interaction, as we have seen, is a process by which individuals "take each other into account" and act appropriately.[7] In the primary group, the members take each other into account as *individuals* with unique qualities, not as faceless units in a crowd. Each is important in and by himself, and one person cannot be substituted for another without destroying, or at least changing, the relationship. Each member of the gang, each personal friend, companion, army buddy, and, above all, each husband, wife, and child is unique and plays his own part in primary group interaction. This does not mean that each member is equally important to the group. It *does* mean that each is a separate personality in this most "human" of all relationships, and is treated as such by the others.

Social interaction depends upon communication. The character of the group similarly depends to a large extent upon the nature of the communication between the members.[8] In the primary group, this process is comparatively informal. Husband and wife communicate in many ways, from a raising of an eyebrow to an inflection of the voice. They often communicate a mood without saying a word or making a gesture. In the primary group, acts and perceptions are equally subtle. Lovers and friends take each other into account in ways not comprehended by outsiders. In the communication network of the primary

---

[6] Ellsworth Faris, "The Primary Group: Essence and Accident," *American Journal of Sociology,* 38:41-50 (July, 1932), p. 50.

[7] Herbert Blumer, "Psychological Import of the Human Group," Chapter 8 in Muzafer Sherif and M. O. Wilson (eds.), *Group Relations at the Crossroads* (New York: Harper & Brothers, 1953).

[8] Jurgen Ruesch, "Synopsis of the Theory of Human Communication," *Psychiatry,* 16:215-243 (August, 1953), p. 243.

group, each person occupies a special position. Only the initiated can grasp the subtleties of this form of interaction.

The study of the primary group has undergone a renaissance in recent years with the emphasis upon the small group. The insights of an earlier generation of social psychologists have been subjected to quantitative verification and many new insights have resulted from the experimental investigation of these miniature social systems. Many small groups, although by no means all of them, are primary in the Cooley sense. Out of these studies have come new and somewhat more sophisticated definitions of the primary group. Such a definition is offered by Shils: "By primary group, we mean a group characterized by a high degree of solidarity, informality in the code of rules which regulates the behavior of its members, and autonomy in the creation of these rules. The solidarity involves a close identification of the members with one another and with any symbols of the group which might have grown up." [9]

Members of primary groups regard each other as ends, rather than as means

---

[9] Edward A. Shils, "The Study of the Primary Group," in Daniel Lerner and Harold D. Lasswell (eds.), *The Policy Sciences* (Stanford: Stanford University Press, 1951), p. 44.

The primary group is its own reward; its major function is to provide a setting for important human activity.

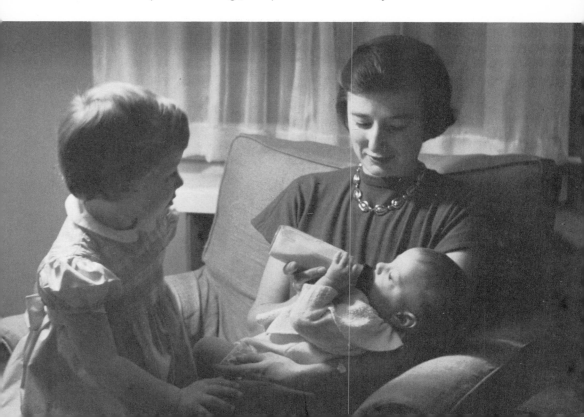

to ends. The ultimate value of a mother, father, brother, sister, husband, wife, or friend cannot be measured by any criteria other than the relationship itself. The primary group requires no other justification than its own existence.[10] Friendship is not valuable because of any concrete gift the friend can bestow, but because the relationship is itself inherently valuable. The love of husband and wife derives its value from the marital interaction itself and not from any secondary benefits. The emotional needs fulfilled by the primary group are important in themselves. They are their own justification.

It follows, therefore, that the primary group is literally its own reward. Peers, friends, lovers, and spouses ask nothing better than to bask in the warmth of their own group. It is not so much what the primary group *does*, although this is important, as what it *is*. As Robert Faris puts it, "To the contented member of the primary group the association itself is a value above the particular activities the group undertakes, and the members care less what they do or where they go than that they do it together." [11] The adolescent "adores" just "playing around" with his peers. The mature man finds deep inner satisfaction in talking quietly with his old friend. The lover approaches the heights of rapture in exchanging endearments with his beloved. And the spouse would rather be with his mate than anyone else in the world. In each of these cases, the most awful fate that could overtake the member is to be deprived of his association with the primary group.

The Social Setting of the Primary Group

The nature of group interaction determines the social setting and vice versa. Village and rural community life is marked, by and large, by primary group relationships, wherein people know each other intimately and react to each other as individuals. In the historical development of western European society, from which our own has evolved, primary group relationships predominated until recently. The same is true of the early history of the United States. The city and urban ways of life, however, are changing the traditional pattern of primary relationships. The nation is becoming an increasingly urban society, marked by urban institutions and by a corresponding decline in the relative importance of the primary group.[12]

It is impossible to establish a strict and watertight series of categories that set off one type of group from another. Human behavior does not lend itself realistically to such compartmentalization. Group relationships rather lie along a continuum, from those that predominate in isolated rural communities to those that characterize large metropolitan centers. In recent years, furthermore, the dweller in the rural community has become less "countrified" than he used

---

[10] Kingsley Davis, *Human Society* (New York: The Macmillan Company, 1949), pp. 295-296.
[11] Robert E. L. Faris, *op. cit.*, p. 175.
[12] Donald Bogue, "Urbanism in the United States, 1950," *American Journal of Sociology*, 60:471-486 (March, 1955).

to be, thanks to modern transportation and mass communication. And the city is not merely the residence of the "urban" population; it is also the center of many of the influences that characterize modern life as a whole.[13] With these reservations, we may contrast some of the *typical* characteristics of group interaction in terms of their "primary group" qualities—or lack of them.

1. *Gemeinschaft and Gesellschaft.* A basic distinction between primary and nonprimary (secondary) relationships is subsumed under the concepts of *Gemeinschaft* and *Gesellschaft.* These two terms mean, roughly, *community* and *society,* and were originally used in their sociological context by the German sociologist, Ferdinand Tönnies. In this sense, *community* refers to an aggregate of persons whose relationships are primary and among whom social control is based largely upon unwritten customs, rather than formal law. The *Gemeinschaft* relationship is typified by the ancient rural community, with its emphasis upon kinship, friendship, and familiarity. The relationships of the *Gesellschaft* are typically those of the large city, where interaction reflects the rational concerns of an impersonal society. Recent studies have indicated, however, that *Gemeinschaft* continues in the large city, especially among working-class families, and that many urban associations are not so impersonal as had previously been supposed.[14] Despite such qualifications, the distinction between the two polar forms holds true in general.[15]

2. *Sacred and secular.* Closely related to the above are the concepts of sacred and secular. "Sacred" is *not* used here in its religious sense, where it is roughly synonymous with "spiritual," "holy," or "divine." Sacred societies are, rather, those "which impress upon their members modes of conduct making for a high degree of resistance to change." Secular societies are those "in which resistance to change is at a minimum or . . . where change in many aspects of life is usually quite welcome." [16] Sacred relationships are essentially primary, and social roles are prescribed by custom and tradition. Secular roles are more open to achievement on the basis of rational considerations. In general, sacred relationships are more common in the rural community and secular relationships in the urban community. The latter is the place where the individual is more "free" to act as he chooses, rather than in accordance with traditional patterns.[17]

3. *Homogeneity and heterogeneity.* Primary relationships are, in a sense, more homogeneous (of the same kind or nature) than nonprimary relationships. The family and church occupy most of the interests of the primary community and bring the members into close and continuous interaction with these

[13] Louis Wirth, "Urbanism as a Way of Life," *American Journal of Sociology,* 44:1-24 (July, 1938).

[14] Wendell Bell and Marion D. Bost, "Urban Neighborhoods and Informal Social Relations," *American Journal of Sociology,* 62:391-398 (January, 1957).

[15] Leonard Blumberg and Robert R. Bell, "Urban Migration and Kinship Ties," *Social Problems,* 6:328-333 (Spring, 1959).

[16] Howard Becker, "Interpreting Family Life in Context," Chapter 1 in Howard Becker and Reuben Hill (eds.), *Family, Marriage, and Parenthood* (Boston: D. C. Heath and Company, 1948), pp. 19 and 34. See also Howard Becker, "Sacred and Secular Societies," *Social Forces,* 28:351-376 (May, 1950).

[17] Redfield makes a similar distinction in his analysis of "folk" and "urban" society. Robert Redfield, "The Folk Society," *American Journal of Sociology,* 52:293-308 (January, 1947).

basic institutions. In the urban setting, however, as Wirth suggests, "the individual acquires membership in widely divergent groups." [18] The primary community in this sense is similar to what Shils calls the "primordial" primary group, which is united by age-old ties of culture, religion, kinship, and "blood." [19] In the large city, on the other hand, the heterogeneity of social contacts means that the urban dweller is freer than his rural counterpart to change his employment, his residence, and his wife.

4. Complete and segmental roles. The dweller in the primary setting knows a limited number of people intimately. He interacts with his whole personality in comparatively few primary groups. In the urban setting, one interacts with a comparatively large number of persons in a partial or segmental capacity. The urban dweller knows the man from whom he buys his morning paper, but only in that specialized role. He knows (or cares) nothing about the rest of the news dealer's life. The urban resident knows many people in these segmental roles, but he rarely knows them well. Such urban contacts are indeed face-to-face but, in Wirth's words, "they are nevertheless impersonal, superficial, transitory, and segmental." [20]

5. Anonymity and familiarity. A related contrast between primary and non-primary interaction reflects the different degrees of knowledge we have about other persons. In the nonprimary setting of the large city, each person is known to comparatively few others, especially when away from his family. Much of the rest of his time is spent as an anonymous individual. Hence such symbolic factors as clothes and other material possessions (cars) are important as guides for others to place him and react accordingly. In the primary setting of the small town, these symbols are not so important, for each person's status is known by such criteria as family, work, and home.[21]

We find, therefore, two broadly different types of group relationship—the primary and the nonprimary. The first is considered in this chapter and the second in the following chapter. These two types of relationship are distinguished by the ties that hold people together and that produce agreement on common group purposes. The primary group derives its unity from members who are basically similar in residence, class, religion, ethnic background, and aspirations. The nonprimary group draws its unity from the rational self-interests of people of different backgrounds, who act cooperatively for the realization of their purposes. A group of lifelong friends illustrates the first type, a Rotary Club the second.[22]

---

[18] Louis Wirth, "Urbanism as a Way of Life," *op. cit.,* pp. 16-17.

[19] Edward A. Shils, "Primordial, Personal, Sacred and Civil Ties," *British Journal of Sociology,* 8:130-145 (June, 1957).

[20] Louis Wirth, "Urbanism as a Way of Life," *op. cit.,* p. 12.

[21] William H. Form and Gregory P. Stone, "Urbanism, Anonymity, and Status Symbolism," *American Journal of Sociology,* 62:504-514 (March, 1957), p. 504. See also Richard Wohl and Anselm L. Strauss, "Symbolic Representation and the Urban Milieu," *American Journal of Sociology,* 63:523-532 (March, 1958).

[22] Robert E. L. Faris, *op. cit.,* p. 156.

The Basic Functions of the Primary Group

Function means the normal and characteristic action(s) that an organism performs. The function of the primary group is, in one sense, as broad as life itself, for social interaction in this setting gives rise to human nature. In a more restricted sense, the functions of the primary group are as follows:

1. *Activity function.* The first function is to provide an organization for interesting and important human activity. In the primary group, many activities are performed because they are pleasant in themselves, and the members enjoy them for their own sake. Husbands and wives, members of cliques and peer groups, and adult friends find pleasure in the characteristic activities of their groups.

2. *Defense function.* A second function of the primary group is to provide a setting in which the person feels protected. In a society becoming increasingly impersonal, the individual needs the moral and emotional support that can be provided by the primary group alone. This need for defense against the outside world is suggested by the fact that a higher proportion of the population is married than ever before.

3. *Personality function.* A third function is to give the child a friendly place in which to develop his personality. Personality evolves in a primary-group setting, and the child learns the customs of the society in a tolerant atmosphere. The adult also requires close and continuous contact with similar groups if he is to remain socially adjusted. The primary group is the principal relationship that prepares the individual for participation in the larger society.[23]

4. *Communication function.* A fourth function is the communication function of the primary group. In the study of mass communications, it has been found that everybody does not react with equal force. Some persons are more enthusiastic television viewers, radio listeners, and newspaper readers than others. The more active ones hand on the information they have acquired to other members of the primary group. In this sense, the primary group is a "communications network," and the individual acquires many of his attitudes on public questions in this way.[24]

The primary group is important in a world that is becoming more impersonal, secular, and rational. In the rural community, the individual is protected by the family, the church, and local groups, which are essentially primary in the sense defined above. These primary ties are restrictive, although most persons are unconscious of the restriction. People live and die in the cozy atmosphere of their native village, where they are enveloped in a web of primary relationships. Throughout most of his history, man has lived in primary communities of this kind. Most of the world *still* lives under these conditions,[25] even though

---

[23] Adapted from Robert E. L. Faris, *op. cit.*, pp. 178-180.

[24] Elihu Katz and Paul F. Lazarsfeld, *Personal Influence: The Part Played by People in the Flow of Mass Communications* (Glencoe, Ill.: The Free Press, 1955).

[25] George A. Theodorson, "Acceptance of Industrialization and Its Attendant Consequences for the Social Patterns of Non-Western Societies," *American Sociological Review*, 18:477-484 (October, 1953).

the cauldron of change is bubbling. The defense function of the primary group has, therefore, been predominant in the experience of human beings until comparatively recently.

The commercial and industrial revolutions have drawn large numbers of persons away from their primary village communities and into the large and impersonal city. They have found freedom in this new environment from the secure but sometimes stultifying atmosphere of the primary community. An eminent psychiatrist has suggested, however, that men do not really *want* this freedom, at least to the extent it has been granted them. Deep in their personalities, they miss the primary group that gave them emotional security, even as it confined them and limited their horizons. In a blind and unconscious attempt to recapture this lost security, millions of men and women have sought the soothing submission of totalitarian movements. The fascist, communist, and other totalitarian groups emphasize many of the same primary qualities that modern man has lost or is fast losing. These parties are agents of the great movement of "escape from freedom." [26]

The primary group is not necessarily marked by continuous cooperation. Competition and even conflict are an important part of primary-group interaction. The family is often the scene of conflict between husband and wife, parent and child, brother and sister. Children in the neighborhood play group may be jealous of each other and strive bitterly for prestige. Daily contacts in the adult group may involve intense animosities, rendered more acrimonious by the fact that the members see each other every day. In spite of latent hostilities, however, the primary group presents a united front against outsiders. The bickering family, the discordant gang, and the gossiping neighborhood group will close ranks against hostile action from the outside.

Primary-Group Forms and Functions

Form and function are closely related. The form a group takes is determined by the functions it performs. We shall illustrate the relationship of form and function in certain typical primary groups, among them the group of army buddies, the peer group, the clique, and the gang.

1. The army group. The defense function of the primary group is illustrated in the army. Soldiers spontaneously form groups with their comrades. These groups provide an informal relationship in a setting that is otherwise highly formalized. The army is a large, bureaucratic organization, in which the individual is subject to arbitrary authority. In an effort to defend themselves against this authority, enlisted men turn to others of similar rank. These group ties are strong while they last, and the men read each other's mail, borrow money from each other, share parcels from home, and confide their most intimate secrets. The soldier strongly identifies himself with this group of his peers. His feeling

---

[26] Erich Fromm, *Escape from Freedom* (New York: Holt, Rinehart & Winston, 1941).

may be limited to the informal group of buddies or transferred to the formal unit of the platoon, company, regiment, or division.[27]

The primary group thus defends its members against the arbitrary authority of their officers in particular and the army in general.[28] The group also performs a central function for the army as such. The primary group sets standards of behavior for the soldier and sustains him in combat situations. In so doing, it bolsters his courage and gives him standards of bravery that he tries to uphold. He strives to achieve his combat objective so that he will not let the *group* down, rather than because of hatred for the enemy or love of his own country. The group extends its respect to the man who carries through and withholds it from the one who betrays the group by his failure. The primary group is more important to morale than the abstract symbols of the army, the state, or the political cause (democracy) for which the war is presumably being fought. The soldier pays lip service to these symbols, but his behavior is largely motivated by the immediate and tangible presence of his fellows.[29]

2. The peer group. The primary group takes other forms with other functions. Another important form is the peer group, which may be defined as "an aggregation of people of approximately the same age *who feel and act together.*" [30] In this sense, most neighborhood groups are peer groups, inasmuch as they tend to involve boys or girls of the same age and approximately the same social status. In some schools, furthermore, each class is a peer group because the members share both age and social similarities. In other schools, the class is *not* a peer group because the children come from different social levels. The peer group is not as small as typical primary groups, but it has many of their characteristics.

The central consideration in the peer group, as in any group, is *social interaction*. Peer group members interact in numerous ways. In a study of the adolescent society, a large sample of boys and girls from ten different high schools were asked the following question: "What do you and the fellows (girls) you go around with here at school have most in common—what are the things you do together?" For the boys, the following activities (in this order) were most common: participating in organized outdoor sports, dating or going to dances together, going to the movies together, "hanging around together," engaging in unorganized outdoor sports (hunting, fishing), eating lunch together, and taking part in school clubs. For the girls, the activities were very different, with organized outdoor sports naturally of less importance. The most common form of interaction among girls was dating or going to dances together, followed by going to the movies together, participating in school clubs and other school-

---

[27] Edward A. Shils, "Primary Groups in the American Army," in Robert K. Merton and Paul F. Lazarsfeld (eds.), *Continuities in Social Research* (Glencoe, Ill.: The Free Press, 1950), pp. 16-25.

[28] For a further discussion of the role of the adult peer group in this connection, see William M. Evan, "Peer-Group Interaction and Organizational Socialization: A Study of Employee Turnover," *American Sociological Review*, 28:436-440 (June, 1963).

[29] *Ibid.*

[30] Robert J. Havighurst, *Human Development and Education* (New York: Longmans, Green and Company, 1953), p. 47. (His italics.)

The peer group trains the child to get along with his fellows; members of a Little League baseball team here get together for a game.

related events, eating lunch together, having parties together, and engaging in unorganized outdoor activities.[31]

In these forms of interaction, the peer group provides the social setting for personality development. The high school, with its adolescent culture, is the forum in which boys and girls learn group behavior patterns. The boys' predominant interest is athletics, the girls' is the opposite sex. As Coleman wryly notes, "boys are interested in sports and girls are interested in boys." [32] Hence the principal (although not the only) road to social success for boys is interscholastic athletics, which bring them prestige, and glory to the school. The principal avenue of prestige for girls is to be attractive to boys. The adolescent peer group thus places a premium upon *doing* for boys and *being* for girls.

The peer group and the adolescent culture are clearly increasing in importance in our society. These elements are, furthermore, assuming many of the functions formerly performed by the family. In contemporary urban society, the family deals with a comparatively small range of activities; especially limited are those that are interesting to the adolescent. Parents are woefully ignorant of such important matters as the latest style of dress, the current favorites among the popular songs, and the popular movie and television actresses. The adolescent naturally turns to the peer group and the mass media for instruction in these fields. The distance between generations is great in any society because of the inevitable disparity in age and role. In modern urban life, these differences are accentuated. The family loses and the peer group gains.[33]

The peer group performs such functions as the following: (*a*) It trains the child to get along with his fellows. (*b*) It develops a rational conscience and

---

[31] James S. Coleman, *The Adolescent Society* (Glencoe, Ill.: The Free Press, 1961), p. 14, Table 6.

[32] *Ibid.*, p. 13.

[33] David Riesman, *et al., The Lonely Crowd* (New Haven: Yale University Press, 1961).

(with the family) gives the child a scale of values. (*c*) It teaches the social attitudes appropriate to the age and sex status of the child. (*d*) It helps the child to attain emotional independence from his family.[34] In an earlier day, most of these functions (except the last) were performed by the family alone. Now, however, in a variety of fields, the adolescent turns more and more to the peer group instead of to the family. The peer group is not organized (except informally) to carry out these educational functions, and the implications of this shift are perplexing.[35]

3. *The clique.* The clique is another and related form of primary group. It is found among different age groups, but its functions are especially important at the high-school level. In his study of the community of Elmtown, Hollingshead offers a penetrating analysis of this group. He defines the clique as: ". . . an informal group composed of a minimum of two to about twenty persons. It tends to be age- and sex-graded within a relatively narrow range of prestige positions. . . . Cliques are the smallest organized units within a [social] class, but there are many cliques of different ages within the class."[36] In general, the clique is composed of persons from the same peer group, but it is smaller and more compact than the peer group. During his high-school years, most of the waking hours of the adolescent are spent with members of a clique. He walks to school with them, talks with them between classes, whispers to them during study hall, and goes to basketball games with them.

The clique is formed when two or more persons come together in close friendship. The relationship involves joint participation in activities and mutual acceptance. "Perhaps the most characteristic thing about the clique," continues Hollingshead, "is the way its members plan to be together, to do things together, go places together."[37] The "things" they do and the "places" they go are much the same as those indicated above for the peer group. Boys play games together, girls date and go to dances together. This element of "togetherness" within the clique means a great deal to the members, who depend upon it for friendship, confidence, and emotional support. The clique is thus a primary group in the most intimate sense, with an unspoken but firmly established set of common norms and values.

The clique is its own board of admissions, and the boy or girl is admitted or dropped by the consent of the others. To be a member of the "leading crowd" is one of the highest ambitions of the entering high-school freshman, although few ever attain this exalted status. In Coleman's study, cited previously, he asked a number of students what it took to get into the leading crowd at their school. For boys, the desirable attributes were as follows, in approximately this order. First was a good "personality," which meant the quality of being friendly and "nice" to the other kids. Then came a good "reputation," closely

---

[34] Havighurst, *op. cit.,* pp. 47-63.
[35] Coleman, *op. cit.,* p. 312.
[36] August B. Hollingshead, *Elmtown's Youth* (New York: John Wiley & Sons, Inc., 1949), p. 80, footnote.
[37] *Ibid.,* p. 205.

followed by athletic ability, good looks, good grades, good clothes, a car, money, and finally, to come from a good neighborhood. For girls, "personality" was by far the most important quality for acceptance, even more so than for boys. Next came good looks and a good "reputation" (i.e., successful with boys but not sexually permissive), followed by good clothes, being "friendly," dressing neatly, having money, getting good grades, and, bringing up the rear again, coming from the right neighborhood.[38]

The clique performs an important emotional function. During his high-school years, the adolescent has a strong need to be loved and respected by his peers. The clique satisfies this need. Even if the boy or girl fails to "make" the leading clique, the chances are good that he or she will gain acceptance into *some* clique which will perform the same function. During this period, the adolescent is in the process of emancipation from the values of childhood and from many (although by no means all) of those of the parental family. He has not yet identified with the values of adult society. He is therefore living in a sort of marginal, never-never land, whose standards, expectations, and behavior patterns are transitional, but which are nevertheless of crucial, although temporary, importance for him.[39] He seeks the support of his peers who are in the same general situation. The clique provides a strong measure of such security.

If that security is lacking and the adolescent is excluded from *all* significant clique participation, his self-feeling is impaired and he feels badly about himself. As we shall see in a later chapter, the individual's conception of *himself* reflects his judgment of the opinions of *others* toward him. Boys and girls who do not belong to the leading crowd or to any crowd at all feel rejected by a society that places a high premium upon such acceptance. By a cruel coincidence, those who care the most are hurt the most. As Coleman puts it, "The students most involved in the school and most identified with it—those for whom school means most—are the ones upon whom exclusion from the leading crowd has its greatest impact. Those least involved in school, the ones who can take it or leave it, are least likely to be hurt by its social system." [40] At this time of life, rejection by one's peers is especially hard to take.

4. The delinquent gang. The delinquent gang is another type of primary group that has received extensive study. The functions of this group are more controversial than those of the army group, the peer group, and the high-school clique, inasmuch as gang activities are defined as deviant by the larger society. In many areas of the large city, the gang is the most important influence in the life of the adolescent boy. He incorporates the deviant values into his own personality and looks to his fellow gang members for support and approbation in a hostile world. The gang is (ordinarily) a conflict group, and the enemy ranges from the rival gang in the next block to the entire structure of organized society. In their interaction within the gang, the members are drawn

---

[38] Coleman, *op. cit.*, p. 40, Figure 2.9.
[39] *Ibid.*, p. 138.
[40] Coleman, *op. cit.*, p. 228.

together by a common loyalty, which is the quality most highly prized by the group.[41]

The delinquent gang lives in, and contributes to, what has been called a "delinquent subculture"—that is, a pattern of group expectations stressing antisocial and illegal behavior. The delinquent subculture is viewed as "nonutilitarian, malicious, and negativistic" by members of the middle class.[42] This means that much delinquent behavior is meaningless in its goals (nonutilitarian), is cruel and vicious toward others (malicious), and serves no useful purpose except perhaps that of the members themselves (negativistic). Insofar as the delinquent gang may be said to have any "function," it is to provide status for the lower-class boy who cannot gain status in the middle-class world. Negro and Puerto Rican boys in the noisome slums of New York and Chicago thus seek from the gang recognition that they cannot receive from the larger society.[43]

Delinquent gangs take different forms, depending upon their composition, structure, and goals. Among these forms are the following:[44]

(a) *The criminal gang.* In this group, the basic goal is to gain money by illegal means. Theft, robbery, and extortion (with or without incidental violence) are the principal activities of this type of gang. Members cooperate to reach goals that are primarily pecuniary. Such goals are basically no different from those of other individuals and groups in a materialistic society. Only the means of the gang are different from those of law-abiding persons. The criminal gang is the "traditional" form of delinquent group that has long been an integral part of the life of the large city.

(b) *The conflict gang.* In this group, the goals shift from the illegal acquisition of money to the perpetration of gratuitous violence. This gang is a conflict group pure and simple. Its aim is to inflict violence upon rival gangs or upon individual members of the general public who are so unfortunate as to come in contact with these juvenile marauders. This gang is a more recent addition to the urban scene than the criminal gang, and is built largely, although not entirely, upon racial and ethnic distinctions. Negroes,[45] Puerto Ricans, Italians, and other racial and ethnic groups constitute the principal, although not the exclusive, membership. The conflict gang is perpetually embroiled either in a hot or cold war with other gangs. The quality most prized by this group is reckless courage.

(c) *The retreatist gang.* This group, as the name signifies, concentrates upon "retreating" from a society that despises and rejects them. Drugs are the princi-

---

[41] The classic study of the gang is Frederick M. Thrasher, *The Gang* (Chicago: University of Chicago Press, 1927).

[42] Albert K. Cohen, *Delinquent Boys: The Culture of the Gang* (Glencoe, Ill.: The Free Press, 1955), p. 25.

[43] *Ibid.*, p. 121. See also Martin R. Haskell, "Toward a Reference Group Theory of Juvenile Delinquency," *Social Problems*, 8:220-230 (Winter, 1960-61).

[44] The following is adapted from Richard A. Cloward and Lloyd E. Ohlin, *Delinquency and Opportunity* (Glencoe, Ill.: The Free Press, 1960), p. 1.

[45] In one study, it was found that most "conflict-oriented" gangs were Negro. James F. Short, Jr., Ray A. Tennyson, and Kenneth I. Howard, "Behavior Dimensions of Gang Delinquency," *American Sociological Review*, 28:411-428 (June, 1963), p. 425.

In many areas of the large city, the gang is the most important influence in the life of the adolescent boy; here a gang surveys the passing scene in Harlem.

pal means of such a retreat, and the members may commit other deviant acts in order to get these desired commodities. The important goal is the temporary state of stimulation, euphoria, or oblivion derived from the consumption of the different stimulants or depressants, depending upon which type of drug is used. Participation in these retreatist activities is widespread among Negro adolescents, although membership is not exclusively confined to this minority group. Discrimination against the Negro, and his isolation from the larger society, result in a disproportionate number of drug addicts among this group.[46]

The gang, finally, may not be a group at all. In an interesting report on conflict gangs in New York City, Yablonsky argues persuasively that the gang is what he calls a "near-group." By this he means that the gang lacks the structure, organization, and leadership of a "true" group. Near-groups, in his estimation, have the following qualities that make them ineligible for true group status: "(1) diffuse role definition, (2) limited cohesion, (3) impermanence, (4) minimal consensus of norms, (5) shifting membership, (6) disturbed leadership, and (7) limited definition of membership expectations." [47]

[46] Harold Finestone, "Cats, Kicks, and Color," *Social Problems*, 5:3-13 (July, 1957).
[47] Lewis Yablonsky, "The Delinquent Gang as a Near-Group," *Social Problems*, 7:108-117 (Fall, 1959), p. 109.

Commenting upon this approach, Pfautz suggests that the delinquent gang is, rather, a form of collective behavior or "expressive social movement," which is neither true group nor mob but something in between. Gang behavior for him represents an "attempt on the part of adolescents living in disorganized, lower-class urban slums to act together in the face of social unrest." [48] Whether "true group" or "near-group," however, the gang has many primary qualities and performs a variety of primary functions for its members. In this sense, the gang is a form of face-to-face, intimate, and primary relationship that strongly influences the lives of its members.

5. *The corner boys.* Another function of the primary group is illustrated in a study of a street corner gang by William F. Whyte that has become a sociological classic.[49] This function is the simple but basic one of giving a *position* to the individual—that is, recognizing him as a person with an accepted place in an operating group. The gang was called the Nortons and its members lived in a slum area of Boston where the population was composed largely of second generation Italian-Americans. The time was the Great Depression of the 1930's. Unemployment was endemic in the slums of every big city, and Cornerville was no exception. Few of the young men had jobs or any regular means of livelihood. Although most of the Nortons were well into their twenties, they still lived at home. Or rather they ate and slept there and spent the rest of their time on the corner or in the lunchrooms, pool halls, and barber shops in the immediate neighborhood. They had nothing much to do all day, but even this abundant leisure was spoiled by their lack of money. Hence they were obliged, in a sense, to "consume" each other, for the only commodity they had in abundance was the friendship generated by the group itself.

The structure of the corner gang, Whyte remarks, "arises out of the habitual association of the members over a long period of time." [50] Social interaction is clearly seen in the growth and continued operation of the Nortons, beginning in their early boyhood and continuing into their twenties and even their thirties. In better times, the gang relationship would have been broken sooner, as the boys (men) got regular jobs, married, and began to raise families. Under such conditions, they would not have continued to need the gang to give them recognition, security, and affection. For the Nortons, however, "The stable composition of the group and *the lack of social assurance* on the part of its members contribute(d) toward producing a very high rate of social interaction within the group." [51]

The Norton gang was thus, in a very real sense, the most important social structure in the world of its members. As Italians in an Irish-dominated slum, the Nortons were marginal in an ethnic sense. As unemployed males, they were marginal in an economic sense. And as grown men still living at home, with no

---

[48] Harold W. Pfautz, "Near-Group Theory and Collective Behavior: A Critical Reformulation," *Social Problems,* 9:167-174 (Fall, 1961), p. 174.

[49] William F. Whyte, *Street Corner Society* (Chicago: The University of Chicago Press, 1955), enlarged edition.

[50] *Ibid.,* p. 255.

[51] *Ibid.,* p. 256. (Italics added.)

wives or families of their own, they were marginal in the most fundamental sense of all. No wonder they turned to each other for self-confidence and self-assurance. The leader of the gang was a great man among the Nortons, but nowhere else. The rank and file were no great shakes among the Nortons, but even this lowly place was better than nothing. When a man excelled on a particular day at bowling, boxing, or baseball, he received a heartening recognition from the gang. No matter how negligible his rank was away from Cornerville, he at least had a *position* in the gang. Here and here alone he knew where he stood and was recognized as a person in his own right. This status was all he had, but it was something.

The Dysfunctions of the Primary Group

The primary group is necessary to the individual and society alike. It does not follow, however, that primary relationships are ideal for *all* social interaction or that primary interaction should characterize *all* groups. Primary relationships can have dysfunctions—that is, activities that interfere with the operation of other elements in the society, from individual members of the particular group to the larger society itself. Therefore, in a large and complex society, many relationships should be nonprimary (secondary) so that the necessary business can be conducted in an orderly and efficient manner. The policeman who releases a friend who has violated the law, the instructor who gives a high grade to a student merely because of a personal relationship, the judge who throws a case out of court because the defendant is a friend of a friend, and the army officer who plays favorites among his men—these are intrusions of primary relationships into situations where they are not appropriate.[52]

By the same token, life would not become utopian if all relationships were miraculously changed into primary ones and society became literally one big, happy family. The primary group has its dysfunctions as well as its functions, its liabilities as well as its assets. Many situations arise in modern society where primary relationships are inappropriate at best and harmful at worst. In large bureaucratic structures, so necessary to contemporary social organization, impersonality is more appropriate than intimacy, routine more important than spontaneity, and division of labor more necessary than versatility. Societies and subsocieties composed of tight networks of primary relationships are often more intolerant of differences, more resistant to change, and less receptive to freedom than societies where relationships are more casual. We may examine some of the *dysfunctions* of primary group relationships.

1. Restriction. The dysfunctions of the primary group are often the reverse of its functions. This is clearly illustrated in the family, the most intimate primary group of all. As we have seen, this group provides pleasure, defense, and tolerance for its members, qualities necessary to the development and maintenance of personality. At the same time, the family may, in Olmstead's words,

---

[52] Ellsworth Faris, "The Primary Group: Essence and Accident," *op. cit.*

"restrict, inhibit, or even smother the individual in its close embrace." [53] This was especially true of the family of the nineteenth century, when the patriarchal father exerted a benevolent authoritarianism over his wife and children and often stifled and warped their personalities in the process. The literature of this period, from *The Way of All Flesh* to *The Doll's House*, is full of the desperate attempts of sons, daughters, and wives to escape the restriction of their families and live their own lives. The emotional problems of these domestic dramas were given scientific immortality by the researches of Freud.

The authoritarian, father-dominated family has largely given way to the equalitarian family, especially among the middle classes. In some respects, however, patriarchal dominance has been replaced by the gentler but equally powerful authority of the mother. As Green has cogently suggested, the middle-class mother may smother her child with affection and then, as punishment, threaten to deprive him of this affection.[54] An even more drastic effect of such all-embracing maternal affection is suggested by the shattering appellation óf "Momism," applied to the restrictive relationship between mother and son. Some psychiatrists, indeed, maintain that the high rate of psychoneurotic illness among American soldiers in World War II was one result of this smothering maternal affection. In her efforts to protect her son from the vicissitudes of life, the American mother was, in this view, doing him a grave disservice. The primary group thus, in effect, may restrict rather than enhance the personality of its male children.[55]

2. Conformity. The adolescent peer group illustrates a second possible dysfunction of the primary group. This is the fostering of conformity, complacency, and conservatism in the adolescent. As we have seen, peer groups play an important part in developing such indispensable qualities as getting along with others, learning one's position in society and the behavior associated therewith, and emancipating oneself from the (often) stultifying embrace of the parental family. But while the adolescent is immersing himself in the cozy little world of his peer group, he may also dismiss or ignore virtually everything that does not come within its purview. Between the ages of 12 and 18, the adolescent belongs to a succession of such primary groups, whose fervor is often only slightly less than that of the most doting of mothers. This voluntary limiting of horizons means that the average adolescent accepts a strict conformity as the price of acceptance by his fellows.[56]

This conformity is symbolized by a haunting little story told by David Riesman in *The Lonely Crowd*. The story concerned a fourteen year old boy who was taking piano lessons. Unlike most of his peers, he not only *enjoyed* playing the piano but was *good* at it, so good that he was voluntarily playing the "classics" for his own pleasure. His mother, however, was not enchanted with this

---

[53] Michael S. Olmstead, *The Small Group* (New York: Random House, Inc., 1959), p. 49.

[54] Arnold W. Green, "The Middle-Class Male Child and Neurosis," *American Sociological Review*, 11:31-41 (February, 1946).

[55] E. A. Strecker, *Their Mothers' Sons* (Philadelphia: J. B. Lippincott Company, 1946).

[56] Cf. Matilda W. Riley and Samuel H. Flowerman, "Group Relations as a Variable in Communications Research," *American Sociological Review*, 16:174-180 (April, 1951).

precocious evidence of musical talent. She warily told the interviewer that she was closely rationing her son's hours of practice and was not letting him spend more than a limited time every day at the keyboard. She insisted, instead, that he spend more time in wholesome outdoor activity—preferably playing football. "I hope," she added wistfully, "to keep him a *normal* boy." By "normal," she meant "like everyone else." As a modern mother, she was keenly aware of the importance of acceptance by the group. She wanted her boy to conform, and to be accepted by his peers.[57]

3. *Reaction.* A final dysfunction of primary relationships is to foster reaction, or resistance to social change. This situation is most apparent in societies where a rigid class structure is maintained by a network of "primordial" primary relationships. In these societies, ignorance, superstition, and intolerance often render people hostile to changes that threaten their ancient prerogatives. This reactionary spirit is not merely a form of enlightened self-interest, whereby those in high places consciously resist innovations that undermine their age-old privileges. Equally conservative are most members of the lower social orders, who resist intellectual, industrial, and educational changes that might conceivably weaken their own hereditary shackles. Such people often love their primary bonds and cannot conceive of life without them. *Gemeinschaft* and slavery are preferable to *Gesellschaft* and freedom.

In our own society, mass communication and mass culture are helping to break down this primary-group parochialism. This process is occurring at varying rates of speed in different regions and among different groups within the same regions. In general, those areas that are the least exposed to newspapers, books, radio, television, and motion pictures cling most tenaciously to the primary relationships of a caste-like society. In the long drawn-out agony of desegregation in the South, the states that are most rural, least educated, and least exposed to the mass media offer the most ferocious resistance to integration. In a given area, furthermore, men and women with the highest education and the broadest exposure to mass communications are most willing to accept the implications of desegregation.[58] In breaking down primary resistance to such changes, "Mass media, the extension of education and professionalization tend to equate the rates at which different classes and regions are exposed to changing standards." [59]

The Reference Group

In concluding our discussion of the primary group, we may examine some of the implications of another aspect of group relationships, namely, the *reference* group. This is not a particular *type* of group, but rather a way of looking at the relationship between the individual and *any* group, primary or otherwise.

---

[57] Riesman, *et al., op. cit.,* p. 77. (Italics added.)

[58] Melvin M. Tumin, *Desegregation* (Princeton: Princeton University Press, 1958).

[59] Joseph R. Gusfield, "Mass Society and Extremist Politics," *American Sociological Review,* 27:19-30 (February, 1962), p. 29.

A reference group is one to which the individual *refers* and with which he identifies himself, either consciously or subconsciously. The central aspect of the reference group is psychological identification.[60] In short, a reference group is "that group whose outlook is used by the actor as the frame of reference in the organization of his perceptual field." [61]

The reference group is the product of a complex society. In a simple, homogeneous society, the individual belongs to a comparatively small number of groups (largely primary), and his behavior is largely determined by them. In our own society, the individual is confronted with a variety of groups that influence his behavior on different levels and to which he owes varying degrees of allegiance. In certain instances, his face-to-face groups are not as important as his reference groups. The neighborhood group in the urban community may be comparatively unimportant to the middle-class person, as compared to such reference groups as professional societies, political parties, or college alumni groups. The physician identifies himself with his professional group, with its particular standards, rather than with his local community group.[62]

In a dynamic mass society, each person assumes the point of view of several reference groups. Some of them seem very desirable to him, others not so desirable. In his interaction with these groups, the individual tries to maximize his satisfactions and minimize his deprivations, as he draws closer to some groups, withdraws from others. In this sense, social interaction is constantly changing, "with some persons moving in the direction of increased psychological membership, some in relative equilibrium, and others gradually drifting toward decreased psychological membership." [63]

These reference groups may be business, professional, religious, recreational, racial, or ethnic in origin, and they are often connected through the mass media of communication. Social interaction in these groups occurs by remote control, as it were; the doctor reads the *Journal of the American Medical Association*, the baseball fan reads the sports pages, and the religiously minded person keeps in touch through his own church journal. Men and women interact with a view, consciously or unconsciously expressed, to increasing their emotional gratifications through their contacts with these groups.

The norms, attitudes, and values of these reference groups are important, even though the members do not come in physical contact. These groups "structure" the mental world of the individual, in the sense that they furnish organized perspectives and ways of looking at society. Much of this book will be concerned with group behavior in a mass society. In this analysis, one of the crucial problems is "that of ascertaining how a person defines [a given] situa-

[60]Muzafer Sherif, "The Concept of Reference Groups in Human Relations," Chapter 9 in Muzafer Sherif and M. O. Wilson (eds.), *Group Relations at the Crossroads* (New York: Harper & Brothers, 1953), p. 206.

[61] Tamotsu Shibutani, "Reference Groups as Perspectives," *American Journal of Sociology*, 60:562-569 (May, 1955), p. 565.

[62] Robert K. Merton and Alice S. Kitt, "Contributions to the Theory of Reference Group Behavior," in Merton and Lazarsfeld (eds.), *Continuities in Social Research, op. cit.*, pp. 53-59.

[63] Jay M. Jackson, "Reference Group Processes in a Formal Organization," *Sociometry*, 22:307-327 (December, 1959), p. 325.

tion, which perspective he uses in arriving at such a definition, and who constitutes the audience whose responses provide the necessary confirmation and support for his position.[64]

The identification between the individual and the reference group may be conscious, as one thinks of himself as an American even though far from his native shores. It may be unconscious, as he reacts to situations in terms of religious standards that were inculcated long ago and whose origins he has forgotten. Identification may be partially conscious and partially unconscious, as the individual associates himself with a particular social class.[65] In each case, the person interacts with a group that is not physically present. He may be in one group situation (such as a play group) but he may be reacting to an entirely different group (such as a religious group). The symbolic character of human communication means that man may respond to the symbols of one group while physically in another.[66]

The reference group is not synonymous with the membership group. The individual may identify himself with groups of which he is not a member, but of which he aspires to be a member. The ambitious clerk may identify himself with the board of directors of the bank. He interacts on a face-to-face basis with his fellow clerks, but he may think of himself in more exalted company. Identification with groups of which one is not a member is characteristic of a society where the opportunities for advancement are great and the choice of group participation is wide. In a simpler society, the individual rarely identifies himself with groups to which he does not belong, but is content with his own position. This may be a lowly one, but he is at least sure what it is.

This sense of personal identification may be lacking in a complex society. The person may identify himself with two or more groups whose standards conflict. A member of a minority group, for example, may identify himself with the majority, but he may be unable to make the identification completely. His ties to the minority group (his membership group) are still strong, even though he tries to identify himself with the higher status group (his reference group). Furthermore, he may be rejected by the majority group and thus find that his identification is rebuffed. In his inability to be accepted by the reference group, he becomes a "marginal man." [67]

Modern society is full of marginal men, whose reference groups are not the same as their membership groups. They aspire to a status that is not theirs at birth and must be laboriously achieved. Millions of persons entered this country as immigrants and remained marginal to membership groups in the Old World and reference groups in the new. Complete transition to the new reference groups sometimes takes two or three generations, during which the marginal men continue to suffer from feelings of insecurity. Members of lower-income groups similarly identify themselves with upper-income groups. In some

---

[64] Shibutani, "Reference Groups as Perspectives," *op. cit.*, p. 569.

[65] Neal Gross, "Social Class Identification in the Urban Community," *American Sociological Review*, 18:398-404 (August, 1953).

[66] Sherif, "The Concept of Reference Groups in Human Relations," *op. cit.*, pp. 204-207.

[67] Everett V. Stonequist, *The Marginal Man* (New York: Charles Scribner's Sons, 1937).

instances, this subjective identification has eventually led to actual participation in these exalted groups. In other cases, it has not. Success in making the transition from the membership to the reference group has been known as the "American Dream." Failure to make this transition has often led to insecurity, frustration, and conflict.

The reference group sets the goals to which the individual aspires. In the early years of life, membership and reference groups are usually the same, as the child learns the goals of his family or other primary group. In later years, many of these initial goals are still deep in his personality, but they may be supplanted by others derived from reference groups. The reference group is an object of aspiration, and people conceive of the future in terms of groups to which they aspire. In a society marked by upward movement in the social scale, this aspect of the reference group is important.[68] The young man starting out in business may identify himself with the select group of successful men who own Cadillacs.

In this sense, one may think of himself as a great artist, soldier, doctor, or businessman, although he is actually none of these. The individual thus interacts with a reference group on an indirect basis, although he does not belong to it in any formal sense. Despite such a lack of formal group affiliation, the reference group still influences him through personal identification. He feels himself one with the group and responds to many of its goals, even though he has never "joined" it in any way except symbolically.[69]

The reference group is, in summary, "a group with which the individual feels identified, the norms of which he shares and the objectives of which he accepts."[70] The reference group provides many of the standards that guide behavior, even when the standards are contrary to those of earlier membership groups. The boy who identifies himself with a criminal gang will try to follow its standards, even when they conflict with those of his family. The delinquent boy "refers" himself to the gang, even though he "knows" that he is acting in conflict with the membership groups of his family, school, and church.[71] To understand the behavior of the individual, we must therefore know his reference groups as well as his membership groups. Only in this way can we fully understand the interaction between the individual and the group.

In this chapter, we have examined the most intimate form of social interaction—that of the primary group. Although this group looms large in human experience, we must not lose sight of the other major forms of social interaction. The nonprimary or secondary group is the most general term for this form, which also includes many types of institutional and bureaucratic struc-

---

[68] Ralph H. Turner, "Reference Groups of Future-Oriented Men," *Social Forces*, 34:130-136 (December, 1955).

[69] Anselm Strauss, "Concepts, Communication, and Groups," Chapter 4 in Sherif and Wilson, *op. cit.*, pp. 112-113.

[70] Eugene L. Hartley and Ruth E. Hartley, *Fundamentals of Social Psychology* (New York: Alfred A. Knopf, Inc., 1952), p. 480.

[71] Muzafer Sherif and Hadley Cantril, *The Psychology of Ego-Involvements* (New York: John Wiley & Sons, Inc., 1947), p. 291.

tures. We are, first of all, members of families, friendship groups, peer groups, and cliques. But we also belong to business organizations, churches, service clubs, political parties, and educational institutions. Social interaction reaches out from the primary group into these and other nonprimary situations. We must retain a sense of perspective and realize that, important as it is, the primary group is merely a part (albeit a central part) of the larger and more complex reality of society. The role of primary groups cannot be fully understood merely by examining what goes on within them. Full understanding of social reality must extend beyond the intimate confines of the primary group.[72]

---

[72] Edward A. Shils, "The Study of the Primary Group," *op. cit.*, p. 69.

SELECTED BIBLIOGRAPHY

Cloward, Richard A., and Lloyd E. Ohlin, *Delinquency and Opportunity.* Glencoe, Illinois: The Free Press, 1960. This is a study of primary groups in a delinquent subculture. The latter is described as one "in which certain forms of delinquent activity are essential requirements for the performance of the dominant roles supported by the subculture." Hence primary group behavior in this setting is strongly influenced by delinquent role-expectations.

Coleman, James S., *The Adolescent Society.* Glencoe, Illinois: The Free Press, 1961. This significant study of the adolescent culture patterns in a number of high schools throws a great deal of light on the norms of various groups—notably the adolescent peer group and the clique. In addition, the study points up the anti-intellectualism of the adolescent culture which, in effect, "forces a scholar to choose between being *selfish* by studying hard, and being *unselfish* by working for the glory of the school in its interscholastic games."

Cooley, Charles Horton, *Social Organization.* New York: Charles Scribner's Sons, 1909. In this sociological classic, the author defines and analyzes the primary group and indicates its importance in social organization. In recent years, the "rediscovery" of the primary group has emphasized many of the early insights of Cooley.

Faris, Ellsworth, "The Primary Group: Essence and Accident," *American Journal of Sociology*, 38:41-50 (July, 1932). This analysis supplements that of Cooley (above) and qualifies some of the earlier statements of the nature and essential qualities of the primary group. All face-to-face groups, for example, are not primary; all primary groups are not face-to-face.

Faris, Robert E. L., "Development of the Small-Group Research Movement," Chapter 7 in Muzafer Sherif and M. O. Wilson (eds.), *Group Relations at the Crossroads.* New York: Harper & Brothers, 1953. This is an important statement of the historical development of research in the small (and primary) group, together with an analysis of this form of interaction.

Katz, Elihu, and Paul F. Lazarsfeld, *Personal Influence: The Part Played by People in the Flow of Mass Communications.* Glencoe, Illinois: The Free Press, 1955. This is an empirical study of several related fields of communication. The primary group is seen as an "interpersonal" network of communication between the mass media and the general public.

Olmstead, Michael S., *The Small Group.* New York: Random House, Inc.,

1959. In this excellent analysis of the small group, the primary and secondary group are examined at considerable length. The author makes the important point that, whereas *most* primary groups are small groups, *all* small groups are not primary.

Shils, Edward A., "Primary Groups in the American Army," in Robert K. Merton and Paul F. Lazarsfeld (eds.), *Continuities in Social Research.* Glencoe, Illinois: The Free Press, 1950. This essay analyzes the data on the primary group that grew out of the studies conducted during World War II and reported in Samuel A. Stouffer, *et al., The American Soldier.* Princeton: Princeton University Press, 1949. The primary group plays a basic role in morale by establishing a personal relationship that stands between the enlisted man and organized authority.

————, "The Study of the Primary Group," in Daniel Lerner and Harold D. Lasswell (eds.), *The Policy Sciences.* Stanford: Stanford University Press, 1951. This essay is another step in the renaissance of the primary group and its acceptance as a central form of social interaction.

Yablonsky, Lewis, *The Violent Gang.* New York: The Macmillan Company, 1962. This is a case study of a New York gang whose principal function is to engage in periodic conflicts with other gangs, marked by gratuitous violence on both sides. The book also offers a general theory of the behavior of such groups—or rather "near-groups," as the author calls them. The author transmits the stark reality of the interaction within the gang, as he gives us transcripts of tape recordings in which the members plan their next "rumble."

5 *Secondary Groups*

The Nature of the Secondary Group

The primary group is not the only form of group relationship. The secondary group supplements and even at times supplants the primary group. As the name suggests, the secondary group is less intimate, personal, and inclusive than the primary group. This secondary group includes many relationships entered voluntarily and purposively, in contrast to the primary relationships of the family where the individual has little or no choice. No such definitive statement of the nature and functions of the secondary group compares with that given the primary group by Cooley. The secondary group, indeed, is often defined in a negative sense, as involving that form of interaction that is *not* primary. The secondary group is assuming greater importance, however, as the individual lives more of his life with comparative strangers with whom he interacts on an impersonal level.

In contrast to the primary group, members of the secondary group regard each other as means to ends, rather than as ends in themselves. The salesman views a potential customer in terms of the impending sale, rather than of warm personal friendship. One customer has no intrinsic value as distinguished from any other customer, as long as the essential relationship is maintained. Each member of a secondary group expects something from it, quite apart from the pleasure of the interaction. In the primary group, substitution of one person for another is difficult and often impossible. Husband, father, and friend are unique; they cannot be replaced.

The secondary group is further characterized by the concept of *contract*, a rational relationship entered into by two or more parties, with the mutual duties and obligations clearly stated. Modern society is marked by an increasing emphasis upon *contract*, as contrasted with the primary relationship of *status*.[1] In the secondary group, the personal liability of each member is limited by the terms of the contract, whereas the liability of the primary group member is virtually unlimited. When two persons marry, they enter into a contractual relationship, but they also agree to a great deal more. They obligate themselves to a lifetime of undetermined liability, the terms of which they cannot possibly know in advance.

The individual enters a secondary group with separate and specialized parts of his personality. This interaction is common in the metropolitan community and reflects the various special interests that occupy the many-sided modern individual. Commenting upon this type of social interaction, Wirth suggested that, even though contacts in the city may be face-to-face, they are at the same time partial and superficial. In other words, urbanites interact with each other in "highly segmental roles."[2] In a society marked by a growing emphasis upon secondary relationships, the individual becomes correspondingly fragmented. He reacts with one segment of his personality rather than with the entire personality as in the primary group. The task of developing and maintaining an integrated personality under such conditions may be a difficult one.[3]

It is hard to distinguish in all cases between primary and secondary groups. Human relationships seldom lend themselves to such rigid categories, and in many instances one type merges imperceptibly into another. Primary and secondary qualities may be considered along a continuum. A group of relatives and friends represents one end of the continuum and a buyer and seller the other. In between is a variety of group relationships, some more primary than others. Furthermore, secondary groups often attempt to develop the intimacy and

---

[1] Henry Sumner Maine, *Ancient Law* (10th ed.) (London: John Murray, 1906).

[2] Louis Wirth, "Urbanism as a Way of Life," *American Journal of Sociology*, 44:1-24 (July, 1938), p. 12.

[3] Ernest W. Burgess, "Social Factors in the Etiology and Prevention of Mental Disorders," *Social Problems*, 1:53-56 (October, 1953).

sense of participation of the primary group. Business organizations try to engender and maintain the friendly spirit. In this sense, says Riesman, "much time in the office ... is ... spent in sociability: exchanging office gossip ('conferences'), making good-will tours ('inspection'), talking to salesmen and joshing secretaries ('morale')." [4]

In like manner, educational and religious groups strive to inculcate a sense of primary-group concentration, so that their members will display the same devotion to the school or church that they display toward the family or friendship group. This does not mean that all of the problems of our society would be automatically solved if, by some magic, secondary interaction were suddenly changed into primary. As we have indicated, many functions can best be performed by secondary groups and voluntary associations. When the primary note is introduced into relationships that do not warrant it, the result is often more dysfunctional than functional. Both primary and secondary groups have their place in modern society. The functions of one cannot adequately be performed by the other.[5]

Until recently the secondary group has received surprisingly little attention, when we consider the importance of this type of interaction. One study indicated that the degree of participation in secondary groups varies in terms of position in the social structure. The higher the income of the family, the greater the participation of its members in secondary groups. Persons from the upper-income groups belonged to a number of secondary groups in the metropolis, whereas those in the lower-income groups had neither the interest nor the leisure to share this rich group life.[6]

These findings were confirmed by other studies. One study dealt with participation in secondary groups (voluntary associations) by working-class families in a medium-sized industrial city. A large number of persons were found to have no secondary group participation at all, and confined their leisure activities entirely to their families. Three-fifths of the men and four-fifths of the women did not participate in any formal secondary group, and two-fifths of both sexes did not even have any friendship group outside their immediate family and relatives.[7]

These and related studies of secondary groups suggest several interpretations. (a) They confirm the continued importance of the primary group (especially the family), even in urban communities where secondary groups are most plentiful. (b) They indicate that the secondary group is comparatively unimportant among the urban population in the lower-income groups.[8] (c) They

---

[4] David Riesman, et al., The Lonely Crowd (New Haven: Yale University Press, 1961), abridged edition, p. 136.

[5] Cf. Edward Gross, "Some Functional Consequences of Primary Controls in Formal Work Organizations," American Sociological Review, 18:368-373 (August, 1953).

[6] Mirra Komarovsky, "The Voluntary Associations of Urban Dwellers," American Sociological Review, 11:686-698 (December, 1946).

[7] Floyd Dotson, "Patterns of Voluntary Association Among Urban Working-Class Families," American Sociological Review, 16:687-693 (October, 1951). Also John C. Scott, Jr., "Membership and Participation in Voluntary Associations," American Sociological Review, 22:315-326 (June, 1957).

[8] Leonard Reissman, "Class, Leisure, and Social Participation," American Sociological Review, 19:76-84 (February, 1954).

suggest that the stereotype of the American people as "joiners" (of secondary groups) must be revised in view of the fact that this behavior seems to be confined largely to middle- and upper-income groups. (*d*) They imply that the adolescent associations in the high school clique are not continued after marriage, when the group association is limited to the family. (*e*) They demonstrate that the persons who *do* participate in secondary groups are extremely active in their membership, making up in the multiplicity of their contacts what they lack in numbers. In short, a comparatively small segment of the middle- and upper-class population belong to a great many secondary groups, and the majority of the lower classes do not belong to any.[9]

The Voluntary Association as a Secondary Group

Social interaction occurs within and between groups of all levels and sizes. The sociologist has traditionally concerned himself largely with small and informal groups, such as the family, the gang, the clique, and the peer group. This preoccupation may reflect an unconscious value judgment, in terms of which the *Gemeinschaft* relationship is regarded as the norm and the *Gesellschaft* relationship as an undesirable departure from the norm. The primary group, furthermore, offers a deceptive simplicity, that may have led to its selection in preference to larger and presumably more complicated groups. Whatever the combination of factors, most sociological research and speculation has been

---

[9] Dotson, *op. cit.*, p. 693.

A voluntary association is a form of secondary group in which the members come together voluntarily to accomplish specific tasks or perform specific functions.

directed at the primary group rather than the various forms of the secondary group.[10]

One manifestation of the secondary group is the voluntary association. The nature of this group may be divined from its title—a *voluntary association* of persons to accomplish a specific task or perform a specific function. Members of the association come together because they want to, not because they are born into it or are forced to join it. This element of willing union in the voluntary association typifies the theory and practice of democracy. It is no accident that this type of group is characteristic of western democracies in general and the United States in particular. The individual is under no compulsion to enter a voluntary assocation; he does so because he believes that he can derive some tangible or intangible benefit.[11]

The voluntary association includes a variety of large groups that are so much a part of the scene that Americans take them for granted. Especially in the urban community and among the middle and upper classes, voluntary associations flourish like the green bay tree. Modern life is so complicated that people need (or think they need) special groups to fill many special functions, ranging from stamp collecting to temperance reform. In his occupation, his church, his leisure-time pursuits, his political activities, his veteran's status, and his "sociable" behavior, the modern urban individual joins with hundreds, thousands, or millions of likeminded citizens in voluntary associations.

Many of the functions of the voluntary association are similar to those already indicated for the secondary group. In its relationship to the structure of modern democratic society, the association has other more general functions. Among them are:[12]

1. Distribution of power. The voluntary nature of the association means that it is, within limits, open to anyone who wishes to join. Certain limitations arising from inferior class status, education, and income do, in fact, exist,[13] but in general membership is freer than in any other society. Much of the political, economic, social, and cultural power is therefore distributed among large numbers of free citizens, acting in voluntary associations. Power is kept out of the hands of a few, whether elected representatives, appointed officials, or wealthy property owners.

2. Feeling of participation. The distribution of power gives a feeling of participation in democratic living and an accompanying sense of satisfaction. The member of a voluntary association, whether its function is slum clearance or consumer cooperation, has a sense of *personal* involvement in the aims and purposes of the association. He feels that he has a hand in getting things that

---

[10] Arnold M. Rose, "Voluntary Associations Under Conditions of Competition and Conflict," *Social Forces,* 34:159-163 (December, 1955).

[11] Arnold M. Rose, "A Theory of the Function of Voluntary Associations in Contemporary Social Structure," Chapter 3 in *Theory and Method in the Social Sciences* (Minneapolis: University of Minnesota Press, 1954), pp. 50-51.

[12] The following is adapted from Rose, "A Theory of the Function of Voluntary Associations in Contemporary Social Structure," *op. cit.,* pp. 50-52.

[13] Reissman, "Class, Leisure, and Social Participation," *op. cit.*

interest him done, and that he is, within limits, master of his own fate. The voluntary association thus *personalizes* many of the problems of modern life.

3. *Direction of social change.* Voluntary associations are characteristic of a society in process of change. These groups are rarely found in static or feudal societies, where relationships continue much the same from generation to generation. When the citizen participates in one of these associations, he is under the impression that he is modifying a certain segment of society in a direction that he considers desirable. In a changing society, new problems and needs are constantly arising, and the voluntary association provides a mechanism for meeting these needs in a democratic fashion.[14]

Voluntary Associations in America

"In no country in the world," observed a sympathetic visitor to the United States, "has the principle of association been more successfully used, or more unsparingly applied to a multitude of different objects, than in America. . . . The Americans," he continued, "make associations to give entertainments, to found seminaries, to build inns, to construct churches, to diffuse books, to send missionaries to the antipodes; in this manner they found hospitals, prisons, and schools. If it is proposed to inculcate some truth or to foster some feeling by the encouragement of a great example, they form a society." [15]

This perceptive observation on the American mores might have been written yesterday. It was, however, written some 130 years ago. The author was a young Frenchman named Alexis de Tocqueville, who came to America, was impressed by what he saw (although not always favorably), and predicted with startling insight many of the directions that this country has followed since. Among other things, he pointed to a tendency to come together in voluntary associations to satisfy the special needs of a society in which the family, church, and local community were comparatively weak. The subsequent growth of voluntary associations has reflected this lack of traditional institutional ties, plus the mobility of the frontier, the democracy of the people, and the growing urbanization of the nation.[16]

Voluntary associations are "those social structures of the community which have very limited but clearly specified purposes (excluding the pursuit of private profit), to which people belong deliberately and from which they may resign." [17] We have already considered these structures briefly as forms of secondary groups that people join in order to reach specific goals. These goals are of two general types: ". . . (1) those for the sociable or expressive purposes of the members themselves (such as sports groups or literary societies); and (2)

---

[14] Rose, "A Theory of the Function of Voluntary Associations in Contemporary Social Structure," *op. cit.*
[15] Alexis de Tocqueville, *Democracy in America*, Volume II (edited by Phillips Bradley) (New York: Alfred A. Knopf, Inc., 1945), p. 106. The original English edition of this book was published in 1840.
[16] Rose, "A Theory of the Function of Voluntary Associations in Contemporary Social Structure," *op. cit.*, pp. 50–52.
[17] *Ibid.*, Chapter 4, "Voluntary Associations in France," p. 73.

those actively directed toward an outside purpose (such as social welfare or social reform groups)." [18] Social interaction in contemporary urban society is increasingly marked both by interaction *within* these voluntary associations and *between* two or more groups.

Voluntary associations are found on every hand. Page after page of the classified directories of metropolitan telephone books is devoted to them. Their "clearly specified purposes" cause persons to join labor unions, fraternal associations, benevolent groups, service clubs, consumer cooperatives, university alumni organizations, societies for the prevention of cruelty to animals, racial cooperation associations, scientific societies, bowling clubs, bird-watching societies, ladies aid groups, neighborhood improvement associations, hospital auxiliaries, and chambers of commerce. Some of these organizations promote activities that are pleasant in themselves (bird watching). Others are designed to produce some specific change in the external environment (racial friendship). Whether for "sociable" or "outside" purposes, voluntary associations are an integral part of the American scene.

From the American Legion to the National Association of Manufacturers, from the League of Women Voters to the Women's Christian Temperance Union, and from the Boy Scouts of America to the United Automobile Workers of America—the list of voluntary associations is long and the fields of interest are varied. In one computation, the number of *national* voluntary associations in the United States runs into some five thousand, and the list is admittedly incomplete.[19] The number of voluntary associations on a local level staggers the imagination. In view of this proliferation of interest groups, it is no wonder that Americans have been called a nation of joiners.

The evidence for this latter statement is impressive. On a national level, the fraternal orders, such as the Masons and the Knights of Columbus, claim a total attendance of approximately 20 million. More than 1,500 chapters of national fraternities and 600 chapters of sororities flourish in the colleges and universities. Every city worthy of the name has a local chapter of one or more of the "service clubs," such as the Rotary, Kiwanis, and Lions. The three million members of the National Federation of Women's Clubs belong to some 14,000 different local member organizations. The American Legion, Veterans of Foreign Wars, and American Veterans Committee among them include a majority of the 14 million men and women mobilized in World War II. The nation supports more than 1,500 national trade associations, 4,000 chambers of commerce, 100,000 women's organizations, and 70,000 local labor unions.[20] The bulk of the latter are now included in the 15 million members of the combined American Federation of Labor and Congress of Industrial Organizations. In thousands of voluntary associations, the American people exercise their constitutional right

---

[18] *Ibid.*

[19] Rose, *Theory and Method in the Social Sciences, op. cit.*, p. 52, footnote 2.

[20] Robin M. Williams, Jr., *American Society: A Sociological Interpretation* (New York: Alfred A. Knopf, Inc., 1951), pp. 466-467.

to gather in groups of their own choosing to advance their own version of life, liberty, and the pursuit of happiness.

The Role of Voluntary Associations

Associations play a prominent role because a secular society demands them. In a fluid, mobile, and specialized society, voluntary associations are the principal means of getting many things done. Furthermore, they give the individual a sense of participation. In Warner's words, the association is "the perfect social instrument for those Americans who wish to be private citizens and free individuals and yet, at the same time, public men who are socially bound in their daily lives." [21] Men and women enter voluntary associations, play an active or passive role according to their inclinations, and then drift away into the vast anonymity of the city.

Voluntary associations and social institutions are related but not synonymous. Institutions are spontaneous patterns that arise in all societies about fundamental group needs. Rearing a family, socializing the child, earning a living, controlling the group, interaction with other groups, and propitiating the supernatural powers are some of the functions performed by social institutions. Voluntary associations, on the other hand, ordinarily involve private, rather than manifestly public, interests and hence differ from institutions in degree of importance of the society.

The values at the heart of social institutions are the "infinite" values of a society.[22] These values are vital in and of themselves, and need no other justification than their own existence. Creation of human life, training of children, and identification with a higher power are at the very basis of society. Voluntary associations ordinarily grow up about values that are more marginal to social welfare. Nevertheless, voluntary associations may consider their activities central to society, as well as to the well-being of their members. Associations of cat-fanciers or trade organizations for the sale of children's comics can, with very little difficulty, persuade themselves that their interests are crucial to society. Viewed impartially, however, the average voluntary association is on a different level of importance from the social institution.

Institutions are universal, in that they are found in all societies in one form or other. Associations are the products of a certain type of society at a certain period in its development. Primitive and folk societies have ordered patterns of group activity that can readily be identified as institutions. These societies do not, as a rule, have many voluntary associations. They are too small, too homogeneous, and too static to develop the need for them.[23] Furthermore, folk societies do not ordinarily have the same conception[24] of organized group action for

---

[21] W. Lloyd Warner, *American Life: Dream and Reality* (Chicago: University of Chicago Press, 1953), p. 191.

[22] William R. Catton, Jr., "Exploring Techniques for Measuring Human Values," *American Sociological Review*, 19:49-55 (February, 1954).

[23] Robert Redfield, "The Folk Society," *American Journal of Sociology*, 52:293-308 (January, 1947)

[24] Francis E. Merrill, *et al.*, *Social Problems* (New York: Alfred A. Knopf, Inc., 1950), Chapter 4.

the solution of social problems as do western democratic societies. Social institutions are very old in human experience. Voluntary associations are comparatively recent and reflect the needs of a secular and changing society.

The Setting of Voluntary Associations

Voluntary associations arise in a unique social setting, one that man has never before seen. This setting is exemplified in the United States, although the association is also found in many similar societies. The most important characteristic of American society as the cradle of the voluntary association is its *newness*. Several societies of the Old World share with America the proud heritage of political democracy. But they are *old* in the sense that they have a continuous culture whose roots lie in feudalism and beyond. In these societies (for example, France) the traditional institutions of the extended family, church, and local community have maintained their vigor and continue to provide a sense of personal identification. Hence the *need* for voluntary associations is not so great in Europe as in the new and emerging culture of America.[25]

A new culture is also more flexible than an old culture. The patterns are not so firmly entrenched in the personality, nor have they acquired a virtual life of their own as in an old society. A new culture is not so heavily structured, which means that the ways of doing things are less definite and traditional. The early settlers in America brought a culture that was primarily Anglo-Saxon. But they met a new set of conditions and had to modify the culture accordingly. One of the forms of this adjustment was the voluntary association.

The role of the frontier in American society was therefore important in establishing the voluntary association.[26] The traditional institutions were, virtually without exception, weakened by the mobility of a frontier society. The patriarchal family could no longer exert its former influence when the children moved away from the parental roof and took up new land in the west.[27] The central government was unable to control people who were far out on the frontier and who were, furthermore, convinced that the best government was the one that governed least. The church lost much of its control, as the Protestant denominations encouraged their members to worship as individuals. The voluntary association of today is the result of three centuries of atomization (breakup) of the ties of the traditional institutions.

"Why," therefore, "are Americans a nation of joiners? In part," the Kluckhohns[28] answer their own question, "this is a defense mechanism against the excessive fluidity of our social structure. Because of the tension of continued struggle for social place, people have tried to gain a degree of routinized and

---

[25] Rose, *op. cit.*, Chapter 4, "Voluntary Associations in France," pp. 103-113.

[26] Frederick J. Turner, *The Frontier in American History* (New York: Henry Holt and Company, 1921).

[27] de Tocqueville, *op. cit.*, Volume II, Chapter 8.

[28] Clyde Kluckhohn and Florence Kluckhohn, "American Culture: Generalized Orientations and Class Patterns," Chapter 20 in Lyman Bryson, *et al.* (eds.), *Conflicts of Power in Modern Culture* (New York: Harper & Brothers, 1947), pp. 249-250. Quoted by Rose, *op. cit.*, "A Theory of the Function of Voluntary Associations in Contemporary Social Structure," p. 62.

recognized fixity by allying themselves with others in voluntary associations." In an old society, people have a sense of belonging that gives them emotional security. They know that they belong to *something*—to the extended family group, to the all-embracing church, and to the fixed local community and its institutions. In a mobile society, much of this identification is lost. The members seek to regain it, in part at least, through voluntary associations.

This search is not always successful. One of the characteristic aspects of our society, indeed, is a continued "quest for community." [29] This quest reflects the inability of the traditional institutions, *plus* the voluntary associations, to give the same sense of belonging that the average man (presumably) had in an earlier day. Individualism is apparently not enough. Modern man needs more than freedom if he is to live a full and satisfactory life. Participation in voluntary associations is one expression of this new freedom, whereby man directs his attention toward the most efficient satisfaction of his desires. But man is much more than a rational animal. He is also a highly emotional animal, who needs to belong deeply and fully to something. His widespread acceptance of modern totalitarian movements may be one expression of his "escape from freedom." [30]

Participation in Voluntary Associations

Participation in voluntary associations varies between class groups. This is equivalent to saying that the type of need differs from one social level to another. In general, working-class groups do not actively participate in voluntary associations. Participation is largely confined to the middle and upper classes, who constitute the membership of most of the associations. In Yankee City, Warner and his associates found this differential participation exemplified. Within the upper class, approximately 72 per cent of the people belonged to associations, as compared with 64 per cent of the upper-middle class, and 49 per cent of the lower-middle class. Among the working classes, only 39 per cent of the "upper-lower" class and a mere 22 per cent of the "lower-lower" participated in voluntary associations.[31]

Information on a national scale discloses very much the same general pattern, which may be summarized as follows. (1) Nearly half (47 per cent) of all the families in the United States belong to no voluntary association whatever. (2) Approximately a third (31 per cent) of all families belong to only one such group. (3) Slightly more than a fifth (21 per cent) of all families belong to more than one voluntary association. (4) Membership in such organizations is much more characteristic of white persons than of Negroes. (5) Participation is proportionately highest among Jewish families, less so among Protestant families, and still less so among Catholics. (6) Urban and rural-nonfarm families are more apt to belong to voluntary associations than are rural-farm families. (7) Membership is "directly related to socio-economic status, as measured by

[29] Robert A. Nisbet, *The Quest for Community* (New York: Oxford University Press, 1953).

[30] Erich Fromm, *Escape from Freedom* (New York: Rinehart & Company, Inc., 1941).

[31] Warner, *American Life: Dream and Reality, op. cit.,* p. 193.

level of income, occupation, home ownership, interviewer's rating of level of living, and education."[32]

The working classes do not feel at home in associations whose activities are devoted to social welfare, civic duty, and higher culture. They do not have the background to participate on an equal basis with persons of higher educational attainment. Women whose husbands work at semi-skilled labor feel a wide social gap between themselves and women whose husbands are professional men or business executives. Like other forms of social behavior, participation in associations is learned. The average lower-class person seldom has the opportunity to learn.[33]

The voluntary associations in which lower-class persons participate are therefore largely confined to labor unions, fraternal orders, and church groups. The union is playing a steadily increasing role as a recreational and welfare association, in addition to acting as an agent for collective bargaining.[34] The church continues to play a part in the recreational life of many underprivileged groups, to whom religion is a way of life as well as a means of contact with the supernatural. Both Protestant and Catholic members of the working classes tend to confine their outside activities to religious associations, and to their own families and immediate circle of friends.[35]

The middle classes make up the bulk of the membership of voluntary associations in the urban community, with the exception of those indicated above. Middle-class persons are conscious of the importance of upward mobility; one of the ways to such advancement is through voluntary associations. The young professional man joins a service club to meet important people. His wife takes an active part in the Parent-Teacher's Association for much the same reason.[36] Similarly, the clerk joins a bowling club and his wife a Ladies Aid Society. A good record with the Community Chest or the School Board is useful to the rising young businessman. We do not imply that participation is motivated wholly, or even largely, by utilitarian considerations. At the same time, participation in worthy groups seldom handicaps the middle-class person.[37]

Such participation is, furthermore, an evidence of the *involvement* of the individual or family in the community. Persons who own their own homes, have children in school, and take an active interest in community welfare constitute the bulk of the membership of voluntary associations. One index to such involvement is political activity. In a study of a single voluntary association (one seeking to advance public recreation), it was found that the members were: (a)

[32] Charles R. Wright and Herbert H. Hyman, "Voluntary Association Membership of American Adults: Evidence from National Sample Surveys," *American Sociological Review*, 23:284-294 (June, 1958), p. 294.

[33] John M. Foskett, "Social Structure and Social Participation," *American Sociological Review*, 20:431-438 (August, 1955).

[34] Nelson N. Foote, "The Professionalization of Labor in Detroit," *American Journal of Sociology*, 58:371-380 (January, 1953).

[35] Leonard Reissman, "Class, Leisure, and Social Participation," *American Sociological Review*, 19:76-84 (February, 1954).

[36] See Joan W. Moore, "Patterns of Women's Participation in Voluntary Associations," *American Journal of Sociology*, 66:592-598 (May, 1961).

[37] Robin M. Williams, Jr., *American Society: A Sociological Interpretation* (New York: Alfred A. Knopf, Inc., 1951), pp. 471-472.

more likely to *be* voters than were non-members; (*b*) more likely to *remain* voters; and (*c*) more likely to *become* voters if they had previously been non-voters. Voluntary associations thus have an active role in stimulating political activity.[38]

American society provides a fertile ground for the proliferation of voluntary associations. This in itself is essentially a *passive* factor in their growth. The relationship is also an *active* one, in that our society actively encourages the development of voluntary associations. The Protestant ethic has been an important factor and has provided much of the philosophical justification. From Martin Luther's day to the present, Protestantism has been sympathetic to the spirit of individualism implicit in the voluntary association. If a traditional institution is not satisfactory, the American is encouraged to find a few like-minded friends and form a group of his own. In religion, business, and government, this trend has been apparent. The law has made it easy to incorporate for any reasonable purpose and has placed a minimum of restrictions upon the activities of the voluntary association.[39]

Voluntary associations in American society are, in summary, made possible by "a permissive power-structure and are encouraged by diversity of interests and values, by the weakening of organic groupings, and by organizational complexity. . . . Impetus . . . is also given by the shared values of equality and individualism." [40] Added to these contemporary factors is historical precedent, which has made the voluntary association synonymous with a free society. In the urban community and throughout the country as a whole, the interaction of these associations with each other and with the institutions of the family, church, and government is increasingly important.

The Interaction of Voluntary Associations

Social interaction is the process whereby two or more persons "take each other into account" and react in an appropriate manner.[41] Social interaction is based upon communication, which may be physical, oral, written, or by any form of meaningful gesture. The most characteristic type of human interaction is the exchange of significant symbols. Through language and other symbolic acts, man not only stimulates others but himself as well. Human beings react to their own symbols at the same time as they react to those of other persons. The essence of social interaction is its reciprocity, as each influences the other and is influenced in turn.

The interaction of voluntary associations was carefully studied by Warner and his associates in their survey of Yankee City. In this context, interaction is

---

[38] Herbert Maccoby, "The Differential Political Activity of Participants in a Voluntary Association," *American Sociological Review*, 23:524-532 (October, 1958).

[39] Williams, *op. cit.*, pp. 469-470.

[40] *Ibid.*, p. 472.

[41] Herbert Blumer, "Psychological Import of the Human Group," Chapter 8 in Muzafer Sherif and M. O. Wilson (eds.), *Group Relations at the Crossroads* (New York: Harper & Brothers, 1953).

what the members do in their group capacity. After observing some 5,800 events (activities) of 357 different associations, Warner classified their activities into 19 types. In order of number of times observed, these activities were: drama and talent exhibitions, listening to speeches, organization (rules, minutes, voting), eating, fundraising, various forms of ritual (ceremonies), gift-making and gift-taking, sedentary games, hospitality, contests, athletic games, craft and skills, socials, outings, teaching and learning, and social dancing.[42]

Social interaction occurs in certain recurrent forms, which are known as social processes. Park and Burgess have isolated four major forms of social interaction—namely, competition, conflict, accommodation, and assimilation.[43] To these we may add cooperation. We have previously considered social interaction largely between two or more persons. Interaction also involves groups or social systems. Institutions and voluntary associations are among the important groups whose interaction accounts for much of the dynamic quality of modern society.

1. Competition between corporations. Competition is a struggle between two or more social units for limited ends. In a study of voluntary associations, Rose has extended this definition of competition to: "the existence within the same community of at least two independent groups whose primary functions are the same and the recognition by the leaders of at least one of these groups that their goals are the same as those of the other group." [44] No matter how ruthless competition may allegedly be, it is still carried on in accordance with the laws and the mores. The goals for which the members compete are determined by the society itself, and they may range from a million dollars to a scroll of paper. Competition is a dynamic force, in that the desire to compete more effectively causes groups to change their ways and thus change social relationships.

The scarce goals for which voluntary associations compete include power, prestige, and money. In the case of the corporation, the final goal is money, even though other and intermediate goals ("a larger share of the market") may be widely mentioned. In a capitalistic social system, the final criterion of success is profit. Money is the most impersonal of all goals.[45] Competition for money involves changes in technology, which may determine the competitive ability of a given group.[46] Other dynamic elements in corporation practice arising from competition include changes in structure (administrative organization), changes in management-labor relations, and changes in relationships to government (lobbying).

---

[42] Warner, *op. cit.,* p. 197, Table 4.

[43] Robert E. Park and Ernest W. Burgess, *Introduction to the Science of Sociology* (Chicago: University of Chicago Press, 1924).

[44] Arnold M. Rose, "Voluntary Associations Under Conditions of Competition and Conflict," *op. cit.,* p. 160.

[45] Nicholas J. Spykman, *The Social Theory of Georg Simmel* (Chicago: University of Chicago Press, 1925), p. 251.

[46] William F. Ogburn, "Technology and the Standard of Living in the United States," *American Journal of Sociology,* 60:380-386 (January, 1955).

2. *Cooperation between welfare agencies.* Cooperation is a form of social interaction in which two or more persons or groups unite toward a common goal. Cooperation allows all or most of the units to gain the same or equal goals, whereas in competition it may be all or nothing. In the development of American society, competition has been stressed, often to the virtual exclusion of cooperation. As voluntary associations have grown in size and power, however, cooperation has become more important, if only for mutual survival. Large industrial corporations can no longer simply compete with labor unions for a limited return, for the latter have become so powerful that they must be treated as equals. Cooperation for mutual advantage is becoming the order of the day.

In the field of voluntary associations, cooperation is illustrated among private social welfare agencies. These voluntary associations are partially denominational, with Protestant, Catholic, and Jewish organizations coexisting in all the large cities. The goals of these associations are the intangible but important ones of increasing human welfare and decreasing human suffering. The rewards are equally intangible and are virtually unlimited. Social problems in a modern, urban society can never be completely eliminated. The different associations cooperate by specializing in particular fields; one specializes in family case work, another in psychiatric social work, and a third in basic research. Cooperation also occurs in the methods by which each agency refers cases to the other, in city-wide councils, and in exchanging information.[47]

3. *Conflict between interest groups.* When two individuals or groups come in conflict, their interaction becomes conscious and personal. Rose has defined group conflict in associational terms as "the existence within the same community of at least two groups whose primary functions are opposed to each other and the recognition by the leaders of at least one of these groups that this opposition exists." [48] The goals of conflict change from the acquisition of scarce values (as in competition) to the injury, incapacitation, or even annihilation of the opposing groups. In conflict, the *similarities* between human beings are minimized or ignored. The *differences* between men—whether racial, ethnic, religious, or economic—are emphasized. In the development of American society, voluntary associations have for the most part reflected the peaceful processes of competition and cooperation. In certain instances, however, conflict has been the basis of the social interaction.

Conflict associations may also promote a special interest—whether race, social class, or religion. Conflict groups flourish in times of insecurity and stress, such as the Great Depression of the 1930's and the years immediately before World War II. Some of the groupings in the prewar years were open propaganda agencies for foreign nations. Others operated under presumably native auspices, but in reality received financial support from the Axis Powers. Most of these "hate associations" united on the theme of anti-Semitism, but they

---

[47] Nelson N. Foote and Leonard S. Cottrell, Jr., *Identity and Interpersonal Competence* (Chicago: University of Chicago Press, 1955), Chapter 4.

[48] Rose, "Voluntary Associations Under Conditions of Competition and Conflict," *op. cit.*, p. 160.

were only slightly less vociferous in their attacks on Negroes and alleged "leftists." Social interaction took other forms than conflict, as they competed with each other for members and cooperated, deliberately or not, to further the cause of the Axis. Associations based upon fear, hatred, and suspicion have happily been comparatively rare on the American scene. Most associations have been primarily concerned with *integrating*, rather than *dividing*, the society.[49]

4. *Accommodation and racial tolerance groups.* In accommodation, the conflict situation is temporarily relieved and the erstwhile opponents settle down to an uneasy peace. The latent tensions are still there, but the adversaries have adjusted as best they can to the truce, cold war, or armed neutrality. Modern society abounds in accommodative interaction between voluntary associations. The settlement of a strike involves an accommodation between two competing or conflicting groups. Political parties often declare a tacit truce on foreign policy, after they have been at each other's throats during a bitter presidential campaign.

The most spectacular and far-reaching example of accommodation is in the field of race relations. The caste system in the South is an informal and extralegal device for bringing about accommodation between racial groups. The whites in the past encouraged certain types of Negro leaders, whose function was indicated by the title of "accommodating leadership."[50] These leaders accepted the permanent subordination of the Negro and tried to induce their people to do likewise. The elaborate system of racial "etiquette" in the South, with its defined patterns of speech, manner, and deportment, was another traditional accommodative device.

Many of these accommodative devices are in the process of modification under the continuing impact of social change. The South is undergoing massive changes: (*a*) from rural to urban living, (*b*) from agriculture to a more diversified economy, (*c*) from relative isolation to a greater integration with the rest of the country, (*d*) from a comparatively "tradition-directed" to an increasingly "other-directed" society (to use Riesman's terminology), (*e*) from relative poverty to relatively greater wealth, and, above all, (*f*) from widespread under-education to a rising level of education for both races—these changes have modified the century-old caste structure almost beyond recognition.[51] At the same time, the character of Negro leadership has drastically changed, from the old-time "accommodating" posture to a more militant one. Many of these new Negro leaders are highly educated, notably in the ministry and education, and they have led their people into increasingly active efforts to better their status. Many of the most intelligent and enlightened white leaders have,[52] in

---

[49] Leo Lowenthal and Norbert Guterman, *Prophets of Deceit* (New York: Harper & Row, 1949).

[50] Gunnar Myrdal, *An American Dilemma* (New York: Harper & Row, 1944) Volume II, Chapter 34, "Accommodating Leadership."

[51] Charles U. Smith, "Race, Human Relations, and the Changing South," *Phylon*, 23:66-72 (Spring, 1962).

[52] James W. Vander Zanden, "Accommodation to Undesired Change: The Case of the South," *The Journal of Negro Education*, 31:30-35 (Winter, 1962).

their turn, "accommodated" themselves to the changing trends, even though they have been none too happy about it.

In a dynamic society, social interaction goes on all the time between groups, associations, and institutions. This interaction is one of the principal factors making the society dynamic. Competition, cooperation, conflict, accommodation, and assimilation occur simultaneously, as the various groups attempt to gain more power, prestige, and members. Each of these processes is apparent in the organized behavior of every secondary group, although some groups stress one type of activity more than others. Conflict groups do not fight all the time; they cooperate with other conflict groups, accommodate themselves to organizations more powerful than themselves, and compete with other organizations for members.

Interaction between groups occurs through human beings, acting in their roles as group officers, members, and functionaries. Voluntary associations are not endowed with life, and their activity is always human activity. The Anti-Defamation League, for example, is devoted to increasing religious *tolerance* and, in the process, is perforce obliged to fight religious *intolerance*. The fighting is done by persons acting as members, officers, and directors of the organization. In these roles, they commit the association to various forms of social interaction with the ultimate end of raising the status of minority groups. In social processes, therefore, groups interact by individuals taking other individuals into account.

Social Trends and Secondary Groups

In this chapter, we have examined a somewhat more diffuse form of social system—namely, the secondary group. In contrast to the comparatively small size and clear-cut ends of the primary group, the secondary group is large in numbers, heterogeneous in composition, and (sometimes) vague in goals. Its membership is not so restricted nor are its purposes so fundamentally simple as those of the primary group. In a pluralistic, mass society, however, the secondary group performs a variety of functions that cannot be performed either by the relatively short-lived primary group or by the more traditional social institution. Many secondary groups enable individuals to participate meaningfully in the activities of the mass society who otherwise would be unable to do so. This participation is, as we have seen, more common in the middle class and upper-middle class than in the lower class. Restricted as it is, however, participation in secondary groups (political, welfare, recreational, reform, educational) gives a strength and depth to social interaction that would otherwise be lacking.[53]

The most characteristic form of secondary group is the voluntary association. In recent years, sociologists have increasingly turned their attention to this

---

[53] Joseph R. Gusfield, "Mass Society and Extremist Politics," *American Sociological Review*, 27:19-30 (February, 1962).

type of group. Their researches have added greatly to our knowledge of social interaction on the nonprimary, or secondary, level. Many of these findings have been incorporated into the present chapter. Certain observers of the mass society have ventured the gloomy pronouncement that modern man is being steadily crushed by the ponderous organizations of big government, big business, and big labor. Other observers have suggested, however, that voluntary associations help to mediate between "the isolated individual and massive power" and thereby retain a degree of autonomy for the human being.[54]

The functions that voluntary associations perform and the interests they further are neither so deep nor so universal as those of primary groups and social institutions. These latter groups are found in all societies and are necessary to organized social life as such. Voluntary associations are necessary, however, to life in a democratic society as presently constituted. The rationality, segmentalization, and efficiency of the voluntary association are indispensable to the performance of many tasks that people consider important. As long as people maintain the present variety of their interests, and as long as they desire to carry out these interests freely—so long will the voluntary association be an important part of the social scene.

The voluntary association, as noted, is an instrument of social change. The flexibility of this group is such that it can direct its activities into new channels more efficiently than the traditional institutions of family, church, and government. Furthermore, new needs arise in fields as varied as the exploitation of a new invention, the protection of a minority group, or the promotion of a new political program. In a dynamic society, with its constant technological and social innovations, a high degree of adaptability is more necessary than ever before. This role is filled, in part at least, by the voluntary association.

The future of the secondary group is closely related to the degree of freedom in a society. Voluntary associations reflect the ability of like-minded persons to band together to further their special interests. This general relationship was stated many years ago by Durkheim. "A democratic nation," he said, "can be maintained only if, between the State and the individual, there is intercalated [interposed] a whole series of secondary groups near enough to the individuals to attract them strongly in their sphere of action and drag them, in this way, into the general torrent of social life."[55]

The freedom to come together in voluntary associations may be restricted in two ways. (1) The association may fall under the control of the state, in the real or alleged interests of the society as a whole. In this way, labor unions, professional groups, and the press are controlled by the totalitarian state. (2) The association itself may become so large and powerful that new groups cannot arise. In this sense, corporations, labor unions, and communications industries may become so strong that new associations cannot be formed. This situa-

---

[54] Scott Greer and Peter Orleans, "The Mass Society and Parapolitical Structure," *American Sociological Review*, 27:634-646 (October, 1962).

[55] Emile Durkheim, *The Division of Labor in Society* (Translated by George Simpson) (Glencoe, Ill.: The Free Press, 1947), p. 28.

tion produces a form of private monopoly by limiting the number of new associations and further curtailing the democratic process.

Unless there is a fundamental change in American society, however, the ability to unite in secondary groups will continue to be one of our most precious possessions. As the rate of social change increases, the flexibility offered by the voluntary association will be more and more necessary. By inclination and necessity, this form of secondary-group relationship will serve as an important response to new situations. Even as they did in the days of Tocqueville, therefore, the American people will continue to "make associations" for many purposes.

SELECTED BIBLIOGRAPHY

Bell, Wendell, and Marion D. Bost, "Urban Neighborhoods and Informal Social Relations," *American Journal of Sociology*, 62:391-398 (January, 1957). In this study, members of voluntary organizations in urban neighborhoods reported that they had several close friends who were also members. These findings suggest that such organizations are not as formal and impersonal as is often assumed and that many primary relationships occur in the setting of the voluntary association.

Gordon, E. Wayne, and Nicholas Babchuk, "A Typology of Voluntary Associations," *American Sociological Review*, 24:22-29 (February, 1959). In this context, the "typology" of voluntary associations refers to such factors as the ease or difficulty of joining, the status conferred by membership, and the types of functions performed by various groups.

Komarovsky, Mirra, "The Voluntary Associations of Urban Dwellers," *American Sociological Review*, 11:686-698 (December, 1946). This is one of the first studies of differential participation in voluntary associations in the urban community. Most of the participation was found among the middle and upper classes, with the working class showing a strong reluctance to take part. Subsequent studies have, in the main, confirmed these conclusions.

Maccoby, Herbert, "The Differential Political Activity of Participants in a Voluntary Association," *American Sociological Review*, 23:524-532 (October, 1958). There is a close relationship between participation in voluntary associations and political activity. In this study of a single association, participants were more likely to be voters than were non-participants. Voluntary associations are seen as "stimuli" to participation in the political activity of the larger society.

Moore, Joan W., "Patterns of Women's Participation in Voluntary Associations," *American Journal of Sociology*, 66:592-598 (May, 1961). This article compares the participation of middle- and upper-class women in voluntary associations. The author concludes that such participation has different functions. For middle-class women, these functions are "primarily to help adapt the woman herself to changes in the family life-cycle in a minimally disturbing way; for the upper class it [participation] plays a role of significance to the entire class."

Rose, Arnold M., *Theory and Method in the Social Sciences*. Minneapolis: University of Minnesota Press, 1954. Chapters 3 and 4 of this collection of sociological essays contain important analyses of the nature and functions of voluntary associations.

————, "Voluntary Associations Under Conditions of Competition and Conflict," *Social Forces*, 34:159-163 (December, 1955). This is one of the few empirical studies of voluntary associations in action, as distinguished from studies of participation in these groups. As the title indicates, the processes of competition and conflict are observed in terms of their influence upon the organizational structure.

Scott, John C., "Membership and Participation in Voluntary Associations," *American Sociological Review*, 22:315-326 (June, 1957). In a medium-sized New England community, the role of the voluntary association is examined in detail. The study bears out the hypotheses advanced in earlier investigations (notably that of Komarovsky) that participation is largely confined to the middle and upper-middle classes, who make up for their relative lack of numbers by their interest and enthusiasm.

Warner, W. Lloyd, *American Life: Dream and Reality*. Chicago: University of Chicago Press, 1953. Chapter 9 of this book is entitled "Associations in America." It deals with the role of voluntary associations in the community, with particular reference to Yankee City, the New England city which Warner and his associates studied in the late 1930's and 1940's.

Wright, Charles R., and Herbert H. Hyman, "Voluntary Association Memberships of American Adults: Evidence from National Sample Surveys," *American Sociological Review*, 23:284-294 (June, 1958). This is a significant addition to existing knowledge of voluntary associations. As the subtitle indicates, the data were taken from national surveys, thus getting a nation-wide sample for the first time. With almost half (47 per cent) of all families in the United States indicating that they belonged to *no* voluntary association, the assumption that Americans are a "nation of joiners" must be revised.

6 *Group Norms*

The Nature of Group Expectations

Man is a social animal who interacts with other social animals through symbolic communication. He lives his life in contact with other men in a variety of group relationships. He is controlled by group pressures when he is acting as a human being and not as an animal. His *social* behavior is therefore socially determined, whereas his *physical* behavior (digestive, respiratory, eliminative) is only remotely modified by group interaction. In the present chapter, we shall examine how man is controlled and how his behavior is determined by group norms. To understand the varied implications of this control, we must understand the nature of group *expectations.* Depending upon the circumstances, these socially sanctioned patterns of behavior are called norms, folkways, mores, or laws.

In the process of group interaction, members develop certain expectations. This means exactly what it says: that members of a group *expect* that other members will act in a certain way under certain conditions. When one person greets another, for example, he expects that the salutation will be returned in the manner appropriate to the group setting. When the other's behavior conforms to this expectation, each continues on his way with a (minimal) feeling of well-being because the brief interaction has gone according to expectation. If the second person should respond to the conventional greeting with a vulgar gesture, the greeter will be shocked, frustrated, and probably angered. The other is thus failing to react in the expected manner.[1]

We have here the basic element of social interaction, as the process whereby two or more persons are in meaningful contact. Each takes the other into account and governs himself accordingly.[2] In the group, interaction occurs over a considerable period, and the members work out certain expectations that are unique to the relationship. In a larger sense, a given society (or social system) works out expected forms of behavior that enable members to anticipate the behavior of others and adjust their own behavior accordingly.

These forms of expected behavior become common group property. The individual who participates intimately in the group will acquire its characteristic expectations and they will determine his own reaction to future situations. Social expectations not only involve the individual's idea of what the other will do, but also his idea of what he himself should do. When two or more persons are in interaction, their behavior is a partial expression of their expectations of their own, as well as others', behavior. The student learns that certain things are expected of him by his friends and certain others by his teachers. What he actually *does* in given situations is in part a result of the relative intensity of these expectations. The tendency is to follow the expectations of his fellows, rather than those of his teachers, in cases of conflicting expectations.[3]

Group life is made up of a network of such expectations. Some are even simpler than the above example of the social salutation. Other expectations involve a complex series of reciprocal responses. When a man asks a woman to marry him, he sets in motion a chain of expected responses, of whose nature and complexity he is only dimly aware. Members of a family learn to anticipate certain attentions and responses from each other. These expectations vary from one society to another, and the members of the American family have very different expectations from those of the Chinese family. The family in our society is char-

---

[1] Talcott Parsons and Edward A. Shils (eds.), *Toward a General Theory of Action* (Cambridge: Harvard University Press, 1951), p. 51.

[2] Herbert Blumer, "Psychological Import of the Human Group," Chapter 8 in Muzafer Sherif and M. O. Wilson (eds.), *Group Relations at the Crossroads* (New York: Harper & Brothers, 1953).

[3] Richard Videbeck and Allan P. Bates, "An Experimental Study of Conformity to Role Expectations," *Sociometry*, 22:1-11 (March, 1959). Cf. also Clay V. Brittain, "Adolescent Choices and Parent-Peer Cross-Pressures," *American Sociological Review*, 28:385-391 (June, 1963).

acterized by a greater informality than is present in other groups, but the expectations are still there. Each member is taught to expect definite acts and sequences of acts from every other member.

The family is also the group through which many of the broader expectations of society are transmitted to the child. These expectations range in importance from matters of etiquette to such fundamental questions as a belief in God, monogamous marriage, and private property. Informal education in the family and later in other groups is the process of interaction by which these patterns of related expectations are inculcated in the individual so that he will never forget and rarely question them. Such secondary groups as the school, the church, and the labor union assist in the educational process by imparting some of the expectations of the larger society. If the person is to act efficiently in his group setting, he must be familiar with its expectations. In this sense, adjustment to society means an understanding of and adjustment to its expectations.[4]

The Role of Social Interaction

The expectations of the group thus evolve and are maintained through social interaction.[5] The most important single characteristic of this interaction is its mutual or reciprocal character. The individual is made aware not only of his own expected behavior but of the expected behavior of others toward him. Action is thus constantly oriented toward the expected action of the other(s). It is this quality that distinguishes social action from physical action. The individual may react violently when he barks his shins upon a stone wall, but his action is not predetermined by any expected reaction on the part of the wall. Action between two human beings, however, always carries with it an expectation of similar or appropriate response from the other person. As Parsons suggests: "It is the fact that expectations operate on *both* sides of the relation between a given actor and the object of his orientation which distinguishes social interaction from orientation to nonsocial objects." [6]

Group expectations are not always uniform. The individual may not need to conform *exactly* to the expectations of others. In many forms of interaction, the expectations cover only the *general* form of reciprocal response and do not prescribe precisely what each actor will say or do. The social expectations surrounding a high school date, for example, are highly ritualized, with both parties expected to respond to the actions of the other in a socially approved fashion.[7] The exact forms of such mutual response, however, depend upon the personalities and the situation. At the same time, there is a "range of toleration" within which the boy and the girl are expected to operate, violable at the risk of social disapproval. The group provides the general setting of reciprocal

---

[4] Peter M. Blau, "Structural Effects," *American Sociological Review*, 25:178-193 (April, 1960).

[5] Franklin J. Shaw and Robert S. Ort, *Personal Adjustment in the American Culture* (New York: Harper & Brothers, 1953), pp. 26-27.

[6] Parsons and Shils (eds.), *Toward a General Theory of Action, op. cit.*, p. 15.

[7] Margaret Mead, *Male and Female* (New York: William Morrow & Company, 1949), Chapter 14.

responses within which the actors are expected to remain, even though the exact pattern of response permits some leeway.[8]

Social interaction is never completely uniform. Every individual is subject to different forms of interaction as he progresses from infancy to adulthood. The expectations of the larger society are seldom transmitted consistently to everyone. The child learns the society's expectations through his own family, which has its own interpretation of many of them. Expectations therefore vary slightly from one group to another, even though they are essentially similar. The social experience of two persons is never exactly the same, even though they are reared in the same family. The interpretation of group expectations is always subject to some variation, and no two individuals have the same pattern.

In these terms, each person may be viewed as a number of fragmentary persons. This internal cast of characters is made up of the patterns of expectations that each person follows in the various groups of which he is a member. Each group calls out a different combination of expectations and the individual acts differently in different settings. We are different persons, in a sense, in the classroom than at a fraternity dance or a football game. In each case, we try to live up to our conception of the expectations of others. We have learned that cer-

[8] Talcott Parsons, *The Social System* (Glencoe, Ill.: The Free Press, 1951), pp. 234-235.

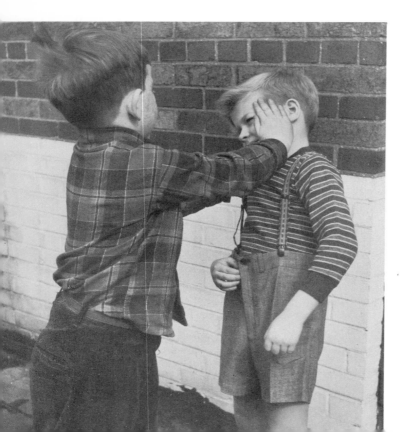

In social interaction, members of a society expect that other members will behave in a certain way under certain conditions; this little boy fails to act as he is supposed to.

tain responses are expected of us in the family and others in the peer group. In each group setting, our behavior is organized according to the expectations of others. We accept most of these expectations uncritically and follow them because it is the easiest thing to do.[9]

The Normative Aspect of Group Expectations

As social expectations evolve through social interaction, they take on elements of right and wrong, of what ought and ought not be. In short, they become social *norms*, namely group expectations with moral overtones. According to Sherif: "The term 'social norm' is a sociological designation referring ... to all products of group interaction which regulate members' behavior in terms of the expected or even the ideal behavior. A norm denotes not only expected behavior but a *range of tolerable behavior,* the limits of which define deviate acts." [10] Some group expectations carry a stronger normative content than others, as we shall see in our analysis of the folkways and mores. Human behavior has meaning largely in normative terms. Patterns of expectations are defined by the group, and the individual gradually acquires the norms of his society.[11]

Norms evolve from group interaction. When a new group is formed, new norms arise from the interaction of the members. These norms are *new products* and not merely the sum total of the norms of the individuals. Group norms cannot be anticipated from the expectations of the individual members. In a number of experimental group situations, the emergence of new norms has been observed. The group interaction is unique and hence the product is always something new.[12] When a number of boys form a neighborhood gang, the group norms are neither the total nor the average of the norms of the participants. Considerable similarity does exist, it is true, between the norms of various groups in the same neighborhood of the city. But there is always some difference between norms because each group interaction is unique.[13]

Norms help to make human behavior predictable.[14] If we know the norms of a group, we can predict what the members will do in some (but not all) of the situations governed by the group. Members of a family can predict the behavior of the husband, wife, and children in terms of the norms of the family group and those of the larger subculture and culture. Persons reared in the Deep South absorb certain normative expectations on racial discrimination, and hence many aspects of their behavior can be predicted from a knowledge of these norms. Each person acquires the norms of his society from a variety of sources—the family, the play group, the church, the school, and the mass

---

[9] Parsons and Shils (eds.), *Toward a General Theory of Action, op. cit.,* p. 154.

[10] Muzafer Sherif, "Integrating Field Work and Laboratory in Small-Group Research," *American Sociological Review,* 19:759-771 (December, 1954), p. 763. (His italics.)

[11] Talcott Parsons, *Essays in Sociological Theory Pure and Applied* (Glencoe, Ill.: The Free Press, 1949), p. 169.

[12] Muzafer Sherif, *The Psychology of Social Norms* (New York: Harper & Brothers, 1936).

[13] Sherif, "Integrating Field Work and Laboratory in Small-Group Research," *op. cit.,* p. 767.

[14] Michael S. Olmstead, *The Small Group* (New York: Random House, Inc., 1959), pp. 88-93.

media. Whatever the source, the similarity of norms makes social interaction (within certain limits) predictable. People know in general what to expect of others and themselves. Life becomes meaningful to them in these terms.[15]

In his classic studies of social expectations in children's groups, Piaget found that the child is unable to make up new norms until he can understand group interaction. The young child initially follows the rules and regulations (expectations) given to him by his parents. He applies these old expectations to a new group experience until he is able to realize the nature of the group. He gradually understands that human beings interact on the basis of mutual expectations that grow out of group situations. Only then is he able to make up new rules to govern behavior in the new setting. When norms have been formulated in the new group situation, they are accepted by the members and serve as guides to future behavior. The children then become concerned with the enforcement of the group norms that they themselves have established. They expect to follow the new rules themselves and expect the others to do likewise.[16]

The Individual and the Norm

"A norm," says Homans, "is a statement made by a number of members of a group, not necessarily by all of them, that the members ought to behave in a certain way under certain circumstances." [17] By conforming to the *norms*, the group member receives certain benefits, the most important of which is acceptance. He is rewarded by the approbation of the other members and often by his own. This feeling is very gratifying to the person, whether or not he is consciously aware of the reason for his feeling. A number of experimental studies have indicated that ". . . if an individual desires to attain, or maintain, an intimate relationship with others, if he wants to 'get somewhere' either within a group or via a group, he must identify himself with the opinions and values of these others." [18] In short, he must conform to the group norms.

The normative aspects of behavior constitute a major difference between human and animal behavior. Man is (presumably) the only animal that sets up norms by which he judges both his own behavior and that of others. These norms are accepted as the proper method of behavior, and the individual conforms to them because it is expedient to do so. Certain norms have a strong content of morality, and the person follows them because it is his moral duty. The norms do not always represent the "ideal" patterns in a particular society, but rather those that are widely accepted. The Sermon on the Mount states the highest ideal of Christian behavior, but the majority of persons in our society are not expected to follow these teachings literally. Saints and Saviours have a

---

[15] Parsons and Shils (eds.), *Toward a General Theory of Action, op. cit.*, pp. 105-106.

[16] Jean Piaget, *The Moral Judgment of the Child* (London: Kegan Paul, 1932).

[17] George C. Homans, *Social Behavior: Its Elementary Forms* (New York: Harcourt, Brace & World, Inc., 1961), p. 378.

[18] Elihu Katz and Paul F. Lazarsfeld, *Personal Influence: The Part Played by People in the Flow of Mass Communications* (Glencoe, Ill.: The Free Press, 1955), pp. 52-53.

code of expectations that is, by definition, higher than that of the ordinary person.

Products of group interaction cannot be directly experienced with the senses. We cannot see a social norm *as such*, inasmuch as it consists of the expectations of what each actor in a social situation is supposed to do. We cannot weigh the social norms relating to sexual behavior, family relationships, national loyalty, or belief in God. We can merely observe what people *do* in these situations. Uniformities in behavior can be observed and the norms inferred from the behavior. What people do and say (or what they refrain from doing and saying) in various group situations are the data that can be observed and measured. The scientific reality involves both the behavior and the inferences that can be drawn from it. Social norms constitute a basic reality in social interaction.[19]

The most intimate relationship between the individual and the group occurs on the normative level. As stated by Sherif, "the individual becomes a group member to the extent that he internalizes the major norms of the group, carries on the responsibilities, and meets expectations for the position he occupies." [20] This process may be seen in long range in the socialization of the individual from infancy to adulthood, as he gradually incorporates the norms of the larger society into his personality. The process may be seen in short range in the initiation of a boy into a neighborhood gang, as he learns the expectations of the group and acts accordingly. The individual's feeling of self-respect is closely identified with the group norms. When he follows these expectations, he feels content and secure. When he deviates from them, his self-feeling suffers accordingly.[21]

The primary group is the most important agency in the preservation of group norms. The child learns most of the basic norms of his society from the family. He continues to experience the norms in other primary relationships. In the play group of the child, the clique of the adolescent, the friendship group of the factory worker, or the group of army buddies, the evidence has shown that these groups *reinforce* the norms. Interaction is an active force in this process, and the group disciplines its deviants and tries to insure conformity in those who remain loyal to it. The person who wishes to remain a member in good standing tries to adapt himself to the group norms, as he understands them. His attitudes toward himself depend in part upon the attitudes of others toward him. These attitudes are in turn related to his continued conformity to the normative patterns of behavior.

Deviations from the Norm

The average person does not follow the norms of the group at all times. Norms are the products of group interaction and often seem to benefit the group rather than the individual. It is sometimes boring, irritating, or inconvenient to

---

[19] Marion J. Levy, Jr., *The Structure of Society* (Princeton: Princeton University Press, 1952), p. 114.
[20] Sherif, "Integrating Field Work and Laboratory in Small-Group Research," *op. cit.*, p. 763.
[21] Parsons, *Essays in Sociological Theory Pure and Applied, op. cit.*, p. 169.

follow the norms, and people may deviate from these expectations when they think they can get away with it. We have examined some of the theoretical implications of deviance in Chapter 3, with particular reference to the role of communication in this process. We will indicate in more concrete terms some of the aspects of deviation from group norms.[22]

The tendency to deviate is not confined to modern society. It is also found in isolated, primitive societies, where the informal group control is presumably very strong. Among the Trobriand Islanders, Malinowski found that many of the more burdensome customs were evaded when the individual believed (rightly or wrongly) that he could escape detection. The group norm relating to exogamy, for example, prohibited sexual intercourse and marriage between members of the same clan. Group sanctions against such behavior were, in theory, very drastic and even involved suicide by the guilty party if he were discovered and publicly insulted. If no such public gesture took place, however, nothing much was done about this violation of the sexual norm and the culprits were allowed to go their illicit ways in peace. Even in such a tightly knit society as that of the Trobriands, the norms do not function "automatically" to insure obedience. Deviation can and does occur on a wide scale when it is convenient.[23]

In the same primitive society, systematic methods of evading other norms have arisen. Even those with supernatural (magical) sanctions can be broken, provided one makes use of other supernatural (counter-magical) sanctions. A man who wishes to violate the norm against adultery may thus enlist magical practices to estrange the affection of a wife from her husband and induce her to look favorably upon him (the prospective seducer). In much the same way, magic may be used to commit acts against the normative structure: "to destroy the crops, to thwart a fisherman, to drive the pigs into the jungle, to blight bananas . . . [or] to spoil a feast."[24] The institutions of Trobriand society are based upon norms that forbid these and other malicious practices. At the same time, there are systematic and institutionalized methods of evading these norms.[25]

The systematic deviation from group norms is by no means limited to primitive societies. Indeed, it is probably more widely practiced in complex social systems, where the informal methods of social control are weak and the formal methods are not widely accepted. In our own society, a variety of normative standards are systematically evaded by persons who simultaneously affirm the importance and sanctity of the norm. This is, in effect, a form of unconscious social hypocrisy, in which people say one thing and do another. Among the common evasions of important norms are the following:

---

[22] For an excellent discussion of this behavior, see Albert K. Cohen, "The Study of Social Disorganization and Deviant Behavior," in Robert K. Merton, et al., (eds.), Sociology Today (New York: Basic Books, 1959), pp. 461-484.

[23] Bronislaw Malinowski, Crime and Custom in Savage Society (London: Routledge & Kegan Paul, Ltd., 1926), Part II, Chapter 1, "The Law in Breach and the Restoration of Order."

[24] Ibid., p. 82.

[25] Ibid., pp. 81-82.

1. The affirmation of premarital sexual chastity and the large-scale indulgence in premarital sexual relationships.

2. The statement of equality before the law for all men and the prevalence of racial, religious, and ethnic discrimination.

3. The ethical conception of truth and the presence of certain practices in advertising, ranging from exaggeration to outright misrepresentation.

4. The lip service given to honesty in government and the widespread practice of political corruption.

5. The emphasis upon honesty in intellectual and academic activities and the practice of cribbing and copying.

6. The professional codes of doctors and lawyers and the practices of fee-splitting and ambulance-chasing.[26]

In these and other forms of deviation, one constant element appears. This is the discrepancy between cultural goals and the approved means of reaching them. The man who seeks sexual pleasure outside of marriage, the corrupt politician who illicitly seeks money and power, the student who tries to pass an examination by cheating, and the criminal who gets money at the point of a gun instead of by working—each of these persons is trying to reach a social goal by illegitimate means. In so doing, he is deviating from the norms which society expects its members to follow. We are, in short, dealing with "pressures toward deviant behavior arising from discrepancies between cultural goals and approved modes of access to them." [27]

As a result of this discrepancy between means and ends, the deviant person rejects one norm or group of norms. He may do this deliberately, as when the criminal plans an armed robbery. The student rejects another set of norms when he copies another's paper because "everybody else does it." The corrupt politician may similarly rationalize his behavior in various ways. However conscious or unconscious the motivation, the deviant is rejecting, in Dubin's words, "at least one facet of the social system." [28] Most deviants confine their rejection to a particular group of norms; few, if any, reject the entire pattern of society. The bank robber who obeys the traffic laws, is kind to his mother, and is a faithful husband scrupulously follows the norms in these fields. His rejection is limited to the norms relating to private property.

Reasons for Deviance

Deviance occurs for various reasons. Some deviant behavior takes place because the individual does not consider the norm very important. Many traffic violations fall in this category. Other such behavior arises from the fact that all the

---

[26] Adapted from Robin M. Williams, Jr., *American Society: A Sociological Interpretation* (New York: Alfred A. Knopf, Inc., 1951), pp. 357-366.

[27] Richard A. Cloward, "Illegitimate Means, Anomie, and Deviant Behavior," *American Sociological Review*, 24:164-178 (April, 1959), p. 164.

[28] Robert Dubin, "Deviant Behavior and Social Structure: Continuities in Social Theory," *American Sociological Review*, 24:147-164 (April, 1959), p. 163.

members of the society do not understand the norm very well. The lower-class person is not aware of many of the niceties of etiquette that are part of the expected behavior of upper-class people. Other norm violations reflect class differences in the norms themselves, as seen in the case of sexual behavior.[29] Still other deviance reflects the handicaps of lower social economic position and antisocial behavior on the part of the parents. In one study, children of deviant fathers showed an unusually high rate of deviance themselves. The sequence of deviance from one generation to the next is summarized as follows: "Anti-social fathers have (a) low occupational achievement with consequent low social status, and (b) a disproportionately high rate of anti-social children." [30]

In many situations, the norms do not evoke a single type of response, but rather a range of permitted responses. In this sense, some degree of flexibility of behavior is permitted, and the individual can act in various ways without deviating from permissible behavior. A study of student attitudes about cheating disclosed considerable variation as to the types of acts that the students approved, depending upon the circumstances. The norm in this case was flexible rather than rigid, and the range of expectations was rather wide. The degree of norm flexibility naturally varies between different types of behavior, for example, between murder and cheating on examinations. In certain realms of behavior, the norms allow considerable variation in order to facilitate group interaction.[31]

The reactions of the group to deviance range from irritation, through fear, to hatred, depending upon the importance of the norm. The group may punish the deviant in various ways. The other members may avoid him, restrict their relations with him, make fun of him, expel him, or put him to death.[32] In the majority of cases, however, the group punishes the deviant through his own sense of guilt, shame, and remorse. These reactions are characteristically and intensely human. The individual may not follow a norm (for example, that relating to sexual behavior), but it influences his behavior nevertheless. If the norm were not present, the deviant would not suffer pangs of conscience because he has evaded it. The group establishes the standards, even though the majority of individuals may, in one or more respects, fail to live up to them. The norm exists in the personality of the individual and serves as a standard by which he judges his own behavior.[33]

Deviant behavior reflects a still more basic human quality—*individuality*. No man is ever fully "socialized" in the sense that he is completely and unequivocably in tune with the norms and values of his society. In a penetrating article

[29] Alfred C. Kinsey, *et al.*, *Sexual Behavior in the Human Male* (Philadelphia: W. B. Saunders Company, 1948).

[30] Lee N. Robins, Harry Gyman, and Patricia O'Neal, "The Interaction of Social Class and Deviant Behavior," *American Sociological Review*, 27:480-492 (August, 1962), p. 492.

[31] Samuel A. Stouffer, "An Analysis of Conflicting Social Norms," *American Sociological Review*, 14:707-717 (December, 1949).

[32] Robert E. L. Faris, "Development of the Small-Group Research Movement," in Muzafer Sherif and M. O. Wilson (eds.), *Group Relations at the Crossroads* (New York: Harper & Brothers, 1953), p. 175.

[33] For a further discussion of deviation, see Robert A. Dentler and Kai T. Erikson, "The Functions of Deviance in Groups," *Social Problems*, 7:98-107 (Fall, 1959).

addressed to this theme, Dennis Wrong has called attention to what he calls "The Oversocialized Conception of Man." [34] This conception (or rather misconception) assumes that men automatically "internalize" group norms and then eagerly respond to these "expectations" in an effort to maintain a favorable self-image. Within certain limits, as we have suggested, this is an adequate explanation of the relationship between human behavior and social order. But it is not *completely* adequate.

There is always an element of individual perverseness in every human being that reflects his personal uniqueness, if nothing else. The interests of the individual are never exactly the same as those of the group, no matter how carefully he has been socialized. Sexual drives are perhaps the most obvious motivations for man's deviant actions. Material interests are another. Desire for power over others is a third. As a result, self-interest is often stronger than group interest. Each of us is indeed a *social* animal, but none of us is a completely *socialized* one. The difference is more than a mere play on words. We internalize the norms, but we remain individuals. As a result of his individuality, man is more than a "disembodied, conscience-driven, status-seeking phantom." [35] His saving quality of individualism will always make him something of a deviant.

The Folkways as Group Norms

The folkways are literally the "ways of the folk"—norms that arise in social interaction and are handed down from one generation to the next. The classic analysis of these group expectations was made more than half a century ago by William Graham Sumner.[36] He began his study of the folkways with the fundamental fact that man must act in order to live. He has needs that must be met in some fashion if the group is to survive. He is constantly faced with situations that require action, whether or not there is any precedent to guide him. Man will meet a new situation with a trial-and-error attempt to do *something*, to reach his goal as best he can. If this attempt is moderately successful in meeting the need, it tends to be adopted by the group and becomes the accepted way. The folkways are simply the accumulated patterns of expected behavior that have arisen to meet the recurrent situations of social interaction.[37]

The folkways seldom result from rational deliberation. Still less do they continue because of their essential rationality. They are, instead, characteristically irrational and subservient to the past. In Sumner's words, "The folkways . . . are not creations of human purpose and wit. They are like products of natural forces which men unconsciously set in operation . . . which are handed down by

---

[34] Dennis H. Wrong, "The Oversocialized Conception of Man in Modern Sociology," *American Sociological Review*, 26:183-193 (April, 1961).

[35] *Ibid.*, p. 193. See also Lewis A. Coser, "Some Functions of Deviant Behavior and Normative Flexibility," *American Journal of Sociology*, 68:172-181 (September, 1962).

[36] William Graham Sumner, *Folkways* (Boston: Ginn and Company, 1906).

[37] *Ibid.*, Chapter I. Cf. Parsons and Shils (eds.), *Toward a General Theory of Action, op. cit.*, Chapter 1.

tradition and admit of no exception or variation, yet change to meet new conditions, still within the same limited methods, and without rational reflection or purpose." [38] Folkways become normative and the individual follows them for fear of possible sanctions if he does not.

The folkways include thousands of group expectations that have arisen in the cumulative life of a society. Representative folkways are rules of eating and drinking, forms of salutation and departure, details of dress, ceremonies and rituals of polite deportment, rules of behavior in business, and conduct expected in such institutional settings as the church, school, and family. Some of the folkways are collected in books of etiquette. Most of them, however, never attain the dignity of print, but exist in unwritten and implicit form in the social heritage. They constitute one part of the pattern of expectations by which the group instructs the individual. Acting through group interaction, the folkways exert a strong social force, and in this way influence individual behavior.[39]

The folkways constitute the "right" (that is, the normative) way to respond to various situations. "There is," says Sumner, "a right way to catch game, to win a wife, to make one's self appear, to cure disease, to honor ghosts, to treat comrades or strangers, to behave when a child is born, on the warpath, in council, and so on in all cases which can arise." [40] In a simple society, the "right" way is widely understood and most people follow it without hesitation. In a complex society, there may be several "right" ways, each followed by a particular group. Persons are exposed to this variety of norms and expectations and become understandably bewildered. In the modern urban community, with its conflicting norms, one is often confused as to which way to behave.

The folkways are maintained because they are old, familiar, and easy. This does not mean that they *never* change. The folkways are, indeed, subject to what Sumner called a "strain of improvement" toward the more efficient achievement of group goals. Folkways that are clearly incompatible with these goals cannot continue indefinitely, although they often linger on long after their functional utility has disappeared. In social interaction, human beings are continually experimenting, even though the experimentation may be largely unconscious. Changes in the folkways are often painfully slow, and generations come and go with little apparent innovation. If the frustration from an unsatisfactory response is too great, however, the folkway will gradually change and the "strain of improvement" will become apparent.[41]

The folkways are subject to another general tendency, one that Sumner called the "strain of consistency." This means that they tend to develop in approximate consistency with each other and thereby give internal cohesion to the society. The folkways grouped about the great institutions of church, state, family, and economic system maintain a certain basic consistency, so that one set of folkways does not depart drastically from the others. This consistency means in

---

[38] Sumner, *op. cit.*, p. 4.
[39] Ruth Benedict, *Patterns of Culture* (New York: Penguin Books, Inc., 1946), p. 2.
[40] Sumner, *op. cit.*, p. 28.
[41] Sumner, *op. cit.*, pp. 5-6.

our society that the major institutions have such values in common as democracy, capitalism, and Christianity. Folkways alien to these values would not be accepted by most of the people. The "strain of consistency" is never completely realized, especially in a dynamic society. The *tendency* in this direction, however, is a characteristic of the folkways.[42]

We may therefore think of the folkways in their entirety as "a great mass of usages, of all degrees of importance, covering all the interests of life, constituting an outfit of instruction for the young, embodying a life policy, forming character, containing a world philosophy, . . . and sanctioned by ghost fear so that variation is impossible. . . ."[43] The folkways, the mores, and the laws are the principal normative elements defining individual participation in group interaction. The origins of many of the folkways are lost in the mists of time; these expectations continue to be handed down and accepted because they have "always" been so. In this way, the folkways provide their own justification. They are true because they have "always" been true.

The Mores as Group Norms

Group expectations have varying degrees of normative value. Some are clearly more important than others. The penalty for deviation from some norms is greater than from others. It is not a matter of overwhelming importance, for example, if a man fails to remove his hat when addressing a woman. He is expected to make such a gesture of politeness, but he is not clapped into jail if he fails to carry out this or any other folkway. Such an expectation carries some normative power, but it is still marginal to social welfare. Other expectations, however, *are* important to social welfare. Among them are those patterns relating to the family, the state, property, and human life. These expectations are called *mores.*

The mores have been defined by Sumner as "the folkways, including the philosophical and ethical generalizations as to societal welfare which are suggested by them, and inherent in them, as they grow."[44] Distinctions between folkways and mores are often arbitrary, since many are so marginal to group welfare that they make a clear line of demarcation impossible. A working definition, however, is usually made between these two types of expected behavior. In practice, men place greater stress upon some norms than upon others. In some fields, there is a wide range of tolerable behavior and the individual has considerable freedom. In other fields, the range is narrower. An approximate distinction is drawn in all societies between, say, murder and social etiquette, and there is usually a strong agreement on the distinction.

The mores contain group expectations that are ordinarily taken for granted. People are not usually aware of the mores until they are faced with abrupt

---

[42] *Ibid.*
[43] *Ibid.,* p. 67.
[44] *Ibid.,* p. 30.

changes in them. In times of rapid social change, the mores may no longer be suitable to the new situation. In the decade of the 1930's, the traditional mores of individual initiative were seriously questioned by mass unemployment. In the decade of the 1940's, the mores of individual freedom became more precious because of the threat to their existence from the Fascist powers. The decade of the 1950's was faced with the danger of Soviet imperialism, and this situation made persons aware of the mores of liberty. Group expectations embodied in the mores are seldom questioned until a major crisis arises.

The term "mores" is the plural of the Latin word *mos*, which means custom. Mores forms the root of the English word "moral," thus literally referring to any act or belief in accord with customary group expectations. An act is moral if it is customary, immoral if it is not. In popular parlance, "morality" has become largely confined to one phase of behavior—that pertaining to sex relations. The immoral person is therefore one who has violated the sex mores. This is an arbitrary limitation. Immorality applies with equal justification to the violation of any set of mores. A man may be immoral in his business dealings, in his treatment of his family, and in his callousness toward the unfortunates in society. These and other actions are defined by the mores, and their violation equally endangers group welfare.

In a small and comparatively simple society, the mores tend toward uniformity throughout.[45] In a large and complex society, the mores vary between social classes and subcultures. The mores of the lower class in this country, for example, differ from those of the middle and upper classes regarding premarital sex relationships.[46] Significant class differences also appear concerning thrift and saving, with the middle class more insistent upon these virtues than the lower class.[47] The consumption of alcohol is a violation of the mores of many middle-class persons in rural communities, in sharp distinction to the attitudes of most groups in the large city.[48] In these and many other respects, the mores differ within a dynamic and heterogeneous society.

Folkways become mores through a change in emphasis and definition. Certain folkways may take on the sanctity of mores merely because they are old. The way of the ancestors becomes the only right way and any change is rebellion. The welfare (real or supposed) of the group is the crucial consideration, no matter how the judgment has been reached. If the group defines a particular norm as important to its welfare, it *is* important, no matter how trivial it may appear to outsiders. The society is the only agency that can judge the validity of its own norms. There is no international supreme court to define the mores of different societies.

In our society, the norms relating to monogamous marriage, the worship of

[45] Benedict, *Patterns of Culture, op. cit.,* Chapters 4, 5, 6.

[46] Kinsey, *et al., Sexual Behavior in the Human Male, op. cit.,* Chapters 10, 11.

[47] Allison Davis, "Child Rearing in the Class Structure of American Society," in *The Family in a Democratic Society* (New York: Columbia University Press, 1949).

[48] John Dollard, "Drinking Mores of the Social Classes," Lecture 8 in *Alcohol, Science, and Society* (New Haven: *Quarterly Journal of Studies on Alcohol,* 1945).

the Christian God, the rights of private property, and the practice of demo-cratic government are some of the central mores.[49] The numerous written and unwritten prohibitions against murder, rape, incest, theft, sexual license, polyg-amy, and treason are further group expectations that have assumed the status of mores. These judgments may be either positive or negative. They may be stated either as *thou shalt* or *thou shalt not* do this or that. The mores involve sins of omission as well as commission. As the child participates in the primary group, he learns the mores of his society.

The Mores and Group Sanctions

The mores are enforced both by positive sanctions and by *taboo*. The latter concept refers to a prohibition against acts forbidden by the mores. Taboo involves behavior that under no circumstances should be performed. Among primitive societies, taboos are sustained by fear of ghosts or other forms of supernatural retribution, whereas in our society they reflect religious, ethical, or welfare doctrines. Even in primitive societies, however, taboos are not always strictly observed. Social control is ordinarily more complete in such societies than in our own, but primitive man is still an individual. He has desires that run contrary to the norms of the group and he often attempts to satisfy these desires, even though they are forbidden by the most sacred taboos.[50]

Taboos are products of the ages, and deal with acts long regarded as harmful to the group. In this category are certain forms of sexual relations (incest), physical aggression against members of the ingroup, betrayal of the group (treason), and other forms of behavior that cannot be permitted if organized society is to continue. The taboo is not so much an expression of rational thought as of deep feeling against certain behavior. Punishment for the viola-tion of a taboo includes ostracism, banishment, imprisonment, imposed suicide, and death.[51]

The mores are developed, established, and perpetuated by ritual. We are fa-miliar with ritual in connection with religion, whereby certain mores are drama-tized in ceremonies sanctioned by time. Ritual is also important in other situa-tions. In this sense, ritual is any formal and ceremonious pattern of action prescribed by the group and having symbolic significance. Every basic institu-tion has ritualistic ceremonies, in which the members perform symbolic acts that impress upon them the seriousness of the relationship. Religion, government, the school, the army, and many voluntary associations employ ritual to rein-force their norms.[52]

The interaction by which a child learns the mores likewise has many charac-teristics of ritual. The child repeats by rote the group norms as held out to him

---

[49] John Gillin, "National and Regional Cultural Values in the United States," *Social Forces*, 34:107-113 (December, 1955).

[50] Malinowski, *op. cit.*, pp. 98-99.

[51] Sumner, *op. cit.*, pp. 30-31.

[52] W. Lloyd Warner, *American Life: Dream and Reality* (Chicago: University of Chicago Press, 1953), pp. 197-198.

by his parents. By the time he can think for himself, these norms have become such an intimate part of his personality that he does not question them. The essence of ritualistic learning is that it admits of no exception; ritual is essentially unthinking, whether practiced in the church or the family. Ritual involves signs and symbols that are emotionally loaded. Under the spell of ritual, the individual learns to defer to authority and submit to tradition.[53]

The mores may vary in accordance with different group situations.[54] The same act may be against the mores under certain conditions and in agreement with them under other conditions. The deliberate taking of human life is usually a serious moral offense. In time of war, however, it is considered praiseworthy. The change has occurred in the setting and the definition, not in the act itself. This difference is even more significant when viewed in long-term perspective. Such varied activities as dueling, capital punishment for minor theft, witch burning, religious torture, infanticide, prostitution, and many other forms of behavior repugnant to modern society have at one time been defined as correct by the dominant mores of Western society.

The relativity of the mores has been characterized by Sumner's trenchant phase—"The mores can make anything right."[55] In literal truth, they can. Standards of right and wrong of a given people at a given time have no other basis than the mores. These norms constitute the sole *secular* standards of good and bad. The average person has no other basis for judging his own or another's behavior than the mores themselves. These standards have become so integral a part of his personality that he cannot think in any other terms. From the haughty eminence of their own mores, people are always prepared to pass judgment on the behavior of others. Every group makes these judgments in terms of their own mores, which may appear equally wrong to the foreigners whom they judge so blithely. Each society believes in the essential validity of its own mores.[56]

Sumner concludes: "We must conceive of the mores as a vast system of usages, covering the whole of life, and serving all its interests; also containing in themselves their own justification by tradition and use and want, and approved by mystic sanctions until, by rational reflection, they develop their own philosophical and ethical generalizations, which are elevated into 'principles' of truth and right."[57] The mores arise, like the folkways, from the need for action in life situations. The philosophical implications usually arise *after* the mores are established, and some form of rational justification is believed necessary. For the great mass of people, the mores are absolute truth. There are no accepted provisions for questioning the ultimate validity of the mores. The very

---

[53] Sumner, *op. cit.*, pp. 60-62.

[54] Austin L. Porterfield and Jack Gibbs, "Law and the Mores," *Sociology and Social Research,* 37:223-229 (March-April, 1953).

[55] Sumner, *op. cit.*, Chapter 15, "The Mores Can Make Anything Right."

[56] See Harold T. Christensen, "Cultural Relativism and Premarital Sex Norms," *American Sociological Review,* 25:31-39 (February, 1960).

[57] Sumner, *op. cit.*, p. 79.

act of questioning would imply that they might not be correct. Such an implication is unthinkable to most people.

In primitive, isolated, and preliterate societies, social control is based almost wholly upon the folkways and mores. These societies are so cohesive that the informal expectations provide all the necessary sanctions. In Redfield's words, "Men act with reference to each other by understandings which are tacit and traditional. There are no formal contracts or other agreements." [58] The choice of alternate forms of behavior is limited, and the average person has no source of social approval or disapproval other than the folkways and mores. Hence he seldom engages in behavior that presents any *permanent* danger to the established moral order.

The Laws as Group Norms

In advanced societies, the concept of law emerges from the mores. The mores have regularity, a quality they share with the law. The mores define social relationships; so does the law. The mores and the law both involve sanctions. The difference between the mores and the law is primarily one of the type of sanctions. The law involves physical coercion by an individual or organization whose function is so defined. As stated by an expert in primitive law, the distinction is as follows: "Law is distinguished from mere custom in that it endows certain selected individuals with the privilege-right of applying the sanction of physical coercion, if need be." [59] A normative expectation becomes legal if its omission or commission is met by physical force, or the threat of such force, by a socially constituted authority. Behavior punished by the informal sanctions of the mores may be the same as that punished by the laws. The difference lies in the enforcement.[60]

The *law* thus supplements and enforces the mores. The law may be viewed in two general senses, namely, *customary* law and *enacted* law. The first merely formalizes the customary sanctions of the mores, whereas the second is enacted by organizations established for this purpose. Customary law is composed of "the traditional conceptions of rights and obligations and the customary procedures whereby these rights and obligations are assured." [61] Customary law provides some form of accepted group sanctions when a moral infringement occurs. Punishment is vested in certain members of the society or in special groups convoked for this purpose. The chief sanctions are provided by the mores, and the legal machinery is at first merely an extension of the informal moral order.[62]

As a society grows more complex, an increasing formalization of the law be-

---

[58] Robert Redfield, "The Folk Society," *American Journal of Sociology,* 52:293-308 (January, 1947), p. 300.

[59] E. Adamson Hoebel, *The Law of Primitive Man* (Cambridge: Harvard University Press, 1954), p. 276.

[60] *Ibid.,* p. 28.

[61] Redfield, *op. cit.,* p. 30.

[62] Sumner, *op. cit.,* pp. 55-56.

comes necessary. A permanent organization (court) is established to interpret the laws still embodied in the mores and to apply these precedents to new situations. The mores are arranged (codified) so that they can be applied with greater efficiency to emerging conditions. Customary law is rephrased and some of the ambiguities are removed. A science of the law as an organized body of normative expectations begins to emerge. General principles arise about the mass of customary law and an effort is made to increase the consistency of these principles. Respect for the past is still so strong, however, that no attempt is made for a long time to change the sense of the mores, let alone introduce new conceptions into the body of the law.

This is essentially the process whereby the English common law evolved and became incorporated into our legal system. In this sense, says Sumner, "Legislation . . . has to seek standing ground on the existing mores, and it soon becomes apparent that legislation, to be strong, must be consistent with the mores." [63] Law must conform to existing moral judgments if it is to be obeyed. If the masses consider the law either too strict or too lax (in terms of the mores), they will fail to obey it. The mores differ from one subculture to another, and laws suitable to one subculture may be unsuitable to another. The Prohibition Amendment reflected the mores of large sections of the rural population, and drinking was (and still is) considered by them as morally wrong. But legal prohibition was not in tune with the mores of the metropolitan community, where the law was made virtually inoperative.

As society becomes still more complex, customary law alone is unsatisfactory for social control. Customary law is then supplemented by *enacted* law. The latter is a considerable departure from the idea that the only valid law comes from the mores. The legislative branch of the government is entrusted with enacting new laws to cover new situations. Some of these legislative enactments grow out of the mores, or at least embody principles already laid down in the mores. Others deal with responses to new technological innovations, such as motor vehicle laws. Despite the fact that traffic law violations involve, directly or indirectly, both large loss of life and large property damage, these acts are not ordinarily regarded as socially reprehensible. One of the reasons for this comparative public indifference is the recent origin of such laws and their lack of support in the mores. The person who commits murder evokes the outraged moral sentiments of the group; the speeder who kills someone in an automobile accident is usually regarded as an unfortunate victim of circumstances beyond his control. [64]

Enacted law is ordinarily more flexible than customary law. The latter is bound by the mores and tends to exert a conservative influence over social change. Enacted law has become an important mechanism whereby a democratic society adjusts to the changing conditions of its economic and social structure. [65]

---

[63] *Ibid.*, p. 55.
[64] H. Lawrence Ross, "Traffic Law Violations: A Folk Crime," *Social Problems*, 5:231-241 (Winter, 1960-1961).
[65] Porterfield and Gibbs, *op. cit.*, p. 22.

Such legislation as the Social Security Act of 1935 (with subsequent amendments), the National Labor Relations Act, the Civil Rights Act of 1964, and the various state Fair Employment Practices acts are formal enactments that have anticipated, rather than followed, changes in the mores. The widespread enactment of progressive legislation is thus a bulwark of democracy. The legislation changes the behavior of millions of people. In a comparatively short time, new feelings and emotions (mores) develop about such enacted legislation. The innovation has been accepted and the mores have changed.[66]

Not all behavior carries the sanctions of the folkways, the mores, or the laws. Much of the ordinary behavior of modern, urban society is not expressly defined and hence bears no normative implications. Many familiar daily actions, from brushing one's teeth in the morning to going to bed at night, fall into a category of *permissive* behavior, with few explicit moral judgments. In this large and amorphous realm, the individual is comparatively free to do as he wishes, without evoking either positive or negative sanctions.

The range of such permissive behavior is greater in complex societies than in primitive or folk societies. The primitive society is far from being a group of automatons, but its activities are ordinarily more closely bound by the mores than is the case in an urban, complex society. In the latter setting, the person can do as he pleases in a variety of activities that are forbidden by custom in "sacred" societies.[67] In this sense, the popular conception of complete "freedom" in primitive societies is an illusion. From the cradle to the grave, custom defines the behavior of the primitive man. This custom is not always obeyed, but it is nevertheless always there.

In this chapter, we have surveyed the nature and functions of group norms. These patterns arise from group interaction and are perpetuated in the same way. The norms carry an element of right and wrong, good and bad, acceptable and unacceptable. These group expectations include the folkways, the mores, and the laws; and the members of the society are constrained in varying degrees and in different ways by these normative patterns. The norms are not universally obeyed in any society, primitive or civilized, and various methods have grown up to evade them. Whether honored in the breach or the observance, however, the mere presence of the norm has an important effect upon behavior. Man is a norm-making animal.

---

[66] Harry V. Ball, George E. Simpson, and Kiyoshi Ikeda, "Law and Social Change," *American Journal of Sociology*, 67:532-540 (March, 1962).

[67] Howard Becker, "Sacred and Secular Societies," *Social Forces*, 28:361-376 (May, 1950).

SELECTED BIBLIOGRAPHY

Angell, Robert C., *Free Society and Moral Crisis*. Ann Arbor: University of Michigan Press, 1958. The grave theme of this important book is moral order and moral integration in a society. This integration is based upon norms and reflects the degree to which they are obeyed. The author views the good society as "one in which leaders are working through many kinds of institutional groups to achieve the adjustments in the moral web that are both suitable to the conditions and consonant with common values."

Ball, Harry V., George E. Simpson, and Kiyoshi Ikeda, "Law and Social Change," *American Journal of Sociology,* 67:532-540 (March, 1962). This article is a reëxamination of Sumner's position with regard to law and social change. The master's central thesis is that the way to change the mores is to change the rituals, not vice versa.

Blau, Peter M., "Structural Effects," *American Sociological Review,* 25:178-193 (April, 1960). In this important article, the author presents both a theoretical and an empirical analysis of the relationship between group norms and the personalities of the members. The thesis is that these norms are, in a sense, *external* to the value patterns of any of the group members, taken individually.

Dubin, Robert, "Deviant Behavior and Social Structure: Continuities in Social Theory," *American Sociological Review,* 24:147-164 (April, 1959). A significant contribution to the literature of group norms and the deviation therefrom is made in this long, closely reasoned essay. The central position is that deviation represents a rejection of "at least one facet of the social system."

Homans, George C., *Social Behavior: Its Elementary Forms.* New York: Harcourt, Brace & World, Inc., 1961. Among the "elementary forms" of social behavior that are discussed in this perceptive analysis are the norms. The latter are the statements by members of a social system that it is desirable to act in a certain way under certain conditions. The *actual* behavior may or may not coincide with the expressed ideal.

Kinsey, Alfred C., *et al., Sexual Behavior in the Human Male.* Philadelphia: W. B. Saunders Company, 1948. Also, *Sexual Behavior in the Human Female.* Philadelphia: W. B. Saunders Company, 1953. In these two volumes, the late Dr. Kinsey and his associates offer extensive statistical data on the observance of and departure from a basic normative pattern in our society.

Malinowski, Bronislaw, *Crime and Custom in Savage Society.* London: Routledge & Kegan Paul, Ltd., 1926. In this anthropological classic, the normative patterns of a primitive people (those inhabiting the Trobriand Archipelago near the coast of New Guinea) are explored at length. The author demonstrates conclusively that the uniformity of behavior among the Trobriands is not as great as is believed to exist among primitive peoples generally. Both spontaneous and deliberate violations of the norms continually occur.

Sherif, Muzafer, "Integrating Field Work and Laboratory in Small-Group Research," *American Sociological Review,* 19:759-771 (December, 1954). Beginning with his early experimental work on social norms (1936), the author has made many important contributions to the psychological aspects of group expectations and the way they arise from group interaction.

Sumner, William Graham, *Folkways.* Boston: Ginn and Company, 1906. In this great pioneer study, the author introduces the concepts of the folkways and the mores and establishes the theoretical foundations for many other basic ideas in the field of social norms.

Wrong, Dennis H., "The Oversocialized Conception of Man in Modern Sociology," *American Sociological Review,* 26:183-193 (April, 1961). This illuminating article takes a long, hard look at the process whereby "man becomes tractable to social controls." The author suggests that the theory of first internalizing social norms and then seeking a favorable self-image by conforming strictly to these expectations is perhaps a bit oversimplified.

CULTURE AND

PERSONALITY *Part Two*

7 *Culture*

Culture and Social Interaction

The basic reality of society is two or more persons in meaningful interaction. In the first section, we explored some of the implications of this central fact: first with reference to the nature of social interaction, then in terms of the group forms reflecting this process, and finally with respect to the control exerted over the group members by the normative expectations that issue from social interaction. Society exists in and through social interaction, as human beings react to others and in turn are influenced by them. Each member learns to take into account the behavior of others and in so doing learns to make the appropriate response. Social interaction is thus *reciprocal*, and each member governs his behavior in terms of the expectations of others.

In the present section, we shall undertake a more extensive analysis of the conditions under which social interaction takes place, as well as an examination of the products of this process. The first important concept in our study is that of society (or the group) in interaction. The second central concept deals with the outgrowth of that interaction. The product of group interaction is its culture. The group may vary in size from a small group to an entire society, but the principle is the same.[1]

Society comes first and culture after. Culture issues from society in interaction. During the hundreds of thousands of years when *homo sapiens* was passing through his various developmental sequences, it may be logically assumed that at some time he existed in society but without culture. After the early beginnings of culture, the process became cyclical, with societies evolving cultures which in turn influenced the interaction in the societies. At the present time, of course, every society has a culture that has been handed down from earlier generations and that affects the ongoing process of interaction. But both logically and historically, society precedes culture.[2]

We may provisionally define culture as the learned behavior shared by the members of a society. We shall consider the nature of culture more fully below, but in this sense it is apparent that it arises in and is transmitted by the group. Society and culture are related but not synonymous. Society is the group in interaction and culture is the product. Neither can be fully understood without the other, either in theoretical terms or in terms of a functioning society. The actions of human beings in society are determined in large part by the symbolic meanings implicit in the culture. The culture provides appropriate responses to the needs of the interacting members of a society. In brief, "Interaction makes possible the development of culture on the human level and gives culture its significance in the determination of action." [3]

Social interaction occurs between two or more persons and in an environment composed of still other persons. This means that the behavior of each person is determined both by the physical presence of others and by the socially prescribed bases upon which they act. The element of time is important because the past influences the thoughts and actions of each of us, operating through the heritage of the group. In this sense, we are the heirs of the great traditions of Christianity, democracy, and the other tenets of our society. These traditions form part of the setting within which we interact with others. Culture is incorporated in the individual personality and thereby sets limits for action. Culture is also part of the "external" environment to which we respond because of the expectations of others. In this sense, culture "is present in persons, shaping

---

[1] Michael S. Olmstead, *The Small Group* (New York: Random House, Inc., 1959), Chapter 6, "The Culture of the Group."

[2] David Bidney, *Theoretical Anthropology* (New York: Columbia University Press, 1953), p. 104.

[3] Talcott Parsons and Edward A. Shils (eds.), *Toward a General Theory of Action* (Cambridge: Harvard University Press, 1951), p. 17.

their perceptions of events, other persons, and the environing situation in ways not wholly determined by biology and by environmental press." [4]

This book is based upon society and culture. In the course of our exposition, other basic concepts will emerge. In a very real sense, however, society and culture are the cornerstones to the understanding of social behavior. Man is *both* a social and a cultural animal, and his behavior can be fully grasped only in this double context. During his social development in a particular cultural setting, he develops a personality that has certain qualities in common with other members of the society, as well as certain qualities unique with him. As we continue our analysis, other aspects of the ongoing society will necessitate other concepts for understanding. Among these are personality, status and role, social stratification, social institution, and social change. It may fairly be said, however, that the study of sociology, as here advanced, rests upon the conceptual foundation of society and culture. [5]

Definitions of Culture

There are many definitions of culture. We shall indicate some of the representative definitions of this central concept in order to suggest its richness and manifold implications. We shall then suggest a synthetic definition that combines the principal insights of this important and many-sided term.

1. The classic definition of culture was given many years ago by the anthropologist E. B. Tylor. He stated that "culture ... is that complex whole which includes knowledge, belief, art, morals, law, custom, and any other capabilities and habits acquired by man as a member of society." [6] This definition includes such nonmaterial products of group life as folkways, mores, and laws, which emerge from social interaction and carry a normative content. In addition, there are the material elements that constitute such an important aspect of culture and that, in the form of artifacts ranging from arrowheads to automobiles, represent the most obvious products of society. Finally, there are the meaningful relationships between the parts of culture and the symbolic interpretations placed upon them. Customs, material objects, and meaningful relationships comprise the principal elements of culture.

2. The symbolic aspects of culture are stressed by another anthropologist, Leslie A. White: "Culture is an organization of phenomena—acts (patterns of behavior); objects (tools, things made with tools); ideas (belief, knowledge); and sentiments (attitudes, 'values')—that is dependent upon the use of symbols. Culture began when man as an articulate, symbol-using primate, began. Because of its symbolic character ... culture is easily and readily transmitted from one human organism to another." [7] The history of culture is, in a sense,

---

[4] A. L. Kroeber and Clyde Kluckhohn, *Culture: A Critical Review of Concepts and Definitions, Papers of the Peabody Museum of American Archaeology and Ethnology,* 47:3-223 (1952), p. 186.

[5] Pitirim A. Sorokin, *Society, Culture, and Personality: Their Structure and Dynamics* (New York: Harper & Row, 1947), p. 63.

[6] E. B. Tylor, *Primitive Culture* (London: John Murray, 1871), p. 1.

[7] Leslie A. White, "Culturological vs. Psychological Interpretations of Human Behavior," *American Sociological Review,* 12:686-698 (December, 1947), p. 693.

the history of man as a human being. For hundreds of thousands of years, culture in some form has been continuously transmitted. Some elements have been lost, others have been changed, still others have been added. But culture itself has gone on. "Culture is, therefore," concludes White, "a symbolic, continuous, cumulative, and progressive process." [8]

3. In his definition of culture, Coon stresses its learned quality. He suggests that we may view culture as "the sum total of the ways in which human beings live, transmitted from generation to generation by learning." [9] The variety of elements included in culture is indicated by his statement that "it includes the relations between people in pairs and in groups, man's work activities involving actual materials, and his expenditure of energy in the realm of symbols, including speech, music, the visual arts, and the human body itself." [10] Culture subsumes everything learned, as distinguished from those elements inherited in the germ plasm. Man is an animal that learns symbolically and transmits the products of this learning from generation to generation. The cumulative product is the culture.

4. The intellectual quality of culture is suggested by Bidney. "A culture," he says, "consists of the acquired or cultivated behavior and thought of individuals within a society, as well as of the intellectual, artistic, and social ideals and institutions which the members of the society profess and to which they strive to conform." [11] In this sense, culture is a product of society and is acquired by man in social interaction. The acquisition of culture is primarily an *intellectual* process, and the material aspects become meaningful only in terms of the mind. It is through meaningful communication in the form of language and other symbolic acts that the individual first learns his culture and then transmits it to the coming generation. "Man is by nature a cultural animal," says Bidney, "since he is a self-cultivating, self-reflective, self-conditioning animal and attains to the full development of his natural potentialities only insofar as he lives a cultural life." [12]

5. In his conceptual pattern, Parsons considers culture as a basic constituent of a "system of action." Culture is for him an emergent of social interaction and is a guide to behavior in subsequent interaction. In this sense, culture is closely related to society on the one hand and personality on the other. Culture comes out of social interaction and is an important constituent in personality. The individual incorporates the culture of his society and develops a personality that is more or less adjusted to the demands of that society. [13]

6. This relationship between society, culture, and personality is likewise stressed by Linton: "A society is an organized group of individuals. A culture is an organized group of learned responses characteristic of a particular

[8] *Ibid.*
[9] Carleton S. Coon, *The Story of Man* (New York: Alfred A. Knopf, Inc., 1954), p. 5.
[10] *Ibid.*
[11] Bidney, *Theoretical Anthropology, op. cit.,* p. 30.
[12] *Ibid.,* p. 126.
[13] Parsons and Shils, *op. cit.,* Chapter 1. also Sorokin, *op. cit.,* Chapter 3, "Generic Structure of Sociocultural Phenomena."

society. The individual is a living organism capable of independent thought, feeling, and action, but with his independence limited and all his resources profoundly modified by contact with the society and culture in which he develops." [14] In our own discussion, we shall refer constantly to this threefold and reciprocal relationship between society, culture, and the individual.

7. A further conception of culture is that of Kroeber. In a famous essay first published in 1917, he spoke of culture as "superorganic" in character; that is, existing over and above any specific (organic) individual. By this he meant that culture is held by individuals, but that its existence is independent of any particular individual. The system of meaningful symbols that make up a language illustrates the superorganic quality of culture. The language of a society is not dependent upon the life of any single member. If *all* the members were suddenly wiped out, together with all written records, the language would presumably come to an end. Under ordinary conditions, however, the language is passed on from individual to individual and group to group as a "superorganic product." [15]

8. The most extensive examination of the concept of culture has been made by Kroeber and Kluckhohn. They first studied the history of the word *culture* and its meaning in various linguistic settings. They then surveyed the definitions of culture under the following headings: descriptive, historical, normative, psychological, structural, and genetic. Following this, they investigated the various statements about culture, dealing with its nature, components, and properties, as well as the relations between culture and psychology, culture and language, and culture and society. The definitions alone number 164, not counting the various statements *about* culture that number in the thousands. The extent of this literature suggests the importance of the concept of culture for the social scientist.[16]

In summarizing their own ideas, Kroeber and Kluckhohn have not attempted to add a 165th definition of culture, but rather to indicate their own thinking in this field. They suggest that: "Culture consists of patterns explicit and implicit, of and for behavior acquired and transmitted by symbols, constituting the distinctive achievement of human groups, including their embodiments in artifacts. The essential core of culture consists of traditional (i.e., historically derived and selected) ideas and especially their attached values; culture systems may, on the one hand, be considered as products of action, on the other hand as conditioning elements of further action." [17]

On the basis of these and related definitions, we may formulate our own conception of culture. Culture, therefore: (*a*) is the characteristically human product of social interaction; (*b*) provides socially acceptable patterns for meeting

---

[14] Ralph Linton, *The Tree of Culture* (New York: Alfred A. Knopf, Inc., 1955), p. 29.

[15] A. L. Kroeber, *The Nature of Culture* (Chicago: University of Chicago Press, 1952). The article on "The Superorganic" is reprinted here as Chapter 3. Other statements of Kroeber are reprinted in Part I, "Theory of Culture."

[16] Kroeber and Kluckhohn, *Culture: A Critical Review of Concepts and Definitions, op. cit.,* Parts II and III.

[17] *Ibid.,* p. 181.

biological and social needs; (c) is cumulative as it is handed down from generation to generation in a given society; (d) is meaningful to human beings because of its symbolic quality; (e) is learned by each person in the course of his development in a particular society; (f) is necessarily a basic determinant of personality; and (g) depends for its existence upon the continued functioning of the society but is independent of any individual or group.

Characteristics of Culture

Culture exists in the minds or habit patterns of the members of a society. Culture is visible in the behavior of individuals, as they engage in various forms of learned behavior. There are degrees of visibility of cultural behavior, ranging from the regularized activities of persons to their internal (and often unconscious) reasons for so doing. Boys and girls of high school age, for example, engage in behavior that is regularized by the teen-age culture in which they participate. Their reasons for dating, dancing, and related behavior are equally cultural although not so visible. Many of the boys and girls may be having a date because they wish to appear popular, not because of any special affection for their temporary companion. This wish for social approval is part of the cultural behavior learned by the boy and girl, even though it is not as apparent as their physical behavior.[18]

These two aspects of behavior have been characterized by Kluckhohn as the "explicit" and the "implicit" culture. The *explicit* culture comprises "those regularities in word and deed which may be generalized straight from the evidence of the ear or eye." [19] The similarities in the behavior of teen-agers at a dance are part of the explicit culture, since they constitute behavior that can be analyzed directly from the sensory evidence. On the explicit level, the adolescent cultural behavior can be generalized from regularities in dress, mannerisms, and conversation.

The *implicit* culture, in Kluckhohn's words, "is an abstraction of the second order. Here the anthropologist infers least common denominators which seem ... to underlie a multiplicity of cultural contents ..." [20] On this level, the cultural motivations may be assumed from the variety of behavior of the teen-agers in question. The implicit wish for social approval is a culturally induced motivation that may be inferred from the group behavior.

Culture is an abstraction. The basic reality is human behavior and the products of that behavior. We cannot see culture as such; we can only see human behavior. This behavior occurs in regular, patterned fashion and from this regularity we infer the existence of something that we call culture. We shall consider culture patterns later. Here we merely indicate that human beings act in accordance with *systems* or forms of group expectations. The forms can be

---

[18] Margaret Mead, *Male and Female* (New York: William Morrow & Company, 1949), Chapter 14.
[19] Clyde Kluckhohn, "The Study of Culture," Chapter 5 in Daniel Lerner and Harold D. Lasswell (eds.), *The Policy Sciences* (Stanford: Stanford University Press, 1951), p. 88.
[20] *Ibid.*

inferred from the action; they cannot be envisaged as such. We can see people eating, drinking, working, marrying, fighting, and engaging in many other forms of social interaction. When we examine these activities, we see that they are not individualized and random, but instead assume definite forms. The *systems* of activity are abstractions that the observer draws. The participants are rarely aware of the patterned nature of their behavior.[21]

In this sense, culture may be viewed simply as "regularities of behavior in the members of a particular society."[22] Culture is not a force, operating by itself and independent of the human actors. There is an unconscious tendency to reify culture—to endow it with life and treat it as a *thing*. Culture is a creation of society in interaction and depends for its existence upon the continuance of society. In a strict sense, therefore, culture does not "do" anything. It does not "cause" the individual to act in a particular way, nor does it "make" the normal individual into a maladjusted one. Culture should not, strictly speaking, be the subject of a transitive verb. It is logically incorrect to abstract culture from human behavior and then say that the culture "causes" the activity we have just observed. Culture, in short, is a human product; it is not independently endowed with life.[23]

Culture is the source of much, but not all, of the uniformity of human behavior. Folkways, mores, and the rest of the normative group expectations are examples of culture. They are generated in social interaction, transmitted to the new generation, and constitute a previously defined set of responses. The child finds his ways of behaving already worked out for him, and he must follow these ways if he is to be a successful member of the group. The society derives the benefits of uniformity in the behavior of its members, and this would be impossible without culture. Each individual acquires the uniformities that are necessary both to his adaptation to the group and the ultimate survival of the society.

The majority of persons judge other cultures in terms of their own. The values of each culture constitute the only criteria of the folkways and mores of another. The person reared in a culture stressing Christianity, monogamy, and capitalism tends to regard Mohammedanism, polygamy, and communism as both pernicious and "unnatural." This general tendency is known as *ethnocentrism*—the act of regarding one's culture as the center of the universe and hence as the basis for all comparisons with other cultures.[24]

Forms of Culture

We have previously considered culture as the regularities assumed from observing human behavior. In this sense, culture is intangible and cannot be directly

---

[21] Parsons and Shils, *op cit.*, p. 39.

[22] Philip H. Bagby, "Culture and the Causes of Culture," *American Anthropologist*, 55:535-554 (October, 1953), p. 539.

[23] David Bidney, "On the Concept of Culture and Some Cultural Fallacies," *American Anthropologist*, 46:30-44 (January-March, 1944).

[24] William Graham Sumner, *Folkways* (Boston: Ginn and Company, 1906), p. 13.

experienced by the senses. In another respect, however, culture is tangible and *can* be experienced by the senses. This is due to the fact that regularities of behavior give rise to physical products. The many material elements in the physical framework of society fall in this latter category. In our society, automobiles, razors, shoes, pencils, radios, houses, trains, and hydrogen bombs suggest the vast conglomeration of material products growing out of cultural interaction. The infinite variety of these material elements is indicated in the catalogue of a mail order house, where thousands of forms of the most complex material culture the world has ever known are displayed.

Material culture is clearly the product of man. No one would presume that the automobile sprang full-blown from the brow of some supernatural power. The automobile is the product of a long line of cultural innovations, each adding something to the product. These innovations can be traced in a continuous line, beginning with the wheel and ending with the latest model. Man alone wrought with hands and brain to produce the cultural developments that culminated in the automobile. The physical results of these mental processes are there for everyone to see. Material culture is the externalization or physical manifestation of the interaction of human beings.[25]

Nonmaterial culture likewise has a human source. We have considered the process whereby folkways, mores, laws, and other normative expectations arise from social interaction. These "ideological" uniformities are often associated with supernatural powers, which provide many of the sanctions for the norms. The group expectations constituting the present social codes grew out of cumulative experience in very much the same sense as the invention of the wheel culminated in the automobile.

The nonmaterial aspects of culture do not, it is true, always show the consistency of development of many material aspects. Some contemporary norms are not demonstrably superior to those of two thousand years ago, whereas the automobile is patently superior to the oxcart as a means of transportation. The human aspect of culture, however, applies to all of these manifestations. Man makes his culture with his mind. Some aspects remain in psychological form and others are physical.

Culture, therefore, has two forms or levels, both products of meaningful interaction. All culture is, in the final analysis, a pattern(s) of regularized human behavior. Social interaction is the source of this behavior. The *first* level of culture is the material and includes all the artifacts (material objects) in a particular system. The *second* level is the nonmaterial or "ideological," and includes the meanings, values, norms, and relationships. These are *levels* of culture, not different types.[26] The fundamental basis of culture is found in the human mind, and the physical manifestations have meaning only in terms of these mental patterns. Ideas are the real foundation of culture. Material objects are useless without the knowledge of how to use them.

[25] Sorokin, *op. cit.*, p. 313.
[26] *Ibid.*

The meanings attached to the different levels of culture are thus more important than the physical forms. The things that count are the ideas, ideals, techniques, and regularized relationships between human beings. Culture patterns are essentially *mental*, in that they are regularities of behavior found among socialized human beings. In the study of prehistoric cultures, the material artifacts are the sole evidence remaining of the way of life of these long-dead societies. Hence the stone axes and other material remains are the only basis for reconstructing the culture. Group expectations do not have an independent existence as such after the group has gone. They can only be inferred from the physical remains. The key to a culture, whether the society has long since vanished or is still very much alive, is to be found in the meanings which alone give relevance to the physical elements.

The patterns of meanings of a culture are passed on through the group and are inculcated in each individual by social interaction. Every pattern originally emerged from human beings acting in groups. Subsequent groups conserved these expectations and invested them with social sanctions. Still other groups passed them on from one generation to the next. This process began long before man learned to write down his group norms in order to perpetuate them for posterity. The process will continue as long as man survives on the earth. Cultural expectations are not the exclusive property of any man or group; they exist independently of any individual. As they exist in the mind of each member of a society, they constitute the *social heritage*.[27]

Qualities of Culture

The concept of culture is perhaps the most important single contribution of the social sciences to the understanding of society. It has other characteristics that make it significant. Some of them have been anticipated in the preceding discussion; others will be discussed later in more detail. These characteristics of culture may be brought under a single general heading.[28]

1. The learned quality. Culture is learned behavior and is not present in the biological equipment of the human being. It includes the group expectations that the individual learns during his social conditioning. Man engages in symbolic and meaningful interaction with others in a group setting, and thereby learns the uniformities of behavior that we call culture.

2. The transmissive quality. Culture can be transmitted from one generation to the next, and, in this sense, it is cumulative. Man can build upon the achievements of preceding generations; he need not start anew every generation. Different aspects of culture are cumulative in different ways, with language following a different course from technology.[29] In the process of transmission, the

---

[27] Kroeber, *op. cit.*, p. 129.

[28] The following is adapted from George P. Murdock, "The Cross-Cultural Survey," *American Sociological Review*, 5:361-370 (June, 1940).

[29] Harvey C. Moore, "Cumulation and Cultural Processes," *American Anthropologist*, 56:347-357 (June, 1954).

regularities of behavior assume an existence independent of any particular individual or group.

3. *The social quality.* In the discussion of the group, we indicated that its members share certain expectations that assume a normative quality. This illustrates the social quality of culture, in that the expectations are products of group interaction. Behavior assumes a uniformity with respect to the activities pertaining to the group. Each organized group has its own culture comprising, among other things, these normative expectations.[30]

4. *The ideational quality.* The group habits that constitute the culture come to be viewed as ideal patterns of behavior, to which the members are supposed to conform. Considerable disparity exists between the ideal and the practice, but the existence of the ideal is generally understood. This quality of culture distinguishes it from individual habits with no ideational content.

5. *The gratifying quality.* Culture satisfies human needs and thus has a gratifying quality. These needs may be biological, as hunger and thirst. They may also be sociocultural, in that they arise through group interaction and are transmitted in the same way. The need to fall in love and marry is a sociocul-tural product that the individual learns in our society.[31] Just as individual habits persist only if they satisfy some conscious or unconscious individual needs, so the social habits of culture must satisfy group needs. Continued failure to do so means the eventual disappearance of a pattern of culture.

6. *The adaptive quality.* Culture must also adapt to forces outside itself. The most obvious form of such adaptation involves the geographical environment; people must be able to feed, clothe, and house themselves by adapting to their surroundings.[32] This does not mean that the environment "determines" the direction of culture, but merely that culture must adjust to the geographical necessities if it is to continue. Culture must also adapt to *itself*, in the sense that its different aspects are continually changing.[33] The family must therefore adapt to the automobile, and governments must adapt to the hydrogen bomb. Man lives in and through culture, and he is the most adaptive of all the animals.

7. *The integrative quality.* The parts of a culture tend to form a consistent whole. In Sumner's words, there is a "strain of consistency" among the various parts of a culture.[34] This integrative tendency is very apparent in a simple and isolated society, where extraneous elements are rare and the constituent elements in the culture do not change rapidly. Integration is not so apparent in a

---

[30] Muzafer Sherif, "Integrating Field Work and Laboratory in Small-Group Research," *American Sociological Review*, 19:759-771 (December, 1954).

[31] Robert F. Winch and Thomas and Virginia Ktsanes, "The Theory of Complementary Needs in Mate Selection: An Analytic and Descriptive Study," *American Sociological Review*, 19:241-249 (June, 1954).

[32] Betty J. Meggers, "Environmental Limitation on the Development of Culture," *American Anthropologist*, 56:801-824 (October, 1954).

[33] William F. Ogburn, *Social Change* (rev. ed.) (New York: The Viking Press, 1950).

[34] Sumner, *op. cit.*, pp. 5-6.

complex and heterogeneous culture, whose constituent elements are in constant change. Within wide limits, however, all cultures show such tendencies, for without a minimum of cultural integration the society would not stay together.

Common Problems of Culture

Man has certain basic needs in all societies. In the effort to satisfy these needs, common cultural forms evolve. In every society a number of necessary jobs must be done by people acting in culturally prescribed ways. This universality reflects the need of all men to adjust: (a) to their own physical and psychological necessities; (b) to the demands of the physical universe; and (c) to the reciprocal demands of other persons. The exact forms of the adjustments differ from one society to another, but the general similarities remain. These similarities constitute the "common denominator of cultures." [35]

This common denominator may be explained in terms of the principles of human learning. These are the same in all members of the human species and involve the following factors:

1. *Drive or impulse.* This factor refers to the drives of hunger, thirst, sexual satisfaction, and other impulses that man shares with his fellow mammals. These drives are not, however, sufficient by themselves to explain the underlying similarities in culture.

2. *Stimulus or cue.* This factor refers to certain general stimuli that arise from social interaction in all societies. Among these problems are caring for the young, dealing with the external environment, and controlling the actions of men in society.

3. *Habit.* This factor involves "the tendency of any learned response to be repeated under similar conditions of drive and stimulus." [36] When human beings have worked out reasonably satisfactory responses to the basic drives and stimuli, they tend to repeat these responses under similar conditions. The responses (folkways) become incorporated in the culture.

4. *Limitation of potential responses.* The final factor underlying the basic similarities of culture is the limitation of the potential responses that man can make to his various impulses and cues. Although man is the most adaptable of all the animals, his reactions (and therefore the number of cultural responses) are nevertheless limited.[37]

All societies have certain common problems to solve. The similarities are more important than the differences. These problems have been considered under the framework of the "universal culture pattern," a concept introduced by Clark Wissler. The elements in his universal culture pattern are: Speech, Material Traits, Art, Mythology, Social Systems, Religion, Property, Govern-

---

[35] George P. Murdock, "The Common Denominator of Cultures," in Ralph Linton (ed.), *The Science of Man in the World Crisis* (New York: Columbia University Press, 1945).

[36] *Ibid.*, p. 138.

[37] The above analysis was adapted from Murdock, *op. cit.*, pp. 137-138.

ment, and War.[38] This concept is a convenient abstraction that makes it possible: (a) to grasp the functional quality of culture; (b) to appreciate the underlying similarities of culture; and (c) to analyze various societies and their constituent cultures.

The universal culture pattern has been elaborated by an enormous scholarly labor conducted through the years at Yale University. This project is called the Human Relations Area Files and is a catalogue and cross-reference of the cultures of several hundred contemporary primitive societies, plus those of various modern nations and other societies that are no longer existent. The survey contains some sixty-nine aspects of culture, ranging from language to capital-goods industries, and from entertainment to health and welfare. This list differs from Wissler's universal culture pattern in that all societies do not have all of the elements included in the survey.[39]

The structure of particular elements of the universal culture pattern varies from society to society, even though they perform the same general functions. There are many forms of family structure in the world, despite the fact that the family is one of the "universals" in the universal culture pattern. The latter is, in effect, a system of classification that reflects the fact that all cultures have elements in common. Murdock says: "The true universals of culture . . . are not identifies in habit, in definable behavior. They are similarities in classification, not in content. They represent categories of historically and behavioristically diverse elements which nevertheless have so much in common that competent observers feel compelled to classify them together." [40]

Further uses have been made of the mass of material in the Human Relations Area Files. In one study, all the aspects of culture were classified under four general headings in a sort of composite universal culture pattern. These headings comprise the following: (a) the productive arts (technical and economic activities); (b) the regulative arts (social control and government); (c) the personal expressive arts (direct human experience); and (d) the institutional expressive arts (family and church). For any given society, a composite culture profile can be constructed on the basis of these classifications, using the information contained in the Files.[41] The similarities and differences between societies or groups of societies may thus be statistically measured.[42]

The Nature of Culture Patterns

Culture is thus a complex whole, the uniquely human product of social interaction. It has both material and nonmaterial forms, but its most characteristic

---

[38] Clark Wissler, *Man and Culture* (New York: Thomas Y. Crowell Company, 1923), p. 74.

[39] George P. Murdock, *et al., Outline of Cultural Materials* (3rd rev. ed.) (New Haven: Human Relations Area Files, Inc., 1950).

[40] Murdock, "The Common Denominator of Cultures," *op. cit.*, p. 125.

[41] Edward Rose and Gary Willoughby, "Culture Profiles and Emphases," *American Journal of Sociology*, 63:478-490 (March, 1958).

[42] See also Linton C. Freeman and Robert F. Winch, "Societal Complexity: An Empirical Test of a Typology of Societies," *American Journal of Sociology*, 62:461-466 (March, 1957).

aspects exist in symbolic form in the human mind. These common intellectual elements mean that the behavior of the members of a society assumes certain regularities, in thought as well as action. Culture also is patterned; that is, arranged in regular systems of ordered behavior that channel human activities. Culture patterning refers to "the relation of units in a determinate system, the interrelation of parts as dominated by the general character of wholes." [43]

The simplest element in culture is the trait. A culture is composed of thousands of individual traits, each the result of human activity. Culture traits may be either material or nonmaterial. A nail or a shoe string is a material trait; a religious act is a nonmaterial trait. The latter category includes folkways, mores, and other normative sanctions, as well as the great amorphous group of undefined acts. The dividing line between the two in practice is largely one of perspective. Both reflect the regularity of behavior. Material traits have some custom, technique, or behavior sequence related to them. Man cannot live by material traits alone. Neither can he live without them.

Culture traits are rarely found in isolation. They ordinarily combine with other-related traits, forming a dynamic interrelationship. Individual traits have meaning only in relation to other traits and to their combination. Each trait bears a functional relationship to the others and can be understood only in this relationship. This group of functionally related traits is known as a culture pattern or configuration. The pattern, not the individual trait, is the basic functional unit of culture. The individual seldom learns individual or isolated traits, but rather learns the practices and expectations of his culture in the form of patterns. Patterns are learned as units and not piecemeal in terms of their constituent parts.[44]

The concept of the culture pattern provides a basic insight into the reasons why group behavior is ordered and regular. Without the tendency to form patterns, regularity in social behavior would be impossible. Individuals would react in random and haphazard fashion to their biological and visceral drives, and ordered society could never arise. The individual components of culture, whether material or nonmaterial, however, are not sufficient in themselves to explain the regularity of social behavior. Human behavior is patterned, and these patterns are transmitted (learned) as each generation acquires the group ways of life. The concept of individual habit alone is not sufficient to account for this regularity. Clusters of group habits (culture patterns) are the basic elements in organized society.

In the process of socialization, the individual learns the appropriate culture patterns involving such varied behavior as eating breakfast, going to school, playing football, having a date, and getting married. Each society and, to a certain extent, each class has its own set of patterns which it imposes upon the individual and thus assures, within limits, a minimum uniformity of behavior. The sanctions that form the moral basis of these patterns are the folkways,

---

[43] Clyde Kluckhohn, "The Study of Culture," Chapter 5 in Daniel Lerner and Harold D. Lasswell (eds.), *The Policy Sciences* (Stanford: Stanford University Press, 1951), p. 97.

[44] A. L. Kroeber, *The Nature of Culture* (Chicago: University of Chicago Press, 1952), p. 5.

mores, and other normative expectations. When the members of a group are following the same basic expectations, a degree of uniformity and predictability is observable in their behavior. They are, in other words, following the same culture pattern.[45]

As an example of a familiar culture pattern, we may take the game of baseball. In the hundred years since its "invention," baseball has accumulated a stock of patterned behavior that has become part of the heritage of every American boy. Formal and informal rules form the basis of this pattern. The huge physical investment represented by organized baseball, with its parks, its coaching and scouting systems, and its valuable players are material manifestations of this pattern. Publicity is also part of the process by which interest is maintained during the long playing season and even more during the months of winter hibernation. The final and indispensable element in the baseball pattern is the millions of devoted fans who support their team through thick and thin. They flock joyfully to the parks when they have the time and the resources, and there munch peanuts and revile the umpire at their pleasure. These and many other elements constitute the culture pattern of baseball.

The Study of Culture Patterns

Culture patterns are intangible and exist only in the minds and habits of human beings. The person who enters another society—whether primitive or advanced—for the purpose of studying its culture cannot experience the patterns with his senses. All he can see is human behavior, occurring in more or less regular fashion. In the final analysis, culture is an abstraction from observed and regularized behavior. This statement is even more apparent in culture patterns than in culture in general. Human beings engage in behavior that, upon continued observation, is found to have regularity. This regularity is the pattern. The sociologist or cultural anthropologist is chiefly concerned with patterns rather than with the individuals who carry them out.[46]

Our foreign observer, attending a high-school dance in the United States, would be at a loss to explain much of the behavior of the teen-age participants. At first glance, our observer might assume that the actions were highly spontaneous, individualistic, and (perhaps) somewhat abandoned. On closer observation, however, the dancing, the conversation, and the hand-holding follow strict regularities. Boys and girls who were acting spontaneously could never reach such uniformities of behavior all by themselves. As he became increasingly familiar with teen-age culture, our hypothetical observer would begin to realize that this behavior, at first seemingly so individualistic, was in reality as stylized as a primitive fertility rite. These adolescents dress, speak, dance, and think in accordance with uniform cultural pressures. As these regularities take

---

[45] John J. Honigmann, *Culture and Personality* (New York: Harper & Brothers, 1954), p. 24.

[46] Talcott Parsons and Edward A. Shils (eds.), *Toward a General Theory of Action* (Cambridge: Harvard University Press, 1951), p. 39.

shape in the mind of the observer, he becomes aware that he is seeing a culture pattern in action.[47]

The existence of a culture pattern means that uniformities in behavior exist in a given society at a given time. These uniformities are limited in time and space. Many of those currently observed in our society were not present a generation ago, nor will they be present a generation hence. Limitations are equally apparent in terms of space. Some of the patterns of our society are not found among other societies, whether primitive or advanced. As we have seen, broad cultural uniformities *do* exist between societies, insofar as all of them have some form of language, government, family system, and economic organization.[48] But the specific forms that evolve to meet a society's many needs are subject to wide variation. The regularities of behavior that constitute culture patterns exist in individual societies.

The evolution of the culture pattern is thus from "facts to patterns." The observer first notes the occurrence of many acts by the members of a society. As these acts fall into recurrent categories, the observer becomes increasingly aware of regularities of behavior in a variety of fields, from toilet-training to technology. When a number of such acts take the same form, he may make a tentative generalization concerning the behavior in question. The generaliza-

[47] Geoffrey Gorer, *The American People* (New York: W. W. Norton & Company, Inc., 1948), Chapter 4, "Love and Friendship."

[48] George P. Murdock, "The Common Denominator of Cultures," in Ralph Linton (ed.), *The Science of Man in the World Crisis* (New York: Columbia University Press, 1945), pp. 123-142.

A culture pattern means that certain uniformities of behavior exist in a society; here Moslems are at prayer in a mosque.

tion regarding, say, the ceremonies attending the passage from childhood to maturity describes the pattern. The motivations for such behavior exist in the conscious and unconscious mental processes, where they have been implanted by the learning process. The pattern formed by *many* such individual acts exists, in final analysis, in the mind of the observer.[49]

We have spoken as if culture patterns consisted solely of inferences drawn from physical acts. In practice, this constitutes only one category of patterned behavior. There are at least three distinct, although clearly related, aspects of such behavior.

1. Physical behavior. This category includes all of the physical actions of the members of a given society that assume socially prescribed regularity. The many forms of daily activity, from eating and drinking to propitiating the supernatural powers, fall under this heading.

2. Verbal behavior. Language is a second form of patterned behavior. The group assigns meanings to symbols and instructs its members in the relationships between them. Language is patterned behavior in the most literal sense.

3. Material artifacts. Material objects in a society are the products or appendages of culture patterns. The presence of money or any other exchange symbol may thus indicate the existence of a complex economic pattern; charred bones in a prehistoric campsite are evidence of the pattern of roasting meat. In recent thinking, there has been a growing tendency to exclude material objects from the concept of culture pattern and to include what Linton calls the "patterns for objects."[50] These patterns are inferences drawn from material objects.

Culture patterns may also be viewed in terms of their function in group life. Many patterns have such obvious functions as earning a living, raising the young, and communicating with the supernatural. Other patterns do not have such clear objectives. Unconscious motivations may cause the members of a group to follow a particular pattern. The patterned behavior of dating in our society may have the function of finding a mate and thereby founding a family. At another level, however, the function of dating may be to enhance the psychological satisfactions of both parties. The man and woman may be seeking to satisfy in marriage certain emotional needs, of whose existence they may be only dimly aware. These needs may be *complementary*, in that a woman who unconsciously wishes to be dominated seeks a man who will satisfy this need.[51] This function is a far cry from the conscious desire to marry and have children. The dating pattern performs the function, after a fashion, of fulfilling both types of satisfactions.

Culture patterns vary with respect to the degree of standardization and the social media involved in the learning process. In a primitive society, regularity of behavior results from word-of-mouth learning and example, as the child learns the expected ways of thought and action proper to his status. He has

---

[49] Honigmann, *Culture and Personality, op. cit.,* pp. 93–96.
[50] Ralph Linton, *The Tree of Culture* (New York: Alfred A. Knopf, Inc., 1955), p. 37.
[51] Robert F. Winch and Thomas and Virginia Ktsanes, *op. cit.*

before him the example of his elders, and he learns the basic patterns of the group by observation, conscious training, and unconscious imitation. The elementary patterns of the culture are present in the behavior of persons in his immediate environment. Under such conditions, the learning process is simple, direct, and strong. The raw material of personality is there for all to see.[52]

In a large and amorphous society such as our own, regularity of behavior is the result of mass media of communication, in addition to the more intimate efforts of the primary group. Radio, television, the comics, and the movies play an important part in cultural patterning. Many of the behavior patterns of the adolescent generation directly reflect the mass media. The adolescent peer group assumes many of its attitudes and behavior patterns from these forms of communication. The adolescent learns how to dress, talk, dance, and amuse himself from these sources. As localized patterns have broken down, culture patterning has become increasingly standardized under the impact of mass communication.[53]

National Patterns of Culture

The largest *functional* unit in our analysis is the national pattern of culture. This is an intricate mosaic of all the individual patterns, held together by a few over-all patterns that are accepted, in approximately the same form, by the members of a society. We are familiar with the modern nation as a cultural unit, as American culture is distinguished from French, German, Italian, or Swedish culture. In some cases, the nation transcends cultural boundaries, for such units as the Soviet Union, India, and China contain many widely different cultures, held together by more or less rigorous administrative ties.[54] In general, however, national states and national culture patterns are roughly coterminous, at least in western European civilization.

The existence of large patterns of culture has long been empirically accepted. In ancient times, the Egyptians, Greeks, and Romans acted upon the assumption that the various societies with which they came in contact, in peace and war, had certain broad characteristics that set them off from others.[55] In more recent times, the common-sense belief in the existence of cultural differences between national states has become an important part of the folk heritage. The intuitive acceptance of these differences, indeed, constitutes the principal basis for ethnocentrism, as Americans, Frenchmen, Germans, and (more recently) Chinese, Indonesians, Burmese, Egyptians, and Nigerians are convinced that their own culture is superior to that of any other. This situation has stimulated

---

[52] Ruth Benedict, *Patterns of Culture* (New York: Penguin Books, Inc., 1946), Chapter 8, "The Individual and the Pattern of Culture."

[53] David Riesman, *et al., The Lonely Crowd* (Doubleday & Company, 1953), Chapter 4.

[54] Maurice L. Farber, "The Problem of National Character: A Methodological Analysis," *Journal of Psychology*, 30:307-316 (1950).

[55] Ralph Linton, "The Concept of National Character," in Alfred H. Stanton and Stewart E. Perry (eds.), *Personality and Political Crisis* (Glencoe, Ill.: The Free Press, 1951), p. 134.

many studies in this general field, with the ultimate purpose of eliminating, or at least mitigating, the cultural tensions that lead to war.[56]

It is one thing to sense these broad differences between national states. It is quite another to demonstrate the nature of these differences and reduce them to workable terms.[57] Among the difficulties in delimiting national culture patterns are: (*a*) the fact, as noted, that some nations include a number of different culture patterns—for example, the Soviet Union contains entire cultures as divergent as the Ukranian and Mongolian; (*b*) the fact that culture patterns change, so that the national pattern of a country like Japan was not the same in the pre-industrial nineteenth-century period as it is today; (*c*) the fact that nations contain many subcultures, which often make it difficult to distinguish the universal cultural elements, if any; (*d*) the fact that the policy makers who administer a nation may act in ways that are not those of the rank and file members of the society; (*e*) the fact that certain cultural products (literature and art) are produced by a small and presumably atypical segment of the population and hence may not be representative of the broad, underlying pattern of the common people.[58]

The scientific (as distinguished from the impressionistic) study of cultures as more or less self-contained units began with the anthropologists, who have investigated hundreds of such comparatively small and integrated societies. Many of these unitary studies of cultures reflect the work of Ralph Linton and Abram Kardiner, an anthropologist and a psychoanalyst, respectively. They have combined these two disciplines, plus the insights and methods of several others, in an effort to demonstrate: (*a*) the existence of broad cultural uniformities within each society; and (*b*) the impact of these uniformities upon personality. In these studies, they emphasized early childhood experience, especially in such matters as feeding, toilet-training, weaning, and the like. They also made use of the various projective techniques in the repertoire of the clinical psychologist, such as the Rorschach and Thematic Apperception Tests, with their accompanying insights into the structure of the personality.[59]

The paramount fact that emerges from these and other anthropological studies is that culture patterns actually *do* differ from one society to another. Summarizing these general conclusions, Linton suggests that: "The existence of different personality norms for the members of different small, culturally homogeneous societies seems to be well established. Objective techniques for the study and detection of such norms are fairly well developed. Although the work leading to these results has been done almost exclusively on the so-called primitive societies, it seems highly probable that the same techniques can be

---

[56] Otto Klineberg, *Tensions Affecting International Understanding* (New York: Social Science Research Council, 1950).

[57] Emily M. Nett, "An Evaluation of the National Character Concept in Sociological Theory," *Social Forces*, 36:297-303 (May, 1958).

[58] Farber, *op. cit.*

[59] Ralph Linton, *The Cultural Background of Personality* (New York: Appleton-Century-Crofts, Inc., 1945); Abram Kardiner, *The Individual and His Society* (New York: Columbia University Press, 1939); Abram Kardiner, *The Psychological Frontiers of Society* (New York: Columbia University Press, 1945).

applied to the study of culturally homogeneous societies within modern nations." [60] Hence the theoretical basis for postulating national patterns of culture would seem to be empirically established.

The psychocultural techniques developed by the anthropologists have also
been employed in the study of national patterns of culture. The composition
and dimensions of the patterns are, as it were, inferred from the personality
structures of the (presumably) typical members of the society. More specifically, personality is studied not only in terms of biologically inherited factors
but also in terms of "the intra-personal representation of the culturally and
socially transmitted mechanisms for regulating, distributing, and controlling
the tensions of these innate need-systems." [61]

A number of national patterns have been subjected to various hypotheses
concerning the relationships between the organization of systems of biological
needs and the resultant configurations of personality. La Barre has made extensive observations of the character structure of the Japanese and Chinese.[62] Ruth
Benedict has likewise studied the national pattern of the Japanese, a work
inspired by the urgent military desire to understand the culture of one of our
principal enemies in World War II.[63] Some of the culture patterns of eastern
Europe have also been examined in terms of their expression in personality,
with particular emphasis upon the techniques of child-rearing. Certain personality traits of Polish and Russian children (and later adults) are thus said to
reflect the methods of swaddling employed in these two cultures by the peasant
family.[64]

The culture of the Soviet Union has been the subject of the most intensive
study of any national pattern in the decades following World War II. The
Armed Forces have been concerned with the Soviet Union as an actual enemy in
the Cold War and a possible enemy in a thermonuclear war. Hence the goals of
these studies have often been as much military as scientific. The studies of the
Soviet pattern have perforce been conducted "at a distance" since, with negligible exceptions, American social scientists have not been allowed in the country.
Most of the subjects who presumably incorporate in their personalities the basic
elements of the Soviet pattern have been persons who, for one reason or another, have emigrated from the Soviet Union. Some of these persons left their
native land two decades ago. Despite these difficulties, some very important
work has been done in this dynamic culture pattern.[65]

---

[60] Linton, "The Concept of National Character," *op. cit.*, p. 144.

[61] Henry V. Dicks, "Observations on Contemporary Russian Behavior," *Human Relations*, 5:111-175 (1952), p. 113.

[62] Weston La Barre, "Some Observations on Character Structure in the Orient: The Japanese," *Psychiatry*, 8:319-342 (August, 1945); Weston La Barre, "Some Observations on Character Structure in the Orient. II. The Chinese. Part One," *Psychiatry*, 9:215-237 (August, 1946); Weston La Barre, "Some Observations on Character Structure in the Orient. III. The Chinese. Part Two," *Psychiatry*, 9:375-395 (November, 1946).

[63] Ruth Benedict, *The Chrysanthemum and the Sword* (Boston: Houghton Mifflin Company, 1946).

[64] Ruth Benedict, "Child Rearing in Certain European Countries," *American Journal of Orthopsychiatry*, 19:342-350 (April, 1949).

[65] Alex Inkeles, *The Soviet Citizen: Daily Life in a Totalitarian Society* (Cambridge: Harvard University Press, 1959).

The American Culture Pattern

In a famous passage, Ruth Benedict characterized the tendency of different societies to emphasize different cultural elements. "The cultural pattern of any civilization," she says, "makes use of a certain segment of the great arc of potential human purposes and motivations, just as . . . any culture makes use of certain selected material techniques or cultural traits. The great arc . . . is far too immense and too full of contradictions for any one culture to utilize even any considerable portion of it." [66] Each society stresses certain patterns, sometimes to the virtual exclusion of others. Broad similarities exist between cultures, but each one is unique.

The American culture pattern therefore comprises the elements that Americans have selected out of the "great arc of potential human purposes." This is the combination of cultural factors that makes America like no other society. The American pattern is not necessarily more desirable or more conducive to

---

[66] Benedict, *Patterns of Culture, op. cit.,* p. 219.

Each society emphasizes some culture patterns and minimizes others. Americans are fond of competitive athletics, as typified by professional baseball, "the national pastime."

human welfare than any other. It is merely different. It stresses different values.[67] Out of all the possible combinations of culture patterns, this society has selected certain ones to emphasize and others to neglect. Pattern and emphasis both seem best to us because they are a part of us.

The traditional source of information in this field has come from the descriptions of travelers. The informal study of the American culture pattern conducted some 125 years ago by Alexis de Tocqueville remains one of the classic analyses by a foreign observer.[68] In the brief history of this country as an independent nation, it is estimated that several thousand persons, with varying degrees of sympathy, understanding, and insight, have observed American culture and generalized in writing upon it.[69]

The description of American culture has also occupied Americans.[70] We cannot consider all of these efforts here, although, in a sense, much of the subsequent description and analysis in this book deals with this general subject. We may merely indicate some of the broad elements that have emerged from the interaction of American society. The characteristics of American culture are the result of the selectivity of this society. In our analysis, we shall follow the lines set down by Robert S. Lynd,[71] whose researches in American culture make him eminently qualified to generalize in this elusive field.[72]

1. The American pattern is casual. The patterning of any culture is, by the nature of the cultural process itself, essentially unplanned. The American pattern is more casual than most, and the very concept of planning is anathema to many persons. The Puritan heritage, the frontier spirit, and the capitalistic ethic are among the factors that have stressed the individualism of the culture and the belief that a minimum of central authority is desirable.

2. The American pattern is uneven. As Ruth Benedict points out, every society stresses some patterns of culture more than others. American culture devotes a great deal of attention to making a living and the acquisition of property. In this emphasis, it shows a comparative neglect of such patterns as religion, art, welfare, and large kinship groups.

3. The American pattern is unequal. American culture is also marked by what Lynd has called "extreme differences in power." This power varies between individuals, corporations, voluntary associations, and other social units. Our society has alternated between: (*a*) encouraging the competition that leads

---

[67] Cora Du Bois, "The Dominant Value Profile of American Culture," *American Anthropologist,* 57:1232-1239 (December, 1955).

[68] Alexis de Tocqueville, *Democracy in America* (edited by Phillips Bradley) (New York: Alfred A. Knopf, Inc., 1945). The first English edition of this book was published in 1840.

[69] H. S. Commager (ed.), *America in Perspective: The United States Through Foreign Eyes* (New York: Random House, Inc., 1947).

[70] "The U.S.A. as Anthropologists See It," *American Anthropologist, Volume* 57 (December, 1955), entire issue.

[71] Robert S. Lynd, *Knowledge for What?* (Princeton: Princeton University Press, 1939), Chapter 3.

[72] Robert S. Lynd and Helen M. Lynd, *Middletown* (New York: Harcourt, Brace and World, 1929); Robert S. Lynd and Helen M. Lynd, *Middletown in Transition* (New York: Harcourt, Brace and World, 1937).

to monopolistic concentrations of power, and (*b*) discouraging such concentrations through antitrust legislation.

4. *The American pattern is mobile.* American culture is based upon a high degree of mobility. This mobility is of two related types: (*a*) *horizontal*—where the individual moves frequently from place to place; (*b*) *vertical*—where the individual moves up or down in the social scale. These aspects of mobility are interrelated, since physical movement often accompanies efforts to rise in the social scale. Business executives who reach positions of authority are highly mobile, for they must be ready to move when the opportunity for a better job comes along.[73]

5. *The American pattern is urban.* A basic trend in American society has been the movement from the farm to the city and from there to the metropolitan area. More than 115 million persons in the United States live in the 216 standard metropolitan areas, and the way of life of the metropolis is becoming typical of the nation as a whole. Culture patterns are increasingly *urban* patterns, as the influence of the city extends even to the minority still living on farms.

6. *The American pattern is oriented toward the future.* A strong tendency of the Protestant ethic is the postponement of present satisfactions for the sake of future satisfactions. The most obvious form of this behavior is to save money— to refrain from enjoying present satisfactions in order to enjoy those that will presumably come later.[74] In a broader sense, Americans have always believed in the perfectibility of man, the improvement of society, and the increase in material comfort in the future.[75]

7. *The American pattern is youth-centered.* It has often been said that America is a young man's country. This has been true in both a literal and a figurative sense. The age level of the population has been considerably lower than in most European countries, partially because of the high birth rate and partially because of the large numbers of young adults who came to this country from abroad. In the figurative sense, America has also been a young man's country because it was a large and undeveloped continent, open for exploitation by the young, the hardy, and the daring. The cult of youth has remained in different aspects of the culture pattern; both men and women strive to remain young and regard old age as the time when life is essentially over.

8. *The American pattern is a mass pattern.* The mass culture comprises those patterns of belief and behavior that are held by most persons in all walks of life. The mass culture is, in part, originated and communicated through mass media that can make a comic strip character into a folk hero and a radio crooner into everybody's sweetheart. The mass culture is by its very nature less permanent than those patterns centered about the family, church, and state. In

[73] W. Lloyd Warner and James C. Abegglen, *Big Business Leaders in America* (New York: Harper & Row, 1955), Chapter 4, "The Private Worlds of Mobile Men."

[74] Louis Schneider and Sverre Lysgaard, "The Deferred Gratification Pattern: A Preliminary Study," *American Sociological Review*, 18:142-149 (April, 1953).

[75] Du Bois, *op. cit.*, pp. 1233-1234.

American society, however, social interaction is increasingly carried on through the mass culture.[76]

In this chapter, we have examined the nature of culture and its tendency to form patterns. In every society, there are consistent forms of response to a variety of recurrent situations—from eating to marrying, from playing to worshiping. These regularities are the culture and the latter tends to form regular sequences or patterns. We have indicated the way in which culture emerges from social interaction, and some of the characteristics of this emerging phenomenon. Culture takes both material and nonmaterial forms, but the latter are the essential elements. Fundamental needs of man in all societies are met by the ordered behavior that is culture. Culture patterns vary in different societies, with primitive peoples learning largely by word-of-mouth and more advanced peoples learning (partially) by such complex agencies as the mass media. The largest functional unit in the study of culture is the national pattern, whose qualities we observed both in theory and in the form it has taken in the United States.

---

[76] Bernard Rosenberg and David Manning White (eds.), *Mass Culture* (Glencoe, Ill.: The Free Press, 1957). We shall consider the mass society and its culture in Chapter 24 below.

SELECTED BIBLIOGRAPHY

Benedict, Ruth, *Patterns of Culture*. New York: Penguin Books, Inc., 1946. This is an outstanding contribution to a popular understanding of the nature and implications of culture. The author has analyzed several primitive societies, with cultures very different from our own, and has shown how each of these patterns calls out behavior that differs widely from that found in contemporary American society.

Bidney, David, *Theoretical Anthropology*. New York: Columbia University Press, 1953. In this analysis of the theory of culture, the author says some significant things about the relationships between society and culture. Written on an advanced level, this book is recommended to the student who wishes to know more about the nature of culture.

Jahoda, Marie, "A Social-Psychological Approach to the Study of Culture," *Human Relations*, 14:23-30 (February, 1961). In this thoughtful essay, the author makes the important point that "Culture patterns and the values and beliefs of an individual can, but need not, coincide." The adjustment of each individual is, in part at least, a function of the degree to which this coincidence occurs.

Kaplan, Bert (ed.), *Studying Personality Cross-Culturally*. New York: Harper & Row, 1961. This symposium brings together a number of essays on the general subject of culture and, more specifically, the relationships between culture and personality.

Kluckhohn, Clyde, "The Study of Culture," Chapter 5 in Daniel Lerner and Harold D. Lasswell (eds.), *The Policy Sciences*. Stanford: Stanford University Press, 1951. A leading authority on the theory and "practice" of culture indicates the importance of this concept to the "policy sciences."

Kroeber, A. L., "The Delimitation of Civilizations," *Journal of the History of*

Ideas, 14:264-275 (April, 1955). An elder statesman in anthropology discusses some of the factors distinguishing one culture (civilization) from another, with particular emphasis upon those activities that are overtly creative.

————, and Clyde Kluckhohn, *Culture: A Critical Review of Concepts and Definitions, Papers of the Peabody Museum of American Archaeology and Ethnology,* 47:3-223 (1952). This is the most extensive survey ever made of the concept of culture, including its various definitions, its history, and its relationship to society.

Linton, Ralph, *The Tree of Culture.* New York: Alfred A. Knopf, Inc., 1955. In this posthumous work, an original and stimulating thinker presents a boldly conceived and well-written history of the development of culture throughout the world.

Lipset, Seymour M., and Leo Lowenthal (eds.), *Culture and Social Character.* Glencoe, Illinois: The Free Press, 1961. In this wide-ranging book, a number of scholars representing disciplines in both the social sciences and the humanities examine the work of David Riesman, with particular reference to his insights on the nature of culture and its relationship to social character.

Murdock, George P., "The Common Denominator of Cultures," in Ralph Linton (ed.), *The Science of Man in the World Crisis.* New York: Columbia University Press, 1945. The author examines the principles of learning in connection with the universal culture pattern. He then suggests that the similarity of these (learning) principles among all men accounts in part for the presence of the pattern.

8 *Personality and the Group*

Personality and Social Interaction

Culture is the fund of patterned and shared experience established and perpetuated by social interaction. It comprises the collective aspects of personality in a society. In his social development, the individual comes in contact with many different groups. These groups are the bearers of culture, and the individual acquires most of his patterned behavior from them. He engages in social interaction with these persons and, by taking them into account, slowly acquires his personality. In our society, the learning situation involves first the family, then the peer group, and later the church, school, and the other formal

151

agencies. Each of these groups is a miniature society, and the child learns different aspects of culture from them.

Personality is the third major element in our analysis. Our first concern was with *society*, with particular emphasis upon its group aspects. We then examined *culture* as the product of group interaction and observed the patterned form that culture takes. We turn now to the individual and the *personality* that he acquires in his social and cultural setting. These three major concepts are so interrelated that they can be separated only in theory, not in practice.[1] Each person incorporates into his personality the culture patterns he has learned from his interaction in various groups. Indeed, personality has been called the subjective aspect of culture.[2]

Social interaction is crucial to the formation of personality in another sense. The most intimate and "personal" aspect of the personality is the self, the entity that sets each individual off from every other individual. This uniquely personal thing is the product of interaction with others in a series of group settings. We acquire our attitudes toward ourselves largely through the attitudes of others toward us. We are modest, vain, confident, or timid largely because of the attitudes we think others have toward us. This conception of the self is the core of the personality. We cannot form this conception by ourselves, but must learn it from others. In this sense, complete personal individuality has been called an "illusion," inasmuch as the self cannot be isolated from others.[3]

The human being has an hereditary equipment that enables him to learn the behavior expected by the society. The way in which he participates in social relationships determines his personality. The extreme plasticity of his biological heritage permits him to modify his responses to meet the most diverse cultural expectations. This heritage differs from one individual to another, and no two persons receive exactly the same genetic combination. These hereditary differences are important in determining the basis of personality, but they properly constitute the subject matter for the biologist and the psychologist. As sociologists, we are primarily concerned with the social and cultural influences that combine with the biological base to form the complete personality. We shall therefore direct our discussion to the role of social interaction and its cultural products in the formation of personality.[4]

The average person understands this process of interaction only imperfectly. He does not realize that his own personality or that of his friend is the product of years of learning in different sociocultural settings. When someone shows an unhappy failing for drink, fast living, or delinquent behavior, our observer often attributes these activities to hereditary factors. He may examine the family of the transgressor for signs of similar behavior. If he finds (or thinks he

---

[1] Pitirim A. Sorokin, *Society, Culture, and Personality* (New York: Harper & Row, 1947).

[2] Ellsworth Faris, *The Nature of Human Nature* (New York: McGraw-Hill Book Company, Inc., 1937), p. 278.

[3] Harry Stack Sullivan, "The Illusion of Personal Individuality," *Psychiatry*, 13:317-332 (August, 1950).

[4] Cf. A. I. Hallowell, "Personality Structure and the Evolution of Man," *American Anthropologist*, 52:159-173 (1950).

finds) such "evidence," he concludes that "blood will tell." For many people, the only possible explanation for such behavior is that the person was "born" that way. The influence of social interaction is either ignored or minimized.[5]

Personality is, however, a social product and must ultimately be defined in social terms. The derivation of the word provides an important clue to its nature. Personality comes from the Latin word *persona*, the masks worn by the actors in the Roman theater. When the actor wished to become another person, he would change masks and thereby acquire a different "personality." The term gradually came to be applied to the social roles that the individual plays, both off and on the stage. From this comes the sociological definition of personality: "the sum and organization of those traits which determine the role of the individual in the group."[6]

In this sense, personality is based upon the conditions under which the individual participates in social interaction. This process begins the moment he is brought into the world as a helpless little animal, endowed with the possibilities for becoming a human being but requiring extensive social relationships to bring out these possibilities. These relationships include the loving attentions of his mother, his friendly struggles with playmates, the instruction of his teachers, and his physical conflicts on the athletic field. The process of interaction is central to this development. Personality arises and continues to exist in interpersonal relations.[7]

Personality and Socialization

The process whereby personality is acquired through social interaction is known as *socialization*. Every society is faced with the necessity of making a responsible member out of each child born into it. The child must learn the expectations of the society so that his behavior can be relied upon. He must acquire the group norms in order to take the behavior of others into account. In the process of socialization, he learns the reciprocal responses of the society, so that he can anticipate the behavior of others toward himself, as well as his own behavior toward others. The society must socialize each member so that his behavior will be meaningful in terms of the group norms and predictable to the other members. A minimum of conformity is fundamental to ordered social interaction. Socialization is the process by which this conformity is assured.[8]

Socialization and the acquisition of personality are thus two aspects of the same process. Socialization emphasizes the process in terms of society and the necessity for responsible, meaningful, and predictable behavior by the members. From the standpoint of the individual, this process stresses the way in

---

[5] Harry Stack Sullivan, *The Interpersonal Theory of Psychiatry* (New York: W. W. Norton & Company, Inc., 1953).

[6] Robert E. Park and Ernest W. Burgess, *Introduction to the Science of Sociology* (Chicago: University of Chicago Press, 1924), p. 70.

[7] Edward Sapir, "Personality," in *Encyclopedia of the Social Sciences*, Volume 12 (New York: The Macmillan Company, 1934), p. 85.

[8] Talcott Parsons, *The Social System* (Glencoe, Ill.: The Free Press, 1951), Chapter 6.

which each person acquires his personality from his group contacts. The needs of the individual and the group are reciprocal, although not necessarily synonymous. The group ordinarily demands a higher degree of conformity than the individual is willing to accept. A certain amount of deviance is found in every society, no matter how homogeneous and closely knit.[9] Without a minimum of similarity between the aims of the individual and those of the group, however, neither is able to function adequately.

In the process of socialization, the group teaches various expectations to the individual. These expectations range from food habits to patterns of religious worship, from sexual attitudes to definitions of spending and saving, and from toilet-training to world philosophy. The individual is influenced by various patterns of expectations, depending upon the dimensions of the group that is socializing him at the moment. Some of these patterns are common to everyone in the society of the United States. Others are peculiar to certain racial or ethnic groups within the society. Others reflect the outlook of a broad social class, as lower-class patterns differ from those of the middle class in a number of respects. Still other patterns are unique to the particular peer group, adolescent clique, or family with which the individual interacts.

In the present section and in those that follow, we shall be concerned with socialization from various points of view. Socialization has direct implications for the general study of personality. It has an equally immediate bearing upon Negro personality in the caste setting of the United States, where the Negro child perforce learns different responses from those the white child learns. Socialization likewise is closely related to differences between social classes. Social institutions in general, and the family in particular, are the principal agents of socialization. In short, society has a variety of agencies of socialization through which the individual learns the values, norms, and cultural expectations.

The process of socialization may be clarified by indicating briefly the range of expectations involved in it. These elements include the following:[10]

1. The basic disciplines. The first type of socialization in point of time involves the basic physical disciplines. The child learns such things as what to eat and how to eat it, under what circumstances he may release the tensions of bowel and bladder, and the degree to which he must control the emotions of love, hatred, and fear. In his early years, he is also socialized with regard to sexual behavior, as that important activity is viewed in his partcular group setting. An understanding of these and other physical and emotional disciplines is indispensable to making the child a responsible and predictable member of society.

2. The accepted aspirations. Society is also concerned with imparting the basic goals, aspirations, and values to which the child is expected to direct his

---

[9] Bronislaw Malinowski, *Crime and Custom in Savage Society*, Part II (London: Routledge and Kegan Paul, 1926), Chapter 1.

[10] Leonard Broom and Philip Selznick, *Sociology* (New York: Harper & Row, 1955), Chapter 4.

behavior for the rest of his life. In this context, he learns the accepted criteria of success, whether based upon money, political power, artistic achievement, scholarly endeavor, religious piety, or a combination of these and other values. He learns the levels to which he is expected to aspire, and learns that these aspirations are limited by such fortuitous factors as the color of his skin, his name, his religious faith, or the social status of his parents. In this aspect of socialization, the society imparts to its maturing members the goals that are important and the way one goes about attaining them.

3. *The necessary skills.* At the same time that he learns the accepted goals of his society, the child begins to acquire the necessary skills for reaching them. He learns, first of all, how to speak and thus assures his ability to communicate with others, first by speaking and then (perhaps) by reading and writing. All other skills are based upon this rudimentary ability to communicate symbolically. After that come the techniques he must have to act as a responsible member of society. These techniques reflect the way of life of the society and the place of the individual in it. The skills necessary for the Trobriand child differ widely from those required by the child in urban America. A considerable difference also exists between the skills of a working-class child and those of an upper-middle-class child in the same society. Whatever they are, these skills are an important part of the equipment imparted to the individual by socialization.

4. *The appropriate roles.* A final element in socialization is the acquisition of the appropriate social roles that the individual is expected to play. For present purposes, a social role may be considered as the pattern of expected behavior relative to a certain function or position in society. This concept is so important in socialization and personality formation that we are devoting an entire chapter to it. Indeed, Parsons defines socialization *as such* as "the acquisition of the requisite orientations for satisfactory functioning in a role." [11] We shall use the concept of socialization in a considerably broader sense, but social roles nevertheless remain central to this process. As males, females, husbands, wives, sons, daughters, parents, children, students, teachers, worshipers, ministers, voters, workers, and managers, accepted social roles must be learned if the individual is to play a functional and predictable part in social interaction.

Socialization is both *conscious* and *unconscious*. The group may deliberately instill the appropriate expectations in the child so that he will act in a responsible manner throughout his life. The mother who teaches her child how to talk and walk, and how to eat his spinach, offers an example of conscious socialization. The elaborate educational machinery of our society, from the nursery school to the graduate school, is the most obvious institutional medium of conscious socialization. Wherever and whenever one individual deliberately imparts a cultural pattern to another, socialization is taking place. The individual may learn imperfectly, incompletely, and inadequately. But the process of transmission is the important consideration, as each person slowly becomes a more complete member of the group.

---

[11] Parsons, *op. cit.*, p. 205.

The unconscious aspects of socialization are even more numerous, complex, and pervasive. The child learns most of his disciplines, aspirations, skills, and roles without realizing that he is doing so. Merely by interacting with others, he becomes socialized in a variety of ways. The play group socializes the child with its own norms. The high school clique imparts its ideals and behavior patterns to its members with no visible difficulty. The delinquent gang instills norms that deviate from those of the larger society. Members of the gang learn these deviant patterns as easily as other adolescents learn the norms of society as a whole.

Communication and Social Interaction

Social interaction takes place through symbolic communication. We have already considered some of the implications of this process in Chapter 2. The transmission of learned behavior is impossible without some form of symbolic communication. A symbol is a word, sign, object, or gesture accepted by a group and standing for something else. A word is a symbol that may stand for an idea, emotion, experience, object, or imaginary condition. The meaning of a verbal symbol may range from that of a word like *pencil* to such complex implications as are involved in words like *God*, *liberty*, or *justice*. Ability to communicate through abstract symbols is the basis for social interaction. This ability is also fundamental to the development of personalty.[12]

The faculty of communicating through symbols is uniquely human. Animals communicate by cries and gestures, but their action is not symbolic. Wolves can warn each other of approaching danger. Sheep can communicate emotional states, and collectively can work themselves into a panic over real or suspected danger. Other animals can communicate on various sensory levels, whether by cries, smells, or sounds. But man is the only animal that is able to transfer meanings by symbols. Language is thus a basic adjunct to the development of personality.

Language symbols have certain *general* characteristics shared by all societies. These common elements are as follows:[13]

1. They are systematic. Language symbols are systematic because they represent systems of meanings. One part of the system cannot be understood without the others. The word for "husband" is meaningful only in terms of a system of symbols containing a word for "wife." The child develops his personality by learning the systems of meanings of his culture.

2. They are inherently social. Language symbols derive meaning from mutual agreement by members of the society. They evoke approximately similar reactions in the person who uses them and in the person to whom they are addressed. Social interaction is possible only when language symbols mean the

---

[12] Patrick Mullahy, "A Philosophy of Personality," *Psychiatry*, 13:417-437 (November, 1950).

[13] The following is adapted from Alfred R. Lindesmith and Anselm L. Strauss, *Social Psychology* (rev. ed.) (New York: The Dryden Press, 1956), p. 56.

same things to different persons. The child learns to associate words with the appropriate elements in his expanding environment.

3. *They are voluntarily produced.* Language symbols can be produced by the individual at any time, whether alone or in the company of others. Man can stimulate himself by language, in much the same way as he can stimulate others. The child continues the process of socialization by talking to himself when others are not present. In this way, he learns to identify himself with the group meanings.

Personality development is marked by an increasing facility in communication. The beginnings of language are apparent about the tenth month, when the child's hitherto meaningless cries begin to assume recognizable form. The word *mama* is traditionally the first word in the vocabulary of the English-speaking child. This symbol represents the most important object in his environment. The affectionate sympathy of the mother endows many of the child's random vocal gestures with meaning. She senses by his tone whether he wants a drink, a change of clothing, or is merely bored. In this way, she provides the principal liaison between the child and his environment. When he imperiously summons her by calling "mama," he is enjoying his first symbolic control of his world.

The solicitude of the mother is usually not shared by others. The child must develop his vocabulary if he is to communicate with anyone besides his mother. These limits are gradually expanded, and by the age of two he has a vocabulary of 250 words. His personality constantly changes as his interpersonal contacts increase. His broadening horizon becomes a part of himself, as he learns first that things have names and then that they are related. First nouns and then verbs form the general order of linguistic development, as the child learns to participate more fully in society.[14]

As the expansion of his vocabulary continues, the child also begins to acquire the normative expectations of his society. The folkways and mores gradually assume significance for him, and he learns to distinguish right from wrong in terms of the definitions of his culture. In order to formulate his reactions to his expanding world, he must first state them to himself. Before he can tell his mother about his fight on the playground, he must first phrase this experience in abstract and symbolic terms. This process of formulation and telling is an education in itself and heightens the experience in his own mind. In this way, the adventures of each day become a part of his expanding personality.

This self-stimulation through language is an important part of personality development. The child can review in his own mind the encounter he has had with a friend or anticipate the one he is about to have with an enemy. In each case, he sets off an emotional response and thereby adds to his experience. Reading is a process in which the child enlarges his experience and his personality through language symbols. The child who grows up in a literate household

---

[14] Arnold Gesell, *et al., The First Five Years of Life* (New York: Harper & Brothers, 1940), Chapter 8, "Language Development."

and early acquires a wide vocabulary is a different person from the one reared in a home where the symbolic experience is poorer. Each person can directly experience only a small part of his total environment. He must learn about most of it through communication. The person who communicates with others by reading, writing, or talking incorporates ever larger segments of the world into his personality.

Personality and the Social Self

The central element in the world of every individual is himself. In this sense, every person spends his life in a prolonged love affair with himself. This does *not* mean that he is "selfish," in the usual sense of the term. It *does* mean that for every person, no matter how "unselfish," his own self is the most important consideration. He wishes to be well thought of by others and is constantly striving to gain this end. Many of his emotional difficulties result, directly or indirectly, from the feeling that he is scorned, despised, or rejected by those whose opinion he values.[15] We shall subsequently examine some of the implications of this relationship between the ideas that we have of ourselves and those held by others. Suffice it to indicate here that each man's judgments of himself are the most crucial he holds.[16] Man is human because he can act toward himself as he thinks others might act. The essence of his "humanness" consists in the possession of a self.[17]

Each individual has a unique set of genetic characteristics and a unique personal history. The paradoxical aspect of this uniqueness and individuality, however, is that *the self is a social product.* The individual is obliged to look at himself through the eyes of others. He views himself in terms of their reactions to him, as he perceives these reactions. In other words, the self arises in social interaction and continues through this process. That is, *"The individual's conception of himself emerges from social interaction and, in turn, guides or influences the behavior of that individual."* [18] Without early and continuous interaction with other persons, the self would never emerge. In the most literal sense, therefore, the self is dependent upon society.[19]

This aspect of the self has been demonstrated by a number of empirical studies, in which the attitude of the individual toward himself was compared with the conceptions of others toward him or his interpretation of these conceptions. A significant series of correlations emerged between these self-appraisals and

---

[15] William R. Rosengren, "The Self in the Emotionally Disturbed," *American Journal of Sociology,* 66:454-462 (March, 1961). Elton F. Jackson, "Status Consistency and Symptoms of Stress," *American Sociological Review,* 27:469-480 (August, 1960).

[16] Simon Dinitz, *et al.,* "Delinquency Vulnerability: A Cross Group and Longitudinal Analysis," *American Sociological Review,* 27:515-517 (August, 1962).

[17] Herbert Blumer, "Society as Symbolic Interaction," Chap. 9 in Arnold M. Rose (ed.), *Human Behavior and Social Processes* (Boston: Houghton Mifflin Company, 1962), p. 181.

[18] John W. Kinch, "A Formalized Theory of the Self Concept," *American Journal of Sociology,* 68:481-486 (January, 1963), p. 481. (His italics.)

[19] The pioneer in the interactionist theory of the self was George H. Mead. The chief source of this approach remains his *Mind, Self and Society* (Chicago: University of Chicago Press, 1934).

the reflected appraisals of others. Each person thus views himself through the eyes of others. "The results of this research," the authors of one study conclude, "lend empirical support to the symbolic interactionist view of self-conception. Our findings," they continue, "indicate that the response, or at least the attitude, of others is related to self-conception; but they also indicate that the subject's perception of that response is even more closely related." [20]

The child therefore does not have a self at birth. The self is not present in the germ plasm in the same sense as blue eyes, curly hair, or a fair skin. The child acquires a social self through interaction with others. The self reflects the group situations in which he participates. The most important of these groups is the family. Here the child comes in contact with others during his most impressionable years and takes the attitudes toward himself of those who matter most. The elements of the self that arise in this situation are the most basic. They constitute the core of the self and remain a central part of it through life. [21]

In this way, the person perpetuates the attitudes directed at him when he was a child. In Sullivan's words, "the peculiarity exists that one can find in others only that which is in the self." [22] The individual who grows up without affection from others will later find difficulty in giving it to others. He will express his own negative self-feelings by finding fault with others, disparaging their efforts, and generally attacking their personal prestige. His own self-appraisal may have arisen in the beginning because, as a child, he was never sufficiently loved, appreciated, or made to feel secure in his attitude toward himself. He is condemned to express this low self-appraisal in his subsequent reactions with other persons. He looks at the world through the emotional atmosphere of distrust that he himself generates. [23]

The self is thus "a subject which is its own object." Each person loves himself, hates himself, praises himself, blames himself, and punishes himself. Both the subject and the object of these verbs is the self. The attitude toward the self, furthermore, varies according to the group context. The football player may be sure of himself on the field and unsure of himself in the classroom. The child is "self-confident" when his mother is near, but collapses in a panic when she is not. The self is a product of interaction in a number of group situations. If the *general tone* of these situations throughout the early years has been friendly and affectionate, the general orientation of the self will tend to be secure; if not, insecure.

The subjective and objective aspects of the self have been viewed by Mead and others in terms of the pronouns *I* and *me*. The former is the subject of the self-attitudes, the latter is their object. The "I" is the active part of the self, the

[20] S. Frank Miyamoto and Sanford W. Dornbusch, "A Test of Interactionist Hypotheses of Self-Conception," *American Journal of Sociology,* 61:399-403 (March, 1956), p. 403. See also David A. Goslin, "Accuracy of Self-Perception and Social Acceptance," *Sociometry,* 25:283-296 (September, 1963).

[21] Bingham Dai, "A Socio-Psychiatric Approach to Personality Orientation," *American Sociological Review,* 17:44-49 (February, 1952).

[22] Harry Stack Sullivan, *Conceptions of Modern Psychiatry* (Washington, D. C.: The William Alanson White Psychiatric Foundation, 1947), p. 10.

[23] *Ibid.,* p. 11.

part that does things on its own, as it were. The "me" reflects the expectations and judgments of others. As stated by Foote and Cottrell, the "I" refers to "the active, assertive, and emergent features of human behavior, not reducible to standard roles in conventional situations." The "me" is "the vested and organized experience of the community as incorporated within personal conduct." [24] Cultural expectations are embodied in the "me," whereas the "I" is more unique and individual.

The two parts of the self are in constant interaction. The "I" holds attitudes about the "me," and the latter reflects the judgments of others toward the "I." This dialogue is a basic part of the conscious and unconscious mental life of every individual. These self-attitudes give rise to what Sullivan has called the "Good-me" and the "Bad-me." The "Good-me" is the part of the self that reflects affection, tenderness, and generally pleasant treatment from others. This aspect is related to the mother, who is ordinarily the first one to give the child affection. She is the one who first loves him and thus causes him to love himself. The encouragement of these self-attitudes by the mother explains in large part the sentiments that the average person has toward her all his life.[25]

The "Bad-me" reflects the dissatisfaction arising from lack of affection from the mother or from other "significant others" in the environment. One of the basic elements in the "Bad-me" is *anxiety*, arising from the feeling of the person that those nearest and dearest to him do not love him. The person may be timid and insecure because of a basic anxiety in his interpersonal relations. People ordinarily try to avoid thinking and talking about the "Bad-me," because it makes them unhappy to do so. They prefer to think about the "Good-me," for this image gives them pleasure. Both the "Good-me" and the "Bad-me" reflect the judgments of others toward the self, or at least the individual's interpretation of these judgments. Both happiness and unhappiness reflect this dual aspect of the self.[26]

The two aspects of the self embodied in the "I" and the "me" represent an act that only a human being can perform. Man is the only species that can hold an attitude toward himself. Cows presumably do not worry about their immortal souls. Dogs make no discernible attempt to justify the ways of God to dogs. Man's conception of himself is one of the principal elements that raise him above the level of the beasts. His capacity for infinite suffering and infinite exaltation both arise from his possession of a self and from the "reflected appraisals" that set its tone. In this sense, man is an animal with a social self.

The Emergence of the Self

The infant is the center of his own universe. His wants are satisfied as soon as he makes them known. He has a high degree of control over his environment,

---

[24] Nelson N. Foote and Leonard S. Cottrell, Jr., *Identity and Interpersonal Competence* (Chicago: University of Chicago Press, 1955), p. 58.

[25] Sullivan, *The Interpersonal Theory of Psychiatry, op. cit.*, pp. 161-162.

[26] *Ibid.*

which initially consists largely of his family. During his early weeks, his behavior is completely selfish, in the sense that he seeks only to satisfy his own drives. The world offers little or no frustration and his wishes are law. This situation does not continue very long, and frustrations sooner or later arise. The infant is unable to receive food, warmth, affection, or physical attention at the precise moment that he wants them. At this point, he encounters for the first time the "reality" of the universe. He gradually learns that he must adjust to other persons and take them into consideration.

The development of the social self arises through this emerging interaction. The infant is not sensitive to the opinion of others, but as he grows older he becomes increasingly aware of them. At first a blind, unthinking little tyrant, he soon learns that other persons exist, who must be humored and manipulated. Only by taking others into account can he receive the affection that is so necessary to his emotional well-being. In this sense, "the self is a system within a personality, built up from innumerable experiences from early life, the central notion of which is that we satisfy the people that matter to us and therefore satisfy ourselves. . . ."[27]

In the development of the self, the child learns the norms of his group. These expectations are learned in the early interaction between the child and those who matter most to him. The mother is the principal instrument of this development, and the child wishes to please her above all others. She imparts to him many of the basic norms, and he incorporates them into the fabric of his per-

---

[27] Sullivan, "The Illusion of Personal Individuality," *op. cit.,* p. 328.

The first and most important object in the world of the infant is his mother.

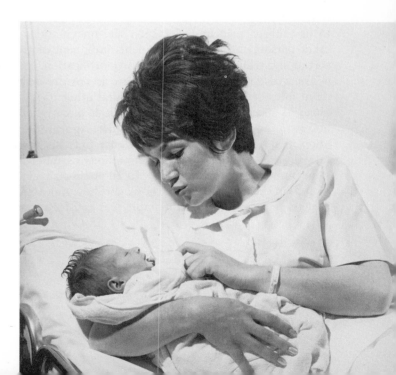

sonality. In order to make the child obey these normative patterns, the actual presence of the mother is necessary at first. She must be physically there to register approval or disapproval to the child and thereby reinforce the norms in his emerging personality.[28]

As he grows older, however, the child begins to judge himself in terms of the norms that his mother (or mother substitute) has given him, even though she is no longer present. She may, indeed, have been dead for many years, but the self-judgments she has given him remain at the core of his personality. This process of self-judgment is called the *conscience* (or the superego), and the maturing individual judges his actions by the standards learned in his early years.

These standards are in the form of "symbol systems"—that is, related patterns of words that embody the value judgments of the culture. These symbol systems involve such profound questions as moral judgments, religious beliefs, and sexual attitudes. They go far to determine the way the individual views the world and his place in it. This process of self-judgment is partly conscious and partly unconscious. Many times, the person is not even aware of the source of self-judgments and tends to view them as innate. There is no doubt, however, that conscience arises in the person through social interaction.[29]

In his penetrating analysis of the role of social interaction in the emergence of the self, Cooley hit upon the happy phrase, "the looking-glass self," to indicate this relationship. He based his discussion on the couplet, "Each to each a looking glass/Reflects the other that doth pass." The person figuratively observes his image in the looking glass. He imagines the reaction of others to this image and is satisfied or ashamed as a result. Cooley has characterized this reflected image of the self as follows: "A self-idea of this sort," he says, "seems to have three principal elements: the imagination of our appearance to the other person; the imagination of his judgment of that appearance; and some sort of self-feeling, such as pride or mortification. . . ."[30]

The girl getting ready for a dance is not dressing for herself alone. She is more interested in what the boys (and other girls) will think of her appearance. As she looks into the mirror, she is already anticipating the reactions of others to the face that looks back at her. Appearance is an important consideration in self-judgments. As one scholar puts it, "the self is established, maintained, and altered in social transactions as much by the communication of appearances as by discourse."[31] In all our social relationships, we are similarly wondering what others think of us and how our actions affect them. If we feel that these judgments are favorable, our self-feeling is one of pride or satisfac-

---

[28] Gregory Bateson, "Cultural Determinants of Personality," in J. McV. Hunt (ed.), *Personality and the Behavior Disorders*, Volume II (New York: The Ronald Press, 1944), Chapter 23.

[29] Talcott Parsons, "The Superego and the Theory of Social Systems," *Psychiatry*, 15:15-25 (February, 1952).

[30] Charles Horton Cooley, *Human Nature and the Social Order* (New York: Charles Scribner's Sons, 1902), p. 152.

[31] Gregory P. Stone, "Appearance and the Self," Chapter 5 in Arnold M. Rose (ed.), *op. cit.*, p. 117.

tion. If we fear that these judgments are unfavorable, we experience uneasiness or mortification. In everyday life, we continually "present" ourselves to other persons and, in so doing, strive to present a favorable impression.[32] Self-judgments depend in large part upon our perception of the judgments of others toward us. In this way, the self emerges and develops in continuous interaction with others.

The Self and the Other

We thus derive our self-attitudes by projecting ourselves into the minds of others. This process is known as "taking the role of the other." The individual puts himself in the place of the other and tries to imagine what he would think under similar circumstances. Consciousness of the self arises when the child starts to take the role of other persons and view himself as (he believes) they do. Many childhood games are based on the child taking the role of others toward himself. He takes the role of his mother and praises himself. He takes the role of his brothers and sisters and plays imaginary games with himself. He takes the role of a policeman and arrests himself. In this process, he gradually begins to see himself as others see him.[33]

The ability to take the role of the other corresponds roughly to what the psychologists call "empathy," the emotional identification of one person with another. One person takes the role of the other and responds emotionally in the process, thereby exhibiting an "empathic response." This type of response is basic to all social interaction, for the individual must enter into some kind of emotional identification with the other if he is to communicate with him. The person who is insensitive to the responses of others is lacking in "empathic ability," or the ability to take the role of the other. In other words, ". . . the processes by which the self emerges and functions depend heavily upon the empathic responses. 'Reflected appraisals' and 'taking the role of the other' in responding to one's own actions and impulses mean the same kind of operation which includes the incorporation in one's own reactive system of the responses of another." [34] In this process, the self interacts with other selves.

The empathic responses are subject to wide individual variations. Some persons have the ability to participate fully in the emotions of others. They are warm, expressive, out-going, and optimistic. They are sympathetic to the reactions of others, because they can participate in these reactions. Other persons are lacking in empathic ability and are correspondingly rigid, diffident, and inhibited. They keep to themselves because they cannot participate in the responses of others. They do not make friends easily and their social relationships are limited and formal. They cannot give themselves fully to another, for

---

[32] Erving Goffman, *The Presentation of Self in Everyday Life* (New York: Doubleday Anchor Books, 1959), "Introduction."

[33] Mead, *Mind, Self, and Society, op. cit.*

[34] Leonard S. Cottrell, Jr., and Rosalind F. Dymond, "The Emphatic Responses," *Psychiatry*, 12:355-359 (November, 1949), pp. 356-357.

they are unable to put themselves in the other's place. These differences in empathic response are relative, insofar as every human being possesses some ability to take the role of the other. Otherwise, he would be incapable of communicating with his fellows.

As he takes the role of the other, the child begins to hold internal conversations with himself. These conversations involve the "significant others" in his environment—the persons who matter to him. His mother is ordinarily the most "significant other" in his early experience, although the father may play an important role in discipline. In an ingenious study, Henry found that (male) persons who perceive their *mothers* as playing the most important disciplinary role in the family tend to blame themselves strongly in later life. On the other hand, males who perceive their *fathers* as playing the principal disciplinary role tend to blame others rather than themselves. In these and other subtle ways, the early interaction of the child with different members of his family appears to have an effect upon his social self.[35]

The child learns to anticipate the responses of significant others by putting himself in their place. He expects affection from his mother and, ordinarily, from the other members of his family. As he grows older, however, he realizes that others will not necessarily have the same affectionate feeling for him. In the development of his self, he learns to adapt his behavior to the expected behavior of others.[36]

The social self is thus the *object* of self-attitudes as well as the *subject*. The self arises in interaction with others, and the individual looks at himself through their eyes. He feels happy or sad as he evokes praise or blame from those whose roles he takes in his imagination. By taking the role of others toward himself, he develops self-attitudes. In Mead's words, "The individual . . . enters his own experience as a self or individual . . . only in so far as he first becomes an object to himself just as other individuals are objects to him or in his experience; and he becomes an object to himself only by taking the attitudes of other individuals toward himself within a social environment . . . in which both he and they are involved." [37]

The "others" that make up this audience may be of different kinds. The others may be there in person or far away; they may be living or dead; they may be specific individuals or a vague but nevertheless very real "they"; they may include one's parents, friends, colleagues, or superiors; and they may even be as yet unborn, as the bride thinks of her unborn children and the artist dreams of posterity. These inferences of others' attitudes may or may not be correct. It is clearly difficult to anticipate the reactions of one's unborn children or those of the literary or artistic public in fifty years. It may be almost as difficult to anticipate the attitudes of someone who is face-to-face with us at the moment. The important consideration, in any event, is the variety of the "others" to whom we

---

[35] Andrew F. Henry, "Family Role Structure and Self-Blame," *Social Forces*, 35:34-38 (October, 1956).
[36] Ralph H. Turner, "Self and Other in Moral Judgment," *American Sociological Review*, 19:249-259 (June, 1954).
[37] Mead, *op. cit.*, p. 138.

respond in our imagination and whose real or imputed attitudes determine our own self-feeling.[38]

In modern society, the individual interacts with a wide variety of others—some intimately, others indirectly, and still others remotely. A member of a learned profession takes the role of several levels of others, who are all more or less directly related to him in his performance of his professional activity. The doctor, for example, takes the role of his clients (patients) and endeavors first to find out what is the matter with them and then cure them. At the same time, the doctor also takes the role of his professional colleagues, whose judgments are vital to his self-image. He also takes the role of members of related occupations, although their judgments (whether real or in his imagination) are not as important to him as are those of his medical colleagues. Relatives and friends of his patients also enter into the category of "others," as do members of the community who hold attitudes about him as a doctor, neighbor, and citizen. His self-conception is thus a complex product of the attitudes of these and other persons (e.g., his own immediate family)—or of his perception of these attitudes.[39]

In his early experience, the child learns to take the role of his mother, his father, and his brothers and sisters. Then his horizon broadens and he takes the role of a teacher, a policeman, or a soldier. A further development occurs when he begins to play games with other children. To play his role properly, he must understand the roles of the others. As he learns to act within a more complex pattern of expectations, his self becomes correspondingly more complex. At first, these games are spontaneous and the children work out the rules as they go along. The process becomes more complicated when they play a formal game. These organized patterns are vital for the child, for they are (at the moment) his most important business. The rules of the game are his moral precepts. His attitudes toward these rules (and himself as a part of them) go far toward determining his later attitudes toward moral codes in general.[40]

This stage of role-taking may be illustrated by a football game. Each player has different parts (roles), established by the rules of the game. Each one must be aware of the parts of the others as well as his own. He responds in his imagination to these roles, and in so doing he stimulates himself. Every member of the team must be similarly aware of, and responsive to, the roles of the others. The action of each player depends upon his knowledge of all the roles that collectively constitute the rules of the game of football.

The self grows by similar cooperative activities, all taking different forms in different societies. Chinese boys obviously do not play football to develop the cooperative attitudes basic to the social self. Every society has its own group activities in which a definite series of reciprocal responses is expected of every-

---

[38] Anselm L. Strauss, *Mirrors and Masks: The Search for Identity* (Glencoe, Ill.: The Free Press, 1959), pp. 34-35.

[39] Everett C. Hughes, "What Other?", Chapter 6 in Arnold M. Rose (ed.), *op. cit.*, p. 125.

[40] Robert J. Havighurst, *Human Development and Education* (New York: Longmans, Green and Company, 1953), p. 54.

one. In this way, each maturing individual learns to take the role of the other toward himself and thereby develops his own self.[41]

The Self and the Generalized Other

The most complex stage in the development of the social self arises when the individual begins to take the role of society as a whole (or a significant segment of it) toward himself. Mead calls this "taking the role of the generalized other." In a narrow sense, the generalized other refers to the roles, attitudes, and expectations of all the other persons in a particular social situation, such as an organized game. In a broader sense, it refers to the organized culture patterns of the entire society. The generalized other includes the folkways, mores, values, and other normative elements in a culture. The child slowly becomes conscious of these expectations and begins to judge himself in these terms.[42]

The generalized other is not the same for all persons. Each one has different self-attitudes toward the basic concerns of life, even though general similarities do exist among all persons reared in the same society. In a simple society, the generalized other is homogeneous, and all the members are able to view their own behavior in much the same light. Studies of primitive societies have confirmed this general similarity of basic philosophy, at least until the pattern is broken by the introduction of alien cultures.[43]

This homogeneity is lacking in our society, which is so complex that each child merely receives a part of the total normative expectations of the culture. The literature on social class indicates clearly that the generalized other each child incorporates into his personality is different. Persons reared in middle-class environments have very different attitudes from lower-class persons toward such diverse aspects of the generalized other as sex norms[44] and attitudes toward personal aggression.[45] There appear, indeed, to be significant differences between social classes in attitudes toward the self. Persons in the middle and upper classes show greater aggression against the self than do those in the lower class. The aggressions of the latter appear to be more strongly directed against other persons than against the self.[46]

The concept of the generalized other as developed by Mead should, therefore, be modified to take account of this heterogeneity. Instead of one homogeneous generalized other, there are many generalized others within the same society. The child is exposed to one or more of these generalized others, but not to all of them. He incorporates into his personality the version of his social class

---

[41] Cf. Manford H. Kuhn and Thomas S. McPartland, "An Empirical Investigation of Self-Attitudes," *American Sociological Review,* 19:68-76 (February, 1954).

[42] George Herbert Mead, *op. cit.,* p. 162.

[43] Ruth Benedict, *Patterns of Culture* (New York: Penguin Books, Inc., 1946).

[44] Kinsey, *et al., op. cit.,* p. 347.

[45] Allison Davis, "American Status Systems and the Socialization of the Child," *American Sociological Review,* 6:345-354 (June, 1941).

[46] Samuel Z. Klausner "Social Class and Self-Concept," *Journal of Social Psychology,* 38:201-205 (November, 1953).

or subculture, as mediated to him by his parents, brothers and sisters, peer groups, and similar agencies. This version becomes the "significant" other as far as he is concerned and may differ in many important respects from that held by others. The standards by which the individual judges himself when he takes the role of the generalized other are subject to considerable variation within the same complex society.[47]

The peer group is important in defining and incorporating the version of the generalized other to which the individual responds. As we have seen in Chapter 4, the peer group is a group of boys and girls of about the same age who have the same general attitudes. In the development of his social self, the child or adolescent is continually interacting with a series of such groups. He learns from them many of the norms that serve as reference points for his self-attitudes. In his study of the adolescent society, Coleman indicates the crucial role of the peer group at the high-school level. Adolescents, he says, "are looking to each other rather than to the adult community for their social rewards." [48] Given the choice between observing the adult norms (studying) and the adolescent norms (being an athlete), their choice is usually in favor of the latter.[49]

In a number of respects, therefore, the peer group is more important than the parents in establishing the version of the generalized other to which the adolescent responds. In the field of religion, for example, one study indicated that the attitudes of the peer group are more influential than those of the family in defining behavior.[50] In another study, these cross-pressures are further explored, with the tentative conclusion that adolescent choices (in this case, those of girls) depend upon the character of the alternatives presented. That is to say, in behavior involving social values that are changing rapidly, the adolescent girls tend to follow the peer group. In behavior involving more permanent values, they tend to follow the values of their parents.[51]

The process by which the child incorporates the generalized other is complex and gradual. The infant has no abstract moral values, but is instead extremely egocentric. He has no feeling for, nor consideration of, other persons and must learn to take, first, the role of the other and, later, that of the generalized other. His attitudes are highly personal and are largely concerned with the behavior of other persons toward himself. His conception of abstract moral principles comes later. The child learns early in life that he must not strike his younger brother, and vice versa; these are interpersonal relations that affect him directly. It takes him much longer to learn that society has many other norms that have nothing directly to do with him. The degree to which such gen-

---

[47] Harry Stack Sullivan, *Conceptions of Modern Psychiatry* (Washington: William A. White Foundation, 1947), pp. 95-96. Cf. also Leonard S. Cottrell, Jr. and Nelson N. Foote, "Sullivan's Contribution to Social Psychology," Chapter 6 in Patrick Mullahy (ed.), *The Contributions of Harry Stack Sullivan* (New York: Hermitage House, 1952).

[48] James S. Coleman, *The Adolescent Society* (Glencoe, Ill.: The Free Press, 1961), p. 11.

[49] *Ibid.*, p. 310.

[50] Bernard C. Rosen, "Conflicting Group Membership: A Study of Parental-Peer Group Pressures," *American Sociological Review*, 20:155-161 (April, 1955).

[51] Clay V. Brittain, "Adolescent Choices and Parent-Peer Cross-Pressures," *American Sociological Review*, 28:385-391 (June, 1963).

eral principles of morality are accepted varies between individuals. Some persons never grasp these essential elements of the generalized other.

Social Interaction and the Generalized Other

The gradual acquisition of the generalized other as a part of the personality is indicated in the development of language habits. The child of two or three has not yet begun to take the role of the generalized other and hence does not think of himself as a member of a cooperative society. The words most commonly used at this age are *I, me, my*, and *mine*. Verbs are in the imperative mood, as the child demands the attention of others in his immediate environment. The use of self-words and imperative sentences decreases as he grows older and learns that there are others in the world, whose wishes must also be considered.[52] At four or five, he begins to play simple games requiring an awareness of others and an ability to take their roles. He begins to look to others for praise or blame; in order to gain these benefits for his expanding self, he must play the game according to the rules. As the social self emerges, "selfishness" declines.

The concept of the generalized other may be further illustrated by attitudes toward private property. When two boys struggle over a baseball glove, each may invoke the concept of private property in defense of his own interests. One boy insists that he found the glove and that it therefore belongs to him. The other maintains that his father bought it for him, that he laid it down for a moment, and that it is indubitably his property. They are both invoking the abstract attitude toward private property that is a central part of the generalized other in our society. They agree on the importance of private ownership, but they disagree on the circumstances under which each can appeal to this concept. Each is taking the role of the generalized other toward himself as well as toward his adversary.

Society is based upon such general attitudes toward the home, religion, property, democratic government, and the like. The individual incorporates these principles into his social self by taking the role of the generalized other toward himself. The responses to this process, says Mead, ". . . give him what we term his principles, the acknowledged attitudes of all members of the community. He is putting himself in the place of the generalized other, which represents the organized responses of all the members of the group."[53]

The social self is the core of the personality. The self develops in interaction with other persons, as the individual learns to take the role of the other toward himself. This interaction is marked by imaginary projection into different levels of experience. In his early experience, the child takes the role of the other in a simple and direct sense. He acts toward himself as mother, father, brother, sis-

---

[52] Arnold Gesell, *et al., The First Five Years of Life* (New York: Harper & Brothers, 1940), Chapter 8, "Language Development."

[53] George Herbert Mead, *op. cit.,* p. 162.

ter, and member of the peer group. As he learns to play games, he learns to take the role of several other persons, as well as that of a pattern of group expectations (the rules). The self enters the final stage of development when the individual begins to take the role of society in general (or a significant part of it) toward himself. He then judges himself in terms of the normative aspects of the culture. Throughout the rise of the social self, the relationship between the self and other persons is close and continuous.

As the core of the personality, the social self has an important relationship to individual stability. Marked inconsistency in self-attitudes seems to produce feelings of insecurity, rejection, and (possibly) disorganization. Persons whose attitudes toward themselves vary widely from the attitudes of others toward them have difficulty adjusting to the group. In one study of rejected children, it was found that "adolescents who perceive themselves differently from the way they are perceived by their group . . . are likely to be accorded a low degree of acceptance by the others." [54] Group interaction depends upon an essential similarity between the self-conceptions of each of the members and the conceptions of others toward them. By the same token, individual emotional stability is based in large part upon such a similarity.

The relationships between self-judgments and other-judgments have been further indicated in two forms of problem behavior—mental illness and juvenile delinquency. These forms of behavior differ as to the combination of factors that bring them about. They appear to have some similarity, however, in terms of the self-attitudes of those involved. In one study, personal disorganization in mental illness is seen as a function of the individual's conception of himself, which in turn is related to the conceptions of others toward him. Persons with sharply inappropriate self-conceptions thus appear to be more subject to some forms of mental illness than those whose self-conceptions are more appropriate.[55] In a series of studies of juvenile delinquency, the self-structure was found to be related to behavior when the boy was exposed to antisocial influences. In summary, "a good self concept, undoubtedly a product of favorable socialization, veers slum boys away from delinquency, while a poor self concept, a product of unfavorable socialization, gives the slum boy no resistance to deviancy, delinquent companions, or delinquent subculture." [56]

The social self that emerges from this complex process is a unique product. The criticism is sometimes made that the interpersonal concept of the self destroys the uniqueness and individuality of each human being. Nothing could be farther from the truth. In the first place, the uniqueness of each person is assured by the biological unity of the organism, whereby each individual has a unique combination of genes. In the second place, and more germane to the

---

[54] David A. Goslin, *op. cit.*, p. 296.

[55] Simon Dinitz, *et al.*, "Integration and Conflict in Self-Other Conceptions as Factors in Mental Illness," *Sociometry*, 22:45-55 (March, 1959). See also William R. Rosengren, "The Self in the Emotionally Disturbed," *op. cit.*

[56] Simon Dinitz, *et al.*, "Delinquency Vulnerability: A Cross Group and Longitudinal Analysis," *American Sociological Review*, 27:515-517 (August, 1962), p. 517.

interactional approach, is the fact that each self develops in a series of different group settings. Patterns of interaction by which the self evolves are different for every individual. Even identical twins in the same family interact uniquely with others inside and outside the family and develop different selves.

The interactional approach to personality emphasizes the individuality and uniqueness of each person. The social process is similar for everyone, in that each person uses symbolic communication, although even here complete language uniformity does not exist. Each individual nevertheless takes the role of the other and the generalized other toward himself and further participates in the same *general* process.

Despite these general similarities, according to Mead, "every individual self has its own peculiar individuality, its own unique pattern, because each individual self . . . reflects in its organized structure a different aspect or perspective of this whole social behavior pattern from that which is reflected in the organized structure *of any* [*other*] *individual self* within that process." [57] Each person participates in the social process and develops a self by taking others into account. The ultimate product of each individual experience is a unique human being.

---

[57] George Herbert Mead, *op. cit.,* p. 201. (My italics.)

SELECTED BIBLIOGRAPHY

Cooley, Charles Horton, *Human Nature and the Social Order.* New York: Charles Scribner's Sons, 1902. This book contains one of the earliest and most intuitive discussions of the social nature of the self, built around the famous concept of "the looking-glass self." The author was a pioneer in this field, and many of his original insights have only recently been explored in some of their implications.

Dinitz, Simon, *et al.,* "Delinquency Vulnerability: A Cross Group and Longitudinal Analysis," *American Sociological Review,* 27:515-517 (August, 1962). This study examines the general hypothesis that "a good self concept is indicative of a residual favorable socialization and a strong inner self, which in turn steers the person away from bad companions and street corner society . . . ."

Goffman, Erving, *The Presentation of Self in Everyday Life.* New York: Doubleday Anchor Books, 1959. This brilliant book deals with the relationships between social interaction and the self. More specifically, the author analyzes the circumstances in which the individual, consciously and unconsciously, projects a favorable impression of himself to other people.

Goslin, David A., "Accuracy of Self Perception and Social Acceptance," *Sociometry,* 25:283-296 (September, 1962). This article examines some of the differences between rejected and accepted children in terms of the similarities and disparities between self-ratings and peer-ratings. Children whose attitudes toward themselves differ widely from the attitudes of their peers toward them tend to be rejected by the group.

Hughes, Everett C., "What Other?", Ch. 6 in Arnold M. Rose (ed.), *Human*

Behavior and Social Processes. Boston: Houghton Mifflin Company, 1962. This perceptive essay views the concept of "taking the role of the other" in a fresh light. "One of the complications of civilized life," the author remarks in this connection, "is that one is confronted with a variety of 'others', some of whose directions are not compatible with those of some others."

Kinch, John W., "A Formalized Theory of the Self Concept," *American Journal of Sociology,* 68:481-486 (January, 1963). The basic postulates of the interactionist theory of the self are stated in this article. The essence of the theory is that "the individual's self-concept is based on his *perception* of the way others are responding to him." (My italics.)

Mead, George Herbert, *Mind, Self and Society* (edited by Charles W. Morris). Chicago: University of Chicago Press, 1934. These notes, compiled from Mead's lectures and published writings, constitute the most important single source for the analysis of the social self. Mead explores at length the subtle implications of such concepts as taking the role of the other and that of the generalized other.

Merrill, Francis E., "The Self and the Other: An Emerging Field of Social Problems," *Social Problems,* 4:200-207 (January, 1957). This essay advances the hypothesis that relationships between the self and the other are an increasing source of social problems in contemporary society. Among such self-other problems are marriage relationships, racial contacts, religious prejudice, and mental illness.

——, "Stendhal and the Self: A Study in the Sociology of Literature," *American Journal of Sociology,* 66:446-453 (March 1961). In Stendhal's great novel, *The Red and the Black,* the social self of the hero, Julien Sorel, is analyzed as emerging from a complex process of role-taking.

Shibutani, Tamotsu, *Society and Personality.* Englewood Cliffs, New Jersey: Prentice-Hall, Inc., 1961. The subtitle of this book is "An Interactionist Approach to Social Psychology." As such, it deals with the relationships between social interaction and personality, with particular emphasis upon the evolution of the social self.

Stoodley, Bartlett H. (ed.), *Society and Self: A Reader in Social Psychology.* Glencoe, Ill.: The Free Press, 1962. The editor of this reader has gathered a wide and eclectic collection of articles that "explore the significance of social structure for the individual enterprise." In these terms, the book offers perhaps the widest selection of empirical analyses of the social self available in a single volume.

Strauss, Anselm L., *Mirrors and Masks:* The Search for Identity. Glencoe, Ill.: The Free Press, 1959. This book offers a striking series of insights into the nature of the social self as it evolves in social interaction. The self is pictured as always changing in the course of the individual's appraisals and reappraisals of the judgments of others.

Sullivan, Harry Stack, *The Interpersonal Theory of Psychiatry.* New York: W. W. Norton & Company, Inc., 1953. The author drew on the work of Cooley, Dewey, and Mead in developing his interpersonal theory of psychiatry. He also added many insights from his own intensive clinical experience. Sullivan was best known as a psychiatrist, but his work also makes an important contribution to social psychology, especially to the theory of the social self.

9 *Personality and Social Structure*

The Structural Basis of Personality

The relationship between personality and social interaction is close and continuous. In the previous chapter, we considered the emergence of personality in terms of the social self, which is both the core of the personality and its most clearly interactional aspect. In the present chapter, we continue the analysis of personality as it arises in the social interaction. The emphasis here is upon the *structural* aspects of personality—that is, upon the patterns of organized social relationships that exist in the society for the purpose of performing certain basic social functions. The principal structural elements are *social roles* and the corresponding *social statuses*. These two elements are reciprocal in that they are, in a sense, different aspects of the same process. A *status* is the position(s) the individual occupies in a society, whereas a *role* is the *ordered* behavior expected by virtue of this position. In the evolution of the personality, the social self is closely related to the statuses of the individual and the roles he plays. The separation in this discussion is merely for the purposes of exposition. In practice, the personality is a functioning whole.[1]

The concept of social structure is therefore useful in understanding the nature of personality. Social structure may be defined as "the over-all pattern or network of social relationships that recur among a designated set of persons."[2] This definition contains several related elements: (*a*) a pattern, network, or configuration that assumes a more or less ordered form; (*b*) social relationships arising in interaction and channeling further interaction; (*c*) recurrence of these relationships, as behavior becomes ordered and predictable; and (*d*) a particular set of persons ranging in size from a small group to a national state. One may speak of the "structure" of a small group or that of a society of several hundred million persons. In the present context, we are using the concept of social structure in the latter sense, as referring to the behavior patterns of an entire society.

Every society has certain functions that must be performed if it is to survive. Among these functions are the procreation of new members, the socialization of these members, the provision of basic goods and services for physical survival, the maintenance of order among the members, and the relationships with other groups or societies. In the performance of these recurrent functions, persons play different parts (roles) and occupy different positions (statuses). Other elements also go to make up the social structure (e.g., norms, values, and other understandings), but roles and statuses are basic to social interaction. The entire pattern of these positions, functions, and understandings composes the *social structure*.[3]

In the course of his socialization, each person incorporates into his personality some (but by no means all) of the social structure. He learns what his position is, what is expected of him because of that position, and the principal norms and aspirations of the society as a whole. The latter elements are roughly equivalent to the "generalized other" of Mead, as discussed in the previous chapter. Social interaction is based upon a common acceptance of these understandings. As Shibutani puts it, "The reality to be observed in the study of social groups is the interaction among people, and the regularities discernible in these interchanges constitute social structure."[4] What each person has learned

---

[1] The interactional theory of personality owes its development to a number of works. Among them are: Pitirim A. Sorokin, *Society, Culture, and Personality* (New York: Harper & Row, 1947); Talcott Parsons, *The Social System* (Glencoe, Ill.: The Free Press, 1951); Harry Stack Sullivan, *The Interpersonal Theory of Psychiatry* (New York: W. W. Norton & Company, Inc., 1953). See also Neil J. Smelser and William T. Smelser (eds.), *Personality and Social Systems* (New York: John Wiley & Sons, 1963).

[2] James M. Beshers, *Urban Social Structure* (Glencoe, Ill.: The Free Press, 1962), p. 19.

[3] Tamotsu Shibutani, *Society and Personality* (Englewood Cliffs, New Jersey: Prentice-Hall, Inc., 1961), pp. 55-56.

[4] *Ibid.*, p. 167.

regarding these regularities makes him an acceptable and predictable member of his society. He conforms to group expectations in order to further his own acceptance. In so conforming, he strengthens the structure of the society. "Social structure," therefore, "consists of a continued flow of coordinated activity in which the participants provide one another with mutual support." [5]

The concept of social structure refers to positions and activities related to the basic problems of a society. The industrial organization produces and distributes goods and services. The family socializes (educates) the new members, a function that it shares with the school. The church provides a link between the group and the supernatural. In these and other ways, the social structure is composed of the generalized patterns of expected behavior. The social structure parallels the "personality structure," as one reinforces the other. Each individual carries within himself, as a basic part of his personality, certain elements common to the structure as a whole. In the following discussion of role and status, the relationships between personality and social structure will be examined in more detail.[6]

The Levels of Personality

A complete discussion of personality includes both the general and the individual elements in this complex biological and social product. In the scientific division of labor, the sociologist has been largely concerned with the general elements, whereas the biologist and the psychologist have studied the individual elements. Before we examine these general elements in more detail, we may indicate the various levels on which personality may be viewed. These levels or determinants constitute four major categories.[7]

1. *Universal determinants.* All human beings have certain common (universal) personality traits merely because they are human. These universals arise from the fact that man is: (*a*) an animal with a distinctive physical and mental equipment; (*b*) a social animal that lives in groups; (*c*) a cultural animal capable of symbolic communication; and (*d*) a biological animal living in a physical world to which he must adjust.[8]

2. *Communal determinants.* All the members of a society have certain traits in common with other members of the same society. Americans share more personality traits with other Americans than with Frenchmen. Membership in a society produces a degree of similarity of personality. The values of a society, the goals it holds out to its members, the roles it prescribes for them, and the common meanings that they share constitute some of the communal determinants of personality.[9]

---

[5] *Ibid.*

[6] Neil J. Smelser and William T. Smelser, *op. cit.*, p. 9.

[7] The following analysis is adapted from Clyde Kluckhohn and O. H. Mowrer, " 'Culture and Personality': A Conceptual Scheme," *American Anthropologist,* 46:1-29 (January-March, 1944), pp. 2-3.

[8] Cf. A. Irving Hallowell, "Personality Structure and the Evolution of Man," *American Anthropologist,* 52:159-173 (1950).

[9] Cf. A. Irving Hallowell, "Culture, Personality, and Society," in A. L. Kroeber (ed.), *Anthropology Today* (Chicago: University of Chicago Press, 1953).

3. *Role determinants.* In every society, certain positions are assigned to individuals on the basis of age, sex, marital status, family, and similar criteria. Each of these positions carries a pattern of common expectations, so that each man has certain personality traits in common with every other man in the society by virtue of their common male role. These patterns are culturally defined, and they constitute some of the most important determinants of personality in any society.[10]

4. *"Idiosyncratic" determinants.* Every individual (except an identical twin) has a unique genetic equipment and each (without exception) has a unique life experience. Hence the various determinants listed above influence each one in a different way. Brothers in the same family have a different order of birth and, therefore, do not have the same roles. The culture is interpreted to each person in a different fashion, the roles are played in a slightly different way, and the statuses are subject to individual variations.

We have briefly indicated the range of factors in personality: from those common to all men (universal), through those common to members of a particular society (communal), and those common to all members of a particular society who occupy certain statuses and play certain roles (role determinants), to those (idiosyncratic) that make each personality unique. These factors are social and cultural in character and do not take into consideration the biological elements in personality. We shall deal here primarily with the social determinants, with particular reference to those arising from the position that the individual occupies in society and the roles he plays as a result.

The Nature of Social Roles

Personality and social structure come together most intimately in the form of social roles. In a sociological sense, personality may be considered as the combination of roles that the individual plays in his structural relationships. A role is a pattern of expected behavior associated with a certain position in a society. The adult male in the contemporary United States, for example, has a pattern of culturally determined behavior ascribed to him merely because of his adultness and maleness. The role is defined by the society in general terms, and the individual ordinarily has little to say concerning the privileges or responsibilities of his role. From earliest infancy, he is offered a progressively changing set of roles appropriate to his age and sex, and he is expected to play them with reasonable persistence and accuracy.[11]

Society may be viewed as a complex and interrelated system of positions. The individual occupies several of these positions, each of which carries certain assumptions about the functions he is supposed to perform. The sociologist is primarily (although not exclusively) interested in the positions and their related

---

[10] Annabelle B. Motz, "The Role Conception Inventory: A Tool for Research in Social Psychology," *American Sociological Review*, 17:465-471 (August, 1952).

[11] Ralph Linton, *The Cultural Background of Personality* (New York: Appleton-Century-Crofts, Inc., 1945).

behavior, rather than in the individuals who happen to occupy them. These positions (statuses) become the role determinants to which we have just referred. As such, both status and role have a central importance to personality. Structure and personality meet at this point. The structure is the collective and objective aspect and the personality the individual and subjective aspect of status and role.[12]

Social roles carry patterns of expectations. The norms (folkways and mores) are also social expectations, but they are more general than roles. The latter, as noted, are attached to a particular position and are more or less independent of the person who happens to be occupying the position at the moment. The doctor has a certain role *as doctor* and not as John Smith.[13] Teachers have clusters of expectations attached to their position, and these expectations guide their behavior in the appropriate roles. Every society has scores of these generalized patterns, and some have many more. When each member of the society acts in accordance with his role(s), the society may be expected to function smoothly.

Roles also carry the idea of reciprocity. They not only comprise the expected behavior of one actor in a situation, but also the behavior of others toward him. The behavior of one person becomes the stimulus for the behavior of the other because each has learned to think and act in this way. The roles of officer and enlisted man offer a formalized example of this reciprocity. Each is expected to act in certain ways toward the other, and the salute symbolizes the nature of the relationship. The army is essentially an authoritarian institution, in the sense that clear lines of authority must be observed at all times. The expectations contained in the roles of officers and men help to make the organization run efficiently.

In his analysis of social structure, Shibutani makes an interesting distinction between what he calls "conventional roles" and "interpersonal roles." By the former, he refers to roles in the sense in which we have been using the term— that is, "representing a pattern of behavior expected of a person in a given situation by virtue of his position in the transaction. . . ."[14] Interpersonal roles, on the other hand, reflect the special expectations that arise from individual participation in "a network of interpersonal relations . . . bound by a set of special claims and obligations."[15] Conventional roles are those of merchant and customer, doctor and patient, lawyer and client, and parent and child. Interpersonal roles are less formalized and reflect the personality traits of the participants in a continued interpersonal relationship. Representative interpersonal roles are those of lover, partner, friend, companion, collaborator, shirker, com-

---

[12] Daniel J. Levinson, "Roles in Formal Organizations," *Journal of Abnormal and Social Psychology,* 58:170-180 (1959).

[13] Cf. Talcott Parsons, "Illness and the Role of the Physician," *American Journal of Orthopsychiatry,* 21:452-460 (1951).

[14] Shibutani, *op. cit.,* p. 46.

[15] *Ibid.,* p. 326.

plainer, and leader. This type of role is most clearly seen in studies of the small group carried on over a considerable period of time.[16]

Conventional roles are the basic structural elements of a society, whereas interpersonal roles arise in individual group situations and vary accordingly. Each society defines the conventional roles its members are expected to play. Interpersonal roles tend to reflect more intimate group situations than do conventional roles. The definition, in either case, is not a deliberate process, but arises in spontaneous interaction and is handed down in the same way. In his analysis of socialization, Parsons states that the acquisition of social (conventional) roles is the most important aspect of this over-all process. Socialization also involves other learning situations, in addition to those related to social roles. Nevertheless, training in conventional role behavior is clearly basic to the total task of making predictable and responsible members of society.[17]

The Dynamics of Social Roles

Roles are therefore dynamic motivating forces in behavior. They are not merely abstract categories but are also determinants of action and therefore of personality. The newly married man regards his wife in terms of the roles that he expects her to play toward him. He has learned these roles from his own family, from persons outside the family, from mass media, such as the movies, and from other sources. His activity in his newly acquired status as husband reflects such factors as: "... his own preformed role concepts, his own expectations regarding the reciprocal roles of his mate, his mate's expectations regarding him, and the degree of correspondence between the two sets of role concepts and expectations. ..." [18] In any case, he is motivated to act in one way or another by his role expectations.

Human life is more than an *individual* venture. It is also a *social* experience. Each person acts out a set of expected roles and looks at other persons in terms of them. In social interaction, each takes the other into account through the roles each is playing at the time. The criminal knows what to expect from the policeman, the patient has learned what to look for in the doctor, and the husband has strong preconceptions concerning the role of his wife. In these different roles, the behavior of each individual is, of course, subject to differences of interpretation. But in many respects each person still knows what to expect. If he did not, if each individual acted entirely without prior socialization (that is, "individually"), organized group life would be impossible.

Social roles are not always consistent. Some are clearly contradictory, and the person is expected to perform contradictory acts by following the expectations of different roles. Some of these difficulties may be personal. A man who has

---

[16] Cf. Clarence F. Sherwood and William S. Walker, "Role Differentiation in Real Groups," *Sociology and Social Research*, 45:14-17 (October, 1960).

[17] Parsons, *The Social System, op. cit.,* p. 205.

[18] Leland H. Stott, "The Problem of Evaluating Family Success," *Marriage and Family Living*, 13:149-153 (Fall, 1951), p. 151.

been devoted to his mother may find it hard to transfer his affection to his wife. Here the roles of son and husband become confused, and the individual may be unable to play either one adequately.[19] In other cases, the contradictions are implicit in the culture. The economic role demands aggressive behavior toward other persons in the competitive world. The expectations of the Christian role, on the other hand, are for humility and gentleness toward others. The majority of persons escape any fundamental difficulty in this respect by playing the economic role to the virtual exclusion of the religious role. The implicit conflict is, nevertheless, there.[20]

Social roles involve varying degrees of compulsion. Some behavior is *required* of the person filling a role, whereas other behavior is expressly *forbidden*. Within these limits, a considerable range of behavior is *permitted*, but not *demanded*, of the individual in his role capacity. The doctor is required to cure the sick to the best of his ability. He is forbidden to put an end to life, even though the patient may be dying in terrible pain of an incurable and inoperable disease. Within these limits, however, considerable discretion is granted as to how he shall play his role as doctor. He may exact high prices for his services or he may treat many people free of charge; he may be a family doctor or a specialist; and he may develop a congenial bedside manner or a brusque aloofness. The basic expectations of the role, however, are produced by the society, or by a group within it, and the individual has little or nothing to say in this definition.[21]

The obligations placed upon the individual by the variety of roles are sometimes conflicting and often difficult. Each person is drawn in a number of directions by the demands of his various roles. As husband, father, breadwinner, churchgoer, and citizen, he has obligations that are mutually incompatible and that force him to pick and choose as to which roles he will follow and which he will ignore. Fortunately for the stability of society, most people most of the time *want* to do what they are *supposed* to do. They wish, in other words, to fulfill their role obligations, either because (*a*) they feel better when they are doing so, or (*b*) they are forced to do so by the expectations of others.[22]

Even under the best of circumstances, however, the person's role obligations are often "over-demanding"—that is, they demand too many different things. One must make some adjustment to these demands if he is to retain his peace of mind. He may act *inconsistently*, in the sense of following the claims of a role under certain circumstances and ignoring them under others. The professed Christian may be gentle and humble in church and grasping and arrogant in his office. The person may *eliminate* some of his role obligations by ceasing to have anything to do with others who demand too much of him. He may

---

[19] Cf. Gerald S. Blum, *Psychoanalytic Theories of Personality* (New York: McGraw-Hill Book Company, Inc., 1953).

[20] Karen Horney, *The Neurotic Personality of Our Time* (New York: W. W. Norton & Company, Inc., 1937), pp. 284ff.

[21] Theodore M. Newcomb, *Social Psychology* (New York: The Dryden Press, 1950), pp. 280-283.

[22] William J. Goode, "A Theory of Role Strain," *American Sociological Review*, 25:483-496 (August, 1960).

erect barriers against intrusions upon his time, as the business executive has several secretaries to keep people from "bothering" him. He may, finally, *select* some roles he enjoys and *reject* others he dislikes, as the husband lets his wife balance the checkbook. In these and other ways, the individual consciously or unconsciously tries to reduce the role strain in his life.[23]

Much of human behavior is organized about social roles. The way we play these roles is an important factor in our personalities. The "internalized role expectations" constitute perhaps the most important single element in the social self.[24] In our self-judgments, as noted, we look to the judgments of others or (more strictly) to our inferences about these judgments.[25] These judgments are based in large measure upon the way we play our principal roles—as husbands, wives, parents, children, friends, colleagues, and business associates. We view ourselves as objects through the eyes of others and in so doing judge ourselves in terms of our performance in these major roles.

We may summarize the basic elements of the social role as applied to the formation of personality. The social role is learned in the course of socialization. The individual "internalizes" (absorbs) the basic values that go with the role and give it meaning. The role involves: (*a*) the identification of the personality and the social self with the role, so that the latter becomes an emotional personal experience; (*b*) the definition by the society of the patterned behavior appropriate to situations occurring regularly; (*c*) the reciprocity of these patterns, whereby each role is related to other roles, as the role of husband is related to the role of wife; and (*d*) the self-evaluation by the individual of his comparative success or failure in his role. In this sense, the reaction of the person arises from the "reflected appraisals" of the "looking-glass self." [26]

The Social Setting of the Role

Roles differ between societies and subcultures. Age and sex roles in our society differ from those in primitive societies. Boys of fourteen are considered hardly more than children in our society, whereas in other societies they are ready for the adult role. Girls of twelve in American society are not ordinarily considered of marriageable age, whereas their readiness to assume this role is taken for granted in many other societies. Adolescent and adult roles are not so much matters of age as of social definition, and adulthood is reached much earlier in primitive societies. The role of son or daughter in our society implies a long period of adolescence, during which the adolescent is free to amuse himself without many social responsibilities.[27]

In many primitive societies, childhood and adolescence have different roles

---

[23] *Ibid.*

[24] A. R. Mangus, "Role Theory and Marriage Counseling," *Social Forces*, 35:200-209 (March, 1957), p. 203.

[25] Carl J. Couch, "Self-Attitudes and Degree of Agreement with Immediate Others," *American Journal of Sociology*, 63:491-496 (March, 1958).

[26] Alfred R. Lindesmith and Anselm L. Strauss, *Social Psychology* (rev. ed.) (New York: The Dryden Press, 1956), Chapter 13.

[27] Margaret Mead, *Coming of Age in Samoa* (New York: William Morrow & Company, 1928).

and involve greater responsibilities.[28] The child is often expected to carry water, gather wood, repair nets, cultivate rice, clean fish, grind grain, take care of younger children, and otherwise participate in the serious activities of the society. Under such conditions, the transition from childhood to adulthood is gradual, and the adolescent slowly assumes additional responsibilities until he or she is ready to take the full adult role. In our society, boys and girls are sometimes obliged to assume adult roles before they are emotionally prepared for them. An early marriage often brings a sudden transition from the carefree years of adolescence to the cares of adulthood. The high divorce rate among couples married under twenty years of age suggests that the boy or girl of this age is often unprepared for an adult role.

Social roles bring out or limit behavior, depending upon the different social settings. In our society, adolescents are ordinarily not expected to play significant roles outside of their narrowly prescribed orbit of education and amusement. In an earlier day, youths of eighteen were painting great pictures, writing

---

[28] Margaret Mead and Martha Wolfenstein (eds.), *Childhood in Contemporary Cultures* (Chicago: University of Chicago Press, 1955).

Social roles differ between societies. In this social gathering in Sumatra, the men drink a ceremonial toast and the women and children stand respectfully in the background.

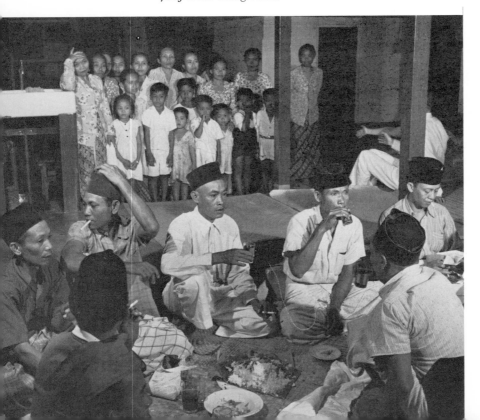

epic poems, serving in royal cabinets, and commanding armies. In contemporary American society, boys of this age are not expected to be concerned with anything more serious than adjusting to their peer group, finding an appropriate date for the Junior Prom, and graduating with reasonable grades from high school. In this case, the society *limits* the potential abilities of the adolescent by not expecting much of him.

The entire repertoire of family roles differs between societies. In many peasant societies, patriarchal roles remain virtually intact from an earlier day. The role of the father still involves dominance in many family relationships, whereas that of the wife entails submission on many matters that would be subject to joint discussion in the United States. When the son and daughter in the peasant society wish to marry, they must gain the assent of the patriarchal father. The mere statement of these roles indicates their disparity with the corresponding roles in our society. The patriarchal family is hardly recognizable in the American scene.

Family roles constitute perhaps the most tightly knit pattern in any society. The child is exposed to these roles from birth, and he learns that his position carries responsibilities and obligations as well as rights and privileges. As a child, the role of son or daughter emphasizes the care lavished by the parent. In later years, these roles carry reciprocal obligations—affectional or economic— toward the parents who nurtured the child in his early years. Roles are *social* phenomena in the most literal sense, for their meaning exists only in relation to other people.

The rapid transition from a rural, agricultural society to an urban, industrial society has brought many role changes in the family. Children can now become economically independent and must no longer look to an inheritance from the father. With approximately one out of every three married women now gainfully employed, the roles of husband and wife have also undergone dramatic changes. The wife who is actively contributing to the support of the family has acquired an equality that was never dreamed of a century ago. The husband can no longer be the arbiter of the destiny of his wife.

The system of family roles inherited from an earlier day is thus in the process of rapid disorganization. Men and women are not performing their roles in accordance with traditional definitions. This inability does not arise from any personal failure, but instead reflects basic changes in society. Wives cannot continue to act solely as homemakers and mothers when society demands millions of women workers. Husbands cannot continue to be dominant when the wife is adding substantially to the family income. Men and women are confronted with situations not of their own making, in which traditional roles no longer apply. They are forced to improvise their behavior instead of following accepted roles. Such improvisation is difficult. Disappointment and frustration are the price of failure.[29]

---

[29] Francis E. Merrill, *Courtship and Marriage* (rev. ed.) (New York: Holt, Rinehart and Winston, 1959), Chapter 20, "Frustrated Roles."

The Nature of Social Status

Status is the position a person occupies in society by virtue of his age, sex, birth, marriage, occupation, or achievement. Role is the part he is expected to play in each of a series of statuses. Status and role are reciprocal elements in personality and relate to different components of the functioning whole. Both are social products, for one could not exist without the other. A person can have status only in relation to others; it is not something he can create by himself. As we study the structural aspects of personality, emphasis shifts from role to status and back again. Social interaction determines both the statuses the individual occupies and the corresponding roles he plays.

Linton defines status as "the place in a particular system which a certain individual occupies at a particular time," whereas role refers to "the sum total of the culture patterns associated with a particular status." [30] In his analysis of personality structure, Shibutani speaks of status as "a person's standing in a community," and role as "a participant's contribution to an organized enterprise." [31] With certain exceptions which we shall consider later, a person's general status is relatively constant and is ordinarily raised or lowered only gradually. A person plays a number of roles in a single day, however, some of which carry high prestige and others less. In the course of a few hours, a doctor plays his professional role (high prestige), his role as citizen (moderate prestige), and his role as parent disciplining his child (mixed prestige).[32]

Status is, as we shall see, originally *ascribed* on the basis of sex, birth, and age. Status may also be *achieved* on the basis of socially valued behavior in such fields as war, art, science, or commerce. Roles are reflections of status and represent their dynamic aspects. Status is an important element in personality, both objectively and subjectively. The *objective* (actual) status of the individual may not be as important as the *subjective* (imagined) definitions by others and himself. Self-attitudes are based upon status, and the image a person has of himself reflects his perception of the judgments of others.[33]

Status refers to positions in *all* the systems of society, not just to the *prestige systems*. Both the president of the bank and the office boy have certain positions in the occupational system and possess appropriate statuses. The rights, duties, and prerogatives of the president are more complex than those of the office boy. But each pattern is a product of social interaction and invokes certain recognizable expectations in the participants. The self-judgments related to each status are, as noted, significant elements in the personality. But the concept of status, *as such*, carries no necessary value judgments.[34]

The value judgments rest in the valuation that society places upon certain

[30] Linton, *The Cultural Background of Personality, op. cit.*, pp. 76-77.
[31] Shibutani, *op. cit.*, p. 219.
[32] *Ibid.*
[33] Manford H. Kuhn and Thomas McPartland, "An Empirical Investigation of Self-Attitudes," *American Sociological Review*, 19:68-76 (February, 1954).
[34] Ralph Linton, *The Study of Man* (New York: Appleton-Century-Crofts, Inc., 1936), p. 114.

statuses and roles. Some roles are obviously more highly valued than others, and receive a proportionately greater share of money, prestige, special favors, and other scarce goods and services. Every society has certain functions it considers important, and it rewards the persons who perform these functions. Our own society values the roles of business executive, industrialist, salesman, and entertainer. These roles are rewarded accordingly. Our society does not place a high valuation upon the roles of minister, teacher, scholar, artist, and (ordinarily) soldier.[35] In other societies, these roles are highly valued and remunerated accordingly. Many ambitious young men aspire to roles with high valuation, and comparatively few seek those where the valuation is more modest. In this way, the society brings out certain qualities in its members and restricts others.[36]

The person has status in several different groups. The high school boy has one status on the football field, another in the classroom, and a third at home. The adult male has one status as a worker, another as a father, another as a club member, and still another as a church-goer. He plays successively the role of businessman, parent, colleague, and deacon. Each position involves a different status, which in turn evokes an appropriate role. In our society, economic status dominates the others. The respect connected with high economic standing often sets the tone for the personality. A man may be a poor father, an unfaithful husband, and a disloyal friend. But if he is successful in making money, his failure in his other roles may be forgotten.

In recent decades, Americans have become increasingly self-conscious about the symbolic manifestations of status. In highly stratified and traditional societies, the status of a given individual is known to his fellows, either directly or through his dress, speech, or other outward and visible signs. In the dynamic society of contemporary America, however, many of these traditional indices of status no longer apply. We shall consider this problem in more detail in Chapter 14, where we deal with social class differentials and the related symbols. Suffice it to indicate here that Americans are always on the lookout for some tangible evidence to demonstrate their high social status. These status symbols include clothing, houses, automobiles, cabin cruisers, and private swimming pools. Their purpose, in part at least, is to impress one's friends, neighbors, and acquaintances with one's exalted social position.[37]

The Forms of Social Status

There are two principal forms of status, *ascribed* and *achieved*. Linton refers to them as follows: "*Ascribed* statuses are those which are assigned to individuals without reference to their innate differences or abilities. They can be predicted and trained for from the moment of birth. The *achieved* statuses . . . are those

---

[35] Bernard Barber, *Social Stratification* (New York: Harcourt, Brace and World, 1957), p. 7.

[36] Erich Fromm, *The Sane Society* (New York: Holt, Rinehart & Winston, Inc., 1955), pp. 78-79.

[37] William H. Form and Gregory P. Stone, "Urbanism,, Anonymity, and Status Symbolism," *American Journal of Sociology*, 62:504-514 (March, 1957).

requiring special qualities, although they are not necessarily limited to these. They are not assigned to individuals from birth but are left open to be filled through competition and individual effort." [38] The over-all patterns of status and role are thus partially established at birth and partially achieved later.

Societies differ as to the number and importance of the statuses that are ascribed and those that may be achieved. In primitive or feudal societies, most of the statuses are ascribed, and the place of the individual is ordinarily fixed by the accident of birth. In democratic and industrialized societies, greater importance is attached to achieved status. Substantial rewards are held out to those who are successful in the competition for achieved status. The United States has always been proud of the predominance of achieved over ascribed status.

Society places various limits upon the achievement of status. Even in our own society, status achievement is not as free as many would like to think. Race and ethnic background are important limitations, with the most spectacular such restriction applied to the Negro. Until recently, he has been largely limited to menial jobs. A study of achievement motivation among various racial and ethnic groups disclosed that widespread differences existed between Jews and white Protestants on the one hand and Italians and Negroes on the other. The first group tended to have higher motivation to gain status than the second. Social class is also important in this difference of motivation, with Jews and white Protestants tending, on balance, to have a somewhat higher class status than Italians and Negroes. Those with low ethnic and class status have a lower motivation to rise in the social scale than those with high status in these respects.[39]

At different stages in his life, the individual occupies different ascribed statuses. His status as a child differs from his status as an adolescent. After he has reached maturity and presumably "put away childish things," he acquires other statuses. The seven ages of man, as depicted by Shakespeare, illustrate the typical progression, from the infant mewling in the nurse's arms, through the schoolboy creeping unwillingly to school, to the old man "sans everything." All societies have some division of status on the basis of age; as the individual inexorably passes through life, he finds that each period has its ascribed privileges and responsibilities. Age provides a fundamental basis on which society ascribes different statuses to its members, largely without regard for their individual abilities.

Each status has its role. Society expects different behavior from persons holding different statuses. Girls are expected to play with dolls and display an early interest in the home and the family; boys are expected to scorn such feminine activities and concentrate on manly sports and games. The responses that are expected of boys and girls are inculcated at an early age. Recent studies indicate that preschool boys are taught to be less dependent and more aggressive than

---

[38] Linton, *The Study of Man, op. cit.,* p. 115.
[39] Bernard C. Rosen, "Race, Ethnicity, and the Achievement Syndrome," *American Sociological Review,* 24:47-60 (February, 1959).

girls. The latter tend to identify themselves more strongly with their mothers than is the case with boys. These early differences in masculine and feminine roles are not always taught deliberately, but they are consistently present in the culture patterns.[40]

The United States represents the triumph of achieved over ascribed status. The social structure in this country did not have the dead weight of ascribed status to overcome as was the case in western Europe. Furthermore, a new continent awaited the exploitation of its resources, with few hereditary factors to interfere. Men of humble birth became millionaires; the log cabin was the birthplace of presidents; and farm boys became captains of industry. This ability to rise in the social scale and reach the heights of achieved status is known as the American Dream.

The present status of the American Dream is open to considerable question. Some persons maintain that it is virtually impossible to overcome the handicaps of lower-class background and rise to a position of high status in the business world. Others are equally vehement in insisting that the way to the top is still open to men of ability and initiative. We shall not attempt to explore this problem at any length here, but shall consider the trends in social mobility in Chapter 15. Briefly, the situation appears to be that the majority of men who occupy positions of authority come from the upper levels of society. The backgrounds of business leaders were recently investigated in an extensive study. Two-thirds of them came from families whose status was well above the average for the country as a whole. More than half of these leaders were sons of owners or executives and another 14 per cent were sons of professional men.[41]

High family status is thus an important (perhaps *the* most important) factor in business success today. Boys whose fathers are leaders of business and industry have a considerable initial advantage over those whose fathers are white-collar workers, farmers, or laborers. At the same time, the fact that a third of the business elite *did* come from lower-status backgrounds indicates that the American Dream *in individual cases* is still far from dead. Sons of laborers, farmers, and white-collar workers can still make their way to the top in American business, *provided* they can get a higher education. This latter factor is becoming increasingly indispensable to the achievement of status, especially for those who must make their own way without benefit of family help.[42]

On a broader scale, other changes are apparent in status in this country. In the first fifty years of the present century, the proportion of unskilled workers declined from 15 to less than 10 per cent of the population. At the same time, semi-skilled workers increased from 15 to 20 per cent of the population. This change reflects the mechanization of industry and the consequent increase in the number of persons tending machines, rather than working with pick and

---

[40] R. R. Sears, *et al.*, "Some Child-Rearing Antecedents of Aggression and Dependency in Young Children," *Genetic Psychology Monographs*, 47:135-234 (May, 1953).

[41] W. Lloyd Warner and James C. Abegglen, *Big Business Leaders in America* (New York: Harper & Row, 1955), p. 14.

[42] *Ibid.*, Chapter 3, "The Royal Road: Higher Education."

shovel. In this shift from unskilled to semi-skilled labor there is an upgrading in occupation (and indirectly in status) of a considerable segment of the population.[43]

The Adjustment to Social Status

The normal functioning of a society depends upon the widespread acceptance of status and role. Persons who depart consistently from the roles considered appropriate to their status are viewed with suspicion, for they present grave difficulties to social stability. People must act substantially as they are expected to act or social interaction becomes chaotic. Girls who consistently dress in boys' clothes and play boys' games are frowned upon by their elders. Boys who play the role of girls are regarded even more dubiously. Adults who consistently act as children are usually placed in mental institutions. Each society has roles considered appropriate to the various statuses.

Departure from these roles is viewed as social deviation. Whether deliberately or not, the deviant is unwilling or unable to play the roles and occupy the statuses to which society has assigned him. He may be a criminal, prostitute, embezzler, drug addict, alcoholic, homeless man, or chronically unemployed, but in each case his behavior represents a consistent departure from one or more of his expected roles. In this way, he rejects the norms related to his particular status. This rejection is usually confined to one set of norms; the embezzler usually obeys the traffic laws and the homeless man ordinarily believes in the capitalistic system.[44] A study of the worker who loses status, indeed, indicated that he is *more* conservative in many respects than the one who keeps his status. The worker who goes down in the socio-economic scale maintains a strong belief in the economic order and the class structure that has arisen about it.[45]

Even those who rise in the social scale cannot always adjust to their new status. Wives of successful businessmen are often unable to play the roles demanded by the hard-won success of their husbands. Women from lower social levels whose husbands have become business leaders often have difficulty in growing along with them. This situation may cause frustration and resentment in the wives, the husbands, or both. In some instances, the husband "solves" the problem by keeping his wife in the background, never entertaining at home, and generally separating his business life as completely as possible from his family life. Some wives are content to play this secondary role, others are not. Role changes from one social class to another are often difficult to make.[46]

---

[43] Ely Chinoy, "Social Mobility Trends in the United States," *American Sociological Review,* 20:180-186 (April, 1955), p. 183.

[44] Robert Dubin, "Deviant Behavior and Social Structure: Continuities in Social Theory," *American Sociological Review,* 24:147-164 (April, 1959).

[45] Harold L. Wilensky and Hugh Edwards, "The Skidder: Ideological Adjustments of Downward Mobile Workers," *American Sociological Review,* 24:215-231 (April, 1959).

[46] Warner and Abegglen, *op. cit.,* Chapter 6.

Maladjustment to ascribed status is apparent in other situations, because some women are unable to act in the manner expected of them. Some women are temperamentally unsuited to the traditional role of wife and mother. They may seek a career in business or the professions, to which they consider their education, talent, or both eminently entitle them. Educated women are often inadequately prepared for the roles of mothers and housekeepers, which will be their lot and which (parenthetically) most of them unconsciously desire.[47] In a society as complex as our own, statuses are often incompatible and conflicting. Women are told that they are the intellectual equals of men and are educated accordingly, only to learn that their major adult status will be that of wife and housekeeper.[48]

Other women may actively seek a career because they are unwilling to devote themselves exclusively to the roles of wife and mother. If they do not marry, they may pay for their success in a professional role by psychological frustrations. In one study, unmarried career women who had moved upward in the status scale had a disproportionate number of psychosomatic and nervous illnesses, as compared with a control group of career women who were not upwardly mobile. The mobile women were motivated by strong drives to leave their previous position and occupy a higher status. Such women had an early history of rejection by parents and other primary groups. The sample in this study is too small to be conclusive, but it does suggest that the adjustment to one's adult status is related to one's early interaction in primary groups.[49]

In more general terms, the relationship between self-feeling and adjustment to status-expectations is very close. When a person is unable to live up to these expectations, he may develop feelings of anxiety. As we have noted, role-expectations constitute an important part of the social self. Failure to adjust to these expectations weakens the fabric of the self.[50] The man who is unable to earn a decent living, the wife who is unable to bear children, and the child who cannot do his school work all fail in a basic role. When this failure becomes pronounced and prolonged, the person may become mentally ill.[51]

The Sexual Basis of Status

The influence of ascribed status upon personality may be illustrated by the most spectacular example of this process—namely, the ascription of personality characteristics on the basis of sex. Other examples involve such factors as occupa-

---

[47] Arnold M. Rose, "The Adequacy of Women's Expectations for Adult Roles," *Social Forces*, 30:69-77 (October, 1951).

[48] Mirra Komarovsky, *Women in the Modern World* (Boston: Little, Brown and Company, 1953), Chapter 4, "The Homemaker and Her Problems."

[49] Evelyn Ellis, "Social Psychological Correlates of Upward Social Mobility Among Unmarried Career Women," *American Sociological Review*, 17:558-563 (October, 1952).

[50] Simon Dinitz, A. R. Mangus, and Benjamin Pasamanick, "Integration and Conflict in Self-Other Conceptions as Factors in Mental Illness," *Sociometry*, 22:44-55 (March, 1959).

[51] A. B. Hollingshead, *et al.*, "Social Mobility and Mental Illness," *American Sociological Review*, 19:577-584 (October, 1954).

The traditional ascription of status and role is changing, as women work side by side with men in office, factory, and store; here a group of business men and women await elevator in the lobby of an office building.

tion[52] and social class,[53] but the sexual ascription is the most important. In every society, certain personality traits are selected and then ascribed largely or exclusively to males or females, *merely because of their maleness or femaleness.* This selection is not deliberate or planned, but arises in the slow and spontaneous manner of the folkways and mores. Each individual at birth has certain traits that may be defined as either masculine or feminine by his society. Many of the traits that have "always" been considered as sex-linked are now realized to be, at least in part, the product of assigned status and role.[54]

Society thus "elaborates" the biological differences between the sexes. This means that the obvious differences between men and women are taken as the basis for ascribing a variety of other differences, some of them cultural in origin. The fact that men procreate and women bear children is an inescapable biological condition. The assumption that men are "naturally" more capable of understanding politics, painting pictures, or practicing a profession, however, is an unwarranted addition to this biological fact. The traditional beliefs concerning the differences between the sexes are based upon many such gratuitous elaborations on the central fact of sexual differentiation. Many aspects of these beliefs go back to Biblical times, when the patriarchal family was the principal institution defining status and role.

The patriarchal definitions assumed that men were "naturally" imperious, dominant, aggressive, and generally fitted to wrestle with the complex affairs of a masculine world. Women were assumed to be constitutionally timid, submissive, and generally unfitted to cope with life outside the home. These assumptions have had the support of organized religion and unassailable public

---

[52] Everett C. Hughes, "Personality Types and the Division of Labor," in Ernest W. Burgess (ed.), *Personality and the Social Group* (Chicago: University of Chicago Press, 1929).

[53] Robert J. Havighurst, "Social Class and Personality Structure," *Sociology and Social Research,* 36:355-363 (July-August, 1952).

[54] Margaret Mead, *Male and Female* (New York: William Morrow & Company, 1949).

opinion. "Masculine" traits have accordingly been cultivated for thousands of years in boys and "feminine" traits in girls. The biological basis of these statuses and roles has seemed as natural as the stars. The close correlation between sexual status and personality traits was considered axiomatic, one of the few things that remained fixed in a changing world.

These ascribed statuses have undergone drastic changes in recent decades. Statistics on the gainful employment of women offer the most irrefutable evidence that the traditional personality traits ascribed to the female sex were not based upon unalterable genetic factors. The biological characteristics of women have not changed since the Victorian Age, but the society in which women live *has* changed radically during the same period. The role of women has been revised since the days when they were considered capable only of bearing children, caring for the home, and attending divine services. Many secondary personality differences between the sexes are disappearing as men and women sit side by side in the classroom, office, or factory.[55]

The influence of society in ascribing personality traits to each sex is strikingly illustrated in studies of primitive societies. The most conclusive of these studies was made of three small tribes on the island of New Guinea in the South Pacific. In one of these societies, the prevailing personality for both men and women is cooperative, gentle, and "maternal." Male and female both have the personality attributed in our society to the female. In a second tribal society, both sexes are aggressive, driving, and domineering. They display the personality traits that our society attributes to the more "masculine" among the males. In the third society, the roles of the sexes are almost completely turned around. The women are dominant and aggressive and the men are submissive and gentle. The "normal" roles of the sexes are thus reversed. In terms of the status-ascription of our society, the women are "men" and the men are "women."[56]

Many differences between the sexes are thus the products of social conditioning, especially during the plastic years of childhood.[57] In this connection, Margaret Mead states that "Standard personality differences between the sexes are ... cultural creations to which each generation, male or female, is trained to conform."[58] Woman and human female are far from synonymous. "Human female" is a biological phenomenon, whereas "woman" is a social product.[59]

Inconsistencies in Social Status

"Much of the behavior of man," says Shibutani, "consists of acting in a manner designed to preserve or enhance his social status."[60] Each man is concerned

---

[55] Talcott Parsons, "Age and Sex in the Social Structure of the United States," *American Sociological Review*, 7:604-616 (October, 1942).

[56] Margaret Mead, *Sex and Temperament in Three Primitive Societies* (New York: William Morrow & Company, 1935).

[57] Cf. Meyer Rabban, "Sex-Role Identification in Young Children in Two Diverse Social Groups," *Genetic Psychology Monographs*, 42: 81-158 (August, 1950).

[58] Margaret Mead, *Sex and Temperament in Three Primitive Societies, op. cit.*, pp. 280-281.

[59] Simone de Beauvoir, *The Second Sex* (New York: Alfred A. Knopf, Inc., 1953).

[60] Shibutani, *op. cit.*, p. 270.

with his self-image, which reflects the status to which he is assigned by friends, peers, and society as a whole. This relationship between status and personality has its roots in the structure of the social self, as we saw in the previous chapter. This viewpoint also looks ahead to the later discussion of social stratification—that is, problems of caste and class. As Goffman has so delightfully described, much of our everyday behavior is dedicated to the crucial task of maintaining our status and thereby our sense of personal worth. In this dramatic performance, each person consciously and unconsciously tries to put himself in situations where he will be viewed in a favorable light and to avoid those in which the contrary is true. The individual who can convince his audience that he should be taken at his own evaluation is, in these terms, a happy and contented man. Consistent inability to produce a believable performance often means anxiety, frustration, and unhappiness.[61]

The relationship of status and personality has been examined on several levels. In one study, a number of persons were examined in terms of their "status crystallization"—i.e., the consistency among different status criteria. Status was defined in terms of income level, occupation, education, and ethnic background. Persons who measured low in status crystallization and thus high in status inconsistency were lower in one or more of the above classifications. This latter category included college professors (low in income level), Hollywood actors (low in formal education), Jewish businessmen (low in ethnic status), and Protestant clergymen (also low in income level). The personalities of these men of such diverse backgrounds were found to have certain common qualities because of their status inconsistency. This similarity was especially marked in political attitudes, with all four groups tending to have "liberal" attitudes and voting records.[62]

On such questions as government health insurance, price controls, and extension of governmental powers, the four groups showed a surprising consistency in espousing the liberal (*not* radical) position. The explanation offered by Lenski for these similarities is that each group was not completely secure in *all* aspects of its status. In purely economic terms, their statuses differed as between college professors and Protestant clergymen on the one hand and Hollywood actors and wealthy Jewish businessmen on the other. A certain amount of frustration is apparent among all of these groups because of the inconsistency between one or more of their various statuses. These men presumably wished to be treated on the basis of their highest status, but were instead widely treated on the basis of their *lowest*. Hence they suffered frustration and wished to reform certain aspects of the status quo. College professors wished to be treated as highly educated persons, not as comparatively underpaid white-collar workers. Hollywood actors wished to be treated as rich and influential

---

[61] Erving Goffman, *The Presentation of Self in Everyday Life* (New York: Doubleday Anchor Books, 1959), Chapter 1.

[62] Gerhard E. Lenski, "Status Crystallization: A Non-Vertical Dimension of Social Status," *American Sociological Review,* 19:405-413 (August, 1954).

citizens, not as men who had never finished high school. And so on down the list of inconsistent statuses.[63]

Further studies have explored the complex relationships between status and personality. Jackson has examined the "stressful impact of status inconsistency upon the individual," using occupation, education, and racial-ethnic background as different dimensions (aspects) of status. His purpose was to discover the effects upon men and women of discrepancies between these three dimensions of status. He found that persons whose racial-ethnic status was higher than their occupational or educational status seemed most prone to symptoms of psychological stress. Persons of old English or old American stock, for example, often showed marked symptoms of stress if they worked at low-status occupations or lacked a college education. One possible explanation for these stress symptoms, Jackson suggested, is that "A person whose achievement ranks are inferior to his ascribed rank is likely to view his situation as one of personal failure." [64] Other relationships appeared between status inconsistency and stress symptoms, and marked differences were also found between men and women in this respect. The basic conclusion of the study was that social status has several dimensions and these dimensions affect the personality if they are inconsistent. "The fact that is disturbing," Jackson concludes, "implies that occupation, education, and racial-ethnic origin are experienced as separate and distinct status dimensions in America today." [65]

In a long and thoughtful review of the relevant material, Kleiner and Parker further explored the thorny problem of status and personality. They were especially interested in the relationships between status position, social mobility, and aspiration on the one hand and mental illness on the other. They reviewed a number of relevant studies and found that many of the data were conflicting. Their findings point to the importance of what they call "mobility orientation" or the "discrepancy between achievement and aspiration." Persons with high aspirations and low achievement, they suggested, may be more prone to mental disorders than those whose aspirations are not so high or whose achievements so low. Low achievement is, by definition, characteristic of persons with low status, which may account for the high prevalence of mental illness among lower socioeconomic groups. In a society such as our own, where everyone is (theoretically) expected to achieve high status, a marked discrepancy between aspiration and achievement may become highly stressful. Anxiety, frustration, and unconscious retreat from the world may follow such a discrepancy between what people actually are (status) and what they would like to be.[66]

Another study in this complex area dealt with the relationships between so-

[63] Gerhard E. Lenski, "Social Participation and Status Crystallization," *American Sociological Review*, 21:458-464 (August, 1956).

[64] Elton F. Jackson, "Status Consistency and Symptoms of Stress," *American Sociological Review*, 27:469-480 (August, 1962), p. 477.

[65] *Ibid.*, p. 480.

[66] Robert J. Kleiner and Seymour Parker, "Goal-Striving, Social Status, and Mental Disorder: A Research Review," *American Sociological Review*, 28:189-203 (April, 1963).

cial status and "anomia." [67] The latter concept, derived from the French word *"anomie,"* means a state of normlessness, hopelessness, discouragement, and disorganization which is often characteristic of persons who have, for one reason or other, failed to achieve their goals in life.[68] Many, although by no means all, of these goals are related to status. In their study, Simpson and Miller examined the "status-inconsistency" hypothesis and the "social failure" hypothesis and concluded that these did not give complete explanations of personality maladjustment. This incompleteness of explanation, they say, is especially evident in the case of persons occupying the same status, some of whom succumb to mental illness and others of whom do not. Simpson and Miller suggested what they call an "attitude exposure" hypothesis to explain the differences in the occurrence of mental illness between persons in the same status. Anomia, they postulated, is more prevalent among persons who have in the past been exposed to the "anomic" attitudes of lower-status groups. Such persons learn self-attitudes from members of lower-status groups, where hopelessness and frustration are more prevalent. In short, "Since low status and anomia go together . . . this means that each low-status attribute increases the probability that one's associates are anomic. Therefore," conclude Simpson and Miller, "the social environment of a low-status person exposes him to an anomic climate of opinion." [69]

In this chapter, we have explored some of the structural aspects of personality, with particular emphasis upon status and role. The hierarchy of statuses and roles is extremely complex in American society, whereas that of many primitive societies is comparatively simple. In our society, furthermore, the traditional expectations associated with the various statuses are in many cases no longer consistent with the way of life. The individual may be obliged to adjust an old role to fit a new situation, as the working wife must adapt her traditional role of wife and mother to the exigencies of office, shop, or factory. The emphasis upon achieved over ascribed status is another factor in the determination of personality. The number and variety of possible statuses open to the individual are very large. The role determinants of personality tend to vary accordingly. Under these conditions, many inconsistencies in status appear in the same person. For reasons beyond his control, he may occupy a high status in certain respects and a low one in others. The effects of this situation upon his self-image, and hence upon his personality structure, are often unfortunate.

---

[67] Richard L. Simpson and H. Max Miller, "Social Status and Anomia," *Social Problems*, 10:256-264 (Winter, 1963).

[68] Dorothy L. Meier and Wendell Bell, *"Anomie* and Differential Access to the Achievement of Life Goals," *American Sociological Review*, 24:189-202 (April, 1959).

[69] Simpson and Miller, *op. cit.,* p. 264.

SELECTED BIBLIOGRAPHY

Friedan, Betty, *The Feminine Mystique.* New York: W. W. Norton & Company, Inc., 1963. This book examines a considerable portion of the vast literature on the status and role of women in modern society, with particular reference to the forces that make for the acceptance by women of the traditional "feminine" role, instead of considering themselves as individuals.

Henry, Andrew F., "Family Role Structure and Self-Blame," *Social Forces,* 35:34-38 (October, 1956). The relationships between the individual and his parents are examined in this brief but perceptive article, with particular reference to the disciplinary role. Men whose mothers are the chief source of discipline tend to blame themselves to a greater extent than do those whose fathers are the major disciplinary agents.

Kleiner, Robert J., and Seymour Parker, "Goal-Striving, Social Status, and Mental Disorder: A Research Review," *American Sociological Review,* 28:189-203 (April, 1963). This article contains a review of some of the extensive research that has been done in recent years on the relationships between social status, social mobility, and motivation on the one hand and mental illness on the other. The authors conclude that a relationship between these sets of variables exists, with mobility orientation (i.e., goal-striving behavior) as perhaps the main unifying thread.

Lenski, Gerhard E., "Status Crystallization: A Non-Vertical Dimension of Social Status," *American Sociological Review,* 19:405-413 (August, 1954); ——————, "Social Participation and Status Crystallization," *American Sociological Review,* 21:458-464 (August, 1956). In these two perceptive articles, the concept of "status crystallization" is used in approximately the same sense as "status consistency." The study explores some of the political implications of the lack of "crystallization" among certain groups that measure high in some types of status and low in others.

Mangus, A. R., "Role Theory and Marriage Counseling," *Social Forces,* 35: 200-209 (March, 1957). ——————, "Family Impacts on Mental Health," *Marriage and Family Living,* 19:256-262 (August, 1957). These two articles are an outstanding contribution to the theory of social role. Among other insights, the author suggests that "The internalized role expectations which converge upon a given person constitute that person's social self."

Mead, Margaret, *Male and Female.* New York: William Morrow & Company, 1949. The roles of male and female are examined in a number of primitive societies as well as our own. The author conclusively demonstrates that many of the traits hitherto regarded as sex-linked are the result of ascribed status and the corresponding role-expectations.

Merrill, Francis E., *Courtship and Marriage* (revised edition). New York: Holt, Rinehart and Winston, 1959. This textbook offers a discussion of social interaction in dating, courtship, and (especially) marriage, in which the concepts of status and role form the conceptual framework.

Rabban, Meyer, "Sex-Role Identification in Young Children in Two Diverse Social Groups," *Genetic Psychology Monographs,* 42:81-158 (August, 1950). This study seeks to determine whether "sex role . . . is not only shaped by cultural factors, but is also channeled by social class membership delineating subcultures within a society." The conclusion is that both cultural and subcultural (class) influences are important in determining sex roles.

Simpson, Richard L., and H. Max Miller, "Social Status and Anomia," *Social Problems,* 10:256-264 (Winter, 1963). This study seeks to explain why some persons who occupy a particular social status become mentally ill whereas others do not. The hypothesis advanced is that of "attitudinal exposure," which maintains that "among people currently at the same status level, those with more past exposure to the anomic attitudes of lower-status groups will be more anomic" (i.e., maladjusted).

Smelser, Neil J., and William T. Smelser (eds.), *Personality and Social Systems*. New York: John Wiley and Sons, 1963. This book contains an extensive selection of scientific articles dealing with the relationships between personality and social systems. In their analysis, the authors employ the concept of *personality* as focusing upon the individual "as a system of needs, feelings, aptitudes, skills, defenses," whereas *social systems* focus on "certain relations that emerge when two or more persons interact with one another."

10 *Personality and Culture*

Cultural Aspects of Personality

The group is the bearer of culture. Group interaction in a cultural setting gives meaning to the world of the individual. These meanings are incorporated into his personality. The human being at birth is very plastic and can develop in many directions, depending upon the cultural setting. Each society takes certain culture patterns as the norm and directs the socialization of its members accordingly.[1] In the present chapter, we shall examine some of these cultural aspects of personality. In this analysis, we shall be concerned with "what happens to

---

[1] Ruth Benedict, *Patterns of Culture* (New York: Penguin Books, Inc., 1946).

195

personality by virtue of an individual's membership in enduring groups whose members follow socially standardized ways of acting, thinking, and feeling." [2]

Personality takes shape by socialization in a particular cultural environment. In this process, social approval goes to the child who follows the accepted culture patterns, and disapproval goes to the child who does not. Every society makes conformists of its members, since nonconformity is difficult and sometimes dangerous. The child begins to conform at an early age and, by so doing, increases pleasure, minimizes anxiety, and generally makes life easier for himself. He learns the culturally approved adjustments to the world first from his mother and later from others. By following these expectations, he gains the love of those persons who are important to him and thereby enhances his own security.[3]

This does not mean that the child is the passive recipient of cultural influences. Nor does it mean that the culture places a uniform stamp upon each personality. The relationship is much more complicated. Individuals differ in intellectual endowment, temperament, and physical characteristics. Furthermore, each group has its own interpretation of the culture and the many culture patterns. The latter also vary between social classes and subcultures. Each individual, therefore, has a unique biological equipment and a unique history of social interaction. Despite this fact of individual personality, certain uniformities remain between persons who participate in the same culture. These uniformities are the basis for the scientific study of culture and personality.[4]

Culture and personality are not two separate and independent entities, but are in reality two aspects of the same thing. They are part of the same unified process whereby human beings adjust to their geographical environment, their social groups, and themselves. This relationship between culture and personality is dramatized by the description of culture *in* personality, rather than culture *and* personality. In the words of one anthropologist: "Personality and culture . . . are not different or mutually exclusive entities; they are part and parcel of the same process of interaction. Both personality and culture reside in the individual or, to put it differently, they *are* the individual as modified by learning." [5] Each individual interacts with other individuals from the moment of birth. In this process, each acquires a personality. The particular version of personality is thus a (partial) product of the cultural influences upon the individual.

In each society, the problems of socialization are different.[6] Some societies are easier to adjust to than others, for the demands of the culture upon the individual vary. Each society has a unique historical development, set of institutions, and pattern of cultural roles. The emotional problems of meeting these

---

[2] John J. Honigmann, *Culture and Personality* (New York: Harper & Brothers, 1954), p. 3.

[3] Harry Stack Sullivan, "The Illusion of Personal Individuality," *Psychiatry*, 13:317-332 (August, 1950), p. 328.

[4] Honigmann, *op. cit.*, p. 28.

[5] Melford E. Spiro, "Culture and Personality," *Psychiatry*, 14:19-46 (February, 1951), p. 43.

[6] See Dennis Wrong, "The Oversocialized Conception of Man in Modern Sociology," *American Sociological Review*, 26:183-193 (April, 1961).

cultural demands are ordinarily greater in a complex and dynamic society than in a simple and static one. In our own society, these demands are often both exacting and inconsistent. In the present chapter, we shall contrast different societies with our own in terms of the demands to conform made upon individual members. Each society exacts a minimum of conformity from its members, but the difficulty of socialization varies with the nature of the culture.[7]

The logic of the culture and personality approach may be stated as follows. "Man," says Slotkin, "inherits a limited repertory of responses. Most of his responses," he continues, "are learned; and the majority of these are learned from others, i.e., culturally acquired. Consequently," he concludes, "it is to be expected that the individual's responses, *abnormal as well as normal*, are greatly influenced by his cultural milieu. And cultures vary tremendously." [8] Although the theory may thus be stated simply, the sociologist and anthropologist run into complications when they attempt to apply it to actual human beings. In the pages that follow, we shall present some of the implications of this approach to culture and personality. In so doing, we shall try not to lose sight of the forest (the theory) for the trees (the varieties of cultural behavior).

Culture and Basic Personality Type

Culture presents uniformities that affect the behavior of the members of a society. Members of the same society have many elements in common that distinguish them from members of other societies. These constitute the *communal* determinants of personality that we considered in the preceding chapter. Such determinants range in importance from matters of etiquette to attitudes toward society and the universe. The way children are reared is an important such personality determinant. A society that enforces a general code of severity will produce one type of personality, whereas one where the parents spoil the child will produce another. These and many other elements constitute a pattern that has been called the "basic personality type" for a particular society. The same general elements are found in the personalities of all the members.[9]

The basic personality type is a product of socialization in a particular society. The central forum of this process is the family. The roles making up the family are the most powerful the individual will encounter during his life. His own personality, furthermore, is at its most plastic during his early family relationship. This combination of demanding roles and infant plasticity gives rise to the similarities included in the basic personality type. In Parsons' words, basic personality is "a function of socialization in a particular type of system of role relationships with particular values." [10]

---

[7] Reinhard Bendix, "Compliant Behavior and Individual Personality," *American Journal of Sociology,* 58:292-303 (November, 1952).

[8] James S. Slotkin, "Culture and Psychopathology," *Journal of Abnormal and Social Psychology,* 51:269-275 (1955), p. 274. (My italics.)

[9] Ralph Linton, *The Cultural Background of Personality* (New York: Appleton-Century-Crofts, Inc., 1945), pp. 129ff.

[10] Talcott Parsons, *The Social System* (Glencoe, Ill.: The Free Press, 1951), p. 228.

The basic personality type is not a rigid norm, but rather a general pattern of belief and behavior toward which members of a society tend to gravitate. The basic personality type in the United States differs from that in France, Germany, the Soviet Union, or the island of Bali. The person reared in American society has cultural values and understandings that distinguish him from the person reared in a society with a different pattern of norms and expectations. Differences also exist within the same society, based upon class, caste, religion, or economic status. But all the members of the same society are exposed to certain *typical* cultural experiences that produce broad similarities in personality. As formulated by Linton, "the fact that personality norms differ for different societies can be explained on the basis of the different experience which the members of such societies acquire from contact with their cultures." [11]

These uniformities are especially apparent among small, isolated, primitive societies, whose cultures are homogeneous and where the individual is ordinarily exposed to a single basic personality pattern. In a large and heterogeneous society, the situation is more complicated, with various subcultures adding their distinctive definitions to the over-all culture. The personality of the American Negro, for example, is different from that of the white person in many respects, for the world of the Negro is subject to strains and inconsistencies that are largely unknown to the white man. Prejudice and discrimination toward the Negro vary between sections and between social classes. The over-all impact of these attitudes of white society is important in setting the basic pattern for the Negro personality.[12] In spite of these and other variations, however, certain fundamental uniformities still exist. These uniformities make Americans what they are, despite differences in race, creed, or social status.

The most important single determinant of the basic personality type is the set of culturally determined patterns for dealing with the child. The socialization of children is a process of learning the acceptable cultural adjustments. The family hands on to the child the patterns of the culture as it (the family) understands them, and in this way teaches the child to cope with the physical and the social world. In a society where the mother cares for the child with gentle kindness, the latter will tend to grow up with a different basic personality than in a society where the relationship is more casual. In matters of eating habits, toilet training, physical punishment, sexual development, personal aggression, control of basic impulses, and emotional responses, the family interprets the general culture patterns to the receptive child.[13]

The basic personality type reflects the impact of culture in several ways: (*a*) *content*—the actual behavior patterns handed down to the child are the most obvious way in which each culture forms a basic personality type; (*b*) *interpretation*—the adult who transmits the pattern determines the way in which the

---

[11] Linton, *op. cit.*, p. 145.

[12] Abram Kardiner and Lionel Ovesey, *The Mark of Oppression* (New York: W. W. Norton & Company, Inc., 1951).

[13] Allison Davis, "American Status Systems and the Socialization of the Child," *American Sociological Review*, 6:345-354 (June, 1941).

child will interpret both his own behavior and that of others; and (c) *organization*—the culture determines the way learned behavior is organized and the form it takes in the mind of the child. In our own society, much of this learning occurs through the mother, and the moral judgments subsequently reflect, consciously or unconsciously, the image of the mother.[14]

In many respects, the basic personality type constitutes the fundamental pattern of the adult personality. The personality is subject to elaboration and development through adolescence, maturity, and, indeed, until the end of life. At the same time, experiences that happen in the early years are important to personality, and these happenings have a basic similarity within each society. This is the period when the "patterning" of personality is most apparent. Patterning is an active verb that indicates "the process, originating with a group or a community, whereby an individual's personality is modified, limited, or standardized." [15] Each society has its own way in which this standardization occurs during the early years of life.

Culture and the Normal Personality

Society singles out certain general patterns for its members from all the possible forms of behavior. In this way, it sets the standards for normal and abnormal conduct; these standards vary between periods and between societies. Behavior defined as "normal" in one society is "abnormal" in another. Acceptance in the culture patterns, as in the mores, can make almost anything right.[16] A given act must be culturally defined before it has meaning. In the course of history, practically every form of behavior that we now consider abnormal has been accepted by some society as both normal and desirable. Every society makes its own norms, and personality at any time reflects these norms.

The sociological definition of normality recognizes this wide range of behavior. This definition is a statistical one, in which the normal is equal to the most usual or the most frequent in a given society at a given time. The "normal" personality does not depart drastically or consistently from the behavior of the majority of persons living under similar cultural conditions. Society is vitally concerned with "normality" in this sense, and the process of socialization is directed toward this end.

The group requires members whose behavior can be relied upon, not only in emergencies but even more in day-to-day activities. Social interaction, as we have seen, is based upon this element of predictability. From the intimate small group of the family to the large and heterogeneous group of the national state, the "normal" personality is the one whose activities are reliable and predictable.

---

[14] Gregory Bateson, "Cultural Determinants of Personality," Chapter 23 in J. McV. Hunt (ed.), *Personality and the Behavior Disorders,* Volume II (New York: The Ronald Press, 1944), p. 729.

[15] Honigmann, *Culture and Personality, op. cit.,* p. 170.

[16] William Graham Sumner, *Folkways* (Boston: Ginn and Company, 1906).

The concepts of status and role further suggest the implications of this approach to personality. In the process of social interaction, the behavior appropriate to a particular status emerges in the form of a role. The normal person is the one who plays the roles that his group considers appropriate for him. He does what is expected of him and his conduct can therefore be relied upon. His self-attitudes and the attitudes of others toward him are substantially in accord. Each individual lives through his relationships with others; if these relationships are distorted, interrupted, or disorganized, his personality will suffer.[17]

The functional relationship between culture and the normal personality may be clearly seen in the case of the psychotic ("insane") person. The latter lives in a world of his own, a world different from that of normal men and women. He may suffer from persistent delusions of grandeur, in which he imagines himself to be the Pope or the President of the United States. In any case, his own conception of his role conflicts with that held by others, and the normal cultural expectations no longer apply for him. He is unable to take the role of others toward himself, and his interpersonal relations may break down completely. In this case, he suffers from acute social isolation, which is in itself an "abnormal" condition.[18]

Other forms of departure from the norm are not so striking. Many persons depart from conventional group expectations in one respect or another. Some of these eccentricities are tolerated, especially in large cities, where such individuals can usually find kindred spirits. Such behavior may be considered bizarre, but not sufficiently abnormal for the person to be ostracized, incarcerated, or executed. Only those individuals who consistently and spectacularly run counter to organized group expectations are defined as abnormal. The great majority follow the expected patterns and are therefore adjudged normal persons.

The concept of *deviance* is useful in considering the relationship between culture and the normal personality. The deviant is the person who departs from group norms and whose behavior therefore cannot be adequately predicted. His departure from conventional expectations may reflect a variety of factors, ranging from ignorance of the norm, through boredom with the constraint exerted by it, to a deliberate desire to advance his own interests at the expense of the group. All societies face the problem of deviance, from the small and homogeneous society of the Trobriand Islands[19] to the large and heterogeneous society of the United States.[20] The *degree* of deviance, however, varies widely

---

[17] Harrison L. Gough, "A Sociological Theory of Psychopathy," *American Journal of Sociology*, 53:359-366 (March, 1948).

[18] Melvin L. Kohn and John A. Clausen, "Social Isolation and Schizophrenia," *American Sociological Review*, 20:265-273 (June, 1955). See also John A. Clausen, "The Sociology of Mental Illness," Chapter 22 in Robert K. Merton, Leonard Broom, and Leonard S. Cottrell, Jr. (eds.), *Sociology Today* (New York: Basic Books, Inc., 1959).

[19] Bronislaw Malinowski, *Crime and Custom in Savage Society*, Part II (London: Routledge & Kegan Paul, Ltd., 1926), Chapter 1.

[20] Robin M. Williams, Jr., *American Society: A Sociological Interpretation* (New York: Alfred A. Knopf, Inc., 1951), pp. 357-366.

between societies, with our own offering a spectacular example of large-scale deviance in many respects.

The deviant in our society may violate group norms with respect to such behavior as sexual acts, attitudes toward property, family relationships, religious observances, respect for human life, and governmental loyalty. The prostitute, the criminal, the bigamist, the murderer, and the revolutionary are among the deviants in modern society. These persons are by no means "insane," in the sense that they are cut off from normal interaction with others; they have merely violated one or more important group norms and hence are considered as deviants.[21]

A society can tolerate a certain amount of deviation in its members, although such behavior is ordinarily viewed with suspicion. In a small group, the members may attempt to bring the erring brother back into line by increasing their interaction with him and thus pointing out the error of his ways.[22] If persuasion fails, the group may curtail its relationships with the deviant, in ways ranging from avoidance to ostracism or even banishment. In extreme cases, such as those involving murder, incest, treason, or offenses against the gods, the larger society may punish the deviant by death.[23] Depending upon the importance of the norm, a society has a number of devices for maintaining conformity in its members.

Cultural Variation and Personality

Personality is thus considered normal or abnormal on the basis of its conformity to the standards of a particular culture at a particular time. The variations between cultures are so great that it is difficult (if not impossible) to find a consistent pattern of personality that would be normal in all societies at all times. Sapir has commented upon this relative conception of normal behavior by pointing out that the "norm" is extremely elastic and that one of the principal functions of the study of man is to underscore this fact. Furthermore, he indicates, "personalities are not conditioned by a generalized process of adjustment to 'the normal' but by the necessity of adjustment to the greatest possible variety of idea patterns and action patterns according to the accidents of birth and geography."[24] The "normal" individual is the one who lives in Rome and does as the other Romans do.

The definition of abnormality (like that of normality) differs from one society to another, and behavior defined as abnormal in one may not be so re-

---

[21] John J. Honigmann, "Toward a Distinction Between Psychiatric and Social Abnormality," *Social Forces*, 31:274-277 (March, 1953).

[22] Stanley Schachter, "Deviation, Rejection, and Communication," *Journal of Abnormal and Social Psychology*, 46:190-207 (April, 1951).

[23] Robert E. L. Faris, "Development of the Small-Group Research Movement," Chapter 7 in Muzafer Sherif and M. O. Wilson (eds.), *Group Relations at the Crossroads* (New York: Harper & Row, 1953), p. 175.

[24] Edward Sapir, "Cultural Anthropology and Psychiatry," *Journal of Abnormal and Social Psychology*, 27:229-242 (October-December, 1932), p. 235.

garded in another. In terms of sexual deviation, epilepsy, artificially induced social isolation, or delusions of grandeur, individuals have made adequate and even highly satisfactory adjustments to some societies, despite the fact that this behavior is considered abnormal in our own. We may briefly explore some of these situations by way of indicating the elasticity of the "normal."

1. Cultural norms and sexual abnormality. In our society, normal sexual relations are by definition those between adult members of the opposite sex. The homosexual is a social outcast, and is the subject of mingled derision, scorn, and pity. He fails to carry out the role expectations of his sex, and hence is regarded as a deviant and undesirable person. His deviation is viewed as a menace to the organized expectations of society, and every effort is made to eliminate, or at least minimize, his behavior. Such fragmentary evidence as we have suggests that homosexual behavior is considerably more widespread in our society than most persons would like to admit.[25] Despite (or perhaps because of) this fact, homosexuality is a deviation that is feared and scorned.

Homosexuality is not similarly regarded in all societies. In the Athens of Pericles, this form of sexual behavior was widely practiced and had widespread social acceptance among the upper classes. In certain contemporary primitive societies, the homosexual is regarded with a sort of veneration, as constituting a link between the natural and the supernatural, the normal and the divinely abnormal. In these societies, he is often given the status of *shaman* or religious leader. At some time in his life, the future shaman apparently undergoes a religious transformation, when he communes with the spirits and simultaneously changes his sex. Homosexuality is not the norm in these societies, but still it is not viewed with the same horrified distaste as in our own. Norms of sexual conduct are culturally defined, with different norms evoking different behavior.[26]

2. Cultural norms and social withdrawal. Complete social withdrawal is regarded in our society as a personal tragedy. This condition arises from a breakdown in communication between the individual and the group. The self-absorption demanded by Buddhistic religious training in India represents a condition that for us would be the most unfortunate of all roles. The candidate is trained to remove himself as completely as possible from other persons, not in the physical sense of withdrawal but in the mental sense of losing himself in a trance-like state. In our society, such a condition is defined as pathological, whereas in India it is widely regarded as an enviable and holy state.[27]

A similar disparity of definition is seen in our own society at different times. In the Middle Ages, the self-imposed isolation of the saint was viewed with great veneration. Saint Simeon Stylites spent twenty years perched high upon a pillar, where his contemplation of the eternal truths was uninterrupted by any

---

[25] Alfred C. Kinsey, *et al., Sexual Behavior in the Human Male* (Philadelphia: W. B. Saunders Company, 1948).

[26] Benedict, *op. cit.,* pp. 243-245.

[27] Franz Alexander, "Buddhistic Training as an Artificial Catatonia," *Psychoanalytic Review,* 18:129-145 (April, 1931), quoted by Otto Klineberg, *Race Differences* (New York: Harper & Brothers, 1935), p. 293.

mundane considerations. Saint Francis of Assisi gave away all his worldly possessions and dedicated himself to a life of renunciation. Thousands of ordinary persons took the monastic vows of poverty, chastity, and obedience and devoted their lives to meditation and good works. The behavior of the saint would at the present time be considered as definitely abnormal. In terms of participation and withdrawal, social attitudes vary from one epoch to another.

3. *Cultural norms and personal delusions.* In our society, there is supposed to be a reasonable consistency between the role a person conceives himself as playing and that which he actually plays. When the discrepancy between these roles becomes too glaring, the person is considered dangerous to ordered social relationships. Persistent delusions of grandeur are symptoms of personal abnormality, although they may not have the same significance in societies with different norms. Similarly, men who identify themselves with the winds, the heavens, and the mountains are adjudged candidates for mental hospitals in the United States.

Among certain tribes of Northwest Coast Indians, however, similar delusions constitute normal behavior for the chiefs, who are considered by themselves and others as very great men. These chiefs devote long and eloquent speeches to the glorification of themselves and their prowess, in which they try to leave no doubt in the minds of the listeners as to their superhuman powers. The oratory that resounds about the banquet halls of these chieftains would in our society be heard only in the corridors of mental hospitals, where the less violent psychotics are allowed to exchange experiences. The chiefs may or may not be convinced of the truth of their own claims to grandeur. The point is that any person in our society who speaks of himself in such consistently grandiose terms is mentally suspect.[28]

Cultural Participation and Personality

The average person is also in constant communication with others. Serious interruptions in this process are injurious to personality. Man must continually renew his social relationships if he is to continue as an adequate member of society. Interruptions or distortions in this interaction suggest the abnormal personality. Communication may be interrupted by anxiety, fear, or other emotional conditions. Whatever the cause, interpersonal relationships are unsatisfactory. We may indicate some of the ways in which inadequate communication impairs cultural participation and hence personality.[29]

1. *Mental deficiency and communication.* Personality grows through participation in symbolic communication. A minimum of mental ability is necessary for such participation. Different levels of ability allow varying degrees of participation: (*a*) The *moron* is slightly below "normal" in intelligence and is handicapped only in the more subtle shades of meaning and in situations in-

---

[28] Benedict, *op. cit.*, Chapter 6, "The Northwest Coast of America."
[29] Harry Stack Sullivan, *The Interpersonal Theory of Psychiatry* (New York: W. W. Norton & Company, Inc., 1953), p. xii.

volving complex personal adjustments. Morons can play fairly adequate roles in many simple situations and can function adequately under circumstances where the difficulty of choice is not great. (*b*) The *imbecile* is incapable of playing a normal role in the group, although he *can* care for his own rudimentary bodily needs. His mental age remains on the level of a child of three to seven years, which means that he is unable to grasp any but the simplest symbolic meanings. (*c*) The *idiot* cannot even play a minimum role in society. He has a mental age of less than three years and will never advance further. He is apparently unable to take the role of the other in any but the simplest relationships, and the role of the generalized other is altogether beyond his powers. The idiot is scarcely a human being in any recognizable sense, and his personality remains on the most elementary level.

The nature of the social environment is also a determinant of "normal" personality development. Some environments are more complex than others and require a correspondingly higher mental complement. The moron may make a satisfactory adjustment to a simple environment. As long as he stays there, he is all right. When some external crisis, such as a war, dislodges him from his familiar surroundings, he may be unable to adjust. Isolation from cultural participation is thus a matter of degree. The person who is "normal" (adequately adjusted) in one environment may be "abnormal" (maladjusted) in another.

The relationship between personality, mental deficiency, and communication has been explored in recent years. It was formerly assumed that the inability to communicate was *solely* due to heredity, and that nothing whatever could be done about it. Recent research has indicated that the ability to play an adequate role in the group may be developed to a certain extent by training and other environmental (cultural) factors. This improvement applies primarily to persons defined as morons, rather than to those of lower mental powers. In a number of studies, persons formerly adjudged to be feeble-minded developed considerably in mental ability when given sympathy, understanding, and adequate training.[30]

2. *Mental derangement and communication.* Mental derangement is the impairment of a hitherto normal mind by physical or social factors. The mentally deranged person is unable to maintain meaningful contact with other members of the group. His world is also marked by social isolation, although in a different sense from that of the mentally deficient. The psychotic (mentally deranged) person continues to use the words he learned in his personality development. These words may not, however, mean the same thing to him as to the normal person. We cannot consider here the processes whereby this progressive isolation takes place. Suffice it to state that the most common forms of mental derangement are characterized by a high degree of social isolation.[31]

The nature of this isolation is suggested in a number of ways. In sections of

---

[30] Don C. Charles, "Ability and Accomplishment of Persons Earlier Judged Mentally Deficient," *Genetic Psychology Monographs*, 47:3-71 (February, 1953).

[31] Robert E. L. Faris, "Cultural Isolation and the Schizophrenic Personality," *American Journal of Sociology*, 40:155-164 (September, 1934).

the large city having unusually high rates of schizophrenia, various indices of social isolation were found. Among these indices were: the names of fewer neighbors were known; fewer personal friends and acquaintances were had; more homes were rented than owned; there was less membership in such secondary groups as lodges or fraternal organizations; a higher degree of unemployment and a higher job turnover were indicated; fewer contacts outside of the local area were found; and fewer visits were made with friends. In these and other ways, persons living in areas with high rates of schizophrenia indicated that their cultural participation was less intensive than that of persons in areas where the rates were lower. To be mentally healthy, the individual must retain fruitful contact with the group.[32]

In a study of mental disorders in New Haven, Connecticut, there emerged a definite connection between sociocultural environment and the incidence of different types of mental difficulty. In the areas where the lowest class lived, the rate of schizophrenia was *eleven* times as high as in the areas inhabited by the highest class. The latter, on the other hand, was more prone to neurotic disorders than were the members of the lower classes. In short, "the neuroses are concentrated at the higher levels and the psychoses at the lower end of the class structure." [33] The assumption is that there is a pronounced difference in social isolation between the different areas. Members of the lower class are thus (presumably) more isolated from cultural contacts than are the upper classes.

Social isolation appears to work reciprocally with schizophrenia. Many of the original symptoms of the disease reflect the initial isolation of the person from the group. The lonely and introverted adolescent early develops inadequacies in his social relationships, first in his family and later in his peer groups. As he grows older, these symptoms further alienate him from other persons. The lack of cultural participation is accentuated by the evolving nature of the mental difficulty itself. His personality becomes increasingly abnormal as the barrier widens between himself and others. In other words, "social isolation is . . . a sign that the individual's interpersonal difficulties have become so great that he is no longer capable of functioning in interpersonal relationships." [34]

3. *Racial and ethnic factors in communication.* Difficulties in communication may also follow the interruption of participation that is not due to any physical or mental impairment. These difficulties pertain to large segments of the population whose complete cultural participation is impaired by ethnic background, religious discrimination, and racial stigmata. In a significant study of the vertical mobility rates of various ethnic and racial groups, Rosen found that these groups differed widely in terms of their motivations and aspirations toward gaining higher status. One of the factors in the relatively low motivation of

---

[32] E. Gartly Jaco, "The Social Isolation Hypothesis and Schizophrenia," *American Sociological Review,* 19:567-577 (October, 1954), pp. 575-576.

[33] August B. Hollingshead and Frederick C. Redlich, "Social Stratification and Psychiatric Disorders," *American Sociological Review,* 18:163-169 (April, 1953), p. 167.

[34] Kohn and Clausen, "Social Isolation and Schizophrenia," *op. cit.,* p. 273.

such groups as Italians, French Canadians, and Negroes is the barrier to cultural participation experienced (in varying degrees) by these populations.[35]

The result of this barrier is most apparent in the personalities of 21 million Negroes in the United States. Skin color deprives more than 10 per cent of the population of this country of their proportionate share in the cultural heritage, irrespective of their individual abilities. These deprivations range all the way from the elementary right to the safety and security of the person to the right to practice a profession and hold office. These discriminations vary from one section to another, but even in the North there are differences in housing, employment, social and religious activities, and political behavior. Only in public education does the Negro in the North approach theoretical equality with the white.

In other sections of the country, the Negro is subject to various barriers to cultural participation. He is handicapped by unequal educational facilities, discrimination in public and private schools, housing restrictions, restricted rights to health services, segregation in public transportation, limited access to many forms of public accommodations, and discrimination in areas of "social" relationships. Recent decisions of the Supreme Court have declared virtually all of these forms of discrimination unconstitutional, but they nevertheless continue to exist without change in many areas. As a result, the Negro suffers from a feeling of rejection by the society as a whole. Insecurity and self-hatred are attributes of many Negroes that can be attributed to their minority status.[36]

Cultural Conflict and Personality

The individual in our society is subject to conflicting cultural expectations. Some groups expect him to act in one way, others in another. His family may have one set of expectations, whereas his school, his church, and his business have others. In some respects, these expectations coincide; all, for example, will agree on the sanctity of private property. But in many other respects they may disagree; the church may emphasize spiritual values above those of the market place, at the same time that business is organized about monetary values. Many other contradictions mark the pattern of American culture. The individual absorbs these contradictory attitudes, and they become part of his personality. Most people are able to reconcile these conflicting expectations—some are not.[37]

Personality conflict takes a variety of forms. Even among those who conform to the customary patterns in every important respect, some conflicts are apparent. The individual need not be a deviant to be confused. Many of his personal difficulties arise because he has absorbed the values of his culture *too well*.[38]

---

[35] Bernard C. Rosen, "Race, Ethnicity, and the Achievement Syndrome," *American Sociological Review*, 24:47-60 (February, 1959).

[36] Clemmont E. Vontress, "The Negro Against Himself," *Journal of Negro Education*, 23:237-241 (Spring, 1963).

[37] For an illuminating discussion of this problem, see Jules Henry, *Culture Against Man* (New York: Random House, 1963).

[38] Karen Horney, *The Neurotic Personality of Our Time* (New York: W. W. Norton & Company, Inc., 1937).

His confusion reflects the inconsistency of the culture, not any weakness or incapacity on his part. Many juvenile delinquents are merely expressing the American values of initiative, material wealth, and preoccupation with the main chance. These values conflict with others that stem from Christianity and the brotherhood of man, but the second are obscured by the first. The delinquent is acting out some of these aggressive forms of group expectations and in so doing is in harmony with an important aspect of his society and culture.

Personality conflict thus reflects cultural inconsistency. Cultures with glaring contradictions produce more than their share of personality difficulties. Families whose wants are indefinitely stimulated by advertising but whose purchasing power is limited meet one form of cultural contradiction. Women brought up with the belief that their place is in the home may find the role adjustment difficult when they are forced to go to work to supplement the family income. Members of minority groups who believe the democratic creed of freedom and equality may suffer a rude shock when they are confronted with prejudice and discrimination. The culture of the United States is subject to many such contradictions.[39]

Personality difficulties of this type are more prevalent in dynamic, heterogeneous societies than in comparatively static, homogeneous societies. In the latter, the ideal personality type is easier to attain. The standards of personality are, furthermore, relatively stable and the individual is trained to play a role that will in all probability remain the same throughout his lifetime. In our society, the individual is expected to rise in the social scale and thereby achieve a higher status than his father. In a simple and homogeneous society, the individual aspires to be like his parents, to carry on their status, and to deviate as little as possible from their way of life. These two forms of society—the one relentlessly dynamic and the other placidly static—are reflected in the corresponding stability of the personality. We have committed ourselves to the dynamic, and personalities in our society reflect this choice.[40]

In a dynamic society, the culture prescribes certain roles and goals but at the same time makes it difficult for many persons to attain them. An example of this disparity arises when the individual is unable to become economically self-sufficient, despite the cultural expectation that he do so. Other conflicts arise where the individual is called upon to play two or more contradictory roles. He is expected to compete aggressively and at the same time practice Christian humility toward his fellow men. He is told that he is free to do as he pleases, but at the same time is dependent upon his job. He is taught to value affection above all other things, but is often deprived of this affection.[41] He is encouraged to participate fully in a democratic culture, but he is handicapped by racial, ethnic, and religious barriers.

---

[39] Read Bain, "Our Schizoid Culture," *Sociology and Social Research*, 19:266-276 (January-February, 1935).

[40] Talcott Parsons, "Certain Primary Sources and Patterns of Aggression in the Social Structure of the Western World," *Psychiatry*, 10:167-181 (May, 1947).

[41] Arnold W. Green, "The Middle-Class Male Child and Neurosis," *American Sociological Review*, 11:31-41 (February, 1946).

Large numbers of persons thus lack access to the means of achieving the goals that society sets for them. Because of social class, social isolation, ethnic background, religious preference, or racial heritage, millions of men and women are handicapped in the competition for the good things that society has to offer. To put it another way, their "life chances" are lower than those of the more fortunate persons who have none of these handicaps. The personalities of these unfortunate ones are often marked by "hopelessness, discouragement, despair, and demoralization"—in short by what has been called *"anomie."* [42] In our subsequent discussion of social class and social mobility, we shall have more to say about the related concepts of "life chances" and *"anomie."* Here we merely indicate that differential access to the means of achieving life goals is an important factor in personality conflict.[43]

The majority of persons are able to overcome these and other conflicting patterns. They are able to adjust to modern society, with all its frustrations, inconsistencies, and insecurities. They constitute the great mass of "normal" persons, whose behavior approximates the cultural expectations. Others are not so fortunate. They are the maladjusted, the neurotics, and the psychotics. They have apparently "experienced the culturally determined difficulties in an accentuated form, mostly through the medium of childhood experiences, and . . . [have] consequently been unable to solve them, or . . . solved them at great cost to [their] personality." These unhappy persons are numbered in the millions. They are the "stepchildren of our culture." [44]

Efforts are now being made to adjust the individual to the expectations of his culture, and vice versa. Until recently, the person who was unable to live up to these expectations was considered biologically inadequate and (perhaps) even morally unsatisfactory. The treatment of the maladjusted person was based upon the assumption that he should be fitted to his social role and his personality should somehow be adjusted to the traditional pattern. Charity followed this general point of view, as did the early practice of social work. More recently, the relationships of culture and personality have become more clearly understood. Social roles are coming to be viewed as cultural products and not as divine pronouncements.

In psychotherapy, for example, the doctor may devote his major efforts to clarifying the role(s) of his patient and assisting him in playing them more adequately. The man who is mentally ill may fail to understand his conventional role as husband and thus fail to live up to the expectations of his society. He may also fail in his more intimate interpersonal role and thereby frustrate the expectations of his wife.[45] Marriage is one of the most complex interpersonal relationships we know of, and both husband and wife may need

---

[42] Dorothy L. Meier and Wendell Bell, *"Anomie* and Differential Access to the Achievement of Life Goals," *American Sociological Review*, 24:189-202 (April, 1959).

[43] Ephraim Harold Mizruchi, "Social Structure and Anomia in a Small City," *American Sociological Review*, 25:645-654 (October, 1960).

[44] Horney, *op. cit.*, p. 290. See also Marie Jahoda, "A Social-Psychological Approach to the Study of Culture," *Human Relations*, 14:23-30 (February, 1961).

[45] A. R. Mangus, "Role Theory and Marriage Counseling," *Social Forces*, 35:200-209 (March, 1957).

help in defining and playing their roles.[46] Many (although not all) mental difficulties reflect some degree of failure in role-playing, and this failure affects the attitudes of the patient toward significant others and, above all, toward himself. The "normal" personality, by definition, is able to play his basic roles more or less adequately, as required by the society. The "maladjusted" and the mentally ill, by the same token, need help in this process.[47]

The luminous conception has recently crept into social thinking that the expectations connected with some social roles may be changed, at least in part. Minimum wages, social security, health insurance, old age pensions, mothers' aid, and public housing are some of the techniques whereby the individual is enabled, on a large scale, to carry on his economic and social roles more adequately. These efforts are in their infancy, and many persons will continue to be frustrated by failure to fulfill the expectations of their culture. Social engineering of this kind will doubtless take many hitherto unexpected forms. As the opportunities for the individual to attain the goals of our society are increased, the maladjustments of personality arising from some forms of role failure may be expected to decrease.[48]

In this sense, many social problems may be gradually disappearing. Problems of economic well-being may be on their way to eventual solution—or at least substantial betterment—in the face of continued prosperity, private pension plans, and (above all) federal social security programs.[49] In place of the traditional problems of unemployment and old-age insecurity, however, modern man may be increasingly plagued by problems arising from his interpersonal relations. He may have "enough" money but not enough status. He may attain economic security but lack emotional security. He may have all the food he needs but not all the love he wants. He may live in a good home but be denied membership in a country club. In these and many other ways, modern man may have many ancient problems virtually "solved," only to be bothered by new problems arising out of his relationships with others.[50]

Culture and "Social Character"

The relationships between culture and personality have been examined in different ways and with different frames of reference. One of the most persuasive of these conceptual schemes is that advanced by David Riesman and his colleagues in their seminal book entitled *The Lonely Crowd*.[51] We have referred

---

[46] Nathan W. Ackerman, "Interpersonal Disturbances in the Family: Some Unsolved Problems in Psychotherapy," *Psychiatry*, 17:359-369 (1954).

[47] Cf. John P. Spiegel, "The Social Roles of Doctor and Patient in Psychoanalysis and Psychotherapy," *Psychiatry*, 17:369-376 (1954).

[48] Lawrence K. Frank, "Opportunities in a Program of Education for Marriage and Family Life," *Mental Hygiene*, 24:578-594 (October, 1940).

[49] Jessie Bernard, *Social Problems at Midcentury: Role, Status, and Stress* (New York: Holt, Rinehart & Winston, 1957), p. 75.

[50] Francis E. Merrill, "The Self and the Other: An Emerging Field of Social Problems," *Social Problems*, 4:200-207 (January, 1957).

[51] David Riesman, *et al.*, *The Lonely Crowd* (New Haven: Yale University Press, 1961). Abridged edition with a new foreword.

to this study in various contexts in preceding chapters and shall have occasion to do so in succeeding chapters. The insights expressed in *The Lonely Crowd* are so wide-ranging that they help us to understand aspects of social interaction ranging from the adolescent peer group to the voluntary association and from child-rearing to political behavior. The intellectual antecedents of Riesman's theoretical approach include the works of such scholars as Erich Fromm, Ruth Benedict, Ralph Linton, Karen Horney, Margaret Mead, Geoffrey Gorer, and others to whom we have referred in our analysis of culture and personality. "The Lonely Crowd" has, in its turn, entered the public domain as an intriguing phrase to describe the alienation of modern man in a mass society. This book has, finally, received the ultimate scholarly accolade in the form of erudite polemics among the sociological fraternity, some of which are contained in a symposium appropriately entitled *Culture and Social Character*.[52]

By "social character," Riesman means approximately what we have called "personality" in the sociological or communal sense. Riesman explicitly states that he is concerned only with the social and cultural aspects of the total personality and not with its "inherited temperaments and talents." In our discussion, we have made the same basic distinction between nature and nurture, genetic qualities and learned behavior, and inborn traits and acquired dispositions. This distinction is not always easy to maintain in theory, let alone in practice. But in general the sociological approach to personality deals with those qualities that human beings share with others by virtue of their common membership in the same societies, cultures, classes, minority groups, ethnic groups, peer groups, and families—as well as the roles they play in these and other groups.

In Riesman's terms, "character" refers to "the more or less permanent socially and historically conditioned organization of an individual's drives and satisfactions." By "social character," he means "that part of 'character' which is shared among significant social groups and which . . . is the product of the experience of these groups." [53] Social interaction, as we have seen, occurs in a cultural atmosphere and also gives rise to new aspects of culture. In the sociological sense, personality arises in a sociocultural setting and assumes many of the qualities of that setting.[54] Whether we call the finished product "personality *in* culture" or "social character," we are speaking of essentially the same thing.

In his analysis, Riesman postulates three general stages of society, each with its appropriate social character. These are: (1) tradition-direction, (2) inner-direction, and (3) other-direction. Every individual, with negligible exceptions, initially learns the forms of social character that will make him *want* to do what he is supposed to do. In his original statement, Riesman suggested that the crucial variable in determining the "style" of the society and hence its domi-

---

[52] Seymour M. Lipset and Leo Lowenthal (eds.), *Culture and Social Character* (Glencoe, Ill.: The Free Press, 1961).

[53] David Riesman, *et al., op. cit.*, p. 4.

[54] Pitirim A. Sorokin, *Society, Culture, and Personality* (New York: Harper & Brothers, 1947).

nant social character was the curve of population growth—that is, whether the population was (*a*) stationary, (*b*) increasing, (*c*) declining or about to decline. In a later reformulation of his position, Riesman conceded that the population variable might not be as indicative of the state of the society as he had originally thought. Instead of the stage of the population curve, he indicated that such factors as "economic development, urbanization, and the spread of education" might be more meaningful as indices of social structure and social character.[55] The important consideration for our purposes, however, is not the variable(s) used by Riesman, but the forms of social character that emerge from different social structures, however defined. In this sense, as noted, Riesman advances a grand design of three such forms—each more important than the last for contemporary mass society.

1. *Tradition-direction.* The first form of social character arises in a society that is static, stratified, and obedient to tradition. The culture of such a society provides its members with "ritual, routine, and religion," and people have little incentive to seek new forms for their relationships or new solutions to their age-old problems. The possibilities for choice are strictly limited, and each person ordinarily occupies the statuses and plays the roles of his ancestors. Each man, woman, and child has his or her traditional place in the scheme of things and is not encouraged to change it. Social "adjustment" is thus maximized and social "maladjustment" is minimized, for the directions are clear and the positions well-defined. But the price of such "adjustment" is high, for it involves a dead conformity to the norms that come down virtually intact from the past. Many of the primary-group qualities of the *Gemeinschaft*, which we considered in Chapter Five, are characteristic of a tradition-directed society. The Middle Ages constituted a classic example of tradition-direction, and these societies were shaken from their ancient lethargy by the Renaissance and the Reformation.[56]

2. *Inner-direction.* The second form of social character reflects a society that is changing rapidly. This is one in which there is great individual mobility, and where people are on the move both vertically up the social scale and horizontally from one place to another. This is the society in which the Protestant Ethic of individual choice is strong in such divergent fields as religion, economic activity, and marriage. The "direction" for the typical individual comes from a pattern of abstract principles implanted by his family and other early agencies of socialization. Among these principles are the doctrine of hard work, saving one's money, the postponement of present satisfactions, and a pervasive individualism in virtually every aspect of life. By first incorporating and then responding to these principles, the individual, in effect, controls himself in a way somewhat reminiscent of the Freudian superego mechanism. In striking contrast to the static, tradition-directed society, the dynamic, inner-directed society offers a wide variety of personal choice, in which the individual

---

[55] David Riesman, *et al., op. cit.,* p. xxxi.
[56] *Ibid.,* pp. 9-13.

is encouraged to strike out for himself instead of following the old norms, roles, and values. The adult therefore drives toward his goals with less overt control by others than is the case in the tradition-directed society or, as we shall see, in the other-directed society. In Riesman's words, *"the source of direction for the individual is 'inner' in the sense that it is implanted early in life by the elders and directed toward generalized but nonetheless inescapably destined goals."* [57]

3. *Other-direction.* The third form of social character is the product of a society in which the problems of production have been basically solved and have been replaced by those of distribution. An other-directed society is a self-conscious society in which, to use Riesman's expression, the chief problem is "other people." [58] The economic structure is marked by the employment of fewer people in production and more in white-collar occupations, large bureaucracies, and "service" occupations. In all of these activities, the individual is primarily concerned with interpersonal relationships. He is either selling something to other people, waiting on them in one capacity or another, or concerned with their opinions of him. In most bureaucratic activities, advancement depends in part upon projecting a favorable self-image to one's superiors and at the same time avoiding any threat to them. This society is characterized, furthermore, by a vast increase in leisure and a reliance upon the mass media to pass this leisure painlessly and agreeably.

In the tradition-directed society, the chief source of direction is the small, local, primary group. In the inner-directed society, the principal direction comes from the abstract principles of conduct absorbed early in life from parents, teachers, ministers, and (last, but not least) books. In the other-directed society, the direction comes primarily from one's contemporaries—children's play groups, adolescent peer groups, adult friendship groups, and groups of business associates. These agencies are augmented by the mass media, which transmit the norms and values of the mass society. The other-directed person tries to keep his personal radar set tuned to the wave lengths of his friends, associates, and competitors. As Riesman puts it, the goals of the other-directed person *"shift with that guidance* [i.e., of his contemporaries]; *it is only the process of striving itself and the process of paying close attention to the signals from others that remain unaltered throughout life."*[59] The age of other-direction is the age of conformity.

Culture and "Human Nature"

As we come to the end of our discussion of personality and culture, a nagging question remains. In the face of all of the evident *differences* in personality

---

[57] *Ibid.*, p. 15. (Riesman's italics.)

[58] *Ibid.*, p. xxi.

[59] *Ibid.*, p. 21. (His italics.) For empirical confirmation of Riesman's general position, see Richard Centers, "An Examination of the Riesman Social Character Typology: A Metropolitan Survey," *Sociometry*, 25:231-240 (September, 1962); Waltraud M. Kassarjian, "A Study of Riesman's Theory of Social Character," *Sociometry*, 25:213-230 (September, 1962).

reflecting divergent cultural patterns, are there any basic *similarities* over and above these differences? Is there, in short, any scientific truth in the traditional aphorism that "human nature is the same the world over?" This is perhaps the thorniest question in the field of personality, and one which we can only raise here. The problem involves such semantic questions as the definition of "human nature" and "personality," as well as the determination and measurement of such basic similarities, if any, among all human beings.

In the scientific study of personality, the emphasis rested for a long time with the bioligical determinists, who viewed the genetic factors as all-important and virtually ignored the cultural factors. In recent decades, the pendulum has swung the other way, especially among many cultural anthropologists and sociologists. In the present chapter, we have examined some of the latter approaches—notably, those involving the basic personality type, the "normal" personality, the deviant personality, and the like. In recent years, however, certain eminent social scientists (notably the late Robert Redfield) have raised the broad question of the universality of certain personality traits that transcend cultural differences.[60] In so doing, Redfield is following the insights of Cooley who, more than a generation ago, devoted himself to essentially the same problem.[61]

In a perceptive essay on this theme, Redfield spoke of the "universally human" qualities and of "universal developed humanity." He defined the latter as "those states of mind which commonly and persistently appear in any normally endowed adult in whatever society he may be reared." [62] These states of mind are clearly related to the "universal determinants" of personality, which we reviewed in the last chapter.[63] Redfield was speaking primarily, however, about the general psychological similarities found among all men, which are sometimes called the "sentiments." All human beings, for example, share such sentiments as guilt, shame, consciousness of self, awareness of the not-self, apprehension of danger, fear of death, ethnocentrism, awareness of time, and ideas of morality. In view of these and other universal sentiments, Redfield ventured the hypothesis that "the rules of conduct, in the societies the world has known so far, have their modality, their tendency toward a very general similar conduct." [64]

If "human nature" were *completely* the subjective aspect of culture, as some persons maintain, such common attributes would be manifestly impossible in the face of the evident differences between cultures. Those whose personalities evolved in, say, the Navajo and modern American cultures, would then be unable to take each others' roles and understand each other in any meaningful

---

[60] Robert Redfield, "The Universally Human and the Culturally Variable," *Journal of General Education*, 10:150-160 (July, 1957).

[61] Charles Horton Cooley, *Social Organization* (New York: Charles Scribner's Sons, 1909); *Human Nature and the Social Order* (New York: Charles Scribner's Sons, 1922).

[62] Redfield, *op. cit.*, p. 158.

[63] Clyde Kluckhohn and O. H. Mowrer, "Culture and Personality: A Conceptual Scheme," *American Anthropologist*, 46:1-29 (January-March, 1944).

[64] Redfield, *op. cit.*, p. 160.

way. Their sentiments would be so divergent that they could never communicate at all. But in practice this is not the case. Despite the culturally induced dissimilarities between members of different societies, people do in practice take each other's roles, presumably because of their common humanity. This does not mean, of course, that *every* member of *every* society has sufficient empathy to put himself in the place of persons from other societies. The murderous antipathies on both sides of the Iron Curtain suggest that ethnocentrism is very hard to overcome. But *some* members of opposing societies, no matter what their ideological differences, are able to cross the cultural barriers and take the role of the other.[65]

If basic similarities in "human nature" *do* exist, the next question is what causes them. What "universal" situation or situations are found among all societies? Cooley answered, in effect, that the *primary group* is the universal determinant. All men, he contended, spend their early years in some primary group(s), in which they learn to take the role of other members under conditions of intimacy, sympathy, and cooperation. Given the same (or similar) patterns of interpersonal relations during the most plastic years, some similar sentiments inevitably develop in every human being.[66] These qualities are not genetic in the same sense as skin color and shape of the head. The genetic potentiality for primary-group experience is obviously necessary, but it must be developed through interpersonal relationships. In the primary-group setting, the person (generally) receives warmth, affection, and emotional security and at the same time learns the universal human sentiments of self-consciousness, rivalry, guilt, and the rest.[67]

This universalist approach to personality is still largely speculative and inferential, for few comparative and empirical studies have attacked this specific problem. Cultural anthropologists have given us hundreds of carefully documented monographs depicting the culturally induced *differences* in personality found for the most part among preliterate societies. We are faced, therefore, with the complex problem of similarity in diversity—that is, with approximately *similar* sentiments arising in widely *different* cultural settings. The problem is made even more complicated by the fact that the same sentiments may, as Shibutani points out, be expressed in quite different ways. The specific expressions are the products of culture, even though apparently motivated by psychological factors (sentiments) that transcend culture.[68] In our own society, for example, persons seek to demonstrate their high status by such symbolic manifestations as large automobiles, swimming pools, and weekend retreats. In other societies, where status is more secure, many persons scorn such ostentatious displays and demonstrate their status by such intangible evidence as intellectual attainment, artistic appreciation, and refinements in manners. The simi-

---

[65] Tamotsu Shibutani, *Society and Personality* (Englewood Cliffs, New Jersey: Prentice-Hall, Inc., 1961), pp. 393-400.

[66] Cooley, *Human Nature and the Social Order, op. cit.*, p. 152.

[67] Ralph Linton, *The Tree of Culture* (New York: Alfred A. Knopf, Inc., 1955), p. 30.

[68] Shibutani, *op. cit.*, pp. 395ff.

larity remains, however, that both groups enjoy the marks of respect from their fellows, even though the expression may be very different.

The "universal developed humanity" of which Redfield speaks may, in the final analysis, reflect the development of the social self. According to this reasoning, the individual learns the universal sentiments in the process of taking the roles of significant others in the primary group. Some form of family, friendship group, and play group appears in all societies and forms the setting in which the individual first learns to take the role of others and, later, of the generalized other. The interpersonal relationships arising about the self may give us the clue to the psychological qualities found in all normal human beings, no matter what their cultural conditioning. As he sees himself through the eyes of others, the individual learns to see them as he himself would like to be seen. He wishes to be loved, nurtured, and respected; at the same time he fears loss of love, deprivation of emotional support, and ridicule by his fellow human beings. These sentiments are all related, more or less intimately, to the social self as seen through the eyes of others. Other sentiments are less clearly related to the self, such as attachment to one's group or a belief in a supernatural power, but the self still is not far distant from the sentiments of patriotism and religion.[69]

It is possible, therefore, that all men have certain sentiments in common, in addition to the genetic qualities which they share because they are all members of the same species. Summarizing the consideration of these similarities is the theory that the "unity of mankind arises not only from the fact that all men are biologically of the same species but also from the fact that certain recurrent patterns of interpersonal relations are inevitable. A common human nature," in short, "becomes discernible in the typical sentiments that are formed as each person develops stable orientations toward his intimate associates." [70] Despite the divisive effect of culture, the similarities between human beings may be more significant than the differences.

In the present chapter, we have explored some of the *communal* and *universal* aspects of personality. The former derive from the culture which the individual shares with other members of his society, whereas the latter *may* arise from the (universal) interpersonal relationships of the primary group. We considered the basic personality type as one approach to the cultural aspect of personality, stressing as it does the similarities in child-rearing within the same society. We also surveyed briefly some of the implications of normality and deviance, as these judgments reflect the cultural setting. Barriers to cultural participation because of impaired communication were also considered. The impact of culture upon personality with respect to the conflicting expectations placed upon the individual was still another concern. We concluded our discussion with a glance at the possibility of a universal "human nature" that is

[69] *Ibid.*, pp. 397-398.
[70] *Ibid.*, p. 401. For further discussion of this question, see Anthony F. C. Wallace, "The Psychic Unity of Human Groups," Ch. 3 in Bert Kaplan (ed.), *Studying Personality Cross-Culturally* (New York: Harper & Row, 1961).

shared by all persons, irrespective of culture. This latter quality may derive from common sentiments and self-attitudes that reflect the participation of all men in the interpersonal relationships of the primary group.

SELECTED BIBLIOGRAPHY

Benedict, Ruth, *Patterns of Culture*. New York: Penguin Books, Inc., 1946. This important and well-written book considers, among other things, the relationships between several primitive cultures and the personality patterns of the people. Different cultures call out different forms of social behavior, so that a response that is "normal" in one society is "abnormal" in another.

Clausen, John A., "The Sociology of Mental Illness," Chapter 22 in Robert K. Merton, Leonard Broom, and Leonard S. Cottrell, Jr. (eds.), *Sociology Today*. New York: Basic Books, Inc., 1959. The sociologist is interested in mental illness from the point of view of the processes that impair the ability of the individual to carry out his various roles. The sociological approach also deals with the way the disorganized person is perceived and treated by the society.

Cloward, Richard A., "Illegitimate Means, *Anomie,* and Deviant Behavior," *American Sociological Review*, 24:164-176 (April, 1959). Much of the deviant behavior in our society reflects the discrepancies between the goals held out by the culture and the approved means of reaching them. This article explores some of the relationships between deviance, goals, and means of access.

Hallowell, A. Irving, "Culture, Personality, and Society," in A. L. Kroeber (ed.), *Anthropology Today*. Chicago: University of Chicago Press, 1953. In this essay, the author presents a critical evaluation of the work in culture and personality carried on by anthropologists, social psychologists, psychiatrists, and others.

Hollingshead, August B., and Frederick C. Redlich, *Social Class and Mental Illness*. New York: John Wiley & Sons, Inc., 1958. This monograph reports on an extremely significant research project at Yale University, dealing with the relationships between social stratification and the incidence, perception, and treatment of mental illness.

Honigmann, John J., *Culture and Personality*. New York: Harper & Row, 1954. This was the first textbook devoted exclusively to the emerging field of culture and personality. The author is an anthropologist and has assembled and organized an impressive body of information from the related fields bearing upon these relationships.

Kohn, Melvin L., "Social Class and Parental Values," *American Journal of Sociology*, 64:337-351 (January, 1959). This study examines the related hypotheses that social classes are "subcultures of the larger society, each with a relatively distinct value-orientation and that values really affect behavior."

Linton, Ralph, *The Cultural Background of Personality*. New York: Appleton-Century-Crofts, Inc., 1945. This little book examines the individual, society, and culture, with particular emphasis upon the emergence of personality from the interaction of these and other variables. Linton develops here many of the insights which he outlined in his earlier work, *The Study of Man* (1936).

Redfield, Robert, "The Universally Human and the Culturally Variable," *Journal of General Education*, 10:150-160 (July, 1957). In this short article, the late Robert Redfield raised a profound question—namely, are there any "universal" personality traits that transcend cultural differences between societies? In this sense, Redfield referred to universal similarities of "sentiment" and not merely those of genetic equipment available to all normally endowed adults the world over.

Singer, Milton, "A Survey of Culture and Personality Theory and Research," Chap. 1 in Bert Kaplan (ed.), *Studying Personality Cross-Culturally*. New York: Harper & Row, 1961. This is an extensive presentation of the developmental trends in the study of culture and personality. The author opens his exposition (p.9) with the following statement: "Until a few years ago the field of culture and personality theory and research was considered an American heresy in anthropology. Today it is no longer a heresy, and in a few more years it will no longer be distinctively American."

Spiro, Melford E., "Social Systems, Personality, and Functional Analysis," Chap. 2 in Bert Kaplan (ed.), *Studying Personality Cross-Culturally* (above). This essay in culture and personality theory devotes itself to the problem of social control—i.e., the process whereby individuals learn the shared cultural assumptions, and thereby behave in accordance with the norms of a society.

Wrong, Dennis, "The Oversocialized Conception of Man in Modern Sociology," *American Sociological Review*, 26:183-193 (April, 1961). This article should be read by every student of culture and personality as a healthy corrective against the erroneous assumption that personality is merely the mirror-image of culture. Wrong calls our attention to the salutary fact that each person has certain anarchistic qualities, reflecting both his genetic impulses and his social training, that make him an *individual*.

SOCIAL

STRUCTURE *Part Three*

11 *Population*

Population and Society

Society is composed of people in interaction, and culture is developed and transmitted by the same process. The two basic concepts of this book thus rest upon population, the elemental raw material of society. The study of population deals with such matters as the number of people, the dynamics of human growth, the birth and death rates, age and sex composition, and social mobility. We cannot consider these matters in detail, but we shall indicate some of the implications of population as they apply to society and culture. Society is directly affected by the growth, composition, and distribution of population. The cultural products of society in interaction are likewise influenced by these same factors.[1]

The central fact of human life is procreation. The extent to which procreation is exercised in a given society is called the *fertility* of the population. This concept is contrasted with *fecundity*, which is the biological ability of the human female to reproduce. These concepts are by no means synonymous, and fecundity is everywhere limited by various factors. Most of these limiting factors are *cultural*, rather than *biological*, and fertility is therefore a reflection of the culture. Among the cultural factors are the state of the technology, the standard of living, the attitudes toward marriage and the family, the value placed upon children, and religious definitions.[2]

Fertility has become of increasing interest to a wide variety of persons in the decades following World War II. Sociologists, government officials, political leaders, social planners, and members of the educated public have recognized the crucial role of fertility. Commenting upon this interest, a leading authority concludes that *"There is an increasing realization that the problematic factor in population growth today is the fertility rate."* [3] International migration is of negligible effect on population growth in most countries. Mortality rates have declined to low levels in some underdeveloped countries and are in the process of decline in many others, as science, medicine, and applied technology have drastically reduced the death rates. But the birth rate remains high in most countries (with the striking exception of Japan), and future rates of growth will increasingly depend upon fertility.[4]

The close relationship between population and society goes back to ancient times. The physical safety—even the survival—of a given tribe or people was directly related to its numbers. Every man was a potential fighter, and the group with the largest number of able-bodied men was in a favorable position in the struggle for survival. The ancient Hebrews provided the most pertinent documentation of this position in the Old Testament. It is no accident that the admonition to be "fruitful and multiply" was part of the doctrine of a people living precariously among hostile nations. Every additional Hebrew was one more man to bear arms or one more woman to bear children.

Certain general relationships between population and social structure emerge. Population affects the structure of the society and vice versa. Among these relationships are the following:[5]

1. Technological factors. There is a close relationship between the stage of technology and the numbers of the population. Such major technological advances as the "invention" of agriculture and the steam engine have played a

---

[1] For an extensive and authoritative study of population, see Philip M. Hauser and Otis Dudley Duncan (eds.), *The Study of Population* (Chicago: The University of Chicago Press, 1959).

[2] Frank Lorimer, *Culture and Human Fertility* (Paris: United Nations Educational, Scientific, and Cultural Organization, 1954).

[3] Ronald Freedman, *The Sociology of Human Fertility* in *Current Sociology*, Vols. 10/11, No. 2 (London: Basil Blackwell), published for UNESCO, 1963, p. 35. (His italics.)

[4] *Ibid.*

[5] The following discussion is freely adapted from Frank Lorimer, "Issues of Population Policy," *Annals of the American Academy of Political and Social Science*, 237:193-203 (January, 1945).

central role in population growth. In general, these advances have meant that a smaller number of people can produce the raw materials necessary to support the rest of the population. A spectacular growth in world population has resulted from technological advancement, although in the advanced industrial countries this growth is slowly leveling off. Both in terms of past development and future trends, technology and population are closely related.[6]

2. *Rural-urban factors.* Large families are characteristic of populations living on farms and under rural conditions. Sons and daughters are economic and social assets, since they provide the free labor of the household economy and serve as symbols of status for the family. When modern sanitation and medicine (technological factors) are introduced to colonial and predominantly rural peoples, the immediate result is a rapid increase in population. High birth rates continue and death rates are drastically reduced. These technological innovations in turn bring about revolutionary changes in the productive relationships and social structure of the formerly undeveloped societies.[7]

3. *Traditional factors.* In societies where social control is still largely vested in the mores, the birth rate is traditionally high and the ideal family is usually a large one. This is the society which Riesman has called "tradition-directed," where the members of the group try to follow exactly in the footsteps of their ancestors, and the perpetuation of the species is virtually synonymous with the perpetuation of group sanctions.[8] In societies of this type, the stage of technological knowledge is low and the death rate is as high as the birth rate. The society is thus engaged in a constant struggle for physical survival.

4. *Secular factors.* The gradual decline in traditional and sacred elements in a society is followed by an increase in the rational and secular elements. Social change is no longer feared and comes to be accepted, first as inevitable and then as desirable.[9] Secular societies often encourage the artificial limitation of population and move toward a stabilization of growth. Among the general characteristics of secular societies are "education, city life, industrial employment, employment of women outside the home in non-agricultural occupations, revolutionary social movements, popular participation in democratic processes, the spread of inventions, and the advance of science." [10]

5. *Planning factors.* A final relationship between population and society is the degree of social planning and the prevailing attitude toward the purposeful direction of human affairs. Control of population growth is one of the most difficult forms of social planning. Cultural and social factors combine to make any deliberate change in reproductive behavior difficult to accomplish. Reproductive behavior is more than a simple individual response to a biological urge; it is deeply imbedded in the culture pattern and cannot be changed without

---

[6] William F. Ogburn and Meyer F. Nimkoff, *Technology and the Changing Family* (Boston: Houghton Mifflin Company, 1955), Chapter 12, "Technology and the Future of the Family."

[7] George A. Theodorson, "Acceptance of Industrialization and Its Attendant Consequences for the Social Patterns of Non-Western Societies," *American Sociological Review,* 18:477-484 (October, 1953).

[8] David Riesman, *et al., The Lonely Crowd* (New Haven: Yale University Press, 1961), Chapter 1.

[9] Howard Becker, "Sacred and Secular Societies," *Social Forces,* 28:361-376 (May, 1950).

[10] Lorimer, "Issues of Population Policy," *op. cit.,* p. 198.

extensive modifications in the pattern. Efforts by governmental or other agencies either to increase or to limit family size have not been notably successful.

Planning in this area is, in final analysis, conducted by families. Knowledge of methods of family limitation is widely disseminated in the United States, although differences continue to exist among religious and racial groups. Most married couples are aware of the desirability (to them) of family planning, as well as the most efficient methods to bring this about. A careful study of behavior in this vital area concluded that: "Family limitation is now almost universally approved and is practiced widely and effectively by the white couples who need it." [11] The American people are coming more and more to share a common set of values about the desirable size of the family (two to four children) and the most effective ways to realize these values.[12]

Population Trends

The growth of population was infinitely slow throughout most of the life of man as a differentiated species. This growth was handicapped by the rudimentary cultural resources of early man. The hundreds of thousands of years of the Paleolithic (Old Stone Age) were marked by small population groups, miserably attempting to wrest a bare living from a hostile environment. The Neolithic Revolution marked the first time that the human species reached a stage in cultural evolution where an increase in population was possible. The discovery of agriculture, the domestication of animals, and the invention of pottery and textiles were among the factors that combined to bring about a greater density of population in the Neolithic (New Stone Age). From that time on, the rate of cultural evolution and the complexity of the culture base slowly increased, giving man a greater control over his environment and a corresponding increase in numbers.[13]

The rate of population growth was still comparatively slow until approximately 300 years ago. In the year 1650, there were perhaps 500,000,000 people in the world, as compared with an estimated 3,200,000,000 in 1962.[14] In the past three centuries, the population of the world has increased approximately six times. The annual rate of growth was greater in the last 150 years than in the first 150 years of this span, with the decade 1950-1960 showing the highest rate of all. In the century 1650 to 1750, the annual rate of growth was about four per 1,000 population; in the century 1750 to 1850, the rate rose to five per 1,000 population; in the century 1850 to 1950, the annual rate increased to eight per 1,000 population.[15]

---

[11] Ronald Freedman, Pascal K. Whelpton, and Arthur A. Campbell, *Family Planning, Sterility, and Population Growth* (New York: McGraw-Hill Book Company, Inc., 1959), p. 401.

[12] *Ibid.*, p. 402.

[13] Kingsley Davis, "The World Demographic Transition," *Annals of the American Academy of Political and Social Science*, 237:1-11 (January, 1945).

[14] Kingsley Davis, "Population," *Scientific American*, 209:63-71 (September, 1963).

[15] Philip M. Hauser, "World Population Trends," *Sociology and Social Research*, 39:73-80 (November-December, 1954), p. 74.

The decade of the 1950's had an estimated annual rate of growth for the world population of 1.8 per cent. This rate is such that it is impossible to sustain it for any prolonged period or, as Kingsley Davis puts it, "for more than a moment of geologic time." [16] Commenting further on the present rate, Davis warns that "If the human population were to continue to grow at the rate of the past decade, within 100 years it would be multiplied sixfold." [17] This growth is occurring at a differential rate as between the nonindustrial ("underdeveloped") nations and the industrial nations. In the period from 1930 to 1960, the population of nonindustrial nations as a class grew approximately *twice as fast* as that of the industrial nations.[18]

The nineteenth and early twentieth centuries saw the rise and expansion of the Industrial Revolution, basic modifications in farming throughout a large part of the world, tremendous improvements in hygiene and sanitation that cut the adult death rate, and great strides in medicine that lowered the infant mortality rate. These and other factors contributed to the above increase in world population, a trend that was hardly slowed by wars, epidemics, and contraception. In the past 150 years, the world has experienced a change in industrial technology, business relationships, agricultural methods, political organization, transportation, and communication such as it had never undergone in all its previous history.[19] One of the accompaniments of this series of events was a rise in population beyond anything before imagined.

This increase led to changes in the social structure of Western Europe and America. The most spectacular single manifestation of this growth was the rise of new cities and the expansion of those already existing. The invention of the steam engine made it possible for millions of persons to live and work in a single urban center. The form and structure of the family underwent a change: more and more persons were crowded into small urban apartments; the number of children decreased and changes occurred in the functions that had formerly been performed by the family. The other institutions began to assume an increasingly urban and secular aspect. The burgeoning of the population that had characterized the first century of industrialization began to slow down. In societies with a fully developed industrial pattern, both the death rate and the birth rate were progressively lowered.[20]

The increase in the population of Western Europe during the eighteenth and nineteenth centuries was accompanied by massive overseas migration. The white man moved in large numbers into sections of the world formerly inhabited solely by other races. This movement intensified consciousness of skin color and other racial differences and, along with other factors, gave rise to the doctrine of *racism*.[21] In their migration to the four corners of the world, the white

---

[16] Davis, *op. cit.*, p. 63.

[17] *Ibid.*

[18] *Ibid.*, p. 68. See also Dudley Kirk, "Dynamics of Human Populations," *Eugenics Quarterly*, 2:18-25 (March, 1955).

[19] Wilbert E. Moore, *Social Change* (Englewood Cliffs, N.J.: Prentice-Hall, Inc., 1963), Chapter 1.

[20] Hauser, *op. cit.*, pp. 76-77.

[21] Ruth Benedict, *Race: Science and Politics* (rev. ed.) (New York: The Viking Press, 1945).

men also brought their advanced technology and superior medical knowledge. This enabled them to bring about a rapid decrease in the death rate of the colonial peoples by improving sanitation, reducing infant mortality, and establishing better transportation.

The Western culture pattern embodying the limitation of fertility through contraception, however, was received with much less enthusiasm by the ancient societies of the Far East. At the present time, about one-third of the human race has some degree of voluntary control over the size of the family. India and China are not among the peoples that exercise this control, and as a result the greatest *absolute* population growth in the proximate future will probably occur in Asia. As one population expert puts it, "The future of the species may well hinge on how rapidly Asians acquire the small-family patterns now adopted in the West . . ." [22] The balance of population growth appears to be shifting from Europe and America to the lands bordering on the western Pacific. The social consequences of this trend are incalculable.

Population in the United States

The history of the United States has been marked by a constant growth of population. The most spectacular increase reflected the millions of immigrants who came to these shores. More important in the long run, however, was the consistent excess of births over deaths. This situation was facilitated by virtually unlimited natural resources of an undeveloped country, where high fertility responded to the atmosphere of abundance.[23] We may examine some of the social and cultural factors that combined to bring about this sustained increase.[24]

1. *Land.* The land was rich, plentiful, and for generations practically free for the taking.

2. *Marriage.* The opportunity for land and economic independence encouraged early marriage.

3. *Family.* Children were an asset on the frontier and continued to be on the farm.

4. *Health.* Farm dwellers were relatively isolated and hence free from many of the infectious and contagious diseases found in the city.

5. *Food.* Famine was never remotely probable in a country with such natural resources.

6. *Religion.* In the early years, the Protestant faith strongly encouraged large families, an attitude heartily seconded by the Roman Catholic faith of the later immigrants.

7. *Philosophy.* The philosophical outlook and general social attitudes of the American people were optimistic, a factor that led to high fertility.

---

[22] Kirk, *op. cit.*, p. 25.

[23] Philip M. Hauser and Conrad Taeuber, "The Changing Population of the United States," *Annals of the American Academy of Political and Social Science*, 237:12-21 (January, 1945).

[24] The following is adapted from Edward B. Reuter, *Population Problems* (Philadelphia: J. B. Lippincott Company, 1937), p. 53.

8. *Immigration.* More than thirty million immigrants, most of them young adults in the most reproductive years, have come to this country since its founding.

9. *Contraception.* Contraceptive information was not widely disseminated until recently, and artificial checks on conception have been lacking.

10. *Residence.* Throughout the nineteenth and early part of the twentieth centuries, the bulk of the population was rural and followed the tendency toward large families that accompanies this way of life.

The growth of the population of the United States was a response to these and related factors. The continued prosperity of this country has been closely tied in with the expansion of the domestic market, uninhibited by trade barriers and other internal restrictions. The size of the population is an important economic consideration for the nation as a whole, as well as for the communities constituting it. Every city vies with every other for the title of "biggest and best," as this increase means higher real estate values, more tax revenue, more voters, and more customers.

Those enterprises that manufacture or distribute automobiles, refrigerators, washing machines, and television sets are especially interested in the number of families, since these and other consumer durable goods are ordinarily sold one to a family. The manufacturers and distributors of food, clothing, and entertainment likewise welcome a large population, since this means greater profits. Business has been geared to an expanding population in the United States and continues to look to this growth to maintain its expansion.

The trends in the growth of population in this country have been spectacular. In the first thirty years of our national existence, from 1790 to 1820, the population increased by approximately 150 per cent. This rate continued during the period from 1820 to 1850. From 1850 to 1880, the rate declined to 116 per cent, and from 1880 to 1910 it declined still further to 80 per cent. The next thirty years, from 1910 to 1940, saw the rate of growth further decrease to 43 per cent.[25] In the decade 1950 to 1960, the population (including Alaska and Hawaii) increased by 19.06 per cent, and in the thirteen-year period from 1950 to 1963 the percentage increase was 24.6 per cent. In the latter period, the numerical increase in the population was approximately 37,206,000 people. These trends are shown in Table 1.[26]

The Birth Rate

The most common measure of the birth rate is the "crude birth rate," that is, the annual number of births per 1,000 of the population. Various refinements have been made upon this concept—notably the number of births per 1,000 married women of childbearing age—but for present purposes the crude birth

---

[25] Warren S. Thompson, *Plenty of People* (New York: The Ronald Press, 1948), pp. 8-9.

[26] Bureau of the Census, *Current Population Reports: Population Estimates*, "Estimates of the Population of the United States, By Age, Color, and Sex: July 1, 1963," Series P-25, No. 276 (November 19, 1963), Table A.

rate is satisfactory. The birth rate depends upon many factors, among them:

1. The marriage rate. The birth rate is directly related to the marriage rate, which in turn is dependent upon a number of technological, economic, and cultural factors.

2. The age composition. The birth rate is also related to the age composition of the population, that is, whether or not it is predominantly a "young" population, with a high proportion of women of childbearing age.

3. The proportion married. This is not synonymous with the marriage rate (above) in any one year, but refers rather to the proportion of women of childbearing age (15-44 years) who are married. A society with a high proportion of married women in this age group will tend to have a higher crude birth rate than one in which a smaller proportion of these women is married.

4. The social climate. The birth rate also reflects a complex group of social, cultural, and psychological factors that might be called the "social climate" of fertility. During the decade of the Depression, this climate was conducive to a low birth rate, especially among the classes with the knowledge and ability to limit conception.[27] In the twenty years from 1940 to 1960, the social climate underwent a striking change in the direction of higher fertility.

Accurate data on the birth rate in the United States have been available only since 1933, when birth registration became effective in all states. Estimates of the birth rate prior to that time were based upon the number of women and children at the successive ten-year censuses. Such data indicate that the crude birth rate began to decline in the nineteenth century, from an estimated 40.0 per 1,000 population early in that century to approximately 30.0 in 1900, culminating in an all-time low point of 16.6 in 1933.[28] A decline in the birth rate is not necessarily synonymous with a decline in population, provided the death

---

[27] The most extensive study of the social climate of fertility was conducted in Indianapolis. See P. K. Whelpton and Clyde V. Kiser (eds.), *Social and Psychological Factors Affecting Fertility* (Four Volumes) (New York: Milbank Memorial Fund, 1946, 1950, 1952, and 1954).

[28] Department of Health, Education, and Welfare, National Office of Vital Statistics, "Annual Summary for 1949: United States, by State," *Monthly Vital Statistics Bulletin,* Volume 12, No. 13 (March 31, 1950).

Table 1.   Changes in the Population, by Age: 1950 to 1963 (Numbers in thousands. Total resident population, including Alaska and Hawaii)

Age	July 1, 1963		April 1, 1960		April 1, 1950	
	Population	Per cent	Population	Per cent	Population	Per cent
All ages	188,531	100.0	179,323	100.0	151,326	100.0
Under 5	20,722	11.0	20,321	11.3	16,243	10.7
5 to 13	34,515	18.3	32,726	18.2	22,281	14.7
14 to 17	13,470	7.1	11,155	6.2	8,443	5.6
18 to 24	17,744	9.4	15,604	8.7	15,926	10.5
25 to 34	22,154	11.8	22,818	12.7	23,878	15.8
35 to 44	24,502	13.0	24,081	13.4	21,535	14.2
45 to 64	37,856	20.1	36,058	20.1	30,724	20.3
65 and over	17,567	9.3	16,560	9.2	12,295	8.1

Source: Bureau of the Census, *Current Population Reports: Population Estimates,* "Estimates of the Population of the United States, By Age, Color, and Sex: July 1, 1963," Series P-25, No. 276 November 19, 1963), Table A.

rate declines more rapidly. This has been the case in the United States, where the population has continued to increase long after the birth rate turned downward, as a result of the continued excess of births over deaths.[29]

In the late 1930's, there was a pronounced upturn in both the business cycle and the marriage rate, shortly followed by an increase in the birth rate, which rose to 18.9 per 1,000 population in 1941. The immediate postwar period saw the rate reach 26.5 in 1947, the highest figure in recent years. In the first half of the decade of the 1950's, the rate hovered about the 25.0 figure. This was followed by a slight decline in the second half of the decade and the early years of the decade of the 1960's. In 1961, the birth rate stood at 23.6 per 1,000 of the population; during this year, some 4,329,000 babies were born.[30] These shifts in the birth rate (shown in Table 2), demonstrate fluctuations in *fertility* in response to social and cultural changes. The *fecundity* of the female population (the biological ability to bear children) obviously underwent no change during this period.

This increased fertility was especially marked among women who were 35-44 years old in the latter part of the 1950's. Many of these women had experienced their years of greatest fertility during the war and postwar years when (as we have just seen) birth rates were high. In 1957, the Bureau of the Census reported that women of this age group (35-44) had already had more children, on the average, than the age group 45-49. This was, the Bureau notes, the first time that an age group still in its reproductive years had borne more children than an age group that had completed its childbearing period. These gains in fertility in the 35-44 age group[31] reflect the tendency of the average woman to

---

[29] P. K. Whelpton and Clyde V. Kiser, "Trends, Determinants, and Control in Human Fertility," *Annals of the American Academy of Political and Social Science*, 237:112-122 (January, 1945).

[30] Bureau of the Census, *Current Population Reports: Population Estimates*, "Estimates of the Population of the United States and Components of Population Change: 1940 to 1962," Series P-25, No. 250 (July 3, 1962), Table A.

[31] Bureau of the Census, *Current Population Reports: Population Characteristics*, "Fertility of the Population: March, 1957," Series P-20, No. 84 (August 8, 1958), Table A.

Change, 1950 to 1963		Change, 1960 to 1963		Change, 1950 to 1960	
Number	Per cent	Number	Per cent	Number	Per cent
+37,206	+24.6	+9,208	+5.1	+27,997	+18.5
+4,479	+27.6	+401	+2.0	+4,078	+25.1
+12,234	+54.9	+1,789	+5.5	+10,445	+46.9
+5,027	+59.5	+2,316	+20.8	+2,712	+32.1
+1,818	+11.4	+2,140	+13.7	−322	−2.0
−1,724	−7.2	−664	−2.9	−1,060	−4.4
+2,967	+13.8	+421	+1.7	+2,546	+11.8
+7,132	+23.2	+1,799	+5.0	+5,334	+17.4
+5,272	+42.9	+1,007	+6.1	+4,265	+34.7

Table 2. Rates of the Components of Population Change: 1940 to 1961
(Rate per 1,000 of the mid-year population, for the population of
the United States including Armed Forces abroad)

Calendar year	Rate of natural increase	Birth rate	Death rate	Net civilian immigration rate
1961	14.3	23.6	9.3	1.9
1960	14.4	23.8	9.4	1.8
1959	14.9	24.3	9.4	1.6
1958	15.0	24.5	9.5	1.7
1957	15.7	25.2	9.5	1.6
1956	15.8	25.1	9.3	2.3
1955	15.6	24.9	9.3	2.0
1954	16.0	25.2	9.1	1.8
1953	15.3	24.9	9.6	1.6
1952	15.4	25.0	9.6	1.5
1951	15.1	24.8	9.7	2.2
1950	14.3	23.9	9.6	2.0
1949	14.8	24.5	9.7	2.2
1948	15.0	24.8	9.9	1.9
1947	16.4	26.5	10.1	1.6
1946	14.2	24.1	9.9	1.1
1945	9.4	20.5	11.0	1.2
1944	9.9	21.3	11.4	1.5
1943	11.8	22.7	10.9	1.1
1942	11.8	22.2	10.4	0.6
1941	9.7	20.3	10.6	0.4
1940	8.6	19.4	10.8	0.6

Source: Bureau of the Census, *Current Population Reports: Population Estimates,* "Estimates of the Population of Change: 1940 to 1962," Series P-25, No. 250 (July 3, 1962), Table A.

have more children, rather than any large rise in the proportion in this age group who are married.

In the year 1957, the entire group of women of childbearing age (15-44) in the United States had borne 22 per cent *more* children, on the average, than women in the same age group in 1950. Measured in terms of the average number of children per 1,000 women, the figure rose from 1,395 in 1950 to 1,696 in 1957 and 1,746 in 1960.[32] There were significant fertility differences in terms of education; women with fewer years of education had more children than women with more years of education. This inverse correlation between education and fertility continued the ratio found in earlier years. In 1957, every 1,000 women with less than six years of formal education had 2,583 children, as compared with 1,335 children for every 1,000 women with 4 years or more of college.[33]

Fertility differentials reflect a variety of factors. The Bureau of the Census has made an ingenious status index comprising: (*a*) education of women, (*b*) occupation of husband, and (*c*) income of husband. These three elements are all indicative of social status, but the combined index gives a more meaningful

[32] Data for 1960 are taken from Bureau of the Census, United States Census of Population, 1960, United States Summary, *General Social and Economic Characteristics,* Final Report, Washington, 1962, Table 81.

[33] Bureau of the Census, *Current Population Reports: Population Characteristics,* "Fertility of the Population: March, 1957," *op. cit.,* Table 4. Other fertility differentials are discussed in Chapter 19, "The Community."

classification than any one of them taken singly. In status 1, the educational criteria were 1 year or more of college or 4 years of high school. The occupation of the husband for this status was professional, technical, managerial, or proprietary. The income was $5,000 or more. The fertility rate of women in status 1 in all three characteristics was approximately two-thirds as high as that for women in status 3 in all three characteristics (0-7 years of elementary school; factory workers, service workers, or laborers; and income under $3,000). In terms of the number of children ever born, each 1,000 women in status 1 in all three characteristics had 2,071 children and those in status 3 had 2,979 children.[34]

The Social Climate of Fertility

The birth rate in the United States is increasingly subject to voluntary restriction by contraception and other means. With control of fertility possible, the birth rate reflects changes in attitudes toward children, as well as other factors that constitute the "social climate" of fertility. In the decades immediately prior to World War II, the social climate favored the restriction of fertility, especially among the middle classes. This climate reflected factors as varied as the growing economic burden of children in urban society and the desire to retain youth and beauty as long as possible. The social climate changed in the period 1940-1960, and the increased fertility of the urban middle classes was a response to this new situation.

The general nature of the social climate affecting fertility has been investigated by Whelpton and Kiser in the Indianapolis study, to which we have previously referred.[35] This study, however, related to the Depression years, when fertility was widely restricted. The "new" social climate of the 1950's and 1960's is the subject of an intensive investigation by Mishler and Westoff, also conducted under the auspices of the Milbank Memorial Fund. This study calls for an examination of the fertility histories of a sample of 1,500 native white women, residing in the 271 counties defined by the Bureau of the Census as being in the Standard Metropolitan Statistical Areas. The basic criterion of the sample is that each woman shall have given birth to a second child approximately six months before the first interview.[36]

The central interest of this study of the social climate of fertility is in the various sociopsychological factors responsible for fertility performance—in the present study, the birth of a third child. These factors have been tentatively classified under three headings:

1. *Person variables.* The first category refers to psychological factors within the parents themselves that reflect their own personality needs. One hypothesis is that "excessive and unsatisfactory needs for emotional support from other

---

[34] *Ibid.,* Table B.
[35] Whelpton and Kiser, *Social and Psychological Factors Affecting Fertility, op. cit.*
[36] Charles F. Westoff, Elliot G. Mishler, Robert G. Potter, Jr., Clyde V. Kiser, "A New Study of American Fertility: Social and Psychological Factors," *Eugenics Quarterly,* 2:229-233 (December, 1955).

persons will tend to be incompatible with desires for additional children."
That is, parents who themselves have strong needs for emotional support will
presumably have comparatively little desire for the additional emotional complications attending a third child. Another hypothesis is that "personal involvement in or identification with an extra-familial social role will tend to be
incompatible with desires for further children." The role of (further) parenthood may be less important if the parents are successful in roles outside the
family, such as the economic or professional.[37]

2. *Family group variables.* This category attempts to discover the relationship between fertility and the structure of the family group itself. For example,
there is the "extent to which the social organization of the family group will be
able to absorb adequately the stresses and strains of an additional child." These
variables include the way husbands and wives share the burdens of family life,
the delegation of responsibility, and the adjustment of the family to its various
problems. The hypothesis is that families with a strong organization will, other
things being equal, have more children than those with a weak organization.[38]

3. *Social setting variables.* The third group of variables thought to be related to fertility performance involves the social setting of the family in a variety of group contexts. This factor includes such considerations as: "(a) the relative benevolence of the environment; (b) the relative stability of the social
settings with which family members are involved; and (c) the degree of control which is available to the family over the type and extent of involvement
with its various social settings." The hypothesis is that families whose members
feel secure in their jobs, their group relationships, their social status, and in the
general "benevolence" of their world will be more fertile than those who view
their environment with apprehension, anxiety, and hostility.[39]

As a result of recent social and cultural changes, a new climate of fertility
seems to be emerging. This climate is marked, as noted, by increasing agreement among all classes of the population on the desirability of a family with
from two to four children. Some difference is still apparent between religious
groups, with Catholics desiring somewhat larger families than Protestants. Religious differences as such, however, appear to be decreasing, as consensus on
family size grows more pronounced. The American people are strongly "famil-
istic" in their values, in the sense that they consider the family (with several
children) as a central value. If this social climate continues and the American
people continue to be strongly oriented toward a family of 2-4 children, the
population will continue to increase rapidly in the proximate future.[40]

---

[37] *Ibid.*, p. 232.
[38] *Ibid.* For an account of the background, samples, design, and methodology of this study, see Charles
F. Westoff, *et al., Family Growth in Metropolitan Areas* (Princeton: Princeton University Press, 1961).
This is the first of two volumes.
[39] *Ibid.*, pp. 232-233. See also Elliot G. Mishler and Charles F. Westoff, "A Proposal for Research on
Social Psychological Factors Affecting Fertility: Concepts and Hypotheses," *Current Research in Human
Fertility* (New York: Milbank Memorial Fund, 1955), pp. 121-150.
[40] Ronald Freedman, Pascal K. Whelpton, and Arthur A. Campbell, *op. cit.,* pp. 401-404.

The Death Rate

The death rate is the other side of the population equation.[41] The death rate measures the extent to which the numbers of the population are subject to the annual attrition of death. The crude death rate is based upon the same conception as the crude birth rate—namely, the number per 1,000 of the population. The crude death rate is also subject to variations reflecting the age composition of the population, with a relatively "old" population tending to have a higher death rate (other things being equal) than a relatively young one. The death rate, furthermore, reflects such factors as sanitation, health, diet, famine, epidemics, and war. Although death must eventually come to all men, the manner and time of its coming are to some extent dependent upon culture and social structure.

Population growth depends upon variations in both birth and death rates. If the birth rate is high, the expected rate of population increase may be cut or even turned into a negative figure by an extremely high death rate. If the birth rate is low, population growth may still occur at a relatively rapid rate, provided the death rate is even lower. Nations that have undergone drastic decreases in the death rate and have maintained high birth rates have increased rapidly in population over a comparatively short time. Such a situation is apparent in India, where the death rate has been sharply cut by Western methods of hygiene and sanitation, but where the mores giving rise to high birth rates have remained comparatively untouched. In many of the countries of western Europe, there was a lag of half a century or more after the death rate had begun to decline before there was any significant decline in the birth rate. Under such conditions, the population increased rapidly.

Throughout most of the history of mankind, the death rate has been very high. A large proportion of all babies died within a few days, weeks, or months of birth. Many of those who survived this earlier period subsequently succumbed to such "childhood" diseases as scarlet fever, measles, and diphtheria. To these "normal" risks of life were added periodic epidemic visitations of bubonic plague, typhus, or pneumonic plague. It is no wonder that historic death rates were high by modern standards. At the beginning of the nineteenth century, the crude death rate in the United States was probably as high as 25.0 per 1,000 of the population, as compared with the current rate of approximately 9.3 per 1,000, which is one of the lowest ever recorded in this country. The difference between a current *death rate* of 9.3 and a *birth rate* of 23.6 (as noted) explains the great increase in population during the postwar decades.

This decrease in the death rate in the Western countries is the result of developments in medical knowledge, economic organization, and transportation that have been greater in the past century than in all previous history com-

---

[41] For a detailed study of this subject, see Harold F. Dorn, "Mortality," Chapter 19 in Hauser and Duncan (eds.), *op. cit.*

bined.[42] The diseases that can be held in check by public health, sanitation, and improved medical knowledge have rapidly decreased in importance as causes of death. Those arising from the degeneration, decline, or decay of the organs of the body have become increasingly important. Medical advancement in certain respects has reduced the death rate almost as far as it can go unless there is an important breakthrough in the treatment of the degenerative diseases.

With the decrease in the death rate has come an increase in longevity. Under conditions of mortality prevailing in 1879-1894, the expectation of life at birth in the United States was only 34.0 years. At the present time, the expectation of life at birth is approximately 70.0 years.[43] In the intervening period, more than 30 years have been added to the expectation of life at birth for the average person. It is important to understand the relationship between the *increase* in longevity and the *decrease* in infant mortality. The rise in life expectancy from 34 to 70 years does not mean that persons in middle and later years are living 36 years longer than they did three-quarters of a century ago. It means that babies born today have a better chance of reaching their "allotted" three-score and ten years because their chances of living through the first years of life are greater.

The reduction in infant mortality reflects such factors as: improvements in prenatal care, increased medical knowledge, better diets, and the growing number of childbirths in hospitals, rather than at home. The first figures in the United States for infant mortality were for 1915; they showed a rate of 99.9 deaths for every 1,000 live births. In other words, one out of ten children failed to live through their first year, with most of them dying in the first weeks. In 1935, this figure had been reduced to 55.7 per 1,000 live births and by 1950 it had fallen to 29.2. In the period since 1950, the rate has declined slightly, but the trend of the decline has leveled off. In the years from 1954-1959, the rate fluctuated between 26.0 and 26.9. In 1960, the last year for which complete data are available, the mortality rate for infants under 1 year stood at 26.0 deaths per 1,000 live births.[44]

The death rate has been affected by technological and industrial changes, in addition to those in the field of health. The latter were made possible in part by the rise in industrial productivity, which increased the standard of living, furnished the resources for public sanitation, and generally made the lot of mankind physically easier. The results of the Industrial Revolution were coupled with those accruing from the agricultural revolution, which increased the yield of crops, added to soil fertility, and improved the number and quality of livestock. Technological factors were also apparent in the increased facilities for transportation and communication, which removed the possibility of fam-

[42] Davis, "Population," *op. cit.*

[43] Department of Health, Education, and Welfare, *Vital Statistics of the United States, 1960*, Vol. II, Section 2, Washington, 1963, Table 2-4.

[44] Department of Health, Education, and Welfare, *Vital Statistics of the United States, 1960*, Vol. II, Section 3, "Infant Mortality," Washington, 1963.

ine in the Western world. The decline in the death rates in the past century gives witness to the tremendous cultural advances in health and well-being.[45]

The conditions characteristic of the countries of western Europe as late as the eighteenth century still prevail throughout large sections of the world. These are the nonindustrialized or "underdeveloped" countries, in which more than a billion people live under conditions of health, hygiene, and transportation that give rise to death rates as high as 30.0 per 1,000 of the population.[46] In India, these conditions are already in the process of change, whereas in China improvements are still in an embryonic state. In the latter country, as in many other underdeveloped countries, a decrease in the death rate would shortly introduce a rapid increase in population, unless this decrease were accompanied by a corresponding decrease in the birth rate. Such a decrease in fertility in China appears unlikely at the present time.

Composition of the Population

The composition of the population refers to the different elements constituting the body of the people. As stated by Hawley, the term "composition" calls attention to "the existence of various internal differentials which influence the comparability of populations or of demographic phenomena. Strictly speaking," he continues, "composition refers to the distribution within a population of one or more individually carried traits or attributes." [47] Among these "traits" or "attributes" are age, sex, race, and marital status. We shall consider the population of the United States in terms of these four categories.

1. Age. We have already mentioned an important aspect of the age composition of the population—the fact that the American people are growing older. In 1850, 52.5 per cent of the people were under 20, as compared with 34.4 per cent in 1940. At the other end of the life cycle, the America of 1850 had only 2.6 per cent of its population over 65; in 1940, 6.8 per cent were in this category; and in 1962 the percentage had increased to 9.3.[48] The large number of births during the 1950's kept the percentage of old people in the population from increasing still further. In a little more than a century, the United States thus changed from a young nation to one increasingly middle-aged. The median age of the population rose from 22.9 years in 1900 to 28.6 years in 1963. (See Table 3.) This means that approximately half of the people were younger than 28.6 years in 1963 and half were older, with the median at the mid-point of the curve.[49] The numerical composition of the population by age, sex, and color on July 1, 1963 is shown in Table 4.

---

[45] Davis, "Population," *op. cit.*

[46] Cf. Leo F. Schnore, "Social Problems in the Underdeveloped Areas: An Ecological View," *Social Problems,* 8:182-201 (Winter, 1960-1961).

[47] Amos H. Hawley, "Population Composition," Chapter 16 in Hauser and Duncan (eds.), *op cit.,* p. 361.

[48] Bureau of the Census, *Current Population Reports: Population Estimates,* "Estimates of the Population of the United States, By Age, Color, and Sex: July 1, 1950 to 1962," *op. cit.,* Table A.

[49] *Ibid.,* Table D.

Table 3. Median Age of the Population: 1900 to 1963 (As of July 1, except as noted: Total resident population)

Year	Age (years)	Year	Age (years)
United States:		Conterminous United States (Cont.)	
1963	28.6	1954	30.4
1962	28.9	1953	30.5
1961	29.2	1952	30.5
1960 (April 1)	29.5	1951	30.4
		1950 (April 1)	30.2
Conterminous United States:			
1959	29.7	1940 (April 1)	29.0
1958	29.9	1930 (April 1)	26.5
1957	30.1	1920 (Jan. 1)	25.3
1956	30.3	1910 (April 15)	24.1
1955	30.3	1900 (June 1)	22.9

Source: Bureau of the Census, *Current Population Reports: Population Estimates*, "Estimates of the Population of the United States, By Age, Color, and Sex: July 1, 1963," *op. cit.*, Table D.

The aging of the population presents grave problems in the form of increasing needs for old-age security, medical care, and the like. The United States Public Health Service recently outlined some of the health problems of this age group. The proportion of persons over 65 with chronic illness (for example, heart disease, cancer, arthritis, and diabetes) is approximately twice as high as that of persons under 65 (77 per cent versus 38 per cent). Stated somewhat differently, although persons over 65 constitute only 9.3 per cent of the population, they constitute more than 55 per cent of those with limitations arising from chronic illness. The financial aspects of this problem are likewise acute. An estimated 82 per cent of persons over 65 with family incomes of less than $2,000 have limitations due to chronic illness.[50]

[50] U.S. Government Printing Office, *Basic Facts on the Health and Economic Status of Older Americans,* A Staff Report to the Special Committee on Aging, United States Senate, Washington, 1961, p. 1.

The aging of the population presents increasing needs for old-age security, medical care, and adequate housing.

The burgeoning contingents of young people, at the other end of the age scale, generate problems of a different sort. The babies born after World War II are now in their late teens. The number of young people reaching the age of 18 was about 2,750,000 in 1961, and at that time was expected to reach 3,750,-000 by the mid-1960's (specifically, in 1965), as the babies born in 1947 came of college age.[51] The facilities for college and university education are today being taxed to accommodate what in some schools is an overload of students— in most, capacity attendance—and this situation will continue into the decade of the 1970's.[52] This latter assertion can be made with assurance, inasmuch as these young people are already born and very much in evidence. Predictions concerning the number of persons reaching college age by the early 1980's are subject to greater error, since many of them are still to be born. We do not know whether the social climate will be as favorable to fertility during the latter half of the decade of the 1960's as it was from 1945 to 1965.

The population has thus been growing at a disproportionate rate at both ends of the age spectrum. A higher proportion of the population is under 18 *and* over 65 (combined) than ever before. These persons are, broadly speaking, wholly or partially dependent upon those in the "productive" years—that is, from 18 to 64 years of age. A measure of this situation is known as the "dependency ratio"—that is, the number of "dependents" under 18 *and* over 65 for every 100 persons 18 to 64 years of age. In 1963, this ratio was 84, as compared with 64 in 1950 and 60 in 1940. In other words, for every 100 persons in the "productive" years in 1963, there were 84 "dependents," an increase from 60 only 23 years before. In both economic and social terms, these trends in age composition have far-reaching implications for this country.[53]

2. *Sex.* The sex composition of the United States was, until 1950, marked by a slight excess of males over females. In 1900, the sex ratio was 104.4 males per 100 females; by 1950, it had declined to 98.6. By 1963, the ratio had shrunk still further to 96.6 males per 100 females. These trends are shown in Table 5. The principal factors in this long-term trend were as follows: (*a*) the decline in immigration, which in its heaviest period during the early part of the present century was preponderantly male; (*b*) the higher mortality rates for men than for women; and (*c*) the increase in the size of the peacetime armed forces during the decade of the 1950's. The average age of females is also considerably higher than that of males; the median age for females in 1963 was 29.7 years, as compared with 27.4 years for males.[54] This disparity reflects the greater life expectancy of women and their predominance in the older age brackets.

3. *Race.* The nonwhite population of the United States is composed largely of Negroes. A number of persons of Mexican descent are also included in this

[51] Ewan Clague, "Demographic Trends and Their Significance," in *The Changing American Population*, A Report of the Arden House Conference, published by Institute of Life Insurance, New York, 1962, p. 13.
[52] Joseph S. Davis, "Implications of Prospective United States Population Growth in the 1960's," *Milbank Memorial Fund Quarterly*, 39:329-349 (April, 1961).
[53] Bureau of the Census, *Current Population Reports: Population Estimates*, "Estimates of the Population of the United States, By Age, Color, and Sex: July 1, 1963," *op. cit.*, p. 2.
[54] *Ibid.*

Table 4. Estimates of the Total Population of the United States including Armed Forces Abroad, by Age, Color, and Sex, July 1, 1963*

Date and age	All classes			White			Nonwhite		
	Total	Male	Female	Total	Male	Female	Total	Male	Female
All ages	189,278,000	93,369,000	95,909,000	167,134,000	82,593,000	84,542,000	22,144,000	10,777,000	11,367,000
Under 5	20,722,000	10,554,000	10,168,000	17,542,000	8,961,000	8,581,000	3,180,000	1,593,000	1,587,000
5 to 9	20,012,000	10,171,000	9,841,000	17,153,000	8,742,000	8,411,000	2,859,000	1,429,000	1,429,000
10 to 14	18,000,000	9,153,000	8,848,000	15,540,000	7,922,000	7,619,000	2,460,000	1,231,000	1,229,000
15 to 19	15,536,000	7,872,000	7,664,000	13,631,000	6,922,000	6,709,000	1,905,000	950,000	955,000
20 to 24	12,600,000	6,315,000	6,285,000	11,096,000	5,582,000	5,514,000	1,503,000	733,000	771,000
25 to 29	10,971,000	5,449,000	5,522,000	9,649,000	4,826,000	4,823,000	1,322,000	623,000	699,000
30 to 34	11,385,000	5,625,000	5,760,000	10,043,000	5,002,000	5,041,000	1,343,000	623,000	719,000
35 to 39	12,343,000	6,054,000	6,289,000	10,983,000	5,422,000	5,561,000	1,360,000	632,000	728,000
40 to 44	12,261,000	5,989,000	6,272,000	10,989,000	5,387,000	5,602,000	1,271,000	602,000	670,000
45 to 49	11,234,000	5,501,000	5,733,000	10,119,000	4,970,000	5,148,000	1,115,000	530,000	585,000
50 to 54	10,255,000	5,018,000	5,237,000	9,262,000	4,538,000	4,724,000	993,000	480,000	513,000
55 to 59	8,866,000	4,307,000	4,558,000	8,046,000	3,906,000	4,141,000	819,000	402,000	418,000
60 to 64	7,528,000	3,585,000	3,943,000	6,860,000	3,259,000	3,601,000	668,000	327,000	341,000
65 to 69	6,242,000	2,866,000	3,376,000	5,756,000	2,638,000	3,118,000	486,000	228,000	258,000
70 to 74	5,093,000	2,284,000	2,809,000	4,695,000	2,101,000	2,594,000	399,000	184,000	215,000
75 to 79	3,404,000	1,486,000	1,918,000	3,162,000	1,373,000	1,789,000	242,000	113,000	129,000
80 to 84	1,826,000	756,000	1,070,000	1,687,000	692,000	995,000	139,000	64,000	75,000
85 and over	1,002,000	385,000	617,000	922,000	351,000	571,000	80,000	34,000	46,000
Under 1	4,075,000	2,080,000	1,995,000	3,423,000	1,752,000	1,671,000	652,000	328,000	324,000
1 to 4	16,647,000	8,474,000	8,173,000	14,118,000	7,209,000	6,910,000	2,529,000	1,265,000	1,264,000
5 to 13	34,515,000	17,547,000	16,968,000	29,662,000	15,120,000	14,542,000	4,853,000	2,427,000	2,426,000
14 to 17	13,480,000	6,843,000	6,637,000	11,798,000	6,003,000	5,796,000	1,681,000	840,000	841,000
18 to 21	11,129,000	5,615,000	5,514,000	9,783,000	4,946,000	4,837,000	1,345,000	669,000	677,000
14 and over	134,041,000	65,268,000	68,773,000	119,930,000	58,512,000	61,419,000	14,111,000	6,757,000	7,354,000
18 and over	120,561,000	58,425,000	62,136,000	108,132,000	52,509,000	55,623,000	12,429,000	5,916,000	6,513,000
21 and over	112,059,000	54,134,000	57,926,000	100,660,000	48,730,000	51,931,000	11,399,000	5,404,000	5,995,000
65 and over	17,567,000	7,777,000	9,790,000	16,221,000	7,155,000	9,066,000	1,346,000	622,000	724,000
Median age	28.5	27.4	29.7	29.5	28.3	30.6	22.2	21.3	23.1

* Figures represent the sum of the total resident population and Armed Forces stationed outside the United States. Figures have been rounded to the nearest thousand; hence, the sum of parts may differ slightly from the totals shown. Medians are based on the unrounded figures.

Source: Bureau of the Census, *Current Population Reports: Population Estimates*, "Estimates of the Population of the United States, By Age, Color, and Sex, July 1, 1963," *op. cit.*, Table 1.

Table 5. Sex Ratio of the Population, by Age: 1940 to 1963 (As of July 1, except as noted. Males per 100 females. Total resident population)

Year	All ages	Under 15 years	15 to 24 years	25 to 44 years	45 to 64 years	65 and over
United States:						
1963	96.6	103.5	98.7	95.7	94.4	79.4
1962	96.7	103.5	98.4	95.6	94.8	80.6
1961	96.9	103.5	98.4	95.7	95.2	81.6
1960 (April 1)	97.1	103.4	98.3	95.7	95.7	82.8
Conterminous United States:						
1958	97.2	103.5	97.3	95.5	96.2	84.4
1956	97.3	103.5	96.0	95.4	97.0	86.2
1954	97.2	103.5	93.7	95.1	97.9	87.6
1952	97.4	103.6	93.1	95.2	98.9	88.7
1950 (April 1)	98.6	103.7	97.6	96.4	100.0	89.7
1940 (April 1)	100.7	103.0	98.5	98.5	105.2	95.5

Source: Bureau of the Census, *Current Population Reports: Population Estimates*, "Estimates of the Population of the United States, By Age, Color, and Sex: July 1, 1963," *op. cit.*, Table F.

category, as well as small groups of American Indians, Chinese, Japanese, Filipinos, Puerto Ricans, and miscellaneous categories. On July 1, 1963, the white population numbered 166,454,000 and the nonwhite 22,078,000. In terms of percentages, the white population constituted 88.3 per cent of the total and the nonwhite 11.7 per cent. For a number of years, the nonwhite population made up about 10.0 per cent of the total, but in recent years it has increased somewhat more rapidly than the white. From 1950 to 1963, the nonwhite population grew by 42.0 per cent, whereas the white population increased by only 26.0 per cent. These differentials of growth were especially marked for the youngest age groups. Recent trends in these categories are shown in Table 6.[55]

The over-all proportion of nonwhites has, however, *decreased* since the first census was taken in 1790. At that time, Negroes numbered an estimated 19.3 per cent of the total population (compared with 11.7 per cent of nonwhites in 1963). Since the first census, both racial groups have increased rapidly in numbers but, until recently, the *rate* of increase was lower for Negroes than for whites. The natural increase of the white population was, moreover, heavily supplemented by immigration, whereas the immigration of Negroes has been negligible since the Civil War. The Negro population remains heavily concentrated in the South, but the *relative* concentration is changing as a result of Negro migration to the big northern cities.

4. Marital status. A final aspect of population composition is marital status. We shall examine the social and cultural implications of marriage in Chapter 18 in connection with our discussion of the family as a social institution. We are concerned here with the demographic aspects of marital status. In 1962, the male population 14 years of age and over had the following marital statuses: 25.3 per cent were single; 69.2 per cent were married; 3.4 per cent were widowed; and 2.1 per cent were divorced. Of the total number of males over 14

[55] Bureau of the Census, *Current Population Reports: Population Estimates*, "Estimates of the Population of the United States, By Age, Color, and Sex: July 1, 1963," *op. cit.*, Table H.

years of age, some 74.7 per cent had *ever* married; of this group, 63.6 per cent had married once and 11.1 per cent had married more than once. In the same year, the comparable figures for women were as follows: 19.6 per cent were single; 65.3 per cent were married; 12.5 per cent were widowed; and 2.7 per cent were divorced. Of the total number of females over 14 years of age, 80.4 per cent had *ever* married; of this group, 68.8 per cent had married once and 11.7 per cent more than once. These relationships are shown in Table 7.[56]

The marriage state is highly popular with the American people and has grown steadily more so in recent decades. In 1890, 61.2 per cent of the males 14 years of age and over and 59.4 per cent of the females were married.[57] These percentages may be compared with the aforementioned 69.2 per cent of the males and 65.3 per cent of the females in 1962 who were married. Among the factors bringing about this relative increase in marriage for both men and women were: (*a*) the decreasing age of first marriage; (*b*) the increasing proportion of the population that *ever* marries; and (*c*) the growing proportion of persons who marry after widowhood or divorce. Despite the gloomy pronouncements of many amateur critics, marriage apparently is here to stay.

Distribution of the Population

The distribution of the population refers to the physical location of the people, including the manner in which they got there. We shall briefly examine the distribution of the population of the United States in terms of: (*a*) regional distribution; (*b*) rural-urban distribution; and (*c*) recent trends in internal migration. The final category refers to the process whereby the distribution of population is continually modified and new patterns of concentration are set up.

---

[56] Bureau of the Census, *Current Population Reports: Population Characteristics,* "Marital Status and Family Status: March, 1962," Series P-20, No. 122 (March 22, 1963), Table 1.

[57] Bureau of the Census, *Current Population Reports: Population Characteristics,* "Marital Status and Family Status: March, 1959," Series P-20, No. 96 (November 23, 1959), Table B.

Table 6. Changes in the White and Nonwhite Population, by Age: 1963 to 1960 (Numbers in thousands. Total resident population)

| | White | | | | | |
| | July 1, 1963 | | April 1, 1960 | | Change, 1960 to 1963 | |
Age	Population	Per cent	Population	Per cent	Number	Per c
All ages	166,454	100.0	158,832	100.0	+7,622	+4
Under 5	17,542	10.5	17,359	10.9	+183	+1
5 to 13	29,662	17.8	28,341	17.8	+1,321	+4
14 to 17	11,790	7.1	9,779	6.2	+2,011	+20
18 to 24	15,588	9.4	13,686	8.6	+1,903	+13
25 to 34	19,509	11.7	20,144	12.7	−635	−3
35 to 44	21,879	13.1	21,564	13.6	+315	+1
45 to 64	34,263	20.6	32,656	20.6	+1,607	+4
65 and over	16,221	9.7	15,304	9.6	+917	+6

Source: Bureau of the Census, *Current Population Reports: Population Estimates,* "Estimates of the Population of the United States, By Age, Color, and Sex: July 1, 1963," *op. cit.,* Table H.

1. Regional distribution. The nation is divided by the Bureau of the Census into four regions: the Northeast; the North Central; the South; and the West. The Northeast region includes New England and the Middle Atlantic divisions; the North Central region is divided into East North Central and West North Central; the Southern region is divided into South Atlantic, East South Central, and West South Central; and the Western region is composed of the Mountain and Pacific divisions. A recent estimate (1962) by the Bureau of the Census indicated the following population distribution; the Northeast had an estimated 45,914,000 people; the North Central had 52,415,000; the South had 57,299,000; and the West 30,194,000. The total population of the United States at the time of this estimate was 185,822,000.[58]

2. Rural-urban distribution. The United States is steadily becoming more urbanized, and the percentage of the population living on farms is decreasing. In 1870, only 25.7 per cent of the population was listed as urban and 74.3 per cent as rural. In 1940, some 56.5 per cent was classified as urban (living in places, of 2,500 or more residents, incorporated as cities, boroughs, or villages); 20.5 per cent as rural-nonfarm (living in rural areas but not actually on farms); and 22.9 per cent as rural-farm (living on farms).[59] By the end of the decade of the 1950's, only 12.0 per cent of the population was listed as rural-farm, according to this definition. This represented 21,172,000 persons out of a total population of 176,264,000 as the country entered the 1960's.[60]

Migration from the farm to the city was especially pronounced in the 1940's

[58] Bureau of the Census, *Current Population Reports: Population Estimates,* "Estimates of the Population of States and Selected Outlying Areas: July 1, 1962," Series P-25, No. 272 (September 20, 1963), Table 1.

[59] Bureau of the Census, *Current Population Reports: Population Characteristics,* "Internal Migration in the United States: April, 1947 to April, 1948," Series P-20, No. 22 (January 28, 1949).

[60] Bureau of the Census, *Farm Population,* "Estimates of the Farm Population of the United States: April, 1950 to 1959," Series Census-AMS (P-27) (December 28, 1959), Table 1.

| Nonwhite | | | | | |
| July 1, 1963 | | April 1, 1960 | | Change, 1960 to 1963 | |
Population	Per cent	Population	Per cent	Number	Per cent
22,078	100.0	20,491	100.0	+1,586	+7.7
3,180	14.4	2,962	14.5	+218	+7.4
4,853	22.0	4,385	21.4	+468	+10.7
1,681	7.6	1,376	6.7	+305	+22.1
2,156	9.8	1,919	9.4	+237	+12.4
2,645	12.0	2,674	13.0	−28	−1.1
2,623	11.9	2,517	12.3	+106	+4.2
3,593	16.3	3,402	16.6	+191	+5.6
1,346	6.1	1,256	6.1	+90	+7.2

Table 7. Marital Status by Age and Sex, for the United States, Civilian Population, March 1962 (Numbers in thousands.) *

Year, marital status, and sex	Total, 14 years and over	14 to 19 years Total	14 to 17	18 and 19	20 to 24 years	25 to 29 years	30 to 34 years	35 to 44 years	45 to 54 years	55 to 64 years	65 to 74 years	75 and over
MALE												
Total	62,129	8,750	6,308	2,442	5,096	5,162	5,600	11,764	10,317	7,730	5,154	2,556
Single	15,708	8,489	6,274	2,215	2,669	1,103	573	992	799	596	308	179
Married	43,019	253	33	220	2,393	3,965	4,868	10,444	8,936	6,539	4,104	1,517
Wife present	41,218	231	24	207	2,260	3,802	4,706	10,024	8,547	6,236	3,979	1,433
Husband married once	35,323	231	24	207	2,214	3,559	4,250	8,725	7,131	5,027	3,080	1,106
Wife absent	1,801	22	9	13	133	163	162	420	389	303	125	84
Separated	1,004	6		6	78	101	92	239	231	155	69	33
Other	797	16	9	7	55	62	70	181	158	148	56	51
Widowed	2,128	8				8	15	73	207	357	639	829
Divorced	1,274		1	7	34	86	144	255	375	238	103	31
Ever married	46,421	261	34	227	2,427	4,059	5,027	10,772	9,518	7,134	4,846	2,377
Married once	39,541	261	34	227	2,378	3,789	4,535	9,312	7,859	5,695	3,814	1,898
Married more than once	6,880				49	270	492	1,460	1,659	1,439	1,032	479
Per cent												
Total	100.0	100.0	100.0	100.0	100.0	100.0	100.0	100.0	100.0	100.0	100.0	100.0
Single	25.3	97.0	99.5	90.7	52.4	21.4	10.2	8.4	7.7	7.7	6.0	7.0
Married	69.2	2.9	0.5	9.0	47.0	76.8	86.9	88.8	86.6	84.6	79.6	59.4
Wife present	66.3	2.6	0.4	8.5	44.3	73.7	84.0	85.2	82.8	80.7	77.2	56.1
Husband married once	56.9	2.6	0.4	8.5	43.4	68.9	75.9	74.2	69.1	65.0	59.8	43.3
Wife absent	2.9	0.3	0.1	0.5	2.6	3.2	2.9	3.6	3.8	3.9	2.4	3.3
Separated	1.6	0.1		0.2	1.5	2.0	1.6	2.0	2.2	2.0	1.3	1.3
Other	1.3	0.2	0.1	0.3	1.1	1.2	1.2	1.5	1.5	1.9	1.2	2.0
Widowed	3.4					0.2	0.3	0.6	2.0	4.6	12.4	32.4
Divorced	2.1	0.1		0.3	0.7	1.7	2.6	2.2	3.6	3.1	2.0	1.2
Ever married	74.7	3.0	0.5	9.3	47.6	78.6	89.8	91.6	92.3	92.3	94.0	93.0
Married once	63.6	3.0	0.5	9.3	46.7	73.4	81.0	79.2	76.2	73.7	74.0	74.3
Married more than once	11.1				1.0	5.2	8.8	12.4	16.1	18.6	20.0	18.7

Year, marital status, and sex	Total, 14 years and over	14 to 19 years			20 to 24 years	25 to 29 years	30 to 34 years	35 to 44 years	45 to 54 years	55 to 64 years	65 to 74 years	75 and over
		Total	14 to 17	18 and 19								
FEMALE												
Total	67,166	8,916	6,157	2,759	5,869	5,484	5,884	12,477	10,729	8,287	6,076	3,444
Single	13,134	7,843	5,924	1,919	1,717	535	443	660	691	564	441	240
Married	43,846	1,052	233	819	4,038	4,750	5,151	11,006	8,626	5,573	2,935	715
Husband present	41,218	920	193	727	3,726	4,436	4,833	10,391	8,192	5,289	2,761	670
Wife married once	35,791	909	191	718	3,557	4,112	4,308	8,922	6,792	4,367	2,275	549
Husband absent	2,628	132	40	92	312	314	318	615	434	284	174	45
Husband in Armed Forces	299	55	5	50	92	55	36	50	6	5		
Separated	1,433	42	15	27	139	175	190	382	279	127	80	19
Other	896	35	20	15	81	84	92	183	149	152	94	26
Widowed	8,399	7		7	15	32	76	352	974	1,872	2,605	2,466
Divorced	1,787	14		14	99	167	214	459	438	278	95	23
Ever married	54,032	1,073	233	840	4,152	4,949	5,441	11,817	10,038	7,723	5,635	3,204
Married once	46,191	1,062	231	831	3,958	4,550	4,802	10,021	8,206	6,302	4,621	2,669
Married more than once	7,841	11	2	9	194	399	639	1,796	1,832	1,421	1,014	535
Per cent												
Total	100.0	100.0	100.0	100.0	100.0	100.0	100.0	100.0	100.0	100.0	100.0	100.0
Single	19.6	88.0	96.2	69.6	29.3	9.8	7.5	5.3	6.4	6.8	7.3	7.0
Married	65.3	11.8	3.8	29.7	68.8	86.6	87.5	88.2	80.4	67.2	48.3	20.8
Husband present	61.4	10.3	3.1	26.4	63.5	80.9	82.1	83.3	76.4	63.8	45.4	19.5
Wife married once	53.3	10.2	3.1	26.0	60.6	75.0	73.2	71.5	63.3	52.7	37.4	15.9
Husband absent	3.9	1.5	0.6	3.3	5.3	5.7	5.4	4.9	4.0	3.4	2.9	1.3
Husband in Armed Forces	0.4	0.6	0.1	1.8	1.6	1.0	0.6	0.4	0.1	0.1		
Separated	2.1	0.5	0.2	1.0	2.4	3.2	3.2	3.1	2.6	1.5	1.3	0.6
Other	1.3	0.4	0.3	0.5	1.4	1.5	1.6	1.5	1.4	1.8	1.5	0.8
Widowed	12.5	0.1		0.3	0.3	0.6	1.3	2.8	9.1	22.6	42.9	71.6
Divorced	2.7	0.2		0.5	1.7	3.0	3.6	3.7	4.1	3.4	1.6	0.7
Ever married	80.4	12.0	3.8	30.4	70.7	90.2	92.5	94.7	93.6	93.2	92.7	93.0
Married once	68.8	11.9	3.8	30.1	67.4	83.0	81.6	80.3	76.5	76.0	76.1	77.5
Married more than once	11.7	0.1		0.3	3.3	7.3	10.9	14.4	17.1	17.1	16.7	15.5

Source: Bureau of the Census, *Current Population Reports: Population Characteristics,* "Marital Status and Family Status: March 1962," Series P-20, No. 122 (March 22, 1963), Table 1.

* In this report, the "civilian population" includes about 978,000 members of the Armed Forces in 1962 and 547,000 in 1950 living off post or with their families on post but excludes all other members of the Armed Forces. In reports in Series P-25, the civilian population excludes all members of the Armed Forces. Per cent not shown where less than 0.1.

and 1950's. In the period from 1950 to 1959, the farm population decreased from 16.6 per cent of the total population to 12.0 per cent, as noted. Over a longer period, the farm population has decreased in even more spectacular fashion. In 1910, one out of every three persons lived on a farm; in 1950, this ratio was one out of six; and by 1959 it had fallen to one out of eight. The latter figure includes all those persons who were still listed in 1959 as farm residents (see below), even though some earned their living in other ways.[61]

In the Census of 1960, the definition of the farm population was modified to include *only* those persons living on farms and actually working them as such. Specifically, after 1960 the farm population consists of "all persons living in rural territory on places of 10 or more acres if as much as $50 worth of agricultural products were sold from the place in the reporting year." [62] This rigorous definition excludes several million persons formerly enumerated as living on "farms," but whose principal source of livelihood was elsewhere. In terms of the new definition, the farm population is thus reduced still further. In 1962, the farm population totaled 14,313,000 persons or only 7.7 per cent of the population of 185,937,000. These data are shown in detail in Table 8.[63]

This movement from the land has been brought about by a number of related factors. Among these were: (*a*) developments in technology, whereby per cap-

---

[61] *Ibid.*
[62] Bureau of the Census — Department of Agriculture, *Farm Population*, "Estimates of the Farm Population of the U.S.: April, 1962," Series Census-ERS (P-27), No. 33 (March 14, 1963), P. 4.
[63] *Ibid.*, Table 1.

Table 8. Population of the United States, Including Armed Forces Overseas, and Farm Population: April 1950 to 1962 (Numbers in thousands)

Farm population definition and year	Total population including Armed Forces overseas	Farm population	
		Number of persons [a]	Per cent of total population
New definition:			
1962	185,937 [b]	14,313 [c]	7.7
1961	183,025 [b]	14,803 [c]	8.1
1960	180,007 [b]	15,635 [c]	8.7
Old definition:			
1960	180,007 [b]	20,541 [b]	11.4
1959	176,358	21,172	12.0
1958	173,367	21,388	12.3
1957	170,496	21,606	12.7
1956	167,509	22,362	13.3
1955	164,607	22,438	13.6
1954	161,761	22,099	13.7
1953	159,012	22,679	14.3
1952	156,421	24,283	15.5
1951	153,691	24,160	15.7
1950	151,132	25,058	16.6

[a] April-centered annual averages, except for 1950.
[b] Includes Alaska and Hawaii.
[c] Rural farm population; includes Alaska and Hawaii.

Source: Bureau of the Census, Department of Agriculture, *Farm Population*, "Estimates of the Farm Population of the United States: April 1962," Series Census-ERS (P-27), No. 33 (March 14, 1963), Table 1.

ita agricultural production has increased; (*b*) greater economic opportunity in the cities; (*c*) dissatisfaction with life in the village and open country. Young people migrate to the city in search of jobs, adventure, and love—not necessarily in that order. This is especially true of young women, for the farm lacks the opportunities for its daughters that it offers to its sons. In the city, girls find jobs as stenographers, secretaries, clerks, and personal service operatives, and in light manufacturing. Most of them are (consciously or unconsciously) also looking for a husband, although their statistical chances of finding one are less in the city than on the farm. The nonfarm population has only about 93 males for every 100 females; on the farm, there are about 108 males for every 100 females (1962).[64]

The racial composition of the rural population is also significant. Of the 14,313,000 rural-farm persons, 2,148,000 were listed as nonwhite and 12,165,-000 as white. In percentage terms, this means 15.0 per cent of. the rural-farm population is nonwhite and 85.0 per cent white. The nonwhite rural population is a young population. An estimated 43 per cent of this group is under 14 years of age, as compared with 28 per cent in the same age group among the white rural population.[65] This disparity reflects the higher fertility rate of nonwhites in recent years. The proportion of the nonwhite population under 14 years of age in the nation as a whole increased by 61 per cent from 1950 to 1962, as compared with an increase of 39 per cent in the same age group among the white. This increase in nonwhite fertility—both rural and urban—makes for a disproportionately high ratio of dependent children among this population.[66]

3. *Internal migration.* The distribution of the population is partially determined by internal migration, which is also called horizontal (as distinguished from vertical) mobility. People move about for various reasons and in response to a number of factors. Among these factors are: levels of employment in different parts of the country, differentials in wages and living standards, and such noneconomic factors as climate and legend, as in the case of California and Florida.[67] Factors relating to employment, however, are perhaps the most important single element in mobility. During the depression of the 1930's, internal migration reflected the search for *any job at all*, whereas during World War II and the postwar decades millions of people moved in search of *better jobs*. Whatever the motives, the three decades of social change from 1930 to 1960 brought an unprecedented shift in the distribution of the population.

Social mobility is an important characteristic of a dynamic society. This process is discussed at length elsewhere in this book, notably in Chapter 19 (The Community) and Chapter 20 (Human Ecology). We are concerned here with

[64] *Ibid.,* p. 2.

[65] *Ibid.*

[66] Bureau of the Census, *Current Population Reports: Population Estimates,* "Estimates of the Population of the United States, By Age, Color, and Sex: July 1, 1950 to 1962," *op. cit.,* p. 4.

[67] Charles T. Stewart, Jr., "Migration, Population, and Distance," *American Sociological Review,* 25:347-356 (June, 1960).

the general trends in social mobility and with its regional implications for the distribution of the population. The most important *single* generalization about internal migration in the United States is that approximately one out of every five (20.0 per cent) of all persons over 1 year old moves at least once every year. This over-all percentage has remained virtually constant in recent years. Mobile persons are defined as those "who were living in a different house in the United States at the end of the period [of a year] than at the beginning of the period." [68] In round numbers, approximately 35 million persons were in this mobile category in a recent year.[69]

The regional differences in mobility follow the same general pattern as other aspects of population distribution. That is, the highest mobility was found in the West, where 28.1 per cent of the population reported one or more moves. The South was next, with a mobility rate of 22.3 per cent. The North Central region was next with 18.2 per cent, and the Northeast was last with a mobility rate of 14.0 per cent. On balance, the Northeast, the North Central, and the South (in that order) are all losing population by out-migration, with more people leaving each of these regions than entering them every year. The West continues to be a heavy gainer through in-migration. In the period from 1953 to 1961, the West showed an *average* annual number of in-migrants of 766,000 and an average annual number of out-migrants of 503,000, leaving a net average annual increase of 263,000 from this source.[70]

In this chapter, we have explored some of the facts of population growth, development, composition, and distribution, with particular reference to the United States. We have examined these demographic factors in terms of the concept of social interaction, which is the central theme of this book. Population is viewed in sociological terms as one of the raw materials of interaction, and in many ways it is the most basic. In the interactional frame of reference, we considered such questions as birth and death rates; the composition of the population in terms of age, sex, race, and place of residence; and the distribution of the population in terms of region, rural-urban residence, and internal migration. Society and culture are inextricably related to the raw material of population. People in interaction are the stuff of society.

---

[68] Bureau of the Census, *Current Population Reports: Population Characteristics*, "Mobility of the Population of the United States: March, 1960 to March, 1961," Series P-20, No. 118 (August 9, 1962), p. 8.

[69] *Ibid.*, p. 1.

[70] *Ibid.*, Table D.

SELECTED BIBLIOGRAPHY

Bureau of the Census, *Current Population Reports, Population Characteristics,* Series P-20. The Bureau of the Census and the Department of Health, Education and Welfare are the principal federal agencies whose function it is to compile, arrange and distribute statistical information on population in the United States.

Davis, Joseph S., "Implications of Prospective United States Population Growth in the 1960's," *Milbank Memorial Fund Quarterly*, 39:329-349 (April, 1961). The rapid increase in population in the United States during the current decade will have implications for a variety of social problems and the necessary social planning to meet them. From educational requirements to medical care for the aged, these trends will require vast expenditures of time and money.

Davis, Kingsley, "Population," *Scientific American*, 209:63-71 (September, 1963). In this authoritative article, a leading demographer surveys the trends in world population in the early years of the decade of the 1960's. He is particularly concerned with the implications of contemporary rates of growth, and warns that these rates, if continued unchecked, will lead to catastrophe.

Department of Health, Education and Welfare, National Office of Vital Statistics, *Monthly Vital Statistics Bulletin*, published monthly, with annual summaries. These bulletins are the official source of statistics on birth rates, death rates, infant mortality, marriage rates, and divorce rates. In recent years, both the scope and the accuracy of the statistical information disseminated by the Bureau of the Census and the Department of Health, Education, and Welfare (formerly the Federal Security Agency) have greatly improved.

Freedman, Ronald, *The Sociology of Human Fertility*. In *Current Sociology*, Vols. 10/11 (London: Basil Blackwell, 1963). Published for UNESCO. The author of this report is an authority on human fertility (see below). In the present survey, he reviews the literature on this explosive subject. Literally hundreds of empirical studies have been made in recent years on fertility trends in different countries, areas, and regions. This report provides an extensive bibliography of this research.

Freedman, Ronald, *et al.*, *Family Planning, Sterility, and Population Growth*. New York: McGraw-Hill Book Company, Inc., 1959. This is an important empirical study, whose subject matter is indicated by the title. The American people are growing closer together in the vital area of family planning, both with regard to the desirability of this planning and the number of children they wish to have as a result.

Hauser, Philip M., and Otis Dudley Duncan (eds.), *The Study of Population*. Chicago: University of Chicago Press, 1959. This massive treatise is one of the most authoritative and inclusive analyses of population currently available. The editors contribute a number of introductory chapters on demography as a science. The various contributors deal at length with such topics as the development and current status of demography; the elements of demography (composition, distribution, fertility, mortality of population); and the relationships between demography and such disciplines as human ecology, geography, genetics, economics, and sociology.

Kirk, Dudley, "Dynamics of Human Populations," *Eugenics Quarterly*, 2:18-25 (March, 1955). This article is a survey of world population trends and should be read in conjunction with Hauser and Duncan (above). The present article provides a rounded picture of the broad developments in population growth and indicates some of the pressing problems arising in this field.

Lorimer, Frank, *et al.*, *Culture and Human Fertility*. Paris: United Nations Educational, Scientific, and Cultural Organization, 1954. This is an exhaustive survey of the role of social structure and "culturally defined values" in the population experience of societies all over the world. Much of the information is drawn from anthropological studies of "primitive" peoples. This book is the most extensive examination ever made of the relationships between culture (in the broad sense) and fertility.

Milbank Memorial Fund, *Milbank Memorial Fund Quarterly*. New York. This is the most important scholarly publication in the United States devoted solely to the scientific study of population problems.

12 Race

Race and Society

Race is a biological term referring to certain physical similarities among large groups of persons that are transmitted through the mechanisms of heredity. Races may be defined as "populations which differ in the frequencies of some gene or genes." [1] People differ in terms of such biological qualities as color of the skin, color of the eyes, texture of the hair, stature, and proportions of the body. Each of these traits is determined by a number of genes, which are the living units governing

---

[1] L. C. Dunn and Th. Dobzhansky, *Heredity, Race and Society* (rev. ed.) (New York: The American Library, 1952), p. 118.

heredity. Groups of people look alike because they have some of these genetic units in common. A race is therefore a group of persons who resemble each other because of their common genetic heritage. Races differ from one another in terms of the "relative commonness of some of their genes." [2]

The sociologist is interested in group relations, culture patterns, social structure, and other elements produced or modified by social interaction. He would thus apparently have scant interest in a phenomenon so clearly biological as race. But race is also an important factor in social relationships because of the definitions of the physical differences separating human populations. Such relationships as social stratification, discrimination, and segregation are rationalized on the ground that one race is superior to another. It has yet to be conclusively demonstrated, however, that any one racial group is biologically superior to any other as a cultural agent.

The scientific evidence, therefore, is against any assumption of racial superiority. But human beings are neither rational nor scientific in their judgments. They tend to think in terms of stereotypes, ideologies, slogans, myths, and other terms that offer emotional security. Race is one of the most prevalent grounds for such emotional thinking. Hence the average person pays little attention to the judgments of the scientists in connection with racial differences, even when he is exposed to this information. The man on the street acquires his attitudes on such matters from his culture, as these attitudes reflect the structure of his society. Value judgments about race and racial differences are deeply imbedded in our social structure. Race has become a "symbol of social and economic status." [3]

Many of the institutions in our society are based upon the tacit assumption that one racial group is *biologically* superior to another in assimilating and contributing to culture. Children first learn these attitudes from their parents and the other primary agents of indoctrination. As they grow older and come in contact with institutional structures (schools, churches, governments) based upon the suppositions of racial inferiority, these attitudes are reinforced. Whatever the scientific facts, the majority of persons act *as if* members of the white race were, at all times and under all conditions, biologically superior to members of the Negro race.[4] In this sense, racial differences are social facts, and race plays an important role in human behavior.

The institution of human slavery and the subsequent legalized discrimination against the Negro were founded on the assumption that the black man is innately inferior to the white man. It is difficult to rationalize the permanent domination of one group over another on any other ground than the hereditary inferiority of the subject group.[5] The doctrine that all men are created free and equal must therefore be amended to read that all *white* men are so created. The Negro has been placed in a special category because of his alleged hereditary

---

[2] *Ibid.*, p. 125.

[3] Carleton S. Coon, *The Story of Man* (New York: Alfred A. Knopf, Inc., 1954), p. 214.

[4] William E. Bittle, "Racial Myth and Social Action," *Phylon*, 16:232-240 (Third Quarter, 1955).

[5] Gunnar Myrdal, *An American Dilemma* (rev. ed.) (New York: Harper & Row, 1963).

inferiority. These allegations serve as the rationalization for what has been essentially a caste system. We shall consider the forms and implications of this caste structure in Chapter 13. We merely indicate here that race is an important determinant of social relationships and hence comes within the purview of sociology.[6]

Race and Social Interaction

Race has an isolating effect upon social groups. Social interaction is modified and confined by the indelible marks of race. The Negro is assigned to a separate category, where he is unable to participate in social interaction to the same extent as the white man. In the South, the Negro must still go to inferior schools, sit in restricted parts of street cars and other public conveyances, and live in segregated areas of the community. These practices have all been declared unconstitutional by decisions of the United States Supreme Court, notably that of May 17, 1954, relative to segregation in the public school system.[7]

But segregation nevertheless continues to be the rule rather than the exception throughout most of the southern states. In the fall of 1963, there were 6,197 school *districts* in the 17 states where schools were segregated before the Supreme Court decision. Of this total, an estimated 3,053 *districts* had been desegregated by 1963 in the sense that whites and *some* Negroes attended school together. These figures alone are misleading, however, because a large (and undetermined) percentage of these districts permitted only *token* integration (desegregation), with a handful of Negro children attending previously all-white schools. The absolute *number* of Negro children in integrated schools is not known, but it is estimated at less than 10 per cent of the total. Otherwise stated, some 90 per cent of *all* Negro children in the South and border states were still attending segregated schools almost ten years after the Supreme Court decision.[8]

Race plays a central role in the formation of personality in both races. The white southerner may conceivably suffer from an *unconscious* feeling of guilt because of his denial to the Negro of rights that are part of the democratic heritage of America.[9] The personality of the Negro is even more completely determined by the role that the "mark of oppression" (his race) forces him to play in the larger society. His status is conditioned by his skin color and his role grows out of his inferior status.[10] The culture of the Negro group as a whole is a partial product of this status, with its lower economic opportunities, inadequate housing, social discrimination, and limitations placed upon possible

---

[6] E. Franklin Frazier, "Sociological Theory and Race Relations," *American Sociological Review*, 12:265-271 (June, 1947).

[7] L. D. Reddick, "The Great Decision," *Phylon*, 15:194-201 (Second Quarter, 1954).

[8] *Southern School News* (September, 1963), p. 1.

[9] Cornelius L. Golightly, "Race, Values and Guilt," *Social Forces*, 26:125-139 (December, 1947).

[10] Abram Kardiner and Lionel Ovesey, *The Mark of Oppression* (New York: W. W. Norton & Company, Inc., 1951).

goals. This status in turn gives rise to inferiority feelings, personal instability, and repressed aggression in the personality of the Negro.[11]

Racial thinking is also important in interaction between nations and peoples and has corresponding implications for international security. The nations of Africa and the Far East are on the march, both in developing the new technology and in evolving a sense of nationalism. These nations are peopled by dark-skinned persons, who are regarded by many white persons as innately inferior. Discrimination practiced in the United States has been used against this country in the Cold War, and this war is increasingly being fought in the minds of people who are "colored."

A further general element in social interaction arises from the misunderstanding of the concept of race. The average person tends to confuse "nation" and "race" and consequently assumes that the cultural characteristics of nations are somehow hereditary. He thus refers to the Germans as a "race" and in the same breath speaks of the "racial" (biological) traits of their hereditary enemies, the French. The Germans, French, Italians, and Americans are not *races*, but *nations*, and the differences between them are not biological but cultural. Contemporary thinking and acting on international relations are muddled by this confusion and by the failure to distinguish between biological and cultural differences. Social attitudes, statuses, and roles are based upon such misconceptions. Social action is taken on the assumption that these misconceptions are facts.[12]

The idea of race plays still another part in social interaction. This influence involves the various myths that mark racial thinking and acting in the United States. Among these prevailing racial myths are: (a) that discrimination is directly "caused" by the belief that nonwhite races are inferior; (b) that equality between the races can be achieved by segregation and the concept of "separate but equal"; (c) that it is impossible ever to change racial thinking and acting in the South; (d) that laws have no effect upon racial behavior and hence that we cannot "legislate beliefs"; (e) that violence is inevitable in any change; and (f) that we must "make haste slowly" in dealing with the explosive problem of racial interaction.[13]

Each of these ideas has been shown to be false, at least in the sense that they are widely believed to represent the scientific facts of human behavior. We cannot demonstrate here the scientific refutation of all of these myths, but can only indicate some of the fallacies. The myth of "separate but equal" is clearly false and is tacitly recognized as such even by most segregationists. The myth about the absolute rigidity of the southern racial norms has been disproved by the changes actually going on in the large industrial centers. Here the more impersonal contacts of urban life are gradually breaking down many of the caste bar-

---

[11] Kenneth B. Clark, "The Social Scientist as an Expert Witness in Civil Rights Litigation," *Social Problems*, 1:5-10 (June, 1953).

[12] Christen T. Jonassen, "Some Historical and Theoretical Bases of Racism in Northwestern Europe," *Social Forces*, 30:155-161 (December, 1951).

[13] Joseph Lohman and Dietrich C. Reitzes, "Note on Race Relations in Mass Society," *American Journal of Sociology*, 58:240-246 (November, 1952).

riers that originally arose in a rural setting.[14] The myth of inevitable violence is similarly disproved by the peaceful integration of the educational systems in such urban centers as Louisville, Kentucky and Washington, D. C.

Mixture of Races

This is not the place for an extended discussion of the evolution of races and their subsequent mixture. The crucial fact is that the present races evolved from a single species, *Homo sapiens*, and that all men today belong to that species. Evidence for this statement is the fact that races have always intermingled wherever they have lived close to each other for any prolonged period. Inter-breeding that is "genetically effective" occurs only rarely between different species, especially under natural conditions. No other species exists today with which man could interbreed.[15] If the races were different species, they would not have intermingled as they have done in the past and will increasingly do in the future. In short, "All men belong to the same species" and "Mankind is a biologically meaningful entity." [16]

The present racial groups, furthermore, were virtually the same at the beginning of recorded history as they are now. The origins of *Homo sapiens* from an infinitely long process of evolutionary development; the mobility of this undifferentiated species over the surface of the earth; the tendency toward variation through mutation; the operation of natural selection; the fixation of certain genetic traits through inbreeding; the operation of social selection in further fixing other characteristics—these are some of the presumed steps in the development of the racial groups as we know them today.[17] The exact nature of these processes, the parts of the world where they took place, and the contacts between the racial groups during their evolution—these and many other vital matters remain shrouded in silence.[18]

Race mixture is the exchange of genes between members of different racial groups. This process has been greatly accelerated in recent years, following the increased mobility of the peoples of the world. The development of civilization, with its increase in the speed and ease of transportation, leads slowly but surely to the progressive breakdown of race differences. There is no evidence that this process has produced any *biological* disharmony in the hybrid population. The difficulties of the racial hybrid are *social*, rather than *genetic*. As stated by Herskovits, "There is no reason to suppose that such deficiencies as

---

[14] H. M. Blalock, Jr., "Urbanization and Discrimination in the South," *Social Problems,* 7:146-152 (Fall, 1959).

[15] Theodosius Dobzhansky, *Mankind Evolving: The Evolution of the Human Species* (New Haven: Yale University Press, 1962), pp. 183-184.

[16] *Ibid.,* p. 192.

[17] See Ralph Linton, *The Study of Man* (New York: Appleton-Century-Crofts, Inc., 1936), Chapter 2; Carleton S. Coon, *The Origin of Race* (New York: Alfred A. Knopf, Inc., 1962). Coon differs from most authorities in his assumption of a polyphyletic (from more than one ancestral type) origin of *Homo sapiens.*

[18] See S. L. Washburn, "The Study of Race," *American Anthropologist,* 65:521-531 (June, 1963).

seen in some hybrid populations cannot be referred to the social situations in which these people are found." [19]

The mixture of races has been going on for thousands of years. As a result, there is no such thing as a "pure" race, either now or in the recent past. The concept of a pure race is part of the racial mythology, which assumes the existence of a direct correlation between cultural achievement and racial characteristics. Racial groups clearly differ with respect to the *relative commonness* of certain genes. One will see more tall persons with narrow heads, blond complexions, and blue eyes on the streets of Stockholm than on the streets of Rome. But one will also see many brunettes with dark eyes in Stockholm and many blonds with blue eyes in Rome. There is nothing to suggest that dark-haired Swedes and light-haired Italians are any less entitled to be called Swedes and Italians than their compatriots who conform more closely to the popular stereotypes.

Nor were racial or subracial groups "pure" in the historical past. As Dunn and Dobzhansky point out,[20] "Race mixture has been going on during the whole of recorded history. Incontrovertible evidence . . . shows that even in pre-history, at the very dawn of humanity, mixing of different stocks . . . took place. Mankind has always been, and still is, a mongrel lot." The concept of a "pure" race seems to be an answer to a deep-seated emotional need in some persons to belong to a group that is undefiled by alien influences and therefore "better" than others. When the security of the individual is threatened by unemployment, inflation, or the breakdown of the institutional ties of family, church, and local community, he may unconsciously bolster his self-esteem by identifying himself with a "pure" race.[21]

In biological terms, furthermore, the concept of a pure race is impossible, in the sense of a given population inbreeding for many generations and not permitting outsiders to "contaminate" the stock. "Pure" races would be possible only if "heredity were like a fluid transmitted through 'blood,' and if the hereditary 'bloods' of the parents mixed and fused in their offspring." [22] The popular notions were (and still are) based on the assumption that hereditary qualities *are* transmitted by blood, which thereby assumes a magical quality.

Biological science has conclusively refuted this ancient conception. Science has demonstrated that heredity is transmitted through the genes, which are discrete packages and not a fluid like blood which can be made thicker or thinner. If the blood theory of heredity were valid, brothers and sisters would receive the same blood from their parents and hence would have the same heredity. In reality, of course, brothers and sisters receive different sets of genes and hence are different individuals.[23] A race is not a "community of blood" as is popu-

---

[19] Melville J. Herskovits, "Race Mixture," *Encyclopaedia of the Social Sciences* (New York: The Macmillan Company, 1934), p. 43.

[20] Dunn and Dobzhansky, *op. cit.*, p. 115.

[21] James W. Vander Zanden, "The Klan Revival," *American Journal of Sociology*, 65:456-462 (March, 1960).

[22] Dunn and Dobzhansky, *op. cit.*, p. 116.

[23] *Ibid.*

larly supposed. A race is a group of persons with certain genes in common, but with many individual differences.

Elements of Racial Differences

Race is a biological concept with sociological implications. The only traits that can properly be termed racial are those coming down to large numbers of persons in the genes. A discussion of the most important criteria of racial differences follows.[24]

1. Skin color. The color of the skin is the most obvious distinguishing feature of race. It is also one of the least trustworthy. There is a wide variation of skin color within the same racial groups; members of the "white" race, for example, range in color from very light to very dark. The pigmentation of many Caucasoids is darker than that of many African Negroids.

2. Eye color. This classification is open to many of the same errors and discrepancies as skin color. Color of the eye (or rather of the iris) is satisfactory for comparative purposes only within the Caucasoid race, since all non-Caucasoid peoples have either a dark brown or black iris. Only among the Caucasoid populations are blue, grey, or green irises found in the "pure" racial forms.

3. Stature. This category includes height and weight, as well as the ratios between them. The chief function of this anatomical trait is to distinguish between Pygmy and non-Pygmy peoples, since there is so much overlapping between different racial populations in this respect. Stature is subject to considerable variations because of environmental and dietary differences. A superior diet and standard of living will appreciably raise the height and weight of a given population over several generations.

4. Head shape. The shape of the head is useful in distinguishing between subraces within a single racial group. The cephalic index is the principal measurement of head shape and is found by multiplying the width of the head by 100 and then dividing the product by the length of the head. It was formerly thought that the major racial populations could be distinguished by the extent of long, medium or wide-headedness, but this belief has been questioned in recent years. Hence the Caucasoid, Mongoloid, and Negroid groups cannot be set off from each other accurately on the basis of cephalic index. There is, furthermore, some doubt as to whether these differences are completely genic or whether they are not, at least in part, the result of environmental factors.

5. Body hair. Members of the white race have considerable hair on their bodies, whereas the Negroid and Mongoloid races have less. Wide variation exists between members of the same race, but in general the Caucasoids are more hairy than the other major racial groups. This criterion is an important factor in racial distinction, because dietary changes over a prolonged period

---

[24] The following is adapted from Melville Jacobs and Bernhard J. Stern, *Outline of Anthropology* (New York: Barnes & Noble, Inc., 1947), Chapter 3, "The Living Races."

apparently have but little effect upon the amount of body hair. In contrast to some of the racial criteria mentioned above, therefore, body hair appears to be more completely genic in character and less susceptible to environmental influences.

6. *Hair texture.* The texture of the hair in cross-section under a microscope is an important criterion of racial differences. The major groups apparently run more true to type in this respect than in many others formerly considered to be indisputable evidence of racial differences. In cross-section, straight hair (some Caucasoids, the majority of Mongoloids) appears round; wavy to curly hair (most Caucasoids and other and smaller groups) is slightly oval; and kinky or woolly hair (Pygmy, Negroid, and Melanesian groups) is more oval. This trait is almost completely determined by genes and hence is distinctly "racial" in character, with environment playing a negligible role.

7. *Epicanthic fold.* This trait refers to a fold of skin in the inner upper eyelid, characteristic of the Mongoloid peoples of continental Asia and some smaller groups. The effect of this characteristic is to impart the so-called "slanting" quality to the eyes of the continental Mongoloids, although the actual shape of their eyes does not differ from that of other racial groups. This factor is also affected by the genes and not by environmental influences, and hence constitutes an excellent device for distinguishing some of the Mongoloid groups from other major racial populations.

8. *Blood type.* Human beings also differ in terms of the composition of their blood. There are four principal *types* of blood, known as O, A, B, and AB. These types differ in their tendency to agglutinate or "clump together" when one type of blood is transfused into a person with another type. The technical differences between blood types need not concern us here. The important consideration is that races differ in terms of the *relative* numbers of individuals with each of the four types. Each race has all four types, but the relative distribution is different. Group O is the most common type, group A is likewise common, whereas Groups B and AB are less common, even though they are still found in all races. In summary, "the races differ in blood group type only in a relative way. There are no absolute differences in which one race is all of one blood type and another all of another type." [25]

Other physical criteria have been used to distinguish racial groups, but the above are the most important. Efforts have been made, for example, to distinguish between races on the basis of the size and structure of the brain, but the differences between members of the same racial population are as great as or greater than those between racial populations. The Pygmy population is the only one with consistently smaller brains than any other population. Finally, such alleged racial characteristics as body odor result from differences in diet, hygiene, bathing, and other environmental factors and are not characteristic of racial populations as such.[26]

---

[25] Dunn and Dobzhansky, *op. cit.*, pp. 118-121. (The quotation is found on page 120.)
[26] Jacobs and Stern, *op. cit.*, Chapter 3.

Classification of Races

No single criterion is thus adequate to distinguish one race from another. The *combination* of traits that large population groups have in common is the important consideration. It is difficult to formulate a classification of races that will be reasonably inclusive, acceptable to the experts in the field, and at the same time not too complicated. Many scholars, indeed, would abandon the term "race" altogether and substitute some less controversial term. This would not solve the problem, for some word would have to be invented or adapted to refer to the major population groups. The differences that set these groups off from each other are very real, even though they are misunderstood by the average person.

The classification of races is equally complicated. Early attempts at classification were based upon mental and psychological traits, such as "freedom," "invention," and "tenacity." These characteristics clearly reflect value judgments and, furthermore, have nothing to do with physical qualities transmitted through the genes. Later attempts to classify the races were based upon skin color, which is also inadequate. The shape of the head has been used as the basis for classification by some scholars, but this trait likewise has numerous drawbacks.[27]

The major racial classification system that we shall follow comprises the Caucasoid, Mongoloid, and Negroid, with certain subraces and marginal populations omitted for the sake of greater clarity.

1. Caucasoid. This racial grouping has been variously termed the Caucasian, the Caucasic, or the white. Members of this race are popularly presumed to be white, or at least light, in color, but actually they range from the blond northern European to the dark Hindu. The Caucasoid stock as a whole is characterized by medium to thin lips, lack of epicanthic fold, considerable body hair,

---

[27] Dunn and Dobzhansky, *op. cit.,* pp. 109-112.

Race is a biological term referring to certain physical similarities among large groups of persons that are transmitted through the mechanisms of heredity.

hair of the head ranging from straight to curly, and high, thin noses. In respect to stature, the white race ranges from short to tall. Cephalic index varies from one extreme to the other, with no pronounced tendency to a single head shape. With regard to the subdivisions of the Caucasoid race, considerable disagreement exists among physical anthropologists even as to the number of such subgroups, let alone their exact classification. The following five groups, however, have been so widely publicized among both lay and professional groups that they are included, with the proviso that scientific opinion is by no means unanimous in this respect.

(a) *Nordic.* Nordics are found predominantly among the peoples of northern Europe, especially in the more isolated rural districts of the Scandinavian peninsula. Contrary to popular impression, the majority of Germans are not Nordics in the anthropological sense. This subdivision has an unusually high percentage of blondness, fair skins, blue eyes, long heads, and tall bodies. Nordics comprise the most vocal of all the subdivisions of the white (or any other) race in their claims to distinction on the basis of alleged biological superiority.

(b) *Alpine.* The Alpines possess the other basic characteristics of the white race, and in addition they tend to have round heads, short and stocky builds, and skin that is neither as depigmented (light) as the Nordics nor as dark as the Mediterraneans. This group is found throughout central Europe and includes such varied national and ethnic groups as the Czechs, south Germans, Swiss, some of the Slavs, and many of the Balkan peoples. These groups have constituted the sturdy peasant stock of central Europe for millennia, and successive waves of invading peoples have not substantially modified the basic type.

(c) *Mediterranean.* The Mediterranean group has occupied the shores of the Mediterranean Sea since long before the days of the Romans. Insofar as they can be distinguished from the other subdivisions of the Caucasoid race, the Mediterraneans tend to be slight and comparatively short in stature, with long heads, curly hair, dark eyes, and olive or pale complexions. This group comprises the majority of several of the Latin nations. Their physical traits are especially apparent among the southern Italians, the southern French, the Spanish, and the Portuguese.

(d) *Armenoid.* The Armenoid peoples are found in southeastern Europe and Asia Minor among such national and cultural groups as the Turks, Armenians, Syrians, and others in the Near East. They tend to be dark in color like the Mediterraneans, and their most characteristic feature is a large and convex nose. This feature is often associated exclusively with the Jews (who were originally an Armenoid people), but in reality it marks many other groups with widely differing cultures in this part of the world.

(e) *Hindu.* The people of India constitute the fifth major subdivision of the Caucasoid race. Although they are very dark in color, these people possess the other basic Caucasoid characteristics and are physically very much like the Mediterraneans, from whom they may have partially descended. The exact origins and constitution of this large segment of the Caucasoid race constitute one of the mysteries of physical anthropology. Despite the fact that the conquering Europeans have regarded the Hindus as a colored and (therefore) inferior race, in most respects their genic heritage is Caucasoid.

2. *Mongoloid*. This racial group numbers more than one billion people and is about equal in size to the Caucasoid. Considerable variation exists within this group with regard to many of the characteristic racial traits. The skin color of the Mongoloids, for example, ranges from the saffron yellow of the Chinese to the coppery red of the American Indian. The average is a "yellowish light brown." Hair is straight and black, with comparatively little growth on the face and body. In stature, they range from short to tall. The face is marked by high and projecting cheekbones. As noted, the epicanthic or "mongoloid" fold is a characteristic of the Mongoloid peoples, especially among the Asiatic populations. There are three major groups of Mongoloids, and many subgroups and marginal populations. We shall consider only the major subdivisions.

(*a*) *Asiatic*. This is the largest group and comprises the bulk of the peoples on the continent of Asia, with a total population of more than seven hundred million persons. The Chinese, Japanese, and Koreans are the same basic stock, despite local variations between groups. Their physical characteristics are in general those enumerated above in connection with the generalized Mongoloid racial type. Considerable individual variation exists within each of these racial groups and subgroups. Some Japanese are tall, although their median height is less than the median for a Caucasoid group such as the Scandinavian. It cannot be stressed too often, therefore, that races are not homogeneous.

(*b*) *Indonesian-Malay*. This large group comprises more than one hundred million persons in southeastern Asia and Malaysia. The Mongoloid stock is here intermingled with discernible Pygmy genes from the earlier aboriginal inhabitants of these areas to form a hybrid racial group. The natives of the interior districts of the Malaysian islands have more Pygmy characteristics than those in the coastal regions, who are more predominantly Mongoloid. The latter have straighter hair and are lighter in color than their compatriots farther inland. Some Caucasoid genes are also apparent among the coastal peoples of Malaysia, deriving probably from India.

(*c*) *American Indian*. The third great group of Mongoloid peoples is the American Indian, closely related genetically to the natives of eastern Siberia and the Eskimos of North America. The ancestors of the American Indians were apparently of a generalized Mongoloid stock who came to the North American continent across the Bering Straits an estimated twenty thousand or more years ago. During the subsequent wandering of these peoples, a series of mutations (among them skin color) undoubtedly occurred. These mutations were fixed through inbreeding, which is characteristic of all primitive and isolated peoples. The American Indians tend to be taller than the median height for the Asiatic Mongoloids. The skin of the American Indian ranges in color from yellowish to reddish brown; their eyes are brown; their faces are broad with high cheekbones. The nose is sharp and the hair on the head is jet black and very coarse.

3. *Negroid.* The third major racial stock is the Negroid. The African Negroid constitutes the largest and most characteristic racial group in this category and numbers more than one hundred million persons. In general, the Negroid stock is characterized by very dark pigmentation, woolly or frizzly hair, wide noses, thick lips, projecting upper jaws (prognathism), small ears, relatively little body hair, and long-headedness. This stock is further characterized by the widest range in stature, with the shortest (Pygmy) and the tallest (Nilotic Negro) peoples in the world numbered among the Negroid race. A number of subraces have been distinguished by the physical anthropologists, but these refinements are outside the scope of this description. Considerable hybridization has taken place in Africa in the last few thousand years, with the result that many varieties of color, stature, hair, and other racial characteristics are found.

The Melanesians are a Negroid-like people living on many islands in the South Pacific from New Guinea to Fiji. These peoples possess so many genic traits of the African Negroid that both groups were formerly assumed to have evolved from the same stock and then migrated to their present divergent locations in Africa and the South Pacific. This theory has recently been abandoned, however, on the assumption that such primitive peoples would not have had the technological resources to migrate so far under such conditions. It is now assumed that the connection between the Melanesians and the African Negroids is not genic, but that the physical similarities reflect roughly similar circumstances of environment and culture.[28]

In addition to these major groupings, there are numerous marginal peoples that seem to be a combination of two or more of the basic stocks. These marginal groups defy accurate classification. They include such populations as the Micronesians and Polynesians in the South Pacific, the native Australoids, the various Pygmy groups scattered over the earth, and the hairy Ainu of Northern Japan and the surrounding islands. Some of these types may represent premodern man, with the Australoids, for example, apparently retaining Neanderthaloid or other and earlier human characteristics.

Racial development, as we have suggested, has been marked by prolonged interbreeding between the members of the various races and subraces. During the tens of thousands of years when the modern racial populations were developing, men were not bothered by considerations of racial purity. The result of these processes is the complex amalgam that constitutes our contemporary racial heritage.[29]

Mental Differences and Race

Mankind may thus be divided into several large populations on the basis of traits inherited through the genes. The exact nature of these differences and

---

[28] Jacobs and Stern, *op. cit.*, pp. 50-51.
[29] Dunn and Dobzhansky, *op. cit.*, pp. 128-129.

the resulting classifications are the primary concern of the physical anthropologist and the geneticist. The sociologist is interested in racial differences because of their symbolic relationship to society and culture. Racial differences form the basis for social stratification in many (but not all) societies where such differences are found. Caste stratification, which still exists in the South, rests upon the tacit assumption that differences in intelligence are correlated with differences in facial structure, hair structure, skin color, and the rest of the factors constituting race. We may examine the scientific foundation for this assumption.

The most direct method of settling the crucial question of mental differences would presumably be to employ the testing methods developed by the experts in psychology and education. This was done during World War I and World War II, when millions of men of all races and ethnic origins were examined for military service. The results of these large-scale tests constituted, to put it mildly, inconclusive proof of the doctrine of racial superiority. Without entering into the controversy as to whether intelligence tests measure hereditary ability or hereditary ability *plus* social training, the examinations demonstrated that large numbers of Negroes were higher in "intelligence" than large numbers of whites.

Negroes as a group tested substantially lower than whites as a group in the World War I examinations. But Negroes from some of the northern states had higher scores than whites from some of the southern states. The low scores of the Negroes arose largely from the fact that they were predominantly *southerners*, rather than from any hereditary racial incapacity to assimilate culture. If *all* whites were innately superior to *all* Negroes, it would be manifestly impossible for northern Negroes to score higher than southern whites, always assuming that the tests actually measure hereditary ability alone.[30] During World War II, the United States Army Special Training Units for functional illiterates further demonstrated that learning abilities were similar between Negroes and whites when inequalities in education were eliminated. In this training, Negro illiterates progressed as fast as white illiterates.[31]

Many other tests have been conducted in an effort to learn the nature of racial differences (if any) in intelligence. None has conclusively demonstrated that one race is mentally superior to any other. A wide range of individual variations obviously exists within each race, but this does not apply to one race as compared with another. The most important quality of *homo sapiens* is plasticity, the ability to adjust to new environmental challenges. Man has developed because of his ability to learn from experience and to adjust his behavior accordingly. This quality, Dunn and Dobzhansky conclude, "is true for all races of man and for all climates." [32]

The general relationships between races in terms of mental differences were

---

[30] Cf. Otto Klineberg, *Race Differences* (New York: Harper & Brothers, 1935), Chapter IX.

[31] H. Aptheker, "Literacy, the Negro, and World War II," *Journal of Negro Education,* 14:595-602 (Fall, 1945).

[32] Dunn and Dobzhansky, *op. cit.,* pp. 133-134.

examined some time ago by Franz Boas, who was then the dean of American physical anthropologists. In a statement drawing together all the pertinent data at the time, Boas concluded cautiously that "careful tests reveal a marked dependence of mental differences upon conditions of life and that all racial differences which have been established thus far are so much subject to outer circumstances that *no proof can be given of innate differences.*" [33] Almost three decades later, the American Anthropological Association went on record as confirming the basic equality of the Negroid and Caucasoid races. Specifically, the Association repudiated allegations widely current in the United States "that Negroes are biologically and in innate mental ability inferior to whites," and reaffirmed the fact "that *there is no scientifically established evidence* to justify the exclusion of any race from the rights guaranteed by the Constitution of the United States." [34]

We have considered some of the physical and mental aspects of race. The physical differences often loom large, since they are the symbols of dominance and subordination in our society. On closer examination, however, the *differences* between men are not as great as the *similarities.* Mankind is one, for all practical purposes, in terms of those characteristics that are racially transmitted. Differences of pigmentation, hair texture, eye color, and the rest are comparatively superficial when compared with the fundamental similarities in physical and mental traits. In terms of cultural development, man is divided into many groups. In terms of the potentiality of cultural development, these racial differences are insignificant.

Race and Racism

A further consideration has served as a rationalization for much of the mythology of racial thinking. This is the current status of the major races with respect to technological and industrial culture. The white race occupies a dominant position in this respect at the present time. It is commonly supposed by members of the white race that this dominance is the result of superior hereditary qualities. The yellow race has a considerably lower technological position, and hence presumably falls somewhere between the Caucasoid and the Negroid in native ability. The latter currently occupies a manifestly inferior technological status and hence is allegedly inferior to the other two.

The partisans of the white race thus proclaim their past, present, and future superiority. Those who live in northwestern Europe have for some time been especially vociferous in attributing all manner of abilities to persons with the same pigmentation as themselves. This literature is extensive and varied, ranging from the naïve rationalizations of the lunatic fringe to the impressively doc-

---

[33] Franz Boas, "Race," *Encyclopaedia of the Social Sciences* (New York: The Macmillan Company, 1934), p. 34. (My italics.)

[34] Statement by the American Anthropological Association, quoted in *The New York Times* (November 21, 1961). (My italics.) See also Dobzhansky, *op. cit.,* p. 286.

umented monographs of scholars whose objectivity is open to question. Some of this literature was written for frankly political purposes, whereas other examples were composed with the loftiest scientific motives, at least on the *conscious* level. The *unconscious* motivations are both less creditable and less easily discernible.[35]

These dogmas of superiority are known collectively as racism. This is a pervasive and widely held form of ethnocentrism based on the assumption that "one ethnic or racial group is condemned by nature to hereditary inferiority and another group is destined to hereditary superiority." [36] There is no scientific justification for this dogma, but this minor consideration does not interfere with its widespread acceptance. As one anthropologist puts it categorically, "Racism is based on a profound misunderstanding of culture, of learning, and of the biology of the human species." [37] Nevertheless, the feeling of superiority inherent in racism fills a strong need in the personality, especially when the individual is frustrated, threatened, or otherwise maladjusted. We shall consider some of the social factors that give rise to these attitudes in our discussion of the dynamics of race prejudice.

In northern Europe, the myths of earlier Nordic greatness provided a fertile ground for the later Hitlerian myth of "Aryan" supremacy. The most spectacular example of this position was afforded by the Nazis in Germany, who built an entire way of life about it. Their philosophy was founded upon a mystic faith in the superiority of the fictitious Aryan "race," a category that never existed in any scientific sense. This racist myth was the basis for perhaps the most extensive deliberate mass murders in history—the extermination of some five million Jews, Poles, Russians, and other "non-Aryan" peoples.

The ethnocentric belief that a particular group (usually one's own) is somehow better than all other groups is not new. The Greeks of the Age of Pericles made no bones about the fact that they were infinitely superior to all other known peoples, whom they contemptuously labeled as "barbarians"—that is, non-Greeks. This belief differed in one important respect from the modern concept of racism, however, in that the distinction between the Greeks and all other peoples was *cultural*, rather than *biological*.

The Romans likewise considered themselves manifestly superior to the barbarian peoples to whom they brought Roman law and order. But when a "barbarian" had assimilated the culture of Rome, he was thereby eligible for citizenship and became the equal of every other Roman citizen, whether he lived on the Tiber or the Rhine. Christians were also highly prejudiced during the Middle Ages against all those who did not share their religious beliefs. Once converted, however, the non-Christian became as worthy as anyone else to receive

---

[35] For examples of this position in the United States, cf. Madison Grant, *The Passing of the Great Race* (New York: Charles Scribner's Sons, 1916); Lothrop Stoddard, *The Rising Tide of Color Against White World Supremacy* (New York: Charles Scribner's Sons, 1920).

[36] Jonassen, *op. cit.*, p. 155.

[37] Washburn, *op. cit.*, p. 528.

the infinite Grace of God. The criterion here was religious (cultural), *not* racial.

In the last few centuries, the white man has become a world conqueror. A white skin has become the symbol of the dominant race. A yellow, black, or red skin has denoted submission and (by implication) inferiority as well. In the eyes of the white conquerors and colonizers, their own race was the only one capable of fabricating the complex industrial heritage of the Western world. Hence it was permanently superior. The colored peoples were doomed to permanent subordination because of their hereditary inferiority. The slogan of "The White Man's Burden" was the conventional rationalization for this imperialism, whereby the Caucasoid peoples "reluctantly" bowed to the force of destiny and agreed to rule over the lesser breeds.

Race and Cultural Development

Culture must in final analysis be explained in terms of culture. Geography, biology, and psychology are limiting or conditioning factors, but the primary element in cultural development is culture itself. This point of view applies with special relevance to the relationships between race and cultural development. The attempt to explain the cultural achievements of any group in terms of race is not consistent with the facts. The white race did not invent all or even a majority of the basic elements constituting its various cultures. The nations of Western Europe and America have borrowed many culture patterns from other groups and incorporated them into their own cultures.

In the broad development of culture, racial differences *as such* therefore appear to have little or no influence. In Linton's words, "For the purposes of the study of cultural history and development, all human groups may be taken as equivalent." [38] As noted, the American Anthropological Association recently drafted a resolution dealing with the same question. "The basic principles of equality of opportunity and equality before the law," the resolution stated, "are compatible with all that is known about human biology. All races," concluded the resolution, "possess the abilities needed to participate fully in the democratic way of life and in modern technological civilization." [39] In a scientific sense, the burden of proof remains squarely with those who wish to prove the existence of hereditary racial superiority in mental ability.[40]

The circumstances under which societies invented or borrowed culture patterns, the possibilities for future culture development, and the historical position of each society—these and similar considerations cannot be explained in terms of race. Cultural development follows uniformities of its own that are independent of the pigmentation of the interacting human agents. Furthermore, the cultural process presents cyclical fluctuations. The culture of a par-

---

[38] Linton, *The Tree of Culture, op. cit.*, p. 28.
[39] Statement by the American Anthropological Association, *op. cit.*
[40] Ashley Montagu, *Man in Process* (Cleveland and New York: The World Publishing Company, 1961), pp. 121-122.

ticular society may reach a high peak, and at other times the same people, biologically speaking, are on an entirely different cultural level.

We need only look at the great cultures of Egypt, Mesopotamia, Greece, and Rome to realize that changes in cultural level may occur in the space of a few generations, during which the genic structure of the people changes negligibly, if at all. No matter what the racial composition of the societies, many cultures have periods of extensive vigor, followed by periods of stabilization, stratification, and gradual, sometimes rapid, decline.[41] These changes occur in the culture and the social structure and do not involve any substantial racial modification. The white race occupies a dominant position in the world today, but this has not always been so. When most of the barbarian ancestors of the present Caucasoid peoples were roaming the gloomy forests of northwestern Europe, China already had a culture stretching back thousands of years in orderly succession.[42]

The change in the cultural status of a people without modification of the racial stock is dramatically and unhappily illustrated by the American Indian. However much his culture may have differed technologically from that of the invading whites, the noble red man nevertheless had a number of integrated, organized, and highly structured societies that provided a stable cultural framework of accepted goals, standards, values, statuses, and roles. The basic personality type of the Plains Indian, for example, was proud, haughty, and self-sufficient. Faced with superior numbers and technology, he resisted the white men as long and as bravely as he could.

The conquest of the Plains Indians did not bring about their physical extermination. Thousands still live on, in and about the reservations. But they are no longer the same proud, well-organized, and aggressive people. Their culture has been largely destroyed and with it the way of life they knew. In the space of a few generations, the character structure of the Indian has collapsed. Biologically, he is still the same. Socially, he is very different. Commenting upon this dramatic disintegration, Benedict said that such changes "give the lie to the racists' contention that these patterns are eternal and are biologically perpetuated." [43]

The experience of the American Negro offers a final example of cultural change and biological stability. The ancestors of the Negro for the most part came to this country from the African tribal societies of Nigeria. These societies appear to have been highly developed in many respects, notably in government and social organization.[44] This ancestral culture was completely broken after a few generations in America. The slaves perforce adopted the culture of the white man, but with certain limitations, for they were not allowed to participate

---

[41] Pitirim A. Sorokin, *Social and Cultural Dynamics* (Four Volumes) (New York: American Book Company, 1937-1941).

[42] Cf. Arnold J. Toynbee, *A Study of History* (one-volume edition) (New York: Oxford University Press, 1947).

[43] Ruth Benedict, *Race: Science and Politics* (rev. ed.) (New York: The Viking Press, 1945), p. 133.

[44] Melville J. Herskovits, *The Myth of the Negro Past* (New York: Harper & Brothers, 1941).

on a basis of equality. The only culture the Negro knew became the Anglo-American culture, albeit on a restricted basis.[45]

This marginal cultural position continued for generations after the emancipation of the slaves. It still characterizes the status of the Negro. The result is the backward Negro of the rural South, whose caste position we shall consider in the next chapter. The biological heritage of the Negro did not appreciably change during the tremendous transition in his social status from self-government in Africa to slavery in America. In view of the high level of social organization of the Nigerian cultures, the Negro had the demonstrable ability to create a complex social structure. His lowly status today is the result of his prolonged isolation from active participation in the culture of the white man.[46]

Culture has developed in many streams. Some cultures have been continuous (the Chinese); others have flourished and then declined (the Egyptian). The growth, expansion, and decline of culture has followed its own sequences, and race has had little or nothing to do with it. Instead of race there has been a combination of language, religion, political and military development, technology, economic structures, value systems, and artistic forms. These factors distinguish one culture from another. The development of culture arises through complex and, as yet, little known relationships between these and other components. Race in the biological sense has no place in this pattern.[47]

Peoples who have been more or less permanently outside the main streams of cultural development have been unable to advance, no matter what their racial background. Peoples who have been in the main streams of such development have experienced no difficulty in continuing it. We are now witnessing a movement by the "underdeveloped" peoples of the world to catch up with the technological civilization of the white man. These underdeveloped peoples are largely Mongoloid and (to a certain extent) Negroid in racial stock. There is no reason to believe that they are unequal to the challenge.

The Nature of Race Prejudice

The most dynamic factor in the racial situation is prejudice. Prejudice has been defined as "a hostile attitude toward a person who belongs to a group, simply because he belongs to that group, and is therefore presumed to have the objectionable qualities ascribed to the group." [48] An attitude is a tendency to act in a general way when confronted by a particular person, object, symbol, or situation. Attitudes are important factors in social interaction. They set the initial tone for the interaction, define the general way in which the participants shall act, and continue to modify the action after it has begun.[49] The white south-

---

[45] Ruth Landes, "Biracialism in American Society: A Comparative View," *American Anthropologist,* 57:1253-1263 (December, 1955).

[46] *Ibid.*

[47] A. L. Kroeber, "The Delimitation of Civilizations," *Journal of the History of Ideas,* 14:264-275 (April, 1953).

[48] Gordon W. Allport, *The Nature of Prejudice* (Cambridge, Massachusetts: Addison-Wesley Publishing Company, Inc., 1954), pp. 14-15.

[49] Herbert Blumer, "Attitudes and the Social Act," *Social Problems,* 3:59-65 (October, 1955).

Attitudes of prejudice rest with the prejudiced person; hence the "causes" of prejudice must be sought in the majority group, not in the minority group.

erner is influenced by his attitude toward Negroes in general. He is also influenced by the way he sees himself in relation to an individual Negro. He is, finally, influenced by all he has heard, read, and previously experienced about his own role and that of the Negro as a member of an "inferior" race.

Attitudes of prejudice involve different types of minority groups. A person may be prejudiced against Negroes or Chinese (race prejudice), against Jews or Catholics (religious prejudice), or against Germans or Italians (ethnic prejudice). As culture patterns, each of these clusters of attitudes has a history, in some instances stretching back for thousands of years (anti-Semitism). Each of these patterns, furthermore, involves different cultural values, interpersonal relations, and social structures. Prejudice against the Negro has a background of slavery, in which the Negro was kept (intentionally and unintentionally) in a condition of ignorance, subjection, and dependence. Prejudice against Catholics has emotional connotations stretching at least as far back as the St. Bartholomew's Day massacre and the European Wars of Religion. Prejudice against Jews, finally, involves a complex and highly emotional matrix of religious intolerance, cultural suspicion, and fear of competition.[50]

In this brief discussion, we cannot explore all of the ramifications of these

---

[50] James Parkes, *An Enemy of the People: Anti-Semitism* (New York: Penguin Books, Inc., 1946).

and other aspects of the complex problem of prejudice in American society. We can merely suggest some of the causes of prejudice and its bearing upon social interaction through the personality of the prejudiced person. In the next chapter, we shall examine the impact of prejudice upon the Negro. If prejudice merely remained on the covert (hidden) level of attitudes toward minority groups, it would be interesting in a theoretical way, but it would not carry the crucial overtones for behavior that it does. But prejudice is also *acted out* in the overt form of discrimination, whereby minority groups are denied their rights as citizens, forced to occupy an inferior position in society, and sometimes threatened with physical violence for allegedly failing to observe this position.[51] In the United States, the "acting out" of race prejudice is embodied in a caste-like system of social stratification, which we shall consider in Chapter 13. Prejudice is a state of mind that has widespread implications for social interaction.[52]

Attitudes of prejudice rest with the prejudiced person. Hence the "causes" of prejudice must be sought in the majority group, not in the minority group. The fanatical anti-Semite can only be completely understood by analyzing *his* personal history and that of the Christians, not by examining the alleged qualities of the Jews. The rabid Negro-hater can be fully explained only by studying the social and cultural forces that have formed *him*, not by enumerating the personality traits of the Negro. The central "problem" of prejudice is thus basically not a *Negro* and a *Jewish* problem, but a *white* and a *gentile* problem. Bitterly prejudiced persons are often insecure, frustrated, and aggressive. Their self-image is inadequate and they have a strong (if usually unconscious) need to bolster this image. Their "Bad-Me" is so overpowering that they need a comforting illusion to counterbalance their negative feeling. This illusion is their prejudice.

We must distinguish between the bitterly prejudiced and the merely mildly prejudiced person. The former often has a personal history of frustration and aggression, perhaps originating with his role in the parental family. His position in the social structure, as we shall see, is often lowly and unsatisfactory. He has learned his hostile attitudes early in life and has never had the occasion seriously to question them. He has learned that aggression is permitted against the Negro because of the latter's alleged inferiority. The fact that these racial stereotypes are false is not important. The person needs to believe that they are true. As a result, they literally *are* true for him.

The mildly prejudiced person, on the other hand, is usually more secure. Such persons number by far the largest percentage of any society, even that in which prejudice is endemic. Neither the general environment nor the personality needs of these people are the same as those of the highly prejudiced person. The status of the more tolerant group is more secure and their self-image is on firmer foundations. Such persons do not go out of their way to provoke Ne-

---

[51] See Robert L. Hamblin, "The Dynamics of Racial Discrimination," *Social Problems*, 10:103-121 (Fall, 1962).

[52] For an extensive survey of prejudice and discrimination, see Mabel A. Elliott and Francis E. Merrill, *Social Disorganization* (New York: Harper & Row, 1961), Fourth Edition, Chapter 27 and Chapter 28.

groes, because they do not need to do so. They merely accept the prejudiced attitudes that prevail in their social class, ethnic group, and family circle. In this sense, the mildly prejudiced person is acting as a "normal" human being on the basis of what he has learned. He has been "socialized" along certain lines and it is natural that he should hold the attitudes he does. It would be unusual if, under the circumstances, he held any other.[53]

The bitterly prejudiced person has a different reaction pattern. He may be a white sharecropper whose economic status is precarious and whose standard of living is no higher than that of his Negro neighbors. He may be a white migratory laborer who has been forced off the land and follows the crops every spring from Florida to New York State. In either case, he ends each working year with no more money than when he began it. His children are undernourished and poorly educated. He feels bewildered, weak, and threatened by his environment, which he does not understand. One of his few comforts is that he is white and other people are black. In his status as a white man, he can do things that a black man cannot. This is not much consolation for a life of poverty, undernourishment, and deprivation. But it is better than nothing.

Prejudice and Social Structure

Prejudice thus reflects the social structure. By social structure, we refer here to such factors as the system of social classes, the social roles ascribed to different racial, ethnic, and religious groups, and the patterns of norms and values that justify these and similar relationships. Prejudice does not arise on a large scale unless the social and cultural conditions favor it.[54] Men learn hostile attitudes toward their fellow men under certain social conditions. Among these conditions are the following:

1. *Physical differences.* The most obvious "cause" of race prejudice is the physical fact of race itself. Men are said to be prejudiced because they differ from other men with respect to certain biological qualities. But this presumed "explanation" is really no explanation at all because biological differences *as such* do not necessarily give rise to hostile attitudes. In many societies with a genetically heterogeneous population (Brazil), people live in racial harmony. Furthermore, race prejudice reflects only *certain* biological qualities, such as those possessed by the Negro. These qualities are negatively defined because of the circumstances (slavery and subservience) in which the Negro has been placed. For generations, white children have been taught that a black skin means inferiority. Negro children have learned this, too.

2. *Economic competition.* As slavery was replaced by freedom, race prejudice assumed a different tone. Members of the two races have, in a growing number of instances, come into direct competition for land, jobs, and power. This competition first appeared in the Deep South, as sharecropping became a way of

---

[53] Gordon W. Allport, *op. cit.*, p. 395.
[54] Warren Breed, "Group Structure and Resistance to Desegregation in the Deep South," *Social Problems*, 10:84-94 (Summer, 1962).

life for Negro and white alike. As this form of activity has declined in importance, the area of interracial competition (and conflict) has spread. The South has grown more industrialized and urbanized in recent decades. Economic competition is not, of course, the only reason for race prejudice. But it is significant that the most violent prejudice is often found among the poor whites, who compete most directly with the Negro in the vital area of employment.

3. *Social class.* Closely related to the factor of economic competition is social class. Various studies have demonstrated that authoritarian, highly prejudiced, and bigoted attitudes are found disproportionately among lower-class persons. Such persons are less willing to tolerate conflicting opinions and are more willing to prohibit freedom of speech. The alleged "liberalism" of the working class thus appears to be a myth, at least as far as civil rights are concerned.[55] This segment of the population is subject to the stresses related to low social and economic status—from a high rate of family disorganization to the constant experience of unemployment. Persons continually faced by such deprivations may react by aggression against minority groups, ranging from verbal hostility to outright physical violence. In this respect, the lower-class person is conforming to the prejudiced attitudes of those about him, as well as responding to his personal sense of frustration.[56]

4. *Rural isolation.* In one study of desegregation, it was found that people with the least contact with the mass media were likewise the least willing to accept racial integration in the public schools. In other words, the more psychologically isolated the individual is from the modern world, the less willing he is to give the Negro educational equality.[57] Those whites in the isolated rural areas of the Deep South insist most strongly upon the ritual of racial segregation and react most violently when that ritual is threatened. In a more general sense, areas that maintain close and ingrown primary relationships, as contrasted with more permissive secondary relationships, appear to be the most resistant to innovation. Race prejudice is, in this sense, one way in which the rural southerner tries to hold back the wave of the future.

5. *Social change.* A further structural factor related to race prejudice is social change. This may take such forms as social unrest, war, revolution, rapid industrialization, and extensive social mobility. When stable status relationships are undermined by social change, many persons are insecure and frustrated. People who experience sharp declines in their occupational status during these periods of change often react by aggression against minority groups. This does not mean, of course, that *every* member of a dynamic society develops hostile attitudes toward minorities. It *does* mean that some persons, whose per-

---

[55] Seymour M. Lipset, "Democracy and Working-Class Authoritarianism," *American Sociological Review,* 24:482-501 (August, 1959).

[56] William McCord, Joan McCord, and Alan Howard, "Early Familial Experiences and Bigotry," *American Sociological Review,* 25:717-722 (October, 1960).

[57] Melvin M. Tumin, "Exposure to Mass Media and Readiness for Desegregation," *Public Opinion Quarterly,* 21:237-251 (Summer, 1959).

sonalities are already insecure, may respond to social change by developing or intensifying prejudice against groups that the society defines as inferior.[58]

6. *Conflicting values.* The extent and virulence of race prejudice in the United States is difficult to reconcile with the democratic creed that forms the basis of our society. This creed states unequivocally that all men are created free and equal and that they shall not be deprived of their basic rights without due process of law. The discrepancy between the professed creed and the fact of discrimination is the central theme of a classic study of the race problem, aptly entitled *An American Dilemma.* This study, as we have seen, suggests that race prejudice grew up partially as a *rationalization* for discrimination against the Negro, both during and after slavery. The action (discrimination) thus arose first and was followed by the rationalization (prejudice). Without some such rationalization concerning the inferiority of the Negro, it is maintained, the gap between the American creed and the practice of discrimination would be intolerable to men of good will.[59]

7. *Social learning.* A final structural consideration is the socialization process whereby prejudice is transmitted from generation to generation. Learning takes place through the traditional channels of the family, as well as through other primary and secondary groups. Learning also occurs through the schools, not only in terms of formal subject matter but also by the mere fact of segregation. Attitudes of race prejudice are learned in interpersonal interaction. Both white and Negro children learn these patterns early—the former acquiring the stereotypes of prejudice and the latter the subservient behavior expected of them. We shall consider the effects of this learning process in the following chapter, insofar as these effects have become incorporated in the system of caste stratification. We are interested here in the process whereby the social structure inculcates and perpetuates race prejudice.

In the general social situation where discrimination is practiced, the prejudiced person develops a distinctive cluster of personality traits. We are concerned here with the qualities of the bitterly prejudiced person, rather than with those of the mildly prejudiced. The racial bigot has many of the qualities of the authoritarian personality, as described in an important study by that title.[60] Other related studies have suggested that the racially intolerant person has some or all of the following personality traits.[61]

Insecurity. A basic personal insecurity is perhaps the most important quality of the highly prejudiced person. This feeling may derive from his early years in the family, where he felt himself unloved and rejected. It may also be accentuated in later life by the structural factors considered above. The racial bigot often sees himself as occupying a marginal position in society.

---

[58] Cf. Bruno Bettelheim and Morris Janowitz, *The Dynamics of Prejudice* (New York: Harper & Row, 1950).

[59] Gunnar M. Myrdal, *An American Dilemma* (rev. ed.) (New York: Harper & Row, 1963).

[60] T. W. Adorno, *et al., The Authoritarian Personality* (New York: Harper & Row, 1950).

[61] The following is freely adapted from Arnold M. Rose and Caroline Rose, *America Divided* (New York: Alfred A. Knopf, Inc., 1948).

Aggression. A related trait of the highly prejudiced person is his tendency to engage in aggressive behavior without provocation. The racial bigot will often go out of his way to provoke a racial incident in a restaurant, on a bus, or in a public rest room. He will also turn the conversation to the Negro without any apparent reason. In his obsession with the race "problem," he may be unconsciously trying to salvage some of his emotional security by demonstrating his superiority over the minority group.

Conformity. The highly prejudiced person also tries to enhance his own self-image by a super-conformity to the outward norms of society. By strictly conforming to the conventions of speech, dress, and (above all) belief, he apparently derives comfort from his ingroup membership. One of the most comforting forms of such belief is prejudice toward a helpless minority. The prejudiced person has the cozy sense of hating the outgroup and at the same time loving himself through the ingroup.

Stereotyped thinking. Since prejudice is a cluster of stereotyped (commonplace and patterned) attitudes, it is not surprising that the prejudiced person thinks in stereotyped terms. He is given to repeating slogans, clichés, and other hackneyed phrases about Negroes and their alleged lack of industry, initiative, and intelligence. He is, furthermore, content to accept such stereotypes at their face value, rather than to think for himself.

"Intolerance of ambiguity." Thinking for oneself also raises the possibility that one might be wrong. Such a possibility is intolerable to the bigot. His entire life structure is based upon the dogmatic acceptance of (his own) racial superiority and (the other's) inferiority. If this principle were seriously questioned, his own self-structure would be threatened. In a more general sense, the prejudiced person also has an "intolerance of ambiguity." Questions must be clear-cut and capable of being answered in categorical terms. For him, the world is composed of black and white, in both a literal and a figurative sense.

Lack of empathy. Finally, the highly prejudiced person is lacking in ability to take the role of the other toward himself and view himself as an object. This lack of empathy means that he cannot understand either himself or the other person—in this case the member of the minority group. The bigot is secure in his own self-image as a member of the superior race and he cannot understand how a member of the "inferior" race might feel—or even that the latter might have any feelings at all. The prejudiced person is, in short, unable to see his own behavior through the eyes of others.

In this chapter, we have considered some of the general facts about race as a factor in social interaction. We have stressed the idea that race is a biological term with sociological implications. Despite the fact that there is no scientific justification for the doctrine of racial superiority and inferiority, many persons act *as if* this were an incontrovertible truth, handed down by the heavenly powers and destined to last for all eternity. The most dynamic outgrowth of the relationships between the races in the United States is prejudice. We have examined briefly the nature of prejudice as existing chiefly in the mind of the prejudiced person, rather than in the characteristics of the minority group. Prejudice reflects both the structure of the society and the early experience of the prejudiced person.

SELECTED BIBLIOGRAPHY

Allport, Gordon W., *The Nature of Prejudice. Cambridge,* Massachusetts: Addison-Wesley Publishing Company, Inc., 1954. A noted psychologist gives a balanced account of the nature of prejudice. He is careful to distinguish between relatively "mild" or conventional prejudice and the fanatical prejudice of the bigot, whose attitudes are an indispensable prop to his inadequate self-feeling.

Benedict, Ruth, *Race: Science and Politics* (rev. ed.). New York: The Viking Press, 1945. Race is here discussed in its sociological setting, as a force in political and social behavior. The author reviews the rise of modern racism and indicates that this development took place as a partial result of the world conquests of the white man.

Boas, Franz, "Race," *Encyclopaedia of the Social Sciences.* New York: The Macmillan Company, 1934. The late dean of American physical anthropologists gives an authoritative statement of the nature of race, with particular reference to real and alleged racial differences.

Coon, Carleton S., *The Origin of Race.* New York: Alfred A. Knopf, Inc., 1962. The respected author of this controversial book summarizes his position as follows: "My thesis is . . . that at the beginning of our record, over half a million years ago, man was a single species, *Homo erectus,* perhaps divided into five geographic races or subspecies. *Homo erectus* then evolved into *Homo Sapiens* not once but five times, as each species, living in its own territory, passed a critical threshold from a more brutal to a more sapient state."

Dobzhansky, Theodosius, *Mankind Evolving: The Evolution of the Human Species.* New Haven: Yale University Press, 1962. One of the world's leading geneticists discusses some of the crucial questions of human evolution. His central thesis is stated as follows: "Human evolution has two components, the biological or organic, and the cultural or superorganic. These components are neither mutually exclusive nor independent, but interrelated and interpedendent. Human evolution . . . is the interaction of biology and culture." (p. 18).

Dunn, L. C., and Theodosius Dobzhansky, *Heredity, Race and Society* (rev. ed.). New York: The New American Library of World Literature, Inc., 1952. This is a popular and authoritative statement by two leading geneticists of the nature of race in the biological sense. This dispassionate account of the genetic differences (and similarities) between population groups puts into proper perspective much of the uninformed and emotional discussion of the subject.

Frazier, E. Franklin, "Sociological Theory and Race Relations," *American Sociological Review,* 12:265-271 (June, 1947). A leading authority on race relations outlines some of the sociological knowledge in this explosive field.

Klineberg, Otto, *Race Differences.* New Haven: Harper & Brothers, 1935. The basic thesis of this careful study is that there is no significant difference between races in their ability to absorb and initiate culture. A large volume of work has been done since this book was published, but its major findings have not been refuted. In cultural development, racial potentialities are equal.

Myrdal, Gunnar, *An American Dilemma* (rev. ed.). New York: Harper & Row, 1963. This is the most extensive study ever made of the Negro in the United States. The status of the Negro is examined in the light of the democratic value-premises of our society. The caste position of the Negro violates the equalitarian values of the Founding Fathers.

Simpson, George E., and J. Milton Yinger, *Racial and Cultural Minorities* (rev. ed.). New York: Harper & Row, 1958. This is an excellent and inclusive analysis of the race problem in the United States, with its implications for prejudice and discrimination.

Thompson, Edgar T., and Everett C. Hughes (eds.), *Race: Individual and Collective Behavior*. Glencoe, Ill.: The Free Press, 1958. This reader is an important aid to students at either the introductory or more advanced level who seek added perspective in race relations. The editors offer this perspective by their selections from an unusually broad and catholic range of source materials, including "lore, myths, rationalizations, doctrines, poetry, and social fiction as well as . . . serious scientific studies and reports."

Washburn, S.L., "The Study of Race," *American Anthropologist*, 65:521-531 (June, 1963). This article offers an excellent general statement of the current thinking by anthropologists on such matters as the evolution of the races, the role of culture in this evolution, the concept of racism, and the problem of discrimination. On the latter subject, Washburn remarks succinctly, "We know the price of discrimination is death, frustration, and hatred."

13 *Caste*

The Nature of Social Stratification

A functioning society requires that a multitude of different tasks be performed and that there be some means of controlling and directing the behavior of the members toward the fulfillment of these tasks. Status and role are the most important methods of realizing this purpose. A system of hierarchical ranking by groups is a related way of reaching the same end. Each of the major divisions of the social structure has its own status, privileges, and obligations. Some of these elements are ascribed and others are achieved. Social stratification is the name applied to the resulting system of organization.[1]

[1] Kingsley Davis and Wilbert E. Moore, "Some Principles of Stratification," *American Sociological Review*, 10:242-249 (April, 1945).

Social stratification has been briefly defined as "a pattern of superimposed categories of differential privilege." [2] This definition has several important elements. *First,* social stratification is a cultural pattern, accepted by the members of a society, that assigns them to a general position in the social structure. *Second,* social stratification is superimposed by tradition without the will or even the conscious knowledge of the great majority of the members. *Third,* social stratification involves a system of differential privilege, which means that some groups receive more of the goods, services, power, and emotional gratifications of the society than others.

Social stratification is the product of social interaction. In the course of such interaction in a society over a prolonged period, roles and activities evolve that carry different social evaluations. The warrior, the landowner, the priest, the business man, the scholar, and the bureaucrat play different roles that carry different degrees of social evaluation. Some societies value the warrior, others the scholar, and still others the business man. The privileges given to the performance of these and other roles are perpetuated from one generation to the next. Social stratification is thus "the product of the interaction of social differentiation and social evaluation." [3]

Social stratification is in one sense a system of "institutionalized social inequality" that perpetuates privilege from generation to generation. On an ethical level, many forms of stratification are unjustified, however much they may contribute to the "orderly" functioning of a society.[4] The system of slavery in the United States undoubtedly contributed to the "stability" of the South before the Civil War. The rigid class system of the late Middle Ages in Europe was likewise a stabilizing element in the society of its day. The nobility, the clergy, the urban middle class, and the peasantry were locked in a tightly knit system of differential rewards and privileges. But this did not mean that these forms of stratification were ethically justifiable.

There is even some question of the ultimate *efficiency* of certain aspects of social stratification. The individual may lose interest in his work if his rewards are not commensurate with his efforts.[5] If he is denied access to the valued goals of a society (money, status, power), he may become a deviant and a problem to the society and to himself.[6] Although position in an open society may be largely open to "performance," some persons have a greater initial *chance* to perform than others. Under any system of stratification, some persons have

[2] John F. Cuber and William F. Kenkel, *Social Stratification in the United States* (New York: Appleton-Century-Crofts, Inc., 1954), p. 11.

[3] Bernard Barber, *Social Stratification* (New York: Harcourt, Brace and Company, 1957), p. 2.

[4] Melvin M. Tumin, "Some Principles of Stratification: A Critical Analysis," *American Sociological Review,* 18:387-394 (August, 1953).

[5] Melvin M. Tumin, "Rewards and Task Orientations," *American Sociological Review,* 20:419-423 (August, 1955).

[6] Richard A. Cloward, "Illegitimate Means, *Anomie,* and Deviant Behavior," *American Sociological Review,* 24:164-176 (April, 1959).

more chance than others to demonstrate their abilities to fulfill certain valued roles. The opportunity is often as important as the performance.[7]

In a highly stratified society, only a small number of persons in the upper segments are given the chance to show that they can fill the most "functionally" important roles. In the Middle Ages, the armored knight played perhaps the most "functional" role in the society—at least in the sense of protecting his own people and waging war on others. But only a tiny proportion of the male population was ever given the opportunity to train for this role. Conversely, in our own society, the opportunities are greater for a poor boy to become, say, a doctor, lawyer, scientist, or political leader. Even in such a relatively open society, however, advancement is not equally open to bright young men (and women) of every social level. As Buckley puts it, "for *most* societies throughout *most* of history, 'talent' to fill the most 'functionally' important positions has in point of fact been 'recruited' from a small minority of the total 'potential' talent." [8]

Hence it is incorrect to say that a system of social stratification "automatically" insures the assumption of the most functional (important) roles by the best-qualified persons. No society has ever existed where this situation literally applied—provided we mean by "the best-qualified persons" those whose genetic qualifications are the highest. Everywhere the very *fact* of social stratification itself has meant that "some are more equal than others" [9] in the competition for the most highly rewarded roles. Whatever the ethical implications of this situation, the fact remains that "inequality is ubiquitous in human societies"[10]—at least in such societies as the world has hitherto seen. In some societies, indeed, inequality is rendered virtually self-perpetuating by the fact that status is *ascribed* on the basis of birth. The person born into a low status thus has no chance of raising himself in the system. In other societies such as our own, the stratification system is not so rigid and self-perpetuating, and many people *can* ascend the status scale.[11]

The principal forms of social stratification are class and caste. A *class* is a comparatively permanent group of persons of all ages and both sexes who occupy a common social position in a hierarchical ranking within a given society. A *caste* is a fixed group in a rigid social structure, in which rank is based almost entirely upon hereditary grounds. Members of a class receive their status at birth, but they may lose or alter it by subsequent behavior. Members of a caste also receive their status at birth, but it usually remains fixed regardless of

---

[7] Walter Buckley, "Social Stratification and the Functional Theory of Social Differentiation," *American Sociological Review*, 23:369-375 (August, 1958).

[8] Walter Buckley, "On Equitable Inequality," *American Sociological Review*, 28:799-801 (October, 1963), p. 799. (His italics.)

[9] Cf. Wilbert E. Moore, "But Some Are More Equal Than Others," *American Sociological Review*, 28:13-18 (February, 1963).

[10] *Ibid.* Cf. Melvin M. Tumin, "On Inequality," *American Sociological Review*, 28:19-26 (February, 1963).

[11] We shall examine this situation in Chapter 15, "Mobility."

later achievements.[12] Upward movement in the social scale is possible for a class, but ordinarily not for a caste. The latter forms a "frozen" social hierarchy, whereas classes are more fluid. Members of different castes rarely intermarry. Marriage between classes, although limited, is not impossible.[13]

Caste and class both denote a degree of homogeneity among the members, who often carry on the same general activities and occupy approximately the same social status. In this sense, the concept of status implies a general *group* position, rather than a particular *individual* position. Individual status determines differential rights and duties in detail, whereas membership in a caste or class is a rough sorting device for general preferential rewards and the corresponding obligations. This common status also leads to broad similarities in personality among members of the various classes and castes.[14]

The System of Differential Rewards

Membership in a high caste or class carries real social advantages, such as better occupations, living conditions, and clothing, as well as greater leisure, deference, and power. In effect, such membership means greater returns for less effort. Membership in the lower levels of the stratification system involves equally real disadvantages. Such persons must work harder for less remuneration, financial or otherwise, and have little or no unearned increment by hereditary "right." Society offers to its elites (and withholds from its non-elites) such rewards as: (*a*) perferential treatment in sustenance and comfort; (*b*) humor and diversion; and (*c*) self-respect and opportunities for ego-expansion.[15]

Social stratification thus involves different "life-chances" for the various groups. This term refers to the "varying probability that a person in a given status will achieve some stated objective or suffer some stated disadvantage." [16] Life-chances vary between castes and classes. The chances that a Negro boy will become President of the United States are so slight as to be negligible. The chances that a given white boy will reach the same goal are at least statistically possible. The life-chances of attending college are higher for a boy from upper-middle-class parents than for a boy from the working class, even though the latter's chances of reaching this goal have increased.

The operation of "life-chances" in the stratification system of the United States has been demonstrated by a study of the social origins of the leaders of big business. A comparatively small upper segment of the population accounted for most of the business leaders of the present generation. Approximately two out of every three business leaders are sons of business leaders or professional men. Sons of farmers, laborers, clerks, salesmen, and other lower-class and

---

[12] Kingsley Davis, "A Conceptual Analysis of Stratification," *American Sociological Review,* 7:309-321 (June, 1942).

[13] Marvin Harris, "Caste, Class, and Minority," *Social Forces,* 37:248-254 (March, 1959).

[14] Robert J. Havighurst, "Social Class and Basic Personality Structure," *Sociology and Social Research,* 36:355-363 (July-August, 1952).

[15] Davis and Moore, *op. cit.,* p. 243.

[16] Cuber and Kenkel, *op, cit.,* p. 18.

lower-middle-class individuals constitute the other third of the business leaders. In terms of absolute numbers, however, lower-class persons are much more
numerous in the population than are those in the elite positions. In short,
"sons of big business men ... occupy nearly *eight times* their proportionate
share of elite positions." [17]

In a competitive stratification system such as our own, the chief problem is to
motivate the ablest persons to *assume* the positions of responsibility. The system of differential rewards is the most important such motivating force. At the
same time, there are factors operating against such assumption by those with
the best qualifications. Different racial, religious, and ethnic groups have varying attitudes toward achievement. In a significant recent study, Rosen found
that "achievement motivation is more characteristic of Greeks, Jews, and White
Protestants than of Italians, French-Canadians and Negroes." [18] The former
groups displayed both the desire to achieve higher status and, even more important, the personality traits and self-discipline necessary to do so. The latter
groups were, on balance, lacking in this "achievement syndrome." [19]

In a fixed status system, on the other hand, the chief problem is to motivate
the individual to *remain* in his social position, whatever it may.be. Emphasis
here is upon maintaining the *status quo* and the existing system of rewards and
privileges. The social values stress the importance of staying in one's place, of
playing the role of one's father and grandfather, and of keeping the entire system of status and roles intact. The motivations that societies instill in their
members thus differ on the basis of the stratification systems. The latter vary
from one society to another and are closely integrated with other elements of
the culture. [20]

Among these sociocultural elements are: the size of the society; the relations
with surrounding peoples; the internal division of labor; the functional emphasis of the society (for example, on business or war); the traditions of class solidarity; the presence of minority racial, ethnic, and religious groups; and the
accepted standards of social mobility. The widespread existence of social stratification offers proof of its survival value, if not of its ethical justification. A
certain amount of built-in social inequality would appear to be necessary for the
allocation of different jobs and functions in a society.[21]

This does not mean that the resulting stratification system is *completely* functional. The social importance of a given role cannot necessarily be assumed
from the rewards given to it. For centuries, as noted, the rewards of the landed
aristocracy in Europe were disproportionate to their value to the society. Their
role was primarily that of waging war, either on each other or on some outside
enemy. Many of these activities were obviously dysfunctional to the society;

---

[17] W. Lloyd Warner and James C. Abegglen, *Big Business Leaders in America* (New York: Harper &
Row, 1955), p. 17. (My italics.)

[18] Bernard C. Rosen, "Race, Ethnicity, and the Achievement Syndrome," *American Sociological Review,*
24:47-60 (February, 1959), p. 60.

[19] *Ibid.*

[20] Davis and Moore, *op. cit.*

[21] *Ibid.*, p. 243.

lives, property, and institutions were destroyed or damaged in the endless feudal conflicts. Custom and established power combined to make the role of the aristocracy a highly rewarding one for centuries. There is, in short, no necessary one-to-one relationship between different positions in the stratification system and the ultimate welfare of a society.[22]

The idea of social stratification is repugnant to the average American, who has been spiritually nourished on the heady ideal of the equality of all men. Stratification assumes a number of forms, however, that differ in functional efficiency as well as ethical basis. There is considerable difference between a stratification system based entirely upon heredity and one based largely upon individual ability. As long as many (if not most) of the positions of authority are open to trained talent, both efficiency and social justice will be served. If some form of stratification is necessary for the coordination of group activities, a system based upon ability rather than birth is more closely in accord with American cultural aspirations.[23]

The Bases of Social Stratification

Stratification in human societies appears to have developed from two different sources, although one often merges into the other. The bases of social stratification are: (*a*) social, and (*b*) ethnic. The former involves the growth within a given society of a system of ranked strata, whose members are differentiated by purely "social" factors. This form of stratification is often called "functional" in the sense that certain basic "functions" of any society are allegedly furthered. Among these functions are religion, government, economic activity, and technological development.[24] In the performance of these necessary functions, some roles are more "valuable" than others and, as we have seen, are awarded correspondingly greater rewards and privileges.[25] Much of the controversy that has raged in the sociological literature has involved the ethical and the functional implications of this form of stratification.[26]

Ethnic stratification is found in societies where one ethnic or racial group succeeds in dominating another more or less permanently. Variants of ethnic stratification are found in history and anthropology, ranging from sporadic tribute to outright slavery.[27] In some societies, ethnic stratification seems to have preceded social stratification. The development of the English nobility out of the Norman knighthood of William the Conqueror illustrates this process. The enslavement of the Children of Israel by the Egyptians is an even more

---

[22] Richard L. Simpson, "A Modification of the Functional Theory of Social Stratification," *Social Forces*, 35:133-137 (December, 1956).

[23] W. Lloyd Warner, *et al., Social Class in America* (Chicago: Science Research Associates, 1949), p. 8.

[24] George A. Huaco, "A Logical Analysis of the Davis-Moore Theory of Stratification," *American Sociological Review*, 28:801-804 (October, 1963).

[25] Davis and Moore, *op. cit.*

[26] See Melvin M. Tumin and Arthur Feldman, *Social Class and Social Change in Puerto Rico* (Princeton, New Jersey: Princeton University Press, 1961), Chapter 29, "Theoretical Implications."

[27] Gunnar Landtman, *The Origin of the Inequality of the Social Classes* (Chicago: University of Chicago Press, 1938), pp. 102-106.

familiar example of ethnic stratification. In the egalitarian environment of the contemporary United States, few reputable social scientists attempt to explain (let alone justify) ethnic stratification on "functional" grounds. This form of stratification is so clearly foreign to democratic values that whatever "functional" qualities it may possess in maintaining social order are outweighed by its unethical basis.

It is important to bear in mind, therefore, that stratification is based upon different, albeit related, considerations. Both forms of social stratification involve different statuses and roles and corresponding differences in rewards. In theory, however, the *bases* of these rewards are not the same. *Racial* stratification in the United States differs from *social* stratification among the white population. Both forms involve inequality, but the discrepancy between white and nonwhite is much greater than between whites. Furthermore, the system of class stratification in this country has *some* basis in terms of the differential functions performed by, say, doctors and ditch diggers.

The system of racial stratification (caste), however, has no such functional justification. Under this system, more than ten per cent of the population of the United States is arbitrarily deprived of the right to compete for achieved status. As one sociologist puts it, ". . . social [racial] stratification in the Deep South is not integrative. It impedes the getting of essential work done. Much potential talent is undiscovered, untrained, and unused." [28] The waste of human resources from the caste system in this country is literally beyond conception. No one knows how much ability is left undeveloped by the arbitrary assignment of lower-caste roles to Negroes.

In an even broader sense, it is difficult to justify *either* ethnic or social stratification in strictly functional, let alone ethical, terms. Stratification obviously exists and presumably has always existed, and hence may be justified as keeping a given society functioning. In this sense, however, one may be led to adopt the philosophy that whatever *is* is right—because it is functional. [29] Speaking to this general point, Tumin warns us not to be "beguiled into seeking rational accounts for the existence and continuity of various cultural forms, most of which seem to be accidental products of human social history which arise very much by chance, and persist often simply by virtue of impersonal social drift . . . or by the contrivances of various elites who find the social situation to their liking and wish to preserve it." [30]

A final question may be raised in connection with the functional explanation of social stratification. This is, briefly, whether anyone can objectively determine what roles *are* the most functional—in the sense of making the greatest contribution to the stability and (especially) the survival of a given society. Much of this assertion has heretofore been on a commonsense basis—for exam-

---

[28] Stuart A. Queen, "The Function of Social Stratification: A Critique," *Sociology and Social Research*, 46:412-415 (July, 1962), p. 414.

[29] Cf. Harold Fallding, "Functional Analysis in Sociology," *American Sociological Review*, 28:5-13 (February, 1963).

[30] Tumin, "On Inequality," *op. cit.*, p. 25.

ple, that the function of a merchant is more important to economic survival than that of a peasant and hence should be rewarded accordingly. Similarly, a general (especially in wartime) [31] is presumed to be more important than a private. The comparative importance of hundreds of functional roles has, however, largely been taken for granted, often merely because these roles were already highly rewarded in comparison with other roles. This is clearly reasoning in a circle. One scholar has questioned the assumption that, in the present state of knowledge, the sociologist can empirically draw up a list of roles in order of their functional importance for *any* society, let alone for *all* societies.[32]

Caste in India: A Prototype

The most enduring form of social stratification is the caste system of India. This system began as ethnic stratification and continued as social stratification. The caste system is, in effect, a complex system of inherited social status. Each caste has its own system of rewards, taboos, proscriptions, and occupations, and the members are obliged by the mores to remain in their ascribed statuses and perform their ascribed roles. In this latter sense, Dobzhansky speaks of the

[31] Arthur L. Stinchcombe, "Some Empirical Consequences of the Davis-Moore Theory of Stratification," *American Sociological Review*, 28:805-808 (October, 1963).

[32] Huaco, *op. cit.*, p. 804.

Caste in action in India. A priest places a caste mark upon a member of the upper caste, thereby indicating his superior status for all to see.

caste system as "an experiment on a grand scale that attempted to breed varieties of men genetically specialized in the performance of different functions. To all appearances," he concludes, "such a specialization has not been achieved." [33] Furthermore, it will never be achieved because time is running out on the caste system.

Caste is presumably unchangeable from birth and, according to Indian religious notions of reincarnation, only through rebirth can one enter a higher caste. Castes are endogamous and (in theory at least) no one can marry outside his caste or subcaste. The concept of ritual purity is strong and certain occupations (garbage disposal, cleaning the streets, dealing with corpses) are defiling to the castes forced to engage in them. Mere contact with such "untouchables" is likewise contaminating, and there is a taboo against receiving food and drink from a low caste person.

Embodied in religious teaching, deeply ingrained in the norms, and long incorporated into law, the caste system has stood the test of time. This pattern has been the basis of stratification for hundreds of millions of people for many centuries. The government of the new India is attempting to eliminate many caste barriers and substitute greater equality for its citizens. Such efforts must overcome the inertia of the mores, the sanctions of religion, the force of ritual, and the active resistance of vested interests in the traditional structure. The impact of industrialism will encourage this transition, as occupations are increasingly based on training and ability, rather than caste.[34] The system varies considerably from one part of India to another, and changes are occurring at differential rates of speed in the various parts of the vast subcontinent.[35]

The current effort to modify the Indian caste system is one of the most ambitious attempts at deliberate culture change the world has ever seen. Caste is, in final analysis, a culture pattern. And culture rests in the minds of men.[36] The nature of this complex pattern has been explored in a series of studies of the attitudes, opinions, and stereotypes of six Hindu caste groups. Three of these groups were high caste and three low caste, and a sample of 100 subjects from each group was intensively investigated. The members of each caste learn different attitudes toward each other and themselves. These mental pictures are acquired in the process of socialization and carry the sanctions of tradition, religion, and public opinion.[37]

The self-attitudes of the different groups are especially revealing in this connection. As we have indicated, the self is a social product and the individual acquires his self-feeling by taking the role of the other and viewing himself as an object through the other's eyes.[38] In much the same way, different caste

---

[33] Theodosius Dobzhansky, *Mankind Evolving: The Evolution of the Human Species* (New Haven: Yale University Press, 1962), p. 238.

[34] Noel P. Gist, "Caste Differentials in South India," *American Sociological Review*, 19:126-137 (April, 1954).

[35] Noel P. Gist, "Caste in Transition: South India," *Phylon*, 15:155-164 (Second Quarter, 1954).

[36] Gardner Murphy, *In the Minds of Men* (New York: Basic Books, Inc., 1953).

[37] R. Rath and N. C. Sircar, "Inter-Caste Relationship as Reflected in the Study of Attitudes and Opinions of Six Hindu Caste Groups," *The Journal of Social Psychology*, 51:3-25 (February, 1960).

[38] George H. Mead, *Mind, Self and Society* (Chicago: University of Chicago Press, 1934).

groups look at themselves through the stereotypes that have been a part of the culture for centuries. Lower caste groups have a strong feeling of inferiority and self-abasement, and upper caste groups display a corresponding sense of superiority and self-satisfaction. The attitudes of each group toward the other(s) have a strong resemblance, as upper caste members look at themselves in much the same way as do lower caste members and vice versa.[39] That is, upper caste persons have a high status in their own eyes, as well as in the eyes of lower caste persons. Conversely, the latter think of themselves as lowly and are similarly regarded by members of the upper castes. These traditional attitudes form part of the "generalized other" so eloquently described by Mead, and members of Hindu society acquire their self-feeling partially by regarding themselves through this culture pattern.

Another aspect of this important study dealt with attitudes toward low caste untouchables, both on the part of the high caste members and the untouchables themselves. Members of all caste groups reject the traditional belief that untouchability is a result of the untouchables' own prior depravities, viciousness, and general unpleasantness. On the contrary, the belief was widespread that untouchability was caused by the initial and unlawful assumption of power by upper caste groups, the perpetuation of this power by custom, and other social factors. "This kind of belief," comment the authors of the study, "was more amenable to change than any other belief in the genetic or any other inherent biological or mental defects and deficiencies of the untouchables."[40] Hindus themselves thus believe that caste is the product of cultural and traditional, rather than biological and inherent, factors. In this case, the social structure is, in theory at least, subject to change. Even to its members, the caste system is no longer regarded as an Act of God.

The general pattern of the caste system in India is the classic example of this type of social stratification. In this sense, it may be taken as a conceptual model for other systems designated by the same title. We may enumerate the general characteristics of this model pattern and then apply them to the stratification system in the United States:[41]

1. Membership in the caste is hereditary and unchangeable for life.

2. Marriages must be made within the caste line.

3. Contact with other castes or subcastes in all aspects of life is strictly regulated by the mores.

4. Each caste has its particular customs and often its traditional occupation in which its members must engage.

5. The hierarchy of the caste system is strictly enforced according to its local variations.

---

[39] R. Rath and N. C. Sircar, "The Mental Pictures of Six Hindu Caste Groups About Each Other as Reflected in Verbal Stereotypes," *The Journal of Social Psychology*, 51:277-293 (May, 1960).

[40] R. Rath and N. C. Sircar, "The Cognitive Background of Six Hindu Caste Groups Regarding the Low Caste Untouchables," *The Journal of Social Psychology*, 51:295-306 (May, 1960), p. 305.

[41] These criteria are adapted from Kingsley Davis, *Human Society* (New York: The Macmillan Company, 1949), pp. 378-379.

The Caste System in American Society

The subordination of the Negro in the South is the most important aspect of ethnic stratification in our society. It is also the most important *domestic* social problem. Considerable discussion has arisen among social scientists as to whether or not this system actually constitutes a caste organization of society. Most impartial observers agree on the *facts* of the system; the principal disagreement lies with its *definition*.[42] One sociologist maintains that ". . . the term 'caste system' is applicable at the present time in the southern United States . . . and . . . it can be usefully applied to societies with *systems of hierarchical, endogamous subdivisions whose membership is hereditary and permanent*." [43] There are, of course, striking local differences between this form of organization and that of India.[44] But in terms of the general criteria set forth above, the pattern of race relations in the South does approximate a caste system. Without further discussion of semantics, therefore, we shall examine this form of ethnic stratification *as if it were* a caste system.[45]

This form of segregation and exploitation has grown gradually until it has become deeply imbedded in the culture of the South. The present system of race relations has, in a sense, replaced the pattern of slavery as a means of maintaining the former status order. Under the system still widely in effect, the whites have many of the privileges of the former slave owners, but none of the latters' legal and moral responsibilities toward their slaves. Although the Negroes have, in general, remained comparatively passive in their acceptance of their caste status, there is little valid evidence that they are "content" with it. As Berreman puts it, "A comparison of the realities of caste attitude and interaction in India and the United States suggests that no group of people is content to be low in a caste hierarchy . . . regardless of the rationalizations offered them by their superiors or constructed by themselves." [46]

A number of social, economic, and sexual gains fall to the whites by keeping the Negro in a permanently subordinate position.[47] These gains are more evident in the South than in the North, but they are found to some extent in all sections of the country. The white man traditionally had access to Negro women, whereas the reverse was (and is) unthinkable to the white mores. The white man gains social privileges from a Negro minority performing menial tasks at low wages. The white man likewise enjoys economic gains because the Negro has until recently been kept in subordinate occupations, where he will

---

[42] Edward W. Pohlman, "Semantic Aspects of the Controversy Over Negro-White Caste in the United States," *Social Forces,* 30:416-419 (May, 1952).

[43] Gerald D. Berreman, "Caste in India and the United States," *American Journal of Sociology,* 66:120-127 (September, 1960), p. 127. (My italics.)

[44] For a recent account of caste in India, see "Caste" in *Current Sociology,* Basil Blackwell, London, 1959 (Published for UNESCO).

[45] Oliver C. Cox, *Caste, Class, and Race* (New York: Doubleday & Company, 1948), Chapter 15, "Class and Caste."

[46] Berreman, *op. cit.,* p. 127.

[47] John Dollard, *Caste and Class in a Southern Town* (New York: Doubleday Anchor Books, 1949).

not ordinarily compete with the whites. The gains accruing from this situation were demonstrated by a study of the employment statistics in the 151 Standard Metropolitan Areas with more than 100,000 population in 1950. Summarizing these findings, the author stated: "The data presented here leave little doubt that in 1950 whites in American metropolitan areas which had large Negro populations were benefiting occupationally from the presence and low status of Negroes." [48] In these and many other ways, the caste system provides both tangible and intangible "gains" for the majority group.

We may examine the social structure of the South in terms of the general criteria of the typical caste system. This structure is in process of change throughout the South, with the urban industrial areas changing more rapidly than the rural agricultural areas.[49] Many of the following generalizations must therefore be qualified in terms of these and other differentials.[50] It is impossible, however, to qualify *every* statement in order to take into account the many changes occurring throughout the South and the rest of the United States during the mid-1960's. With this reservation, we shall outline some of the *typical* similarities between ethnic stratification in the United States (with particular reference to the Deep South) and the generalized caste system.[51]

1. Caste membership lasts for life. The Negro in the United States is born into a racially defined lower caste in which, with a few individual exceptions, he must remain for life. Spirituals may indeed promise a happier life in heaven for the Negro freed from the serfdom of caste, but the Negro cannot escape his status on earth as long as he has one "drop" of recognizable Negro "blood." The only way for the individual Negro to escape fully from this status is to cross the color line and "pass" as a white man. Reliable figures on the extent of such "passing" obviously do not exist, although one estimate suggests that approximately 2,500 persons cross the color line more or less permanently every year. The same authority tentatively estimates that there are about 110,000 persons who are "legally" Negroes but permanently pass for white.[52]

The individual Negro may thus, in theory, change his caste, provided he is light enough in color and possesses none of the other recognizable Negro characteristics. This process is more common in the urban and anonymous North than in the rural and race-conscious South. Furthermore, a relatively small number of Negroes marry or mate with members of the white race in the United States. In the proximate future, therefore, there will be no large-scale merging of the races. A careful study, indeed, indicates that the Negro will still be a distinct racial minority two hundred years hence, if the present rate of racial intermixture continues. The caste status of the Negro will doubtless

---

[48] Norval D. Glenn, "Occupational Benefits to Whites from the Subordination of Negroes," *American Sociological Review*, 28:443-448 (June, 1963), p. 447.

[49] H. M. Blalock, "Urbanization and Discrimination in the South," *Social Problems*, 7:146-152 (Fall, 1959).

[50] Cf. Charles U. Smith, "Race, Human Relations, and the Changing South," *Phylon*, 23:66-72 (Spring, 1962).

[51] Davis, *op. cit.*, pp. 378-379.

[52] John H. Burma, "The Measurement of Negro Passing," *American Journal of Sociology*, 52:18-22 (July, 1946).

change in this period. But the group itself will remain as an important minority in the population.[53]

2. *Castes are endogamous.* This statement means that marriage must take place within the caste and that members are not allowed to cross caste boundaries in search of a mate. In the United States, most southern and western states have laws against marriage between Negroes and whites. In addition to these legal prohibitions, the mores are overwhelmingly against such mixed racial unions. There is likewise a strong feeling against miscegenation (racial intermixture) in any form, inasmuch as the "purity" of the white race is presumably violated by sexual contact with the Negro, either in or out of marriage.

This taboo does not, in practice, extend to sexual relations between white males and Negro females. This behavior was accepted under slavery and continues to be tacitly condoned at the present time. In this relationship, as noted, a sexual "gain" accrues to the white man, inasmuch as white males have access both to white and Negro females, whereas Negro males have access only to females of their own race. It has been suggested that members of the white caste may suffer from an unconscious feeling of guilt in this relationship.[54] However this may be, it is clear that the *principle* of endogamy is maintained, inasmuch as the offspring of a mixed mating takes the status of the lower caste. The child of a Negro-white union automatically becomes a Negro.

3. *Castes maintain ritual avoidance.* The avoidance pattern between Negroes and whites, like that of the rest of the caste pattern, enters into all the major relationships. This pattern has been formalized into a culturally enforced web of segregation, whose major function is to maintain the caste barrier and "keep the Negroes in their place." Negroes ordinarily attempt to have as little social contact as possible with whites, since these contacts may lead to unpredictable and often unpleasant results. Life for the Negro may be frustrating and dangerous in the world of the white man, where the ritual patterns of avoidance are not always clear.

The avoidance pattern is most obvious in the case of residential segregation. There is generally a segregated section in all communities with a sizable Negro population, although the forms of segregation vary between rural and urban areas and between North and South.[55] In many of the large cities of the North, the segregated area assumes the characteristics of a ghetto, with inadequate municipal services, unsatisfactory police protection, and crowded and expensive housing. In Chicago, for example, there are nearly 1,000,000 Negroes, of whom some 500,000 live in a concentrated area of the "black belt." In one survey, 53 per cent of the Negro housing was found to be substandard or dilapidated, whereas only 15 per cent of the white housing was so defined.[56]

---

[53] William M. Kephart, "Is the American Negro Becoming Lighter?", *American Sociological Review,* 13:437-443 (August, 1948).

[54] Dollard, *op. cit.,* Chapter VII, "The Sexual Gain."

[55] Frank F. Lee, "A Cross Institutional Comparison of Northern and Southern Race Relations," *Social Forces,* 42:185-191 (January, 1958).

[56] Otis Dudley Duncan and Beverly Duncan, *The Negro Population of Chicago* (Chicago: University of Chicago Press, 1957) pp. 77-79.

Although it is now illegal to enforce segregation by municipal ordinance, "restrictive covenants" have long been written into housing deeds, whereby all but "Caucasians" are kept out. These restrictive covenants were declared unconstitutional by the Supreme Court on May 8, 1948, but segregation continues by "gentlemen's agreement" between property owners and realtors.[57] Rental housing, as distinguished from owned homes, is kept segregated by policies restricting desirable apartment buildings to whites.[58] Even when Negroes have enough money to buy a house or rent an apartment in a desirable neighborhood in the North, they are often forced to pay exorbitant prices for the privilege.[59]

Segregation has thus been prohibited by law and administrative action for a number of years. These changes in law do not appear to have been accompanied by changes in actual practice. Residential segregation actually increased, rather than decreased, during the decade 1940-1950. A nationwide study of 185 American cities disclosed that residential segregation had increased in 129 cities, decreased in 52, and remained the same in 4 cities. This study measured the actual physical process of segregation, rather than attitudes toward this practice. Whatever the changes (if any) in attitudes over this period, the fact remains that segregation increased on a broad front.[60]

The armed forces of the United States have traditionally maintained the policy of ritual avoidance through separate colored units and the allocation of Negroes to menial positions. In 1950, however, President Truman ordered the complete desegregation of the services,[61] and at the present time the army, navy, and air force are virtually completely integrated. Negroes are still heavily under-represented at the officer level, especially in the navy and the marine corps, but this disparity reflects (at least partially) a lack of seniority and training, rather than direct discrimination on the basis of race. The Department of Defense has, furthermore, integrated the schools and other facilities under its direct jurisdiction. Attitudes of prejudice and acts of discrimination have obviously not been eliminated by these and other formal actions of the military authorities. But great advances have nevertheless been made toward equality of treatment and the elimination of ritual avoidance in the armed forces, which have hitherto been among the most conservative organizations in this respect.[62]

Ritual avoidance is also applied to education in the southern states. The Supreme Court decision of May 17, 1954 declared this practice unconstitu-

---

[57] Loren Miller, "Supreme Court Covenant Decision—An Analysis," *The Crisis,* 55:265-266ff (September, 1948).

[58] Arnold M. Rose, *et al.,* "Neighborhood Reactions to Isolated Negro Residents: An Alternative to Invasion and Succession," *American Sociological Review,* 18:497-507 (October, 1953).

[59] See also Nathan Glazer and Davis McEntire (eds.), *Studies in Housing and Minority Groups* (Berkeley: University of California Press, 1959).

[60] Donald O. Cowgill, "Trends in Residential Segregation of Nonwhites in American Cities, 1940-1950," *American Sociological Review,* 21:43-47 (February, 1956).

[61] Clarence Mitchell, "The Status of Racial Integration in the Armed Services," *The Journal of Negro Education,* 23:203-213 (Summer, 1954).

[62] J. Milton Yinger, "Desegregation in American Society: The Record of a Generation of Change," *Sociology and Social Research,* 47:428-445 (July, 1963), p. 433.

tional, but the various states have been reluctant to introduce constructive measures toward desegregation. The traditional theory was based upon the concept of "separate but equal" schools for Negroes, a policy that in practice meant that the latter were forced to accept inferior educational facilities. After the historic decision, desegregation began at different rates and under different conditions in the several states. Some states made sincere efforts to desegregate; others made only token efforts after sustained prodding by the courts; and still others made no effort whatever to obey the law. Several states, indeed, attempted either to postpone integration indefinitely or to evade it entirely by legal means. One after another, these attempts were struck down by the federal courts.

The school year 1964-1965, however, started with the great majority of Negro students throughout the South and the border states still attending segregated schools. Seventeen states and the District of Columbia maintained educational segregation before the 1954 Supreme Court decision. This region contains 6,197 school districts, of which 3,053 had some degree of integration by 1963.[63] Many of these nominally integrated districts, however, had only a few Negro students attending schools with white children. Exact figures are unreported, but it is estimated that 9 out of 10 Negro children were still attending segregated schools throughout the South and border states in the fall of 1963, nearly ten years after the Supreme Court decision. Ritual avoidance in education is still an important aspect of the traditional way of life in the South.

With physical avoidance comes social avoidance. With certain striking exceptions (National Association for the Advancement of Colored People, Congress of Racial Equality, Urban League), Negroes do not participate in voluntary associations with white people. As a result, Negroes form their own associations to further their economic, recreational, and social interests. A recent study in Lincoln, Nebraska (population 130,000) found that the rate of Negro participation in voluntary associations was much higher than that of white persons, especially at the lower-class level. This activity is *exclusive* of both church and union participation, neither of which was counted as a voluntary association for purposes of this study. Some two-thirds of all lower-class Negroes were found to participate in one or more voluntary associations, and the proportion among higher-class Negroes was even greater.[64] This is in striking contrast to the situation among the population of the United States as a whole, where 47 per cent of *all* families belonged to no voluntary association whatever.[65]

At first glance, the high rate of participation among Negroes in voluntary associations would appear to be a sign of intense social interaction. On closer examination, however, this turns out to be merely a further indication of ritual

---

[63] *Southern School News* (September, 1963), p. 1.

[64] Nicholas Babchuk and Ralph V. Thompson, "The Voluntary Associations of Negroes," *American Sociological Review*, 27:647-655 (October, 1962).

[65] Charles R. Wright and Herbert H. Hyman, "Voluntary Association Membership of American Adults: Evidence from National Sample Surveys," *American Sociological Review*, 23:284-294 (June, 1958).

avoidance. Following Myrdal, the authors of the present study (i.e., Babchuk and Thompson) view this widespread participation as *pathological*, rather than healthy. Negroes form and participate in their own organizations because they are forbidden such participation in many of the institutions and voluntary associations in American society. Hence Negroes must seek status, recognition, and self-expression in their own organizations. Together with the church, the voluntary association offers an opportunity for meaningful interaction with other persons that is denied the Negro in the fabric of American life. The average Negro voluntary association is, furthermore, able to accomplish very little as compared with the expressed goals of its members.[66]

4. *Caste determines occupation.* The caste order of society also determines the occupational roles that the inferior caste may fill. This situation has traditionally applied in the South and, to a somewhat lesser degree, in the rest of the country. The Negro has been given the most menial and poorly paid positions. He has also been the last hired and the first fired in many marginal occupations in which both races participate. The Bureau of the Census has published an extensive survey of the occupational status of the Negro on a nation-wide basis. The following generalizations emerged from this study.[67]

(*a*) A larger proportion of Negroes than of whites is in the labor force, with 62 per cent of the former and 57 per cent of the latter in this category. This difference is largely due to the fact that Negroes are employed in large numbers in sharecropping and small farming, where both the very young and the very old can find some sort of employment.

(*b*) Occupational differentials between Negroes and whites are indicated by the fact that only 12 per cent of the former are employed in professional, managerial, and other white-collar occupations, whereas 42 per cent of the whites are in these categories. The percentage of Negroes employed in these occupations, however, increased from 9 to 12 per cent between 1948 and 1955, thus indicating considerable improvement.

(*c*) The above proportions are substantially reversed when we consider the percentages of Negroes and whites in service and other unskilled occupations. These categories employ about 47 per cent of all Negro workers and only about 14 per cent of all white workers.

(*d*) A much higher proportion of Negro women is gainfully employed than is the case with white women. The figures are 44 and 34 per cent, respectively. The principal reason for this differential is the lower average income of Negro male heads of families, which necessitates the gainful employment of the wife.

(*e*) A consistent disparity exists between Negroes and whites in the matter of employment and unemployment. In 1955, Negro workers constituted approximately 20 per cent of the unemployed in the country, although they made

---

[66] Babchuk and Thompson, *op cit.*, p.653.

[67] Bureau of the Census, *Current Population Reports: Labor Force*, "Employment of White and Non-white Persons: 1955," Series P-50, No. 66 (March, 1956). The nonwhite group, as defined by the Bureau of the Census, contains Indians, Japanese, and Chinese, as well as Negroes. The proportion of these other groups is negligible, however, so that the nonwhite figures may be taken, for all practical purposes, as constituting the Negro population.

up only 10 per cent of the labor force. The rate of unemployment among Negroes was thus approximately double that among whites.

The strict caste occupational lines are breaking down slowly. Several factors have been responsible for the increase in the percentage of white-collar jobs from 9 to 12 per cent of the Negro labor force. Among the factors making for the slow amelioration of the occupational status of the Negro are: (a) the pressure of the large industrial unions (AFL-CIO), which have taken a strong stand against discrimination both in the North and in the South; (b) the influence of the large national corporations, which have also attempted to discourage discrimination, although not as militantly as the unions; (c) the labor shortage during and after War World II; (d) the work of the Federal Fair Employment Practices Commission during and immediately after World War II, plus that of the several state commissions modeled after this body.

5. *Caste lines are strictly enforced.* The caste lines between Negro and white in the United States have been enforced by various means, ranging from informal taboos to lynching. It is difficult to generalize here, as in many other aspects of the caste pattern, because of the differences between rural and urban areas and the rapid changes occurring throughout the South. Included in the traditional culture pattern, however, is a system of regulation called "the etiquette of race relations," which arose as a means of impressing upon the Negro his subordinate status in the caste system. This pattern has little or nothing to do with etiquette as generally understood, namely, as comprising traditional forms of politeness. On the contrary, the etiquette of race relations is an elaborate system of deliberate insult, addressed to the Negroes by the whites and understood as such by both groups.[68]

Conversational patterns between the races are carefully stereotyped both in content and in form. A Negro may not begin a conversation with a white person, except in a roundabout way. Serious discussion is not expected, except in unusual cases. The Negro is supposed to employ a ceremonial politeness to the white man, with such forms as "Ma'am" and "Sir" sprinkled liberally through his speech. Conversely, the white man is ordinarily expected to use such derogatory terms as "nigger," "darky," and "boy," or the condescending "auntie" or "uncle." The white man is allowed to lose his temper and swear at or otherwise verbally abuse a Negro; the latter may not respond in kind.[69]

Even the bodily patterns of the Negro in the South have traditionally been expected to follow a calculated pattern of subordination. He is supposed to keep his eyes on the ground, move restlessly about, scrape his feet sheepishly, and otherwise demonstrate his presumed inability to act like a normal adult. The etiquette allows a white man to enter the home of a Negro by the front door and without knocking. He may also leave his hat on and take a seat without invitation. A Negro, conversely, must enter the home of a white man by the

[68] B. W. Doyle, *The Etiquette of Race Relations in the South* (Chicago: University of Chicago Press, 1937).

[69] Arnold M. and Caroline Rose, *America Divided* (New York: Alfred A. Knopf, Inc., 1948), pp. 154-161.

back door, take off his hat, and under no circumstances take a seat without invitation. The entire pattern of etiquette, as traditionally observed, serves to differentiate and isolate the two races and to hinder the establishment of normal social contacts. The inferior position of the Negro is manifested by every stereotyped action in this caste role.[70]

The ultimate enforcement of the caste line is by intimidation, violence, and death. Few white persons are aware of the terror still felt by the Negro in many sections of the South. This terror has been intensified by the furious reactions of many southern whites to the attempts of the Negroes to gain their civil rights —ranging from attendance at integrated schools through eating at hitherto segregated lunch counters to voting in national elections. The American people have often shown a disrespect for law and a tendency to take matters into their own hands. This tradition has been especially evident in Negro-white relationships since the Civil War. The conflicts during the Reconstruction Era, the sporadic race riots in both North and South, the bombing of integrated schools in the late 1950's, the beating of young Negroes in the lunch counter "sit-downs" in 1960, and the bombing of Negro churches in 1963—these are some of the forms of violence that have been used to enforce the caste line.[71]

Caste, Discrimination, and Social Problems

The social situation of the Negro has an important effect upon his behavior. The dominant white population assumes (erroneously) that the behavior of the Negro, like that of the white man, is the result of his race. But behavior of any group reflects their position in the social structure, not their biological qualities as such. Many persons, however, remain fundamentally unconvinced by this statement, for they have seen with their own eyes that many Negroes are dirty, uneducated, diseased, irresponsible, and otherwise lacking in many of those qualities that the white man likes to attribute exclusively to his own race. This commonsense position is correct as far as it goes, but it does not go far enough.

The explanation of the social behavior of the Negro is primarily social, rather than biological. The Negro is dirty because he is unable to afford decent living and sanitary conditions; he is uneducated (or undereducated) because he has been denied all but a minimum of education in the South, where the majority of his race are still located; he is irresponsible because he has seldom been given a chance to exercise responsibility and, hence, has had little incentive to take an active role in the community. In many respects, therefore, he *is* different. But the differences reflect his status and not his racial potentialities or lack of them. In short, the differences reflect discrimination.

---

[70] *Ibid.*

[71] For the historical antecedents of contemporary violence, see Allen D. Grimshaw, "Lawlessness and Violence in America and Their Special Manifestations in Changing Negro-White Relationships," *Journal of Negro History*, 44:52-72 (January, 1959).

In our discussion of race prejudice in the last chapter, we stated that discrimination is the *acting out* of prejudice.[72] *Discrimination* is thus an act or series of acts, whereas *prejudice* is a pattern of hostile attitudes. *Segregation* is a form of discrimination by which the minority group—by force, law, the mores or a combination thereof—is denied full participation in social interaction. Both discrimination and segregation are therefore, in effect, forms of aggression. The latter term refers to a deliberate act or series of acts by one individual whereby another individual suffers some form of physical, social, or psychological injury. The minority group is unable to seek high status in a given society and is instead relegated to a low status.[73] By discriminating against the Negro, the white man causes the Negro to suffer these and other types of injury. In its decision on desegregation in the public schools in 1954, the Supreme Court took this fact into consideration and concluded that the Negro was deprived of his constitutional rights by discrimination.[74]

Discrimination is, furthermore, a *deliberate* act by persons who are aware of what they are doing. Various rationalizations have been advanced by the majority group to the effect that discrimination is not injurious to the minority group. But the injury is there, nevertheless. This does not mean that each act of each member of the majority group in a caste society is deliberately injurious to a member of the minority group with whom he is interacting. It *does* mean, however, that the majority group as a whole is aware that the social structure of a castelike system is unfair. The principle of the golden rule operates here, as elsewhere. As one scholar puts it, the person who consistently discriminates against others would find it difficult to answer "yes" when asked if he himself would like to be treated in the same way.[75]

In the field of social problems, the Negro has a high rate of maladjustment. As a depressed population group, living largely in rural isolation in the South and in urban slums in the North, he has an abnormally high rate of delinquency, crime, prostitution, illegitimacy, family disorganization, venereal disease, and many other social problems. In a study of first admissions to Ohio state mental hospitals, it was found that Negroes as a group had much higher rates than whites as a group. These rates involved such diseases as syphilitic psychosis, alcoholic psychosis, and schizophrenia, the latter being the most prevalent form of mental disorder. The rates for mental disease among Negroes were, in turn, found to be related to such factors as income, occupation, education, and socioeconomic status. Negroes ranked low in these four categories and high in most forms of mental disease.[76]

Many of the indices of deviation cited above relate to persons apprehended

[72] Gordon W. Allport, *The Nature of Prejudice* (Cambridge: The Addison-Wesley Publishing Company, 1954), pp. 14-15.

[73] Robert L. Hamblin, "The Dynamics of Racial Discrimination," *Social Problems*, 10:103-121 (Fall, 1963), p. 103.

[74] Kenneth B. Clark, "The Social Scientist as an Expert Witness in Civil Rights Litigation," *Social Problems*, 1:5-10 (June, 1953).

[75] Hamblin, *op. cit.*, p. 103.

[76] Robert M. Frumkin, "Race and Major Mental Disorders: A Research Note," *The Journal of Negro Education*, 23:97-98 (Winter, 1954).

in a breach of the law or otherwise formally coming to the attention of the authorities. Delinquency and crime are the most obvious examples of this situation. Because of his color, the Negro is highly "visible," both to the police and to the public. Many persons believe the crime rate among Negroes higher than it actually is. In a study of white policemen in Philadelphia, about 90 per cent *overestimated* the Negro arrest rate in their own districts. As the arrest rate increased, the overestimation increased disproportionally. In explanation, it is suggested that "as Negro numbers increase arithmetically, their mass visibility, perhaps up to a certain point, increases exponentially." [77]

The authorities, furthermore, are ordinarily not overly zealous in protecting the civil rights of the Negro. Hence the statistics constitute an unbalanced indication of the extent of social problems among this group. The Negro tends to have an unequal status before the law, especially in the southern states, and may be apprehended, indicted, and convicted more easily and more often than the white offender. This inequality is a further factor in the high statistical rate of Negro problem behavior.[78]

This difference in behavior between the races is, finally, more than merely

[77] William M. Kephart, "Negro Visibility," *American Sociological Review,* 19:462-467 (August, 1954), p. 467.

[78] Rose and Rose, *America Divided, op. cit.,* Chapter VIII. See especially pages 240-253.

Caste in action in the United States. In this picture of a convict camp in the Deep South, all of the convicts are Negroes.

statistical. In proportion to his numbers, the Negro *does* engage in certain anti-social actions to a greater extent than the white man. Many white people are convinced that these figures represent a racial predisposition to delinquent, criminal, and irresponsible behavior, and that Negroes apprehended in such activities are merely obeying some deep, primordial, biological impulse. The statement is made that the high rate of desertion among Negroes in the northern cities is an indication that in family responsibility, as in everything else, the Negro cannot be trusted to live up to his obligations. The high rate of venereal infection is similarly cited as evidence that the Negro is "racially" inclined to sexual promiscuity.

The caste-fixed way of life of the Negro, and not any biological predisposition, gives rise to these indices of personal and family disorganization. The Negro has never completely recovered from the deliberate attempt by the whites during slavery to keep family ties loose so that the slaves could be sold with a minimum of emotional difficulties.[79] The economic marginality of the Negro in the northern cities has further tended to perpetuate this comparative disregard of many of the bonds of family life. The high rate of self-support among northern Negro women signifies that they are more independent of marital permanency than many white women. Hence, desertion is more common and sexual relations more casual.[80]

The divorce rate among Negroes is also consistently higher than among whites, contrary to widespread opinion. Negroes have high rates of family disorganization because they are poor, not because they are Negroes. The social forces that combine to bring about a high rate of family disorganization among the American people as a whole seem to be accentuated in the Negro.[81] The extent of family disorganization from all causes (death, desertion, divorce) is shown by the fact that only 58.0 per cent of nonwhite males were living with their first spouse in a recent year, as compared with 78.0 per cent of white males. The disparity among females was about the same, with 47.5 per cent of nonwhite females currently living with their first spouse, as compared with 68.4 per cent of white females.[82]

As a result of these and other forms of personal disorganization, many Negroes develop a strongly negative self-feeling. As we have indicated, the self is a social product, arising through a process of interaction whereby the self views itself through the eyes of others. As a member of a minority group that is alternately feared and despised, the individual Negro takes on some of the attitudes of the majority group toward himself. From this process of internal interaction, a form of self-hatred often emerges. This feeling expresses itself in many of the forms of deviant behavior suggested above, as well as in others which we

---

[79] E. Franklin Frazier, *The Negro Family in the United States* (New York: The Dryden Press, 1948), Chapter II.

[80] E. Franklin Frazier, "Problems and Needs of Negro Children and Youth Resulting from Family Disorganization," *The Journal of Negro Education*, 19:269-277 (Summer, 1950).

[81] William J. Goode, *After Divorce* (Glencoe, Ill.: The Free Press, 1956), pp. 48-55.

[82] Bureau of the Census, *Current Population Reports: Population Characteristics*, "Marital Status and Family Status: March 1962," Series P-20, No. 122 (March 22, 1963), Table B.

have not mentioned. Although the Negro suicide rate is low, in many *indirect* ways the Negro directs his aggressions against himself or members of his own race. The high Negro rates of mayhem, homicide, and miscellaneous personal violence are one indication of this self-hatred. Another is his gradual self-destruction by alcohol and drugs.[83]

Caste and Personality

The alleged carelessness, lack of ambition, and general shiftlessness of the Negro form another personality pattern presumed to be racial in character. The deliberate movements, the shambling gait, and the assumed air of inertia of the southern Negro are popularly believed to be the direct expression of his African ancestry. These characteristics are in reality the heritage of generations of slavery and the post-slavery limitations placed upon any attempt on the part of the Negro to rise above the caste line. No matter how hard he worked and how diligently he applied himself, the Negro was rarely permitted to occupy a position above that allotted him by the caste system.

This social heritage is slowly breaking down under the impact of industrialism, education, and a reaffirmation of the American creed. As a result, the Negro is gaining more opportunity for self-development and self-improvement. When he is able to work his own farm, manage his own business, practice his own profession, and otherwise improve his position, his "racial" lethargy miraculously vanishes and the Negro becomes an individual human being.

Other personality traits widely alleged to be racially conditioned likewise appear, on closer examination, to reflect social status. The Negro is not biologically endowed with a "sense of rhythm" that manifests itself in his ability to dance and play jazz music. This quality is a development of his religion and other aspects of his way of life. The belief that Negro jazz is a manifestation of the African heritage has long since been abandoned, as observers have demonstrated that this interest has evolved from the caste status of the Negro. Music and religion are two fields in which the Negro has largely been left alone by the whites. Popular music and entertainment remain areas in which the Negro can operate with less hampering by racial prejudice. Many of his creative abilities have therefore been channeled into musical activities.

In popular designations of personality differences allegedly based upon race, the emphasis is usually placed upon the *undesirable* traits of the subject group. Socially desirable or at least not actively undesirable traits are also imputed to race with as little reason. The Negro is often characterized as friendly, trusting, loyal, happy-go-lucky, and with many of the other qualities of a lovable child. Insofar as this characterization has any empirical validity, it may be traced largely to two social factors: (*a*) the long generations of slavery when the Negro was encouraged to develop these childlike traits of subordination to and trust in the dominant caste; (*b*) the corollary fact that the white man has re-

[83] Clemmont E. Vontress, "The Negro Against Himself," *Journal of Negro Education*, 23:237-241 (Spring, 1963).

tained this stereotype of the Negro and the latter assumes this role in deference to the white man's expectations.

In this subordinate status, the Negro is comparatively safe from aggression by the white man. As long as the latter is able to feel superior in every respect, he has no strong urge to put the Negro in his place. The role of the conventional southern "darky" is a part the Negro has learned to play because it has been ascribed to him. This role does not represent any "racial" characteristics as such. Like many other such qualities, it is part of the social system of a caste society, reflected in the personality of the Negro.

The impact of status upon personality is not restricted to lower-class Negroes. The business men, doctors, lawyers, teachers, engineers, and scientists who constitute the "black *bourgeoisie*" are likewise subjected to humiliations and conflicts in their interpersonal relationships. In many ways, these frustrations are more bitterly resented by this group than by the Negro workingmen and farm laborers. Middle-class persons, whether black or white, tend to be more self-conscious about their status, and education makes them more aware of discrimination. The training of the Negro intellectual makes him the equal of the white man, but at the same time he is forced to submit to many of the same restrictions as his lower-class fellows.[84]

The stratification of society is one of the facts of social life. Social stratification may be ignored or denied, but it nevertheless continues to exist as a means of fulfilling the tasks of an organized society. In the present chapter, we indicated the general nature of social stratification as a "pattern of differential privilege," and suggested some of the principal bases upon which stratification arises. The caste system of India is one form of social stratification, and provides a prototype by which other forms of caste stratification are judged.

We then applied the general criteria of caste to the social structure of the southern United States. The elaborate system of statuses and roles traditionally ascribed to members of both races constitutes, for all practical purposes, a caste-organized society. In some respects, this system is giving way slowly but surely to the rush of industrialization, urbanization, and democratic implementation through the courts. In other respects, the change is slowed by the nature of the social structure of the South, which is less pluralistic than other sections of the country. This means that there are fewer organized groups (political parties, labor unions, ethnic groups, and women's groups) through which the mass of the people can engage in public discussion of major issues. Among these major issues are integration, desegregation, and the breakdown of prejudice and discrimination.[85] Hence the traditional caste structure remains virtually intact in many sections of the Deep South, with all of its implications for the institutions, social relationships, and personalities of Negroes and whites alike.

---

[84] E. Franklin Frazier, *Black Bourgeoisie* (Glencoe, Ill.: The Free Press, 1957).

[85] Warren Breed, "Group Structure and Resistance to Desegregation in the Deep South," *Social Problems*, 10:84-94 (Summer, 1962).

SELECTED BIBLIOGRAPHY

Barber, Bernard, *Social Stratification*. New York: Harcourt, Brace and Company, 1957. This is the most complete, authoritative, and thoughtful analysis of social stratification in the literature of American sociology. As such, it is an indispensable source book for all instruction on social stratification, with particular emphasis upon class.

Berreman, Gerald D., "Caste in India and the United States," *American Journal of Sociology*, 66:120-127 (September, 1960). This article compares the caste system in India and the system of race relations in the United States and concludes that, despite obvious local differences, the two have many basic structural similiarities.

Breed, Warren, "Group Structure and Resistance to Desegregation in the Deep South," *Social Problems*, 10:84-94 (Summer, 1962). This article offers a sociological, as distinguished from a psychological, analysis of the Deep South. The author emphasizes such elements as social structure and social process and indicates that, in these terms, desegregation is delayed by the fact that the Deep South has fewer organizations (opposition political party, labor unions, ethnic and religious minority groups) and lower membership than other sections of the country.

Buckley, Walter, "On Equitable Inequality," *American Sociological Review*, 28:799-801 (October, 1963); also "Social Stratification and the Functional Theory of Social Differentiation," *American Sociological Review*, 23:369-375 (August, 1958). These two articles are critical analyses of the concept of social stratification advanced by the so-called "functional" school. The author suggests here that the "chance to perform" is as important as "performance" and that prior position in the stratification system necessarily influences the former as well as the latter.

"Caste," in *Current Sociology*, published for UNESCO by Basil Blackwell, London, 1959. This is an analysis of the caste system in India and a statement of the trends taking place in this ancient and complex social structure. The bibliography is especially valuable, dealing as it does with the recent literature in the field.

Cuber, John F. and William F. Kenkel, *Social Stratification in the United States*. New York: Appleton-Century-Crofts, Inc., 1954. The theory of social stratification is discussed at length in this textbook, with illustrations drawn from the extensive literature of social class in the United States.

Davis, Kingsley, "A Conceptual Analysis of Stratification," *American Sociological Review*, 7:309-321 (June, 1942); Kingsley Davis and Wilbert E. Moore, "Some Principles of Stratification," *American Sociological Review*, 10:242-249 (April, 1945). These two articles provide an extensive theoretical analysis of the nature of social stratification. Many of the ideas originally explored in these essays have subsequently been expanded in other theoretical studies.

Dollard, John, *Caste and Class in a Southern Town*. New York: Doubleday Anchor Books, 1949. This is a study of the relationships of caste and class in a small community in the Deep South, with particular emphasis upon the differential gains accruing to the whites by virtue of the caste pattern. The original study was made almost three decades ago, and many of the caste lines are loosening under the impact of industrial and social forces. Nevertheless, especially in the rural areas, many relationships of subordination and superordination remain virtually unchanged.

Frazier, E. Franklin, *Black Bourgeoisie*. Glencoe, Ill.: The Free Press, 1957. A leading Negro sociologist analyzes the role of the "black *bourgeoisie*" in contemporary American society. The status of these intellectuals, professional men, and businessmen is still largely determined by race rather than by accomplishment. This arbitrarily fixed status gives rise to frustration, insecurity, and self-hatred.

Hamblin, Robert L., "The Dynamics of Racial Discrimination," *Social Problems*, 10:103-121 (Fall, 1962). This article "reports the results of a field survey designed to evaluate and interrelate nine hypotheses about the antecedents of racial discrimination." The "acting out" of racial prejudice in the form of discrimination forms the basis for the continuance of the caste-organized society characteristics of the Deep South and, to a certain extent, of the United States as a whole.

Harris, Marvin, "Caste, Class, and Minority," *Social Forces*, 37:248-254 (March, 1959). This article distinguishes between caste and class in terms of intermarriage and the fixation of status in the hierarchy. Caste groups normally cannot intermarry and their status is fixed in the social structure. On both counts, class groups are more flexible.

Moore, Wilbert E., "But Some Are More Equal Than Others," *American Sociological Review*, 28:13-18 (February, 1963). This article continues the controversy over the "functional" nature of social stratification that began with the article by Davis and Moore (see above) some 20 years ago. In the author's words, the crucial issue continues to be "whether social inequality is a necessary feature of social systems."

Rosen, Bernard C., "Race, Ethnicity, and the Achievement Syndrome," *American Sociological Review*, 24:47-60 (February, 1959). This is a study in vertical mobility and the differences in motivation between different racial, religious and ethnic groups. Achievement motivation is, as might be expected, low among Negroes by virtue of their place in the social structure.

Tumin, Melvin M., "On Inequality," *American Sociological Review*, 28:19-26 (February, 1963). The author of this and other articles dealing with the same theme is perhaps the most vehement opponent of the Davis-Moore concept of social stratification. In his analysis, Tumin asks "Under what conditions do we get more and less of various forms of inequality, and why, and with what consequences for whom?" In his opinion, the sociologist should ask questions of this nature, rather than seek to give rational reasons ("functionalism") to justify past and present social inequality.

14 *Class*

The Nature of Social Class

Social class is the second major form of stratification. Like so-cial caste, class patterns emerge from social interaction over a long period, as statuses and roles arise and are given different evaluations by the society. Class is, indeed, more prevalent than caste. Many societies lack a recognizable form of caste, but few societies are without some form of class structure, however rudimentary. This structure takes the form of a hier-archy, with those groups at the apex of the status pyramid whose roles carry the highest social evaluation. These differen-tial statuses are perpetuated from generation to generation.

Children inherit from parents much of the power, prestige, and privilege that the parents themselves inherited in their turn.[1]

A social class is a segment of a society whose members share the same general status. A class-organized society, in turn, is one "in which the hierarchy of prestige and status is divisible into groups each with its own social, economic, attitudinal, and cultural characteristics and each having differential degrees of power in community decisions."[2] Social class thus *arises* out of social interaction. The feudal system in Europe arose during the early middle ages and the class system of the United States grew out of the complex relationships of a new continent. Social class also *patterns* the direction social interaction will take. Members of different class segments in the United States rear their children, earn their living, and amuse themselves in accordance with different behavior patterns.

In this sense, each class evolves a culture that is, in certain respects, unique. At the same time, the members share many of the patterns of the larger society. Virtually all Americans, from every walk of life, share a knowledge of baseball, believe in the capitalistic system, and try to act as responsible fathers and mothers as defined by the American culture pattern. The values held by members of the various social classes, however, are not exactly the same. In some respects, the middle and lower classes have their own values, which influence the behavior of their members.[3] We shall consider these values in more detail below.

Social class is a complex social phenomenon. A class may, for example, be characteristic of a particular community, region, or national society. Class distinctions may reflect objective criteria, the opinions of persons outside the class, or the consciousness of persons within it. Class status may depend upon pecuniary, occupational, or educational factors. Class may be based upon power, prestige, wealth, or a combination of these and other criteria. The delimitation of class membership is therefore a difficult process. The criteria may be objective and quantitative, as well as subjective and qualitative. In view of these circumstances, social class can be defined from several points of view and in terms that differ in accuracy and measurability.[4]

Among the different approaches to social class are the following:[5]

1. Defined Classes. Classes are culturally defined groups that are formally recognized by society, such as the system of ancient Athens, the structure of Imperial Rome, and the estates of medieval Europe.

2. Cultural Classes. Classes are social segments that have developed subcultural patterns of behavior, thought, and values, which distinguish them from

---

[1] Bernard Barber, *Social Stratification* (New York: Harcourt, Brace and Company, 1957), p. 2.

[2] Walter Goldschmidt, "Social Class in America—A Critical Review," *American Anthropologist,* 52:483-498 (October-December, 1950), p. 492.

[3] Melvin L. Kohn, "Social Class and Parental Values," *American Journal of Sociology,* 64:337-351 (January, 1959).

[4] Raymond B. Cattell, "The Cultural Functions of Social Stratification: I: Regarding the Genetic Bases of Society," *Journal of Social Psychology,* 21:3-23 (February, 1945), p. 4.

[5] Goldschmidt, *op. cit.,* pp. 491-492.

other groups and of which they are highly conscious. Social classes in western Europe illustrate this aspect.

3. *Economic Classes.* Classes are groups engaging in different economic activities or standing in different relationships to the means of production. This is the Marxist conception of social class, in which certain groups own and/or control the instruments of production and certain others have only their labor power to sell.

4. *Political Classes.* Classes may be viewed in terms of political power, with one class having greater differential access to the control of the political machinery. In Great Britain, the upper class has, until recently, exercised a virtual monopoly on political power.

5. *Self-identified Classes.* Classes may be conceived in terms of the psychological identification of their members. At opposite ends of the stratification system, the self-conscious elite and the class-conscious proletariat constitute such representative groups.

6. *Participation Classes.* Classes may be viewed in terms of social ties between the members, wherein sociable contacts, marriage, and similar relationships take place within class boundaries but ordinarily do not cross them. This concept of social class is widely, if tacitly, recognized in the United States.

These approaches are not mutually exclusive. In practice, they tend to overlap. In a dynamic society, furthermore, some class distinctions become increasingly blurred. Members of the working class in the United States acquire many of the material goods (automobiles) that in other societies are still the exclusive property of the upper classes. Even with such reservations, however, certain aspects of class stratification are apparent in the United States. Class is one of the extralegal realities of American life. Nowhere is this fact more clearly documented than in the differential "life chances" of individuals to get ahead. Personal opportunities (or the lack of them) are still largely (although not entirely) determined by the accident of birth. This situation is contrary to the popular folklore, but it nevertheless exists.[6]

As the rough equality of the westward frontier has gradually disappeared, many persons have become aware of class differences and are more self-conscious about their position in the stratification system. This awareness has become evident in a number of forms, among them the increased interest by social scientists in the study of social class. In a single eight-year period, for example, one author cited a partial bibliography of some 333 titles in this field.[7] The specific awareness of class has also appeared among large segments of the American public. Millions of persons have recently gained the good things of life in a material sense, only to discover that they are excluded from participation in cer-

---

[6] W. Lloyd Warner and James C. Abegglen, *Big Business Leaders in America* (New York: Harper & Brothers, 1955).

[7] Harold W. Pfautz, "The Current Literature on Social Stratification," *American Journal of Sociology,* 58:391-418 (January, 1953).

tain "status groups." Whether unconsciously or not, these men and women have become "status seekers." [8]

The Different Aspects of Social Class

The dynamic, heterogeneous, and sprawling society of the United States has no single class system. The society is too complex to make a neat division of social levels that would apply to all sections of the country. This situation is in contrast to many societies of western Europe, where the class structure has evolved through the interaction of many centuries and still differentiates the way of life of different social segments.[9] The United States, on the contrary, has many stratification systems, some found largely in small towns in the Middle West, others peculiar to large manufacturing cities in the Middle Atlantic States, and still others characterizing older communities in the South and Northeast. In some of these systems, class is based largely upon family, in others upon wealth, in others upon racial and ethnic differences, and in still others upon a combination of all these.[10]

The differentiation in status systems has, for example, been explored in terms of the size of the community as the principal variable. Among the conclusions of this study were the following: (1) In communities of all sizes, occupation is closely related to social class, with certain high-status occupations (doctor, lawyer, wealthy business man) widely accepted as denoting membership in the upper class. (2) Smaller communities view community activities and choice of associates as closely related to social class, whereas in larger cities the important factors are types of housing and residence area. (3) Material possessions are more closely associated with class in medium-sized cities (50,000 to 250,000) than in cities that are either larger or smaller. The type of social interaction is related to the size of the city. Different attitudes toward the criteria of class membership emerge from interaction in these social settings, as men and women take each other into account under different conditions.[11]

In view of this dynamic situation, the individual usually does not occupy a single, clearly defined position in the stratification system. Instead, he has a number of statuses, reflecting his position in different groups. One man may be wealthy, highly educated, and have a good professional status, but at the same time may lack high class position because of ethnic or religious origin. Another may have an impeccable ethnic background and high educational attainment, but may suffer from a low income. In an old and continuous society, these multiple statuses eventually become merged into a single class status, so that the

---

[8] Vance Packard, *The Status Seekers* (New York: David McKay Company, Inc., 1959).

[9] Natalie Rogoff, "Social Stratification in France and in the United States," *American Journal of Sociology*, 58:347-357 (January, 1953).

[10] John F. Cuber and William F. Kenkel, *Social Stratification in the United States* (New York: Appleton-Century-Crofts, Inc., 1954), pp. 288-292.

[11] Thomas E. Lasswell, "Social Class and Size of Community," *American Journal of Sociology*, 64:505-508 (March, 1959).

individual is reasonably certain of his position. In a new and dynamic society, the social situation makes for multiple statuses.[12]

The *symbols* of status are thus important in the mobile, anonymous, and secondary-group society, in which an increasing proportion of Americans live. Their lives are spent with persons who do not know them very well and who have to appraise their status in direct and immediate ways. Clothing, houses, clubs, organizations, and (above all) conspicuous signs of wealth are important as status symbols. In all social interaction, people take each other into account in order to appraise the other's behavior and direct their own. In a stable and primary society, such reciprocal appraisal is comparatively simple. Everyone knows where he stands. In a dynamic and mobile society, this process is not so easy. Persons are anxious to impress others with their own status and therefore put their best foot forward by using status symbols that they believe will be impressive.[13]

These status symbols are dramatically illustrated by the automobile. The different makes of automobiles and the various lines, styles, and models within each make indicate the sensitivity of the American people to shades of status. As a person moves from the so-called "lower-priced" makes up through the hierarchy of the medium-priced makes, to the exalted position of the Cadillac, he undergoes a corresponding increase in status. The person who is able to buy one of the highest-priced makes (and especially one with an exotic foreign flavor) has, symbolically, *arrived* in the eyes of many persons and, by reflected self-appraisal, in his own eyes.[14]

Such symbols of status are less important in the older societies of Europe. A member of the hereditary nobility in France may be content with a small and inconspicuous automobile because he (and practically everybody else) is certain of his status. In the United States, very few persons have a completely secure status in all respects and hence there is a great emphasis upon such external evidence as the automobile. Even the "lower-priced" makes, furthermore, are made to resemble the higher-priced ones, so that everyone may have the illusion of being able to buy an expensive car and thus demonstrate his status.

The Reality of Social Class

A class system means that persons have access to differential privileges. It also means that they develop distinctive attitudes, values, and styles of life.[15] As a result of these and other factors, Americans "react toward one another as equals, superiors, and inferiors . . . talk of themselves or their families in relation to other persons and their folks in a frame of reference characterized by

---

[12] Gerhard E. Lenski, "Status Crystallization: A Non-Vertical Dimension of Social Status," *American Sociological Review*, 19:405-413 (August, 1954).

[13] William H. Form and Gregory P. Stone, "Urbanism, Anonymity, and Status Symbolism," *American Journal of Sociology*, 62:504-514 (March, 1957).

[14] Walter Goldschmidt, "Social Class and the Dynamics of Status in America," *American Anthropologist*, 57:1209-1217 (December, 1955), p. 1214.

[15] Melvin L. Kohn, "Social Class and Parental Values," *op. cit.*

rank . . . [and] 'place' others in terms of differentially valued symbols and commonly understood levels of social participation and moral reputation."[16] These relationships are for the most part tacitly sensed, and the individual does not ordinarily think of himself in terms of social class. But whatever they may be called, the presence of such gradations cannot be denied. In the sense of: (a) differential privilege; (b) different life-styles; and (c) tacit self-ranking, the United States is a "class-organized" society, whether we admit it or not.

The class structure in this country, as noted, is subject to wide variations on the basis of region, rural-urban differences, and ethnic differences. In a study of social stratification in New Haven, Connecticut, it was found that this process had increased in recent generations, as the compartmentalization of society has speeded up. The status structure of this heterogeneous industrial city has steadily grown more rigid by the allocation of occupations to different groups and the tendency of ethnic groups to assume permanent places. The Italians and other groups from southern Europe constitute, on the whole, the lower occupational segments, whereas the higher business, professional, and civic roles are filled by persons of Anglo-Saxon background. These gradations are further strengthened by the religious, marital, and recreational institutions, which are themselves based upon class lines.[17]

The emergence of social stratification in the United States has also been characterized in terms of occupation. In the words of one observer, "the most important thing that stands out is that our society has changed from an *employer* society to an *employee* society."[18] An increasing number of persons work for others rather than for themselves, as medium-sized business swallows up little business and is in turn swallowed up by the giant corporation. Self-employed professional men are no longer proportionately as numerous as they once were, as doctors, lawyers, chemists, and engineers become attached to corporate enterprise. This concept of class stratification has been challenged as oversimplifying a complex situation.[19] There is no question, however, of the importance of occupational factors in the over-all determination of the status system.[20]

The reality of the status structure is apparent in other forms. A study was made of 150 working-class and 150 middle-class children to determine whether their class membership had any relationship to the way in which they learned their sex roles. The lower-class child, on the whole, was found to possess more consistent definitions of his adult sex role than the middle-class child. In other words, the lower-class child was given more consistent instruction in the sexual

[16] Carson McGuire, "Social Stratification and Mobility Patterns," *American Sociological Review,* 15: 195-204 (April, 1950), p. 196.

[17] August B. Hollingshead, "Trends in Social Stratification: A Case Study," *American Sociological Review,* 17:679-686 (December, 1952).

[18] Peter F. Drucker, "The Employee Society," *American Journal of Sociology,* 58:358-363 (January, 1953), p. 358. (My italics.)

[19] James B. McKee, "Status and Power in the Industrial Community: A Comment on Drucker's Thesis," *American Journal of Sociology,* 58:364-370 (January, 1953).

[20] Nelson N. Foote, "The Professionalization of Labor in Detroit," *American Journal of Sociology,* 58:371-380 (January, 1953).

behavior that he was expected to display as an adult than was the middle-class child. The instructions given the latter were often confused, inconsistent, and sometimes completely lacking. In this respect, it would appear that the lower class prepares its children more adequately and realistically for the sexual roles they will be called upon to play as adults.[21]

The existence of different patterns of social values is another indication of the reality of social class in the United States. In a study of parental values, Kohn found that significant differences existed between middle-class and lower-class persons regarding the behavior that they desired of their children. Middle-class parents took for granted certain values (orderliness and neatness) that lower-class parents considered desirable but did not take for granted. Middle-class parents valued *internal* standards for their children, wherein the latter would take the role of the other and treat him as they themselves would like to be treated. Lower-class parents, on the other hand, tended to stress *external* controls, in which the children would conform to outside authority and do something (or not) because they were told. In conclusion, Kohn found that "parents are most likely to accord high priority to those values that seem to be both *problematic,* in the sense that they are difficult of achievement, and *important,* in the sense that failure to achieve them would affect the child's future adversely." [22]

The Measurement of Social Class

A variety of techniques has been evolved to measure social class in the United States. In one study, some nineteen different measures or indices of socioeconomic status were compared and evaluated.[23] We shall consider two of the principal methods, each of which illustrates a general approach to class participation. The *first* was developed by W. Lloyd Warner and his associates, who worked out an ingenious procedure whereby the status structure of the community may be measured by various "objective" criteria. The *second* is associated with the work of Richard Centers, who believes that the most significant element in class participation is subjective or psychological. Individual identification with a particular class is thus the most important criterion of participation, and membership in a given class is in effect a function of subjective identification with it.

1. *The Warner Method of Class Participation.* This method was developed by Warner and other scholars whose early orientation was along anthropological lines. They employed many of the same insights and techniques in the study of a sophisticated American community as they had earlier used in a primitive or preliterate community. The investigation of American society was described

---

[21] Meyer Rabban, "Sex-Role Identification in Young Children in Two Diverse Social Groups," *Genetic Psychology Monographs,* 42:81-158 (August, 1950).

[22] Kohn, *op. cit.,* p. 350.

[23] Joseph A. Kahl and James A. Davis, "A Comparison of Indexes of Socio-Economic Status," *American Sociological Review,* 20:317-325 (June, 1955).

as "a practical attempt to use the techniques and ideas which have been developed by social anthropologists in primitive society in order to obtain a more accurate understanding of an American community." [24] The assumption that this procedure necessarily leads to a greatly increased knowledge of the American community and social stratification has been questioned by later scholars.[25] Without prejudicing the discussion, however, we may examine some of the methods used in the Warner studies of class participation.

Warner and his associates developed two principal techniques for establishing the "social class configuration" of a community and for placing various individuals in it. The first of these methods is Evaluated Participation (EP) and the second is Index of Status Characteristics (ISC). Evaluated Participation is based upon class ratings by persons who are familiar with the community and who have been trained in the research method. These ratings involve the following considerations:

a. Rating by matched agreements of several informants as to the class position of many persons.

b. Rating by symbolic placement, wherein an individual is identified with a particular group through certain symbols.

c. Rating by status reputation, based upon traits or activities ranked by informants as superior or inferior.

d. Rating by comparison with other individuals whose social class has previously been determined.

e. Rating by simple assignment to a class.

f. Rating by membership in such institutions and groups as churches, clubs, and cliques.[26]

The Index of Status Characteristics is based upon the socioeconomic characteristics of the members of the community. These elements serve both as the basis for describing the class structure and for placing individuals in it. The Index is composed of the following factors: (*a*) occupation; (*b*) source of income; (*c*) house type; and (*d*) dwelling area. These elements provide an objective supplement to the subjective judgments that constitute the Evaluated Participation method. Together, the two techniques are said to give "a clear understanding of social class in a community and the place of any individual or family in this status structure." [27]

This conception of social class reflects the groups and cliques with which the individual plays bridge, gossips, dances, and dines. Some critics maintain that it minimizes the economic and political elements of social control that characterize particular segments of the society. Social prestige is clearly an important

---

[24] W. Lloyd Warner and Paul S. Lunt, *The Social Life of a Modern Community* (New Haven: Yale University Press, 1941), p. 14.

[25] Harold W. Pfautz and Otis D. Duncan, "A Critical Evaluation of Warner's Work in Community Stratification," *American Sociological Review*, 15:202-215 (April, 1950); Ruth R. Kornhauser, "The Warner Approach to Social Stratification," in Reinhard Bendix and Seymour M. Lipset (eds.), *Class, Status, and Power* (Glencoe, Ill.: The Free Press, 1953).

[26] W. Lloyd Warner, *et al.*, *Social Class in America* (Chicago: Science Research Associates, 1949), Chapter 2.

[27] *Ibid.*, p. 43.

aspect of the class structure, but it is not the only criterion. Equally important is the definition of social class in terms of power. The structure of social class, furthermore, differs between rural, urban, and metropolitan communities. The class stratification of a small town (Warner's Yankee City) does not necessarily apply to the nation as a whole. Social class is also affected by religious and ethnic groupings, and these factors in turn differ between regions.[28]

There emerges from the work of Warner and his associates a sixfold division of Yankee City in terms of class stratification. These categories are as follows: (*a*) upper-upper class; (*b*) lower-upper class; (*c*) upper-middle class; (*d*) lower-middle class; (*e*) upper-lower class; and (*f*) lower-lower class. The nature of these class groups can be inferred from their titles. The upper-upper group comprises the tiny minority with inherited wealth and secure social prestige. The lower-upper includes those with recently acquired wealth but less family "background." The upper-middle class comprises the leading professional members of the community, plus persons with an assured social status that is not, however, as high as that of the class above them. The twofold division of the lower class runs the gamut downward from respectable and hardworking persons who work with their hands to the chronic misfits, the perennially unemployed, and those whose source of income is dubious.[29]

2. *The Centers Method of Class Consciousness.* The second general method of measuring social class is associated with the psychologist Richard Centers, although many scholars before and after him have likewise emphasized psychological awareness of class differences. Instead of the various "objective" criteria of class membership, Centers believes that the most important consideration is class consciousness. In this term, he includes not only the awareness of membership in a particular social stratum, but also certain related attitudes, values, behavior patterns, interests, and ideologies. He defines social class in the following terms: "Class . . . can well be regarded as a *psychological* phenomenon in the fullest sense of the term. That is, a man's class is a part of his ego, a *feeling on his part of belongingness to something*; an *identification* with something larger than himself." [30]

The importance of subjective status characteristics in the delimitation of class membership has been indicated by other investigators. The fact that a given individual is a doctor, a salesman, an automobile worker, or a farmer is clearly fundamental to his general position in the status hierarchy. Equally important is the way he looks at himself, his attitudes toward others, and the values he holds, consciously or unconsciously, as a result of his status participation. This approach does not involve any concept of militant class consciousness in the Marxist sense, in which one class conceives of itself as inevitably opposed to

---

[28] Paul K. Hatt, "Stratification in the Mass Society," *American Sociological Review*, 15:216-222 (April, 1950).

[29] W. Lloyd Warner and Paul S. Lunt, *The Status System of a Modern Community* (New Haven: Yale University Press, 1942), Chapter I.

[30] Richard Centers, *The Psychology of Social Classes* (Princeton: Princeton University Press, 1949), p. 27.

other classes. The emphasis here is upon the psychological aspects of social interaction in a class-organized society.[31]

This aspect of class membership is seen in a study of textile workers in Paterson, New Jersey, a community with a long history of labor organization and social stratification based upon occupation. The community is by no means typical of the United States as a whole, precisely because of the related facts of union participation, labor conflict, and class identification. The study is important, however, as a case study of an American community in which the sense of belonging to the working class is strong, with a correspondingly low expectation of personal mobility out of this class.[32] In a later study by the same authors, the relationships between class consciousness and different variables were further explored. The authors suggested that the textile workers might better be described as "job-conscious" or "wage-conscious," rather than as "class-conscious" in any fundamental sense.[33]

Another study of working-class consciousness, this one conducted in Detroit, indicated that union membership and class consciousness among *white* workers had a definite impact upon their voting behavior. White men belonging to unions or otherwise indicating awareness of working-class membership tended to vote for liberal or reform candidates to a greater extent than those without such attitudes. Among Negro workers, however, race was the crucial factor in voting behavior. The great majority of Negro voters, whether or not they belonged to unions or were otherwise class-conscious, tended to support the liberal candidate. The caste status of the Negroes as a group seemed to be more important than their working-class affiliations.[34]

In establishing his own criteria for class membership, Centers stresses occupation as perhaps the most important single factor. Other criteria are "beliefs and attitudes, education, family, money, character and morals, personality, manners, achievements, 'whether or not he works with his hands,' and intelligence." [35] Many of these factors are based upon occupation or at least reflect it, but this is not the only consideration. Members of the working class, Centers maintains, look upon themselves in occupational terms, but they also have other attitudes, ideals, goals, and points of view that distinguish them, in their own minds, from other classes.[36]

The techniques of the psychological studies conducted by Centers and others are too specialized to concern us here. The approach is based primarily upon self-identification, and the respondents are asked, either directly or indirectly,

[31] Ivan D. Steiner, "Some Social Values Associated with Objectively and Subjectively Defined Social Class Memberships," *Social Forces*, 31:327-332 (May, 1953).

[32] Jerome G. Manis and Bernard N. Meltzer, "Attitudes of Textile Workers to Class Structure," *American Journal of Sociology*, 60:30-35 (July, 1954).

[33] Jerome G. Manis and Bernard N. Meltzer, "Some Correlates of Class Consciousness Among Textile Workers," *American Journal of Sociology*, 69:177-184 (September, 1963).

[34] John C. Leggett, "Working-Class Consciousness, Race, and Political Choice," *American Journal of Sociology*, 69:171-176 (September, 1963).

[35] Centers, *op. cit.*, p. 91.

[36] Richard Centers, "Social Class, Occupation, and Imputed Belief," *American Journal of Sociology*, 58:543-555 (May, 1953).

what class they *think* they belong to. The original question was directed by Centers to a presumably representative sample of persons throughout the country, as follows: "If you were asked to use one of these four names for your social class, which would you say you belonged in: the middle class, lower class, working class, or upper class?" A national cross-section of white males responded in these terms: 3 per cent said that they belonged to the upper class, 34 per cent to the middle class, 51 per cent to the working class, and 1 per cent to the lower class. An additional 1 per cent averred that they did not believe in social classes. Most Americans thus seem to be aware of the existence of social class.[37]

In studies of this kind, the phrasing of the question is important. A question phrased with one set of terms will tend to elicit a very different set of replies from one phrased in different terms. In an earlier survey conducted by *Fortune* magazine, the respondents were given the choice of identifying themselves with the upper, middle, or lower class. It is not surprising that 79 per cent chose the middle class, in preference to the toplofty "upper" class or the overly humble "lower" class.[38] When Centers offered the term "working class," he did not prejudge the result. A majority (51 per cent) of the sample did not hesitate to identify themselves with this level. In more recent studies, as noted, the investigators have preferred to ask their questions indirectly and let the respondents themselves supply the identification. A more realistic result is thus obtained.

Whatever the techniques of measurement, the existence of social class is clear. We shall devote the rest of this chapter to an analysis of some of the differences between the various segments of the American population. In so doing, we shall tentatively postulate a class hierarchy consisting of three major groups—the upper class, the middle class, and the working class. Each of these groups has its own subcultural patterns—that is, cultural elements that distinguish one group from another and tend to influence the personalities of the members.[39] These differences are not nearly so great as in societies with a long history of stratification. Social classes in this country have more behavior patterns in common than they have differences, in contrast to the countries of western Europe where historical differences are still very pronounced. Despite widespread similarities, however, certain recognizable class differences are apparent in the United States.[40]

The Upper-class Subculture

At the top of the social hierarchy is the upper class, which Warner estimated as comprising less than 5 per cent of the population.[41] The equalitarian tradition

[37] Centers, *The Psychology of Social Classes, op. cit.*, p. 76-77.

[38] "The People of the United States—A Self Portrait," *Fortune* (February, 1940).

[39] Cf. J. Milton Yinger, "Contraculture and Subculture," *American Sociological Review*, 25:625-635 (October, 1960).

[40] Gideon Sjoberg, "Are Social Classes in America Becoming More Rigid?" *American Sociological Review*, 16:775-783 (December, 1951).

[41] Warner and Lunt, *The Social Life of a Modern Community, op. cit.*, p. 88.

in the United States has worked against the development of a formally recognized and accepted upper class, such as is found in European countries with cultures otherwise somewhat similar to our own (England). With the exception of New England, Philadelphia, and parts of the Old South, this nation has never developed a highly class-conscious upper class with a distinct subculture. Throughout most of our history, the upper class has been roughly synonymous with the wealthy, although this popular identification may be undergoing a change.

In his important study of the upper class, Baltzell distinguishes between the *elite* and the *upper class*. The first is an individual designation; the second refers primarily to families. In his words, "The *elite* concept refers to those *individuals* who are the most successful and stand at the top of the *functional* class hierarchy." [42] The upper class, on the other hand, refers to "a group of *families* whose members are descendants of successful individuals (elite members) of one, two, three or more generations ago".[43] Elite individuals are highly successful in their chosen occupational roles, whether business, law, medicine, religion, education, government, or the fine arts. The criterion of elite membership is *productivity* in whatever activities are honored by the society. The descendants of some of these elite individuals constitute the top groups in the social hierarchy from generation to generation and hence constitute the upper class.[44]

The relationship between the elite and the upper class in this sense is symbolized by the two publications, *Who's Who in America* and the *Social Register*. The former contains biographical sketches of leading *individuals* in the United States—men and women who have made productive contributions to society in their occupational roles. Leaders in business, education, government, science, religion, the military, entertainment, art, literature, and music are among the prominent persons listed in *Who's Who*. The type of information considered pertinent by the publishers for purposes of defining elite status is as follows: "Name, occupation, date and place of birth, full name of both parents, education and degrees, marital status—including name of spouse, date of marriage, and the full names of any children—occupational career, military experience, directorships and trusteeships, honorary societies and associational memberships, fraternal organizations, religious and political affiliation, club memberships, publications, and . . . home and business addresses." [45] Such listing is based wholly upon attainment, as defined by the publishers, and cannot be bought or otherwise obtained through influence. It is, in short, the most valid designation of elite status available in the United States.[46]

The *Social Register*, on the other hand, is frankly an upper-class publication.

---

[42] E. Digby Baltzell, *Philadelphia Gentlemen: The Making of a National Upper Class* (Glencoe, Ill.: The Free Press, 1958), p. 6. (His italics.)

[43] *Ibid.*, p. 7. (His italics.)

[44] *Ibid.* Cf. Harold D. Lasswell, *et al., The Comparative Study of Elites* (Stanford: Stanford University Press, 1952) for a somewhat different concept of elites.

[45] *Ibid.*, pp. 25-26.

[46] Baltzell, *op. cit.*, p. 8.

It contains those families that possess sufficiently exalted social status to warrant their inclusion in a self-consciously upper-class compendium of this kind. Families are listed following their own application, which is sponsored by several other individuals or families who are already inscribed in this select group. "Social acceptability" is the major criterion for such membership, which usually means at least two or three generations of inherited wealth, education, and culture, plus acceptable religious and ethnic background. There is a separate volume of the *Social Register* for each of the following metropolitan areas: New York, Chicago, Boston, Philadelphia, Baltimore, Cleveland, Pittsburgh, Cincinnati-Dayton, Buffalo, St. Louis, San Francisco, and Washington, D.C. In a recent year, some 38,000 families were listed in these twelve volumes. This figure may be compared with the approximately 35 million family units in the United States at the time. The percentage of upper-class families to the total family population was thus approximately one-tenth of one per cent.[47]

It is one of the tenets of a popular democracy that it has no upper class. Everyone, according to this belief, belongs to the middle class, except for a few unfortunate, shiftless, or vicious persons who constitute a lower class. A moment's reflection will convince one of the falsity of this position from a sociological, if not from an ideological, standpoint. If we observe American society from a functional point of view—as a going operation—we can see that the upper class performs a number of basic social functions. These have been stated by Baltzell as follows: "(1) to maintain a continuity of control over important positions in the world of affairs; (2) to provide a primary group social organization within which the informal aspects of the normative order—the folkways and mores—may operate as effective agents of social control; (3) to provide an autonomous power in the community as a protection against totalitarian power; and, finally, (4) to provide a more or less primary group social world within which the younger generation is socialized."[48]

Of these four functions, the first is the most obvious. The upper class in American society effectively controls many (although not all) of the decision-making functions in the world of big business, big industry, and big banking. The normative function of this class is one of keeping its own members in line and assuring their conformity to the norms of the class. The stronger the upper class, the more binding its norms upon its members. A strong upper class, whose power is rooted in business and industry, is furthermore a counterbalance against the usurpation of political power, either coming from inside or from outside the country. The upper class will attempt to maintain the *status quo*, which means holding on to their own power as society is now constituted. Finally, the role of socialization involves the transmission of the subculture of the upper class to its younger members.[49]

This transmission takes place on several different levels. During infancy and early childhood, the learning process rests largely with the upper-class family.

[47] *Ibid.*, pp. 28-29.
[48] Baltzell, *op. cit.*, p. 60.
[49] *Ibid.*, pp. 60-61.

In adolescence, the upper-class boy attends one of the exclusive boarding schools in New England, which have been founded to educate the young in the traditions of their class. In late adolescence, the educational process is continued at one of the Ivy League colleges, notably Harvard, Yale, and Princeton. Here the upper-class boy joins the right clubs, meets the right people, and makes the right connections that will stand him in good stead in later life. In boarding school and college, furthermore, the upper-class boy from Boston or Philadelphia meets others of the same social level from Chicago and San Francisco, thereby tightening the bonds of a national, as distinguished from a local, upper class. The socialization process is continued into adulthood, as the scion of the upper class follows his peers into investment banking, commercial banking, the brokerage business, manufacturing, and (more recently) advertising. The cycle is completed when the young man meets the daughter of another upper-class family at a debutante party and they get married and start another family.[50]

In his classic description of the leisure class, written more than sixty years

[50] *Ibid.*, pp. 64-65.

The patronage of the arts has been a traditional, although not exclusive, activity of the upper class. The annual deficits of the Metropolitan Opera in New York City are paid by upper-class music-lovers.

ago, Veblen described many of the gaudy characteristics of the upper class as it then existed. Social stratification was in its early stages, at least on a national scale, and the railroad, packing, and oil barons were largely self-made men (elite individuals) who held great economic power.[51] The degree of ostentation that prevailed at the turn of the century, satirized so savagely by Veblen, has been replaced by a more restrained attitude toward "conspicuous consumption" among the upper-class descendants of the early elite. The upper class is now largely composed of the third and fourth generations of these elite families of the late nineteenth century, reinforced by the shipping, banking, and trading families of an even earlier day. These families are highly educated and public acceptance of their upper-class status is largely taken for granted. Hence they no longer feel obliged to indulge in vulgar expenditures to insure their position.

The emphasis upon the dress, manners, and recreation of the upper class that was begun by Veblen has been continued by subsequent writers. The result has been that the more superficial characteristics of upper-class subculture have been stressed, often to the virtual exclusion of the important functions that this class performs in American society. Bridge-playing, art-collecting, dog-showing, sportscar racing, wine-drinking, and sailboating are significant aspects of upper-class life, but emphasis upon these "charming idiosyncrasies" (the phrase is Baltzell's) tends to obscure the functional role of this class in American life. The upper class, in short, is the most important single element in the "power elite," whose members make many of the vital decisions in the United States.

This segment is a true "elite" in the sense of individuals who are outstandingly successful in their chosen fields. Numbered among the "power elite" are leaders in industry, business, government, and the military. The first two (industry and business) have traditionally constituted the elite in America, whereas government has not been a major source of recruitment for this segment. The military professions have, except in time of war, enjoyed comparatively slight attention as influential activities. The Cold War and the huge military budgets of recent decades, however, have shifted an unprecedented degree of power into the hands of the directors of the "garrison state"—to use Lasswell's graphic term. In most cases, however, the newer roles of government and military leadership have not formed the basis of the sort of permanent family dynasty that produces an upper class.[52]

The upper class has a quasi monopoly on national economic power through its ownership or (more recently) its control of the large corporations that dominate many phases of our economic life.[53] The ownership and control of wealth —especially "old" wealth that has been in the family for several generations— carry with them many of the symbolic tokens of social esteem. We are not assuming that every wealthy family is *ipso facto* a member of the upper class. We

[51] Thorstein Veblen, *The Theory of the Leisure Class* (New York: The Macmillan Company, 1899).

[52] C. Wright Mills, *The Power Elite* (New York: Oxford University Press, 1956).

[53] Adolph A. Berle, *Power Without Property* (New York: Harcourt, Brace and Company, 1959).

are assuming, however, that the majority of the upper-class families are found among the wealthy. In terms both of self-image and popular identification, there is a strong relationship between wealth and upper-class membership.

The business elite is largely, although not completely, self-recruiting. In other words, the majority of American business leaders come from upper-class families. In their study of American business leaders, Warner and Abegglen indicated the extent of this self-perpetuation. In this connection, they stated that "two of every three leaders of American business come from families whose economic and social positions were well above the average for the nation." [54] If we restrict the upper class to the tiny segment comprising the top 1 to 5 per cent of the social hierarchy, the degree of self-recruitment is even higher. The old adage of three generations from shirt-sleeves to shirt-sleeves has lost much of its validity in the day of the irrevocable trust fund. Whatever the ability or lack of ability of upper-class sons, the parents usually make ample provision that their children shall remain in their privileged positions.

The upper class is still primarily recruited from the "Old Americans," whose ancestors came to this country several generations ago. These groups were predominantly of Anglo-Saxon stock and Protestant faith, and the *Social Register* is still largely composed of families with these ethnic and religious characteristics. In recent years, elite individuals (as distinguished from upper-class families) have been increasingly recruited from groups with other ethnic, cultural, and religious backgrounds. The rapid exploitation of the country, the increase in population, and the rise of new industries have made this form of vertical mobility increasingly possible for talented and aggressive persons of southern and eastern European backgrounds and Catholic and Jewish religions. In many ways, these able, industrious, and productive individuals have benefited spectacularly from the American Dream.[55] In the sense of gaining access to the upper class as families, however, this upward mobility has still not progressed very far.[56]

The traditional distrust for politics and politicians in this country has meant that upper-class persons have not, on the whole, entered this field in the sense of devoting themselves to government as a career. In many countries where social stratification is more pronounced, political power is a recognized function of the upper class. The role of the upper class in England is in this respect sharply different from that prevailing in this country. In the United States, the upper class has been content to control the machinery of government from behind the scenes, leaving the actual office-holding largely to professional politicians.

The outstanding exception to this rule in recent decades was, of course, Franklin D. Roosevelt. The scion of an old New York family, educated at Groton and Harvard, where he belonged to the best upper-class clubs, Roosevelt was a great political leader. In this role, he embodied the social, economic,

---

[54] Warner and Abegglen, *op. cit.*, p. 14.
[55] Hollingshead, "Trends in Social Stratification: A Case Study," *op. cit.*
[56] Baltzell, *op. cit.*, pp. 395-396.

and political changes that swept the country during the decades of the 1930's and 1940's. Insofar as he appeared to challenge the power and status of the upper class, Roosevelt was called a "traitor to his class," even though the long-range effects of New Deal reforms strengthened the basic institutions of the country and with them the power of the upper class. In recent years, Rockefeller in New York, Saltonstall and Lodge in Massachusetts, Dilworth and Clark in Pennsylvania, and Adlai Stevenson in Illinois have been among the members of the old upper class who have taken an active part in politics on a national scale. With certain conspicuous exceptions (Rockefeller, Lodge, and Saltonstall), the majority of the above (and other) upper-class political figures have been Democrats, rather than Republicans, and have been strongly identified with political and economic reform movements.[57]

The comparative absence of class consciousness in the European sense in this country has meant that the upper class, as a group, has not been in the public eye to the same extent as in many western European democratic nations. Members of the upper class in the United States have for the most part been unwilling to identify themselves with such a class, at least publicly, because the equalitarian tradition has been against it. In many respects, furthermore, the subculture of the upper class verges imperceptibly into that of the upper-middle class. Between the "lower-upper" and the "upper-middle" classes of Warner, there is no such sharp dividing line as that setting off the bourgeoisie from the landed aristocracy in Europe. In this as in so many other respects, the class structure of the United States is a continuum, in which the position of each class is marked off by small degrees from those on either side.[58]

The Middle-class Subculture

It is thus difficult to separate the middle class in its upper levels from the upper class and in its lower levels from the working class. From a financial point of view, some of the middle class enjoy a greater income, both earned and unearned, than some of the upper class. At the other end of the scale, many persons in skilled manual occupations earn more than clerks and school teachers, who are clearly middle class in other respects. The middle class includes the men and women who operate much of American small business and keep the books for big business. Many of these men and women hope to achieve membership in the upper class, if not by themselves at least through their children. The traditional symbol of the middle class is the white collar.[59]

Occupation is probably the most important single determinant of social class, in a society where the emphasis has been strong upon work as the central function of existence. In terms of occupation, the middle class comprises small-business owners and managers, store and factory managers, salesmen, office

---

[57] Baltzell, *op. cit.*, p. 39.

[58] Gerhard E. Lenski, "American Social Classes: Statistical Strata or Social Groups?" *American Journal of Sociology*, 58:139-144 (September, 1952).

[59] C. Wright Mills, *White Collar* (New York: Oxford University Press, 1951).

workers, professional men, and farmers who own their own land. In terms of psychological identification, the middle-class person tends to identify himself with small and medium-sized proprietorships, managerial roles, white-collar occupations, salesmanship, farm ownership, and some of the more skilled manual occupations. The middle class also associates itself with property, even though many of its members have comparatively little personal property and only a marginal relationship, if any, to productive property. The genteel character of the middle-class occupation is often as important as the remuneration; many persons continue in white-collar positions rather than accept higher-paying but less honorific jobs at manual labor.[60]

Other and more subtle factors differentiate the subcultures of social classes. These elements in turn differ as between region, religion, and ethnic group, so that it is difficult to generalize about the middle class from a single sample or even several samples.[61] With these reservations, we may indicate some of the ways in which the middle-class family differs from the lower-class family.

One such difference involves techniques of and attitudes toward child rearing. In such matters as breast-feeding, weaning, bowel and bladder training, father-child relations, occupational expectations, age of assuming responsibility, and relative strictness or permissiveness of training, the class patterns differ considerably. Middle-class children are fed on schedule; lower-class children, when they are hungry. Toilet training is begun earlier and enforced more strictly in the middle-class family than in its lower-class counterpart. Discipline is stricter in the middle-class family, and the latter allows the child less freedom than does the lower-class family. In short, the middle-class child is "subjected earlier and more consistently to the influences which make a child an orderly, conscientious, responsible, and tame person."[62]

The middle-class mother attempts to train her child so that he will not indulge in practices that she, as a representative of her class, considers bad for his morals or health. Many precocious manifestations of the sexual impulse fall in this category and are therefore curbed as far as possible.[63] Some of these admonitions are unclear and contradictory, with the result that the middle-class child learns a sex role that confuses him when he grows up. This confusion may be the source of many neuroses in the middle class, as the adult tries to reconcile two conflicting definitions of behavior in his sex relationships.[64]

Other studies suggest still other class differences in child rearing. In one such study, middle-class mothers were found to be more "permissive" toward their children than lower-class mothers. This means that the former allow their children more freedom to criticize them (the parents), are less apt to be strict and

---

[60] *Ibid.*, Chapter 11.

[61] Robert J. Havighurst and Allison Davis, "A Comparison of the Chicago and Harvard Studies of Social Class Differences in Child-Rearing," *American Sociological Review*, 20:438-442 (August, 1955).

[62] Allison Davis and Robert J. Havighurst, "Social Class and Color Differences in Child-Rearing," *American Sociological Review*, 11:698-710 (December, 1946), p. 707.

[63] Allison Davis, "American Status Systems and the Socialization of the Child," *American Sociological Review*, 6:345-354 (June, 1941).

[64] Rabban, "Sex-Role Identification in Young Children in Two Diverse Social Groups," *op. cit.*, p. 152.

consistent in their punishment, are more responsive to crying, and permit more insolence and verbal aggression by the children against the parents.[65] The presumably undesirable effects of such permissiveness (spoiling) on the children have often been cited by child psychologists and parents. The effect upon the parents may be almost as devastating. Permissive parents have little life of their own, no freedom from their children, and slight opportunity for clean, quiet, and spotless homes.[66] Middle-class mothers are, finally, more conscious of the opinions of others and tend more strongly than lower-class mothers to listen to "experts," friends, and other mothers.[67]

The renunciation of sexual gratification before marriage is also part of a broader pattern of middle-class subculture. This pattern involves the principle of deferred gratification, whereby the individual is expected to deny himself present satisfactions for the sake of greater future satisfactions. Saving money is the most obvious form of such behavior, as the person denies himself the present satisfaction of spending so that he may have greater future satisfaction from the money he has saved. There appears to be some difference between middle-class and lower-class persons in this respect. The former tend to believe that they should save for the future. The latter are often more inclined to spend what money they have and even borrow to enjoy such present satisfactions as automobiles, television sets, and electric washing machines.[68]

This general pattern of renunciation may, however, be disappearing as a middle-class norm. Millions of middle-class persons are currently in debt for the purchase of the consumer durable goods that are such an important and tangible evidence of the good life. A recent study indicates that the deferred gratification pattern is no longer (if indeed it ever was) an exclusively middle-class norm. This study examined the tendency to postpone gratification of five adolescent needs (affiliation, aggression, consumption, independence, sex) among a sample of 338 male high-school students in Wisconsin. The study found some evidence "in support of a general deferred gratification pattern," but failed to find evidence "that this is a peculiarly middle-class normative pattern." [69] Regardless of their starting point in the class hierarchy, persons who are going to achieve higher status in our society apparently must defer gratification of some of their immediate needs.

The attitude toward the self is closely allied to the attitude toward personal gratification or its postponement. In one study, a difference emerges between the self-attitudes of middle- and lower-class persons. The former tend to disci-

---

[65] Martha Sturm White, "Social Class, Child-Rearing Practices, and Child Behavior," *American Sociological Review*, 22:704-712 (December, 1957).

[66] Robert O. Blood, Jr., "Consequences of Permissiveness for Parents of Young Children," *Marriage and Family Living*, 15:209-212 (August, 1953).

[67] Martha Sturm White, *op. cit.* Cf. Richard A. Littman, Robert C. A. Moore, and John Pierce-Jones, "Social Class Differences in Child Rearing: A Third Community for Comparison with Chicago and Newton," *American Sociological Review*, 22:694-704 (December, 1957).

[68] Louis Schneider and Sverre Lysgaard, "The Deferred Gratification Pattern: A Preliminary Study," *American Sociological Review*, 18:142-149 (April, 1953).

[69] Murray A. Straus, "Deferred Gratification, Social Class, and the Achievement Syndrome," *American Sociological Review*, 27:326-335 (June, 1962), p. 335.

pline themselves and show a strong degree of aggression toward the self; this may take the form of self-blame, self-distaste, and even self-hatred. Lower-class individuals show insecurity in dealing with other persons and direct their aggressions against others rather than against themselves. The differences in training between the two social levels seem to produce these differences, as the middle-class child is trained to control his behavior by a sense of guilt and other types of self-punishment. The lower-class child is more apt to engage in aggression against other persons.[70]

The middle class is also more active in secondary groups and voluntary associations than is the lower class. The allegation that Americans are a nation of joiners should therefore be amended to apply to the middle class and especially its upper-middle segment. The latter groups dominate the organized life of the community and provide much of the leadership for these organizations. The lower class restricts its participation to family, church, and union groups. Faris contends that the United States is becoming a middle-class nation in these terms, as lower-class people are slowly drawn into the larger structure of organized society. In his words, the meaning of this trend is that "the complex organization which civilized man lives by continues to grow and to embrace more fully the hitherto less organized strata at the lower income and educational levels." [71] Whatever the long-range evidence for such a trend, however, the present disparity between social classes is striking.[72]

Class differences in participation may be partially explained by the concept of role behavior. The person learns a series of roles as a result of his position in the social structure. The lower-class person often finds that his participation in voluntary associations is not congenial because of such factors as lack of education, type of occupation, and, perhaps, prejudice of middle-class persons. These barriers are especially true of lower-class wives who feel keenly their own lack of the advantages that are accepted as a matter of course by middle-class wives. The member of the lower class is rarely able to surmount this combination of circumstances that define his role behavior at an early age.[73]

The middle-class person, finally, tends to have a different attitude toward achievement than either the member of the lower or upper class. The latter has already achieved, or been born into, a high status, whereas many lower-class persons appear to lack the incentive to gain a higher status. In the large and amorphous segment of the population comprising the middle class, however, a belief in the importance of success in general and one's own in particular is strong. Achievement is thus a basic component of the self-attitudes of many members of the middle class. We shall consider these differential aspirations

---

[70] Samuel Z. Klausner, "Social Class and Self-Concept," *Journal of Social Psychology*, 38:201-205 (November, 1953).

[71] Robert E. L. Faris, "The Middle Class from a Sociological Viewpoint," *Social Forces*, 39:1-5 (October, 1960), p. 5.

[72] Leonard Reissman, "Class, Leisure, and Social Participation," *American Sociological Review*, 19:78-84 (February, 1954).

[73] John M. Foskett, "Social Structure and Social Participation," *American Sociological Review*, 20:431-438 (August, 1955).

between classes in the following chapter, which deals with social mobility. We merely indicate here that the middle class appears to have a strong motivation toward such behavior.[74]

The Working-class Subculture

The third major element in the class structure is that large segment variously called the working class, the lower class, and, by the Marxists, the proletariat. It is difficult to characterize this class with even approximate accuracy in the United States, as indeed is the case with the other major strata of our dynamic society. These difficulties are compounded by the fact that many of the studies of the working class include a wide social spectrum ranging from skilled workers to the chronically unemployed and unemployable.[75] In terms of Warner's classification, these persons subsume both the "upper-lower" and the "lower-lower" classes. Under these conditions, absolute precision of exposition is impossible. For the most part, however, we shall follow Miller and Riessman in

---

[74] Bernard C. Rosen, "The Achievement Syndrome: A Psycho-cultural Dimension of Social Stratification," *American Sociological Review*, 21:202-211 (April, 1956).

[75] Joseph A. Kahl, *The American Class Structure* (New York: Holt, Rinehart and Winston, Inc., 1959), pp. 205ff.

The middle class is active in voluntary associations, as illustrated by this service club banquet in a local YMCA gymnasium.

defining the working class as "regular members of the non-agricultural labor force in manual occupations."[76] In these terms, the working class comprises factory workers, service workers, skilled and unskilled artisans, truck drivers, factory operatives, and others who work with their hands.[77]

The white collar has traditionally separated the middle class from the working class. Like many such criteria, this one no longer prevails, at least with its former symbolic quality. The higher scale of living currently available to many members of the working class has gone a long way toward reducing the distinction between classes, at least in terms of goods and services available. In an earlier day, white-collar workers had a higher income than manual workers and class distinctions were partially maintained by this fact. In recent years, however, manual workers have overtaken white-collar workers. A study made a few years ago indicated that manual workers averaged three dollars per week *more* than white-collar workers in the nation as a whole.[78] The mass production of consumer durable goods and the increase in take-home pay for manual workers have further decreased class differences away from the job.

The working class in the United States, as we have seen, has never developed the class-consciousness that marks it in many European countries. Identification with the organized working class (proletariat) brings little prestige in a society that stresses upward mobility above everything else. A high level of class consciousness, indeed, is more characteristic of the uprooted and exploited members of organized labor than of the more settled workers. In a study of 375 blue-collar workers in Detroit, Leggett found that: "Contrary to Marx's expectations, uprooted workers are found to express a higher level of class consciousness than the prepared, partially because the uprooted bring with them fewer skills and experiences that might help them to deal effectively with their new environment."[79]

Until recently, there has been comparatively little scientific study of the subculture of the working class in the United States. For the most part, emphasis has been upon the middle class and its characteristic culture patterns. Two studies, however, one by Miller and Riessman (to which we have already referred)[80] and the other by Cohen and Hodges[81] have thrown considerable light upon the subculture of this large and little-known segment. In their thoughtful analysis, Miller and Riessman develop what they call the "themes" of working-class culture—that is, its general value-pattern. In so doing, they refer to the

[76] S. M. Miller and Frank Riessman, "The Working Class Subculture: A New View," *Social Problems*, 9:86-97 (Summer, 1961), p. 88.
[77] Centers, *The Psychology of Social Classes, op. cit.*, p. 99.
[78] Robert K. Burns, "The Comparative Economic Position of Manual and White-Collar Employees," *Journal of Business*, 27:257-266 (1954).
[79] John C. Leggett, "Uprootedness and Working-Class Consciousness," *American Journal of Sociology*, 68:682-692 (May, 1963), p. 692. By "uprooted workers," Leggett refers to migrants from rural backgrounds who lack the necessary education, training, and skills to cope with an industrial environment.
[80] Miller and Riessman, *op cit.*
[81] Albert K. Cohen and Harold M. Hodges, Jr., "Characteristics of the Lower-Blue-Collar-Class," *Social Problems*, 10:303-334 (Spring, 1963).

stable culture of the regular working class, rather than to the unstable culture of the segments lower on the social scale. The latter include certain minority groups (Negroes and Puerto Ricans) whose inadequate education, skills, and training combine with prejudice to put them near the bottom of the class structure.

Among the "themes" of stable working-class culture are the following: (*a*) traditionalism (emphasis upon family and religion); (*b*) inadequacy of education; (*c*) lack of liberalism (especially on civil liberties and foreign affairs); (*d*) striving for security rather than for status and prestige; (*e*) anti-intellectualism and distrust of abstract ideas; (*f*) emphasis upon personal rather than general qualities; and (*g*) desire for excitement through sports, gambling,[82] sensational news, and the ownership of new cars and television sets.[83] Many of these themes are opposed to those of middle-class culture, and the blue-collar worker does not *necessarily* wish to rise to middle-class status. In this view, some working-class values differ in kind as well as in degree from those of the

---

[82] Irving K. Zola, "Observations on Gambling in a Lower-Class Setting," *Social Problems*, 10:353-361 (Spring, 1963).
[83] Miller and Riessman, *op. cit.*

Faced with a world he cannot control, the lower blue-collar worker often seeks excitement through gambling.

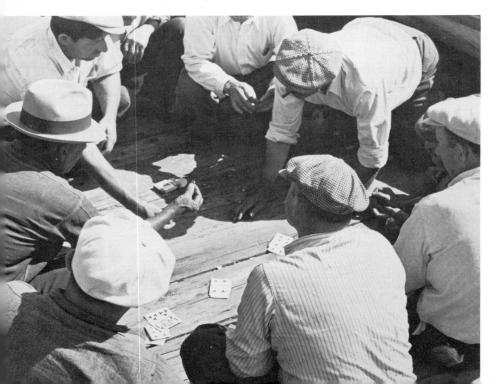

middle class. Many working-class persons, therefore, have no desire to attain middle-class status as long as they can enjoy the values of their own subculture.

In their study of the working class, Cohen and Hodges deal with the lower blue-collar class—that is, the lowest segment of the social structure. They offer a series of perceptive generalizations based upon an examination by Hodges of social class among persons living on the San Francisco Peninsula. We may summarize some of their findings on the life-situation of the lower blue-collar class and the ways in which its members try to adapt to this situation. The life-situation involves the following elements: (*a*) a *simplification* of the experience world, whereby the blue-collar worker unconsciously tries to reduce this world to proportions that he can understand; (*b*) a sense of *powerlessness* because of his inability to manipulate his environment so that he can reach his goals; (*c*) a feeling of *deprivation* because his resources are so far below his felt needs, especially in a society with unlimited aspirations; and (*d*) a feeling of *insecurity* because he never knows when deprivation will strike.[84]

Faced with such a world, the lower blue-collar member tries to work out a way of life that will minimize his anxiety and maximize his security. Since he cannot control the larger world, he must rely on his family and friends. Together they constitute a network of interpersonal relationships in which each aids the other. This aid takes the form of material assistance and emotional assurance of status and worth. "Kinship, neighboring and adolescent peer group relationships," as Cohen and Hodges put it, are the principal agencies of the pattern of mutual assistance. This primary group interaction is especially marked among lower blue-collar wives, who hold the family together emotionally and often economically as well. In short, the authors maintain that "in the lower blue-collar class there is more nearly *exclusive* dependence upon particularistic ties, primarily kin and secondarily peer, than in the other classes. . . ."[85]

A number of other understandings and insights have emerged from these and other studies of the nature of working-class and lower-class subculture. Some of these characteristics have been previously mentioned, but it will be helpful to bring them together. Many of these studies do not always distinguish clearly between the stable working class and the lower blue-collar class, and a certain amount of confusion inevitably results. In our enumeration, we shall try to keep these referents clear, although this is sometimes impossible because of the nature of the data. We shall deal with these subcultural characteristics under two general headings—the *behavioral* and the *ideological*. The first refers to what lower-class persons actually *do*, whereas the second refers to their attitudes, feelings, and ways of looking at themselves and the world. These distinctions are not rigid, for each interacts upon, and merges into, the other. Nevertheless, it may be helpful to view the working-class subculture in these terms.

---

[84] Cohen and Hodges, *op. cit.*, pp. 305-307.
[85] *Ibid.*, p. 313. (Their italics.)

Behavioral Characteristics

1. Sex behavior. In the first volume of his monumental study, Kinsey concluded that the comparative data "constitute some of the best evidence yet available that social categories (classes) are realities in our Anglo-American culture." [86] The subculture of the lower class, as measured largely by educational attainment, has strong patterns favoring complete sexual experience in the early or middle teens and before marriage. The lower the class (educational) level, the earlier such experience begins and the greater the frequency with which it occurs.

2. Child rearing. In a variety of fields connected with the feeding, toilet training, and disciplining of children, the lower-class family shows a greater permissiveness than the middle-class family. The lower-class family tends to feed the child when he is hungry rather than at fixed intervals, and is less concerned with personal hygiene, as in the case of toilet training.[87] The lower-class child expects and receives corporal punishment to a greater extent than the middle-class child. The latter is often punished by the withdrawal of affection by his parents or by the threat of such action.[88]

3. Communication. The lower class is less articulate than the middle class in the matter of communication. The symbolic participation in social interaction is on a more rudimentary level with the lower-class person. He is less able to take the role of the listener and communicate in abstractions; when he tells a story, he speaks in terms of what happened to *him*, without bothering to put himself in the place of the other. He is, furthermore, comparatively insensitive to differences in perspective between himself and the listener, and often fails to realize that his story is neither understandable nor interesting to the other person.[89]

4. Consumer expenditures. In the Cohen and Hodges study, the lower blue-collar worker spent approximately 20 per cent *more* on consumer durable goods (automobiles, television sets, washing machines) than did the *upper* blue-collar worker. This discrepancy is all the more striking because the upper blue-collar worker has a median family income that is approximately 30 per cent *higher* than his more free-spending compatriot. A higher percentage of lower blue-collar workers, furthermore, own Cadillacs than do *any other level* in the class hierarchy. The majority of these Cadillacs are probably secondhand or third-hand, but the fact remains that this status symbol is more important to the marginal worker than to any other segment of the *entire* population. At the same time, the house, garden, and lawn of the lower blue-collar worker are often in a state of disrepair, abandon, and (sometimes) downright squalor. The explanation of these and other discrepancies in consumption patterns would take us

---

[86] Alfred C. Kinsey, *et al.*, *Sexual Behavior in the Human Male* (Philadelphia: W. B. Saunders Company, 1948), p. 335.

[87] Davis and Havighurst, "Social Class and Color Differences in Child-Rearing," *op. cit.*

[88] Arnold W. Green, "The Middle-Class Male Child and Neurosis," *American Sociological Review*, 11:31-41 (February, 1946).

[89] Leonard Schatzman and Anselm Strauss, "Social Class and Modes of Communication," *American Journal of Sociology*, 60:329-338 (January, 1955).

too far afield. We can only note that the lower blue-collar worker tends to concentrate upon a few conspicuous status symbols at the expense of other types of consumer expenditures.[90]

5. *Social participation.* In the realm of group activities, the lower-class person confines his activities to his immediate family and, to some extent, to religious or union activities. The multiple group membership of the urban community is, on the whole, not for him, perhaps because of shyness, lack of education, or general indifference. He leaves the leadership of these voluntary associations to the middle class and prefers to remain among persons of his own social level. This very lack of communication means that the lower-class person is handicapped in upward mobility, since he lacks both the knowledge and the acquaintanceship with members of the class above who might help him on his climb.[91]

6. *Family decision-making.* The lower blue-collar family appears to be a curious blend of matriarchal and patriarchal dominance. The mother makes many family decisions, especially those dealing with spending money and taking care of the children. At the same time, the men studied by Cohen and Hodges heartily agreed with the statement that "Men should make the *really important* decisions in the family." [92] This apparent inconsistency may be partly explained by a rigid division of labor, whereby the wife makes decisions in her sphere and the husband in his. It may also reflect the man's belief that he *should* play the dominant role but that, through lethargy or indifference, he is content to let the woman assume most of the actual authority. Only occasionally, so this argument runs, does the man arbitrarily assert his authority to show his wife, his children, and (especially) himself who is boss. He wants to convince himself that the real authority belongs to him and that he can exert it whenever he wishes. Most of the time, however, his wife runs the family.[93]

7. *Family disorganization.* Contrary to widespread popular opinion, the family life of the working class is no more stable than that of the middle and upper classes. Lower-class families are subject to many stresses and strains merely because of their poverty, and these tensions take their toll in family disorganization. A study of divorced males in Iowa found that divorce is much more common in the lower social and economic groups than it is in the upper socioeconomic levels of the population.[94] Another study concluded that "the cumulative evidence seems overwhelming that there is a rough *inverse correlation between economic status and rate of divorce.*" [95] Lower-class status and poverty present difficulties for marriage interaction, and these difficulties are apparent in the high divorce rate among this segment of the population.

---

[90] Cohen and Hodges, *op. cit.*, pp. 330-331.

[91] Genevieve Knupfer, "Portrait of the Underdog," *Public Opinion Quarterly,* 11:103-114 (Spring, 1947).

[92] Cohen and Hodges, *op. cit.*, pp. 326-327. (My italics.)

[93] *Ibid.*

[94] Thomas P. Monahan, "Divorce by Occupational Level," *Marriage and Family Living,* 17:322-324 (November, 1955), p. 324.

[95] William J. Goode, "Economic Factors and Marital Stability," *American Sociological Review,* 16:802-812 (December, 1951), p. 803. (His italics.)

8. Personality disorganization. There are also differences between social classes in the form and extent of personality deviance and disorganization. The social environment in which the person lives affects both the organization and disorganization of his personality. In a series of studies conducted in New Haven, Connecticut, Hollingshead and Redlich concluded that, in general, the neuroses predominate in the upper social levels and the psychoses in the lower social levels. Members of the lower classes have a disproportionate share of the more serious forms of mental illness, which suggests that the frustrations and insecurities of their way of life are great.[96] In a study of the interaction of social class and deviant behavior, another group of authors found that personality deviance leads to low social status, as well as vice versa. Antisocial (deviant) fathers have low social (class) status, as well as a disproportionately large percentage of deviant children. The latter, in turn, have low social status when *they* get to be adults. Deviance and low status thus interact upon each other.[97]

Ideological Characteristics

1. Concept of the self. There also appear to be differences between classes with regard to the concept of the self. The lower-class person is, on the whole, less able to view himself objectively through the eyes of the other. The superego (conscience) seems to be stronger in the middle-class than in the lower-class person, with a corresponding difference in feelings of guilt. The Kinsey data suggest that these differences are especially pronounced in sex behavior, with the lower-class person less prone to excessive guilt feelings from lapses from conventional morality. The self is, finally, more frequently an object of aggression by the middle-class person, whereas the aggressions of the lower-class person are more often directed outward against others.[98]

2. Status anxiety. It has been widely assumed that the middle class is exclusively concerned with striving for status and that the lower class is virtually free from the anxiety accompanying this quest. Recent studies, however, question this assumption and indicate that working-class persons also suffer from problems of status. This suffering may, in certain instances, be even greater than in the middle class because the status of the lower-class person is (by definition) considerably lower. Tensions in the lower-class child are indicated in one study by "(*a*) concern about the social status of his family; (*b*) concern over his ability to perform up to expected levels, particularly in school; (*c*) rejection of his family . . . ; and (*d*) . . . nervous behaviors indicative of general anxiety." [99]

---

[96] August B. Hollingshead and Frederick C. Redlich, *Social Class and Mental Illness* (New York: John Wiley & Sons, Inc., 1958), p. 210.

[97] Lee N. Robins, Harry Gyman, and Patricia O'Neal. "The Interaction of Social Class and Deviant Behavior," *American Sociological Review,* 27:480-492 (August, 1962).

[98] Klausner, "Social Class and Self-Concept," *op. cit.*

[99] William H. Sewell and A. O. Haller, "Factors in the Relationship Between Social Status and the Personality Adjustment of the Child," *American Sociological Review,* 24:511-520 (August, 1959), p. 519.

3. *Pessimism.* A strong sense of pessimism runs through the reactions of the lower blue-collar class in the Cohen and Hodges study. The world of the lower-lower class is (not surprisingly) viewed as a bleak and uncertain place, where nothing is sure except unhappiness and disaster. The objective situation of this class is unsatisfactory, and their adaptation to this situation does not help much. That is, the position of the member of the lower blue-collar class is worsened "by his *adaptation to* that insecurity and powerlessness, by a style of life marked by improvidence, unsteady work habits, and other characteristics calculated to insure his continued occupancy of what Knupfer calls his 'underdog' status."[100] A vicious circle is established, involving insecurity, pessimism, improvidence, and subsequent failure. The latter condition, in turn, confirms the initial attitude that life is going to turn out badly anyway.

4. *Misanthropy.* Cynicism and distrust of others constitute the syndrome of misanthropy. Lower blue-collar class people believe that others are out to cheat you, that you have to watch out for yourself, and that all men are basically selfish. Most people, in short, are "no good." This pattern reflects the obvious fact that persons in this class *are* exploited because of their lack of power. Hence it is natural that they should be distrustful of others and prone to believe the worst about their fellow men. Furthermore, the lower blue-collar class is ignorant of the larger world of the learned professions, government officials, the police, and big business, all of which are regarded as mysterious agencies whose activities bring only harm to the poor man. In desperation, the latter concentrates upon a few persons who are in the same position as himself and whom he believes he can "trust"—his family, his friends, and his neighbors.[101]

5. *"Extrapunitiveness."* This quality refers to the tendency of the lower blue-collar class to direct their aggressions (punitiveness) against others rather than against themselves. We have referred to this quality in *1* above, in connection with attitudes toward the self. More specifically, lower-class people tend to blame others when things go wrong, instead of blaming themselves. There is, of course, an obvious explanation for this extrapunitiveness, inasmuch as many of the frustrations and insecurities of the lower blue-collar worker *are* attributable to other persons—or to impersonal forces over which the poor man has no control. Unemployment is the most obvious such condition, and many conscientious workers are periodically laid off through no fault of their own. At the same time, many persons will blame others for difficulties brought on by their (the lower blue-collar workers') own fecklessness, lack of foresight, and carelessness. Their sense of social reality tends to become blurred.[102]

6. *Authoritarian tendencies.* Working-class people also seem to be neither as democratic nor as liberal as many middle-class observers have hopefully believed. Indeed, Lipset indicates that working-class persons have, on balance, more authoritarian tendencies than do middle-class persons. On such matters as tolerance of conflicting opinions, willingness to permit freedom of speech,

---

[100] Cohen and Hodges, *op. cit.,* p. 322. (Their italics.)
[101] *Ibid.,* pp. 323-324.
[102] *Ibid.,* pp. 325-326.

assembly, and voting, and participation in democratic activities, working-class people have more totalitarian attitudes than do middle-class people. A number of factors in the working-class subculture contribute to this lack of democratic liberalism. Among these predisposing factors are: "low education, low participation in political organizations or in voluntary organizations of any type, little reading . . . economic insecurity, and authoritarian family patterns." [103]

7. *Prejudice.* Closely related to authoritarian tendencies and extrapunitiveness is racial and religious prejudice. Indeed, prejudice against out-groups in general and Negroes and Jews in particular appears to be part of the authoritarian personality syndrome (pattern of traits).[104] One study of a small sample of lower-class boys suggests that their prejudice was a "reflection of the general set of attitudes characteristic of the American lower class." [105] These boys were for the most part either openly antagonistic ("those dirty niggers are trying to take my job away") or prejudiced ("Jews? Well, they are all right except that they try to gyp you."). The life of lower-class persons is, on balance, marked by many more frustrations, insecurities, and deprivations than that of middle-class and upper-class persons. These difficulties are most evident on the socioeconomic level, but they are also apparent, as we have indicated, in the personal, family, and community life of the lower class. The resulting prejudice may be an unconsciously motivated attempt to strike back at the frustrations of the environment by aggression against minority groups.

In this chapter, we have examined the nature of social class, with particular reference to its manifestations in the contemporary United States. Social class is characterized by the differential distribution of rewards and privileges among the members of a society. The resulting statuses are not as permanent as those of caste, but they nevertheless have an important influence upon the life chances of the individual to gain the basic goals of the society. Social class has been measured by such objective indices as membership in particular groups, rating by informants, and association with persons of a recognized status. It may also be indicated by such subjective criteria as attitudes, values, interests, ideas, and self-identification.

The egalitarian tradition of the United States is so strong that Americans rarely admit that they live in a class-organized society. Most people prefer to think of this country as one in which virtually everyone (except certain minority groups) belongs to an amorphous segment known as the "middle class." When Americans *do* think about class differences, they usually define them in terms of monetary distinctions. This is neither a particularly delicate nor reliable measure of class membership, inasmuch as many members of the "working" class now earn more than many members of the "middle" class. More subtle criteria

---

[103] Seymour M. Lipset, "Democracy and Working-Class Authoritarianism," *American Sociological Review,* 24:482-501 (August, 1959), p. 489.

[104] Cf. T. W. Adorno, *et al.,* *The Authoritarian Personality* (New York: Harper & Row, 1950).

[105] William McCord, Joan McCord, and Alan Howard, "Early Familial Experiences and Bigotry," *American Sociological Review,* 25:717-722 (October, 1960), p. 721.

of class membership have recently been deduced from empirical studies in this field. In terms both of actual behavior in different life situations and of the ideological reactions toward these situations, American society has many characteristic features of social class.

SELECTED BIBLIOGRAPHY

Baltzell, E. Digby, *Philadelphia Gentlemen: The Making of a National Upper Class*. Glencoe, Ill.: The Free Press, 1958. This is one of the rare sociological studies dealing with the elite in American society. As the title indicates, the author analyzes the factors, both historical and contemporary, that produce a member of a recognized upper class. The role of education, both at the preparatory school and college levels, is especially important in the production of gentlemen.

Barber, Bernard, *Social Stratification*. New York: Harcourt, Brace and World, 1957. In this definitive analysis of social stratification, the author discusses at length the nature of social class in the United States and Europe. Three kinds of social class indicators are examined: (*a*) verbal evaluation (what people say); (*b*) patterns of association (with whom people interact); and (*c*) symbolic indicators (possessions, status symbols, and other consequences of different social roles).

Centers, Richard, *The Psychology of Social Classes*. Princeton: Princeton University Press, 1949. This is a study of social class in the United States, with emphasis upon the identification of the individual with a particular class. The author is closely identified with the physchological position in this respect.

Cohen, Albert K., and Harold M. Hodges, Jr., "Characteristics of the Lower-Blue-Collar-Class," *Social Problems*, 10:303-334 (Spring, 1963). This long and perceptive essay reports on a study by the junior author of the "lower-blue-collar-class," which corresponds roughly to Warner's "lower-lower class." The study deals with behavior patterns of this segment and their attitudes toward themselves and the world.

Hollingshead, August B., and Frederick C. Redlich, *Social Class and Mental Illness*. New York: John Wiley & Sons, Inc., 1958. This book is an important contribution to the literature of social class, as well as to that of mental illness. The study reveals that there is a significant relationship between the class position of the individual and the kinds of mental disease from which he suffers, the diagnosis of these diseases, and the treatment that he receives.

Kohn, Melvin L., "Social Class and Parental Values," *American Journal of Sociology*, 64:337-351 (January, 1959). Social classes are seen as subcultures of the larger society. Each class has its own pattern of values, which are important in motivating behavior. Differences between middle-class and lower-class values are explored in the article, which also throws an interesting light upon the forms of social control of the two groups.

Leggett, John C., "Uprootedness and Working-Class Consciousness," *American Journal of Sociology*, 68:682-692 (May, 1963). Also "Working-Class Consciousness, Race, and Political Choice," *American Journal of Sociology*, 69:171-176 (September, 1963). A sample of 375 blue-collar workers in Detroit provided the basic data for these two articles, which add greatly to our knowledge of class consciousness (or the lack of it) among urban industrial workers.

Lipset, Seymour M., "Democracy and Working-Class Authoritarianism," *American Sociological Review*, 24:482-501 (August, 1959). In this study, the subculture of the working class is analyzed in terms of the factors that predispose its members to authoritarian attitudes. Among these factors are: lack of education, lack of reading, economic insecurity, and low participation in the voluntary organizations of democratic government.

Manis, Jerome G., and Bernard N. Meltzer, "Some Correlates of Class Consciousness Among Textile Workers," *American Journal of Sociology*, 69:177-184 (September, 1963). The authors re-examine the data reported in an earlier study (1954) concerning the nature of class consciousness in an eastern industrial city with a long tradition of labor organization. They conclude in the current article that textile workers are more "job-conscious" or "wage-conscious" than "class-conscious" in any militant sense.

Miller, S. M., and Frank Riessman, "The Working-Class Subculture: A New View," *Social Problems*, 9:86-97 (Summer, 1961). In this thoughtful article, the authors question some traditional assumptions about the working class and its subculture. The article is especially valuable for its analysis of certain "themes" of working-class life—that is, the *meaning* of working-class life, rather than its mere description.

Sewell, William H., "Social Class and Childhood Personality." *Sociometry*, 24:340-356 (December, 1961). This article expresses considerable skepticism regarding much of the literature on social class and personality. The author reviews some of this literature and then suggests that, although *some* relationship between class and childhood personality undoubtedly exists, the correlation is relatively low.

Warner, W. Lloyd, Marchia Meeker, and Kenneth Eells, *Social Class in America*. Chicago: Science Research Associates, 1949. This book explains at length the theory of social stratification and the methodology of the Warner studies of social class in the American community.

15 Mobility

The Nature of Social Mobility

The class structure of the United States is a dynamic system of comparatively impermanent groups. This situation is in contrast to the structure of many of the nations of western Europe, where clearly defined classes still bear witness to centuries of evolution of different culture patterns. In this country, the belief in free and unrestricted upward movement in the social scale has been one of the bases of the American Dream. This country has seen the most spectacular such movement in history. Millions of peasants and small artisans have come from Europe and, within their own lifetimes or those of their children, have moved substantially upward on the status ladder.

This process is known as social mobility or, more strictly, as *vertical* mobility. It refers to the movement of individuals upward or downward in the social structure, with a consequent gain or loss in status. The positions to which these persons move have been given different values by society.[1] As defined by Barber, social mobility refers to "movement, either upward or downward, between higher or lower social classes; or more precisely, movement between one relatively full-time, functionally significant social role and another that is evaluated as either higher or lower. This movement," he continues, "is to be conceived as a process occurring over time, with individuals (and their family units) moving from one role and social class position to another because of what has happened to them in various kinds of social interaction." [2] Mobility arises in social interaction, as each individual reacts to others in a changing series of social roles.

In this sense, mobility "provides the individual with more or less of the benefits which his economy and society have to offer." [3] An Italian immigrant's son becomes a lawyer; a Jewish boy from the East Side becomes a doctor; and the son of a Greek fruit peddler becomes an engineer. In each case, a change in role between father and son provides the latter with more of the good things of life. The roles of lawyer, doctor, and engineer require initiative, training, and self-sacrifice. Persons are motivated according to a complex variety of factors to work toward new roles, with their higher status and greater rewards. The good things of life are scarce and individuals must compete, conflict, and cooperate with others to gain them.[4]

Mobility may be considered in several different senses, among them: (*a*) as a change in occupation that involves a consequent change in status; (*b*) as a promotion within the same occupational group; (*c*) as the accumulation of seniority within a given occupation; (*d*) as a change in occupation from one generation to another, as from father to son .[5] A more inclusive conception of mobility, involving both objective and subjective factors, is suggested by Westoff and others. Among these factors are the following: (*a*) changes in occupation between the husband on the one hand and his own father and his wife's father on the other; (*b*) number of job changes of the husband; (*c*) changes in the husband's income and that of the family; (*d*) number of changes of residence since marriage; (*e*) attitudes of the wife toward getting ahead, including such factors as her willingness to leave her friends and to have her husband take a job with less security but more opportunity; (*f*) attitudes of the husband to-

[1] Seymour M. Lipset and Reinhard Bendix, *Social Mobility in Industrial Society* (Berkeley: University of California Press, 1959), pp. 1-2.

[2] Bernard Barber, *Social Stratification* (New York: Harcourt, Brace and Company, 1957), p. 356.

[3] S. M. Miller, "The Concept of Mobility," *Social Problems*, 3:65-73 (October, 1955), p. 66.

[4] Bernard C. Rosen, "Race, Ethnicity, and the Achievement Syndrome," *American Sociological Review*, 24:47-60 (February, 1959).

[5] Theodore Caplow, *The Sociology of Work* (Minneapolis: University of Minnesota Press, 1954), pp. 59-60.

ward getting ahead and his willingness to sacrifice in order to do so; and (g) the level of the husband's satisfaction with this occupation and status.[6]

Social mobility is the dynamic aspect of social stratification.[7] Social mobility in the United States has been conditioned by several related factors: (1) The majority of immigrants to this country were peasants, artisans, or small merchants in Europe. They migrated for the express purpose of escaping the ascribed class society of the Old World and finding a new home where traditional ascriptions did not apply. (2) A rich and virtually unoccupied country was a powerful equalizing force upon such class distinctions as *were* brought to this country. The status of the individual was largely determined by his own abilities and good fortune. (3) The frontier gradually closed and was succeeded by a rapid industrialization that enabled many to lift themselves to important positions in the economic and social system. Class stratification and social mobility have thus been part of the same dynamic process.

Few immigrants came to this country with many material possessions. The limited technical skills needed to fashion a new nation out of the forest and the prairie could be learned by almost any man. The frontier reinforced the equalitarian attitudes of an immigrant people.[8] The sparse communities in the West evinced little interest in the social origins of newcomers, provided they were not Negroes, Orientals, or Indians. On the farmlands and on the plains, individual initiative and ability, not hereditary class, were the prime considerations. A virtually unrestricted system of vertical mobility grew out of this experience. The Horatio Alger story of rags to riches reflected sober reality for a great many persons.[9]

The present status and future possibilities of this inspiring story are variously viewed by social scientists. We shall discuss the trends in social stratification in some detail below. We merely wish to state here the question in broad, theoretical terms. The fundamental issue may be phrased in two ways: (1) Is the stratification *increasing*, with a resulting solidification of class differences? (2) Is the rate of social mobility *decreasing*, with a consequent decrease in the chances of the individual to rise from one social level to another? These two questions are closely related, since they deal with achieved versus ascribed status and individual opportunity to rise to social and economic heights.[10]

The answer to this general question is extremely complex. It depends upon such factors as: (a) the definition of mobility—that is, whether we are speaking of changes between father and son or changes within the same generation; and (b) the changes in the "opportunity structure"—that is, whether or not the society is providing proportionately more occupations that carry high rewards

---

[6] Charles F. Westoff, Marvin Bressler, and Philip C. Sagi, "The Concept of Social Mobility: An Empirical Inquiry," *American Sociological Review*, 25:375-385 (June, 1960), Table 2.

[7] John F. Cuber and William F. Kenkel, *Social Stratification in the United States* (New York: Appleton-Century-Crofts, Inc., 1954), Chapter 15.

[8] Frederick J. Turner, *The Frontier in American History* (New York: Henry Holt and Company, 1921).

[9] Cf. Gustavus Myers, *History of the Great American Fortunes* (New York: The Modern Library, 1936).

[10] Gideon Sjoberg. "Are Social Classes in America Becoming More Rigid?", *American Sociological Review*, 16:775-783 (December, 1951).

and prestige. Some observers suggest that social mobility in both senses is declining and that the class structure is becoming correspondingly more rigid.[11]

Other observers maintain that the social structure (especially the access to white-collar jobs) is actually more fluid than it used to be.[12] Still others state, on the basis of careful research, that the rate of occupational mobility from father to son is about the same as it was at the turn of the century.[13] We shall consider these trends in more detail below. We may simply state here that the evidence for *either* position (increase *or* decrease) is somewhat inconclusive. The frankest answer to this basic question is that *we do not know* at the present time if social mobility is increasing or decreasing in the United States.[14]

The Factors in Social Stratification

The conception of a *completely* classless society in the United States, either now or in the past, is a fiction. Social stratification in some measure has always existed and will presumably continue to exist. Differential status has been with us since the first English settlers landed on the New England coast more than three hundred years ago. The degree of social stratification is *relative*, and in this respect our own structure has unquestionably been more fluid than that of any other society with a comparable culture. Many changes have taken place in this structure during the past century that have, on balance, probably slowed down the *rate* of vertical mobility and formalized many cultural differences between the classes. We do not know exactly what is happening in this respect at the present time. We *do* know that certain changes have occurred in the class structure in the past century, and we can examine some of these general tendencies in the light of certain long-range social trends.

1. The closing of the frontier. The frontier offered an unparalleled opportunity for individuals to start on an equal footing in the race for status and security.[15] Millions of acres of rich land were an initial force for social equality. In general, the Anglo-Saxons and Scandinavians reached the rich farm country of the Middle West before the immigrants from southern and eastern Europe. The latter had no choice but to settle in the cities, even though they would have preferred to settle on the land. The frontier could not remain open indefinitely, and those who came first were the most fortunate. They set the tone for upward mobility in this country. The problem of the frontier was one of timing, with differential status falling to the settlers roughly in the order of their arrival.

[11] J. O. Hertzler, "Some Tendencies Toward a Closed Class System in the United States," *Social Forces*, 30:313-323 (March, 1952).

[12] Gerhard E. Lenski, "Trends in Inter-Generational Occupational Mobility in the United States," *American Sociological Review*, 23:514-523 (October, 1958).

[13] Natalie Rogoff, "Recent Trends in Urban Occupational Mobility," in Paul K. Hatt and Albert J. Reiss, Jr. (eds.), *Reader in Urban Sociology* (Glencoe, Ill.: The Free Press, 1951).

[14] Ely Chinoy, "Social Mobility Trends in the United States," *American Sociological Review*, 20:180-186 (April, 1955).

[15] Walter Goldschmidt, "Social Class and the Dynamics of Status in America," *American Anthropologist*, 57:1209-1217 (December, 1955), pp. 1213-1214.

2. *The curtailment of immigration.* In the century from 1830 to 1930, an estimated 40 million persons came to the United States. Many of them settled on the moving frontier where, as noted, they acquired status and land. Many more settled in the large industrial cities, where they found employment in industry. This steady stream of newcomers provided unskilled labor at the bottom of the status structure and pushed the native born toward the top. Many of the latter entered the clerical, sales, service, and other white-collar occupations of an expanding business structure. These occupations were defined as middle-class, so this change represented upward mobility, even though the income was often no greater than that of manual workers. The prestige of the white over the blue collar was such, however, that millions of persons considered that they had changed their class. This flood of immigration came to a virtual stop in 1924, and with it much of the upward pressure.

3. *The increased fertility of the upper classes.* A more recent factor making for increasing stratification has been the growing fertility of the middle and upper classes. For a long time before World War II, the comparatively low birth rate of the upper-middle classes meant that they were not bearing enough children to replace themselves in the next generation. This failure was estimated at 20 per cent, which meant that every five persons in the upper classes produced only four descendants in the next generation to occupy their inherited status. This factor was a powerful force making for upward mobility, as these vacant positions in the status structure were occupied by persons from the lower levels. In the decades since World War II, however, the birth rate of these groups has increased, leaving less room at the top. Sons of middle- and upper-middle-class families are becoming sufficiently numerous to retain the status positions of their parents. This is a significant factor in slowing down the rate of mobility.[16]

4. *The concentration of corporate control.* High status in American society has meant the ownership and control of wealth. In a period when an individual could start a business with his own limited resources, ownership and control of wealth were at least theoretically open to everyone. In recent decades, however, industry has become larger, and its control has become vested in a comparatively small elite. The number of persons *owning* stock in the large corporations has greatly increased in recent years, but this factor has not been synonymous with *control*. For millions of middle-class investors, ownership means the periodic receipt of a dividend and the privilege of voting for or against the management. The old concept of ownership and control has undergone considerable change. In a study of this relationship, Berle and Means found that the majority of large corporations were controlled by persons who owned only a small percentage of the stock. Hence there was a sharp distinction between *ownership* and *control*, with the nominal owners (the mass of

---

[16] Cf. C. F. Westoff, "Differential Fertility in the United States: 1900 to 1952," *American Sociological Review,* 19:549-561 (October, 1954).

stockholders) having virtually no voice in the affairs of the corporation.[17] The members of the corporate control groups constitute a new and powerful elite.[18]

5. *The evolution of ethnic barriers.* During its first two centuries as a separate society, America was essentially homogeneous in its ethnic base. There were, it is true, small ethnic and religious minorities, but most of the people were English in culture and Protestant in religion. Ethnic factors had little influence upon such class stratification as then existed. In the past century, however, millions of persons of non-Anglo-Saxon culture have settled in this country, and ethnic differences have become increasingly important as a basis for social stratification. Members of certain minority groups find tacit barriers against their upward movement in the status structure, even though they may be economically successful. In individual cases, these barriers can be, and are, surmounted, but they still set off one segment of the society from another. In some large industrial communities, ethnic stratification appears to be increasing, rather than decreasing, in recent decades.[19]

Two general factors, constituting general tendencies (6) and (7) in this analysis of the changing class structure, remain—*The break in the skill hierarchy*, and *The changing role of education.* These factors are so important that we are devoting detailed sections to them. The break in the skill hierarchy refers to changes in manufacturing techniques and the resultant necessity of more training to fill managerial positions. In these terms, it is increasingly difficult for a working-class boy to enter a factory as an apprentice, rise to the position of skilled workman, become a foreman, and eventually own the factory. In the second instance, the importance of education in social mobility is becoming greater. Both general and technical education are necessary for managerial positions.

6. *The break in the skill hierarchy.* We may consider the situation of a young man of working-class parents who is starting to work in a factory today. In many of the mass-production industries, the rudimentary skills needed to operate a machine can be learned in two or three weeks. The skill of the mechanic and artisan has in many cases been replaced by the skill built into the machine. The worker becomes an adjunct to the machine under these conditions. He is an easily replaced part in a process that, although it is dependent upon a mass of anonymous individuals as such, needs his individual skill less and less. This is a drastic departure from the long and gradual road from apprentice to master craftsman and, possibly, foreman and owner. As the modern worker grows older, there is often no increase in skill, but merely a diminution of vitality and pro-

[17] Adolf A. Berle and Gardiner C. Means, *The Modern Corporation and Private Property* (New York: The Macmillan Company, 1932). See also Adolf A. Berle, *Power Without Property* (New York: Harcourt, Brace and World, 1959).

[18] W. Lloyd Warner and James C. Abegglen, *Big Business Leaders in America* (New York: Harper & Row, 1955).

[19] August B. Hollingshead, "Trends in Social Stratification: A Case Study," *American Sociological Review*, 17:679-686 (December, 1952).

dutivity. Many skilled operators remain, of course, but large numbers of workers are side-tracked permanently on the semiskilled level.[20]

The role of the shoe-machine operator in Yankee City illustrates this situation. The progress from apprentice to skilled worker to owner was, in theory at least, formerly open to any able and ambitious boy. Under present conditions in many highly mechanized industries, there is "a break in the skill hierarchy." The unskilled young man who has gone to high school can go only so far in the factory system before he runs into the barrier of education. He may still rise to the position of foreman, whose function is largely that of getting the most work out of the rest of the men, but he can ordinarily go no further.[21]

The engineering and managerial roles are increasingly filled by men from another world than that of the boy from the working-class family. Most men in the higher statuses in the occupational hierarchy of the shoe factories of Yankee City come from business or managerial backgrounds. They have the advantage of long and expensive training that is difficult for members of the working class to acquire, no matter what their innate abilities. The day when the untrained but able mechanic could rise to run the shop and then own the factory is not completely over. But it is not as common as it used to be. In this sense, "Occupational and social status are to an important extent self-perpetuating. They are associated with many factors which make it very difficult for individuals to modify their status." [22]

The increasing role of the machine may be considered in another light. Many functions that were formerly performed by unskilled hand labor are now performed by machines. This has brought about an important change in the composition of the labor market. In the four decades from 1910 to 1950, the proportion of *skilled* workers in the United States remained approximately the same. The proportion of *unskilled* workers declined from 15 to approximately 10 per cent, and *semiskilled* workers increased from 15 to 20 per cent. This change in the occupational status of millions of workers may or may not be defined as upward mobility. It clearly represents an upgrading from unskilled to semiskilled status, with an accompanying increase in the scale of living. These families did *not*, however, make the jump from blue collar to white collar, the traditional symbol for a change in social class.[23]

The break in the skill hierarchy has also been interpreted as indicating a change from "an employer society to an employee society," with a consequent freezing of status.[24] This is an oversimplification of a complex series of social, industrial, and status trends. Some of the traditional channels of upward mobility have become partially blocked, but others have arisen to take their places.

---

[20] Cf. Reinhard Bendix, *et al.*, "Social Origins and Occupational Career Patterns," *Industrial and Labor Relations Review*, 7:247-261 (January, 1954).

[21] W. Lloyd Warner and J. O. Low, *The Social System of the Modern Factory* (New Haven: Yale University Press, 1947).

[22] Bendix, *et al.*, *op cit.*, p. 260.

[23] Ely Chinoy, "Social Mobility Trends in the United States," *op. cit.*, p. 183.

[24] Peter F. Drucker, "The Employee Society," *American Journal of Sociology*, 58:358-363 (January, 1953).

Labor organizations, especially in the great mass-production industries, constitute one such new channel of vertical mobility. These large-scale structures are bringing about profound modifications in a number of fields, ranging from industrial administration to social stratification.[25]

The large union has several hundred thousand members, which means that many managerial posts are open within the organization itself. A variety of functions requiring skill, technical training, and education are needed to carry on the work of the union, and the latter naturally turns to its own members and the sons of members to fill these posts. The importance of these giant labor organizations in the automobile, steel, rubber, glass, textile, and other mass industries has meant that managerial and administrative skills are needed by the spokesmen of organized labor.[26]

Organized labor has become commensurate in strength with the giant corporation, the pressure groups of the farmer, and even government itself. This development has opened up a new horizon of social mobility to hundreds of thousands of members of the working class. In terms of social mobility, this development has been described as trying "so to reconstruct industry as to assure to every man in it a career." [27] Part of this career is within the growing structure of the union itself and part of it is in the industry, where the union is attempting to minimize some of the barriers in the skill hierarchy and other obstacles to upward mobility. This trend is still in its early stages and is confined to a few of the more progressive industrial unions, but the future possibilities of this trend for the class structure are very great.

7. *The role of education.* American society has always prided itself upon the comparative fluidity of its social organization. One of the chief instruments making for this fluidity was (and is) education. In the past, higher education was required primarily for entry into a limited number of the liberal professions, such as those of doctor, lawyer, teacher, and minister. Many of the higher-status roles in business and industry, however, were available to men with comparatively little education. The self-made man was traditionally the one with little or no education but who nevertheless rose to be a captain of industry. This situation is changing, and education is becoming essential for a variety of roles. Education is now the most important agency whereby a young man with ability but limited resources can rise from the class of his parents. The role of education in social mobility is increasing.

The reason for this increased importance of education is clear. The culture has grown more complex in recent decades, and the individual requires a longer time to learn it. In a simple, agrarian society, the knowledge and skills for adequate adjustment were not difficult to learn. Individuals with unusual native ability and strong motivation could forge to the top without much for-

---

[25] George H. Hildebrand, "American Unionism, Social Stratification, and Power," *American Journal of Sociology*, 58:381-390 (January, 1953).

[26] Nelson N. Foote, "The Professionalization of Labor in Detroit," *American Journal of Sociology*, 58:371-380 (January, 1953).

[27] *Ibid.*, p. 373.

mal training, a process that is becoming increasingly rare. In the technical, urban, industrial society of today, the mere ability to adjust requires training in skills that were not even known in an earlier day. The man who wishes to rise in social level must have both general and specialized training that can only come through formal education.

Education thus provides an opportunity for ambitious members of the middle and (occasionally) the lower class to acquire the necessary training to rise in business or the professions. A recent study of leaders of big business found that 57 per cent had graduated from college, as compared with only 32 per cent a generation before. This trend will unquestionably continue, and the generation of business leaders 25 years from now will have an even larger proportion of college graduates. In the same study, approximately two out of every three business leaders came from families in the upper-middle and upper classes. For these men, college was the expected thing. For the third who rose from a lower status background, college was not so easy, although even more important. Whatever the initial class background, higher education is becoming virtually indispensable to business success.[28]

The free play of the educational process is limited by class factors. Despite the extensive scholarship programs in the colleges and universities, many young men and women with outstanding talents are still denied educational opportunities because of their class position. In a national study made some years ago, 15 per cent of the population of the college age group 17-21 were enrolled in institutions of higher learning. It is estimated that approximately 32 per cent of the same age group have the intellectual ability to complete a liberal arts education. The supposition is that the major factor keeping the other 17 per cent from realizing their individual capacities was social class.[29] The percentage of the population in college has increased greatly since this study was made. Under present conditions, an estimated 47 per cent of all high-school graduates enter (although do not necessarily graduate from) college.[30] Despite this increase in over-all enrollment in recent years, a large (although undetermined) number of working-class youths are still eliminated from competition for achieved status.

The colleges and universities have attempted to remedy this situation by offering scholarships to able young people from the lower-middle and working classes. Many private institutions of higher learning find it necessary to offer financial aid to from 35 to 40 per cent of the student body if academic standards are to be maintained. This means that upward mobility through higher education is increasingly a problem of endowment and financial aid, the former provided by private sources and the latter distributed by the institutions themselves. A combination of rising costs and decreasing revenues from tuition has,

---

[28] Warner and Abegglen, *op. cit.*, p. 47.

[29] President's Commission on Higher Education, *Higher Education for American Democracy* (Washington, 1947), Volume I, p. 41.

[30] Bureau of the Census, *Current Population Reports:Population Characteristics*, "School Enrollment: October 1962," Series P-20, No. 126 (September 24, 1963).

in turn, forced these institutions to seek new sources of funds. Some of these funds have come from gifts from large corporations for general educational purposes or scholarship aid. Forward-looking business leaders realize that future leaders will be recruited largely through the colleges and universities. These institutions are, in effect, training grounds that provide hundreds of thousands of potential executives at no cost to the large corporation. The more efficient the educational institution is in offering its facilities to all talented young men, the more the corporations themselves will benefit. Vertical mobility through higher education is as important to the nation as to the large business organizations that dominate the economic structure.

The position that we have just discussed has been accepted without question by most laymen and social scientists alike. At least one scholar, however, has raised a "skeptical" note on the relationship between education and social mobility. In a study of data from England, Sweden, and the United States, Anderson suggests that "education is but one of many factors influencing mobility and it may be far from a dominant factor." [31] *Intelligence*, rather than *education* as such, is in his judgment the crucial factor in upward mobility. He cites evidence to the effect that "from two-thirds to three-fourths of the mobility in the United States was congruent with 'intelligence' differentials." [32] Education, he continues, has a number of functions in a society, such as the continuance of the cultural heritage, that are not directly related to preparation for a higher vocation. It follows from this reasoning that mobility may be independent of education, but *not* independent of intelligence. [33]

The hypothesis we are entertaining is true insofar as an individual lacking a certain degree of intelligence cannot profit by higher education. He may, of course, *retain* a high socioeconomic status if he is so fortunate as to be born to upper-class parents. By the same token, a lower-class boy cannot rise through higher education if he lacks the necessary intelligence to stay in college. The important consideration, however, is the working-class boy with high intelligence, who, without higher education, could never reach certain high status occupations (doctor, lawyer, engineer) that require graduate training. In this sense, education is clearly an indispensable prerequisite to vertical mobility.

Differential Attitudes Toward Social Mobility

The discussion up to this point has reflected the tacit assumption that virtually everyone in our society has a driving ambition to rise in the social scale. This, indeed, is the traditional American ideology, widely accepted by the general public and, until recently, by students of social stratification as well. There is some doubt, however, of the universality of this desire for upward mobility, at

[31] A. Arnold Anderson, "A Skeptical Note on the Relation of Vertical Mobility to Education," *American Journal of Sociology*, 66:560-570 (May, 1961), p. 569.
[32] *Ibid.*
[33] A. Arnold Anderson, "Intelligence and Occupational Mobility," *Journal of Political Economy*, 60:218-239 (June, 1952).

least as it has been popularly conceived of in the Horatio Alger literature. We may examine such evidence as there is in this connection. Briefly, it appears that there are differential attitudes toward social mobility among members of the several classes, with the middle class showing a stronger motivation toward upward mobility than the lower class.

We may first examine the situation with regard to the working class. There is some evidence that large numbers of this group have shifted their objectives, both for themselves and their children, and have become resigned to remaining in the "blue-collar" class, provided certain other satisfactions are forthcoming. In one study of automobile workers, who are among the highest paid of all manual workers, many were found to have changed their ultimate goals from occupational advancement to job security, plus such material symbols of the good life as expensive automobiles, new houses, and television sets. The auto workers define these gains as "getting ahead" and thereby satisfy their aspirations for status. This substitution of material possessions for upward mobility may be a realization by the working class, however well paid, that their chances of reaching the middle class are slight.[34]

In another study of automobile workers, many of the same attitudes toward social mobility appeared, although the interpretation is somewhat different. In the second study, the workers likewise did not have much faith in their own chances of leaving the working class. At the same time, they were not reconciled to this apparent denial of the American Dream. Instead of complete resignation, these men still hoped that they or their children could start a small business and thereby leave the anonymity and impersonality of the assembly line. Any such drastic action, however, meant abandoning the security and high pay of their present jobs. Most of the men shrank from such a move. They continued to indulge in day dreams to satisfy their own unresolved dilemma between the hope of an increase in status and the realistic acceptance of the fact that they would probably never achieve it.[35]

Two swallows do not make a summer, and we cannot generalize widely upon two comparatively small samples of the working class. Nevertheless, there *does* appear to be a difference in the aspiration level of various segments of the American people. These attitudes may be merely a realistic realization that the "life chances" of the working class to rise to high status are not as favorable as those of the middle class and, certainly, of the upper-middle class. The educational possibilities for children in the lower class, as we have indicated, do not compare with those for middle- and upper-class children. Similarly, differences in family status influence life chances for advancement, a consideration that is known to the members of the working class.

The attitudes of the *middle class* toward social mobility have been explored in an ingenious and penetrating study by Bernard C. Rosen. The thesis he set

---

[34] Ely Chinoy, "The Tradition of Opportunity and the Aspirations of Automobile Workers," *American Journal of Sociology*, 57:453-459 (March, 1952).

[35] Robert H. Guest, "Work Careers and Aspirations of Automobile Workers," *American Sociological Review*, 19:155-163 (April, 1954).

out to examine empirically is that "social classes in American society are characterized by a dissimilar concern with achievement, particularly as it is expressed in the striving for status through social mobility." [36] The orientation toward such achievement, he suggests, is a function of two related elements: (a) *achievement motivation*, which "provides an internal impetus to excel"; and (b) *value orientations*, which "define and implement achievement motivated behavior." These psychocultural factors are both necessary to status achievement—the one moving the individual to excel and the other organizing his behavior so that he can do so. [37]

The sample used in the study was the total male sophomore population of two large public high schools in the area of New Haven, Connecticut. These boys were arranged in five status groups, based upon (a) the occupation and (b) the education of the chief family wage earner, usually the father, plus (c) the area of the city in which the family lived. [38] The subjects were given two tests, one a projective test measuring achievement motivation and the other a questionnaire measuring cultural values. Boys in the different social strata showed wide differences in achievement motivation, with the middle-class subjects having consistently higher scores in this respect. Some 83 per cent of the boys in the two upper classes (of whom the bulk were "middle"-class) had high motivation scores, as compared with only 23 per cent in the lowest class. [39]

Achievement motivation is only part of the differential basis of social mobility. The other factor in the study is value orientation, which helps to implement the behavior. In the questionnaire intended to bring out these orientations, the following general factors were included: (a) attitudes toward mastering, or being mastered by, the physical and social environment; (b) attitudes toward time and the consequent emphasis upon enjoying present satisfactions or planning for the future; and (c) attitudes toward the parents and the conditions under which the individual would seek independence, even if it meant moving away from his parents in search of better opportunities. As with achievement motivation, the different classes demonstrated striking differences in value orientation. In the two upper classes, 77 per cent of the boys scored high on the value scale, as compared with only 17 per cent of high scorers in the lowest class. [40]

In a subsequent study, Rosen reported on differential attitudes among various racial and ethnic groups. Members of these groups live in virtually different worlds, with the more favored persons learning both the motivations and the techniques for attaining upward mobility and the less favored showing a corresponding lack of these traits. In general, Rosen found that the "achievement syndrome" is more common among Greeks, Jews, and White Protestants

---

[36] Bernard C. Rosen, "The Achievement Syndrome: A Psychocultural Dimension of Social Stratification," *American Sociological Review*, 21:203-211 (April, 1956), p. 204.

[37] *Ibid.*

[38] Cf. August B. Hollingshead and F. C. Redlich, "Social Stratification and Psychiatric Disorders," *American Sociological Review*, 18:163-169 (April, 1953).

[39] Rosen, *op. cit.*, p. 206.

[40] *Ibid.*, p. 208.

than among Italians, French-Canadians, and Negroes. The former groups combine a desire to rise in the social scale with a willingness to sacrifice in order to do so. It is, of course, difficult to separate class from ethnic factors in this respect. Persons with low ethnic status tend (although not always) to have low class status. These two factors combine to limit their effective desire for upward mobility.[41]

Several recent studies have dealt with attitudes toward social mobility in different contexts. Continuing his investigations in this field, Rosen turned his attention to the role of the family in achievement motivation. He examined the role of four demographic factors (family size, birth order, mother's age, and social class) in motivating the individual to achieve a higher status position. He found that the social class of the family has an important bearing upon achievement motivation, with boys in Classes I, II, and III (with I as the highest) having higher motivation than those in Classes IV and V. Family size is also a factor, with boys from small families having higher motivation than boys from large families, although here also class factors are important. Similarly, the influence of birth order and mother's age must be considered in the light of the other variables. In summary, Rosen states that these four demographic factors, singly and collectively, are clearly relevant to achievement motivation, but that "their effects are complicated, interconnected, and interdependent upon one another, and difficult to assess individually." [42]

Other studies have examined more specialized aspects of achievement motivation or its equivalent. Ellis and Lane brought to light some of the social mechanisms that lead lower-class boys to seek higher education as a means of mobility. Such impetus most clearly originates in the parental family, and the mother seems to be a more important motivating force than the father. In some cases, a high-school teacher is a "structural support" for upward mobility, and in other cases some other adult in the community performs the same function. Lower-class boys need both encouragement and aid from adults outside of the family if they are to implement their desire for upward mobility. In many cases, lower-class parents want their sons to have a higher education, but they do not know how to go about helping them get it. It is here that teachers and other adults can give concrete and tangible aid.[43]

The role of deferred gratification is a final element in achievement motivation. As we have seen, deferred gratification is the tendency to put off present gratifications (sexual, financial, independence) for the sake of greater future rewards.[44] It was formerly supposed that this tendency, with its obvious implications for *successful* upward mobility, was largely confined to the middle

---

[41] Bernard C. Rosen, "Race, Ethnicity, and the Achievement Syndrome," *op. cit., p.* 60.

[42] Bernard C. Rosen, "Family Structure and Achievement Motivation," *American Sociological Review,* 26:574-585 (August, 1961), p. 585. See also Stanley Schachter, "Birth Order, Eminence, and Higher Education," *American Sociological Review,* 28:757-768 (October, 1963).

[43] Robert A. Ellis and W. Clayton Lane, "Structural Supports for Upward Mobility," *American Sociological Review,* 28:743-756 (October, 1963).

[44] Louis Schneider and Sverre Lysgaard, "The Deferred Gratification Pattern: A Preliminary Study," *American Sociological Review,* 18:142-149 (April, 1953).

class, whose members saved their money, postponed marriage, and remained close to their parents until ready to launch out on their own. A recent study, however, has called this assumption into question. Among a sample of 338 high-school boys, the above tendency was found *at all social levels* and appeared to be a personal prerequisite for achievement, rather than one directly related to original class position.[45]

The Effect of Upward Mobility

We have hitherto considered upward mobility as if it were an unqualified advantage for everyone concerned. The folklore of American culture has always maintained the right and, indeed, the duty of every person to rise in the social scale as rapidly and completely as possible. It has been suggested, however, that a very high rate of mobility may contribute to the instability of society in certain respects. A highly mobile society may have many persons who are uncertain of their roles and who thereby contribute to social instability. A society with less mobility, on the other hand, may have the advantage of greater structural stability and individual security.[46]

For the individuals involved, there are many social and psychic costs of upward mobility. Some of these costs are obvious, as men and women break under the strain of a consistent drive for "success." Other costs are more subtle and take the form of the "combativeness, frustration, (and) rootlessness" that many persons find so unpleasant in our society.[47] Even in the midst of plenty, many persons apparently lead lives of alienation and quiet desperation.[48] In their efforts to get ahead and their chagrin at failing to do so, they may become neurotic, alcoholic, or overly aggressive. Whether successful or not in their drive for status, many such persons are unpleasant spouses, inadequate parents, and unsatisfactory friends.[49]

In the course of his upward movement, the mobile man must leave behind many people and places. He must first leave behind the place of his birth, with all its physical and familial associations. He must leave his family of orientation and the friends of his childhood and youth. He must leave the ways of thinking and behaving that characterized many of his earlier associations, and he must learn, if he can, new ways of thinking and behaving appropriate to his new status. In short, "mobility may be seen as a continual process of departing-arriving-departing. . . ."[50]

---

[45] Murray A. Straus, "Deferred Gratification, Social Class, and the Achievement Syndrome," *American Sociological Review*, 27:326-335 (June, 1962).

[46] Dennis H. Wrong, "The Functional Theory of Stratification," *American Sociological Review*, 24:772-782 (December, 1959).

[47] Seymour M. Lipset and Reinhard Bendix, *op. cit.*, p. 285.

[48] Melvin Seeman, "On the Meaning of Alienation," *American Sociological Review*, 24:783-791 (December, 1959).

[49] Dorothy L. Meier and Wendell Bell, *"Anomie* and Differential Access to the Achievement of Life Goals," *American Sociological Review*, 24:189-202 (April, 1959).

[50] Warner and Abegglen, *op cit.*, p. 63. See also Eugene Litwak, "Occupational Mobility and Extended Family Cohesion," *American Sociological Review*, 25:9-21 (February, 1960).

We have long been familiar with the folk stereotype of the successful and mobile individual. His progress has been pictured in glowing terms, as he first amasses a fortune and then offers his family the luxuries he was denied as a boy. The reverse of this inspiring picture is seldom presented. The man with sufficient drive and psychic energy to make this status change is often a ruthless, driving, and self-centered person, whose aggressions are channeled primarily against his business competitors. These aggressions may also be directed against his own family—either his wife or children or both. Hence there is often a disproportionate amount of personal and family disorganization among these new elite members.[51]

The status system in our society is, furthermore, not one but many. The individual may enjoy a high status in certain fields and suffer from low status in others. The upwardly mobile man may be wealthy, powerful, and respected in the business world, but at the same time he may be handicapped by ethnic, cultural, or religious prejudice. His various statuses may not be consistent, and he may suffer from the psychological effects of low status in some respects while enjoying the benefits of wealth and power in others. In one study, the effects of such differential status were noted. Members of minority groups who had gained material rewards were still badly adjusted and suffered from self-blame, self-distrust, and even self-hatred because they were not accepted in all respects.[52]

The problem of status inconsistency has also been explored by Jackson, with particular reference to its stressful impact upon the individual. He defined status *consistency* as "the degree to which an individual's rank positions on important societal status hierarchies are at a comparable level." [53] He then postulated three dimensions of status consistency—namely: occupation, education, and racial-ethnic background. The study then examined the frustration and uncertainty of the individual whose statuses in these respects were *inconsistent*. Different statuses carry different role-expectations, and the individual may not be able to satisfy these contradictory expectations. Hence his sense of *frustration*. He is uncertain of what to expect of others and of what they can expect of him. As a result, "self-blame may result from status inconsistency." [54]

The study bore out empirically the general hypothesis of stress symptoms in persons suffering from status inconsistency. For example, men whose racial-ethnic status was high (Anglo-Saxon stock) but whose occupational status was low (semiskilled, unskilled, or service occupations) were likely to suffer various psychological symptoms indicating stress. Their low *achieved* status was inconsistent with their high *ascribed* status. Other status inconsistencies likewise indicated distinctive symptoms of stress. Jackson concluded that "Both moderate

---

[51] August B. Hollingshead, "Class Differences in Family Stability," *Annals of the American Academy of Political and Social Science*, 172:39-46 (November, 1950).

[52] Gerhard E. Lenski, "Status Crystallization: A Non-Vertical Dimension of Social Status," *American Sociological Review*, 19:405-413 (August, 1954).

[53] Elton F. Jackson, "Status Consistency and Symptoms of Stress," *American Sociological Review*, 27:469-480 (August, 1962), p. 469.

[54] *Ibid.*, p. 470.

and sharp status inconsistency are psychologically disturbing for the individual." [55] In this country, persons experience several dimensions of status. Self-conceptions are therefore more precarious than in societies where status is more clearly established.

The effect of upward mobility is further suggested in a study of unmarried career women. A sample of mobile unmarried career women was compared with one of nonmobile career women. There appeared to be a relationship between the early history of the mobile women and their later mobility. There was evidence of rejection by parents and other primary-group members during childhood and adolescence. The nonmobile career woman showed no such history of rejection. In summary, . . . "upward social mobility is likely to be an outgrowth of basically neurotic drives resulting from unsatisfactory early primary group relations, and . . . mobility leads to a continuation of superficial, impermanent primary group relations and other overt manifestations of emotional maladjustment." [56]

Additional light has been thrown upon this aspect of social mobility by a study of aspiration level as related to experience in the parental family. Some 350 college undergraduates were queried regarding their level of occupational aspiration, in terms of the jobs or professions that they would like to achieve. These results were correlated with data from questionnaires concerning the subjects' relations with their parents. In this latter category were such factors as: ". . . degree of attachment, amount of conflict, frequency of confiding in parents, feelings of rejection, parental favoritism . . . sibling rivalry, childhood happiness, and coercion by parents through disapproval and unfavorable comparisons." [57]

The evidence from this study also indicated a positive correlation between high aspirational levels and *unsatisfactory* parental relationships. Students who were "high" aspirers had been rejected by their parents to a greater extent than those who were "low" aspirers. Some 42 per cent of the "high" aspirers, for example, stated that they had experienced feelings of not being wanted by their fathers, as compared with 24 per cent of the "low" aspirers indicating such feelings. In short, "Unsatisfactory interpersonal relationships in the family of orientation were significantly related to high aspirational levels and satisfactory relationships were related to lower aspirational levels." [58]

The search for status through occupational mobility may thus result from anxiety produced by unsatisfactory childhood experiences. The child who suffers from feelings of rejection may develop anxiety that drives him to seek success through upward mobility. He may achieve the emotional satisfaction that

---

[55] *Ibid.*, p. 479.

[56] Evelyn Ellis, "Social Psychological Correlates of Upward Social Mobility Among Unmarried Career Women," *American Sociological Review*, 17:558-563 (October, 1952), p. 563.

[57] Russell R. Dynes, Alfred C. Clarke, and Simon Dinitz, "Levels of Occupational Aspiration: Some Aspects of Family Experience as a Variable," *American Sociological Review*, 21:212-215 (April, 1956), p. 213.

[58] *Ibid.*, p. 214. Cf. Peter M. Blau, "Social Mobility and Interpersonal Relations," *American Sociological Review*, 21:290-295 (June, 1956).

was denied him in his parental family by attaining success and manipulating other people. Conversely, the child who receives abundant affection in his own family may not have the same need for power and recognition and hence may not aspire to a higher status in his later years. The "happy" and "adjusted" child is the one who, other things being equal, is accepted and loved by his parents. The "unhappy" and "maladjusted" child, on the other hand, may ultimately achieve greater "success."

Social mobility and stratification (status) inconsistency were further examined in a perceptive essay by Bohlke.[59] Many working-class families, he points out, have recently risen in the economic scale to a position equal or superior to that of many middle-class families. But in becoming "new" middle-class families, they have bred large numbers of juvenile delinquents, a situation that is comparatively rare among "old" middle-class families. Bohlke believes that this seeming anomaly arises, at least in part, from what he calls "stratification inconsistency"—a condition "resulting from people being mobile, either upward or downward, in one stratification dimension without a concomitant change in another stratification dimension." [60] These working-class families are upwardly mobile in terms of income, but they still retain many of the working-class values that predispose their children to delinquency. The children may be unable to adapt to the nondelinquent patterns of the "old" middle class, and the latter may also reject these migrants from a lower social stratum. In this case, the problem is not so much one of maladjustment arising directly from successful mobility as it is of inability to change value patterns in the process.[61]

The Effect of Downward Mobility

Social mobility may be even more devastating for the failures. The emphasis upon upward mobility in our society has obscured the fact that a substantial number actually *lose* status during their lifetimes. In a significant study of the urban working class, Wilensky and Edwards found that approximately one out of every five persons was, in their graphic phrase, a "skidder." This means that approximately 20 per cent of the urban working class and perhaps 10 per cent of *all* employed urban persons *fall* rather than *rise* in the social scale in their working lives. The occupational roles at the end of their lives carry less prestige than those that they have at the beginning. These "skidders" are the failures of a status-conscious society.[62]

The stigma attached to such failure is probably greater in our society than in those where upward mobility is not held out as the norm. Fear of failure may evoke feelings of anxiety, especially among Americans. In a study of English and American boys, the latter exhibited strong feelings of generalized anxiety,

---

[59] Robert H. Bohlke, "Social Mobility, Stratification Inconsistency and Middle Class Delinquency," *Social Problems*, 8:351-363 (Spring, 1961).

[60] *Ibid.*, p. 354.

[61] *Ibid.*, p. 358.

[62] Harold L. Wilensky and Hugh Edwards, "The Skidder: Ideological Adjustments of Downward Mobile Workers," *American Sociological Review*, 24:215-231 (April, 1959).

possibly arising from the expectation of upward mobility.[63] It has been generally assumed that status anxiety was greater among middle-class persons than among working-class persons. Recent evidence, however, suggests that children of lower status in the United States exhibit even more symptoms of anxiety than do those coming from the middle class.[64] The cultural expectations of upward movement are strong in American society and cause anxiety in persons of all social levels.

In another study, Meier and Bell examined personal disorganization in connection with the achievement of life goals. This latter process has many characteristics in common with upward mobility. Persons who lack access to the means of gaining their life goals are marked by a psychological condition known as *"anomie"*—that is, "without norms, standards, or values." *Anomie* is characterized by "hopelessness, discouragement, despair, and demoralization," brought on by repeated failure to raise one's status. The study indicated that "socioeconomic status, class identification, age, social isolation, occupational mobility, marital status, and religious preferences, all indicators of life chances, precede in time and cause *anomie.*" [65]

There also appears to be a relationship between upward mobility and mental illness. This relationship is not one of direct cause and effect, but rather one of reciprocity. Mental illness interferes with upward mobility because the mentally ill person is unable to rise. This failure may, in turn, be one of the factors that intensifies the anxiety of the mentally ill. In one study of schizophrenic patients, the latter showed less upward mobility than did matched, non-mentally ill persons. That is, mentally "normal" people of the middle class, the white race, and with more than a grammar school education achieved a higher status than did schizophrenics with the same social characteristics. In the words of the author, there may be "a causal relationship between an individual's attempt to cope with such pressures and his development of mental illness." [66]

This general relationship is further indicated in a study of the mentally ill in New Haven, conducted by a team of sociologists and psychiatrists. The relationships between "status striving, anxiety, and mental health" were examined among persons in the lower economic groups. An important factor in their mental illness was their failure to rise in the status scale as rapidly or as far as they thought they should. Many of the schizophrenic patients believed that their jobs carried no hope of advancement or rise in status. They experienced strong feelings of discouragement, frustration, and anger at the society that had doomed them to a permanently lower status.[67]

---

[63] Joel B. Montague, Jr., "A Study of Anxiety Among British and American Boys," *American Sociological Review,* 20:685-689 (December, 1955).

[64] William H. Sewell and A. O. Haller, "Factors in the Relationship Between Social Status and the Personality Adjustment of the Child," *American Sociological Review,* 24:511-520 (August, 1959).

[65] Dorothy L. Meier and Wendell Bell, *op. cit.,* p. 201. See also Ephraim Harold Mizruchi, "Social Structure and Anomia in a Small City," *American Sociological Review,* 25:645-654 (October, 1960).

[66] Mary H. Lystad, "Social Mobility Among Selected Groups of Schizophrenic Patients," *American Sociological Review,* 22:288-292 (June, 1957), p. 292.

[67] A. B. Hollingshead, R. Ellis, and E. Kirby, "Social Mobility and Mental Illness," *American Sociological Review,* 19:577-591 (October, 1954).

A further refinement has been added to the relationship between social mobility and mental health by Kleiner and Parker.[68] In an extensive review of the voluminous research in this field, they examined three variables—status position, social mobility, and mobility orientation. The latter is a new variable in this complex interaction and the authors define mobility orientation as "the discrepancy between achievement and aspiration." [69] In so doing, they indicate that the important consideration is not achievement *as such*, but rather the disparity between achievement and aspiration. As we saw in the previous chapter, many lower-class persons have low aspirations and hence presumably suffer no great emotional stress when they fail to achieve higher status.[70] But persons with wide discrepancies between what they are and what they want to be may suffer severe mental difficulties.[71]

Downward mobility is more stressful for persons who suffer a drastic *decline* in status position. Men who enjoy an orderly and consistent career tend to make a stable personal, family, and community adjustment.[72] Men who are unable to do so are more vulnerable to the most extreme form of personal disorganization —namely, suicide. In an intensive study of 103 male suicides in New Orleans, Breed found that many of them had severe problems of "work-role performance," instability of employment, and downward mobility. The latter includes both "intergenerational" mobility (occupational level lower than father's) and "worklife" mobility (occupational level at end of life lower than at the beginning).[73] These suicides were, in fact, "skidders" on the socioeconomic scale.[74] In psychological terms, they were sufferers from "*anomie.*"

In his discussion of these 103 suicides, Breed uses the concept of "role performance." As we have seen, our self-conception is in large measure a reflection of our inferences of others' conceptions of us. Crucial to these self-other confrontations is the performance of one's basic roles; perhaps the most crucial male role in our society is that associated with gainful occupation. Failure in this role may shake the foundations of the individual's self-conception and, in extreme cases, may destroy his will to live. Obviously, not all downwardly mobile men kill themselves in shame and frustration. Nevertheless, it is suggested that the chances of such a *dénouement* are increased by failure in the work-role.[75]

---

[68] Robert J. Kleiner and Seymour Parker, "Goal-Striving, Social Status, and Mental Disorder: A Research Review," *American Sociological Review*, 28:189-203 (April, 1963).

[69] *Ibid.*, p. 189.

[70] Albert K. Cohen and Harold M. Hodges, Jr., "Characteristics of the Lower-Blue-Collar-Class," *Social Problems*, 10:303-334 (Spring, 1963).

[71] See also Richard L. Simpson and H. Max Miller, "Social Status and Anomia," *Social Problems*, 10:256-264 (Winter, 1963).

[72] Harold L. Wilensky, "Orderly Careers and Social Participation: The Impact of Work History on Social Integration in the Middle Mass," *American Sociological Review*, 26:521-539 (August, 1961).

[73] Warren Breed, "Occupational Mobility and Suicide Among White Males," *American Sociological Review*, 28:179-188 (April, 1963).

[74] Wilensky and Edwards, *op. cit.*

[75] Breed, *op. cit.*, p. 188.

The Balance Sheet

We have considered the dynamic aspects of social stratification in the form of social mobility. We have indicated some of the factors that have made for social stratification in the United States in the past. Among these factors were: the gradual closing of the frontier, the curtailment of immigration, the increased fertility of the upper-middle classes, the growth of the large corporation, the concentration of corporate control, the rise of ethnic and religious barriers, the changing emphasis upon social mobility, the break in the skill hierarchy in industry, and the differential access to education in a society where education is increasingly necessary for success.

A division of American society into several subcultures has resulted from these and other factors. We have examined the evidence for the existence of these subcultures, even though our society has long denied their existence and is still far from clear as to their nature. The reality of social class in this sense, however, seems incontestable, whether we like it or not. People in the working class *do* live different lives with different culture patterns from people in the upper classes.[76] These distinctions are not so great as in many other countries with a long history of stratification, but they nevertheless exist.

Although we have stated the evidence for the existence of social classes, we have not answered the questions raised by comparing their current rigidity with that of a half century ago. It has been suggested that a dynamic society could not possibly provide the necessary stability and continuity for the evolution of a rigid system of stratification. The classic forms of stratification in Europe arose from different ways of life, standards of values, and patterns of behavior that continued virtually without change for hundreds of years.

No such situation has existed in the United States, nor is it likely to in the future, with social change occurring at an ever-increasing rate. Furthermore, our society is currently undergoing an equalization in many respects related to the mass culture—dress, speech, material possessions, and social rituals. When everyone drives the same automobiles, watches the same television programs, and reads the same mass circulation magazines, many of the psychological distinctions between classes decrease rather than increase.

Social mobility is closely related to social stratification, but the two are not the same. Social classes can exist in well-defined forms, and at the same time large numbers of persons can make the transition from one class to another. If *everyone* made this transition during his lifetime or that of his children, social class would naturally soon cease to have any meaning. In individual cases, such movement continues in our society. This fact does not negate the existence of social class. The *comparative rate* of such mobility is the crucial consideration.

At this point, we are forced to admit that all the facts are not in. We simply do not know, for example, whether "the economic opportunities of the chil-

---

[76] Genevieve Knupfer, "Portrait of the Underdog," *Public Opinion Quarterly*, 11:103-114 (Spring, 1947).

dren of working-class families have increased or decreased since the turn of the century." [77] Various studies throw considerable light on this question. In a careful investigation of the occupational changes from father to son in a single Indiana county, Rogoff concluded that "the likelihood of a son being in an occupational class different from that of his father was *about the same in 1910 and in 1940.*" [78] This would indicate that the class structure has probably *not* grown more rigid in the generation under consideration. During this period, indeed, proportionately *more* jobs opened up in the white-collar category, which would indicate that there was *more* mobility in 1940 than in 1910.

This position is strengthened by a study of occupational mobility between generations in the United States as a whole. Lenski found that, "during the first half of the present century, the rate of inter-generational mobility into white-collar occupations seems to have increased, with the increase being almost wholly attributable to the expansion in the proportion of white-collar jobs and the declining proportion of farmers' sons in the lower stratum. . . ." [79] Changes in economic organization have increased clerical and other white-collar jobs, and the greater productivity of both agriculture and industry has meant that fewer workers can produce more. The white-collar population has grown disproportionately, and this has meant a rise in status for millions of persons.

Other observers are not so sure that the rate of vertical mobility has shown a long-range increase. Chinoy states that ". . . neither inferential analysis based upon historical study nor direct analysis of mobility of groups of individuals can yet indicate whether there has been any change in the rate of vertical mobility in American society." [80] Summarizing the mass of evidence pro and con, Barber concludes that "the safest tentative conclusion is that the amount of mobility has remained *approximately the same* over the last century." [81]

A final remark involves the realm of social values. The question is whether we should continue uncritically to search for more social mobility as an end in itself or whether we should examine the implications of mobility as a means to some more inclusive end. Most persons assume that mobility is a central value and that everything leading to its increase is therefore desirable. This assumption may well be open to question. In the concluding section of their study of social mobility, Lipset and Bendix examine this central question. We should, they believe, "turn away from the quest for more mobility *per se* and concern ourselves with the conditions under which men acquire motivation for achievement . . . [and] instead of identifying greater equality of opportunity with human happiness we should begin to enquire into the dissatisfactions which are endemic in our social life." Included in this enquiry, they conclude, should be "those dissatisfactions which create a drive for achievement and are hence a source of both the assets and liabilities of social mobility." [82]

---

[77] Bendix, *op. cit.*, p. 261.
[78] Natalie Rogoff, *op. cit.*, p. 106. (Her italics.)
[79] Gerhard E. Lenski, *op. cit.*, p. 523.
[80] Chinoy, "Social Mobility Trends in the United States," *op. cit.*, p. 186.
[81] Barber, *op. cit.*, p. 486. (My italics.)
[82] Lipset and Bendix, *op. cit.*, p. 287.

SELECTED BIBLIOGRAPHY

Barber, Bernard, *Social Stratification*. New York: Harcourt, Brace and World, 1957. In summarizing the evidence on social mobility, the author suggests that "the safest tentative conclusion is that the amount of mobility has remained approximately the same over the last century."

Breed, Warren, "Occupational Mobility and Suicide Among White Males," *American Sociological Review*, 28:179-188 (April, 1963). This is a study of 103 white male suicides, gathered from interviews with persons who had known them before their death. The author postulates that the principal variable between life and death in each case was the quality of the "work-role performance" that led to downward mobility.

Chinoy, Ely, "Social Mobility Trends in the United States," *American Sociological Review*, 20:180-186 (April, 1955). This is an authoritative survey of the general trends in social mobility. At the end of the analysis, the author states that sufficient information is not presently available to make any definite statement one way or the other.

Ellis, Robert A., and W. Clayton Lane, "Structural Supports for Upward Mobility," *American Sociological Review*, 28:743-756 (October, 1963). Lower-class boys who seek upward mobility through higher education receive a great deal of their "structural support" from their mothers, rather than their fathers. Other adults in the community, notably high school teachers, also encourage the boys to go to college and help them to realize this ambition.

Guest, Robert H., "Work Careers and Aspirations of Automobile Wokers," *American Sociological Review*, 19:155-163 (April, 1954). This is a study of workers on the automobile assembly line. They are among the most highly paid manual workers in the world, but they are often frustrated at the lack of opportunity for leaving the working class.

Kleiner, Robert J., and Seymour Parker, "Goal-Striving, Social Status, and Mental Disorder: A Research Review," *American Sociological Review*, 28:189-203 (April, 1963). The authors review some of the extensive literature on the relationships of "status position, social mobility, and mobility orientation (i.e., discrepancy between achievement and aspiration) to mental illness." The paper demonstrates the importance of "goal-striving behavior" in precipitating mental disorder.

Lenski, Gerhard E., "Trends in Inter-Generational Occupational Mobility in the United States," *American Sociological Review*, 23:514-523 (October, 1958). According to this important study of national mobility trends, upward changes in status increased during the first half of the century, largely reflecting the rise in the proportion of white-collar jobs in the economy. More opportunities have thus arisen to enter the middle-class status of a white-collar role.

Lipset, Seymour M., and Reinhard Bendix, *Social Mobility in Industrial Society*. Berkeley: University of California Press, 1959. This book contains a number of studies on social mobility, carried on through the years by the authors. Some of the studies were made in Oakland, California, and others report on national trends. This is an important source both of theory and empirical material on this complex subject.

Miller, S. M., "Comparative Social Mobility," *Current Sociology*, published by Basil Blackwell for UNESCO, London, 1960, Volume 9. This is an important compilation of data from 18 nations, dealing with comparative rates of social (vertical) mobility. The author suggests some intriguing hypotheses, notably the possibility that, in some respects, the mobility rate in certain countries (the Soviet Union and France) is actually higher than in the United States.

Rogoff, Natalie, "Recent Trends in Urban Occupational Mobility," in Paul K. Hatt and Albert J. Reiss, Jr. (eds.), *Reader in Urban Sociology*. Glencoe, Ill.: The Free Press, 1951. This is a careful study of occupational mobility in a single Indiana county, which demonstrates that the social structure has not grown more rigid in the period 1910-1940. In the author's words, "the likelihood of a son being in an occupational class different from that of his father was *about the same in 1910 and in 1940*." (Her italics.)

Rosen, Bernard C., "Family Structure and Achievement Motivation," *American Sociological Review*, 26:574-585 (August, 1961). Achievement motivation is examined in the light of four demographic factors—family size, order of birth, mother's age, and social class. The author concludes that these variables are all relevant to achievement motivation, but that their interrelationships are so complex that it is impossible to state which one, if any, is more important than another.

Straus, Murray A., "Deferred Gratification, Social Class, and the Achievement Syndrome," *American Sociological Review*, 27:326-335 (July, 1962). In order to achieve upward mobility, the individual must presumably defer present gratifications for the sake of greater future gratifications. Contrary to earlier studies, however, the author indicates that this quality is not confined to the middle class, but rather characterizes any persons *regardless of class* who hope to rise in the social scale.

Warner, W. Lloyd, and James C. Abegglen, *Big Business Leaders in America*. New York: Harper & Row, 1955. This is a popular account of a study of leaders of big business and the factors related to their mobility or lack of it. Among these significant factors are their mothers, their colleges, and their wives.

Wilensky, Harold L., and Hugh Edwards, "The Skidder: Ideological Adjustments of Downward Mobile Workers," *American Sociological Review*, 24:215-231 (April, 1959). This article presents the other side of the mobility picture. In this study of the factory worker, the "skidder" is the person who goes *down* in the social scale. He is the one who, at the end of his life, occupies a role with less prestige and fewer rewards than when he started. According to the authors, approximately one out of every five urban manual workers is a "skidder" in this sense.

INSTITUTIONS

AND COMMUNITY *Part Four*

16   *Social Institutions*

The Nature of Social Institutions

Social institutions are patterns of behavior grouped about the central needs of human beings. In our analysis of social interaction, we considered the folkways, mores, laws, and other normative expectations that arise out of group life, take on varying degrees of importance, and are transmitted in the social heritage. Most of these forms of prescribed behavior cluster about certain fundamental human needs that are found in all societies and are necessary to ordered social life. These forms serve as guides and directions for behavior. "If one of these clusters has a high degree of specificity and internal cohesiveness," remarks Rose, "it is generally spoken of by social scientists as an institution." [1] These organized patterns of behavior are simple in theory and as complex as life itself in actual practice.

Social institutions are culture patterns directing the ordered behavior of human beings in the performance of their daily activities. The latter include: (a) the socially sanctioned birth and early training of children; (b) group efforts toward physical survival by the production, consumption, and distribution of goods and services; (c) propitiation (and possibly manipulation) of the supernatural powers in directions desired by the group; and (d) social control of the members of the group in their behavior toward each other. Other activities arise in different societies, but these are common to all organized groups.

Each institution is also "a structure of related roles which embodies the common values of a society." [2] The family, the economic system, the religion, and the form of government each comprise a number of reciprocal roles that define the behavior of the individual in his institutional capacity. The institutions of a society are, in turn, connected through the roles that each person plays in the several institutions of which he is a member. In composite form, social institutions make up a large part, although by no means all, of the structure of a society. A significant way to study a society, indeed, is through its institutions.[3]

Social institutions are culture patterns in much the same sense as hundreds of other regular forms of behavior in a society. Institutions are more regularized and formal, and hence differ from other patterns. The needs they answer, the values they serve, and the direction they provide are so important that every society organizes institutional behavior more formally than presumably less important behavior. The ceremonials by which the institutional functions of church, state, family, and other basic institutions are surrounded attest to this process of formalization. The more venerable the institution, the more solemn and elaborate is its body of practices. The ceremonials of the Roman Catholic Church are more formal than those of a small evangelical sect.

Out of this formality of the institutional pattern arises a degree of order and continuity. Members and functionaries of the institution learn these practices and incorporate them into their own personalities. This assures the continuity of the institution and the maintenance of its practices. The more behavior becomes *patterned*, the more deeply ingrained it will be and the better chance it will have for survival. The practices of teen-age culture, the passing fads of dress, and the short-lived patterns of dancing, talking, and behaving peculiar to this age-group are examples of behavior that is not institutionalized. This ephemeral behavior may be contrasted with the solemnities of the marriage ceremony, some of whose practices go back to Old Testament times.

---

[1] Arnold Rose (ed.), *The Institutions of Advanced Societies* (Minneapolis: University of Minnesota Press, 1958), p. 30.

[2] Robert C. Angell, *Free Society and Moral Crisis* (Ann Arbor: University of Michigan Press, 1958), p. 85.

[3] Robert S. Lynd and Helen M. Lynd, *Middletown* (New York: Harcourt, Brace and Company, 1929); Robert S. Lynd and Helen M. Lynd, *Middletown in Transition* (New York: Harcourt, Brace and Company, 1937).

The continuity of institutional practices is further assured by the development of ritual. Behavior becomes ritualized: (a) when it is associated with important cultural values; (b) when it is virtually "automatic"; and (c) when it can be memorized and performed without thinking. Many institutions have ritual behavior, such as the ceremony of the mass and the child's oath of allegiance to the flag. The individual engaging in ritual behavior rarely analyzes its meanings, nor does he find it necessary to grope for words in his recitation. The form and pattern are already established and are handed down from generation to generation by the institution. Heads of state perform ritualistic acts in a variety of forms, such as laying a wreath upon the tomb of the unknown soldier, throwing out the first ball at the opening of the baseball season, and reviewing the victory parade at the end of a war.[4]

The Claims of Social Institutions

Social institutions differ in terms of their claims upon the individual. Some institutions are involuntary, in the sense that the person has no choice in his membership. The parental family is the most obvious example of an involuntary institution, for the child has no choice in his participation. Economic institutions, on the other hand, have a voluntary character, and the individual is free (within limits) to choose a given profession, business, or industry. He does not have the power to depart from the broad economic patterns of his society—for example, he cannot adopt communism in a capitalistic society. Participation in a government is also largely involuntary, and the person has certain rights and obligations (the latter especially apparent in wartime) toward the state under whose flag he lives. Participation in the basic institutions is thus, on the whole, more involuntary than voluntary. Most institutional ties are determined by the accident of birth.[5]

Institutions lay claims upon their members in another sense. Different institutional roles call out different degrees of obligation. In the family, the role obligations are extremely strong, and parents are called upon to give their attention, their strength, and, sometimes, their lives to their children. The reciprocal claims of the family upon the child are not as strong as they formerly were, when grown children were expected to care for their parents in old age. Even so, the family normally places stronger emotional claims upon the individual than any other institution.[6] Parents who violate their major responsibilities to their children may be condemned informally by the community and formally by the state.

The claims of institutions upon their members are also known as loyalties. Individuals hold different attitudes toward the various institutions in their so-

---

[4] W. Lloyd Warner, *American Life: Dream and Reality* (Chicago: University of Chicago Press, 1953), Chapter 1.

[5] Everett C. Hughes, "Institutions," in Robert E. Park (ed.), *An Outline of the Principles of Sociology* (New York: Barnes & Noble, Inc., 1939), p. 320.

[6] Nelson N. Foote and Leonard S. Cottrell, Jr., *Identity and Interpersonal Competence* (Chicago: University of Chicago Press, 1955), Chapter 1.

cial environment. Loyalty to the family is ordinarily strong, at least to the extent of maintaining affectionate relationships toward the parents throughout one's life. The extent of family loyalties may change, however, as the society itself changes. Loyalty to the more remote members of the family (cousins, aunts, uncles, grandparents) is no longer as strong as it was in an earlier day.

Institutional loyalties may conflict, especially in a complex and dynamic society. In wartime, loyalties toward family and nation are in direct conflict, as young men face the prospect of military service. In peacetime, loyalties to church and business may also conflict, although in a somewhat different sense. The man who tries to take literally the admonitions of the Christian creed of love, humility, and cooperation may have difficulty in accepting the business creed of individualism, self-assurance, and competition. Loyalties to political institutions also conflict with those of church and nation, as the party member may be called upon to commit or condone an act involving graft or political corruption that will violate his religious teachings or injure the government institution.

The Interaction of Social Institutions

Social institutions have both *individual* and *collective* aspects. We have spoken largely of the collective aspects, by which we mean the organized patterns of belief and behavior that determine the general responses of a society. These patterns are not dependent upon *any one* family, church, corporation, or government, although they clearly have their existence in the patterned behavior of large numbers of such groups. The *collective* aspects of the family thus continue, irrespective of what happens to any *individual* family. If *all* of the individual family units were wiped out, the institution would cease to exist.

In the subsequent discussion, we should therefore remember that the term institution is used in two senses: (*a*) as referring to general patterns of expectations determining social behavior; and (*b*) as referring to individual groups in which this behavior is, with variations, embodied. We can, therefore, understand both the collective character of the institutional patterns and the fact that they act as social determinants for groups of real people.

The institutions of a society are connected in a close and interdependent pattern. A functioning society needs all of the basic structures operating with at least a minimum of efficiency. The economic system, the government, the religious organization, and the family must all operate adequately if social interaction is to go on. Difficulties in one institution are reflected in the others, for most persons participate in all of the basic structures. Prolonged economic instability is immediately communicated to the family and eventually to the government. Religion provides a normative direction for the members of the society, and without these shared meanings the society could not long endure. Hence no single basic institution is "more important" than any other in social interaction. Each carries out its own functions which, in concert, are necessary to ordered social life.

Institutions are connected through the statuses and roles of the members. The individual is a father, a deacon, a member of the school board, a selectman, and a businessman. In each of these statuses, he plays a role in a basic institution. In another form of institutional interaction, the minister talks to the teacher, the parent to the banker, and the businessman to the legislator. The essence of an institution is the *pattern* of reciprocal roles through which each individual interacts with others in a variety of institutional contexts. Human behavior is the basic reality of social institutions. Patterns are inferred from the behavior. Interaction occurs through the medium of these patterns.[7]

These interconnections may be clearly seen in the family, the most universal of all institutional patterns. The family is immediately apparent in connection with the ownership, transmission, and safeguarding of property. The family is also directly related to the welfare institutions of the society, through the care of the young and, until recently, of the old and the sick. The family is a central religious unit and maintains an intimate connection with the church. The family is the most vulnerable of all the institutions, in that its members are immediately influenced by outside factors, notably those related to technology, business, and industry.[8]

When we say that institutions "interact," therefore, we mean that people interact in their institutional roles. As family members, teachers, businessmen, and citizens, people compete, conflict, accommodate, and cooperate with each other. Their interaction is patterned by their institutional roles, which carry strong expectations of what they shall and shall not do. Each acts with reference to the other in ways that have been previously defined by the institution. No two forms of interaction are *exactly* the same, for parents, teachers, priests, and policemen have their unique personalities that interpret the institutional expectations in a slightly different way. In general, however, the minister and the communicant, the officer and the soldier, and the judge and the criminal know what to expect of each other as they act out the expectations of their institutional roles.

Institutions and the Social Heritage

Social institutions are the great conservers and transmitters of the cultural heritage. This function is an outgrowth of their "general" or superorganic character, in the sense that they are independent of any individual or group of individuals. Institutional patterns live by and through individual personalities, in addition to their formal incorporation in the laws, codes, and archives. The immortality of the pattern consists partially in the fact that all the members do not die at the same time and hence continue the institutional concepts and structures in the living stuff of their personalities. The general pattern of the

---

[7] Robin M. Williams, Jr., *American Society* (New York: Alfred A. Knopf, Inc., 1951), Chapter 13.

[8] William F. Ogburn and Meyer F. Nimkoff, *Technology and the Changing Family* (Boston: Houghton Mifflin Company, 1955).

family is virtually immortal, whereas the life of an individual conjugal family is limited to that of its members.

The process by which institutions retain and transmit the cultural heritage is essentially the same as that by which personality is formed. The child initially plays a receptive role in the family, and in this way receives his largest share of the cultural heritage. In this status he does not originate culture, but only receives it from his family. As he learns to adapt his behavior to the expectations of his mother, father, brothers, and sisters, he acquires many of the important elements of culture that the others have learned in the same way.

In addition to the general patterns of his culture, the child also learns the more specific patterns that pertain to the family. He learns how to be a good son, a good husband, and a good father, as these roles are defined in his society. He learns what is expected of him during the different stages of his family life. These expectations become part of his personality. In this way, he is the personal conservator of an important part of the cultural heritage. The American family of the middle part of the twentieth century lives in and through him.

The culture is transmitted by interaction in an institutional setting. The child interacts with members of his family and takes them into account in terms of their normative expectations. He learns the particular version of the culture held by the members and, by interacting with them, incorporates these norms into his personality. The child develops as a member of a particular interacting group and not as a biological organism following predetermined lines. The affection, response, and cooperation that he receives from his family are important elements in his emerging personality. In this way, personality is partly the product of interaction in the family setting.

Institutions other than the family play more specialized roles in the preservation of the cultural heritage. The school is specifically entrusted with this function, and the roles of pupil and teacher are the principal patterns in the interaction process. These roles are dynamic and reciprocal. The role of the student is to learn, no matter how much he may disguise, deprecate, or ignore it. The role of the teacher is to teach, to instruct the student in the cultural heritage. Next to the family, the school is the most important institutional mechanism engaged in preserving and handing on the knowledge, skills, and techniques of the society.

The church is also an important educational institution, even after many of these functions have been assumed by the school. Acting in collaboration with the family, the church was once the only institution to transmit the social heritage. The church was for centuries the sole repository of knowledge, except for the folkways, mores, and skills handed down through the family. During the Dark Ages, the light of learning was kept burning, albeit dimly, in the religious institutions of western Europe. Since the Reformation, learning has gradually become secularized and has been taken over by the school.

In the performance of their educational functions, the institutions of family, school, and church are closely interconnected. Many general religious beliefs and practices are handed on through the family, rather than through the church, although even here the parents and the Sunday school, for instance, combine to perpetuate the Christian creed. As we shall see in Chapter 18, neither the Protestant[9] nor the Catholic[10] family carries on these activities to the full satisfaction of the respective denominations. This "failure" of the family, however, reflects the increasing secularization of the society in which the members perform their other roles. Blame for the inadequate religious instruction of the contemporary family cannot be heaped upon this institution.

The Functions of Social Institutions

The central aspects of institutions are the functions that they perform and the patterns established to carry out these functions. This conception was embodied in the definition made many years ago by William Graham Sumner. He referred to an institution simply as "a concept . . . and a structure." By a *concept*, he meant the "idea, notion, doctrine, interest" at the basis of the institution and found in some form in all societies. A *structure* was, in Sumner's words, "a framework, or apparatus, or perhaps only a number of functionaries set to co-

[9] Ernest W. Burgess (ed.), *The Adolescent in the Family* (New York: Appleton-Century-Crofts, Inc., 1934), pp. 171-172.

[10] John L. Thomas, S. J., *The American Catholic Family* (Englewood Cliffs, N.J.: Prentice-Hall, Inc., 1956), Chapter 12.

Social institutions conserve and transmit the cultural heritage. This New England college has handed on the cultural heritage for almost two hundred years.

operate in prescribed ways at a certain conjuncture." [11] Concept and structure are parts of a functioning pattern and one cannot be separated from the other. The concepts of the basic institutions embody the purposes and goals of life itself. The structures are the mechanisms established to carry out the concepts.

The concept of the family is to provide a socially accepted framework for the conception, birth, and socialization of children. The structure may range from the large consanguine group found in some societies to the small conjugal unit in our own. The concept of the religious institution is to unite man and the supernatural; its structure may range from the simple Christianity of the Apostles to the elaborate ceremonial and hierarchy of the Roman Catholic Church. The maintenance of order is the concept of government; the massive apparatus of the totalitarian state is one type of structure and the informal leadership of the primitive clan another. As an institution entrusted with transmitting the social heritage, a university may vary in structure from a complex grouped about a series of Gothic quadrangles to Mark Hopkins at one end of a log and a student at the other. In each instance, concept and structure are reciprocal and interrelated.

Many of the basic cultural values of a society are embodied in its institutions. Cultural values are conceptions broadly held and relating to what is desirable and important in a given society.[12] These conceptions relate to physical needs (food, clothing, shelter), social relationships (children, love, companionship), and spiritual aspirations (salvation, forgiveness, divine compassion). Cultural values of this type are of "infinite worth" to human beings, and they are important for their own sake.[13] Social institutions foster these cultural values and provide a framework for realizing them more completely. The very nature of these cultural values is such that human beings cannot realize them by themselves. They must combine with other persons in some form of patterned behavior, collectively known as social institutions.

Values are not equally important. Some are directly related to the basic institutions and some only remotely so. The values of human life, communication with the supernatural, and satisfactory group relationships are clearly related to one or more of the major institutions. Other values, such as recreation, the attainment of luxuries, and the niceties of dress do not have the same institutional connotations. In many questions involving choice (for example, make of automobile), the problem of infinite values does not arise. In questions related to monogamy, private enterprise, and love of country, however, these fundamental cultural values come into play. These values are incorporated into the central institutional patterns.

The functions of social institutions are to provide an ordered and continuous framework for the realization of group values. Moral norms also perform some

[11] William Graham Sumner, *Folkways* (Boston: Ginn and Company, 1906), p. 53.

[12] John Gillin, "National and Regional Cultural Values in the United States," *Social Forces*, 34:107-113 (December, 1955).

[13] William R. Catton, Jr., "Exploring Techniques for Measuring Human Values," *American Sociological Review*, 19:49-55 (February, 1954).

of these functions, but institutions are more complex. Furthermore, the structures of institutions make them more readily apparent and also help to enforce their own norms. The family is an institution and the seventh commandment is a moral norm. The first is both more complex and more efficient than the second in carrying out the values of society. In this sense, the "concept" of Sumner and the "value" of other analysts are very similar. They both indicate the moral ideas at the heart of every institution.[14]

The notion of function deals with the things an institution *does*, the activities it performs in carrying out its underlying concept.[15] The function may be an ideal one, in the sense that it comprises the activities the institution is *supposed* to perform, as contrasted to those it actually *does* perform. The function may also be a real one, in the sense that it refers to the activities of the members while playing their institutional roles. All societies face certain similar problems in order to survive, govern themselves, and transmit the cultural heritage. The solutions to these problems are the major functions of social institutions.

The primary institution historically was the family, and all of the above functions were originally performed by this central structure. From this original unit, other institutions have evolved to meet the more specialized needs of an increasingly complex society. Until comparatively recent times, the family performed many such derivative functions as economic production, a function that fell to it by default because there was no other institutional structure suited to it. The production role of the family is rapidly changing, however, and many of its other functions are being transferred to other agencies.[16]

This transfer involves the family, the church, the economic institution, and the government. The family was the sole "economic" institution during most of the early development of organized society, and all of these activities were once directed in the family setting. During the Middle Ages, many economic functions came to be regulated by the Church, which partially controlled both the price of goods and the price of labor. The concept of the *just price*, as evolved by the Church, was an early attempt to control economic behavior in the interests of society as a whole.

With the rise of capitalism, the development of the market, and the appearance of Protestantism, the regulation of prices and wages became a function of the impersonal forces of the market place. The "invisible hand," as later postulated by Adam Smith, was supposed to bring about justice for all concerned. In modern society, this regulatory function has been partially assumed by the government. In time of peace, the government supports (regulates) the prices of agricultural commodities, and in time of war this regulation is greatly extended. First the family, then the church, then the economic institution, and finally the government have performed this regulatory function.

In the division of labor in the social sciences, government and economics have their own specialists, bodies of knowledge, and conceptual schemes. It is

---

[14] Robert C. Angell, *op. cit.*, Chapter 2, "The Anatomy of the Moral Order."

[15] William F. Ogburn and Meyer F. Nimkoff, *op. cit.*, p. 123.

[16] *Ibid.*, Chapter 6, "Shrinking Functions."

obviously impossible to survey these disciplines here, and we are not even remotely attempting to do so. We are merely suggesting some of the current changes in the *functions* of the major institutions as they operate in the community and the larger society. A central theme is the transfer of functions from the family to other and more specialized institutions.

The Governmental Function

The institution of government is increasingly important in our society. Its functions include a vast range of activities, from the care of widows with dependent children to the production of nuclear energy. The governmental institution is at the center of social change, whatever the ideological objections of many persons. This transfer of function to government reflects the impersonal processes of modern society and not the schemes of a power-hungry bureaucracy. The massive shift from primary (family) control to secondary (governmental) control is part of a fundamental change in the structure of society. The evidence indicates that this change will continue.

This general evolution has been variously defined. One such conceptual framework is that of *Gemeinschaft* to *Gesellschaft*—that is, from the primary community to the formal society.[17] In somewhat different terms, the transition has been described as one from *status to contract*—from a society in which the social roles were largely fixed by custom to one where they are increasingly established by the rational force of contract.[18] As the relative power of the informal controls of the folkways and mores has declined, the formal controls embodied in the laws and other expressions of government have increased. Society is no longer controlled solely by the unwritten expectations of the group; the written commands and formal sanctions of the state have partially replaced the ancient norms.

We may indicate some of the forms in which the transfer of functions from other institutions to government is currently apparent.

1. *From the Family*
   a. Physical protection of the home.
   b. Economic support of the unemployed.
   c. Care of the sick.
   d. Treatment of the insane.
   e. Custody of the aged.
   f. Support of widows and orphans.
   g. Formal education of children.

2. *From the Economic Institution*
   a. Fixing of prices.
   b. Manipulation of credit.

---

[17] Ferdinand Tönnies, *Gemeinschaft und Gesellschaft*, Berlin, 1926.
[18] Henry Summer Maine, *Ancient Law* (10th ed.) (London: John Murray, 1906).

   c. Settlement of labor-capital disputes.
   d. Regulation of securities and commodities exchanges.
   e. Guarantee of bank savings.
   f. Production of electricity.
   g. Subsidization of recreation.
3. *From the Church*
   a. Education of children.
   b. Regulation of conditions for marriage.
   c. Jurisdiction over divorce.
   d. Establishment of grounds for annulment of marriage.
   e. Rise of secular over canon law.
   f. Maintenance of poor relief.

The first basic trend in the governmental institution is the increase in the number and scope of its functions. The second basic trend is the centralization of these functions in the national government. Throughout most of human history, the functions of government were conducted on a local level by persons dealing with those immediately around them. The idea of democratic government in America, as evolved in the latter part of the eighteenth and early nineteenth centuries, assumed such a decentralization. The most important concerns of everyday life were conducted in the local community, or at most in the state capital, leaving to the federal government only those activities that could not be so confined. This pattern of decentralization is the American *ideal* and subsequent trends toward greater centralization have been widely viewed with alarm.

This movement toward centralization has reflected the increasing size of the country and the scope of the problems facing the national government. The local agencies have neither the resources nor the skills to solve many of the problems of the twentieth century, which range from the building of superhighways to the control of crime. The financial limitations of state and local governments were dramatized during the Great Depression of the 1930's, when mass unemployment was too great for them to handle. The rapid centralization of government during this decade was the result of an economic crisis that could not be met in any other way. The decade of the 1940's saw a crisis of a different sort, one that also resulted in the increased centralization of government.

Among the technological factors in this trend have been the developments in transportation and communication. These devices have been both the cause and the effect of centralization. The nation expanded with the railroad and, much later, with the automobile and the airplane. The ease of communication has in turn furthered the centralization of control, because the central government can now maintain contact with remote sections of the country. The agencies of mass communication (radio, television, motion pictures, the press) have indirectly aided this process.[19]

[19] Cf. Wilbur Schramm (ed.), *The Process and Effects of Mass Communication* (Urbana: University of Illinois Press, 1954).

"War," said a brilliant essayist, "is the health of the state." [20] By this paradoxical statement, he meant that the power of the government is greatly increased in wartime and its functions are correspondingly centralized. The executive branch increases its power at the expense of the legislative and judicial branches, as the national crisis makes quick and fundamental decisions more necessary than in the leisurely times of peace. Furthermore, the country is in danger and the emotions of the people are mobilized about the national symbols. Total war affects the entire nation and the people respond with a strong sense of sacrifice. When the country is threatened, men welcome the opportunity to entrust their lives and fortunes to the government.[21]

The centralization of wartime power takes various forms. Some of them are:

1. Control of men. The most obvious form of increased governmental power in wartime is the conscription of young men for the armed forces. This power is, in effect, one of life and death, inasmuch as persons so conscripted may be killed or wounded.

2. Control of industry. Modern war involves total industrial mobilization, whereby the federal government assumes temporary control over the allocation of raw materials and the productive facilities of industry.

3. Control of labor. The increased power of the central government also extends, directly or indirectly, to the control of civilian manpower. Men are directed into industries and occupations where they will presumably be most useful to the war effort.

4. Control of prices. The increase in government expenditures so increases purchasing power that wartime price controls are necessary to avoid a ruinous inflation. The control of prices is another way in which the central government assumes regulatory functions customarily left to the economic institution.

5. Control of wages. The control of wages and salaries is a necessary corollary to the control of prices in order to avoid inflation. Under the capitalistic system, wages are worked out by individual or (more recently) collective bargaining. This process is partially suspended in time of war.

6. Control of capital. The central government increases its control over capital, whether in the form of individual savings or corporate profits. In the first instance, a system of compulsory savings that channels some of the surplus funds into government securities is introduced. In the second instance, corporate profits are partially controlled through excess-profits taxes.[22]

The Educational Function

The educational function has historically been divided between the family and the church. At the present time, education is nominally under the direction of

---

[20] Randolph Bourne, "Unfinished Fragment on the State," in *Untimely Papers* (New York: B. W. Huebsch, 1919).

[21] Cf. Raymond Aron, *The Century of Total War* (New York: Doubleday & Company, 1954).

[22] Cf. Max Lerner, "The State in War Time," in Willard Waller (ed.), *War in the Twentieth Century* (New York: The Dryden Press, 1940).

the state, and hence might be considered one of the functions of government. The emergence of an elaborate system of private and public education has, however, greatly increased its importance as a distinct pattern, and we are therefore listing it as a major institution in its own right. The great community enterprise of tax-supported elementary, secondary, and higher education has assumed a dignity and importance never before found in any society. Education represents both a transfer of function from the older institutions and the rise of a new series of functions that the school is expected to perform.

The extent of these functions is indicated by the enrollment in the nation's educational institutions. In October, 1962, an estimated 48,704,000 pupils from 5 to 34 years of age were enrolled in the schools of the United States. This figure represented 57.8 per cent of the total number of persons in this age group. Of this number, 32,285,000 children 5 to 13 years were in school, representing 95.2 per cent of this group. From 14 to 17 years, 11,740,000 or 92.0 per cent of this group attended school. In the 18 to 19 year group, the number dropped sharply to 2,144,000 or 41.8 per cent. The majority of students in the latter group were in institutions of higher learning. From 20 to 24 years, the number enrolled was 1,725,000, or 15.6 per cent of this age group. From 25 to 29 years, the number dropped to 522,000 (5.0 per cent of the age group), and from 30 to 34 years, a scholarly band of 288,000 (2.6 per cent) were still attending school.[23]

The educational institution exacts a different role from the sexes. In general, the older the age group, the smaller the percentage of girls enrolled in school in comparison with boys. In 1962, some 61.7 per cent of the total number of males aged 5 to 34 years were enrolled in schools; the comparable percentage of females was 54.0. In the age group from 5 to 13 years, the percentages of the sexes in school were exactly equal at 95.2 per cent. In the 14 to 17 year group, the percentages in high school were 93.7 for the boys and 90.3 for the girls. At 18-19 years, when most of this age group who are still in school are entering college, the differences were more pronounced; 51.2 per cent of the boys and 33.7 per cent of the girls were in school in 1962. In the age group 20 to 24 years, the disparity was even more marked; 23.4 per cent of the males and only 9.1 per cent of the females were in colleges and universities. In the postgraduate years from 25 to 29 years, 8.5 per cent of the men and 1.8 per cent of the women were in school. In the age group 30 to 34 years, 3.9 per cent of the males and an earnest 1.4 per cent of the females were still attending school.[24]

The primary function of this elaborate process is to transmit the cultural heritage from one generation to the next.[25] In this sense, education is a conservative force. This statement may seem strange in view of the widespread conception of education as a search for new truth and therefore basically a progressive

---

[23] Bureau of the Census, *Current Population Reports: Population Characteristics,* "Shcool Enrollment: October 1962," Series P-20, No. 126 (September 24, 1963), Table 1.

[24] *Ibid.*

[25] Natalie Rogoff Ramsøy, "Public Education in America: A Research Program," *Sociology of Education,* 37:1-8 (Fall, 1963).

force. This latter aspect, however, is largely confined to the various forms of advanced education, where groups of scholars and students engage in a cooperative quest for truth. Most education is oriented in a conservative, rather than a progressive, direction. Whether conducted by parents, teachers, or religious leaders, education hands on the folkways, mores, ideals, attitudes, values, skills, and institutional patterns of the existing society to the next generation.

We are using the word "conservative" here in the sense of saving or conserving the cultural heritage. We are not using it in the traditional political sense of remaining fixed to the old order of things. Quite the contrary. In a nationwide study of conformity, tolerance, and "liberalism" in the acceptance of new ideas, it was found that the greater the education the more tolerant the person was. Other things being equal, older persons as a group were less tolerant than younger persons, with reference to political, religious, and social nonconformity. This fact reflects the increase in education over the past generation. Within each age group, furthermore, the better educated were more tolerant than the less educated. The flow of information on vital subjects tends to break down the barriers of intolerance.[26]

A social institution, as we have seen, has both a concept and a structure. The

---

[26] Samuel A. Stouffer, *Communism, Conformity, and Civil Liberties* (New York: Doubleday & Company, 1955), Chapter 4.

In the kindergarten, the child first participates in an organized educational experience, through which he learns many of the culture patterns of his society.

concept is the goal or purpose of the institution—what it is supposed to do. In a complex society, there is seldom complete agreement as to the nature of these goals. Education is no exception and the various interest groups in our society have different conceptions of the goal of education. Contrary to the prevailing impression, however, this lack of agreement is nothing new. Approximately 2,300 years ago, Aristotle stated this dilemma in terms that are startling in their modernity: "All people do not agree in those things they would have a child taught, both with respect to improvement in virtue and a happy life; nor is it clear whether the object of it should be to improve the reason or rectify the morals. From the present mode of education we cannot determine with certainty to which men incline, whether to instruct a child in what will be useful to him in life, or what leads to virtue, or what is excellent; for all these things have their separate defenders." [27]

In our own society, these "separate defenders" range all the way from those who believe that education should transmit the bare rudiments of knowledge to those who maintain that it should lead the way to a new social order. In most communities, the educational system is a compromise between these two extremes, with the result that many persons are not satisfied with the role of the school. Those who believe that education should transmit the cultural heritage without change look back nostalgically to the little red school house, with its alleged virtues in inculcating the three R's. Those who think that education should point the way to a new world believe that the school is falling far short of its progressive role as a guide to democratic life.

Society has increased both in complexity and rate of change since formal education became an important institution. As a result, the school is attempting to perform all the functions that it performed a century ago, plus a variety of others. The school is expected to do too much. The average high school maintains the liberal arts program it has given for several generations. In addition, it offers courses in everything from automobile mechanics to marriage and family living. Most of these courses are in the curriculum as a result of the specific demand of an important segment of the community. These groups believe that instruction in salesmanship and shorthand, for example, is as important as training in English literature and solid geometry. In an age when the school is expected to prepare the children of all social classes for "life," it is difficult to state categorically that one branch of knowledge is more "important" than another. When the high school was still largely a college-preparatory institution, its curricular problems were correspondingly easier.[28]

Education is faced with another problem: whether or not the school should attempt to teach moral and spiritual values. At first glance, this question has only one answer, an affirmative one. Of course, the school should transmit the basic ethical and moral values of our culture. At second glance, however, the question becomes more complicated. The traditional separation of church and

---

[27] Quoted by Francis Keppel and Sloan Wilson, "Goals for Our Schools," *Saturday Review*, 38:17-18 (September 10, 1955).
[28] *Ibid.*

state in our society suggests that the primary responsibility for moral values should rest with the family and the church, rather than the school. Furthermore, many persons would interpret a mandate to teach morality as an invitation to turn the schools into churches. Sectarian questions also arise. The various religious groups have differing definitions of ethics and morality. We are not attempting to answer these questions here. We are merely indicating that the role of education in this respect is not a simple one.[29]

We may summarize some of the complexities faced by organized education in the contemporary United States:

1. The content of modern culture has increased tremendously in scope and complexity, and the amount of training necessary to adjust to it has increased proportionately. The individual therefore requires a greater formal training in knowledge and skills than ever before.

2. The increase in the number of achieved, as contrasted to ascribed, statuses means that many young people have no idea what status(es) they will occupy and what role(s) they will play as adults. Hence they must have a more extensive general training in cultural skills so that they can adapt to a variety of different situations.

3. The educational motivation of the child is often low, especially in the lower class, because direct application of knowledge and skills is not readily apparent. This lack of motivation often leads to inadequate effort while the child is in school, as well as early withdrawal by many children.

4. The conflicts in our society between various goals, ideals, and values are reflected in the educational system and in the cultural heritage the child is expected to acquire. These conflicting values include religious definitions, racial discrimination, family disorganization, and labor relations.

5. The complexity of the society is also reflected in the number of fields in which the school is expected to offer instruction. This situation is further complicated by the differences of opinion as to whether the school should stick to a liberal arts curriculum or should attempt to cover the entire field of adjustment to all the "practical" problems of modern life.

6. The difficulties of the educational institution are symbolized by the comparatively low status of the persons connected with it. Society pays lip service to education as the foundation of democracy, but at the same time accords low status and pay to those who devote their lives to training the young.

The Economic Function

The function of the economic institution is to provide physical subsistence for a society. This involves such activities as the production, processing, distribution, and consumption of the goods and services necessary for group survival. Man has developed increasingly complex methods of providing for his necessities and the growing number of his luxuries. In the main stream of cultural evolu-

[29] *Ibid.*

tion, the taming of plants and animals followed a nomadic hunting period, as man settled down to a stable existence based upon herding and agriculture. Many societies in isolated parts of the world never made this transition and remain contentedly in hunting or pastoral cultures. But the great stream of cultural development followed the way of life based upon a settled form of economic production. This resulted from the so-called Neolithic Revolution, which was one of the most important changes in the history of culture.[30]

The importance of the economic and social system based upon agriculture is emphasized when we realize that *no basic change* occurred in the subsistence function from the prehistoric village to the eighteenth-century city. This tremendous interval saw such changes in other cultural spheres as an increased ability to transport goods by wind power, plus an added knowledge of rudimentary hygiene, so that men could live together in larger groups. But the rural and handicraft base of society remained essentially static until the Industrial Revolution in the second half of the eighteenth century.[31]

Mechanical power was then added for the first time on a large scale to the production and distribution of goods. In the past century and a half, more changes have occurred in the economic institution than in the preceding millennia. These changes in the way man makes his living have been communicated to the other institutions. The family, the school, the government, and the church began in the simple culture of an essentially agricultural society. Many of the current difficulties in these institutions reflect their inadequate adjustments to the new economic system based upon an advanced technology.[32]

The development of the economic institution has been accompanied by an increasing complexity in the division of labor. This concept refers to the different functions performed by the members of a society, not only in their economic roles but in their other institutional roles. The division of labor is an important *sociological*, as well as *economic*, aspect of society. The economic role of the individual is basic to many other roles. The importance of the occupation is especially great in those societies that, like our own, stress the economic aspects of group life. In this sense, our society represents the most elaborate division of labor the world has ever seen.[33]

The division of labor involves more than the allocation of functions to the various members of a society. The psychological elements are as significant as the structural. It is important to know that certain persons engage in banking, truck driving, and farming, but it is also important to know how these functions are regarded in the society and the motives that cause the individuals to assume them. Central to the division of labor are such considerations as the prestige of the various activities, their monetary or emotional returns, and the resultant status of the participants.

---

[30] Ralph Linton, *The Tree of Culture* (New York: Alfred A. Knopf, Inc., 1955), Chapter 13.

[31] Lewis Mumford, *Technics and Civilization* (New York: Harcourt, Brace and World, 1934).

[32] Cf. S. C. Gilfillan, "Social Implications of Technical Advance," *Current Sociology*, 1:191-207, UNESCO, Paris, 1953.

[33] Émile Durkheim, *The Division of Labor in Society* (Translated by George Simpson) (Glencoe, Ill.: The Free Press, 1949).

The division of labor also involves social interaction. Competition and cooperation are the principal polar forms of interaction here. By informal group pressure, every society regulates the way its members combine to perform a given activity, as well as the differential compensation that goes to each person. Some societies are marked by a high degree of cooperation, whereby each member works for the common good and receives in return his "just compensation." Other societies are marked by intense competition, and the members are primarily concerned with the personal gain deriving from a particular function, rather than with its relationship to the welfare of the group.

Many (but not all) primitive societies are organized on the first basis, whereas our own operates on the second. In the comparatively simple division of labor in a primitive society, the individual may not sharply distinguish his own interests from those of the group. He starves when the others starve and feasts when they feast. In our society, this organic unity has long since disappeared and has been replaced by a pervasive spirit of individualism. Each person is intent upon his own gain, often made at the expense of others. These patterns of expectations are deep in the mores, and each society operates on the assumption that its own mores are inevitable, just, and right.

Other patterns of societal beliefs reflect other forms of division of labor. In the societies of ancient Greece and Rome, gainful employment was regarded as degrading to free human beings. The necessary economic functions were in large measure performed by slaves, and the citizens devoted their attention to such honorific activities as government, war, and the cultivation of the arts. In the early Christian era, labor was seen as a penalty for original sin, a chore that every man must perform but which was not thereby rendered any more pleasant. Only in comparatively recent times has labor for gain been considered an activity to which every man should devote the majority of his waking hours.[34]

The Protestant Reformation was in large part responsible for this new attitude toward work. In the Calvinist view, work was a sacred calling and the elect of God were those who were unusually successful in these pursuits. This concept was brought to this country by the English colonists and has been a basic part of the American ideology ever since. Such a philosophy was ideally suited to a continent where the resources were there for the taking, and where every man was needed to provide the necessary labor. The United States has been dedicated to this glorification of gainful labor in its subsequent history.[35]

The division of labor may also take the form of a feeling of interdependence and mutual cooperation in a great common activity. The more complex the division, however, the more difficult it is for the average individual to grasp this sense of cooperative enterprise. In modern society, this feeling is often confined to the members of the same nation. Most Americans are conscious, however vaguely, of their participation in the tremendous social entity that is the United States. This mutual interdependence actually stretches beyond the national state

---

[34] William Graham Summer, *Folkways, op. cit.*, pp. 160-162.
[35] J. Milton Yinger, *Religion in the Struggle for Power* (Durham: Duke University Press, 1946), Chapter 4, "Calvinism and the Rise of Capitalism."

and embraces much of the world. So strong are the symbols of nationalism, however, that the realization of this broader division of labor is difficult to attain.

A final general characteristic of the economic institution is the degree of concentration taking place in its corporate structure. Economic power in many fields is concentrated in a small number of giant corporations, and mergers and consolidations are continually reducing this number. In the corporation itself, control is increasingly vested in a few persons, who own only a small fraction of the shares but nevertheless exercise effective control. This trend toward the separation of ownership and control was noted three decades ago,[36] and in the intervening period it has become even more pronounced.[37]

The Religious Function

Religion is the final great social institution that we shall examine. Like the other major structures, religion varies from one society and one period to an-

[36] Adolf A. Berle and Gardiner C. Means, *The Modern Corporation and Private Property* (New York: The Macmillan Company, 1932).
[37] Adolf A. Berle, *Power Without Property* (New York: Harcourt, Brace and World, 1959).

In the Middle Ages, the Church was the great, all-embracing institution. Notre Dame Cathedral in Paris is one of the most impressive examples of the church of that day.

other. Many social functions have been transferred from religion to the other institutions and back again. In certain societies, the religious institution has dominated all the others. Priests have been leading citizens, economic power has been vested in the church, and the state has been closely related with organized religion. In other societies, religion has been relegated to a position of comparative unimportance and the church has, figuratively and often literally, been obliged to beg its bread in the streets.

In some societies, the church has likewise performed many derivative functions, from education to social welfare, and from banking to the patronage of art. In the Middle Ages, the Church was the great, all-embracing, and multifunctional institution, whose activities reached into virtually every phase of life. The Church provided much of the secular government; the light of learning was kept burning in the monasteries; the price of labor was regulated by ecclesiastical decree; the poor, the sick, and the destitute were aided and comforted by the Church; education was conducted in close cooperation with the religious authorities; recreation was sponsored by the same agency; and even warfare was often carried on by religious leaders, operating as agents of the Church militant.

In other societies, the church has been obliged to keep to its central function of providing spiritual guidance. In nations where the separation of church and state has followed a revolution, the church has been neither encouraged nor permitted to assume its former derivative functions. In France, the Revolution of 1789 ushered in a conflict between church and state that still continues. This conflict was marked by the legal separation of these two institutions in the early part of the present century and the subsequent curtailment of many of the educational, economic, and political activities of the Catholic Church.

The ultimate function of religion is to provide a meaning for life. Death faces every man and religion tries to reconcile him to his destiny. The religious institution grows out of that central *concept* and assumes a variety of forms. Even within our own society, the *structure* of religion has varied from the elaborate symbolic ritual of the Catholic Church to the simple ceremonies of many Protestant denominations. The number of functionaries necessary for the religious experience is also subject to variations, with the hierarchy of the Roman Catholic Church and the individual Protestant reading his Bible representing extremes. Despite these structural differences, the essential religious function is to help the individual derive spiritual solace from communion with the supernatural forces.

Religion also provides a foundation for the mores. Many of the mores are far older than the form of organized religion that currently prevails. The mores embodied in the Ten Commandments, for example, are older than organized Christianity and have their origins in the culture of the ancient Hebrews. The moral prohibitions against murder, blasphemy, and adultery can be traced far back into pre-Christian antiquity, where they were enforced by the religions of still earlier peoples. Christianity has provided additional sanctions for these mores and thereby gives them greater power of control. The mores are enforced by group pressure *plus* the sanctions of the divine and the supernatural.[38]

Offenses against the mores thus become offenses against the divine order. The sexual morality of the Hebrews and the early Christians was invested with the force of religion. Violations of these group injunctions became sins—that is, transgressions of the word of God. This relationship has been evident in the history of Christianity. The hostility of the early Church Fathers toward sexual relationships outside of wedlock became incorporated in the moral code of the Western World. This process of investing the mores with religious sanctions occurs in every society, and the moral and the religious become virtually synonymous. More than the mere realization of social welfare is necessary for group members to observe the mores. The additional sanction is provided by religion.

Religion also provides an organized culture pattern by which the individual can meet and, it is hoped, surmount the crises of life. In this sense, crisis implies change and readjustment, as each person must meet new situations throughout his life. The major crises mark a change from one status to another, whereby the individual must learn a new role. This prospect would be both terrifying and confusing if the individual had to face it by himself. Hence the society has worked out appropriate rites to accompany the major changes in status. These rites receive the sanction of organized religion. The forms of these rituals vary from one society to another, but their function is similar. Religion guides the individual through the vicissitudes of life, which are much the same for all men.

The Roman Catholic Church has evolved the most fully developed system of rites to guide and comfort the erring mortal through the major crises. The sacraments of the Church take him from birth to death and prepare the way for his ultimate resurrection. The sacraments are baptism, confirmation, holy Eucharist, penance, matrimony, holy orders, and extreme unction. At each change of status, the individual is offered divine guidance to carry out his new role. The nature and function of the sacraments are officially described as follows: "By baptism we are born again, confirmation makes us strong, perfect Christians and soldiers. The Eucharist furnishes our daily spiritual food. Penance heals the soul, wounded by sin. Extreme unction removes the last remnant of human frailty, and prepares the soul for eternal life. Orders supplies ministers to the Church of God. Matrimony gives the graces necessary for those who are to rear children in the love and fear of God." [39]

The sanctions of organized religion are not universally accepted. Different groups take different attitudes toward religious institutions.[40] One of the characteristics of a dynamic society, indeed, is a lack of consensus concerning the basic values of religion. Some groups attempt to extend the sanctions of religion, whereas others try to restrict these definitions to concerns that are clearly religious. Conflicts over the matters in which religion is sovereign and those in

---

[38] Cf. Joachim Wach, *The Sociology of Religion* (Chicago: University of Chicago Press, 1944).

[39] *The Catholic Encyclopedia*, Volume XIII (New York: The Encyclopedia Press, Inc., 1912), p. 301.

[40] Gerhard E. Lenski, "Social Correlates of Religious Interest," *American Sociological Review*, 18:533-544 (October, 1953).

which the secular government has pre-eminence are apparent in our society. Controversies arise over such issues as contraception, divorce, education, and child labor.

On the basis of these and other disparities between belief and practice, it has been suggested that the "functions" of the religious institution are more difficult to isolate in complex societies than in simpler ones. Many of the functional analyses of religion are based upon primitive societies, whose social structures are in most cases less complex than our own. Hence some of the alleged functions of the religious institution may not apply to our own society. Religious norms and sanctions often pervade every aspect of a small and primitive society. The role of religion in preserving the norms, providing a meaning for life, and surmounting the crises of existence is correspondingly clearer than in our own society.[41]

Some of the reasons for this possible lack of clear-cut religious functionalism in complex societies are as follows: (*a*) The norms of religion lose much of their power if large numbers of persons do not believe in them. Unless one "believes," he is not controlled by religious norms. (*b*) The sanctions of religion are more easily evaded in complex societies than in primitive societies. The individual may follow economic, humanistic, or other secular norms, rather than religious ones. (*c*) The activities of religion are less "precise" in complex societies because of the many other competing institutions, whose power is equal to, or greater than, that of the religious institution. (*d*) The psychological impact of religion may, in certain instances, be more "dysfunctional" than functional in complex societies. Personal guilt, racial hostility, ethnic prejudice, and opposition to liberal thought are some of the possible dysfunctions of the religious institution in this sense.[42]

Organized religion in the United States has been further characterized by the proliferation of its individual institutions. Throughout our discussion of institutions, we have dealt largely with the broad institutional patterns, rather than with individual examples. We have accordingly examined the family, the governmental institution, the school, and the church, rather than individual families, governments, schools and churches. This distinction between the culture pattern and the individual example is especially striking in the religious organization of the United States. In 1963, there were some 258 *different* religious bodies in this country (including the monolithic Roman Catholic Church), with an estimated total membership of 116,109,665.[43]

This variety of religious bodies reflects the trend toward diversity among the Protestant denominations since the Reformation. One of the basic tenets of Protestantism is its strong individualism, embodied in the belief that the individual can communicate directly with God without the mediation of any institution or hierarchy. Hence division and subdivision are contained in the very

---

[41] Allan W. Eister, "Religious Institutions in Complex Societies," *American Sociological Review*, 22:387-391 (August, 1957).

[42] *Ibid.*

[43] *The World Almanac and Book of Facts for 1963* (New York: World Telegram, 1963), p. 705.

nature of Protestantism, and these tendencies have flourished in the free air of America. The result has been the many different religious bodies noted above, some of them embracing no more than a few thousand adherents and others with members in the millions. The freedom of the individual to seek his own salvation is carried to its logical conclusion.

The institution of organized religion, whatever its denominational basis, is faced with a major force in many parts of the world. This is the power of totalitarian government, which by its very nature can brook no interference from an institution whose ultimate sanctions lie outside the state. The conflict between Hitler and the Roman Catholic Church was one aspect of this problem. The continuing conflict between the same Church and the totalitarian countries of eastern Europe is another. The communist governments allow no loyalty to any institution but themselves, and the Catholic Church gives its proximate loyalty to Rome and its ultimate loyalty to God. The sympathies of millions of persons of the Catholic faith in these countries are sorely tried. Many of their cultural loyalties are rooted in their own land. Their religious loyalties have long rested in Rome.[44]

Religion is faced with a final threat that is more powerful even than the combined police power of the totalitarian states. This threat is the rise of secularism. A point of view rather than a specific doctrine, secularism has been gradually increasing in extent and intensity. The basic characteristic of the secular outlook is the belief that human problems are primarily *social*, rather than *religious*. The secular attitude is a worldly attitude, not in the sense of superficial sophistication, but rather in its insistence that human affairs should be governed by reason rather than faith.

The secular attitude has been both caused and affected by the discoveries in physical, biological, and, more recently, social science. This attitude stresses individual liberty and independence of thought, both from arbitrary powers of government and from rigid religious orthodoxy. The secular attitude accepts change as a necessary adjustment to a world that cannot stand still.[45] The ultimate danger to the religious institution, at least as traditionally constituted, is social change. The secular attitude is an expression of this change.[46]

Many of the institutions of organized religion in the United States are trying to adjust to this growing secularism. This effort takes such forms as widening the scope of adult education in the churches, providing various social welfare services, increasing the recreational facilities, and making it possible for young people to meet under church auspices. These activities are highly commendable in themselves, but they are more secular than sacred. Secular values are so pervasive in American culture that the church (of any denomination) may be fighting a losing battle to extend (and even preserve) its sacred values. Mem-

---

[44] Werner J. Cahnman, "Religion and Nationality," *American Journal of Sociology.* 49:524-529 (May, 1944).

[45] Howard Becker, "Sacred and Secular Societies," *Social Forces,* 28:361-376 (May, 1950).

[46] Harold W. Pfautz, "The Sociology of Secularization: Religious Groups," *American Journal of Sociology,* 61:121-128 (September, 1955).

bership in the institutions of organized religion is the highest in the history of the country. This would suggest that sacred values are growing at the expense of secular values. This may or may not be the case. One plausible explanation for the increased identification with religious institutions is "not so much that the American people are becoming more religious as that religion is becoming more like American culture." [47]

In this chapter, we first surveyed some of the characteristics of social institutions, such as their nature and the claims they place upon their members; the interaction of the members in their institutional roles; and the conservative character of institutions as transmitters of the cultural heritage. We also surveyed the functions of social institutions as the activities they perform in carrying out their basic purposes. We then examined the institutions of government and the school, the economic institution, and the church, in terms of the general functions which they perform and the extent to which some of these functions have been transferred from one institution to another. This survey has been suggestive rather than exhaustive. The basic trend appears to be the loss of some traditional functions by the family and the church, and the transfer of these functions to the school, the government, and the economic institution.

---

[47] W. Seward Salisbury, "Religion and Secularization," *Social Forces*, 36:197-205 (March, 1958), p. 204.

SELECTED BIBLIOGRAPHY

Angell, Robert C., *Free Society and Moral Crisis*. Ann Arbor: University of Michigan Press, 1958. This is an important book, which deals with some of the great problems of our time. The central problem, as conceived by the author, is that of moral order and integration. The institutions are the central agencies for maintaining this common body of values in a society.

Chapin, F. Stuart, "Social Institutions and Voluntary Associations," Chapter 9 in J. B. Gittler (ed.), *Review of Sociology: Analysis of a Decade*. New York: John Wiley & Sons, Inc., 1957. In this essay, an authority on social institutions reviews the literature of the decade of 1945-1955. Chapin indicates that much of the research on small-group behavior is also relevant to institutional behavior, inasmuch as institutions provide the settings for much (although by no means all) of this behavior.

Durkheim, Émile, *The Division of Labor in Society* (Translated by George Simpson). Glencoe, Ill.: The Free Press, 1950. This is a classic study of the institutional patterns of a society, with particular reference to the conscious and unconscious demands that they place upon the individual. Many of the insights originally developed by Durkheim have since been incorporated into the body of sociological thought.

Herberg, Will, *Protestant-Catholic-Jew*. New York: Doubleday Anchor Books, 1960 (rev. ed.). This is an extensive and up-to-date analysis of the three great religious groups that constitute the "triple melting pot" of contemporary America. Over and above the religious beliefs of the American people is their firm commitment to the American Way of Life, which is vaguely believed to equate religion with American aspirations in other fields.

Lynd, Robert S., and Helen M. Lynd, *Middletown*. New York: Harcourt, Brace and World, 1929. This book and its successor (*Middletown in Transition*. New York: Harcourt, Brace and World, 1937) have become modern sociological classics. The authors portray a representative American community in terms of its constituent institutions. Although the original study was made more than three decades ago, many of the basic institutional patterns have changed very little in the intervening years.

Rose, Arnold M. (ed.), *The Institutions of Advanced Societies*. Minneapolis: University of Minnesota Press, 1958. This is one of the comparatively few institutional studies of advanced, as contrasted with primitive, societies. The editor has commissioned a number of long and thoughtful essays on advanced national societies, written by nationals of these countries who are trained in the social sciences.

Salisbury, W. Seward, "Religion and Secularization," *Social Forces*, 36:197-205 (March, 1958). In this significant analysis, religion in the United States is seen as increasingly secularized. The society of this country, with its emphasis upon material values, may be setting the tone for *all* institutions, including the religious.

Sumner, William Graham, *Folkways*. Boston: Ginn and Company, 1906. A knowledge of Sumner is essential to an understanding of social institutions. The author advances the most succinct and significant definition of an institution as "a concept . . . and a structure." The book is a mine of cross-cultural information on comparative institutions and their role in primitive and (by implication) advanced societies.

Vernon, Glenn M., *Sociology of Religion*. New York: McGraw-Hill Book Company, 1962. This is an excellent *sociological* study of religion, based upon a conceptual framework of social interaction. In this sense, the book is truly sociological in its orientation, rather than being a survey of religion with occasional "social" overtones.

Wach, Joachim, *The Sociology of Religion*. Chicago: University of Chicago Press, 1944. This is a monumental survey and interpretation of the research on the various aspects of the religious institution throughout the world.

Weber, Max, *The Protestant Ethic and the Spirit of Capitalism* (Translated by Talcott Parsons). London: Allen & Unwin, 1930. This classic study of religion and business deals with the rise of Protestantism and the reciprocal relationships between this religion and the business and trading classes during and after the Reformation in several of the nations of western Europe.

Williams, Robin M., *American Society*. New York: Alfred A. Knopf, Inc., 1951. This is an extensive analysis of the culture and social structure of American society, with particular reference to the main institutional patterns. This book is recommended to the student who wishes to get a comprehensive picture of American institutions.

17 *Bureaucracy*

The Nature of Bureaucracy

As it grows in size and complexity, modern society is becoming increasingly bureaucratized. This means that many institutions are becoming more formal, with an elaborate set of statuses and roles fixed by rational decision, deliberate control, and legal practice. A bureaucracy may be briefly defined as a formal structure that organizes and coordinates the various functions of large numbers of persons engaged in a common activity. Bureaucracies are organizations with a complex division of labor, a high degree of specialization, and an established pattern of authority. Bureaucracy is a characteristic feature of modern life and applies to many, but not all, social institutions and voluntary associations. In short, bureaucracy is a way of getting things done in an organized, systematic, and rational manner in a large and diversified society.

The institutional aspects of bureaucracy have been stressed by many commentators. In this context, bureaucracy is defined by Dimock as "the composite institutional manifestations which tend toward inflexibility and depersonalization. Any institution," continues Dimock, "may prove bureaucratic, and since individuals are moulded by their environments, they also take on bureaucratic coloration." The word "composite" refers to the tone of bureaucratic institutions as such, which reflects the nature of their goals and the ways their members seek these goals. "Bureaucracy," therefore, "is simply institutionalism written large. It is not some foreign substance which has been infused into the life-blood of an institution: it is merely the combination of characteristics found in all [institutions]." [1] When institutions become complex, they tend to assume the characteristics of a bureaucracy.

Bureaucracy is therefore a descriptive and not an abusive term, and merely indicates a certain form of social structure. Bureaucracy is not something one likes or dislikes, but is rather something one tries to understand. Bureaucracy is not confined to government, but applies to large private organizations that have nothing to do with government. The Standard Oil Company of New Jersey is a bureaucracy just as much as the Department of the Interior, and the Metropolitan Life Insurance Company is every bit as bureaucratic as the Department of Commerce. Bureaucracy is thus a fact of life that a growing number of people in our society must face. "A large and increasing proportion of the American people," remarks Blau, "spend their working lives as small cogs in the complex mechanisms of bureaucratic organizations." [2]

These bureaucratic employees work at white-collar occupations as (to cite a few examples) stenographers, typists, file clerks, bookkeepers, salesmen, accountants, draftsmen, and operators of office machines. Others are employed in the factories and assembly plants of large industrial corporations, where they work at various "blue-collar" jobs, ranging in status and remuneration from semiskilled operatives through skilled craftsmen to foremen and supervisors. Whatever the precise nature of their jobs, these members of the corporate hierarchy are essentially bureaucratic employees and are subject to the advantages and disadvantages of this system. The organization in which they spend their working lives may be a branch of government, a corporation, an army, a church, or a political party. Whatever the nature of the organization, however, the roles of the majority of its employees are similar.

The concept of bureaucracy was developed by Max Weber, the German sociologist, and subsequently expanded by other sociologists in Europe and Amer-

---

[1] Marshall E. Dimock, "Bureaucracy Self-Examined," *Public Administration Review*, Vol. IV (1944), quoted in Robert K. Merton, *et. al.* (eds.), *Reader in Bureaucracy* (Glencoe, Illinois: The Free Press, 1952), p. 397.

[2] Peter M. Blau, *Bureaucracy in Modern Society* (New York: Random House, Inc., 1956), p. 2.

ica.[3] In their analyses, these scholars made certain departures from, and added certain refinements to, the concept originally established by Weber. We shall refer to some of these additions below. Our central approach, however, follows that of Max Weber. In his analysis, he advanced a number of related characteristics of what he called the "ideal type" of bureaucracy. He used this term, not in the "moral" or "ideal" sense, but rather in the scientific sense. The "ideal type" refers in this application to the "pure" form of bureaucracy, and is thus a mental construct, a general statement of the characteristics of a typical bureaucracy.[4]

Max Weber further stated that bureaucracies take two general forms—(a) charismatic, and (b) legal-rational. By "charismatic," he referred to "a certain quality of an individual personality by virtue of which he is set apart from ordinary men and treated as endowed with supernatural, superhuman, or at least specifically exceptional powers or qualities."[5] These qualities, by definition, do not belong to ordinary men, but are granted to such persons as great military leaders, political heroes, and religious prophets. Napoleon, Hitler, and Jesus Christ were charismatic leaders, and the concept clearly refers to seemingly magical powers of inspiration and leadership (Napoleon and Hitler) as well as to moral qualities for good (Jesus Christ). One major form of bureaucratic organization arises from these leadership qualities by the process of what Weber calls "the routinization of charisma"—that is, the establishment of charismatic leadership in more or less permanent organizational form.[6] The Napoleonic Empire, the Nazi State, and the Christian Church are examples of this "routinization of charisma."[7] The hierarchical structure of the Roman Catholic Church is the supreme example in the Western world of such a process.

Charismatic bureaucracy is, because of its supernatural nature, considered by its members to be an end in itself and hence not responsible to the larger society. Legal-rational bureaucracy does not have this divine power. It is regarded by both its members and the rest of the society as a means to social welfare and not as an end in itself. Legal-rational bureaucracies can be controlled and their energies directed into channels approved by the society. The Communist party in the Soviet Union is a charismatic bureaucracy. Our Department of Health, Education, and Welfare is a legal-rational bureaucracy.[8] As

---

[3] Max Weber, *Wirtschaft und Gesellschaft*, Tübingen, 1922. The English edition is Max Weber, *The Theory of Social and Economic Organization* (Translated by A. M. Henderson and Talcott Parsons), (New York: Oxford University Press, 1947), especially pp. 329-340; cf. also H. H. Gerth and C. Wright Mills (eds.), *From Max Weber: Essays in Sociology* (New York: Oxford University Press, 1948).

[4] For a critical review of the "ideal type" concept in Max Weber, see Carl J. Friedrich, "Some Observations on Weber's Analysis of Bureaucracy," in Robert K. Merton, *et al.*, (eds.), *Reader in Bureaucracy*, *op. cit.*, pp. 27-33.

[5] Max Weber, *The Theory of Social and Economic Organization, op. cit.*, p. 358.

[6] *Ibid.*, pp. 363-373.

[7] Cf. Paul M. Harrison, "Weber's Categories of Authority and Voluntary Associations," *American Sociological Review*, 25:232-237 (April, 1960).

[8] Helen Constas, "Max Weber's Two Conceptions of Bureaucracy," *American Journal of Sociology*, 63:400-409 (January, 1958).

society grows more secular, legal-rational bureaucracy tends to become relatively more important than charismatic bureaucracy. In the present analysis, we are primarily concerned with the legal-rational form.

This latter type of structure is found in a number of organizations with widely different goals. In Weber's words, the concept of legal-rational bureaucracy "may be applied in profit-making business or in charitable organizations, or in any number of other types of private enterprises serving ideal or material ends. It is," he continues, "equally applicable to political and to religious organizations."[9] The most striking example of legal-rational bureaucracy is the modern state, whether democratic (United States), socialist (Sweden), fascist (Nazi Germany), or communist (Soviet Union). Modern governments, whatever their political values, are so complex that they require an organized staff, precisely conceived duties and responsibilities, and definite rules of authority. Any other system of administration under present conditions would give rise to complete chaos.

The nature of bureaucracy cannot be fully understood without a knowledge of the conditions that produced it. Bureaucracy existed as early as the societies of Greece and Rome,[10] as well as in the China of the Ch'ing Dynasty (1644-1912),[11] but its most characteristic manifestations appeared in Europe after the Reformation. In the centuries between the rise of Protestantism and our own day, the following social conditions either appeared for the first time or became accentuated.[12]

1. Monetary economy. A monetary economy allows a system of stated salaries, regularly paid, which means that the bureaucratic personnel is dependent upon the organization but at the same time has a definite incentive to work hard and faithfully.

2. Large size. The recent historical development of Western Europe and America has been marked by a rapid growth in population and a corresponding growth in the size of governments, armies, corporations, welfare agencies, and virtually every other type of social institution.

3. Capitalistic system. The development of capitalistic enterprise has enlarged the sphere of government and business organizations alike, as a result of which both have been obliged to introduce bureaucratic methods of administration in the interests of greater efficiency.

4. Protestant ethic. The Protestant Reformation developed hand in hand with capitalistic enterprise. Both have stressed rational discipline and dedication to hard work, related ideologies indispensable to the growth of bureaucracy.[13]

---

[9] Max Weber, *op. cit.*, p. 334.

[10] Max Weber, *The Theory of Social and Economic Organization, op. cit.*, pp. 324ff.

[11] Robert M. Marsh, "Formal Organization and Promotion in a Pre-Industrial Society," *American Sociological Review*, 26:547-556 (August, 1961).

[12] The following is adapted from Peter M. Blau, *Bureaucracy in Modern Society, op. cit.*, pp. 36-40.

[13] Richard H. Tawney, *Religion and the Rise of Capitalism* (London: Pelican Books, 1938).

The Bureaucratic Role

Bureaucracy needs bureaucrats to make it go. Bureaucracy forms bureaucrats by imposing role behavior upon them. Institutions are clusters of interlocking and reciprocal roles, each with its obligations, expectations, and qualifications. In some of these institutions, such as the family, the roles are informally constituted, and husbands, wives, parents, and children learn their rights and duties by informal instruction. Bureaucratic roles are more formally established. These roles are codified in meticulous fashion and can be learned and applied to the letter.[14] A characteristic aspect of bureaucracy, indeed, is this learned quality of its roles, so that the bureaucrat always knows, in theory at least, exactly where he stands. We may examine the nature of bureaucratic roles that make up Max Weber's "ideal type" bureaucracy.[15]

1. *Authority.* The bureaucrat is subject to formal authority and must perform definite obligations and carry out prescribed functions during his day's work. His authority is strictly limited and he must not exceed it.

2. *Freedom.* At the same time, the bureaucrat has a considerable amount of freedom from the time he leaves his office in the evening until he reaches it the next morning. He is free to do what he likes after hours, provided he does not break the law or discredit the organization.

3. *Hierarchy.* A bureaucracy is arranged in the form of a hierarchy, with each level having groups of functionaries both above and below it. The head of the bureau is answerable to a still higher authority, who is often an elected (i.e., nonbureaucratic) official.

4. *Competence.* Members have clearly defined spheres of competence. Some of these qualifications are certified before an individual can embark upon a bureaucratic career and others are learned from experience. Each person thus develops a fund of specialized knowledge relating to his office and, in theory at least, the longer he is there the more he knows.

5. *Contract.* Positions are filled by contract and both the organization and the individual are bound by contractual terms. In this respect, the bureaucracy is a secondary group, not a primary group that the individual ordinarily enters by birth or on the basis of emotional needs. The role of the bureaucrat is, in principle, an impersonal one.

6. *Appointment.* The bureaucrat is *appointed* to his post on the basis of his competence, which is often determined by competitive examination. He is not *elected* and hence is not subject to the same electoral hazards as democratic officials. It is impossible to maintain the same degree of bureaucratic discipline among elected officials (e.g., congressmen) as among permanent civil servants for the simple reason that the former are answerable only to the electorate.

---

[14] Reinhard Bendix, "Bureaucracy: The Problem and Its Setting," *American Sociological Review*, 12:493-507 (October, 1947).

[15] The following is adapted from Max Weber, *op. cit.*, pp. 329-336. See also Robert K. Merton, "Bureaucratic Structure and Personality," *Social Forces*, 18:560-568 (May, 1940).

7. *Salary.* Salary is fixed for each grade of the hierarchy. In government bureaucracy, and to an increasing extent in private corporations, the position also carries the right to a pension. Financial security is thus an important element to the bureaucrat and often influences his self-conception. Most men think twice before they will sacrifice the financial security of a lifetime of disciplined work.

8. *Promotion.* Promotion is slow but reasonably sure. It is based largely upon seniority, although exceptional achievement may also be considered. Tenure in office is assured, short of gross negligence in performance. These aspects of the bureaucratic role make for a reliance upon rules and procedures at the expense of initiative and daring.

9. *Procedure.* Bureaucratic procedure is highly regularized. Communication proceeds "through channels" and according to established forms. In general, this leads to efficiency, for without some regular procedure neither the Bureau of Naval Personnel nor the Bell Telephone Company could operate effectively. These forms of communication, however, constitute the combined bureaucratic frustrations known as "red tape."

10. *Discipline.* Bureaucratic personnel are subject to strict, if often benevolent, discipline. Organizational rules are expected to be obeyed and the bureaucrat is expected to do his job, keep the "secrets" of the bureau, and maintain a united front against outsiders. Under such conditions, members internalize their roles and thus discipline themselves.

11. *Rationalism.* Bureaucratic roles are highly rationalized, which means that they are based upon reasoned analysis rather than personal whim. Max Weber referred constantly to this concept of rationalism, which he considered central to legal-rational bureaucracy. Bureaucracy represents the institutionalization of reason and its acceptance as the guiding principle for the realization of human goals. Needless to say, this ideal is never fully reached, for man is far from being a completely rational animal—even if he *is* a bureaucrat.[16]

12. *Office.* The bureaucratic role is an "office," by which Max Weber meant a formally defined position in a social structure. Bureaucratic organization is a hierarchy of such offices, and each member has the power to make decisions in his "official" capacity, rather than as an individual. Military organizations illustrate this principle, and the salute given to the officer is a formal recognition of his rank (office), rather than a tribute to him as an individual.

13. *Career.* Bureaucratic roles are, finally, regarded as careers.[17] The individual is made to feel that he has enlisted "for the duration," which in his case ordinarily means his active working life. He becomes identified with the organization, and his self-conception reflects the judgments of his fellow workers. The bureau, in short, becomes an integral part of him.

Historical conditions in the United States have, until recently, worked

---

[16] Cf. Stanley H. Udy, Jr., " 'Bureaucracy' and 'Rationality' in Weber's Organization Theory: An Empirical Study," *American Sociological Review*, 24:791-795 (December, 1959).

[17] Cf. Harold L. Wilensky, "Orderly Careers and Social Participation: The Impact of Work History on Social Integration in the Middle Mass," *American Sociological Review*, 26:521-539 (August, 1961).

In a large, bureaucratic organization, a person is usually unable to control his working conditions, can seldom express his preferences about his job, and may have trouble maintaining a favorable self-image.

against the development of bureaucracy in the aforementioned sense. The prizes of life have, for the most part, fallen to the successful businessman, industrialist, and politician (as distinguished from bureaucrat), and occasionally to the soldier. A career in government has not, by and large, offered a great inducement to the ambitious young man, although this situation appears to be changing: many more college graduates now seek careers in government than in times past.

The Organization Man as Bureaucrat

A bureaucratic career in big *business*, however, interests the ambitious young American very much. Large organizations in private business, industry, and banking have become increasingly complex, rationalized, disciplined, and hierarchical—in short, more bureaucratic. The young man enters these organizations under the same competitive conditions as he would enter a governmental bureaucracy. He is dependent upon the same types of procedure and is subject to the same chain of command. He hopes for security in the bosom of the corporation during his active life and looks forward to a pension when he retires.

The brightest, ablest, and most ambitious young men compete strenuously for admission to these corporate bureaucracies.

The college graduate who leaves the protecting warmth of alma mater to enter the equally hospitable arms of Procter and Gamble; Batten, Barton, Durstine, and Osborne; the General Electric Company; the General Motors Corporation; or the Chase Manhattan Bank does not think of himself as entering a bureaucracy. Nevertheless, that is exactly what he is doing, even as he enthusiastically affirms his dedication to private enterprise and his corresponding loathing for the welfare (bureaucratic) state. The thousands of junior executives of the great corporations, with their button-down collars and Ivy League suits, are a new generation of bureaucrats. In the words of the Boswell of the Organization Man, these rising executives "have left home, spiritually as well as physically, to take the vows of organization life, and it is they who are the mind and soul of our great self-perpetuating institutions." [18]

The organization man is the product of the trends that have separated the functions of ownership and management. In an earlier day, management was virtually synonymous with ownership, and men operated the property they owned. The separation of ownership and management has been documented by Berle and Means, and this phenomenon is one of the most important developments of our time. The large corporation is managed largely by men who do not own it; the owners (stockholders) have very little to say about major decisions and nothing at all to say about day-to-day operations. [19] The new managers are, in effect, the organization men.

The functions performed by the different levels of the bureaucratic (administrative) hierarchy are difficult to assess, let alone measure. The rising organization man is therefore under the same pressures as the bureaucratic employee in any large organization. His work, salary, and chances of promotion depend upon his ability to impress his superiors—not so much by what he can *do* but by what sort of person he *is*. The latter conception involves such intangible criteria as ability to get along with others, loyalty to the organization, and conformity to its norms and values. The rising young executive who can project such a favorable image of himself will, other things being equal, be promoted. Failure to do so, conversely, means that he will not become a vice-president. [20]

In an effort to impress his own outstanding qualities upon his superiors, the junior executive develops certain protective reactions. *First*, he follows the regulations and refrains from original efforts that might get him into trouble with his superiors. *Second*, he sends communications up the chain of command that will be favorable to himself and at the same time not threaten his superior. *Third*, he conforms to the prevailing corporate norms and follows the accepted

---

[18] William H. Whyte, Jr., *The Organization Man* (New York: Simon and Schuster, 1956), p. 3.

[19] Adolf A. Berle, *Power Without Property* (New York: Harcourt, Brace and World, 1959). The thesis was originally developed in Adolf A. Berle and Gardiner C. Means, *The Modern Corporation and Private Property* (New York: The Macmillan Company, 1932).

[20] William M. Evan, "Organization Man and Due Process of Law," *American Sociological Review*, 26:540-547 (August, 1961).

image of what an executive should be, do, say, and think. *Fourth*, he maintains his conformity in the community and plays it safe outside as well as inside the office. *Fifth*, he carries this "togetherness" into his family life and in so doing helps to rear another generation of conformists.[21]

The future organization man is, in many cases, the student who is reading these pages. A sizeable number of the four million men and women now in college aspire to be organization "men." Many will fail because they will not finish college. Others will go into their fathers' businesses. Still others will enter the professions, although even here the long arm of bureaucracy is reaching out toward the young doctor, lawyer, and engineer. A small and valiant minority will strike out for themselves as entrepreneurs. But the majority of aspiring businessmen want to work for a large corporation. If and when they do, their roles will bear a surprising similarity to that of the bureaucrat as heretofore defined.[22]

1.   The organization man is subject to the same hierarchical table of *authority* as the functionary in any legal-rational bureaucracy.

2.   The organization man may be even less *free* after hours than the government clerk. The new bureaucrat must meet certain corporate requirements as to his style of life, political affiliation, recreation, and (sometimes) his wife. Furthermore, he is expected to take home a full brief case.

3.   The *competence* of the organization man is based, first of all, upon his ability to graduate from a good college with reasonably good grades. He then enters a company training school, where he learns the rudiments of the business. After that, he is sent to the various departments (e.g., sales, accounting, manufacturing) to gain further specialized knowledge.

4.   His relationship to the corporation is based upon *contract*. He is not elected to his job, either by his peers or the general public. He is expected to live up to the terms of his contract and the company, in return, will do the same.

5.   Decisions in the organization are based upon regularized *procedure*. Each position in the corporate bureaucracy has its own responsibilities, and the incumbents can make only certain decisions on their own. Other decisions must be made by those in the higher echelons, up to the president and the board of directors.

6.   The organization man is expected to be loyal to the organization, and is subject to certain *disciplinary* procedures if he fails to live up to his obligations. One of the principal goals of the organization is to inculcate loyalty in its employees, especially those of executive grade, to such an extent that the latter are encouraged to place the company above all other organizational ties.

7.   The activities of the corporation are, by definition, highly *rationalized* in the literal sense of the Weberian concept. The ultimate purpose is the emi-

[21] *Ibid.* Cf. also Melville Dalton, "Informal Factors in Career Achievement," *American Journal of Sociology*, 56:407-415 (March, 1951).
[22] The following is adapted from William H. Whyte, Jr., *op. cit.*, Chapter 6, "A Generation of Bureaucrats."

nently rational one of making a profit for the stockholders and, in the process, insuring higher salaries, larger bonuses, and more generous pension systems for the officers. A pecuniary purpose of this kind is more frankly "rational" than that of a governmental bureaucracy, whose operations are complicated by cloudy and amorphous goals relating to the public welfare.

8.   Each of the stages in the corporate hierarchy is an *office* and the service constitutes a *career*. When the college graduate signs a contract with the Standard Oil Company of New Jersey, he is making a decision that will affect the rest of his life. He is making somewhat the same type of commitment as the career soldier, the priest, or the civil service employee.

The Formal Structure of Bureaucracy

The *function* of bureaucracy is to get things done efficiently. The *structure* of bureaucracy is a formal and institutionalized pattern of roles for bringing this about. These roles are based upon the concept of rational authority and each office has a definite responsibility in initiating and carrying out decisions. Authority in this sense may be said to be "legitimatized." Authority involves the nature of the communications within a formal organization and the way in which these communications are acted upon by the members and functionaries.[23] Authority is thus (*a*) a *relationship* between two or more individuals, based upon (*b*) *voluntary obedience*, and hence is (*c*) a *working pattern* of interaction rather than a plan set down on paper.[24]

Three general spheres of authority may be distinguished. These involve different types of functions and degrees of control over the members and the organization itself.[25]

Technical. The first function involves authority over the technical activities of the bureaucracy and refers to the "materials" that are handled by the members. These materials may be physical, as the blue-collar workers on an assembly line "process" materials in this sense. The materials may also be "cultural," as the personnel of a mass-communication industry turns out messages for transmission. The materials may, finally, be "human," as some members are occupied with "processing" human beings—that is, supervising, instructing, appraising, and promoting the personnel.

Managerial. The second function involves the "mediation" of (*a*) the external relations of the bureaucracy, and of (*b*) its internal affairs. In the first category are relationships with clients (Department of Health, Education, and Welfare) or with customers (Procter and Gamble Soap Company). The second category involves the over-all direction of the internal affairs of the organiza-

---

[23] Chester I. Bernard, "A Definition of Authority," in *The Functions of the Executive* (Cambridge: Harvard University Press, 1938), pp. 163-171, quoted by Robert K. Merton, *et al.* (eds.), *Reader in Bureaucracy, op. cit.*, p. 180.

[24] Peter M. Blau, *op. cit.*, p. 71.

[25] The following is adapted from S. N. Eisenstadt, "Bureaucracy and Bureaucratization," *Current Sociology*, Vol. VII, Paris, 1958, pp. 114-115. (Prepared with the assistance of UNESCO.)

tion—that is, the way in which the members carry out their specialized roles in pursuance of the goals of the organization.

Supervisory. The third function is that of over-all supervision of the entire organization. This supervision is best illustrated by the board of directors of a large corporation. These men have nothing to do with the day-to-day operations of the corporation and are, indeed, expressly chosen from outside the organization. They meet periodically to decide major matters of policy. The trustees of a university perform the same function in higher education, and the school board in primary and secondary education. In each instance, the supervisory group mediates between the bureaucracy (corporation, university, high school) and the larger community whose interests it presumably serves.

Two levels of organization are found in a bureaucracy—the *formal* and the *informal.* Each has its own special type of authority. In his analysis of legal-rational bureaucracy, Max Weber was largely concerned with the first, or formal, organization. Much of the analysis in this chapter has followed, directly or indirectly, in the footsteps of the master. Hence we have largely dealt with the nature of *formal* organization, the roles emerging therefrom, the implications for personality, and the functions and dysfunctions thereof. The formal organization is, however, often supplemented by an informal one that arises from the day-to-day interaction of members and functionaries. We shall consider the formal organization first, then turn to the informal.

On the *formal* level, bureaucratic organization involves the following considerations:[26]

1. The organization is viewed as an instrument for realizing certain goals, such as maintaining ordered relations with foreign powers (Department of State), insuring religious instruction in this world and salvation in the next (Protestant Episcopal Church), and increasing the efficiency of communication (American Telephone and Telegraph Company).

2. Decisions made by members of the organization are based upon rational knowledge and deliberate weighing of alternatives. The Department of State examines the anticipated results of raising the tariff on cotton goods, the Protestant Episcopal Church considers the pros and cons of appointing a Negro bishop, and the American Telephone and Telegraph Company investigates the possibilities of communication by artificial satellite.

3. These decisions are, furthermore, made in accordance with formal procedures, and each level of the bureaucratic hierarchy participates in accordance with its prerogatives. Memoranda, consultations, and specialized information form the basis for these decisions, with the different members contributing technical knowledge or seasoned advice.

4. Rational delegation of authority is the accepted procedure, and deviations therefrom are the result of human error or failure in calculation. Such deviations are recognized, but they are minimized when considering over-all

---

[26] The following is adapted from Alvin W. Gouldner, "Organizational Analysis," Ch. 18 in Robert K. Merton, *et al.* (eds.), *Sociology Today* (New York: Basic Books, Inc., 1959), pp. 404-405.

operations. Rational procedures are presumably so well established that every major contingency is anticipated by the checks and balances built into the organization.

5. The formal organization is, finally, subject to long-range planning, which implies that means and ends are continually weighed in pursuance of organizational goals. The period of planning varies, with a large corporation planning in terms of months, years, and perhaps decades, but with the Roman Catholic Church planning for centuries and, ultimately, for all eternity.

In furtherance of its ends, the formal organization uses a variety of such "rational" techniques as the following:[27]

a. Systematic evaluation of the success of its policies and practices—for example, an advertiser periodically checks on the television rating of his program to see how many people are exposed to his message.

b. Examination of different departments within the organization to see whether, for example, the research division is too large or the sales division too small.

c. Selection of new employees on the basis of psychological tests that allegedly reduce the procurement of personnel to an exact science and separate the potential executive from the rank-and-file.

d. Defense of organizational policies through research, by which device one manager may defend his preconceived notions by showing how "necessary" a particular change may be.

e. Employment of behavioral scientists to conduct market surveys, make studies of group dynamics, and suggest ways of increasing morale. Most of these devices were originally used by business, but some of them have been taken over by churches, social welfare agencies, labor unions, and other non-pecuniary organizations.

Formal organization, then, is dedicated to furthering the stated goals of the bureaucracy. Formal organization includes, in summary, "the systems, policies, rules, and regulations . . . which express what the relations of one person to another are supposed to be. . . . It prescribes the relations that are supposed to obtain within the human organization and between the human organization and the technical organization."[28] In this sense, the principles of formal organization in a legal-rational bureaucracy apply to a governmental agency, a military organization, a corporation, a church, a factory, or a university.

The Informal Structure of Bureaucracy

The bureaucracy also includes an informal organization, evolved by the members to protect themselves against depersonalization by the formal organization. In some cases, as we shall see, the informal organization is encouraged by

---

[27] The following is adapted from Alvin W. Gouldner, *op. cit.*, p. 408.

[28] F. J. Roethlisberger and William J. Dickson, *Management and the Worker* (Cambridge: Harvard University Press, 1939), quoted by Robert K. Merton, *et al.* (eds.), *Reader in Bureaucracy, op. cit.*, p. 255.

the formal. Among the factors giving rise to informal organization are the following:[29]

1. The employee may develop defense reactions, such as daydreaming, aggression toward his fellows, and ambivalent (mixed) reactions toward the company.

2. The employee may become apathetic and indifferent, and his behavior may take such forms as loafing on the job, restricting quotas (see below), and making deliberate errors.

3. The employees may gather in informal groups that sanction the above attitudes and symbolize their lack of self-involvement with the formal organization.

4. The employees may (with or without the cooperation of the management) perpetuate these informal groups and evolve permanent norms, thereby establishing an *informal organization* in the plant or office.

The existence of informal organization has long been intuitively grasped by such literary observers of bureaucracy as Balzac and Kafka. Likewise, foremen, managers, and supervisors have empirically understood these procedures by the rank-and-file employees. The role of the informal organization, however, was not scientifically demonstrated until the classic researches of Roethlisberger and Dickson on the Bank Wiring Observation Room in the Hawthorne Plant of the Western Electric Company in Chicago. The research concerned the informal reactions of the employees to a wage incentive plan established by the company and providing that remuneration be based upon both individual and group production.[30]

This plan was a product of the formal organization of the company and was conceived in accordance with the rational procedures of corporate bureaucracy. In their interaction with one another, however, the men worked out an informal organization that was very different. This organization consisted, in effect, of setting their own informal production limits. An employee who did *more* work than the group thought he should was called a "rate-buster." The one who did *less* than the group norm was called a "chiseler." In each case, the work group set the norms and the employees conformed to this informal pattern, rather than to the formal one set by the management. The formal organization was not completely ignored, but it was definitely modified by informal interaction.

The influence of informal organization in a bureaucratic structure was also demonstrated in studies of the armed forces during World War II. By its very nature, a military organization is both bureaucratic and authoritarian, since its lines of authority are clearly drawn and the individual is constrained on pain of punishment to obey. In an effort to erect a buffer between themselves and formal authority, enlisted men have, from time immemorial, established informal

---

[29] The following is adapted from Chris Argyris, *Understanding Organizational Behavior* (Homewood, Illinois: The Dorsey Press, Inc., 1960), pp. 16-17.

[30] F. J. Roethlisberger and William J. Dickson, *op. cit.*, pp. 255-258.

organizations of their own. The soldier is loyal to his immediate primary group and the norms which it evolves, and he does his best to keep faith with this informal organization. The soldier carries out his combat mission so that he will not let the group down, rather than from patriotism or personal hatred of the enemy. Once again, formal and informal organizations interact to further the ultimate goals of the structure.[31]

Informal organization also performs certain more general functions in the bureaucratic structure. Many of the motivations for informal organization, as we have seen, reflect the desires of individuals to protect themselves against authority, to get around the rules, and to get things done in their own way. Out of these individual interactions emerge more general behavior patterns, which are often tacitly recognized by management as well as the rank-and-file. Many of these emerging patterns represent adjustments to changing circumstances in ways not covered by the rules. These changes are more apparent in business and industry than in government, but to a certain extent they characterize any institutional structure in a dynamic society. No matter how routine the problems may be, they cannot always be met by rigorously "following the book." Individual initiative is always a valuable addition, within limits, to formal organization.

The "theory" of bureaucratic organization is therefore continually supplemented by the "practice" of informal organization. This is especially apparent in large-scale business organizations in American society. Americans have been traditionally suspicious of anything that smacks of arbitrary coercion, whether in public affairs or business activities. Hence men in industrial organizations in this country have been more willing to experiment, to act empirically, and to look for new ways of doing things than have their counterparts in Europe. The "newness" of American society has meant that behavior patterns are not so encrusted with tradition as those of the Old World—whether in government, education, or business enterprise. The comparative absence of social stratification (or the lack of awareness of it) has likewise worked against any tendency to accept uncritically the theory and practice of bureaucracy as set forth by Max Weber and other European scholars, from more highly stratified societies.

Many large-scale enterprises, therefore, have a constant interaction between the formal and the informal. Some of this interaction, as we have seen, is not sanctioned by the management, who often try to make the rank-and-file follow the established procedures. Other such interaction is encouraged by the front office, either tacitly or overtly, because of the added efficiency, *esprit de corps*, and incentive that accompanies it. To further informal interaction, the leaders may: (*a*) have periodic "informal" meetings with their employees to learn what the latter are thinking; (*b*) send down commands for new and "unofficial" action by "tested" personnel; (*c*) permit favored subordinates to depart from formal routines; (*d*) assign "unofficial" roles to chosen personnel so that the

---

[31] Edward A. Shils, "The Study of the Primary Group," in Daniel Lerner and Harold D. Lasswell (eds.), *The Policy Sciences* (Stanford: Stanford University Press, 1951).

latter can experiment without actually changing the formal practices; (*e*) pretend not to see departures from formal behavior when they (the management) believe that such departures are constructive; (*f*) establish informal, two-way channels of communication with rank-and-file personnel; and (*g*) incorporate into the formal organization some of the practices that have been worked out informally.[32]

In any large-scale organization, however, the formal structure must, in the final analysis, continue to dominate the interaction. Concessions are often made in the interests of greater harmony, as well as greater efficiency, but the final decision rests with the formal organization. As Dalton puts it, "First, the formal largely orders the direction the informal takes. Second, it consequently shapes the character of defenses created by the informal. And third, whether the formal is brightly or dimly existent in the blur of contradictions, it requires overt conformity to its precepts." [33] If control does not remain with the formal organization, the advantages of such organization will be minimized and, perhaps, ultimately destroyed. One of the intangible, but very real, qualities of leadership in a large organization is therefore to know when to follow the formal role-structure and when to depart from it. This dynamic interplay between the formal and the informal is essential to the delicate balance between continuity and change in large organizations.

The Dysfunctions of Bureaucracy

The advantages of bureaucracy arise from the fact that a legal-rational structure is necessary in modern, large-scale organization, whether public or private, profit or nonprofit, sacred or secular. As Max Weber pointed out many years before the corporation had reached its present size, capitalistic enterprise would be impossible without bureaucratic organization. He emphasized the interrelationships between capitalism and bureaucratic organization as follows: "On the one hand," he said, "capitalism in its modern stages of development strongly tends to foster the development of bureaucracy. . . . Conversely," he continued, "capitalism is the most rational economic basis for bureaucratic administration and enables it to develop in the most rational form because, from a fiscal point of view, it supplies the necessary money resources." [34]

The United States Steel Corporation would therefore be just as helpless as the United States Government if neither had a formal, hierarchical, structured organization, marked by established authority, a definite chain of command, channels of communication, and a competent and disciplined personnel. Some of these characteristics are more apparent in government than in private organizations, but the bureaucratic essentials are similar. The coordination of the vast and far-flung activities of a large organization, whether church, corpora-

---

[32] The above is adapted from Melville Dalton, *Men Who Manage* (New York: John Wiley & Sons, Inc., 1959), pp. 226-238.

[33] *Ibid.*, p. 237.

[34] Max Weber, *op. cit.*, pp. 338-339.

tion, philanthropic foundation, university, or labor union, would be impossible without some such legal-rational structure as we have outlined. In summary, "The chief merit of bureaucracy is its technical efficiency, with a premium placed on precision, speed, expert control, continuity, discretion. . . ." [35]

The dysfunctions of bureaucracy involve both the difficulties that interfere with the operation of any given bureaucracy and the disadvantages of bureaucratic organization *as such* to society. These dysfunctions are part of the price we pay for the complexity of modern life, whether in the Boy Scouts of America, the United Automobile Workers, or the Ford Motor Company. In many cases, the dysfunctions are merely the other side of the functions. Formality brings rigidity; hierarchy downgrades the individual; procedure means red tape. The bureaucratic role requires that functionaries get their work done as efficiently as possible. This emphasis often becomes an end in itself, rather than a means to a broader end. The bureaucrat may become rigid and stereotyped in his thinking and correspondingly unable to respond to a situation not covered by the regulations.[36]

In his analysis of bureaucracy, Bendix speaks of "authoritarian" and "democratic" structures, by which he refers primarily to different degrees of obedience and authority. Each of these forms has its dysfunctions, arising from the qualities inherent therein. The authoritarian bureaucracy is often marked by conflicting cliques, suspicious of each other, and using spies to see what the other is doing. The bureaucracies of Nazi Germany and the Soviet Union demonstrated this form of dysfunction when carried to its logical extreme, with conflicting groups engaged in a murderous struggle for self-preservation.[37]

A major problem of the democratic bureaucracy is to find and keep able men. Failing this, says Bendix, the bureaucracy may function badly "because the frustrations of administrative work may deter qualified men and because suspicion of authority goes so far as to make efficient policy formulation and execution impossible." [38] He is speaking here primarily of governmental bureaucracy in this country, with its traditional suspicion of political control. As we have seen, no such difficulty arises in recruiting promising young men for large corporate bureaucracies. Thousands of college graduates are only too happy to become organization men.

A general dysfunction of bureaucracy that is common to all large organizations is the lack of correspondence between the emotional needs of the individual and the rational structure of the organization. A mature person has strong needs, among others, to control his immediate environment, to express his individuality, and to maintain a favorable self-image. In a large, bureaucratic organization, these needs are difficult for him to fulfill. He is unable to control his working conditions; he can seldom express his preferences about his job; and he has trouble maintaining a favorable self-image in an impersonal setting.

[35] Robert K. Merton, "Bureaucratic Structure and Personality," *op. cit.*, p. 561.
[36] *Ibid.*
[37] Reinhard Bendix, "Bureaucracy: The Problem and Its Setting," *op. cit.*, pp. 504-505.
[38] *Ibid.*, p. 506.

The rational goals of the organization deal only incidentally with such matters. The organization is impersonal, the self is highly personal, and the twain seldom meet.[39]

Many of the dysfunctions of bureaucracy are symbolized by the concept of "red tape." This phrase carries connotations of endless and pointless delay, avoidance of responsibility, transfer of papers from desk to desk, impersonality carried to the point of brutality, and other components of a Kafkaesque nightmare of bureaucracy. Red tape becomes a social problem when it threatens the values of the person who encounters it. To the one who understands the necessity of bureaucratic procedure, this process is considered at best a desirable quality and at worst a necessary evil. To the one who is delayed and frustrated by rational procedure, red tape is an infuriating problem.

Red tape is defined as a social problem in the following context:[40]

1. It is unnecessary. Red tape is unnecessary, inefficient, and interfering, inasmuch as it is interposed between the individual and his goal. The goal may be borrowing money from a bank, getting a driver's license, or applying for social security benefits.

2. It is an invasion of privacy. Red tape is also seen as an invasion of privacy. The person who must tell the bank why he wants a loan; the soldier who must tell his commanding officer why he wants a weekend pass; and the automobile owner who must fill out an elaborate questionnaire before the insurance company will consider his claim—these examples of red tape are viewed as unnecessary encroachments upon privacy.

3. It is too impersonal. Bureaucracy is a secondary group organized for activity that cannot be adequately performed by a primary group.[41] The resulting impersonality is an added annoyance to the person who wants to be treated in primary-group fashion—i.e., "as a human being." The motorist arrested for speeding, the student accused of cheating, and the clerk who takes the afternoon off and goes to the baseball game all want to be treated as individuals, not as anonymous victims caught in the toils of bureaucracy.[42]

4. It is undemocratic. Red tape is believed to obstruct some persons and not others. The critic naturally believes that *his* goals are the ones that are obstructed. Other people, he insists indignantly, do not have to pay as high taxes as he does; other people get their speeding tickets fixed, whereas *he* gets fined; other people are promoted faster than he is. In each case, he feels that he is being treated "unfairly"—i.e., undemocratically.[43]

5. It makes no sense. Red tape "makes no sense," is "meaningless" and "confused." This sense of meaninglessness reaches the point of madness in the novels of Franz Kafka, where the hero (if that is the word) struggles through an

---

[39] Chris Argyris, *op. cit.,* pp. 14-15.

[40] The following is adapted from Alvin W. Gouldner, "Red Tape as a Social Problem," in Robert K. Merton, *et al.* (eds.), *Reader in Bureaucracy, op. cit.,* pp. 410-418.

[41] Ellsworth Faris, "The Primary Group: Essence and Accident," *American Journal of Sociology,* 38:41-50 (July, 1932).

[42] Robert K. Merton, "Bureaucratic Structure and Personality," *op. cit.,* pp. 368-369.

[43] *Ibid.,* pp. 369-370.

endless maze of bureaucratic procedures, in which he ultimately loses every-thing, including his life.

6. *It is infuriating.* The sensitive sufferer from red tape ends his encounters with bureaucratic procedure in a state of apoplectic frustration. This distress-ing experience happens to some people and not to others. The variable in the situation is the personality of the individual, not the nature of the bureaucratic experience. Some people take red tape in their stride, others are only mildly bored, and still others become livid with fury.

The dysfunctions of bureaucracy may be briefly summarized. A number of different factors, singly or in combination, may either impair the efficient func-tioning of a bureaucracy or cause it to break down completely. Among these factors are: (a) overloading the organization with useless personnel; (b) over-lapping and duplication of functions between different units; (c) political pa-tronage in assigning persons to administrative positions, outside of bureaucratic procedures; (d) inadequately educated and trained personnel; (e) indecision and conflict in establishing policies and carrying them out; (f) insufficient sal-aries to get and keep good men; (g) lack of administrative skills, especially in the higher echelons; (h) internal rivalry by conflicting cliques and factions; and (i) paralysis of activity because of sheer organizational inertia (red tape). Some of these factors are found to a degree in *all* bureaucratic organizations (e.g., internal rivalry); others are peculiar to old, established bureaucratic or-ganizations in advanced countries (e.g., paralysis of activity); and still others apply chiefly to the emerging bureaucracies of underdeveloped countries (e.g., inadequately trained personnel). These and other manifest dysfunctions indi-cate that bureaucratic organization is no panacea.

The Balance Sheet of Bureaucracy

Bureaucracy has an important influence upon both the structure and goals of a society. We may first examine the implications of bureaucracy for the implemen-tation of democratic goals. On the credit side of the ledger, bureaucracy tends to decrease the differences between social classes and to level social gradations based upon birth, race, religion, and ethnic background.[44] In a stratified soci-ety, social privileges are inherited and position depends largely upon birth. The son of a peasant, farmer, small shopkeeper, or industrial worker finds it hard to rise in the class structure. Upward mobility is correspondingly limited. Bureauc-racy provides one of the few ways in which such mobility is possible. During the Middle Ages, the bureaucracy of the Roman Catholic Church was virtually the only mechanism whereby a peasant's son could become the equal (or even the superior) of a scion of the landed aristocracy.

The personnel policies of bureaucracy also contribute to the equalitarian goals of democracy. The individual is, in theory at least, appointed to his posi-tion because of his technical competence, which is based upon such considera-

---

[44] Max Weber, *The Theory of Social and Economic Organization, op. cit.*, p. 340.

tions as native ability and educational advancement. In the federal bureaucracy, Negroes with the necessary competence do not encounter the same degree of prejudice and discrimination as in private industry. The Negro college graduate can enter the bureaucracy on the same basis as his white contemporary. This does not mean, of course, that race prejudice is completely eliminated in the federal (or any other) bureaucracy; most bureau chiefs are still white. But it *does* mean that the impersonal qualifications for bureaucratic service tend to *minimize* the handicap of racial differences.[45]

The armed forces of the United States constitute another bureaucratic organization where substantial progress has recently been made in the minimization of undemocratic practices. The army, navy, and air force have, until comparatively recently, enforced ritual avoidance among their personnel, which meant in practice the maintenance of racially segregated units. In recent years, integration has proceeded rapidly in all three branches of the service, and the segregation of combat units has been abolished. The impetus for these changes has not come from the armed forces *because* of their bureaucratic character. The winds of freedom have blown *from* the society *to* the services, and not vice versa. The point is, rather, that changes of this kind are easier to introduce and make effective because of the bureaucratic nature of the service organizations. Directives introduced from above must be carried out through the chain of command and the various levels of bureaucratic authority.

The administration of large-scale public housing is another field in which bureaucratic organization has minimized, although not eliminated, undemocratic practices. Under recent legislation, apartments built wholly or partially with federal funds are open to all citizens, irrespective of race, religion, or ethnic background. The costs of such housing are so great, the business risks so formidable, and the financial return often so low that public aid is necessary for this type of construction. This aid is administered through the Federal Housing Authority, which is a bureaucratic organization established to carry out the mandate of a democratic society. Without such rational and impersonal procedure, the principles of equality of housing would be impossible to realize. When left to themselves, private persons continue to discriminate against the Negro, in the North as well as in the South.[46]

Equality under the law is another sector in which bureaucracy furthers democratic goals, provided that the directing forces in the society fully believe in these goals. The bureaucratic structure of the federal courts has been the chief bulwark of freedom for the Negro in fields ranging from education to voting and from transportation to recreation. Race prejudice is still strongly entrenched in local communities, especially in the Deep South, and the federal judiciary has been forced to throw the full weight of its authority into the battle for civil rights. The most spectacular single instance of this pressure began with the Supreme Court decision of May 17, 1954 and has continued through

[45] Peter M. Blau, *op. cit.*, pp. 114-115.
[46] Donald O. Cowgill, "Trends in Residential Segregation of Nonwhites in American Cities, 1940-1950," *American Sociological Review*, 21:43-47 (February, 1956).

the long series of federal court actions to secure compliance with this decision. Without the centralization, rationalization, and hierarchical structure of the federal courts, whose power of enforcement stems directly from the President of the United States, the struggle for civil rights in this and other sectors would have been lost before it began.[47]

Bureaucracy also plays an important role in the implementation of social change through invention. This function is directly contrary to the belief of many persons, who uncritically assume that bureaucracy, per se, exerts a reactionary influence upon innovations. The "invention" of the atomic bomb, for example, is popularly supposed to have sprung full-blown from the brains of a long list of scientists, from Einstein to Oppenheimer. In a sense, this is true, but the vast expenditures of money, the prolonged series of experiments, the difficult procurement of materials, and the complicated procedure of testing—all these could never have been possible without a complex bureaucratic organization. Some people, of course, suggest that this vast expenditure of men, money, and materials might have been directed more wisely into other fields. But there is no question that this tremendous scientific innovation, along with many others, would have been impossible without bureaucratic organization.[48]

Bureaucracy is also a basic element in mass society.[49] As such, bureaucracy plays an important role in maintaining the democratic process against the forces making for totalitarianism. Along with mass communication and the equalitarian ideology, bureaucracy helps to relate the individual to the larger society. The man who votes for a national political party, who collects his social security check, or who works for a large corporation, participates in a bureaucratic process that takes him out of his isolation and introduces him to democratic, as distinguished from totalitarian, ideas and practices. The elements of bureaucracy which we have outlined make for political equalitarianism, rather than the extremist politics of Fascism or Communism. The leveling of social barriers, minimization of racial differences, and equality before the law are bureaucratic, as well as democratic, forces in American society. In these and other ways, bureaucracy encourages democracy and discourages totalitarianism.[50]

Despite these manifest advantages, many students of bureaucracy remain strongly ambivalent toward this form of organization. The basic question is the location of ultimate power—whether, in short, bureaucracy is to be "master or servant, an independent body or a tool—and if a tool, whose interests it can be made to serve." [51] For any bureaucracy to carry out its functions in the most rational and efficient manner, it must have a considerable degree of power. Its members, furthermore, must have specialized training, a high level of morale, a knowledge of the rules, and substantial freedom from outside interference.

[47] Peter M. Blau, *op. cit.,* p. 115.
[48] *Ibid.,* pp. 91-92.
[49] See Chapter 24.
[50] Joseph R. Gusfield, "Mass Society and Extremist Politics," *American Sociological Review,* 27:19-30 (February, 1962).
[51] S. N. Eisenstadt, *op. cit.,* p. 100.

The civil service, for example, must have security and tenure and a large measure of autonomy in its hiring and firing or it will become a political football.

The more efficiently the bureaucracy performs its functions, however, the more power it will gather about it. Power struggles may arise between the bureaucracy and its legally constituted managers. The latter may be elected officials of a government or stockholders of a corporation. In extreme situations, a military bureaucracy may refuse to obey the civil authorities, and may overthrow the legal government. The regulation of bureaucracy is a delicate operation. If the regulation is too severe, the bureaucracy may be unable to carry out its goals. If the regulation is too loose, these goals may dominate the society as a whole. The bureaucratic organization then becomes an end in itself, rather than a means to a democratic end.

The basic problem of bureaucracy thus involves the relationship between *bureaucracy* and *bureaucratization*. "Bureaucracy" refers to the continued employment of large-scale, rational, hierarchical organization in the fields of government, business, education, welfare, recreation, and religion. "Bureaucratization" refers to the relative increase in power of these organizations and their dominance over widening spheres of human activity. The problem is one between bureaucracy as means and end. In other words, the primary concern is the relation "between the acquisition of power necessary for fulfilment of what are seen as the society's and the bureaucracy's legitimate function on the one hand and usurpation of such power, displacement of goals, and growing bureaucratization on the other." [52]

Modern society cannot exist without bureaucracy. Social interaction has become so complex that it cannot operate without bureaucratic organization. This is as true in corporate, as in governmental, enterprise. In view of this functional necessity, the problem is one of minimizing the disadvantages of bureaucracy. This is admittedly easier said than done. One way out of this dilemma is to increase democratic participation in organizational behavior.[53] Such participation begins on the local level, where more people could spend more time on politics, public welfare, and education. Increased bureaucratic organization of business and industry has so increased productivity in the advanced countries that men have more leisure than ever before. If they would devote some of this leisure to participation in public causes, the spectre of bureaucratic domination might be exorcised.[54]

In the final analysis, bureaucracy is an instrument for performing certain types of activities in a complex society. As an instrument, bureaucracy by itself does not embody basic value judgments about the nature of the society which it serves. We have indicated some of the ways in which bureaucracy may implement the democratic values of our society. In totalitarian societies, bureaucracy obviously implements undemocratic values. Many totalitarian regimes in West-

---

[52] *Ibid.*, p. 103.
[53] Peter M. Blau, *op. cit.*, pp. 117-118.
[54] Scott Greer and Peter Orleans, "The Mass Society and the Parapolitical Structure," *American Sociological Review*, 27:634-646 (October, 1962).

ern countries have developed and maintained vast bureaucratic structures. Since the turn of the century, German bureaucracy has served the monarchy of Kaiser Wilhelm, the Weimar Republic, the totalitarian Nazi regime, and the postwar West German Republic. Czarist and Communist Russia have both been directed by large bureaucracies.

On the other hand, democratic France has long had one of the most highly developed and trained bureaucracies in the world. Sweden and Great Britain, to name two other countries with a long and cherished tradition of political and social democracy, likewise enjoy efficient and scrupulous governmental bureaucracies. Hundreds of thousands of civil servants faithfully serve the various agencies of government in the United States at the local, state, and federal levels. Bureaucracy is therefore a form of social and institutional structure that can be used for different ends.

SELECTED BIBLIOGRAPHY

Argyris, Chris, *Understanding Organizational Behavior*. Homewood, Illinois: The Dorsey Press, Inc., 1960. The author of this book is a specialist in the systematic study of social organizations. He presents here a theoretical framework and an outline of specific suggestions for the analysis of factories, offices, and similar bureaucratic structures.

Bendix, Reinhard, "Bureaucracy: The Problem and Its Setting," *American Sociological Review*, 12:493-507 (October, 1947). A leading student of modern bureaucracy examines the nature, forms, functions, and pathologies of bureaucratic organizations, with a wealth of illustrations drawn from all types of such organizations.

Blau, Peter M., *Bureaucracy in Modern Society*. New York: Random House, Inc., 1956. In this brief and lucid analysis, the author sets forth the important facts about bureaucracy, both in theory and operation. The book is recommended for the student who wishes to learn more about these (bureaucratic) organizations that are coming increasingly to dominate modern society.

Dalton, Melville, *Men Who Manage*. New York: John Wiley & Sons, Inc., 1959. This is an empirical study of several corporations engaged in different types of business. The author is interested in the extent to which the companies follow the formal organization rigorously and the extent to which they depart from it. Chapter 8 is especially concerned with the "informal" organization.

Eisenstadt, S. N., "Bureaucracy and Bureaucratization," *Current Sociology* (Volume 7). London: Basil Blackwell, 1958 (Prepared with the assistance of UNESCO). This analysis of the nature and trends in bureaucracy is supplemented by an extensive international bibliography. The author returns repeatedly to his crucial question—namely, is bureaucracy to be master or slave?

Gouldner, Alvin W., "Organizational Analysis," in Robert K. Merton, *et al.* (eds.), *Sociology Today*. New York: Basic Books, Inc., 1959. The author gives us a sociological framework for the study of all types of formal organizations in modern life, of which the bureaucratic organization is an important example.

Merton, Robert K., "Bureaucratic Structure and Personality," *Social Forces,* 18:560-568 (May, 1940). This brief article contains a wealth of insights on the role of bureaucracy in modern life, with particular reference to the personality as it evolves in a bureaucratic setting.

Merton, Robert K., *et al.* (eds.), *Reader in Bureaucracy.* Glencoe, Illinois: The Free Press, 1952. This reader is the most extensive single source of information on the sociological study of bureaucracy. The authors range in time from Max Weber to students of bureaucracy in its modern forms.

Roethlisberger, F. J., and W. J. Dickson, *Management and the Worker.* Cambridge: Harvard University Press, 1939. In this empirical study of corporate bureaucracy, the authors made a classic analysis of the evolution of *informal* organizations in the midst of the *formal* organization.

Weber, Max, *The Theory of Social and Economic Organization* (Translated by A. M. Henderson and Talcott Parsons). New York: Oxford University Press, 1947. This is a translation of important sections of the work of one of the great pioneer sociologists. As such, it is the most easily available source in English of Max Weber's definitive analysis of bureaucracy, which has stimulated most of the subsequent work in the field.

Whyte, William H., Jr., *The Organization Man.* New York: Simon and Schuster, 1956. In this popular study, the author has not only contributed a highly descriptive phrase to current usage ("the organization man"), but has given us an original and well-written analysis of the bureaucratic aspects of the large corporation and its impact upon the rising young executive.

18 *The Family*

The Changing Family

The family is the universal institution. It is the most multi-functional of all the institutions, even though in our society many of its former functions have been partially taken over by other institutions. In many societies, the family is still the principal social pattern that can be called institutional. Social control, education, religion, protection, recreation, and the rest of the institutional functions are conducted by the family in these societies. Even in our own, the family performed many of these general functions until comparatively recently. As this society has become increasingly industrialized, urbanized, and secular-

405

ized, the family has lost many of its former functions. In the present chapter, we shall survey this massive change in the oldest social institution, which has affected every man, woman, and child.[1]

The progressive shift in function away from the family has been received unhappily by many persons. The traditional family has assumed an ideal quality in the mores, and any departure is viewed as an infringement upon sacred values. The family of an earlier day, with its rural background, its many children, its multifunctional character, and its patriarchal roles, became the ideal pattern, the family as it "should" be. The contemporary urban family is an obvious departure from this pattern, and it therefore arouses a vague uneasiness in those persons whose values are based upon the family as it used to be.

The accusation has thus been directed at the family that it is falling down on the job, that it is somehow failing to do its duty, whether from deliberate negligence or moral turpitude. The family is, obviously, not justly open to such recriminations because it is neither a *person* nor a *thing*, but a *culture pattern*. The family lives in and through the behavior of its members, who alone are responsible for their actions. Furthermore, the transfer of functions from the family to other institutions has not so much reflected a "failure" of the family as the ability of other institutions to perform certain functions *better* than the family. The traditional large family provided much of the recreation of its members because it was the only organized cultural pattern available for such a purpose. The neighborhood movie is better organized to provide recreation, of a sort, than the most talented family.[2]

Social institutions may be viewed not only as performing certain functions but as fulfilling certain values. The concept of function implies that the needs satisfied by the institution are more or less continuous. The concept of social values means that the possibilities for realizing and enhancing these values are virtually unlimited. As a social institution, the family may be viewed as correcting, ratifying, and extending the values of its members through sharing new experiences with others. The values of consumption, recreation, security, affection, companionship, and the like can be extended indefinitely. As Foote and Cottrell put it: "Family functions have often been transferred to other institutions, not because of the failure of the family to do its duty, but because another could realize the values involved even more fully." [3]

The family in American society has been defined by the Bureau of the Census as "a group of two or more persons residing together who are related by blood, marriage, or adoption." [4] This is the definition used in gathering and compiling census statistics, which constitute the basic quantitative source of knowledge of the family. In functional terms, the family may be viewed as an endur-

---

[1] William F. Ogburn and Meyer F. Nimkoff, *Technology and the Changing Family* (Boston: Houghton Mifflin Company, 1955), Chapter 1, "What Has Been Happening to the Family?"

[2] Nelson N. Foote and Leonard S. Cottrell, Jr., *Identity and Interpersonal Competence* (Chicago: University of Chicago Press, 1955), Chapter 3.

[3] *Ibid.,* p. 99.

[4] Bureau of the Census, *Current Population Reports: Population Characteristics,* "Martial Status and Family Status: March 1962," Series P-20, No. 122 (March 22, 1963), p. 5.

ing relationship of parents and children that performs such functions as the protection, rearing, and socialization of children and the providing of intimate responses between its members. The contemporary family stands or falls on its success in performing these and related functions.[5]

The institutional aspects of the family may be further considered in terms of the "related type parts" constituting the generalized structure of social institutions. The characteristic type parts of the family structure are as follows:[6]

1. Attitudes and behavior patterns. The family is based upon a group of "common reciprocating attitudes of individuals and their conventionalized behavior patterns." Included are such attitudes and emotions as "love, affection, devotion, loyalty, and parental respect." Without these common and reciprocal expectations, the family would lack cultural unity and continuity.

2. Symbolic culture traits. The family also includes various "objects charged with emotional and sentimental meaning to which human behavior has been conditioned." These symbolic elements range from wedding rings to marriage ceremonies, and they are important because, as symbols, they stand for something more basic and meaningful than themselves.

3. Utilitarian culture traits. The family institution also embraces certain physical objects to which the members are attached and which play a utilitarian role in family activities. The home, furniture, and the family automobile are among the elements that make possible the day-to-day life of the group and that, in their turn, assume symbolic meanings.

4. Oral or written specifications. A final element in the institutional structure of the family is a group of "oral or written language symbols which preserve the descriptions and specifications of the . . . interrelationships among attitudes, symbolic culture traits, and utilitarian culture traits." In this category are marriage licenses, birth certificates, and last wills and testaments, all of which bear witness to the institutional nature of the family and the personal crises through which its members must pass.

Marriage and the Family

Marriage and the family are related but not synonymous. Marriage is a relationship between two adults of the opposite sex, whereas the family ordinarily involves two generations—parent(s) and offspring. Marriage is thus "a complex of customs centering upon the relationship between a sexually associating pair of adults. . . . Marriage defines the manner of establishing and terminating such a relationship, the normative behavior and reciprocal obligations within it, and the locally accepted restrictions upon its personnel."[7]

---

[5] See Robert F. Winch, *The Modern Family* (New York: Holt, Rinehart and Winston, Inc., 1963), Revised Edition, Chapter 1.

[6] The following is adapted from F. Stuart Chapin, *Cultural Change* (New York: Appleton-Century-Crofts, Inc., 1928), pp. 48-49.

[7] George P. Murdock, *Social Structure* (New York: The Macmillan Company, 1949), p. 1.

The American people are becoming increasingly enchanted with marriage. This fact is in striking refutation of the gloomy (and erroneous) pronouncements that we are losing faith in marriage. As we indicated in Chapter 11, the proportion of the population married is at a high point. In 1890, when statistics on marital status were first tabulated, 61.2 per cent of the male population 14 years of age and older were married, as compared with 69.2 per cent in 1962. The corresponding percentages for the female population were 59.4 and 65.3.[8] Instead of being dissatisfied with the marital status, as might be inferred from the comparatively high divorce rate, the people of the United States have become more and more delighted with it.

The age at which men and women enter this happy state has declined over the past seventy years. In 1890, the median age at first marriage for men was 26.1 years and for women 22.0 years. Half the persons were above and half below the median figure. In 1962, the median for men was 22.7 years and for women 20.3 years. As shown in Table 9, the greatest change in the median age of marriage for both men and women occurred in the 1940's. In round numbers, approximately half of the men in this country today who will ever marry do so before the age of 22.7 years and half of the women before 20.3 years.[9]

Many of the readers of this book will marry somewhat later than the median figure, since they are presently in college and (often) preparing for graduate work. The majority of men and women in this country, however, do not attend (much less finish) college. They are the ones who bring the median age of marriage down. This decline in recent decades is due to a number of social and technological factors. Among these are: (a) the increase in semiskilled industrial employment, whereby young men just out of high school can earn high wages at an early age; (b) the increase in the employment of women, more than a third of whom work during the first year of marriage; (c) the increase in the income of the population as a whole, which has provided both economic and psychological security and encouraged people to marry young.

The family in our society is a *conjugal* unit—that is, one based upon the central relationship of husband and wife. The family grows out of the marriage of a man and a woman and, except in certain statistical senses, ceases to exist when this union is dissolved. The children born of this relationship are the other principal element of the conjugal family, which is a small, closely knit, and highly emotional group. The other relatives in the conjugal pattern—grandparents, uncles, aunts, and in-laws—play a relatively unimportant role in the family as we know it.

We are so accustomed to think of the family in these terms that any other pattern is both difficult and repugnant to visualize. Another important family pattern, however, is maintained by millions of persons in different parts of the world and is well suited to its cultural setting. We refer to the *consanguine*

[8] Bureau of the Census, *Current Population Reports: Population Characteristics,* "Marital Status and Family Status: March 1962," Series P-20, No. 122 (March 22, 1963), Table 1.

[9] Bureau of the Census, *Current Population Reports: Population Characteristics,* "Marital Status and Family Status: March 1962," *op. cit.,* Table C.

Table 9. Median Age at First Marriage, by Sex, for the United States, March 1960 to 1962, and for Conterminous United States, 1890 to 1959

Year	Male*	Female	Year	Male*	Female
1962	22.7	20.3	1951	22.9	20.4
1961	22.8	20.3	1950	22.8	20.3
1960	22.8	20.3	1949	22.7	20.3
			1948	23.3	20.4
1959	22.5	20.2	1947	23.7	20.5
1958	22.6	20.2			
1957	22.6	20.3	1940	24.3	21.5
1956	22.5	20.1	1930	24.3	21.3
1955	22.6	20.2	1920	24.6	21.2
1954	23.0	20.3	1910	25.1	21.6
1953	22.8	20.2	1900	25.9	21.9
1952	23.0	20.2	1890	26.1	22.0

* Figures for 1947 to 1962 are based on Current Population Survey data supplemented by data from the Department of Defense on marital status by age for men in the armed forces.

Source: Bureau of the Census, *Current Population Reports: Population Characteristics,* "Marital Status and Family Status: March 1962," *op. cit.,* Table C.

family, in which the central relationship is not that of spouses but rather of blood relatives. Linton notes that the consanguine family consists of "a nucleus of blood relatives surrounded by a fringe of spouses," whereas the conjugal family consists of "a nucleus of spouses and their offspring surrounded by a fringe of relatives." [10]

Under the consanguine family system, men and women marry and enter into sexual relationships, but the spouses remain in their parental families, surrounded by persons of their own "blood" (hence the name *consanguine*). This pattern is more permanent and continuous than the conjugal family, since it does not depend for its origin upon the marriage of two persons or for its continuance upon the maintenance of this relationship. In many ways, the consanguine family is more "efficient" than the conjugal. In case of death or divorce, the family goes on and the children are assured of a home. The old persons, furthermore, are not dependent upon their children, but remain within the nucleus of the continuous and permanent family.

The functions of an institution, as we saw in Chapter 16, are the activities performed by its members as they further the purposes of the institution. The family performs a variety of activities in this fashion, including procreation, economic production, consumption, recreation, religious worship, education, and affectionate response. These activities are the *functions* of the family, the things it does or is supposed to do. The heart of any institution lies not so much in its *structure* as in the *functions* it performs and the *values* it enhances. When we say that the family is changing, we mean that it is ceasing to perform certain functions and is concentrating upon others. We shall therefore consider the family in these terms.[11]

---

[10] Ralph Linton, *The Study of Man* (New York: Appleton-Century-Crofts, Inc., 1936), p. 159.
[11] Ogburn and Nimkoff, *op. cit.,* Chapter 6, "Shrinking Functions."

Changing Economic Functions

The broad economic movements of the past century have changed the family from a rural and agricultural institution to one increasingly urban and industrial. The roles of the members have changed correspondingly. In 1870, some 74.3 per cent of the population was listed as rural and 25.7 per cent as urban. In 1962, the *total* farm population comprised only 14,313,000 people, or 7.7 per cent of the total population.[12] The other 92 per cent were either listed as urban or rural-nonfarm; the latter being those who were earning their living otherwise than as farmers, even though some of them continued to live in the open country. We shall consider the composition of the rural, urban, and metropolitan communities in the next chapter. We wish merely to indicate here the extent of the decline in the traditional rural functions of the family. This overall change is the most important the American family has ever undergone in so short a time. Many role changes in related fields follow directly or indirectly from this transition in the socioeconomic base of the family.

In its rural setting, the family was the central unit of both production and consumption. The direct production of goods and services by the family has greatly decreased as a result of changes in the social and economic structure. Only the farm family maintains some of its direct productive functions, in the sense of raising, processing, and selling commodities for the market. As we have seen, less than 8 per cent of all families in the United States are "farm" families in this sense. Relatively speaking, this family retains some aspects of its former economic function, along with some of the other functions whose absence has been viewed with alarm in the urban family. The farm family most closely approximates the traditional "ideal" family and its functions are most nearly those of the family as many persons think it "should" be.

The urban family does not perform a direct productive function, even to the reduced extent of the farm family. Members of the urban family are primarily engaged in working for wages or salaries in order to buy the necessities of life. The shift from the production function is indicated by such indices as the increase in the clothing, canning, and preserving industries, and the growth in the number of restaurants, bakeries, delicatessens, supermarkets, and other stores dispensing food. The increased purchase of canned and frozen food is another indication of the changed production function. Cooking, housecleaning, washing, sewing, and the purchase of food and clothing are among the few productive functions still remaining to the urban family.[13]

A significant change in the division of labor within the family is apparent in the urban, middle-class population. Functions formerly performed by the husband are performed by the wife and vice versa. Many middle-class women now supervise repairs to the house, service the family automobile, purchase such

---

[12] Bureau of the Census—Department of Agriculture, *Farm Population*, "Estimates of the Farm Population of the United States: April 1962," Series Census-ERS (P-27), No. 33 (March 14, 1963), p. 1.
[13] Ogburn and Nimkoff, *op. cit.*, pp. 125-130.

staples as coal and oil, and pay all the bills. Many husbands, conversely, help with the housecleaning, wash the dishes, and change, feed, and bathe the baby —functions formerly included in the role of the wife.[14] These role changes are still largely confined to the middle class, but in the future such modifications may characterize the rural-farm family and the urban working-class family.

Production and consumption are two sides of the same coin. The family consumes whatever it produces, whether in the form of goods, services, commodities, or their equivalent in cash income. Savings are the principal differential between these two functions. We may consider some of the basic trends in consumption, whereby the average family spends the equivalent of its cash income, and sometimes more, in an economy based upon money. The impact of technological development is such that the contemporary American family consumes more and better goods than ever before. This is equivalent to saying that the American family has the highest standard of living in the world.[15]

The median family income in the United States in 1962 was $6,000, the highest figure ever reached. Half of the 47 million families had incomes above $6,000 and half below it. Income is defined by the Bureau of the Census as "the sum of money wage or salary income, net income from self-employment, and income other than earnings, such as net rents, interest, dividends, Social Security benefits, pensions, and public assistance or other governmental payments. Family income represents the combined total received from these sources by all family members during the calendar year."[16] This figure covers money income only, and does not include such items as rent-free housing and commodities produced and consumed on farms. The trends in family income from 1947 to 1962 are shown in Table 10.

The distribution of family income gives a significant indication of the range of family consumption. At the upper end of the income scale, approximately 18 million (39 per cent) of the families had incomes of $7,000 or more in 1962. At the other end, an estimated 9½ million (20 per cent) had money incomes of less than $3,000. At present price levels, these latter families could scarcely be said to live in affluence. In the middle brackets, 9 million (19 per cent) of the families had incomes between $3,000 and $5,000, whereas 10½ million (22 per cent) had incomes between $5,000 and $7,000.[17] The number of families in the different income ranges is shown in Table 11.

Variations naturally exist between families as to the proportion spent for various goods and services. In general, families in the lower income groups spend a larger proportion of their income on food, clothing, and shelter than do those in the upper income groups. As one ascends the income scale, a *decreasing* proportion of the family income is spent for the basic necessities and

[14] E. Gartly Jaco and Ivan Belknap, "Is a New Family Form Emerging in the Urban Fringe?", *American Sociological Review*, 18:551-557 (October, 1953).

[15] William F. Ogburn and Francis R. Allen, "Technological Development and Per Capita Income," *American Journal of Sociology*, 65: 127-131 (September, 1959).

[16] Bureau of the Census, *Current Population Reports: Consumer Income*, "Average Family Income Up 4 Percent in 1962," Series P-60, No. 49 (June 26, 1963), p. 1.

[17] *Ibid.*, p. 1.

an *increasing* proportion for education, recreation (especially automobiles),[18] and clothing. Differences in expenditures also exist between farm and nonfarm families. Farm families spend considerably less for food, clothing, recreation, and reading than do nonfarm families. Conversely, farm families spend more for home furnishings and equipment.[19]

Changing Social Functions

The family has traditionally performed many functions in addition to the economic ones. The family formerly provided a social setting in which (*a*) knowledge, skills, and culture patterns were transmitted; (*b*) the members entertained each other; (*c*) religious training and worship were centered; (*d*) the sick and aged were protected; and (*e*) other related activities were conducted. In a changing society, many of these functions have been taken from the family and allotted to other agencies, some commercial and others governmental. We shall continue our analysis by reviewing briefly some of these changes.

1. *The educational function.* The family was formerly the only educational institution in addition to the church. In an informal sense, the family retains much of this function, especially during the early years of the child. Indeed, as the White House Conference on Children in a Democracy has pointed out, "In

---

[18] In one study of the lower blue-collar worker, however, this class possessed *more* Cadillacs (presumably second or third hand) per capita than *any other* socioeconomic group. See Albert K. Cohen and Harold M. Hodges, Jr., "Characteristics of the Lower-Blue-Collar-Class," *Social Problems*, 10:303-334 (Spring, 1963).

[19] Inter-Agency Committee on Background Materials, National Conference on Family Life, *The American Family: A Factual Background* (Washington, 1948), pp. 73-76.

Table 10. Family Income, 1947, 1950, and 1953 to 1962: Families by Total Money Income, for the United States

Total money income	1962	1961	1960	1959	1958	1957
Number (in thousands)	46,998	46,341	45,435	45,062	44,202	43,714
Per cent	100.0	100.0	100.0	100.0	100.0	100.0
Under $500	2.1	2.4	2.5	2.4	2.6	3.0
$500 to $999	2.1	2.6	2.5	2.7	3.0	3.4
$1,000 to $1,499	3.5	3.6	3.8	4.0	3.9	4.0
$1,500 to $1,999	3.9	4.1	4.2	4.3	4.8	4.5
$2,000 to $2,499	4.3	4.6	4.5	4.6	5.1	5.2
$2,500 to $2,999	4.0	4.1	4.2	4.7	4.7	4.4
$3,000 to $3,499	4.7	4.8	4.9	5.3	5.3	5.7
$3,500 to $3,999	4.5	4.6	4.9	4.8	5.9	6.1
$4,000 to $4,499	5.0	5.4	5.2	5.9	6.9	7.3
$4,500 to $4,999	4.9	5.1	5.3	5.8	6.5	6.8
$5,000 to $5,999	11.5	11.7	12.9	13.2	13.7	14.5
$6,000 to $6,999	10.9	10.2	10.8	11.0	10.7	10.3
$7,000 to $7,999	8.6	9.1	8.7	8.4	} 16.8	16.3
$8,000 to $9,999	12.3	11.6	11.3	10.6		
$10,000 to $14,999	12.8	11.3	10.6	9.1	7.6	6.5
$15,000 to $24,999	4.0	3.6	2.8	2.4	1.9	1.4
$25,000 and over	0.9	1.1	0.9	0.7	0.5	0.5
Median income	$5,956	$5,737	$5,620	$5,417	$5,087	$4,971

Source: Bureau of the Census, *Current Population Reports: Consumer Income*, "Average Family Income Up 4 Percent in 1962," *op. cit.*, Table 1.

spite of the great changes which have occurred in family life . . . there is still no more far-reaching educational institution than the family." [20] In our study of personality, we have seen how the basic group norms are passed on through the family. This is the educational process in its most elementary form.

In a more formal sense, however, the educational function of the family has steadily declined. From prenursery school to the university, the educational structure has expanded until it now takes more of the individual's time and energy than ever before. Society has changed from a comparatively simple agricultural and household economy, in which the basic skills were imparted by the parents, to a complex pattern in which the individual must learn other skills in order to adjust. The school is geared to impart this specialized knowledge and the family is not. The family cannot compete with the school in this respect. The child therefore begins his schooling earlier, spends longer hours every day in school, goes to school more days in the year, and spends more years of his life in school than ever before.

The school has recently assumed another function that was formerly considered the sole prerogative of the family, with the collaboration of the church. This is the function of aiding the child to adjust to the world emotionally as well as intellectually. The school increasingly directs its attention to the "whole person," his relationships to others and to himself. Many school systems maintain elaborate "adjustment" staffs, including clinical psychologists, psychiatrists, and social service workers. Visiting teachers examine the home environ-

---

[20] White House Conference on Children in a Democracy, *Final Report*, Children's Bureau Publication No. 272 (Washington, 1942), p. 26.

1956	1955	1954	1953	1950	1947
43,445	42,843	41,934	41,202	39,929	37,237
100.0	100.0	100.0	100.0	100.0	100.0
3.2	3.4	4.6	4.7	5.8	4.4
3.3	4.3	4.2	3.9	5.7	6.4
4.4	4.9	5.6	4.9	6.2	7.8
4.5	4.9	5.4	5.0	7.0	8.8
5.1	5.5	5.5	5.7	8.9	11.3
5.1	5.5	6.4	6.0	8.9	10.7
6.2	7.4	7.5	7.6	11.7	11.3
6.3	7.2	7.9	8.2	9.0	8.4
8.0	8.2	8.4	8.6	7.9	6.9
6.9	7.3	7.2	7.3	5.7	4.7
13.7	12.7	11.9	13.2	9.0	7.7
9.8	9.5	8.5	8.1	5.2	} 8.9
15.6	12.9	11.1	11.6	5.8	
5.9	4.8	4.4	4.1	} 3.3	2.7
1.5	0.9	1.0	1.0		
0.5	0.5	0.4	0.3		
4,783	$4,421	$4,173	$4,233	$3,319	$3,031

Table 11. Number of Families by 1962 Family Income, for the United States

Family income	Number of families
Total	46,998,000
Under $1,000	1,950,000
$1,000 to $1,999	3,469,000
$2,000 to $2,999	3,901,000
$3,000 to $3,999	4,325,000
$4,000 to $4,999	4,669,000
$5,000 to $5,999	5,424,000
$6,000 to $6,999	5,100,000
$7,000 to $7,999	4,023,000
$8,000 to $9,999	5,804,000
$10,000 to $14,999	6,019,000
$15,000 and over	2,314,000

Source: Bureau of the Census, *Current Population Reports: Consumer Income,* "Average Family Income Up 4 Percent in 1962," *op. cit.,* Table A.

ment of the child and attempt to aid him in his adjustment to the outside world. In a less self-conscious age, this work was done by the family and the religious authorities. The school is redefining its function in an increasingly broad sense.[21]

2. *The recreational function.* The family was formerly the principal arena for the recreation of its members. Even those recreational activities conducted away from home were, directly or indirectly, largely under the auspices of the family. Today much of this has changed, despite the renaissance of home recreation through radio and television. The recreational function has been transferred from the home to the movie theater, the bowling alley, the golf course, and the tavern. This transfer has reflected the same broad social trends that have influenced the other functions. Labor-saving devices and the increasing productivity of industry and agriculture have greatly added to the amount of leisure time. Commercial institutions now compete with the family for the leisure hours of its members. This competition is unequal and the family has steadily lost ground as a recreational institution.

The daily experiences of the various members of the family, furthermore, are so different that each has his own idea of recreation. When the activities of the family were more closely concentrated, the members had a similar background of experience and similar ideas about what constituted a change. In the contemporary family, the mother may desire an evening at the movies as a complete change from her day in the home. The father has been away all day and asks no more than a chance to sit down with the evening paper. The children look to their own age group for recreation, and ordinarily amuse themselves away from home.[22] Commercial recreation offers ample opportunity for all of these tastes.

3. *The religious function.* The family has always had a close working relationship with religion. In the intimate family group, the child is "first intro-

---

[21] Federal Security Agency, Office of Education, *Health Services in City Schools,* Bulletin No. 20 (Washington, 1952).

[22] David Riesman, *et al., The Lonely Crowd* (rev. ed.) (New Haven: Yale University Press, 1961).

duced to the religious inheritance of the particular religious group into which he is born. . . . Here the foundations are laid for the moral standards that are to guide his conduct through life." [23] The growing secularization of society has influenced the members and with them the family relationship itself. In general, organized religion plays a less important role than it did a century ago. When the church undergoes a relative decline in importance, the family proportionately ceases to act as a religion-centered institution. This is true, although in varying degrees, in both the Protestant and the Catholic family.

The changing religious function of the Protestant family was examined some years ago by a White House Conference. The role of the family in church attendance, grace at meals, reading of the Bible, and prayers and devotions was examined. Church attendance (with 85 per cent of the rural and 40 per cent of the urban families participating) was the only religious activity in which more than half of the families acted as a unit. Family reading of the Bible engaged the attention of 22 per cent of the rural and 10 per cent of the urban families, and 38 per cent of the rural and 30 per cent of the urban families reported grace before meals. These activities were all presumably part of the regular ceremonial of the majority of Protestant families in colonial America. [24]

A study of the religious activities of the Catholic family suggests that this institution does not live up to "traditional expectations," either in terms of observances or knowledge of Catholic dogma. The study was made of Catholic children at the time they entered parochial school. A distinction was made in this way between the role of the family and the later role of the school. In terms of observances, the Sign of the Cross was the only one in which more than half (52.9 per cent) of the children had the necessary home training. In terms of dogma, less than one-third (30.6 per cent) of the preschool children were able to explain the meaning of the Crucifix, the most important Roman Catholic symbol. The author of this study concluded that "The religious training of the preschool child at home as measured by . . . the present study falls far short of traditional expectations." [25]

4. The protective function. The traditional family was the principal institution that protected the individual in the various vicissitudes of life. In infancy, childhood, adolescence, and old age, the family protected its members as best it could against the ills of the flesh and the crises of the spirit. The family cared for the infant, losing many in the process, but doing the best it could with its limited medical knowledge. The family received the adult member to its collective bosom when he or she was sick, unemployed, or widowed. The family protected its elders when they became unable to care for themselves. In short, the family was the one group to which the individual could look for protection at each step in the seven ages of man.

This function has also been taken over in large part by other agencies, both

---

[23] White House Conference on Children in a Democracy, *op. cit.,* pp. 185-186.

[24] Ernest W. Burgess (ed.), *The Adolescent in the Family* (New York: Appleton-Century-Crofts, Inc., 1934), pp. 171-172.

[25] John L. Thomas, S. J., "Religious Training in the Roman Catholic Family," *American Journal of Sociology,* 57:178-183 (September, 1951), p. 182.

public and private. Private insurance companies provide financial protection to those who can afford it. The Social Security Act of 1935, as amended, offers a minimum of security to many millions who would otherwise be destitute. Private welfare agencies assume many of the special types of need arising in an urban and industrial society. Life is more complex than it was under the agrarian conditions of the early family, and the problems of protection are correspondingly more extensive. The family does not have the physical facilities, the personnel, or the money to care for its members under present conditions. Its protective functions have inevitably fallen to the welfare agencies. The social trends that brought this situation about will not be reversed. Along with the educational, recreational, and religious functions, the protective function can no longer be adequately performed by the family alone.[26]

As we have examined some of the traditional functions of the family, we have seen that other institutions can realize some of the values more adequately than the family can. Factories can make clothes, shoes, and frozen foods more efficiently. The movies can provide more exciting entertainment. Schools have more skills and resources in handing on the cultural heritage. Government is the only agency equipped to care for the mentally deranged, the feeble-minded, the unemployed, the widow with dependent children, and the aged. The family should not be "blamed" for partially abdicating these functions. The several values can, in part at least, be better served by other institutions.[27]

Continuing Social Functions

In view of this widespread loss of function, one may well ask why the family is still considered the basic social institution. The answer lies in the functions it still performs and the values it continues to serve. These are the biological, affectional, and socializing functions. The *biological* function means that the family provides a socially sanctioned relationship for the birth of children. The *affectional* function means that the family offers love and emotional security in an increasingly impersonal world. The *socializing* function means that the family forms the personality of the child by transmitting to him the informal cultural heritage of the group.

1. The biological function. This function is the cornerstone of society. Organized group life literally depends upon the biological function. The traditional family performed this function more extensively than the contemporary family, although this difference is perhaps not as great as many people believe. The family no longer brings as many children into the world as it formerly did. At the same time, more of the children who are born take a permanent place in the family because of the decline in infant mortality.

---

[26] Wilbur J. Cohen, "Current and Future Trends in Public Welfare," *Social Service Review*, 29:247-259 (September, 1955). Cf. Marvin B. Sussman, "The Isolated Nuclear Family: Fact or Fiction," *Social Problems*, 6:333-340 (Spring, 1959).

[27] Foote and Cottrell, Jr., *op. cit.*, pp. 98-99.

The most spectacular index to the changing biological function is the long-time reduction in the crude birth rate, that is, the number of births per 1,000 of the population. In 1790, the rate was an estimated 55.0; it reached an all-time low of 16.6 in 1933, at the depth of the Great Depression. The birth rate rose slightly to 17.9 in 1940 and continued to rise during and after World War II. In 1947, the crude birth rate was 26.6, and by 1954 it had slightly declined to 25.3 per 1,000 of the population. In 1958, the rate was 24.3 and in 1959 it was 24.0. In 1960, the rate dropped slightly to 23.7, in 1961 to 23.3, and in 1962 to 22.4. For the first nine months of 1963, the birth rate continued to decline gradually, with a provisional figure of 21.9 for this period.[28] On the other hand, the decade of the 1950's saw more than 40 million births in the United States, by far the largest number of any decade in its history.[29] Viewed in this perspective, the biological function is still very active indeed.

The biological function of the family has thus been exposed to two conflicting sets of influences in recent decades, one acting to decrease fertility and the other to increase it. We briefly considered these trends in Chapter 11, where we dealt with certain broad modifications in the fertility of the population. We shall now examine these factors in the functional perspective of the family.

a. Long-range factors. The secular decline in the birth rate began in the nineteenth century and continued with cyclical variations until approximately 1940. Among the social and economic factors in this decline were: (1) the shift in the base of the family from rural to urban; (2) the decrease in the size of the housing facilities of the average family; (3) the importance of material success and the presumed limitations upon this goal by several children; (4) the romantic ideal, which emphasizes youth and glamor, sometimes at the expense of children; (5) the increased education of women, which tends to decrease their fertility; (6) the decline in religious incentives to large families; (7) the increasing employment of married women outside the home; and (8) the spread of the knowledge of contraception throughout the population.[30]

b. Short-range factors. The above factors were among those setting the social climate for decreased fertility in the decades prior to World War II. In the years from 1940-1960, a somewhat different set of factors impinged upon the family, especially among the urban middle classes, and resulted in generally higher fertility. Among these recent factors were: (1) the general material prosperity during and after World War II; (2) the continued high level of employment and consequent economic security; (3) the increased efforts by the federal government and many private concerns to provide security against old age and ill health; (4) the increased employment in bureaucratic positions,

---

[28] Department of Health, Education and Welfare, *Monthly Vital Statistics Report, Provisional Statistics,* "Birth, Marriages, Divorces, and Deaths for September, 1963," Vol. 12, No. 9 (November 22, 1963).

[29] Bureau of the Census, *Current Population Reports: Population Estimates,* "Estimates of the Population of the United States and Components of Population Change," Series P-25, No. 250 (July 3, 1962), Table A.

[30] Ogburn and Nimkoff, *op. cit.,* pp. 113-122. See also Bureau of the Census, *Current Population Reports: Population Characteristics,* "Fertility of the Population: March 1957," Series P-20, No. 84 (August 8, 1958).

where the incentive to upward mobility is perhaps less pronounced; (5) the massive movement from the cities to the suburbs, where child raising is easier and more fashionable; (6) the subsequent emphasis upon community relationships, in which children play an important role; (7) the (possible) decrease in anxiety for the future and the related decision to have more children.

The social climate of fertility is in the process of change. The secular (long-range) trend toward smaller families has been arrested, whether temporarily or permanently we do not know. Many of the fertility factors that were apparent in the 1930's[31] have changed, and a new set of factors is emerging.[32] The overwhelming majority of married couples desire children and make every effort to have them. The decade of the 1950's saw an increasing agreement among all classes of the population regarding the desired number of children. The consensus seems to be for a family of 2-4 children, with some variations of religion and class still existing, but not as widespread as formerly. "All classes of the American population," in short, "are coming to share a common set of values about family size." [33] These values stress a moderately high fertility.

The trend toward increased fertility was, as noted, especially marked during the decade of the 1950's and (to a somewhat lesser extent) during the early years of the 1960's. In 1950, the average family consisted (for statistical purposes) of 3.54 persons. In 1955, the average was 3.60 and in 1962 it was 3.67. This upward trend in turn reflected the increase in the average number of children under 18 years of age per family. In 1950, there was an average of 1.06 children under 18 per family; in 1962 the average was 1.22 per family.[34] In a somewhat different perspective, the proportion of *all* families with four or more children under 18 increased from 6 per cent in 1950 to 10 per cent in 1962. These "large" families constituted approximately 15 per cent of all farm families and 18 per cent of all nonwhite families.[35] The figures for 1962 are shown in Table 12.

2. The affectional function. The second principal function remaining to the family is the affectional one. This function comprises intimate and primary relationships for all the members of the family, parents as well as children. The child first experiences affection in the parental family, as his parents and siblings offer him tenderness, sympathy, and the generalized love found in no other group relationship. Later he seeks other affectional responses as he reaches adult status and starts a family of his own. The contemporary family is initiated in terms of affection, and this constitutes probably the most important single reason for marriage.

---

[31] P. K. Whelpton and Clyde V. Kiser (eds.), *Social and Psychological Factors Affecting Fertility* (Four Volumes) (New York: Milbank Memorial Fund, 1946, 1950, 1952, and 1954 respectively).

[32] Elliot G. Mishler and Charles F. Westoff, "A Proposal for Research on Social Psychological Factors Affecting Fertility: Concepts and Hypotheses," in *Current Research in Human Fertility* (New York: Milbank Memorial Fund, 1955), pp. 121-150.

[33] Ronald Freedman, Pascal K. Whelpton, and Arthur A. Campbell, *Family Planning, Sterility, and Population Growth* (New York: McGraw-Hill Book Company, Inc., 1959), p. 402.

[34] Bureau of the Census, *Current Population Reports: Population Characteristics*, "Household and Family Characteristics: March 1962," Series P-20, No. 125 (September 12, 1963), Table E.

[35] *Ibid.*, Table A.

Table 12. Families by Type, and Number or Own Children Under 18 Years Old, for the United States, Total and Farm: March 1962 (Numbers in thousands. Average not shown where base is less than 200,000)

Type of family, color of head, and residence	Total	Number of own children under 18 years old							Average number of children	
		None	1	2	3	4	5	6 or more	Per family	Per family with children
UNITED STATES										
All families	46,341	20,114	8,322	8,009	5,050	2,681	1,072	1,093	1.35	2.39
Per cent	100.0	43.4	18.0	17.3	10.9	5.8	2.3	2.4		
Husband-wife	40,405	16,657	7,313	7,362	4,637	2,478	975	983	1.41	2.40
Other male head	1,293	1,039	138	70	27	9	8	2	0.34	1.72
Female head	4,643	2,418	871	577	386	194	89	108	1.10	2.30
Nonwhite families	4,453	1,896	717	585	436	313	197	309	1.67	2.91
Per cent	100.0	42.6	16.1	13.1	9.8	7.0	4.4	6.9		
Husband-wife	3,220	1,287	521	437	327	244	158	246	1.78	2.97
Other male head	198	146	29	15	5	2	1			
Female head	1,035	463	167	133	104	67	38	63	1.56	2.82
FARM										
All families	3,490	1,612	516	491	350	207	135	179	1.50	2.78
Per cent	100.0	46.2	14.8	14.1	10.0	5.9	3.9	5.1		
Husband-wife	3,141	1,346	479	482	329	201	129	175	1.60	2.81
Other male head	156	135	11	6	4					
Female head	193	131	26	3	17	6	6	4		

Source: Bureau of the Census, *Current Population Reports: Population Characteristics,* "Household and Family Characteristics: March 1962," Series P-20, No. 125 (September 12, 1963), Table A.

This sentiment often takes the form of romantic love, which brings people into marriage and carries them along for some time thereafter. The average person "falls in love" before he marries, and any other basis for marriage is considered both improbable and unsatisfactory. There is some evidence that romantic love is being supplemented by companionship among certain middle-class and highly educated groups.[36] Be that as it may, it seems clear that the great majority of men and women in our society consider "falling in love" the natural and indispensable prelude to a happy marriage.

Even in societies where mates are chosen by the parents, however, the element of "love" must be taken into account. Young people are often sexually attracted to each other, and some way must be found of dealing with this situation. In our society, as noted, this problem usually solves itself and the young people get married and presumably live happily ever after. In other societies, things are not this simple. Violent sexual attraction between two people who, for one reason or another, cannot marry may disrupt the smooth interaction of the group. Family feuds, bitterness, and hatred may result. In such cases, love turns the world upside down instead of making it go around. Whatever the ultimate solution, "love" is clearly a basic force in social interaction. It must be

[36] Ernest W. Burgess and Paul Wallin, *Engagement and Marriage* (Philadelphia: J. B. Lippincott Company, 1953), Chapter 7.

harnessed, controlled, and directed if it is not to interfere with organized patterns of interaction.[37]

In marriages that are successful through the years, romantic love is gradually succeeded by another and more lasting sentiment, which has been called conjugal affection. This relationship involves companionship, friendship, habit, similarity of values, and the ability to count on the other person in a variety of situations. By its very nature, conjugal affection arises gradually, in contrast to romantic love, which strikes like a bolt from the blue. Whether in the form of romantic love or conjugal affection, however, the giving and receiving of affection is an important function of the family relationship.[38]

In one sense, the affectional function has always been present in the family. Sexual relationships have been a central part of marriage, which has provided the socially sanctioned framework for them since time immemorial. Husbands and wives have always entertained sentiments of respect and affection for each other, and children have been loved and valued. In other times, however, the basic *motives* for marriage were different from those of our own day. Husbands and wives were chosen on the basis of such utilitarian factors as similarity of social class, physical strength, fecundity, and household skills. Physical attractiveness, "personality," vivacity, and "charm" were not valued as they are today.

The affectional function includes sexual relationships as perhaps its most obvious manifestation, although they constitute only one phase of the affectional pattern. The whole subject of sex was previously obscured by a veil of

[37] William J. Goode, "The Theoretical Importance of Love," *American Sociological Review*, 24:38-47 (February, 1959).

[38] Francis E. Merrill, *Courtship and Marriage* (revised and expanded edition) (New York: Holt, Rinehart and Winston, Inc., 1959), Chapter 14, "Conjugal Roles."

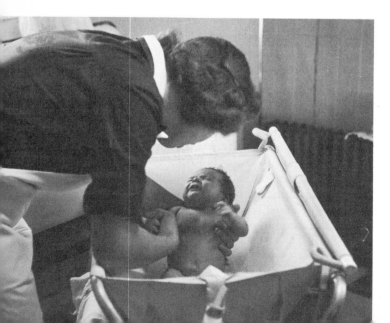

The continuing functions of the family (biological, affectional, and socializing) are symbolized in this picture of mother and child.

taboo and prudery. The popularization (and misinterpretation) of the doctrines of Freud, the increasing freedom of women, and the growing secularization of society have swung the pendulum in the opposite direction. The sexual element is stressed to an unprecedented degree and both the spouses have come to expect more than ever before. "Sexual incompatibility" is widely assumed to be a basic reason for family instability, whereas it is often merely expressive of other and more basic personality differences.

The affectional function includes many other elements, some of them only remotely related to sex. Affection involves the tender intimacies between husband and wife, the sense of mutual identification, and the way in which each spouse physically takes care of the other. This function also includes care of the children during their early years, their emotional security, and the sympathetic identification by the parents with the children. These are sentiments that the family alone can provide. In a world that has grown increasingly impersonal, secular, and alien, the person needs this emotional security if he is to remain healthy and strong.

3. *The socializing function.* The final major function remaining to the contemporary family is that of socialization. This function refers to the part played by the family in forming the personality of the child. The latter is nurtured in the family and receives many of his behavior patterns, attitudes, goals, and values in this way. In a sense, the entire discussion of personality in the earlier chapters was an examination of this function, inasmuch as personality is first molded in family interaction. Hence we shall not repeat the analysis here.

Social Change and the Family

The family cannot remain the same in a changing society. The principal dilemma of the modern family is simply that it is not what it used to be. When we consider that the ideal family is precisely "what used to be," the meaning of this generalization becomes clearer. For many centuries, the family maintained a continuity of functions and patterns, based upon a household economy in a predominantly rural society. The large, agrarian, multifunctional, patriarchal family became the family "as it should be," and any subsequent departure from this pattern has been considered a grave social problem.[39]

The statement is thus often made that "the family is declining." This actually means that *a certain type of family* is declining, and this type is identified with the family *as such*. Such critics fail to realize that there may be other and different forms of the family, each suited to its own social setting.[40] Hence a certain historical form of the family may be in the process of change and eventual decline. But this process is in itself the sign of the appearance of a new form.

---

[39] Francis E. Merrill, "The Study of Social Problems," *American Sociological Review*, 13:251-262 (June, 1948).

[40] Ruth Benedict, "The Family: Genus Americanum," Chapter 9 in Ruth N. Anshen (ed.), *The Family: Its Function and Destiny* (New York: Harper & Row, 1949).

We are now witnessing a transition from one type of family to another, rather than the decline of the family as an institutional pattern.

The traditional family had more children than the modern urban family. The traditional family was a productive unit, whereas the principal economic functions of the modern family are those of consumption. The father had a great deal of power in the traditional family, but in the modern family equalitarian and democratic roles are increasingly apparent. The woman's place in the early family was clearly in the home. Today almost one in every three married women is gainfully employed outside the home. In former times, the family was broken only by death, but the modern family is increasingly broken by divorce or desertion.

One by one, as we have seen, family patterns once considered immutable have changed as society itself has changed. The emerging family tacitly questions many of the verities once considered eternal. This fact is difficult for many persons to understand and even more difficult to accept. Whether we like it or not, however, the new family is here to stay. The family is said to be in the process of change from a stable *institution* to an increasingly unstable *personal relationship*, with institutional overtones.[41] This change is accompanied by doubts, soul-searchings, and insecurities, as the members of the society experience the dislocations in this basic and traditional pattern.

These trends are by no means simple and one-directional in character. Different social situations evoke different family patterns. It has been suggested, for example, that the way of life on the "urban fringe" of the central cities (the metropolitan areas) is giving rise to a new type of family. This pattern differs from the rural-farm family, but it also has many characteristics that distinguish it from the small, companionship family associated with urban areas. The "urban fringe" in this connection refers to the suburbs, satellite communities, and nonfarm territory located immediately outside the metropolitan city, whose inhabitants engage in activities connected directly or indirectly with the central city.[42]

In these fringe areas, the family differs both in structure and function from the family in the central city. These differences take the form of higher fertility, larger families, more persons per family in the labor force, more ownership of homes, less physical mobility, and lower mortality for the fringe family as compared with the family in the central city. In functional terms, the fringe family appears to maintain the traditional family functions more completely than the urban family, as follows: ". . . the economic [function], with employment of mothers as secondary workers; the educational, in the selection of 'better' schools for children; the recreational, in the encouragement of participation of children in selected peer groups and social sets; the religious, in belonging to

---

[41] Ernest W. Burgess and Harvey J. Locke, *The Family* (rev. ed.) (New York: American Book Company, 1955).

[42] E. Gartly Jaco and Ivan Belknap, "Is a New Family Form Emerging in the Urban Fringe?", *American Sociological Review*, 18:551-557 (October, 1953).

and supporting the 'right' churches; and the protective . . . in providing the best care and rearing practices of medical and mental science." [43]

We have briefly examined the contemporary American family in terms of its functions. We have indicated that the economic, educational, religious, and protective functions of this institutional pattern have changed drastically in recent decades, as many phases of these functions have been assumed, in whole or in part, by other institutions. In this sense, the modern American family no longer possesses many of the *functional* reasons for being that traditionally made it a central social pattern. This progressive loss of function has resulted from a series of basic socioeconomic changes that have profoundly modified the world in which the family operates. This loss in turn is the fundamental cause of the instability of the family of today. [44]

The family is becoming an increasingly affectional relationship—using this term in the broad sense of procreation, conjugal affection, and romantic love. The force impelling any given couple to marry is largely personal attraction, which is subject to sudden and inexplicable changes as couples fall in and out of love with each other or with someone else. [45] In a former day, each person was dependent upon the family for his livelihood, education, recreation, protection, and religious instruction. In short, the traditional family was highly "functional" for its members. These old-fashioned ties were solid, and it was virtually impossible to get along without them.

In place of these prosaic but fundamental ties, the modern family is held together in an often unstable equilibrium by a pattern of feelings, emotions, and attractions that are inherently less stable than the functional ties grouped about making a living, building a home, worshiping God, and educating one's children. In place of a functional pattern of reciprocal roles, we have a relationship that is becoming increasingly personal. As Winch puts it: "As functionality diminishes . . . there is a thinning of the . . . relationships between the spouses and a reduction in the degree of their functional importance to each other. As this happens," he continues, "congeniality becomes more important and functionality less important as a determinant of marital stability." [46]

Given this increasing dependence upon the affectional factor, broadly conceived, the individual family is less stable than it formerly was. The reasons for this instability are basically functional, rather than personal. That is to say, family disorganization reflects the broad changes in the functions of the institutional structure, rather than the "personal" qualities of the participants. If the family is sufficiently "functional"—that is, if it performs certain important activities—the spouses will presumably stay together because they *need* this relationship. If the family is *not* sufficiently functional, however, the spouses may find reasons for breaking the relationship on grounds of personal incom-

---

[43] *Ibid.*, p. 556. See also Bernard Lazerwitz, "Metropolitan Community Residential Belts," *American Sociological Review*, 25:245-252 (April, 1960).

[44] Winch, *The Modern Family, op. cit.*, Chapter 22.

[45] Francis E. Merrill, *Courtship and Marriage, op. cit.*, Chapter 3, "Romantic Love."

[46] Winch, *The Modern Family, op. cit.*, p. 703.

patibility. Difficulties in "personality" and temperament have always existed between spouses. But only recently have such problems been grounds for dissolving the family.[47]

Family Disorganization

Throughout most of the history of Western Europe and America, the social setting of the family was basically stable and the family maintained a correspondingly high degree of functionality. These conditions were such as to entrust many of the central phases of human life directly to the family—with the active collaboration of the church. These conditions have changed and the family has changed with them. Many of the old norms still survive, and the instability of the family is accordingly viewed as a social problem.[48] As we have seen, the family is "accused" of somehow failing to do its duty in the manner to which people have become accustomed. This accusation is manifestly inadequate and unjust, since the family is an institutionalized role pattern, not a human being. In this chapter, we have outlined some of the ways in which this role pattern has lost some of its central functions.

The family has thus become increasingly unstable in recent decades. The undesirable aspects of this process are dramatized by the increase in the divorce rate. The large number of desertions constitutes another, although undetermined, indication of the same process. During the period from 1867 (when national statistics were first recorded) to 1948, the population increased by approximately *four* times, whereas the number of divorces increased by almost *forty* times. Measured in terms of divorces per 1,000 of the population, the rate increased from 0.3 in 1867 to 2.8 in 1948, with an all-time high of 4.3 in 1946.[49] Except for cyclical fluctuations during periods of boom and depression, the secular trend in family disorganization through divorce has been upward since the first figures were tabulated.

The decades of the 1940's and 1950's saw spectacular fluctuations in the number and rate of divorces. The height of the postwar divorce period was 1946, when the number of divorces reached the unprecedented total of 610,000 and the rate rose to 4.3 per 1,000 of the population. The rate declined from this peak and became virtually stabilized between 2.1 and 2.4 per 1,000 of the population during the 1950's and early 1960's. In absolute numbers, the figures were 368,000 in 1958, 395,000 in 1959, and 393,000 in 1960.[50]

The return to a dynamic "normalcy" in family stability in the late 1950's and early 1960's saw the divorce rate decrease considerably from the postwar high of 1946. But the rate nevertheless continued at a higher plateau than at any

[47] *Ibid.*, pp. 711-713.

[48] Francis E. Merrill, *et al.*, *Social Problems* (New York: Alfred A. Knopf, Inc., 1950), Chapter 11.

[49] Inter-Agency Committee on Background Materials, National Conference on Family Life, *The American Family: A Factual Background, op. cit.*, Appendix I, Table 8.

[50] Department of Health, Education, and Welfare, Public Health Service, Annual Report, *Vital Statistics of the United States*, Washington, 1962. Figures for divorce in the country as a whole are compiled later than those for births, marriages, and deaths.

time prior to World War II. Family instability appears to be a chronic condition for the proximate future. This prospect is not an inspiring one for many persons. The values of our society continue to be based upon the family as an indissoluble relationship, and any large-scale violation of this value is viewed with alarm. At the same time, moral condemnation of divorce has done little to decrease the rate of family disorganization. The family reflects in its structure the broad social changes that have marked the growing instability of society as a whole.

Social institutions are patterns of roles grouped about basic social needs. The central structural elements in the conjugal family are those of husband and wife. We have considered some of the major changes in the functions performed by the family institution. These functions are largely carried out by persons occupying the statuses of husband and wife and playing the roles appropriate thereto. We may therefore conclude our examination of the contemporary American family by reviewing the statistical data on marital statuses. In this way, we can gain some empirical knowledge of the number of persons playing the principal marital roles. The family status of the American people may therefore be summarized as follows.

In 1962, 69.2 per cent of all males and 65.3 per cent of all females over 14 years of age were married. Some 66.3 per cent of the males and 61.4 per cent of the females had their spouses present at the time of enumeration by the Bureau of the Census. For an estimated 2.9 per cent of the males and 3.9 per cent of the females, their spouses were absent. Of this number, 1.6 per cent of the husbands and 2.1 per cent of the wives reported their spouses as "separated." This number included (a) those with legal separations, (b) those planning to get a divorce and living apart from their husbands or wives, and (c) still others who, in the sober words of the Bureau of the Census, were "permanently or temporarily estranged from their spouse because of marital discord." [51]

The latter group of "separated" couples comprises several million persons. In 1962, there were 1,004,000 men in this category and 1,433,000 women (not counting those whose husbands were in the armed forces).[52] An indeterminate number of these 2,437,000 men and women were in the state of family disorganization known as "desertion." This means that their family relationship had been temporarily or permanently broken by the informal method of one spouse leaving the domicile of the other, either with or without telling the other where he was going or whether he was planning to return. This form of family disorganization was formerly called "the poor man's divorce," but it is by no means confined to the very poor. The role of the deserted wife, especially with younger children, is both ambiguous and desolate. She has no husband and (frequently) no visible means of support.

---

[51] Bureau of the Census, *Current Population Reports, Population Characteristics,* "Marital Status and Family Status: March 1962," *op. cit.,* Table 1.

[52] *Ibid.*

The final enumeration of marital and family status involves those persons that are widowed and divorced. In 1962, some 3.4 per cent of the males (2,128,-000) and 12.5 per cent of the females (8,399,000) were listed as widowed. This disparity between widowers and widows is due in large measure to the greater life expectancy of women over men. Some 2.1 per cent of the males (1,274,000) and 2.7 per cent of the females (1,787,000) were divorced and not remarried.[53] Especially at the younger ages, divorced persons tend to remarry, and a considerable percentage of those listed as divorced at any one time will shortly remarry. They will, however, be replaced by other men and women who are temporarily between marriages. The contemporary family is by its very nature an unstable interpersonal relationship. Some families are broken by divorce and others by desertion. Sooner or later, every family is broken by death.

---

[53] *Ibid.*

SELECTED BIBLIOGRAPHY

Ackerman, Nathan W., *The Psychodynamics of Family Life*. New York: Basic Books, Inc., 1958. This is a significant contribution to the understanding of the family, written by a psychoanalyst with a sociological orientation. The family is viewed as a center of social interaction, and its role both in integrating and disorganizing the personality is thoroughly explored.

Blood, Robert O., and Donald M. Wolfe, *Husbands and Wives*. Glencoe, Ill.: The Free Press, 1960. The subtitle of this book is "The Dynamics of Married Living," and in this way the authors approach the married couple as a field of social interaction. The study is based upon interviews with 731 city families and 178 farm families, and as such presents new factual information, placed in a sound theoretical framework.

Burgess, Ernest W., and Harvey J. Locke, *The Family* (rev. ed.). New York: American Book Company, 1955. The principal thesis of this well-known textbook is that the family is changing from an institution to a personal relationship. In this process, some of the functions formerly performed by the family have been minimized and others have become more important than ever.

Department of Health, Education, and Welfare, Public Health Service, National Office of Vital Statistics, *Vital Statistics-Special Reports*, issued periodically. These bulletins are the official source of statistics dealing with trends in marriage and divorce in the United States. As such, they are indispensable to any quantitative knowledge of the family.

Friedan, Betty, *The Feminine Mystique*. New York: W. W. Norton & Company, Inc., 1963. The "feminine mystique" is the culture pattern embodying the conception that the highest value for women is to maintain and develop their femininity. The author takes violent exception to this traditional ideology and maintains that women should extend their repertoire of social roles with the goal of greater self-development as *human beings—* as well as wives and mothers.

Glick, Paul C., *American Families.* New York: John Wiley & Sons, Inc., 1957. In this statistical study, a family sociologist affiliated with the Bureau of the Census presents a mine of information on various aspects of the family. Much of this information was not previously available in the regular publications of the Bureau.

Goode, William J., "The Sociology of the Family," in Robert K. Merton, Leonard Broom, and Leonard S. Cottrell, Jr. (eds.), *Sociology Today.* New York: Basic Books, Inc., 1959. In common with the other essays in this symposium, the purpose of this one on the family is to formulate the important contemporary problems. The author is a specialist in the family, and his comments on the status of knowledge in this area are significant.

Hill, Reuben, "Sociology of Marriage and Family Behavior, 1945-1956," *Current Sociology,* Volume 7. London: Basil Blackwell, 1958 (prepared with the assistance of UNESCO). In this essay, the author examines the trends in family research during the decade 1945-1956. In addition to his interpretative comments, the international bibliography is valuable for indicating the extent of the changes.

Merrill, Francis E., *Courtship and Marriage* (revised and expanded edition). New York: Holt, Rinehart and Winston, 1959. This textbook is an analysis of courtship and marriage in American society, with emphasis upon the concept of social interaction. The implications of social roles are explored at length, indicating that much marital interaction occurs through the patterned expectations (roles) of husband and wife.

Nye, F. Ivan and Alan E. Bayer, "Some Recent Trends in Family Research," *Social Forces,* 41:290-301 (March, 1963). The authors of this article are primarily concerned with the *methods* of family research, rather than its substantive content. They review some of the methods currently in use by family researchers in extending our knowledge in this important field.

Ogburn, William F., and Meyer F. Nimkoff, *Technology and the Changing Family.* Boston: Houghton Mifflin Company, 1955. Although ostensibly dealing with the relationships between technology and the family, this book actually casts a far wider net. The result is one of the most thoughtful studies of the family that has appeared in recent years. The late Professor Ogburn and his colleague describe technology as the prime mover, which sets in motion far-reaching changes in every aspect of the family.

Waller, Willard, and Reuben Hill, *The Family: A Dynamic Interpretation* (rev. ed.). New York: Holt, Rinehart and Winston, 1951. This is a revision of an original treatise on the family first published in 1938 by Willard Waller. The revision is the work of Reuben Hill and the result is an outstanding contribution to the dynamics of the family. Although the revision is now more than a decade old, much of the analysis of the psychological processes of family interaction is still timely.

Walters, James, "A Review of Family Research in 1962," *Marriage and Family Living,* 25:336-348 (August, 1963). This is an extensive bibliography of research published on the family and related areas during a single year. As such, it should be read in conjunction with the article of Nye and Bayer (above). Taken together, the two give a wide-ranging account of recent trends in both the methodology and substantive areas of family research.

Winch, Robert F., *The Modern Family* (rev. ed.). New York: Holt, Rinehart and Winston, 1963. This distinguished textbook presents a theory of the family and then uses it to analyze the contemporary American family. The author views the family as a social system and examines its structure and functions in this framework. The book also provides a thoughtful analysis of personality as it develops through social interaction in the family setting.

19 | *The Community*

The Nature of the Community

The community has been called "a constellation of institution." [1] This phrase has a number of related sociological implications. Social institutions mean *people*, with biological, psychological, and social needs that the institutions meet.[2] These institutions occupy physical *space*, usually in fairly close contact. The members of the institutions *interact* continuously, sometimes

---

[1] Robert E. Park and Ernest W. Burgess, *Introduction to the Science of Sociology* (Chicago: University of Chicago Press, 1924), p. 493.

[2] Gordon W. Blackwell, "A Theoretical Framework for Sociological Research in Community Organization," *Social Forces*, 33:57-64 (October, 1954).

in their institutional roles and sometimes not. As a result of this interaction, the inhabitants of the community develop rational interests and emotional *bonds* with each other and with the community itself.[3] The physical area defines the limits within which the social interaction occurs. People, space, and interaction are the basic elements of the community.

A community may thus be viewed as a permanent group of persons, occupying a common area, interacting in both institutional and noninstitutional roles, and having a sense of identification with the entity (the community) that arises from this interaction.[4] The central fact of the community is social interaction. People constantly take each other into account in a community setting, whether an obscure village or world metropolis.[5] As they act with reference to each other, they engage in various types of behavior that have been called competition, conflict, accommodation, assimilation, and cooperation. As one author puts it,". . . a community, like a group, is essentially a system of social interaction." [6]

This essential element of interaction has been further developed by Freilich. In working out an "operational" (functional) definition of community, he stresses the relative frequency of interaction of members with each other, as compared with that with persons outside the community. Members of a community exchange information at regular centers, such as the post office or the country store. Much of their interaction depends upon this flow of information. In the course of prolonged interaction, a local culture develops that channels and directs future interaction. Much of this culture is, of course, similar to that of the larger society, but some of it is unique. Every community within a given society has certain broad cultural similarities with every other community. At the same time, some elements are always unique to its own community setting.[7]

Without such interaction, the "community" is merely an "aggregate of dwellings" in which each family lives its own largely self-contained life. Such a situation exists in many of the new factory-made suburbs that have been created as dormitories for young couples. These agglomerations have no organic institutional growth and hence are not, in their initial stages, true communities. They have grade schools but no high schools because the children are not yet old enough. They have supermarkets but few churches. They are places for couples on the move, young people who have few community ties and do not want any. A community is more than an aggregation of families and houses.

The community has been the center of human existence since long before

---

[3] Louis Wirth, "The Scope and Problems of the Community," *Publication of the American Sociological Society*, 27:61-73 (May, 1933).

[4] George A. Hillery, Jr., "Definitions of Community: Areas of Agreement," *Rural Sociology*, 20:111-123 (June, 1955).

[5] Cf. Albert J. Reiss, Jr., "The Sociological Study of Communities," *Rural Sociology*, 25:118-130 (June, 1959).

[6] Irvin T. Sanders, *The Community: An Introduction to a Social System* (New York: The Ronald Press, 1958), p. 120.

[7] Norris Freilich, "Toward an Operational Definition of Community," *Rural Sociology*, 28:117-127 (June, 1963).

historical times. The first settled communities arose in Neolithic times, when the discovery of agriculture made possible fixed homes and continuous social interaction. From its early Neolithic beginnings, the growth of the community was, for a long time, extremely slow. The point at which the *community* became the *city* in this evolution is largely a matter of definition. It is fair to say, however, that the city is a comparatively recent development. The small, rural community has been (and still is in many parts of the world) the characteristic form of human existence.[8]

The Study of the Community

The community has been studied extensively in the United States. The most famous such study was conducted some years ago by the Lynds and resulted in the classic works *Middletown* and *Middletown in Transition*.[9] The Yankee City study comprised a series of investigations of a New England community, carried on by W. Lloyd Warner and associates.[10] A small town in the Midwest, whose pseudonym was Plainville, was the subject of a study by James West, also a pseudonym.[11] August B. Hollingshead carried on extensive investigations in a middle-sized midwestern community that he called Elmtown.[12] The Deep South was the scene of a community study by John Dollard, with particular reference to the caste structure.[13] In these and many other investigations, the sociologist has indicated his interest in the community and his assumption that American society and culture can most clearly be seen in the community.[14]

Communities differ in terms of geographical setting, historical development, economic base, ethnic background, and religious preference. Despite these and other differences between *individual* communities, certain general patterns may be seen. Among them are: (*a*) *The New England Town*—some of the patterns of this community were brought to this country from England by the Puritans who settled New England: (*b*) *The Southern County*—the county, rather than the town, is the basic unit throughout the agrarian South; (*c*) *The Main Street "Service Center"*—this community typically began as a crossroads settlement and continued as a distribution point for the surrounding countryside; (*d*) *The Mill Town*—as the name indicates, this type of community grew up about an industrial plant and is still dominated by it; (*e*) *The Metropolitan*

---

[8] Kingsley Davis, "The Origin and Growth of Urbanization in the World," *American Journal of Sociology*, 60:429-437 (March, 1955).

[9] Robert S. Lynd and Helen M. Lynd, *Middletown* (New York: Harcourt, Brace and World, 1929); Robert S. Lynd and Helen M. Lynd, *Middletown in Transition* (New York: Harcourt, Brace and World, 1937).

[10] W. Lloyd Warner and Paul S. Lunt, *The Social Life of a Modern Community* (New Haven: Yale University Press, 1941). Other volumes in this series depicted various aspects of Yankee City, notably its social stratification.

[11] James West, *Plainville, U.S.A.* (New York: Columbia University Press, 1945).

[12] August B. Hollingshead, *Elmtown's Youth* (New York: John Wiley & Sons, Inc., 1949).

[13] John Dollard, *Caste and Class in a Southern Town* (New Haven: Yale University Press, 1937).

[14] For an excellent interpretive study of the community, see Maurice R. Stein, *The Eclipse of Community* (Princeton: Princeton University Press, 1960).

Agglomeration—the metropolitan community is becoming increasingly characteristic of the American scene.[15]

The community should be distinguished from the society. The latter refers to considerable numbers of persons in more or less continuous interaction who are governed by a common set of institutions. The society is the larger entity and is composed of thousands of communities, ranging in size from the smallest hamlet to New York City. Many of the interests that bind the members of the community are of a local character and arise from the fact that they share the concerns of a specified functional area. The development of the national state has meant that, for all practical purposes, the society is conceived in these terms. American society is viewed as coterminous with the territory under the jurisdiction and effective control of the United States Government and whose people participate in American culture.

Arensberg stresses the interactional conception of the community. "Community study," he remarks, "is that method in which a problem (or problems) in the nature, interconnections, or dynamics of behavior and attitudes is explored against or within the surround of other behavior and attitudes of the individuals making up the life of a particular community." [16] In this sense, the student is not so much interested in the community as a physical unit, but rather in the social interaction taking place within it. This interaction is compared with that of other community settings of a similar type. The purpose of the community-study method is therefore "to use the community as a setting for the exploration, discovery, or verification of interconnections among social and psychological facts and processes." [17]

We shall consider the community under three general headings: the rural community, the urban community, and the metropolitan community. There is an obvious difference between these units in size. but there are also qualitative differences in institutional specialization and social relationships. Increasing urbanization and mobility are combining to break down many of the characteristics that once distinguished the isolated and self-contained village from the cosmopolitan capital. In an earlier day, a remote frontier hamlet differed widely in terms of social interaction and institutional structure from Boston, Philadelphia, and New York. Today, many (but by no means all) of these distinctions are breaking down.

These distinctions are sometimes considered as a continuum, rather than as two or more polar types.[18] In this way, the analysis starts with a remote crossroads village at one end of the continuum and eventually gets to New York City at the other.[19] The thousands of other communities—rural, urban, and

[15] Conrad M. Arensberg, "American Communities," *American Anthropologist*, 57:1143-1162 (December, 1955).

[16] Conrad M. Arensberg, "The Community-Study Method," *American Journal of Sociology*, 60:109-124 (September, 1954), p. 110.

[17] *Ibid.*

[18] Horace Miner, "The Folk-Urban Continuum," *American Sociological Review*, 17:529-537 (October, 1952).

[19] Cf. Richard Dewey, "The Rural-Urban Continuum: Real but Relatively Unimportant," *American Journal of Sociology*, 66:60-66 (July, 1960).

metropolitan—are found somewhere along the line. These intermediate examples are more urban than the most isolated hamlet, but considerably less so than metropolitan New York. Other students of the city have suggested that the rural-urban continuum is not an adequate measuring device because of the increased mobility of large numbers of persons living in physically isolated communities. Such persons may commute daily by automobile to work in a factory that is thirty or forty miles from their homes. Under these conditions, a better distinction between rural and urban communities would be the percentage of residents who work at nonagricultural jobs.[20]

The Rural Community

The rural community is a small constellation of institutions and families focused on a common center and sharing common interests and functions.[21] Some of the members of the rural community live in close proximity to the central institutional cluster. Others live many miles out in the open country, where they maintain more or less continuous contact with the focal institutions. The rural community is less dependent upon a shared physical area than is the urban or the metropolitan community. The important consideration in the rural community is social interaction (cooperation, competition) and common emotional ties. Many members maintain their contacts at long distances and come in to the central point only infrequently. The bonds of common interest are, nevertheless, often stronger and more highly routinized than in larger communities where the members interact in a more restricted physical area.[22]

The rural community has been described in terms of these common interests. "The real community," says Sanderson, "is the devotion to common interests and purposes, the ability 'to act together in the chief concerns of life.' It consists of a recognition upon the part of the individuals and their organizations of a common obligation to the general welfare."[23] In the sense of sharing such institutional interests and sentiments, the majority of rural people belong to *some* community, even though they live on an outlying farm, far from the physical center of community life. Social interaction occurs through the network of primary groups, institutions, and associations that provide the economic, spiritual, political, recreational, educational, health, and sociability needs of the members.

Interaction in the rural community has been further examined by Munch and Campbell. In a study of a rural locality in Wisconsin, they found that the

[20] Charles T. Stewart, Jr., "The Urban-Rural Dichotomy: Concepts and Uses," *American Journal of Sociology,* 64:152-158 (September, 1958).

[21] Cf. George A. Hillery, Jr., "The Folk Village: A Comparative Analysis," *Rural Sociology,* 26:335-353 (December, 1961).

[22] Cf. George A. Hillery, Jr., "Villages, Cities, and Total Institutions," *American Sociological Review,* 28:779-791 (October, 1963).

[23] Dwight Sanderson, "Locating the Rural Community," *Cornell Agricultural Experiment Station Bulletin,* No. 413, Ithaca, New York, 1939, p. 5.

psychological aspects of interaction were as important as the functional. Members of the rural community interact through the conventional institutional patterns of church, store, school, and the rest. But they also interact through such primary groups as the family, the neighborhood group, and the ethnic group. People in rural communities, like people everywhere, are first members of primary groups and then of secondary groups. These two types of groups obviously overlap in the rural community, but the important fact emerging from this study is that the ties of family, kinship, and ethnic group (for example, Swedish, Norwegian, German) tend to determine with whom and in what manner the rural dweller will interact. These primary bonds carry emotional overtones, and people are strongly influenced by such stimuli. Such "collective" or "moral" integration is therefore of central interest in the rural community.[24]

The rural community cannot be exactly defined in terms of numbers. The Bureau of the Census defines as urban all incorporated places of 2,500 inhabitants or more, as well as persons living in unincorporated places of 2,500 inhabitants outside the urban fringe. This does not help us very much in delimiting the rural community in numerical terms or in deciding how many persons live in such communities, since many communities of 2,500 or more are rural in every sociological respect, even though defined for census purposes as urban. Most persons listed as "rural-farm," however, belong to one or more rural communities as just defined, and interact within it. Added to this number is an indeterminate number of "rural-nonfarm" persons who likewise belong to a rural community.[25]

We have considered the rural-urban distribution of the population in Chapter 11. We may briefly repeat the essential features of this discussion in the context of the rural community. The percentage of the population living in rural-farm areas has steadily decreased since the first figures were gathered. In 1870, an estimated 74.3 per cent of the population was listed as rural and 25.7 per cent as urban. Many of the latter were only nominally "urban" in the census definition—i.e., living in communities of 2,500 or more—but for all practical purposes were rural in their way of life and outlook. In 1940, these percentages had changed to 22.9 per cent listed as rural-farm, 20.5 per cent as rural-nonfarm, and 56.5 per cent as urban.[26]

The decrease in the rural-farm population continued through the decade of the 1950's and early 1960's. On April 1, 1962, the rural-farm population constituted only 7.7 per cent of the total population of the United States. Technological improvements in farming have made it possible for fewer persons to raise more food than ever before. The lure of the urban (and especially the metropolitan) community has also depleted the farm population. A

[24] Peter A. Munch and Robert B. Campbell, "Interaction and Collective Identification in a Rural Locality," *Rural Sociology*, 28:18-34 (March, 1963).

[25] Cf. Vincent Heath Whitney, "Changes in Rural-Nonfarm Population, 1930-1950," *American Sociological Review*, 25:363-368 (June, 1960).

[26] Bureau of the Census, *Current Population Reports: Population Characteristics*, "Internal Migration in the United States: April, 1947 to April, 1948," Series P-20, No. 22 (January 28, 1949).

statistical change in the enumeration procedure of the Bureau of the Census still further reduced the percentage of the total population listed as rural-farm. Prior to the 1960 census, persons living in the open country but gaining their livelihood otherwise than by farming (for example, factory laborers and filling-station operators) had been counted as part of the rural-farm population. In the 1960 census, however, the farm population was redefined as "all persons living in rural territory on places of 10 or more acres if as much as $50 worth of agricultural products were sold from the place in the reporting year." [27]

This change in definition decreased the number of the population listed as rural-farm to 7.7 per cent of the total, or 14,313,000 in 1962. According to the old (pre-1960) definition, this number would have been approximately five million persons larger. Exact comparisons are not available, but the change in procedure is estimated to have reduced the total rural-farm population by some 5,400,000 persons *as of 1960*.[28] The reader will note that the figures just cited refer to *1962*. In any event, the basic trends are clear enough. The rural-farm population has been steadily declining as a percentage of the total population. The reclassification by the Bureau of the Census, whereby some five million persons formerly designated as "rural-farm" became "rural-nonfarm" is also more realistic. Such persons, in short, live on farms but are not farmers. Many of the rural-nonfarm population, furthermore, live near one or more urban centers and are, in many respects, as "urban" as if they actually lived in the city. As we shall see shortly, this segment of the population (that is, the "rural-nonfarm") has increased both in numbers and relative importance in the past decade.

The implications of these figures for the rural community are far-reaching. They indicate a broad change in the socioeconomic basis of the United States, from one essentially rural to one increasingly urban. The significance of these statistics in human terms is even more meaningful. In thousands of rural communities, ministers preach to a handful of parishioners; country schools are inadequate because of lack of funds for efficient buildings and competent teachers; and country stores fail as their customers drive to the supermarkets in the nearest city. This stagnation is by no means universal in the rural community. Many rural institutional clusters are still flourishing, but the trends are against them.[29]

A final aspect of the rural community is, therefore, that it is rapidly becoming a part of the larger and essentially *urban* society. The line that formerly separated the country from the city is disappearing. Rural isolation is breaking down under the impetus of better transportation and communication. Radio

---

[27] Bureau of the Census-Department of Agriculture, *Farm Population*, "Estimates of the Farm Population of the United States: April 1962," Series Census-ERS (P-27), No. 33, (March 14, 1963), p.4.

[28] Bureau of the Census-Department of Agriculture, *Farm Population*, "Effect of Definition Changes on Size and Composition of the Rural-Farm Population: April 1960 and 1959," Series Census-AMS (P-27), No. 28 (April 17, 1961), Table A.

[29] For an extensive discussion of these trends, see Mabel A. Elliott and Francis E. Merrill, *Social Disorganization* (Fourth Edition) (New York: Harper & Row, 1961), Chapter 20, "The Rural Community."

and television have put the rural resident in instant touch with the metropolitan center. Hard-surfaced roads and the automobile have placed him within easy driving distance of a larger city. The clothes he buys and the food he eats largely come from the store or supermarket in the neighboring urban center. The occupational structure is changing the gainful activity of many rural persons, as more and more daily commute to work in the city. The mechanization of agriculture is turning many farmers into businessmen, with one eye on the weather and the other on the wheat market. The city is gradually swallowing up the countryside.[30]

In a recent community study, these trends were explored in their broader implications. The object of the study was a rural community of some 3,000 persons in upstate New York. Living in the midst of a society that they were powerless to control, the people of Springdale were nevertheless unwilling or unable to recognize their impotence, and they continued to talk and act as if they were complete masters of their destiny. In an economic sense, the community members shared the traditional values of a Yankee society. At the same time, the prices of the goods and services they bought and sold depended upon outside forces that they could neither understand nor control.[31]

This situation is increasingly typical of the rural community in a mass society. The values to which the people cling are those of a pioneer society, in which individual initiative was seen as the principal determinant of success. The large corporation, government control of agricultural production, and the influence of the mass media are among the impersonal forces that have destroyed the functional basis of this traditional society. But the people of Springdale (and thousands of other rural communities) are, in the authors' words, "unwilling to recognize the defeat of their values, their personal impotence in the face of large events and any failure in their way of life. . . . Instead of facing the issues," the authors continue, "they [the people of Springdale] make compromises and modify their behavior in some cases, and reaffirm their traditional patterns in other cases."[32]

The Urban Community

The urban community is the center of social change. New ideas, techniques, and norms arise in the city.[33] Technology is an important element in the process of urbanization. As men develop new devices to cope with their physical environment, they are able to bring more persons together in the city.[34] Transportation, communication, and industrialization are related to technological innovations that emerge from the city. Men interact with fewer traditional

---

[30] Glenn V. Fuguitt, "The City and Countryside," *Rural Sociology*, 28:246-261 (September, 1963).

[31] Arthur J. Vidich and Joseph Bensman, *Small Town in Mass Society* (Princeton: Princeton University Press, 1958).

[32] *Ibid.*, pp. 313-314.

[33] Nels Anderson, "Urbanism and Urbanization," *American Journal of Sociology*, 65:68-73 (July, 1959).

[34] Paul Meadows, "The City, Technology, and History," *Social Forces*, 36:141-147 (December, 1957).

constraints in the city than in the rural community, and out of this interaction come innovations.[35] It is not without reason that such highly self-conscious societies as the ancient Hebrews warned their people against the contamination of new ideas (heresy) in the cities of Nineveh and Babylon.

The urban community is also the center of social problems, even as it was in ancient times. This situation does not arise from any inherent depravity of contemporary urban dwellers, many of whom are themselves of rural origin. The proliferation of social problems in the urban and (especially) the metropolitan communities reflects the broad social changes that have brought together millions of persons of different racial, ethnic, religious, and cultural backgrounds.[36] Under these conditions, primary controls do not operate effectively, and juvenile delinquency, adult criminality, ethnic conflict, sexual delinquency, family disorganization, alcoholism, and suicide occur to a disproportionate degree. The urban community must spend much time and resources in devising social machinery to cope with these and other forms of social disorganization.[37]

This does not mean that the rural community is devoid of social problems: mental deficiency and derangement, sexual abnormalities, incest, racial discrimination, and religious prejudice are just a few of the problems encountered in the small town and open country. Some of these problems are accentuated by the comparative isolation of the rural community from news of the bracing winds of change, especially as carried by the mass media. In a study of readiness to accept desegregation of the public schools, for example, those persons who were in touch with the mass media were found to be the most willing to accept integration.[38] Institutional inadequacies (churches, schools, health facilities) often increase the severity of social problems in rural areas. Despite the nostalgic myths that derive from an earlier America, the rural community is far from Utopia.[39]

The rural community has existed, in one form or another, at least since early Neolithic times—that is to say, for perhaps ten thousand years. The urban community is much more recent. Compared with other aspects of culture and social structure, indeed, *both* the rural and urban communities are recent phenomena. Language, religion, art, and the family existed for many thousands of years before even the beginnings of the Neolithic village, let alone the urban community. Davis estimates that the first cities (truly urban communities) arose in Egypt, Mesopotamia, and India in the period 6,000 B.C. to 5,000 B.C. These cities were small by modern standards and may have numbered only

---

[35] Don Martindale, "Prefatory Remarks: The Theory of the City," in Max Weber, *The City* (Translated and edited by Don Martindale and Gertrude Neuwirth) (Glencoe, Ill.: The Free Press, 1958).

[36] Leo F. Schnore, "Social Problems in an Urban-Industrial Context," *Social Problems,* 9:228-240 (Winter, 1962).

[37] S. Kirson Weinberg, "Social-Action Systems and Social Problems," Chapter 21 in Arnold M. Rose (ed.), *Human Behavior and Social Processes* (Boston: Houghton Mifflin Company, 1962), p. 421.

[38] Melvin M. Tumin, "Exposure to Mass Media and Readiness for Desegregation," *Public Opinion Quarterly,* 21:237-251 (Summer, 1959).

[39] Elliott and Merrill, *op. cit.,* Chapter 21.

5,000 to 15,000 inhabitants. It was not until the days of the Romans that cities began to have populations numbered in the hundreds of thousands.[40]

The process of urbanization has sociological implications in several related senses: (1) Cities are comparatively recent developments in organized social life, as noted, and they emerged long after the basic institutions and cultural patterns. (2) Cities mark drastic changes in social interaction, and represent a way of life increasingly commercial and industrial. (3) Cities have become centers of growing influence in society, where leaders are made, major decisions are taken, and, more recently, the mass communications are located. (4) Cities represent the "shape of things to come," in the sense that urbanization is still increasing. In the study of the city, we are in the forefront of social change, where we can dimly discern the world of the future.[41]

The urban community may be viewed as a complex system for allocating people to positions in the social structure. The positions are *physical*, in the sense that some persons live in the slums, others in the high-rent districts, and still others in the suburbs. The positions are also *social*, in the sense that status is likewise allocated by the machinery of the metropolitan community. The allocation arises through social interaction, and the urban community is thus a dynamic stage for the social processes of competition, cooperation, conflict, assimilation, and the rest. This general process is described as follows: "In the most fundamental ecological sense, the allocation of persons to positions in a metropolis is dependent upon the supply of persons, the population, and the supply of positions in groups and organizations. It is also dependent upon the supply of . . . institutional services of various kinds, which have become an integral part of the allocation process." [42]

The city may be viewed in *functional* and *statistical* terms. In a *functional* sense, it is simply a "community which subsists by the exchange of manufactured products and services for food and raw materials." [43] The city embodies several functional considerations: (1) The city is itself a *specialized* social system that carries on certain activities of manufacturing, serving, and processing in exchange for raw materials produced by others. (2) The city also involves the *internal* division of labor, with some persons engaged in manufacturing, by hand or machines, others buying and selling goods and commodities, and still others performing services for those otherwise engaged. (3) The city is a center where some leisure is available to a minority of the citizens, who do not have to occupy themselves directly with feeding and sheltering themselves. This leisure is put to creative use, and the city is therefore the home of the arts and sciences.[44]

The functional aspects of the city have been explored by Gibbs and Martin,

---

[40] Davis, *op. cit.*, pp. 429-432.

[41] *Ibid.*, p. 429.

[42] Warren A. Peterson and George K. Zollschan, "Social Processes in the Metropolitan Community," Chapter 34 in Arnold M. Rose (ed.), *op. cit.*, pp. 654-655. The concept of position will be discussed in detail in Chapter 20.

[43] Ralph Linton, *The Tree of Culture* (New York: Alfred A. Knopf, Inc., 1955), p. 118.

[44] Lewis Mumford, *The Culture of Cities* (New York: Harcourt, Brace and World, 1938).

with data drawn from 45 countries. The authors indicate that a large city cannot possibly develop by utilizing the resources in its immediate environment. In the most elementary sense, large numbers of urban persons cannot be fed from farms and truck gardens located in their own back yards. Raw materials for manufacturing similarly must come from a distance. In order to survive, much less grow, therefore, the city must organize means of acquiring the various objects of production and consumption at a distance. This organization, in turn, depends upon a division of labor and a fairly high development of technology. The social systems of the countries in this study range from capitalism to socialism, but this ideological factor is not important in determining the degree of urbanism. The crucial consideration, according to Gibbs and Martin, is *functional*, rather than *ideological*. In their words, "The findings of this study . . . demonstrate consistent relationships among urbanization, the division of labor, the level of technological development, and the dispersion of objects of consumption." [45]

Further light on the functional aspects of the community is given by Jonassen in a comparative study of 88 counties in Ohio. The author abstracted 82 variables from the 88 counties, which included both *rural* and *urban* communities. Hence his variables characterize communities *as such*, not merely urban communities. The author then reduced the 82 variables to 7, which represent *combinations* of related community characteristics that can be used to compare one community with another. These combinations were as follows: (*a*) *urbanism*—a variety of elements ranging from the percentage of employed females to the degree of higher education of the population; (*b*) *welfare*—community organizations for dealing with problems of health, education, and welfare; (*c*) *influx*—relative influx of new residents as illustrated by net population gain, new housing, and increased retail sales; (*d*) *poverty*—presence of a large number of persons on relief and otherwise dependent upon public facilities; (*e*) *"magni-complexity"*—relative degree of industrialization and commercialization, as well as density of population and complexity of governmental structure; (*f*) *educational effort*—expenditures for education and degree of community sacrifice for this purpose; (*g*) *proletarianism*—the presence of "a large proportion of propertyless, relatively poor, low skilled, and poorly paid wage workers." [46]

In a *statistical* sense, the city in the United States was formerly defined as an incorporated place with a population of 2,500 and over. This definition was used by the Bureau of the Census for several decades. In the 1950 Census, however, the classification was revised. As presently defined, the urban population comprises all persons living in: "(*a*) places of 2,500 inhabitants or more incorporated as cities, boroughs, and villages; (*b*) incorporated towns of 2,500 or more except in New England, New York, and Wisconsin, where the term

---

[45] Jack P. Gibbs and Walter T. Martin, "Urbanization, Technology, and the Division of Labor: International Patterns," *American Sociological Review,* 27:667-677 (October, 1962), p. 676.

[46] Christen T. Jonassen, "Functional Unities in Eighty-Eight Community Systems," *American Sociological Review,* 26:399-407 (June, 1961), p. 406.

'towns' is used to designate minor civil divisions of counties; (c) the densely settled urban fringe, including both incorporated and unincorporated areas, around cities of 50,000 or more; and (d) unincorporated places of 2,500 inhabitants or more outside any urban fringe." [47]

This is a dynamic enumeration and takes into account the changing density of the population. This definition has advantages over the previous one, for it is closer to indicating the actual urban population. By including persons living near large cities in the "urban fringe," [48] the new definition incorporates many who are essentially "urban" in livelihood, attitudes, and values. This method is more realistic in treating large urbanized areas as single units, rather than as separate and independent communities. It is also more flexible and can be adapted to future developments. In the dynamic process of urbanization, large satellite rural areas become incorporated into the city, both legally and functionally.[49] The realities of urban growth transcend political boundaries, and the community unit for sociological purposes is the urban cluster, rather than the political subdivision.[50]

In observing the urban community, it is usually assumed that the outlying urban areas have a higher socioeconomic status than the central cities. The central city, so the reasoning goes, is increasingly made up of slums, with their teeming thousands of under-paid and under-privileged workers. The suburbs, on the other hand, are believed to be largely composed of well-to-do persons in the middle and upper classes, who have fled the depressed (and depressing) conditions of the central city. The comparatively small number of wealthy persons in the central city presumably do not compensate for the overwhelming mass of blue-collar workers and lower-middle-class persons. The suburban fringe population, in short, is believed to have a higher income, standard of living, and level of well-being than the central city.

In a significant study of the socioeconomic status of 200 urbanized areas, Schnore found that this common-sense assumption is not *necessarily* true.[51] Some areas on the urban fringe do, in fact, answer to the middle-class and comparatively affluent description. Others do not. As Berger has cogently shown, some suburbs are largely peopled by a blue-collar, working-class population.[52] Furthermore, many satellite cities are industrial in function and have a population that is both working-class and low-income. Hence the assumption of comparative affluence in the suburban fringe is true in some cases but not in others. The basic distinction seems to reflect the age of settlement of the different areas.

---

[47] Bureau of the Census, *Current Population Reports: Population Characteristics,* "Civilian Population of the United States, By Type of Residence: April 1959 and 1950," Series P-20, No. 98 (Rev.) (February 25, 1960), p. 3.

[48] E. Gartly Jaco and Ivan Belknap, "Is a New Family Form Emerging in the Urban Fringe?", *American Sociological Review,* 18:551-557 (October, 1953).

[49] Walter T. Martin, "Ecological Changes in Satellite Rural Areas," *American Sociological Review,* 22:173-183 (April, 1957), pp. 182-183.

[50] Donald J. Bogue, "Urbanism in the United States, 1950," *American Journal of Sociology,* 60:471-486 (March, 1955), pp. 475-477.

[51] Leo F. Schnore, "The Socio-Economic Status of Cities and Suburbs," *American Sociological Review,* 28:76-85 (February, 1963).

[52] Bennett M. Berger, *Working-Class Suburb* (Berkeley: University of California Press, 1960).

In Schnore's words, "Older urbanized areas tend strongly to possess peripheral populations of higher socioeconomic standing than found in the central cities themselves. In contrast, newer cities tend to contain populations ranking higher in education, occupation, and income than their respective suburbs." [53]

The above tendency seems, in turn, to be at least partially a matter of housing. In the *older* urban centers, much of the housing is obsolescent and has been destroyed to give way to low-cost housing developments, which have themselves rapidly become slums. Newer housing developments have arisen in the suburbs and the urban fringe of the older centers and these new projects have been occupied by middle-income and upper-income groups. In the *newer* urban areas, on the other hand, housing at the center of the city is not so old and hence is more desirable for middle-income groups. Many new housing developments in these newer cities are rising far out in the urban fringe, where they are grouped about industrial and commercial organizations. In many such cases, blue-collar workers live near the factories in which they work. [54]

The United States is rapidly becoming one of the most urbanized nations in the world. The people of this country have traditionally conceived of themselves as a nation of independent farmers and small-town dwellers. The city, with its formalized relationships and lack of primary patterns, was seen as the habitat of the European. Under present conditions, however, this country is surpassed in degree of urbanism only by Great Britain and the Federal Republic of Germany among the great nations. Putting it another way, the United States now has the *largest urban population* of any nation in the world. [55]

The Metropolitan Community

The metropolitan community is a constellation of communities grouped about a central city. The metropolitan community is comparatively new. In the present sense, it is largely a twentieth-century phenomenon. Cities have been present for thousands of years, but the metropolitan community reflects modern industrial methods, means of communication, and forms of transportation. [56] Many persons in the subsidiary cities look to the central city for employment and specialized services. Both in absolute numbers of inhabitants and percentages of the total population living in them, metropolitan communities are growing in importance. They represent the shape of things to come. [57]

The metropolitan community has many advantages arising from the large-scale concentration of population and services. Among these advantages are:

---

[53] Schnore, *op. cit.*, p. 82.

[54] *Ibid.*, pp. 82-83. Cf. Theodore R. Anderson and Richard T. Morris, "Spatial Aspects of Social Area Analysis," *American Sociological Review*, 26:392-398 (June, 1961).

[55] Bogue, *op. cit.*, p. 471. See also Thomas O. Wilkinson, "Urban Structure and Industrialization," *American Sociological Review*, 25:346-363 (June, 1960).

[56] Leo F. Schnore, "Metropolitan Growth and Decentralization," *American Journal of Sociology*, 63:171-180 (September, 1957).

[57] Bureau of the Census, *Current Population Reports: Population Characteristics*, "Civilian Population of the United States, By Type of Residence: April 1959 and 1950," Series P-20, No. 98 (Rev.) (February 25, 1960).

The metropolitan community is a constellation of urban communities grouped about a central city; this picture shows the Brooklyn shoreline with Manhattan in the background.

"... low transportation costs, a concentrated market, a joint location for several industries, a large and varied labor supply ..., the opportunity for wholesalers and manufacturers to assemble a wide range of items ..., ready access to financial institutions, and good transportation and communication facilities." [58] As transportation and communication continue to improve, the compact city of the past is rapidly changing. The resultant decentralization may be considered "as a shift toward a new equilibrium that was initiated by the development of new facilities for the movement of persons, commodities, and information." [59]

The increasing importance of the metropolitan community has been recognized by the Bureau of the Census, which introduced the concept of *standard metropolitan area*, later redefined as *standard metropolitan statistical area*. This unit is characterized by the bureau as follows:[60] "Except in New England, a standard metropolitan statistical area is a county or group of contiguous counties which contains at least one city of 50,000 inhabitants or more, or 'twin cities' with a combined population of at least 50,000. In addition to the county, or counties, containing such a city or cities, contiguous counties are included in a standard metropolitan statistical area if, according to certain criteria, they are essentially metropolitan in character and are socially and economically inte-

[58] Donald J. Bogue, "Urbanism in the United States, 1950," *American Journal of Sociology,* 60:471-486 (March, 1955), pp. 478-479.

[59] Leo F. Schnore, "The Growth of Metropolitan Suburbs," *American Sociological Review,* 22:165-173 (April, 1957), p. 173.

[60] Bureau of the Census, *Current Population Reports: Technical Studies,* "Standard Metropolitan Statistical Areas in the United States as Defined October 18, 1963," Series P-23, No. 10 (Dec. 5, 1963), p. 1.

grated with the central city." As so defined, there were 216 standard metropolitan statistical areas in the United States in 1963. The population of these 216 areas in *1960* was approximately 115,800,000, or nearly two-thirds of the population of the country as a whole at that time.[61]

The decade of the 1950's saw a rapid growth in the standard metropolitan statistical areas. The population of these areas increased from 91,568,113 in 1950 to 115,796,265 in 1960, or 26.5 per cent. The population of the country as a whole increased by only 18.5 per cent in this period. Even more striking differentials in population growth were apparent *within* the metropolitan areas themselves. The most spectacular difference was between the rate of growth in the central cities and that in the outlying parts of the areas. The total population of the central cities increased from 52,648,185 in 1950 to 58,441,995 in 1960, or 11.0 per cent. The population *outside* the central cities but *within* the standard metropolitan statistical areas increased from 38,919,928 in 1950 to 57,354,270 in 1960, or 47.4 per cent.[62] Contrary to the widespread impression, this increase was not confined to the suburbs, as ordinarily defined. Much of the gain in population took place in sections of the metropolitan area defined as rural nonfarm—that is, outside of urban communities but definitely not on farms. The growing concentration of the population into metropolitan areas (although not necessarily in the central cities) is part of "the wave of the future."

The five largest cities in the United States present an interesting picture of these general trends. In the 1960 census, New York, Chicago, Los Angeles, Philadelphia, and Detroit led in population, in that order. Their combined population totaled some 17½ million persons, or almost one tenth of the total population of the country in 1960. Despite their commanding size, four out of five of these cities (Los Angeles was the exception) actually *lost* population during the decade from 1950 to 1960. This loss occurred in the central city proper and *not* in the standard metropolitan statistical area of which each city was the focal point. The sharpest loss among the largest central cities was in Detroit with 180,000 or 9.7 per cent fewer people in 1960 than in 1950. New York City suffered a net loss of 110,000 or 1.4 per cent. Conversely, Los Angeles gained more than half a million people, or 26 per cent in the decade under consideration.[63] We may see the extent of these changes in Table 13.

Another striking long-range demographic change in these five central cities was the increase in the nonwhite population (which is predominantly Negro; in New York, the majority of the expanding Puerto Rican population are classified as white). The nonwhite population of Detroit rose from 9 per cent of the total in *1940* to 29 per cent in *1960.* Chicago had a corresponding increase from 8 to 24 per cent, and New York had an increase in the nonwhite population from 6 to 15 per cent of the total in the *two* decades 1940-1960. These

---

[61] *Ibid.*

[62] *Ibid.*, Table 2.

[63] Metropolitan Life Insurance Company, "Population Profile of Our Largest Cities," *Statistical Bulletin* (November, 1961), p. 1.

Table 13. Population of the Five Largest Cities in the United States (Numbers in thousands)

Characteristic	New York	Chicago	Los Angeles	Philadelphia	Detroit
Total population					
1940	7,455	3,397	1,504	1,931	1,623
1950	7,892	3,621	1,970	2,072	1,850
1960	7,782	3,550	2,479	2,003	1,670
Per cent male					
1940	49.3	49.5	48.8	48.8	51.0
1950	48.4	49.1	47.9	48.4	50.1
1960	47.8	48.6	48.3	48.0	48.8
Per cent white					
1940	93.6	91.7	93.5	86.9	90.7
1950	90.2	85.9	89.3	81.7	83.6
1960	85.3	76.4	83.2	73.3	70.8
1950-60					
Natural increase	713	454	261	212	280
White	519	279	189	119	179
Nonwhite	194	175	72	93	101
Net total migration *	−822	−525	248	−281	−460
White	−994	−678	114	−344	−542
Nonwhite	172	153	134	63	82
Age in 1960—per cent	100.0	100.0	100.0	100.0	100.0
Under 14 years	22.6	25.9	25.5	25.2	27.0
14-17	5.2	5.2	5.1	5.6	5.7
18-24	8.5	8.7	8.1	8.7	7.8
25-64	53.2	50.4	51.1	50.1	50.0
65 and over	10.5	9.8	10.2	10.4	9.5
Marital status in 1960					
Ages 14 and over—per cent	100.0	100.0	100.0	100.0	100.0
Single	25.2	24.0	21.7	25.6	22.6
Married	63.4	63.1	63.1	62.3	64.9
Widowed	9.6	9.5	9.2	10.1	8.7
Divorced	1.8	3.4	6.0	2.0	3.8

* Comprises net in-migrants from outside the city, and movement of persons in the armed forces. Minus sign (−) denotes loss.

Source: Metropolitan Life Insurance Company, "Population Profile of Our Largest Cities," *Statistical Bulletin* (November, 1961). Computed by the Statistical Bureau of the Metropolitan Life Insurance Company from data published by the Bureau of the Census and the National Vital Statistics Division of the National Center for Health Statistics.

changes resulted not only from the immigration of hundreds of thousands of Negroes, but also from the flight of large numbers of whites (except in Los Angeles) to outlying regions of the standard metropolitan statistical areas. These racial changes have significant implications for a variety of social problems— ranging from housing to crime and from education to race prejudice.[64]

The Population Differentials

Population is the basic raw material of social structure.[65] In Chapter 11, we considered some of the major differentials in the composition and distribution of population in the nation as a whole. We shall continue this discussion here to

---

[64] *Ibid.*, Table on page 2.

[65] See Amos H. Hawley, "Population Composition," Chapter 16 in Philip M. Hauser and Otis Dudley Duncan (eds.), *The Study of Population* (Chicago: University of Chicago Press, 1959).

include some of the differentials found in various forms of the community. Certain broad distinctions stand out, notably in sex ratio, marital status, employment of women, fertility, and mobility. We are reminded again of the hypothetical rural-metropolitan continuum, with small gradations between different communities along the continuum. The data from the Bureau of the Census are not always strictly comparable, inasmuch as some comparisons involve residents of standard metropolitan statistical areas and persons in "other territory," whereas other comparisons are stated in the more traditional terms of urban, rural-nonfarm, and rural-farm populations.

1. Sex ratio. The urban community has a decided excess of females over males. In 1950, there were 93.6 males per 100 females in the urban communities of the standard metropolitan statistical areas. Some ten years later, this ratio had decreased to 91.5 males per 100 females in the same areas. In the decade of the 1950's, the percentage of males in the general population as a whole also declined, partly because of the higher mortality rate of men and partly because of the increase in the armed forces. In the rural-farm population outside of the standard metropolitan areas, on the other hand, there were 108.2 males per 100 females in 1950, and 105.7 at the end of the decade.[66]

These community differences in the sex ratio may be explained in terms of selective migration. Young people find the city more attractive because of greater economic opportunities, recreational possibilities, and freedom from primary-group constraints. The attraction is proportionately stronger for young women than for young men. The latter have greater economic opportunities in the rural community as farm owners, sons of owners, and laborers. The horizon of the farm girl is limited to housework and marriage. Many young women seek both employment and husbands in the city, where they hope to find work as stenographers, receptionists, or private secretaries. The number of such interesting jobs is limited. With the preponderance of females in the urban population, the number of available husbands is also limited.

2. Marital status. Significant general differences also exist among various community populations in terms of marital status. (*a*) The urban population as a whole has a higher percentage of males *married* than the rural population. Some 69.9 per cent of the urban males over 14 years of age are married, as compared with 67.5 per cent of the rural males. For females, the relationships are reversed. An estimated 64.3 per cent of the urban female population are married, as compared with 69.8 per cent of the rural. (*b*) The percentage of *widowed* males is 3.6 for *both* urban and rural areas, whereas for widowed females the percentages are 12.9 and 10.5, respectively. (*c*) An estimated 2.3 per cent of all urban males are *divorced*, as compared with 1.7 per cent of all rural males. For females, the differences are proportionately greater, with 3.3 per cent of all urban females and 1.5 per cent of all rural females divorced.[67]

---

[66] Bureau of the Census, *Current Population Reports: Population Characteristics,* "Civilian Population of the United States, by Type of Residence: April 1959 and 1950," *op. cit.,* Table C.

[67] Bureau of the Census, United States Census of Population 1960, United States Summary, *General Population Characteristics,* Washington, 1961, Table 49.

The aforementioned comparisons are based upon urban and rural populations as broadly defined by the Bureau of the Census. When comparisons are made between communities of different population concentrations, more striking differences appear. The population living in the urban fringe *inside* the standard metropolitan statistical areas but *outside* the central cities contains the highest proportion of married males, 73.9 per cent. The comparable figure for females in the urban fringe is 69.3, which is next to the rural-farm areas (70.4) for all types of communities.[68] For both males and females, the urban fringe has a high proportion married, a situation that may indeed indicate that a "new" family is emerging in the urban fringe.[69]

When we compare the urban fringe and the central cities, other differences in marital status appear. As noted, 73.9 per cent of urban fringe males are married, whereas in the central cities only 67.3 per cent are in this happy state. The differences between the urban fringe and the central cities are more striking for females, with 69.3 per cent of the former and only 61.4 per cent of the latter married. Broken families, furthermore, are less common in the urban fringe than in the central cities. Some 2.8 per cent of the males in the urban fringe are widowed and 1.7 per cent are divorced; in the central cities the comparable figures are 4.1 per cent (widowed) and 2 8 per cent (divorced). For women, the differences are equally striking. In the urban fringe, 10.3 per cent of the women are widowed and 2.6 divorced, as compared with 13.9 and 4.0 per cent, respectively, in the central cities. The central cities have the highest percentage of divorced women of any type of community.[70]

Several explanations are apparent for this concentration of divorced women in the central cities of the standard metropolitan statistical areas. (*a*) City life is more conducive to divorce than is life in the open country or (apparently) in the urban fringe, and more families in the large urban centers are broken because of this. (*b*) Economic opportunities for divorced women are greater in the city than elsewhere; many divorcees migrate to the city in search of gainful employment. (*c*) The social stigma attached to divorce is not so strong in the large city as it is in smaller communities, a fact that further accounts for the migration of divorced women. (*d*) The latter situation also makes for under-enumeration of divorce in the smaller communities, where many women report their marital status as "widowed" or "married, spouse absent," instead of "divorced." (*e*) The chances for remarriage are better in the city than in the country, since divorced persons (as noted) come to the city to start again with a new partner.

3. *Fertility.* We examined the problem of fertility in Chapter 11, as one of the basic aspects of population. We indicated there that fertility has risen sharply since World War II, as measured by the average number of children per

---

[68] *Ibid.*

[69] Jaco and Belknap, "Is a New Family Form Emerging in the Urban Fringe?" *op. cit.*

[70] Bureau of the Census, United States Census of Population, United States Summary, *op. cit.*, Table 49.

1,000 women aged 15-44.[71] We are primarily interested here, however, in fertility differentials by type of residence and size of community. Throughout most of the history of this country, the rural family has been more fertile than the urban family. This ratio has been complicated by the high fertility of the foreign-born in the large cities, where the reproductive patterns of a peasant Europe have been transplanted to the urban slums. But by and large, the rural family has had more children than the urban. These differences continued through the decade of the 1950's, although the spread was somewhat reduced by the fact that *urban* fertility increased more rapidly in this period than *rural* fertility.[72]

Despite this short-term (1945-1960) differential, the rural-farm areas continue to have the highest fertility. For each 1,000 women who were ever married and who were of childbearing age in 1960, the numbers of children ever born were as follows: 3,008 children in rural-farm areas; 2,559 in rural-nonfarm areas; and 2,179 in urban areas.[73] These differences may be explained by a number of factors. In the long run, changes in traditional attitudes toward family size have been more pronounced in the city than in the country. Restrictions in urban housing, the increasing importance of material success, the demand for a higher standard of living, the idea of happiness (rather than children) as the criterion of marital success, changes in religious observance in the family, and the gainful employment of married women have been among the factors making for these changes. These secular attitudes, combined with a knowledge of contraception, tend to decrease fertility. Such knowledge is more widely disseminated in the city than in the country.[74]

4. Employment of married women. The number of married women in the labor force has fluctuated between 12 and 13 million in recent years. In 1960, the figure stood at 12,365,354, which represented 30.7 per cent of all married women living with their husbands.[75] The increase in the employment of married women during the 1950's was largely confined to those from 35 to 54 years of age. The rate among young married women (under 35) remained fairly constant, for these women were still in the childbearing and child rearing age groups. Middle-aged women have passed this period and today are increasingly seeking, and finding, gainful employment. In a recent year, 43.0 per cent of all married women aged 35-44 years, and 46.5 per cent of those aged 45-54 years, worked outside the home.[76]

Employment differences among urban, rural-nonfarm, and rural-farm women

---

[71] Bureau of the Census, *Current Population Reports: Population Characteristics*, "Fertility of the Population: March 1957," Series P-20, No. 84 (August 8, 1958), Table A.

[72] *Ibid.*, Table 4.

[73] Bureau of the Census, United States Census of Population 1960, United States Summary, *op. cit.*, Table 81.

[74] William F. Ogburn and Meyer F. Nimkoff, *Technology and the Changing Family* (Boston: Houghton Mifflin Company, 1955), pp. 113-122.

[75] Bureau of the Census, United States Census of Population 1960, United States Summary, *General Social and Economic Characteristics*, Final Report, Washington, 1962, Table 82.

[76] Bureau of the Census, *Current Population Reports: Labor Force*, "Marital and Family Characteristics of Workers: March 1958," Series P-50, No. 87 (January, 1959), Table 2.

are also apparent. In the urban population, 32.3 per cent of the married women living with their husbands are in the labor force. This figure compares with 28.4 in rural-nonfarm areas and 21.9 in rural-farm areas.[77] These differences are even more pronounced when it is noted that most of the gainfully employed rural-farm wives are engaged in agriculture and hence remain in or near the home during the working day. The role of the wife who works in an office or factory is very different from that of the one who works on a farm. Employment opportunities for women are more varied in the urban community than in the rural-farm or rural-nonfarm community. Clerical, sales, service, professional, and light manufacturing jobs constitute the principal forms of employment for women. In general, these are essentially urban activities.

When we consider the employment of married women in terms of residence and *color*, other distinctive considerations emerge. Some 31.2 per cent of all white married women in urban communities are gainfully employed, as compared with an astounding 44.1 per cent of nonwhite women living under similar conditions. Among rural-nonfarm women, the employed percentages were 28.0 for white women and 33.3 for nonwhite. For rural-farm wives, the percentages were 21.6 for white and 25.3 for nonwhite.[78] From the farm to the metropolitan center, the nonwhite (mostly Negro) wife plays a proportionately greater economic role than the white wife. The matriarchal character of many Negro families, whereby the wife and mother is the steady breadwinner, is clearly indicated at all community levels.

5. *Mobility.* The American people have always been on the move. The early settlers moving into the country back of the eastern seaboard, the families crossing the Alleghenies into the rich midlands, the newcomers taking up farms on the great prairies, the prospectors toiling through the passes of the Rockies, the men in search of gold in California, the depression migrants of the 1930's in search of work, the migrants after World War II looking for new homes and better jobs in the West—these and many more typify the restless mobility that has marked the American people. Under present conditions, these population movements are less spectacular than they were in an earlier day. But they are even more common than ever before. Mobility is an important characteristic of the community—whether rural, rural-nonfarm, urban, or metropolitan.

The Bureau of the Census defines mobile persons as those "who were living in a different house in the United States at the end of the period than at the beginning of the period." The period is usually one year. Mobile persons are divided into two major categories: (*a*) *intracounty* movers, who are living in a different house but in the same county; and (*b*) *intercounty* movers, who are living in a different county at the beginning and at the end of the period. Intercounty movers are further classified as to whether they migrated within a state or from one state to another. The over-all mobility of the American people

---

[77] Bureau of the Census, United States Census of Population 1960, United States Summary, *General Social and Economic Characteristics, op. cit.,* Table 82.

[78] *Ibid.*

between March 1960 and March 1961 was as follows: 20.0 per cent were living in a different house, of which number 13.7 per cent were still living in the same county and 6.3 per cent had moved from one county to another. In recent years, the yearly mobility rate has varied slightly from 18.6 to 21.0, with an average of 19.7 per cent. No discernible trend has been manifested.[79]

In the year 1960-1961, the greatest mobility was found among the rural-nonfarm population, with 22.1 per cent of this group making one or more moves. The urban population was next, with 19.8 per cent defined as mobile. As might be expected, the least mobile group was the rural-farm, with only 13.6 per cent changing their residence in the period under consideration. Farm *ownership*, as distinguished from farm *labor*, is one of the most physically stable of all occupations, and the rural community maintains the greatest continuity of social relationships because of this elementary fact.[80]

Significant differences in mobility are apparent by size of community *within* the urban and metropolitan categories. Contrary to the general impression, the great metropolitan areas are not as mobile as smaller urban communities. In areas of 3,000,000 or more in 1960-1961, the percentage of mobile persons was 16.9, whereas in cities of 250,000 to 1,000,000 it was 23.2. In cities of 25,000 or more *outside* the standard metropolitan statistical areas, the mobility rate was likewise high at 22.4. In terms of long-range mobility (between states), such cities of 25,000 or more had the highest rate, with 5.0 per cent; conversely, a mere 1.9 per cent of those in cities of 3,000,000 or more made such a move in 1960-1961. Only the rural-farm population, with its 1.3 per cent of interstate migrants, had a lower proportion of long-distance movers than did the large metropolitan areas. These differences may be seen in detail in Table 14.[81]

Trends in Community Development

The future development of the community is still somewhat obscure. As one expert puts it, ". . . urbanism is on the march, and no one is able to say whither or at what cost." [82] It is a reasonable assumption that dynamic changes will continue and that the future will not be the same as the past. The metropolitan community is developing in accordance with its own rhythms, which reflect modern methods of transportation and communication. The city of the past, especially in the Old World, grew up under an entirely different set of conditions.[83] The modern urban community is a dynamic social system, in which people interact in new ways and under conditions never before encountered.

---

[79] Bureau of the Census, *Current Population Reports: Population Characteristics*, "Mobility of the Population of the United States: March 1960 to March 1961," Series P-20, No. 118 (August 9, 1962), p. 1.
[80] *Ibid.*, p. 2.
[81] *Ibid.*, Table 2. For a further discussion of the implications of social mobility, vertical as well as horizontal, see Leo F. Schnore, "Social Mobility in Demographic Perspective," *American Sociological Review*, 26:407-423 (June, 1961).
[82] Nels Anderson, *op. cit.*, p. 73.
[83] Theodore Caplow, "Urban Structure in France," *American Sociological Review*, 17:544-549 (October, 1952).

Table 14. Percentage Distribution by Mobility Status and Type of Mobility of Civilian Population 1 Year Old and Over, by Place of Residence and Color, for the United States: March 1961 (Type of residence represents 1950 classification of territory)

Place of residence and color	Total civilian population	Same house (non-movers)	Different house in the United States (movers)					Abroad on March 1, 1960
			Total	Same county	Total	Within a state	Between states	
ALL CLASSES								
Total	100.0	79.4	20.0	13.7	6.3	3.1	3.2	0.6
Urban	100.0	79.5	19.8	14.2	5.6	2.5	3.1	0.7
In urbanized areas	100.0	80.1	19.2	14.3	5.0	2.2	2.7	0.7
Areas of 3,000,000 or more	100.0	82.4	16.9	13.2	3.7	1.8	1.9	0.7
Areas of 1,000,000 to 3,000,000	100.0	82.7	16.6	11.9	4.7	2.2	2.5	0.7
Areas of 250,000 to 1,000,000	100.0	76.3	23.2	17.3	5.9	2.6	3.3	0.5
Areas under 250,000	100.0	77.6	21.6	15.4	6.3	2.5	3.8	0.8
Not in urbanized areas	100.0	78.0	21.2	13.8	7.3	3.3	4.0	0.8
Places of 25,000 or more	100.0	76.1	22.4	14.6	7.9	2.9	5.0	1.5
Places under 25,000	100.0	78.7	20.7	13.6	7.1	3.5	3.6	0.6
Rural nonfarm	100.0	77.5	22.1	14.0	8.1	4.1	4.0	0.4
Rural farm	100.0	86.1	13.6	9.1	4.5	3.2	1.3	0.3
WHITE								
Total	100.0	79.7	19.7	13.1	6.6	3.2	3.4	0.6
Urban	100.0	80.0	19.2	13.3	5.9	2.6	3.2	0.8
In urbanized areas	100.0	81.0	18.3	13.2	5.1	2.3	2.8	0.7
Areas of 3,000,000 or more	100.0	84.0	15.3	11.8	3.5	1.8	1.7	0.7
Areas of 1,000,000 to 3,000,000	100.0	83.6	15.6	10.8	4.8	2.2	2.5	0.8
Areas of 250,000 to 1,000,000	100.0	77.2	22.3	15.7	6.6	2.9	3.6	0.6
Areas under 250,000	100.0	77.6	21.6	15.2	6.3	2.5	3.8	0.9
Not in urbanized areas	100.0	77.8	21.3	13.7	7.7	3.4	4.3	0.9
Places of 25,000 or more	100.0	76.1	22.3	14.0	8.3	2.9	5.4	1.6
Places under 25,000	100.0	78.4	21.0	13.5	7.5	3.6	3.9	0.6
Rural nonfarm	100.0	77.4	22.2	13.9	8.3	4.3	4.1	0.3
Rural farm	100.0	87.5	12.2	7.6	4.6	3.1	1.4	0.3
NONWHITE								
Total	100.0	76.9	22.7	18.4	4.3	2.0	2.3	0.5
Urban	100.0	75.9	23.6	19.4	4.2	1.9	2.3	0.4
In urbanized areas	100.0	74.8	24.8	20.6	4.2	1.7	2.5	0.4
Areas of 3,000,000 or more	100.0	73.1	26.3	21.3	4.9	2.0	2.9	0.7
Areas of 1,000,000 to 3,000,000	100.0	78.6	21.1	16.8	4.3	1.8	2.5	0.4
Areas of 250,000 to 1,000,000	100.0	71.4	28.4	26.0	2.4	0.8	1.6	0.1
Areas under 250,000	100.0	77.9	21.9	16.4	5.5	2.1	3.4	0.3
Not in urbanized areas	100.0	79.8	19.6	15.4	4.2	2.5	1.7	0.5
Places of 25,000 or more	100.0	76.1	23.4	18.9	4.5	2.5	2.0	0.4
Places under 25,000	100.0	81.3	18.2	14.0	4.1	2.5	1.6	0.6
Rural nonfarm	100.0	79.1	20.3	15.7	4.6	1.6	3.0	0.6
Rural farm	100.0	79.0	20.5	16.2	4.3	3.4	0.9	0.4

Source: Bureau of the Census, *Current Population Reports: Population Characteristics,* "Mobility of the Population of the United States: March 1960 to March 1961," *op. cit.,* Table 2.

The decentralization of the metropolitan community may decrease the relative importance of the central business district. Shopping centers in the suburbs and satellite cities are pointing the way to such a shift in the center of dominance. Many large companies are moving their main offices from the metropolitan centers to the smaller cities or even into the open country. Insurance companies, for example, whose contacts are primarily with their agents in the field, are finding the open country a convenient, economical, and efficient site for their main offices. Other managerial functions, which do not require close proximity to large banks and other credit agencies, are likewise locating in the urban fringe.[84]

The swallowing-up of the rural-farm and rural-nonfarm areas adjacent to the central city is another straw in the wind. This absorption is a result of changes in the metropolitan center, which are communicated to the adjacent areas. "With this continuing 'metropolitanization,'" comments one observer, "selected parts of the satellite rural areas become incorporated legally as well as functionally into the city and their places are taken by other rural areas brought into the city's immediate sphere of influence." [85]

Supermarkets thus stand where corn grew a few years ago; branches of expensive metropolitan shops spring up on filled-in swamps; and electronics companies erect modernistic plants where cattle formerly grazed. Families of all social and economic levels leave the central city to live in the urban fringe. As we have seen, these families are not necessarily drawn exclusively from the middle class and upper-middle class. Many of them work in the newly erected factories and live in blue-collar suburbs.[86] In some parts of the country, notably on the eastern seaboard, metropolitan areas are expanding until they reach the periphery of one or more adjacent areas. Continuous urban and urban fringe areas are arising, with no real rural areas at all. The city is conquering the open country.[87]

Even more rapid than this *physical* incorporation of the open country by the city is its *psychological* incorporation. The relative importance of the metropolitan community is increasing in the United States and all over the world. In this country, the prevailing culture is urban, reflecting many of the changes in social interaction that we have suggested. Institutions are increasingly urban in tone and pattern. Personality is more and more influenced by the mass media, which reflect urban attitudes. We shall consider these influences in Chapter 24. Suffice it to indicate here the general nature of this trend. By listening to the radio, viewing television, reading the mass-circulation magazines, and going to the movies, the rural dweller has greater "psychic mobility" than ever before.[88] He is therefore able to project himself in imagination into a world that is far from the primary community of an earlier day. This ability to take the role of other persons in imagination has, until recently, been more largely an urban than a rural trait. The mass media have given the rural resident a greater empathic ability than he has had in any other era.[89]

The social problems of the future will be increasingly *urban* problems, but in a somewhat different sense than was formerly the case. The traditional ap-

---

[84] Leo F. Schnore, "Metropolitan Growth and Decentralization," *op. cit.*
[85] Walter T. Martin, *op. cit.*, p. 183.
[86] Leo F. Schnore, "The Socio-Economic Status of Cities and Suburbs," *op. cit.*
[87] Glenn V. Fuguitt, "The City and Countryside," *op. cit.*, p. 256.
[88] Joseph R. Gusfield, "Mass Society and Extremist Politics," *American Sociological Review*, 27:19-30 (February, 1962).
[89] Daniel Lerner, *The Passing of Traditional Society* (Glencoe, Ill.: The Free Press, 1958), pp. 50-53.

proach to social problems was largely based, consciously or unconsciously, upon rural values. Many aspects of the behavior of urban persons were regarded as undesirable departures from the norms and hence as social problems.[90] In the future, the urban pattern may increasingly become the norm, rather than the deviation. The urban family, church, school, and government may well be the standards by which other institutions are judged. This change will never be complete, for rural values will remain strongly imbedded in the culture. The trend is, however, in this direction.

Social problems have traditionally dealt largely with persons of underprivileged status in an urban enviroment.[91] Some of these problems are in the course of substantial amelioration, if not eventual solution, in the affluent society of the 1960's. Future social problems will deal with persons from *all* social classes, notably that large and amorphous segment known as the middle class. These emerging problems will involve questions of status and role, self and other, and secondary rather than primary relations.[92] Many persons will feel deprived of status, even though they have a high level of material prosperity. Affection will be as important as affluence. Love will be as valued as a new automobile.[93] Many of these interpersonal problems are those of an urban community, or of a rural community becoming more urbanized. For better or worse, with its problems as well as its advantages, the society of the future will be an increasingly urban one.

---

[90] Francis E. Merrill, "Social Character and Social Problems," *Social Problems*, 3:7-12 (July, 1955).

[91] Cf. Leo F. Schnore, "Social Problems in an Urban-Industrial Context," *op. cit.*

[92] Jessie Bernard, *Social Problems at Midcentury: Role, Status, and Stress* (New York: Holt, Rinehart and Winston, 1957).

[93] Francis E. Merrill, "The Self and the Other: An Emerging Field of Social Problems," *Social Problems*, 4:200-207 (January, 1957).

SELECTED BIBLIOGRAPHY

Arensberg, Conrad M., "The Community-Study Method," *American Journal of Sociology*, 60:109-124 (September, 1954). Also: "The Community as Object and as Sample," *American Anthropologist*, 63:241-264 (April, 1961). In these two articles, the author makes a plea for the comparative method in the study of the community. The forms of social interaction in one community should thus be compared with those in other communities. Among the questions to be asked about a given community are its representativeness, completeness, inclusiveness, and cohesiveness.

Bernard, Jessie, *American Community Behavior* (revised edition). New York: Holt, Rinehart and Winston, 1962. This is an outstanding textbook on problems of the community and the larger society. The author bases her conceptual approach on social interaction, with particular reference to the processes of competition and conflict. In this frame of reference, many aspects of community (and social) organization and disorganization take on new meaning.

Beshers, James M., *Urban Social Structure*. Glencoe, Ill.: The Free Press, 1962. In this analytical study of the urban community, the author defines social

structure as "the over-all pattern or network of social relationships that
recur among a designated set of persons."

Bogue, Donald J., "Urbanism in the United States, 1950," *American Journal
of Sociology,* 60:471-486 (March, 1955). In this long and authoritative
article, the author explores some of the trends in urbanism evident at the
mid-point of the century. He suggests that urban ways and institutions will,
in the future, become increasingly typical of our society as a whole.

Davis, Kingsley, "The Origin and Growth of Urbanization in the World,"
American Journal of Sociology, 60:429-437 (March, 1955). By the ingenious use of historical and other data, the author offers some new and brilliant
hypotheses upon the origins and early development of the city. Viewed in
the long sweep of human development, the city (however defined) is a
comparatively recent way of life.

Fuguitt, Glenn V., "The City and Countryside," *Rural Sociology,* 28:246-261
(September, 1963). This article provides an excellent comparison of the
rural and urban community and the changing relationships between them.
The author cites considerable quantitative data from a variety of sources in
support of his basic hypothesis that the two types of community are becoming increasingly interdependent. The countryside, in short, is becoming
more urbanized.

Gibbs, Jack P., and Walter T. Martin, "Urbanization, Technology, and the
Division of Labor: International Patterns," *American Sociological Review,*
27:667-677 (October, 1962). In this study of urbanization in 45 countries,
the authors establish certain functional prerequisites for the development of
large urban centers. These prerequisites are: a division of labor, a relatively
high level of technological development, and an organization to obtain raw
materials at a distance.

Hillery, George A., Jr., "Definitions of Community: Areas of Agreement,"
Rural Sociology, 20:111-123 (June, 1955). This is an enumeration and
classification of some 94 definitions of community. The common elements
in most of these definitions are: social interaction, physical space, and emotional bond. Also: "Villages, Cities and Total Institutions," *American
Sociological Review,* 28:779-791 (October, 1963). This article continues
the author's analyses of the concept of community, with particular reference
to the "folk village" and city as compared with the "total institution"
(mental hospital, prison).

Mumford, Lewis, *The City in History.* New York: Harcourt, Brace & World,
1961. One of the leading humanistic scholars of our time here continues his
examination of the role of the city in the development of civilization as we
know it. The luminous insights of the author are supported by masses of
historical information gleaned from a number of sources. For the student
who is interested in the broad implications of urban life, this book is indispensable.

Reiss, Albert J., Jr., "The Sociological Study of Communities," *Rural Sociology,*
24:118-130 (June, 1959). This article contains some original insights on
the community and its study — e.g., "A community is an area for the
exercise of status."

Sanders, Irvin T., *The Community: An Introduction to a Social System.* New
York: The Ronald Press, 1958. The central thesis of this textbook is that the
community is essentially a system of social interaction. The book examines
at length some of the implications of this position — namely, the forms of
interaction, the factors in interaction, and changes in interaction at the
community level.

Stein, Maurice R., *The Eclipse of Community: An Interpretation of American*

Studies. Princeton: Princeton University Press, 1960. This is an important contribution to the study of the community. The first part is especially valuable to students because it contains an analysis of several of the most significant community studies made in recent decades. In addition, the author offers some penetrating suggestions on the comparative study of social interaction in the community.

Stewart, Charles T., "The Urban-Rural Dichotomy: Concepts and Uses," *American Journal of Sociology*, 64:152-158 (September, 1958). This article examines critically the concept of "rural-urban continuum," whereby rural areas are viewed as merging imperceptibly into urban along a line or "continuum." The author suggests that this idea is inadequate because of a number of emerging factors, notably the increase in mobility of many rural dwellers.

Vidich, Arthur J., and Joseph Bensman, *Small Town in Mass Society.* Princeton: Princeton University Press, 1958. This brilliant monograph is a departure from the usual study of small towns, in that it views them in their larger social setting. The dweller in the small agricultural community is seen as living in a world he never made, but trying desperately to understand this world with ideas and values from an earlier and simpler society.

Weber, Max, *The City* (Translated and edited by Don Martindale and Gertrude Neuwirth). Glencoe, Ill.: The Free Press, 1958. In this sociological classic, many insights were originally given by Max Weber that were subsequently developed by other students of the city. The long essay by Martindale that prefaces the book is especially valuable for its theoretical analysis of the city, using recent material that was not available to Weber.

Wirth, Louis, "Urbanism as a Way of Life," *American Journal of Sociology*, 44:1-24 (July, 1938). The sociological study of the urban community is the theme of this essay by the late Louis Wirth. The essay is a distillation of many important insights on the nature of city life. Recent empirical studies have questioned some of the generalizations, but for the most part the article remains as a brilliant sociological exposition of the nature of urban life.

20 *Human Ecology*

The Nature of Human Ecology

Social institutions are not distributed at random throughout the community. The institutions of the rural community are grouped in recognizable fashion about a center, with stores, banks, churches, and private houses taking their places in a familiar spatial pattern. The institutions of the metropolis likewise tend to form definite spatial patterns, although their complexity is so great that the form and structure are not readily apparent. Whatever their form, these spatial patterns provide the setting in which social interaction takes place on a more or less continuous basis. Individually and in groups, men communicate, compete, conflict, accommodate, assimilate, and otherwise take each other into account.[1] They carry on these processes of interaction in their various roles as members of families, churches, schools, business, professions, unions, governments, and other institutional groupings.[2]

This pattern of groups and institutions is constantly changing. In the dynamic process of community growth, both the form and the distribution of the major social structures are subject to modification. The central business district invades the areas adjacent to it, light manufacturing encroaches on neighborhoods that previously were exclusively residential, and the metropolitan area expands into suburbs and engulfs satellite cities. Likewise, one ethnic or racial group succeeds another in the slum areas, as Italians, Poles, Negroes, Mexicans, and Puerto Ricans arrive in successive waves and consecutively occupy the least desirable areas. In these and many other ways, human beings and social institutions occupy changing spatial patterns in the community.

The study of these patterns and relationships is known as human ecology. This field deals with such matters as: "... the structure of rural communities, the spatial patterning of cities, distinctive areas of human habitation within a city, social and cultural qualities that characterize and delimit regions, the various processes by which areal patterns arise and change, and the spatial distribution of population [and] institutions...."[3] Human ecology is not so much a separate discipline as *a point of view*, a way of looking at men and institutions in their spatial setting. The frame of reference of human ecology stresses the place of the institutions in the community and their relationships to each other. *Position* is the basic ecological consideration, and many other social relationships grow out of this underlying spatial factor.[4]

The ecological position of the social units emerges primarily from the processes of competition and mobility. In modern urban society, individuals are continually engaged in competitive interaction, whereby they strive to better their economic, social, and cultural positions. In this attempt, they move about within the community and from one community to another and, in the process, occupy new positions. At the same time, they are also conflicting, accommodating, assimilating, and engaging in the other processes of social interaction. The ecological approach, however, stresses the results of competition and reflects the place of the individual, the family, and the institution that emerges from competition and mobility.[5]

Human ecology has its roots in plant and animal ecology, which deals with the relationships of plants and animals to their physical environment. Human

---

[1] George A. Hillery, Jr., "Definitions of Community: Areas of Agreement," *Rural Sociology*, 20:111-123 (June, 1955). See also Irvin T. Sanders, *The Community: An Introduction to a Social System* (New York: The Ronald Press, 1958).

[2] Cf. Conrad M. Arensberg, "The Community-Study Method," *American Journal of Sociology*, 60:109-124 (September, 1954).

[3] James A. Quinn, *Human Ecology* (Englewood Cliffs, N.J.: Prentice-Hall, Inc., 1950), pp. 3-4.

[4] Robert E. Park, "The Concept of Position in Sociology," *Publication of the American Sociological Society*, 20:1-14 (1925).

[5] Robert E. L. Faris, "Ecological Factors in Human Behavior," Chapter 24 in James McV. Hunt (ed.), *Personality and the Behavior Disorders*, Volume II (New York: The Ronald Press, 1944), pp. 736-738.

geography is another forerunner of human ecology, with the stress here again upon the physical, rather than the social, environment. The emphasis in human ecology lies in the spatial position of the individual or institution in the social structure of the community. The central ecological concepts, therefore, deal with place, within which the more intimate social relationships occur. Plants and animals adjust to their physical environment as they find it. Man alone is capable of constructing his social environment. Human ecology is concerned with the spatial forms that this environment assumes.[6]

The development of the study of human ecology represents the work of a number of scholars in the field of sociology and related disciplines. The work of the late Robert E. Park constitutes perhaps the most influential single body of theory bearing on this point of view.[7] Subsequently, Roderick D. McKenzie[8] and Ernest W. Burgess[9] made significant basic contributions to the evolving theory of human ecology. In more recent years, a voluminous literature has arisen, and many studies of the urban community have employed the techniques initially framed by the pioneers in this rapidly evolving field.[10]

A large body of concrete knowledge of the urban community and its constituent institutions has been added to the sociological literature. By the use of ecological methods, insights have been gained into a variety of situations, ranging from land use to mental disorder. In our subsequent examination of the concepts and techniques of human ecology, we shall refer to some of these insights.

In the study of the community, human ecology plays an important, although by no means a definitive, role. Position provides the physical setting within which social interaction occurs. The ecologist is directly concerned with such positional problems as transportation, mobility, and the dynamic distribution of human beings and social institutions. Many of these elements are themselves the result of technological changes, and technology is therefore a casual factor in ecological considerations.[11] But man is also a symbol-using and evaluating animal, whose responses occur on a symbolic level.[12] The ecological point of view is thus of definite, although limited, relevance in the study of the complex interaction within the group, institution, and community. Ecological factors are, in short, *conditioning*, rather than *determining* factors, in that they "set the stage for man, the actor." [13] The central interest of sociology is the actor, rather than the stage.

---

[6] Louis Wirth, "Human Ecology," *American Journal of Sociology*, 50:483-488 (May, 1945).

[7] Robert E. Park, "Human Ecology," *American Journal of Sociology*, 42:1-15 (July, 1936).

[8] Roderick D. McKenzie, "The Ecological Approach to the Study of the Human Community," in Robert E. Park, Ernest W. Burgess, and Roderick D. McKenzie (eds.), *The City* (Chicago: University of Chicago Press, 1925).

[9] Burgess, "The Growth of the City: An Introduction to a Research Project," *The City, op. cit.*, pp. 47-62.

[10] August B. Hollingshead, "Community Research: Development and Present Condition," *American Sociological Review*, 13:136-146 (April, 1948).

[11] E. Gordon Ericksen, *Urban Behavior* (New York: The Macmillan Company, 1954), pp. 92-93.

[12] Christen T. Jonassen, "Cultural Variables in the Ecology of an Ethnic Group," *American Sociological Review*, 14:32-41 (February, 1949).

[13] Wirth, "Human Ecology," *op. cit.*, p. 488.

The Study of Ecological Areas

The concept of the natural area is central to the ecological approach. The natural area has been defined as a geographical area "characterized both by physical individuality and the cultural characteristics of the people" who live in it.[14] The essence of the concept is the word "natural," by which is meant that these areas are the result of natural and unplanned processes of urban growth. They have resulted from the propensities of human beings to cluster in ethnic groups, functional subdivisions, and other types of social patterns. Every urban community has its ethnic or racial areas, its central business district, its areas of high mobility, and its residential areas of different social classes. These areas have not been planned; they have instead resulted from spontaneous social interaction.

The natural area is a natural product in another sense. It seldom coincides with the administrative areas of the community, which are established for purposes of political organization. Natural areas cross the boundaries of precincts, wards, townships, and counties, as families, ethnic groups, factories, and other social units seek their places in the dynamic urban structure. The same precinct, ward, or congressional district contains several distinct natural areas, each with its characteristic human groups.

The natural area is a dynamic product of city growth, whereas the administrative area is more static. The latter is established by legal and formal forces and acquires vested interests. Hence it is difficult to change. The natural area, on the other hand, is constantly changing with the structure of the city, and any efforts to restrict this process are usually unsuccessful.[15] Such problem behavior as delinquency, crime, commercialized vice, family disorganization, and insanity assumes patterns that have little or no relationship to the administrative area.[16]

In the ecological areas of the large city, persons with similar characteristics tend to cluster in definite patterns. In general, these patterns take the form of a "status-value ranking," that is, reflecting such factors as education, income, and occupation.[17] Among the indices used to measure these "status-value" patterns are: "(a) median grade (in school) completed, (b) mean rent, (c) laborers, (d) college graduates, (e) professional workers, and (f) those seeking work." [18]

Some urban areas contain a low percentage of persons with more than a minimum of schooling. These areas also have a low mean rent, a higher pro-

---

[14] Harvey W. Zorbaugh, "The Natural Areas of the City," in Ernest W. Burgess (ed.), *The Urban Community* (Chicago: University of Chicago Press, 1926), p. 223.

[15] Ericksen, *op. cit.,* p. 202-203.

[16] Wirth, "Human Ecology," *op. cit.,* p. 485.

[17] Calvin F. Schmid, Earle H. MacCannell, and Maurice D. Van Arsdol, Jr., "The Ecology of the American City: Further Comparison and Validation of Generalizations," *American Sociological Review,* 23:392-401 (August, 1958).

[18] Calvin F. Schmid, "Generalizations Concerning the Ecology of the American City," *American Sociological Review,* 15:264-281 (April, 1950), p. 281.

portion of laborers than professional workers, and a larger proportion of unemployed. Other areas have different proportions of persons in these "status-value" categories. Position in these ecological areas goes far toward defining the social pattern within which the individual interacts. The general processes of competition and mobility thus set off groups of persons with high ranking in such status-laden terms as education, income, and occupation.[19]

The natural area has status implications in another sense. Persons living in different areas in the large city are very much aware of the status of the local community in which they reside. This status may be high or low, but it is a fact of life and the residents are conscious of it. In a study of a census tract in central Boston, Rose found that people living on Beacon Hill or in the "West End" not only knew the name of their local community but could name most of the boundaries that set it off from other areas. In his words, "it can be said that residents of the area studied regard themselves as living in a named area of the city, and agree on the boundaries of their area in all but one direction."[20] Similarly, such natural areas in Boston and other cities as Back Bay, the South End, Chinatown, Little Italy, Harlem, Little Poland, Back-of-the-Yards, and the like serve to identify the ethnic background and social status of the residents, both in their own minds and in the minds of other persons.[21]

The natural area is not confined to the urban community. The same general approach has been used in the study of rural areas, starting with the pioneer work of C. J. Galpin[22] and continuing through the recent investigations of the rural sociologists.[23] A central interest in most of these studies lies in delimiting the rural community and its constituent areas in terms of the functional relationships between its institutions and the persons living within and without its formal boundaries.[24] The emotional ties that bind the individual to the primary groups of family, neighborhood, and ethnic group, however, are also important in identifying the rural community and its various areas. These ties produce a sort of "moral integration" in the rural community and bring the people closer together through their common membership in face-to-face groups.[25]

In the rural community, the natural environment is more conspicuous than

[19] Schmid, MacCannell, and Van Arsdol, Jr., *op. cit.* See also Scott Greer, "Urbanism Reconsidered: A Comparative Study of Local Areas in a Metropolis," *American Sociological Review,* 21:19-25 (February, 1956).

[20] H. Lawrence Ross, "The Local Community: A Survey Approach," *American Sociological Review,* 27:75-84 (February, 1962), p. 79.

[21] Kevin Lynch, *The Image of the City* (Cambridge: The Technology Press, 1960), cited by Rose, *op. cit., pp.* 78ff.

[22] C. J. Galpin, *The Social Anatomy of an Agricultural Community,* Research Bulletin No. 34, Agricultural Experiment Station, University of Wisconsin, Madison, 1915.

[23] George A. Hillery, Jr., "The Folk Village: A Comparative Analysis," *Rural Sociology,* 26:335-353 (December, 1961); George A. Hillery, Jr., "Villages, Cities, and Total Institutions," *American Sociological Review,* 28:779-791 (October, 1963).

[24] Cf. Albert J. Reiss, Jr., "The Sociological Study of Communities," *Rural Sociology,* 24:118-130 (June, 1959).

[25] Peter A. Munch and Robert B. Campbell, "Interaction and Collective Identification in a Rural Locality," *Rural Sociology,* 28:18-34 (March, 1963).

in the large city. In the latter, the physical surroundings are in part dominated by the social; railroad tracks, express highways, and freight yards cut through and over rivers, hills, and ravines. Ecological distribution in the rural community, on the other hand, may occur in a narrow valley, on the slopes of a sheltering hill, or on the banks of a river. Man exerts an increasing dominance over the topography in the urban areas, whereas this dominance is not so noticeable in the country.

Many of the distinctions between the rural and urban community are, as we saw in the previous chapter, on the process of change.[26] The increased mobility of the rural dweller has changed his relationships to other members of the local community and to people outside of it. In many "rural" areas, men and women commute daily from farms to factories forty or fifty miles away. In their factory jobs, these rural commuters must adjust to the machine in the same way as do the urban industrial workers.[27] Although their residence remains rural, their interaction assumes many urban overtones. Radio and television have further modified their rural "environment," and their residential "position" has accordingly ceased to be a reliable indication of their activities.[28]

The Forms of Ecological Areas

The urban community is the focal point of many, although by no means all, social problems. Social interaction differs from one area to another in the urban community, and many urban problems lend themselves to the ecological approach.[29] The child reared in a delinquency area has different norms and goals from the child whose early life is spent in an area with no delinquent patterns. The status of the homeless man in an area of transition is not the same as that of a settled property-owner in a residential area. The forms of family life in a foreign-born area, with its vestiges of the patriarchal system, differ from those in areas where the family relationship is an equalitarian one. In many such problem situations, the ecological approach has been used with significant success.[30]

1. *Areas of delinquency*. Every policeman, detective, and crime reporter knows, in a rough and empirical way, that some areas of the large city have high rates of delinquency and others do not. Not so generally known is the fact that delinquency has remained high in certain areas for generations, irrespective of the different ethnic and racial groups that have lived there.

---

[26] Walter T. Martin, "Ecological Change in Satellite Rural Areas," *American Sociological Review*, 22:173-183 (April, 1957).

[27] Charles T. Stewart, Jr., "The Urban-Rural Dichotomy: Concepts and Uses," *American Journal of Sociology*, 64:152-158 (September, 1958).

[28] Glenn V. Fuguitt, "The City and Countryside," *Rural Sociology*, 28:246-261 (September, 1963).

[29] Leo F. Schnore, "Social Problems in an Urban-Industrial Context," *Social Problems*, 9:228-240 (Winter, 1962).

[30] For certain statistical reservations concerning the ecological method, cf. W. S. Robinson, "Ecological Correlations and the Behavior of Individuals," *American Sociological Review*, 15:351-357 (June, 1950).

Furthermore, areas of consistently high delinquency are characterized by other indices of social disorganization, such as adult crime, excessive mobility, infant mortality, unemployment, and commercialized vice. Delinquency is a function of the entire urban community, with special emphasis upon the natural areas in which the delinquents live.

In a series of careful ecological studies, Clifford R. Shaw and Henry D. McKay demonstrated the above thesis, first in Chicago and then in other American cities. Their work in Chicago initially covered the decades 1900-1940 and was based upon the spatial distribution of all male delinquents. Area maps showed striking differences in the number of delinquents, with the same areas demonstrating high rates year after year and decade after decade. Shaw and McKay concluded that the consistent association between high rates of delinquency and other forms of community disorganization "not only sustains the conclusion that delinquent behavior is related dynamically to the community but also appears to establish that all community characteristics, including delinquency, are products of the operation of general processes more or less

In the urban community, man increasingly dominates the topography; in this picture of Chicago, the physical environment is overshadowed by the social environment.

common to American cities." [31] Furthermore, the relatively constant rate of delinquency in certain areas, in spite of steady and successive changes in ethnic composition, provides direct and positive proof that the forces producing delinquency are "inherent in the community." [32]

The ecological distribution of urban crime has also been investigated in the city of Seattle, Washington with the mathematical techniques of the behavioral sciences. The following forms of antisocial behavior were examined: suicide, drunkenness, disorderly conduct, vagrancy, sex offenses, larceny, fraud, burglary, and robbery. The indices for these different forms of behavior were, in turn, related to a number of social, economic, and demographic factors. Among the latter were: "population change, population mobility, fertility differentials, housing, population characteristics as reflected by age, sex, marital status, income, education, occupation, and employment." [33].

The findings of this study are too complex to report completely. Some areas, for example, were found to have comparatively weak family life and low social cohesion. These areas had the following qualities: "a high proportion of women in the labor force, low fertility, low proportion of married persons, high percentage of older people and of foreign-born whites, declining or low rate of population growth, high population mobility, lack of home ownership . . . low educational status, low median income, a high proportion of unemployed persons, and a comparatively small percentage of proprietors, managers, and officials." [34] These ecological factors were in turn related to high rates for such forms of criminal behavior as automobile theft, shoplifting, non-residential robbery, and check fraud. Other areas of the city with different combinations of ecological characteristics were found to have different froms of criminal behavior.[35]

Delinquency is primarily a group phenomenon, and most delinquencies are committed by adolescents in groups. The teenager learns delinquent attitudes and techniques from his peers, and these patterns are passed on in the group. In this way, a delinquent subculture arises among lower-class boys, who are unable to gain status in the larger culture dominated by middle-class values.[36] The boy therefore steals, commits sexual delinquencies, and (to an increasing degree) performs acts of wanton physical aggression against other persons. In this way, he acquires status in terms of the values of the delinquent gang. Although he professes to scorn the middle-class culture, the very violence of his reaction suggests that he is not fully committed to the values of the delin-

---

[31] Clifford R. Shaw and Henry D. McKay, *Juvenile Delinquency and Urban Areas* (Chicago: University of Chicago Press, 1942), p. 435.

[32] *Ibid.*

[33] Calvin F. Schmid, "Urban Crime Areas: Part I," *American Sociological Review*, 25:527-542 (August, 1960), p. 530.

[34] *Ibid.*, pp. 535-536.

[35] See also Calvin F. Schmid, "Urban Crime Areas: Part II," *American Sociological Review*, 25:655-678 (October, 1960).

[36] Albert K. Cohen, *Delinquent Boys: The Culture of the Gang* (Glencoe, Ill.: The Free Press, 1955). For a criticism of this position, cf. John I. Kitsuse and David C. Dietrick, "Delinquent Boys: A Critique," *American Sociological Review*, 24:208-215 (June, 1959).

quent subculture. The delinquent boy, in short, lives in a world of conflicting values.[37]

The gang does not change its membership with sufficient rapidity to change the delinquent patterns, which continue regardless of the ethnic composition of the community.[38] The same areas have successively been inhabited by immigrants from Ireland, Italy, Poland, the Deep South (Negroes), and Puerto Rico, but this apparently makes little difference. In this general sense, delinquency is seen as "adaptive behavior on the part of the male children of rural migrants acting as members of adolescent peer groups in their efforts to find their way to meaningful and respected adult roles, essentially unaided by the older generation and under the influence of criminal models for whom the inner city areas furnish a haven." [39] It is in such a context that delinquency is said to be "inherent in the community." The ecological areas provide the setting within which delinquency continues.

2. *Areas of family disorganization.* Family disorganization is a second type of behavior that has been studied by ecological methods. The general thesis is (*a*) that the prevailing patterns in a given ecological area are reflected in the forms of family life; and (*b*) that groups with different goals, aspirations, and values manifest different types and degrees of family disorganization. Within the limits of the metropolitan community, the most extreme variations in family maladjustment are apparent, ranging from areas with high rates of desertion but almost no divorce to those in which the reverse is true. Some of these representative areas are as follows:[40]

(*a*) *Patriarchal-family areas.* These are areas occupied largely by foreign-born industrial workers, whose early years were spent in societies where the partiarchal-family patterns are still strong. These persons are mostly of the Roman Catholic faith, which does not countenance divorce. As a result of these and other cultural factors, these areas are marked by high rates of desertion and practically no divorce. Many husbands desert their wives and thus avail themselves of what used to be called "the poor man's divorce." [41] In this informal way, they free themselves of their family responsibilities without divorce.

(*b*) *Broken-family areas.* A second type of area is that in which most of the wives work and where the family lives in furnished rooms, kitchenette

---

[37] Solomon Kobrin, "The Conflict of Values in Delinquency Areas," *American Sociological Review,* 16:653-661 (October, 1951).

[38] For an original analysis of gang behavior in New York City, see Lewis Yablonsky, "The Delinquent Gang as a Near-Group," *Social Problems,* 7:108-117 (Fall, 1959).

[39] Solomon Kobrin, "The Chicago Area Project—a 25-Year Assessment," *Annals of the American Academy of Political and Social Science,* 322:19-29 (March, 1959), p. 22. For a further examination of delinquency areas, see Roland J. Chilton, "Continuity in Delinquency Area Research: A Comparison of Studies for Baltimore, Detroit, and Indianapolis," *American Sociological Review,* 29:71-83 (February, 1964).

[40] Ernest R. Mowrer, *Family Disorganization* (Chicago: University of Chicago Press, 1939), Chapter V. See also Ernest R. Mowrer, "The Trend and Ecology of Family Disintegration in Chicago," *American Sociological Review,* 3:344-353 (June 1938).

[41] Other data indicate that high rates of desertion are by no means confined to lower-class industrial areas. Cf. William M. Kephart, "Occupational Level and Marital Disruption," *American Sociological Review,* 20:456-465 (August, 1955).

apartments, and apartment hotels. The majority of such "families" consist of husband and wife, and comparatively few of them have children. The forces pushing the spouses from the home are often stronger than those holding them to it. The prevailing form of family disorganization in these areas is divorce. The wife is self-supporting and the economic obstacles to divorce are therefore minimized.

(c) *Matriarchal-family areas.* A third general type of family is found in the residential suburbs outside the corporate limits of the central city. Here most of the husbands commute and the wives play an important role in community activities. The status of the wife is correspondingly high. In such family areas, the divorce rate is relatively high, but there is little desertion. Social status is seriously threatened by desertion, whereas no such stigma is attached to divorce.

(d) *"Fringe"-family areas.* A new type of family may be emerging on the fringe of the central cities of standard metropolitan areas. The "fringe" in this sense includes "suburbs, satellite cities, and any other territory located immediately outside central cities whose labor force is engaged in nonfarm activities." [42] In contrast to the various types of broken-family areas found within the central city, the "fringe" areas demonstrate many aspects of a strengthened and revitalized family, especially with regard to family functions. In summary, the "fringe" family differs from the family of the central city in the following terms: "... higher fertility, larger families, more marriage, more children, greater number in the labor force, more home ownership,

---

[42] E. Gartly Jaco and Ivan Belknap, "Is a New Family Form Emerging in the Urban Fringe?" *American Sociological Review,* 18:551-557 (October, 1953), p. 551, footnote 6.

Delinquency is primarily a group phenomenon, and most delinquencies are committed by adolescents in groups.

greater fluidity, less mobility, lower mortality, more aged persons, lower age at marriage." [43]

3. *Areas of mental disorder.* The combination of ecological, cultural, and interactional forces operating in the urban community is related to another form of problem behavior—that involving various types of mental disorder. The ecological approach is part of the broader sociological approach to mental illness, which concentrates upon the social processes that appear to be related to different types of psychic maladjustment.[44] An eminent student of mental disorder has this to say: "... an investigator making an ecological study of mental diseases, or a mental disease, is concerned with discovering if the incidence of disease, or a given disease, will vary significantly between different temporal, spatial, or social environments. These environments," he continues, "are frequently delimited as social classes, religious groups, occupations, types of families, types of communities, levels of education, historical times, or special environments such as school, military unit, or prison." [45]

Mental illness is the most complicated behavior that has been considered in an ecological context, and we can merely indicate some of the tentative findings. In general terms, the human ecologist has found that "... the probability of becoming psychotic is not random or equal among subgroups of the population ... and persons with different social attributes and affiliations have different rates of psychotic disorders." [46] Such persons, in turn, appear to cluster in different areas of the urban community and thereby form distinctive ecological patterns. In general, the highest rates for certain forms of mental disease are found in and near the central business district; the areas immediately adjacent, with their large transient population of highly mobile persons, have the next highest rates; and the residential areas on the edge of the city have the lowest rates. The rates of first admission to mental hospitals thus show a progressive decrease as one moves from the center of the city toward the periphery.[47]

This generalization applies to commercial-industrial cities, and the same general pattern has emerged in other studies of the same type of community.[48] In cities with another type of ecological structure, however, a different distribution of mental disease emerges. In a city with a political, rather than a commercial-industrial base, one study found that: "The ecological distribution of incidence rates [for mental disorder] differed from the patterns

---

[43] *Ibid.*, p. 557.

[44] John A. Clausen, "The Sociology of Mental Illness," Chapter 22 in Robert K. Merton, Leonard Broom, and Leonard S. Cottrell, Jr. (eds.), *Sociology Today* (New York: Basic Books, Inc., 1959), p. 486.

[45] H. Warren Dunham, "Social Structure and Mental Disorders: Competing Hypotheses of Explanation," *Milbank Memorial Fund Quarterly*, 39:259-292 (April, 1961), p. 262.

[46] E. Gartly Jaco, "Social Factors in Mental Disorders in Texas," *Social Problems*, 4:322-328 (April, 1957), p. 325.

[47] Robert E. L. Faris and H. Warren Dunham, *Mental Disorders in Urban Areas* (Chicago: University of Chicago Press, 1939).

[48] H. Warren Dunham, "The Current Status of Ecological Research in Mental Disorder," *Social Forces*, 25:321-326 (March, 1947).

found in commercial-industrial cities in that no pattern of decreasing rates from the center to the periphery was found." [49]

The latter findings in no way invalidate the ecological approach to the study of mental disorder. In fact, they substantiate this approach by indicating that mental disorder is related to the ecological structure of the city, no matter what that structure may be. The functional differences between cities, as well as those between areas in the same city, appear to be related to mental disorder. The pattern derived from one functional type of city can be extended to others of the same type, but apparently not to other types. Social interaction assumes different forms with different implications for behavior in different ecological settings.

The *fact* that characteristic distributions of mental disorders emerge in different types of cities and in different areas within them is thus well documented. The *causes* of these distributions are not so clear. Some scientists maintain that persons currently suffering from or susceptible to certain mental disorders tend to gravitate to specific areas in the industrial city and thereby increase the rates. This is called the "drift" hypothesis. In their study of New Haven, Hollingshead and Redlich do not attribute much importance to this hypothesis.[50] Others believe that the most prevalent form of mental disorder (schizophrenia) reflects social isolation in a variety of forms. Hence the concentration of schizophrenic disorders in certain areas reflects the numbers of isolated persons found there.[51]

Still other scholars state that the concept of social isolation is plausible as far as it goes, but that it does not explain why *some* persons in these areas become schizophrenic and others in the same area do not.[52] The ecological position of the individual, in this view, sets the framework in which mental disorders arise, but it tells us little of their actual causation.[53] Most ecologists would probably accept this qualification. A related position is taken, finally, by those who believe that the concentration of mental disorders is also a *class* (sociocultural) matter, rather than an exclusively *ecological* (positional) one.[54]

The latter position is illustrated by extensive research studies of mental disease, conducted by scholars at Yale University. These studies were directed primarily at the relationship between position in the class structure and mental disorder. They demonstrate conclusively that members of the *lowest* class groups show the *highest* rates of schizophrenia. In the lowest class in New

---

[49] Ivan Belknap and E. Gartly Jaco, "The Epidemiology of Mental Disorders in a Political-Type City, 1946-1952," *Interrelations Between the Social Environment and Psychiatric Disorders* (New York: Milbank Memorial Fund, 1953), p. 241.

[50] August B. Hollingshead and Frederick C. Redlich, *Social Class and Mental Illness* (New York: John Wiley & Sons, 1958), pp. 244-248.

[51] E. Gartly Jaco, "The Social Isolation Hypothesis and Schizophrenia," *American Sociological Review*, 19:567-577 (October, 1954), pp. 575-576.

[52] David T. Schwartz and Norbett L. Mintz, "Ecology and Psychosis Among Italians in 27 Boston Communities," *Social Problems*, 10:371-374 (Spring, 1963).

[53] John A. Clausen and Melvin L. Kohn, "The Ecological Approach in Social Psychiatry," *American Journal of Sociology*, 60:140-151 (September, 1954).

[54] Hollingshead and Redlich, *Social Class and Mental Illness, op. cit.*

Haven, Connecticut, the incidence of schizophrenia was approximately *eleven times* as high in proportion to numbers as in the highest class.[55] In general, the two class groups occupied characteristic areas in the city, and in this sense the distribution of mental disease followed a recognizable ecological pattern.

Further light is thrown upon the general relationship between ecological position and mental illness by a study of mental disease in 27 local communities in Boston. All of these communities had high concentrations of Italian-born and second-generation Italians. This study found an *inverse* relationship between the density of Italians in a given community and the incidence of both schizophrenia and manic-depressive psychosis. Areas with *many* Italians thus had *fewer* cases of insanity. Large numbers of persons with the same ethnic background apparently provide mutual emotional support and keep people from mental breakdowns. Such persons are presumably freer from the cultural isolation that often culminates in mental breakdown.[56]

The study just discussed, like others in the field, offers a plausible explanation for the differential tendency toward mental disease in different local communities. It does not explain, however, why *some* members of the community succumb to stress and *others* do not. In this latter connection, Kleiner and Parker surveyed the literature and suggested a possible relationship between "status position, social mobility, and mobility orientation (i.e., discrepancy between achievement and aspiration)" and individual cases of mental illness. Persons who have failed to reach their goals feel badly about themselves and this lowering of their self-image may be related to their mental breakdown. A glaring discrepancy between what a person *is* and what he would *like* to be may predispose him to mental illness[57] and even to suicide.[58]

The Dynamics of Ecological Distribution

We have been concerned up to this point with patterns of ecological distribution in the urban community. Taken by itself, this is essentially a static conception, inasmuch as it takes the natural area as an accomplished fact and does not inquire into the forces that brought it about. The ecological point of view, however, is a highly *dynamic* approach to social interaction, and we shall devote the balance of our discussion to an emphasis of this fact. In this sense, indeed, "The metropolitan community can be viewed as a vast processing mill for the allocation of positions, positions which vary according to stages of the life-cycle." [59] This process of allocation is complex, and the literature is

[55] *Ibid.*, Cf. Jerome K. Myers and Bertram H. Roberts, *Family and Class Dynamics in Mental Illness* (New York: John Wiley & Sons, Inc., 1959).

[56] Schwartz and Mintz, *op. cit.*

[57] Robert J. Kleiner and Seymour Parker, "Goal-Striving, Social Status, and Mental Disorder: A Research Review," *American Sociological Review*, 28:189-203 (April, 1963).

[58] Warren Breed, "Occupational Mobility and Suicide Among White Males," *American Sociological Review*, 28:179-188 (April, 1963).

[59] Warren A. Peterson and George K. Zollschan, "Social Processes in the Metropolitan Community," Chapter 34 in Arnold M. Rose (ed.), *Human Behavior and Social Processes* (Boston: Houghton Mifflin Company, 1962), p. 654.

extensive. We may indicate some of the forces that give rise to ecological distribution, with particular reference to the spatial patterning of the community.

1. Mobility. The basic ecological process is mobility. Park and Burgess indicated the importance of mobility when they spoke of a society as "made up of individuals spatially separated, territorially distributed, and capable of independent locomotion." [60] Social mobility has two general forms—*vertical* and *horizontal.* The former means movement up or down in the status hierarchy, whereas the latter means movement from place to place, usually (but not always) within the same status.[61] We have already discussed vertical mobility in connection with the class structure. In the present (and ecological) sense, we are speaking of horizontal mobility, whereby persons move from place to place in an attempt to better their competitive positions.

The urban community is the scene of many such restless movements; some of these are daily and habitual and others are spasmodic and random. Among the results of these movements are "suburbanization, centralization, concentration, segregation, invasion, and succession." [62]. The most common form of movement is the daily commutation from home to job. The extent of this daily mobility has been measured by the Bureau of the Census, which found that about one-seventh of all workers work in a county different from that in which they live. Specifically, 11.5 per cent work outside the county in which they live, and an additional 2.6 per cent work both in their home county and in another county. This figure does not include the large number who live in a suburb outside the central city but in the same county and who daily commute to work. Their movements are extensive, but they are not indicated in the 14.1 per cent of all workers who live and work in different counties.[63]

Horizontal mobility sometimes involves *both* physical movement and a subsequent change in social relationships. Changes in forms of status often accompany this type of mobility. A person may change his home, job, marital status, or religious affiliation. He must also adjust to changing circumstances in the course of his daily, weekly, monthly, and yearly movements.[64] These related modifications in physical position and social status are related to such diverse factors as technological innovations in methods of production (mechanized agriculture) and changing international relations (defense industries).[65] Movement by itself, however, is not as important as the ensuing social con-

---

[60] Robert E. Park and Ernest W. Burgess, *Introduction to the Science of Sociology* (Chicago: University of Chicago Press, 1924), p. 508.

[61] Leo F. Schnore, "Social Mobility in Demographic Perspective," *American Sociological Review,* 26:407-423 (June, 1961).

[62] See Leo G. Reeder, "Social Differentials in Mode of Travel, Time and Cost in the Journey to Work," *American Sociological Review,* 21:56-63 (February, 1956).

[63] Bureau of the Census, *Current Population Reports: Population Characteristics,* "County of Work and County of Residence: September, 1954," Series P-20, No. 60 (August 17, 1955).

[64] Donald J. Bogue, "The Quantitative Study of Social Dynamics and Social Change," *American Journal of Sociology,* 57:565-568 (May, 1952).

[65] Schnore, "Social Mobility in Demographic Perspective," *op. cit.,* p. 421.

tacts. People who move about a great deal develop different life patterns from those who stay at home.

Social mobility also goes beyond the spatial confines of the urban community. Mobility has national, as well as local, implications. We have considered some of these implications elsewhere in connection with: (*a*) major movements of population (Chapter 11), and (*b*) population differentials between communities (Chapter 19). In any one year, approximately 20 per cent of the population are mobile, in the sense that they are living in a different house than they were a year before. In March, 1961, an even 20.0 per cent of all persons 1 year old and older were in this category. Of this number, 13.7 per cent lived in a different house in the same county, and 6.3 per cent were living in a different county. In absolute numbers, some 35,500,000 persons changed their place of residence at least once within a single year.[66]

Social mobility has a varied effect upon social interaction. The mobile person changes his place of residence, his job, and his way of life in order to better himself in an economic, social, and cultural sense. In many cases, he is actually able to do this. At the same time, however, the mobile person in a strange city may be cut off from family, friends, and primary institutions. In these surroundings, he may fall sick, lose his job, or otherwise suffer one of the crises of an urban and industrial society. Under these conditions, he must turn for help to the impersonal agencies of public welfare. The increase in mobility means an increase in public services of this kind.[67]

2. Migration. A second major ecological process is migration. Like mobility, migration has national and international implications, although we are primarily concerned here with its local aspects. Both of these forms of human locomotion involve physical movement, but their nature is essentially different. Mobility is a relatively continuous process, involving a way of life for such intensely mobile persons as the hobo and the migratory-casual worker. The commuter and the traveling salesman are also mobile, inasmuch as their movements are habitual and ordinarily involve no major changes in status. Migration is a movement that may occur only once in the life of the individual or family, but which inescapably alters their way of life.

The movement of an immigrant family from southern Italy to the teeming warrens of the Lower East Side of New York City is a classic example of migration. Members of the migratory unit leave their culture behind them and enter a new culture, to which they adjust as best they can. In so doing, they undergo many changes in status. Place of residence, occupation, family position, and religious affiliation are some of these status modifications. The peasant turned industrial worker must make many adjustments, of which the learning of new work skills is only one. He must accept new physical surroundings;

---

[66] Bureau of the Census, *Current Population Reports: Population Characteristics*, "Mobility of the Population of the United States: March 1960 to March 1961," Series P-20, No. 118 (August 9, 1962), Table 2.

[67] Wilbur J. Cohen, "Current and Future Trends in Public Welfare," *Social Service Review*, 29:247-259 (September, 1955), p. 259.

he must adapt himself to a new social structure; and he must reconcile himself to a system of family relationships in which the patriarchal father is no longer the dominant figure. In short, he occupies a new ecological position and must make the necessary social and cultural adjustments that come with this new position.[68]

In historical times, migration was an enterprise involving whole clans, tribes, and nations. These wandering peoples took their culture with them, and the members of the group did not lose their background of patterned behavior. The modern migrant is in a different situation altogeteher. He leaves behind the network of personal relationships that constitute his own culture base. He tries as best he can to continue these relationships in the ethnic areas of the large American city, where fellow Italians, Poles, or Puerto Ricans constitute small cultural islands in the sea of conventional American society. But as soon as the new migrant steps out of these insulated areas, he has left familiar surroundings. His new status is that of a stranger in a foreign country. In the process of migration, the "cake of custom" is broken, never to be remade.[69]

Migration produces conflict between the culture patterns of the old world and those of the new. These conflicts are apparent in many of the areas of the urban community that we have considered. Areas of delinquency, crime, desertion, and mental disorder are among those in which culture conflict plays an important part.[70] Persons whose early lives are spent in one culture are uncertain of their roles in another. They do not know what is expected of them, and they become what Park has graphically called "marginal men." This type of person has been described as: "A cultural hybrid, a man living and sharing intimately in the cultural life of two distinct peoples . . . a man on the margin of two cultures and two societies, which never completely interpenetrated and fused." [71] Many of the ecological areas of the urban community are peopled by men and women thus spiritually and culturally isolated, even though they may be physically surrounded by thousands of other persons.

The traditional forms of migration in this country have involved the scores of millions who came to our shores from the Old World. The concept of the "melting pot" arose from this situation, wherein the various immigrant strains were hopefully assumed to merge triumphantly to form a new and enriched American culture.[72] The restriction of such immigration in recent decades has modified this picture. The percentage of foreign-born persons is steadily declining, and in a few decades will be negligible. The places of these immigrants in the slums and ghettos of the metropolitan centers have been taken

---

[68] Oscar Handlin, *The Uprooted* (Boston: Little, Brown and Company, 1951).

[69] *Ibid.*, Chapter 1.

[70] Louis Wirth, "Culture Conflict and Delinquency," *Social Forces*, 9:484-492 (June, 1931).

[71] Robert E. Park, "Human Migration and the Marginal Man," *American Journal of Sociology*, 33:881-893 (May, 1928), p. 892.

[72] See Nathan Glazer and Daniel P. Moynihan, *Beyond the Melting Pot* (Cambridge: Joint Center for Urban Studies, Massachusetts Institute of Technology and Harvard University, 1963).

by new swarms of migrants, whose adjustment problems are in many ways even more frustrating then those of the European-born.

These new migrants are the "rural dispossessed," comprising hundreds of thousands of men, women, and children from rural areas who have crowded into the big cities of the North in the past two decades. The most conspicuous of these groups are the Negroes, who have fled the Deep South and found a precarious foothold in the blighted areas of New York, Chicago, Philadelphia, Los Angeles, Detroit, and the other large industrial cities. This influx of Negroes has changed the character of these cities and has added new problems of delinquency, crime, alcoholism, narcotic addiction, desertion, and educational inadequacy to those already present. In the period 1940-1960, the percentage of nonwhites (largely Negroes) increased as follows: in New York, from 6.4 per cent in 1940 to 14.7 per cent in 1960; in Chicago, from 8.3 per cent to 23.6 per cent; in Los Angeles, from 6.5 per cent to 16.8 per cent; in Philadelphia, from 13.1 per cent to 26.7 per cent; and in Detroit, from 9.3 per cent to 29.2 per cent.[73]

The new urban migrants include other groups of the "rural dispossessed"— Puerto Ricans from their island, Mexican-Americans from across the border, and (above all) poor and uneducated whites from the vast depressed areas of the Appalachian highlands. These groups represent different cultural traditions; what they have in common are their rural backgrounds and the difficulties that any rural people have in adjusting to the large city. Most of these migrants are already American citizens, but they are unready to exercise their civil rights because of poverty, ignorance, and isolation from the mainstream of American culture. The large cities have for generations educated the migrants from the Old World, who came to this country imbued with a burning desire for citizenship and participation in the new society. Many of the new immigrants, however, lack the desire for assimilation and upward mobility. Others have the desire but are held at arm's length by a middle-class society. Still others are victims of racial prejudice, compounded by poor housing and substandard education. These new migrants become permanent marginal men in a society that does not seem to want them.

3. *Segregation.* A third form of ecological process is segregation. In many instances, segregation is a direct outgrowth of migration, notably in the case of the Negro in the North. We considered segregation in Chapter 13, as a way of maintaining the caste-avoidance pattern between Negro and white. We shall consider it here in its ecological context, as one of the dynamic processes allocating individuals, families, and institutions to positions in the community. In this sense, segregation involves the involuntary residence of persons and groups in a given area on the basis of racial origin, ethnic background, or economic level. Segregation is an especially complex process because it usually, although not always, carries implicit assumptions of inferiority and superiority.

---

[73] Metropolitan Life Insurance Company, "Population Profile of Our Largest Cities," *Statistical Bulletin* (November, 1961).

Segregation takes four general forms.[74] The *first* is voluntary segregation, in which members of the same cultural, ethnic, or racial group voluntarily interact in adjacent areas. The segregation of the Jews in the ghettos of the Old World was partly of this type, although much of the subsequent pressure for segregation was involuntary and imposed from without.[75] The ethnic communities of the large American city offer a more accurate contemporary example of this form of segregation. Little Italy, little Poland, little Puerto Rico, and similar clusters of persons of like ethnic backgrounds, arise because many bewildered migrants to the metropolis voluntarily live in these communities to be near their cultural compatriots. A *second* type of segregation occurs when the clustering is clearly involuntary, and members of certain racial, ethnic, or religious groups are arbitrarily forced to live in areas and under conditions not of their own choosing. The restrictions upon the Negro, both in the North and the South, are the most spectacular examples of this form of segregation.[76]

A *third* type of segregation is closely allied to the second in that it is also involuntary; it differs in that it is *de facto* rather than *de jure*. This means that segregation exists "in fact," although it is not recognized "in law." This is especially true in education. The large concentrations of nonwhites (mostly Negroes) in the northern cities means that, for all practical purposes, some schools are almost entirely Negro (or Puerto Rican in New York City). These schools are often deteriorated physically, are assigned poor and inexperienced teachers, and are in every way inferior to white schools. Commenting upon this situation, Yinger remarks that "... a significant proportion of the colored children, and the Mexican and Puerto Rican children as well, in the large cities of the North and West, attend schools in which intergroup contact is at a minimum." [77]

A *fourth* form of segregation is one in which the choice of residence is involuntary, but where the reasons for segregation are impersonal. The "enforced" residence of most white persons in slums is the prime example of this form. Such persons are not kept in their residences by arbitrary restrictions, but rather because they cannot afford better housing. Hence the basis for such segregation is, for the most part, economic and impersonal. The family is presumably free to leave the area when it can afford to do so. Taken together, the above types of *involuntary* segregation affect a sizeable minority of the population of this country. Quoting the Commission on Race and Housing, Yinger states that "one-sixth of the American people are to some degree restricted in their choice of residence. Many of them," he concludes, "as a result, are forced into slums." [78]

An extensive empirical analysis of segregation and assimilation in the urban

[74] The following is partially adapted from James A. Quinn, *Human Ecology* (Englewood Cliffs, N.J.: Prentice-Hall, Inc., 1950), Chapter XVff.

[75] Cf. Louis Wirth, *The Ghetto* (Chicago: University of Chicago Press, 1928).

[76] Quinn, *op. cit.*, p. 352.

[77] J. Milton Yinger, "Desegregation in American Society: The Record of a Generation of Change," *Sociology and Social Research,* 47:428-445 (July, 1963), p. 439.

[78] *Ibid.*, p. 435.

community disclosed several significant relationships. (*a*) The degree of residential segregation of any ethnic group is *inversely* related to its socioeconomic status and degree of assimilation. This means that the lower its status and degree of assimilation, the higher the degree of segregation of a particular group. (*b*) The degree of segregation is *directly* related to the "social distance" between the ethnic group and the native stock. Social distance refers to attitudes of acceptance or rejection by the native group. (*c*) The segregation patterns for different ethnic groups are comparatively stable over long periods of time, but they do change as each group lives longer in this country and gradually becomes assimilated to the larger culture. In this sense, segregation is related to the degree of intimate interaction between the ethnic group and the native population.[79]

The most systematic segregation is practiced upon the Negro, who is often forced to live under crowded and expensive conditions in the North and is obliged to live without many basic services in the South. Despite repeated decisions by the Supreme Court, this pattern of segregation continues. In the North, segregation is most marked in housing and after that "in the more desirable jobs, . . . social and religious activities, public facilities, politics, and . . . education." [80] The segregated group is isolated from the main stream of culture and the myth of biological inferiority is perpetuated by lack of cultural contact. Attitudes of frustration, insecurity, and personal instability are engendeded in the minority group by the practice of segregation.[81]

A study of residential segregation during the decade 1940-1950 disclosed that this process was *increasing* rather than *decreasing* in the majority of urban communities. Residential segregation scores were computed for 209 cities in the United States for 1950. In 185 of these cities, comparable scores were available for 1940. The composite segregation score for the cities (on an over-all basis) went up during the decade. Of the 185 cities, segregation increased in 129 cities, whereas it decreased in only 52 cities and remained the same in four cities. Among the comparatively few cities in which segregation decreased was Washington, D. C., where this practice underwent a considerable drop. In most cities throughout the North and West, however, segregation increased during the decade of World War II.[82]

4. Invasion. Invasion is the incursion of one social function or population group upon the area formerly occupied by another function or group. Functional invasion is characteristic of the dynamic urban community, where the central business district encroaches upon adjacent areas, light and heavy industries invade former residential areas, and urban centers swallow up villages and

---

[79] Otis D. Duncan and Stanley Lieberson, "Ethnic Segregation and Assimilation," *American Journal of Sociology*, 64:364-374 (January, 1959).

[80] Frank F. Lee, "The Race Relations Pattern by Areas of Behavior in a Small New England Town," *American Sociological Review*, 19:138-143 (April, 1954), p. 143.

[81] Kenneth B. Clark, "The Social Scientist as an Expert Witness in Civil Rights Litigation," *Social Problems*, 1:5-10 (June, 1953).

[82] Donald O. Cowgill, "Trends in Residential Segregation of Nonwhites in American Cities, 1940-1950," *American Sociological Review*, 21:43-47 (February, 1956).

farms. In each case, an area is invaded by persons and institutions performing other functions. In some of the communities of the Old World, invasion is virtually unknown, as the same functions continue to be performed in the same areas for generations. In the United States, functional invasion is so familiar as to be almost a commonplace.

Invasion takes another and more explosive form, involving changes in residence of different racial, ethnic, or occupational groups. This process is often accompanied by considerable bitterness, and a conflict situation may be generated by the invasion by a minority group of an area hitherto occupied by a majority group. The invasion by Negroes of white residential neighborhoods in many northern cities is an example of this process. Many of the latent tensions in the racial pattern are exacerbated in this way, although a study in Minneapolis suggests that acceptance of Negroes may be increasing.[83]

In the majority of communities, however, racial invasion is marked by continued hostility. Property owners are unwilling to accept the new group for fear of a decline in property values. Various forms of intimidation are introduced, ranging from restrictive covenants (declared unconstitutional) to outright violence. The minority group is victimized in the process, for the members are forced to live under crowded conditions and pay exorbitant rents. Invasion is an inevitable accompaniment of the rapid growth of the modern community, and brings many social problems in its wake.

The general factors that give rise to invasion have been indicated as follows: (a) changes in the numbers of the population; (b) changes in the racial or ethnic composition of the population; (c) changes in commerce or industry that affect the economic status of different groups; (d) residential property taken over for business or recreational purposes; (e) the progressive obsolescence of living quarters in different neighborhoods; and (f) the increase in economic opportunities in the suburbs and consequent large-scale migration to these areas. These factors have one basic similarity, in that they are all related to mobility. In these and other ways, different population groups are set in motion and take over the positions formerly held by other groups.[84]

5. *Succession.* Invasion and succession are closely related. Invasion is the actual intrusion of one function or group into the territory occupied by another. Succession is the end result when one group has finally taken the place of the other. Invasion is thus a process of "becoming," whereas succession is a state of "being" resulting from invasion. Every large city has sections near the central business district that were formerly occupied by fine residences. These areas have been gradually invaded by new functions, of which the first is usually that of furnished rooms. During this transition, the old residents move out, some to the suburbs and others to expensive apartments and residential hotels. After a few years, one function will have largely succeeded another, and the

---

[83] Arnold M. Rose, *et al.*, "Neighborhood Reactions to Isolated Negro Residents: An Alternative to Invasion and Succession," *American Sociological Review*, 18:497-507 (October, 1953).

[84] Harold Gibbard, *Residential Succession: A Study in Human Ecology* (unpublished doctoral dissertation, University of Michigan, 1938), pp. 206-207, quoted by E. Gordon Ericksen, *op. cit.*, p. 214.

rooming-house area will itself be invaded by light manufacturing. The history of the American city can be read in the successive trends in land use in the different areas.[85]

The process of succession, like that of invasion, is more spectacular when it involves different population groups than when it pertains to economic or social functions. The latter are more impersonal and do not generate the same emotional reactions as do movements of ethnic, cultural, and racial groups. The invasion of Negro groups into new areas is usually followed by comparatively rapid succession, whereby the white group leaves the field to the minority. The lower status of the Negro has usually meant that the white residents lose prestige if they remain in their old homes in close proximity to the invaders.[86] Prestige and status are often more important than comfort, accessibility to work, and relative cheapness. In the past, persons threatened with loss of prestige through invasion and succession have fought bitterly to retain the symbols of status.

The most massive and spectacular example of the twin processes of invasion and succession in recent decades is, as we have noted, the movement of southern Negroes into the large cities of the North. We have already commented upon one aspect of this situation, whereby large segments of the Caucasian population (both white- and blue-collar), have fled the central cities in search of housing, status, and schools in the suburbs. Their places in the deteriorating areas and slums have (depending upon the region) been taken by Negroes, Puerto Ricans, Mexican-Americans, and poor whites from the Appalachian highlands. Each of the latter three groups of rural dispossessed has its own problems, but those of the Negro far surpass in complexity those of the others. Large areas at the center of the metropolitan centers have, in effect, become Negro ghettos. The explosive nature of such a situation is accentuated by racial prejudice.

This dynamic process is, however, not completely hopeless. A survey was conducted in Minneapolis of formerly all-white neighborhoods into which a single Negro family had moved. In the past, such a move would have resulted in a panic-stricken flight by white property owners, fearful of loss of status and lowering of property values. This classic pattern was not followed in Minneapolis. The white residents refused to be stampeded into leaving and instead accepted the Negro family. The more direct contacts the white families had with their Negro neighbors, the more likely they were to accept them. Instead of the former processes of conflict and flight, an element of accommodation and stability was achieved. This pattern of acceptance has been followed in a number of residential communities in the North and West.[87]

Succession is also apparent in connection with ethnic (as distinguished from racial) groups. The early decades of the present century were marked by the

---

[85] Walter Firey, *Land Use in Central Boston* (Cambridge: Harvard University Press, 1947).

[86] Harold Gibbard, "The Status Factor in Residential Successions," *American Journal of Sociology*, 46:835-842 (May, 1941).

[87] Rose, *et al., op. cit.*

arrival of millions of immigrants from southern and eastern Europe. These persons were for the most part peasants in the old country and would have preferred to be farmers in the new. By the time of their arrival, however, the desirable farm land was taken up by earlier immigrants and the newcomers were forced to settle in the large cities. Here they assumed definite patterns, as the newest group settled in compact ethnic colonies near the central business district, where they were crowded together in noisome slums. As an individual family became economically successful, it left the ethnic area and branched out into the more desirable and cosmopolitan residential sections. Over the generations, each ethnic group was gradually succeeded by the next one, whose members became in their turn the new hewers of wood and drawers of water.[88]

This process of ethnic succession and (eventual) assimilation has often been pictured as an essentially impersonal and unconscious process. The individuals and families are defined in abstract terms, as ecological units competing for limited goals but without personal awareness of what was going on. This description is oversimplified, for the units in ethnic succession are very conscious human beings. Each person has a set of norms and values that motivate much of his behavior, even though these patterns are not accepted by the larger society. In short, "the residential dispersion of a minority group is due to multiple sociocultural, interrelated factors and can only be understood as part of the group's incorporation into the dominant social system." [89]

In this chapter, we have examined some of the implications of human ecology, insofar as this concept explains the structure of the urban community. We have indicated that the ecological point of view is suggestive, but not exhaustive, in explaining social interaction in the urban pattern. Human beings interacting in groups produce culture, which is structured in the form of institutions. These institutions and their members are distributed in functional positions throughout the community, as the result of social mobility. This distribution has been viewed both in static and dynamic terms: *statically* in terms of natural areas and *dynamically* in terms of the ecological processes that produce the areas.

---

[88] Richard G. Ford, "Population Succession in Chicago," *American Journal of Sociology*, 56:156-160 (September, 1950).

[89] Jerome K. Myers, "Assimilation to the Ecological and Social Systems of a Community," *American Sociological Review*, 15:367-372 (June, 1950), p. 372.

SELECTED BIBLIOGRAPHY

Clausen, John A., and Melvin L. Kohn, "The Ecological Approach in Social Psychiatry," *American Journal of Sociology*, 60:140-151 (September, 1954). The ecological setting is seen as the framework within which social interaction occurs and mental disorders arise. The authors suggest that the ecological approach does not and cannot explain the dynamic, causal factors operating to bring the disorder about.

Duncan, Otis D., and Stanley Lieberson, "Ethnic Segregation and Assimilation," *American Journal of Sociology*, 64:364-374 (January, 1959). This is a careful analysis of the process of ethnic segregation in the urban community, in which the authors propose certain hypotheses to explain the relationships between segregation and other forms of social interaction.

Duncan, Otis D., and Leo F. Schnore, "Cultural, Behavioral, and Ecological Perspectives in the Study of Social Organization," *American Journal of Sociology*, 65:132-153 (September, 1959). In this long and reflective article, the authors make a strong plea for the extension of the ecological approach to the central core of sociology, which is the study of social organization.

Dunham, H. Warren, "Social Structures and Mental Disorders: Competing Hypotheses of Explanation," *Milbank Memorial Fund Quarterly*, 39:259-292 (April, 1961). The author is a trail-blazer in the ecological (and sociological) study of mental disorder (see below). In this long and closely reasoned article, he discusses some of the relationships between social structure and mental illness. He also deals with some of the approaches to this study, among them the ecological.

Faris, Robert E. L., and H. Warren Dunham, *Mental Disorders in Urban Areas*. Chicago: University of Chicago Press, 1939. This monograph reported on a pioneer study of mental disorders in the urban community (Chicago), and as such was an important contribution both to human ecology and social psychiatry. Most of the tentative conclusions in this book have subsequently been critically examined and some modified, but the book is nevertheless a landmark in the field of human ecology.

Martin, Walter T., "Ecological Change in Satellite Rural Areas," *American Sociological Review*, 22:173-183 (April, 1957). This article applies the insights of human ecology to the larger metropolitan community, with particular reference to the adjacent rural areas. In the dynamic process of metropolitan growth, these rural areas are incorporated both legally and functionally into the central city.

Park, Robert E., "Human Ecology," *American Journal of Sociology*, 42:1-15 (July, 1936). The author of this article was the most important single figure in the development of human ecology. This article is one of a number in which he indicated the importance of *position* in the urban community. Many of the later empirical and quantitative studies of ecology are explorations of insights and hypotheses originally raised by Park.

Peterson, Warren A., and George K. Zollschan, "Social Processes in the Metropolitan Community," Chapter 34 in Arnold M. Rose (ed.), *Human Behavior and Social Processes*. Boston: Houghton Mifflin Company, 1962. This essay deals with the metropolitan community "as a vast processing mill for the allocation of persons to positions. . . ." This processing occurs through the major ecological processes of mobility, migration, segregation, invasion, succession, and the rest.

Ross, H. Lawrence, "The Local Comunity: A Survey Approach," *American Sociological Review*, 27:75-84 (February, 1962). This article makes an important contribution to the understanding of the natural areas of the large city. The city is here viewed as a mosaic of local communities (natural areas), recognized as such by their residents and carrying strong connotations of social status (e.g., Back Bay vs. North End).

Schmid, Calvin F., Earle H. MacCannell, and Maurice D. Van Arsdol, Jr., "The Ecology of the American City: Further Comparison and Validation of Generalizations," *American Sociological Review*, 23:392-401 (August, 1958). This article explores the hypothesis that "the social structure of the urban community can be represented by a status-value ranking as determined by such factors as education, income, and occupation."

Schnore, Leo F., "Social Mobility in Demographic Perspective," *American Sociological Review*, 26:407-423 (June, 1961). Social mobility is here discussed in a broad context of demography and human ecology. The author is concerned with ecology in a wide and inclusive sense (see Duncan and Schnore above) and sees mobility as a crucial variable in this study.

Schwartz, David T., and Norbett L. Mintz, "Ecology and Psychosis Among Italians in 27 Boston Communities," *Social Problems*, 10:371-374 (Spring, 1963). Symptoms that bring about psychosis are less stressful among Italians living in local communities with large numbers of their compatriots. Here again the ecological approach is found useful in studying the incidence of psychosis, but, as the authors are quick to point out, this approach by itself is not sufficient to explain *individual* cases.

Shaw, Clifford R., and Henry D. McKay, *Juvenile Delinquency and Urban Areas*. Chicago: University of Chicago Press, 1942. This monograph is one of the classics in the literature of human ecology. It reports on an exhaustive exploration of delinquency areas in the urban community, first in Chicago and later in other cities.

Yinger, J. Milton, "Desegregation in American Society: The Record of a Generation of Change," *Sociology and Social Research*, 47: 428-445 (July, 1963). This authoritative article gives the student a summary, in comparatively brief compass, of the major trends in desegregation in recent decades. The author deals with integration (desegregation) in such fields as housing, education, the armed forces, and public accommodations. His general conclusion is that, on balance, desegregation has made great advances since World War II and gives every present indication of continuing these advances.

COLLECTIVE BEHAVIOR

AND SOCIAL CHANGE *Part Five*

21 Social Change

The Nature of Social Change

This section of the book deals with social change. We have already considered many of the aspects of social change in our analysis of contemporary society. Social change involves such ideas as interaction, movement, growth, and function. These concepts have pervaded the previous discussion, whether specifically dealing with social interaction, the changing context of personality, modifications in the social structure, or the emerging forms of social institutions. It is impossible to analyze the structure of modern society without constantly referring to the changes taking place in behavior, status, role, and the other

481

patterned reactions between the members. In this section, we shall draw these threads together in a discussion of the nature, causes, forms, motivation, problems, and direction of social change.

"The explanation of social and cultural change," remarks Martindale, "is the capstone of a sociological theory." [1] The theory of social dynamics (i.e., social and cultural change) tries to explain how "social forms are created and destroyed." [2] The sociologist is concerned with social forms, structures, and processes—that is, with the way in which groups and their patterned interrelationships emerge, establish equilibrium, and change. The scientist cannot study everything at once and the sociologist often finds it easier to study social structures "in equilibrium" than to explore the dynamic relationships within and among them. [3] This procedure may be rationalized on the grounds of priority or convenience, but the sociologist (and the student) should never lose sight of the fact that this "equilibrium" is a dynamic relationship. [4] From the family to the nation to the world of nations, groups and relationships are continually changing.

Social interaction by its very nature implies change. Human beings never take each other into account in exactly the same way twice. There is always some element of novelty, evolution, and change in each new human relationship. This dynamic aspect of society was grasped by social thinkers as far back as the ancient Greeks, who regarded the eternal flux of man and his institutions with attitudes ranging from resentment to resignation. In recent times, the emphasis upon social change has been more pronounced. Commenting upon the approach of Simmel, one of the pioneer sociologists, a modern sociologist states as follows: "Instead of seeing change as disturbance of a naturally stable thing called society, he [Simmel] sees stability itself as some temporary (although it may long endure) balance among forces in interaction; and forces are by definition capable of being described only in terms of change." [5]

In its most concrete sense, social change means that large numbers of persons are engaging in activities that differ from those in which they, or their parents, engaged some time before. As stated by Gerth and Mills, "By social change we refer to whatever may happen in the course of time to the roles, the institutions, or the orders comprising a social structure: their emergence, growth, and decline." [6] Society is a complex network of patterned relationships in which all the members participate in varying degrees. These relationships change and

---

[1] Don Martindale, *Social Life and Cultural Change* (Princeton: D. Van Nostrand Company, Inc., 1962), p. 31.

[2] *Ibid.*

[3] See Talcott Parsons, "Some Considerations on the Theory of Social Change," *Rural Sociology*, 26:219-239 (September, 1961).

[4] Wilbert E. Moore, "A Reconsideration of Theories of Social Change," *American Sociological Review*, 25:810-818 (December, 1960), p. 817.

[5] Everett C. Hughes, "Foreword" to Georg Simmel, *Conflict* and *The Web of Group-Affiliations* (translated by Kurt H. Wolff and Reinhard Bendix) (Glencoe, Ill.: The Free Press, 1955), p. 9.

[6] Hans Gerth and C. Wright Mills, *Character and Social Structure* (New York: Harcourt, Brace and World, 1953), p. 398.

behavior changes at the same time. Men and women are faced with new situations to which they must respond. These situations reflect such factors as the introduction of new techniques, new ways of making a living, changes in place of residence, innovations in ideas, and social values. Social change thus means modifications of the way men work, rear a family, educate their children, govern themselves, and seek an ultimate meaning in life.

Social change has other implications for social structure. "By social change," says Ginsberg, "I understand a change in social structure, e.g., the size of a society, the composition or balance of its parts or the type of its organization." [7] When social change is taking place, people occupy different statuses and play different roles over a period of time. When we analyze society in terms of its structure, we are viewing it at a particular moment in time. Social interaction takes place continually, and in a structural sense we regard it at a certain instant, as it were.[8] Social change therefore means (a) that given individuals assume different positions in the social structure, and (b) that the positions themselves are subject to change. The important consideration is the element of time.

Social change has basic implications for a dynamic society. Hence it is important to know the extent of the changes in structure. Status and role are among the structural considerations that can be measured. Among the measurable changes in status are: place of residence, marital status, employment, fertility, educational attainment, occupation, level of income, and home ownership. A society in which large numbers of persons change these and other aspects of status is one in which social change is comparatively rapid.[9] Whatever the time interval—whether we are thinking in years, decades, or generations—the United States is one of the most rapidly changing societies the world has ever seen.

A static society, on the other hand, is one in which status and role tend to remain substantially the same from generation to generation. These distinctions are relative; isolated and primitive societies are at one extreme and interdependent and complex societies at the other. No society is completely static, in the sense that no change whatsoever occurs in the social patterns and the behavior they evoke. Likewise, no society is completely dynamic, with all the patterns changing from generation to generation. Our own society is extremely dynamic, but even here many aspects of behavior change slowly.[10] A society in which all behavior changed with the rapidity of, say, nuclear research, would be impossible to live in.

---

[7] Morris Ginsberg, "Social Change," *British Journal of Sociology*, 9:205-229 (September, 1958), p. 205.

[8] Bernard Barber. "Structural-Functional Analysis: Some Problems and Misunderstandings," *American Sociological Review*, 21:129-135 (April, 1956).

[9] Donald J. Bogue, "The Quantitative Study of Social Dynamics and Social Change," *American Journal of Sociology*, 57:565-568 (May, 1952).

[10] William F. Ogburn, "Stationary and Changing Societies," *American Journal of Sociology*, 42:16-31 (July, 1936).

The "Causes" of Social Change

It has been further suggested that modifications in status and role produce stresses and strains that in turn give rise to social change. In a dynamic society, so the argument runs, many persons are unable to adjust to changing roles and hence deviate from the norms. This deviation produces conflict and social change comes about when "conflict or deviation . . . result in a process of disorganization and/or disintegration and necessitate some sort of adjustment." [11] Contemporary society is especially susceptible to such "stress-strain elements," and innovations (changes) accordingly are frequent in highly industrialized and technologically advanced societies. This approach, however, is not especially helpful in understanding the nature and causes of social change, inasmuch as it merely states, in essence, that change and conflict are present and that each brings about the other.

Bock comments that the above point of view (although he was not speaking of this particular article) does little more than state that society is both a "boundary-breaking" and a "boundary-defining" process. In other words, social structures both change and persist through time. Bock then outlines his own position, which is that social change occurs because something *happens*, either within a society or impinging upon it from without. In neither case, however, can change be fully explained from the nature of the social system (group, institution, society) itself. Something must be added, and that "something" is an event or a series of events that happens at a particular time and place.[12]

In his authoritative discussion of the theory of social change, Moore sums up the essential qualities of this process in contemporary society.[13]

1. Frequency of change. Social change is the rule rather than the exception in the modern world. This does not mean that *all* social forms and structures change, but rather that *some* forms and structures and the relationships between them *do* change.

2. Sequence of change. Social change occurs in "sequential chains," with changes in one aspect of society setting off changes in another and so on until the repercussions (for example, nuclear power) are felt all over the world.

3. Planning of change. Social change is far from being entirely haphazard and unpremeditated. In many respects, social planning (or at least deliberate reflection) "causes" or sets in motion social change.

4. Cumulative effect of change. Improvements in technology and communication have been so rapid in recent decades that the cumulative impact of change is greater than ever before, both within single societies and throughout the world.

---

[11] Alvin L. Bertrand, "The Stress-Strain Element of Social Systems: A Micro Theory of Conflict and Change," *Social Forces*, 42:1-9 (October, 1963), p. 5.

[12] Kenneth E. Bock, "Evolution, Function, and Change," *American Sociological Review*, 28:229-237 (April, 1963), p. 237.

[13] The following is adapted from Wilbert E. Moore, *Social Change* (Englewood Cliffs, New Jersey: Prentice-Hall, Inc., 1963), p. 2.

5. *Normality of change.* The net result of the aforementioned factors is that change "affects a wider range of individual experience and functional aspects of societies in the modern world." Every phase of life in modern societies is—to a greater or lesser degree—subject to the expectation of change.

It is important to keep social change in perspective. We are accustomed to think of our society as one in which practically all persons continually change their jobs, their homes, their marital status, and their religious affiliation. This is a slight exaggeration. In terms of the *relative* number of status changes within a given period, the United States may be the most mobile society in history. But this does not mean that structural change is universal. The majority of persons do *not* experience major changes in status every year, or even every five years. Most of them live in the same place with the same wife and work at the same job from year to year. Measured in terms of generations, social change is clearly perceptible in the lives of these average citizens. In any shorter period, however, the bulk of the population does not substantially change. Man is more conservative than we think.

Social change is brought about by a number of factors—technological, industrial, economic, ideological, and religious. No single factor has priority over all others. Some persons insist that technology is the basis of all changes in social relationships. Others are certain that the state of the industrial arts (not the same thing as technology) dominates other aspects of society. Still others maintain that the power relationships between social classes—in the sense of one class owning the instruments of production—are the most important. Ideological and religious factors are also cited as bringing about basic modifications in status and role. Every society is a complex process of social interaction, however, with technological, economic, ideological, and religious overtones. All of these factors, and more, operate in social change.[14]

Most analysts tacitly assume that social change is caused by broad, impersonal factors within the society or affecting it from without. In his closely reasoned analysis, however, Martindale sharply questions this position and maintains that social change, like all forms of social interaction, is basically the work of *individuals.* Sociologists often tend to reify (endow with independent existence) such concepts as group, institution, society, culture, and social process. But human action, Martindale reminds us, is performed by individual human beings. It is true that they are acting in learned, rather than instinctive, fashion; much of the previous discussion in this book has called attention to the learned character of this behavior. But in strict accuracy, Martindale continues, groups and societies do not *do* anything; individuals playing socially acquired roles are the real actors in the human drama. Hence we must look to individuals for the basic "causes" of social and cultural change.[15]

In the course of their interaction, *some* individuals are more important than *others* in initiating, accelerating, or slowing down the rate of social change.

---

[14] For a survey of the various theories of social change, see Gerth and Mills, *op. cit.,* Chapter 13. "Social-Historical Change."

[15] Martindale, *op. cit.,* p. 59.

Daring and imaginative innovators in such fields as religion, science, technology, and government are, in Martindale's view, the real agents in social change. Some of these changes are restricted to a particular field (religion, art), whereas other changes modify an entire society or world society (technology, science). Of all the individuals thus involved in social change, Martindale believes that intellectuals (in the broadest sense) are the most important. They are responsible for the crucial innovations that cause other men to change their statuses, their roles, and their ways of looking at themselves and the world. Martindale summarizes his position as follows: "(1) All social and cultural change is the work of individuals, (2) the major events in human history consist of the formation and destruction of societies and civilizations, and (3) because of their role in forming and justifying communities and civilizations, the intellectuals represent a strategic reference point for the study of these processes." [16]

The question as to what *causes* social change, however, admits of no single answer. Each element in society influences every other. It has been stated, for example, that the steam engine is the most important single instrument in causing the series of changes apparent in modern society. It is true that the steam engine has been used for a number of purposes, from providing power for shoe factories to moving battleships. But the steam engine did not create either the custom of making shoes or that of making war. Alternative ways of performing these functions were present long before the invention of the steam engine. The problem of uncovering *influences* in social change is one thing; that of defining *causes* is quite another.[17]

Social change thus has no single cause. Instead, as Parsons expresses it, there is a "plurality of possible origins of change." Likewise, there is no single and all-embracing *theory* of social change. As we have suggested, persons with particular interests have attempted to base the massive fact of social change upon some unitary cause, such as technological innovation or religious inspiration. None of these theories is sufficiently general or inclusive to encompass the complex reality of social change. In Parsons' words, ". . . we do *not* in the present state of knowledge possess a *general* theory of the processes of change in societies as a whole." [18]

The Nature of Cultural Change

Social and cultural change are not the same thing. Many of the theories attempting to explain *social* change are actually dealing with *cultural* change, often without clearly distinguishing between them. Society is composed of human beings in interaction, and the products of this interaction are institutions, values, statuses, roles, and techniques—in short, culture. Culture is, then, the patterned behavior resulting from social interaction.

---

[16] *Ibid.*, p. 60.

[17] S. C. Gilfillan, "Social Implications of Technical Advance," *Current Sociology*, 1:191-207, UNESCO, Paris, 1953, pp. 202-203.

[18] Talcott Parsons, *The Social System* (Glencoe, Ill.: The Free Press, 1951), p. 534. (His italics.)

These concepts have been explicitly explored by Kroeber and Parsons, whose names have been prominently associated with culture and society, respectively. In a joint article, they suggest that *society* refers to patterned systems of interaction among individuals and groups, whereas *culture* refers to "patterns of values, ideas, and other symbolic meaningful systems" that direct human behavior.[19] It follows that changes in society involve the structures through which human beings interact and the forms that this interaction takes. Changes in culture involve the learned, symbolic, and meaningful behavior that both arises from past interaction and directs future interaction.

Changes in culture include new forms of learning, new dimensions of science, new technological instruments, new dogmas of religion, and new expressions of artistic achievement. These cultural elements are important factors in social change, but they are not the only ones. Changes in physical environment, genetic equipment, and social structure itself also bring about changes in society. In some cases, the latter elements contain cultural overtones, but they are not uniquely cultural.

The principal general elements in *cultural* change are invention and diffusion. *Invention* is the combination of two or more existing culture traits or patterns into something new that is greater than the sum of its parts.[20] The automobile in this sense is a combination of a four-wheeled carriage and an internal combustion engine. In the field of social invention, the American Constitution was a synthesis of (*a*) western European philosophy and (*b*) the experience of the colonists. At the same time, some of the ideological elements in the Constitution go back to ancient Athens.[21]

Diffusion is the movement of a pattern of culture from one society to another or within the same society. It is obvious that without initial invention there would be no diffusion. But without diffusion there would be very little change, since no society by itself produces more than a fraction of its cultural elements. Social isolation implies the comparative absence of diffusion, and this condition breeds cultural stagnation. In order to develop, a society must have *both* invention and diffusion. When barriers are placed in the way of the free diffusion of culture, all societies are the poorer. The products of the human mind from the arts to the physical sciences, require freedom of exchange to develop.[22]

Society and culture are different elements of the same complex and ongoing whole. They are related but not synonymous. Changes in culture bring changes in society and vice versa. The Industrial Revolution came about as a result of changes in the techniques of producing power and manufacturing commodities. These (cultural) changes affected the way of life of subsequent generations in western European society, and the chain reaction is still going on through-

---

[19] A. L. Kroeber and Talcott Parsons, "The Concepts of Culture and of Social System," *American Sociological Review*, 23:582-583 (October, 1958), p. 583.

[20] H. G. Barnett, *Innovation: The Basis of Cultural Change* (New York: McGraw-Hill Book Company, Inc., 1953), pp. 7-8.

[21] Cf. Edward Rose, "Innovations in American Culture," *Social Forces*, 26:255-272 (March 1948).

[22] Edward A. Shils, "Security and Science Sacrificed to Loyalty," *Bulletin of the Atomic Scientists*, 11:106-109 (April, 1955).

out the underdeveloped sections of the world.[23] It is not always possible to distinguish in practice between cultural and social change. In theory, however, this distinction can be made.

In many cases, the traditional patterns of group norms (culture) do not change as rapidly as the processes of social interaction (society). Large numbers of persons engage in social behavior not sanctioned by the cultural norms. In our own society, millions of married women are gainfully employed outside the home as a result of the complex series of cultural and social changes ushered in by the Industrial Revolution. Under the normative expectations that have been traditional for thousands of years, women were confined to the home. The dynamics of cultural change, however, have caused their behavior as working wives in contemporary society to come in partial conflict with the former social norms. The character of social interaction has been changed by technological innovations in the culture.[24]

The interrelationships between cultural and social change are further illustrated in an important recent study of the dynamic world of the Middle East. This world includes a number of distinct and separate societies, of differing degrees of technological advancement and political sophistication. These societies have all been exposed in recent years to the mass media of communication—especially the radio and the motion picture. It is significant that neither of these media requires literacy for comprehension. The majority of the people in many of these countries can neither read nor write. But they can (and do) listen to the radio and watch the motion pictures.[25]

In these two technological devices, we have an example of cultural innovations introducing changes in social interaction. In the dusty market places of the Middle East, millions of illiterate peasants listen to the radio voices of local dictators, calling upon them to rise against their foreign "oppressors," whose identity varies with the whims of the dictator. Revolutionary nationalism is fanned by these radio voices, and the listeners are exhorted to take arms and sweep their enemies into the sea. In a more peaceful, although no less fundamental vein, the motion pictures present scenes of hitherto unattainable luxury to these same unlettered peasants. The movies open a new world to men whose institutions have remained virtually unchanged for centuries.[26]

Changes in culture here bring about changes in society. New techniques of communication produce fundamental changes in the ways men take each other and themselves into account. The mass media increase "psychic mobility" for millions of men and women who, for the first time in their lives, are able to take the roles of other persons in distant lands and with different customs. "The expansion of psychic mobility," says Lerner, "means that more people now

---

[23] George A. Theodorson, "Acceptance of Industrialization and Its Attendant Consequences for the Social Patterns of Non-Western Societies," *American Sociological Review*, 18:477-484 (October, 1953).

[24] Meyer F. Nimkoff, "Technology, Biology, and the Changing Family," American Journal of Sociology, 57:20-26 (July, 1951).

[25] Daniel Lerner, *The Passing of Traditional Society* (Glencoe, Ill.: The Free Press, 1958), p. 50.

[26] *Ibid.*

command greater skill in imagining themselves as strange persons in strange situations, places, and times than did people in any previous historical epoch." [27] With the expansion of the mass media to other backward and underprivileged areas throughout the world, social change of a profoundly revolutionary nature is set in motion. No man can tell where and how these changes will end.

The Nature of Invention

Invention is a combination of previously existent cultural elements that produces something new. This combination may involve ideas about the world of nature, the world of man, or human control of any part of these worlds. Artistic ideas are combined to produce an invention in aesthetics, either in the form of technics (oil painting) or subject matter (abstract painting). Ideas may be combined in moral or ethical standards, with such great religions as Christianity or Mohammedanism serving as examples. Ideas may involve technics for dealing with the physical universe and the production of new goods and services. The latter combination of cultural elements is the only one usually considered under the heading of invention. It is important to realize, however, that the concept is applicable to the entire range of ideas. [28]

Invention has two major sources. The *first* is the existing culture that the inventor has at his disposal, including the entire stock of *ideas* present in the culture and known to him. The inventor obviously cannot make use of ideas that are unknown in his age. Leonardo da Vinci was one of the great universal geniuses of all time. He spent much of his energy attempting, among other things, to produce a flying machine. This attempt was inevitably doomed because the necessary cultural ideas (those combining four centuries later to produce the internal combustion engine) were not developed in Leonardo's day. The basic elements must therefore be present in the culture before the inventor can combine them into something new. [29]

The *second* source of invention comprises what Barnett has called the "non-artificial elements" in the experience of the inventor. [30] These include the phenomena of nature. They also include the inventor himself as a human being. Each inventor possesses certain intellectual attributes common to all men and others that are unique to him. Among the latter elements is that intangible quality known as genius, with which a few persons in a society at any one time are mysteriously endowed. As Martindale reminds us, inventions are made by individuals, not by the impersonal processes of society. The cultural base is fundamental to invention, but without the gifted individual the combination of existing traits would never be made. [31]

---

[27] *Ibid.*, p. 52.
[28] Bernard Barber, *Science and the Social Order* (Glencoe, Ill.: The Free Press, 1952), pp. 194 ff.
[29] Barnett, *op. cit.*, p. 10.
[30] *Ibid.*, pp. 10 ff.
[31] Martindale, *op. cit.*, p. 60.

The larger the cultural base, therefore, the greater the chances that the various elements will be combined to form new ones. The development of material culture was agonizingly slow throughout most of human history. Many thousands of years were necessary to bring about rudimentary refinements in the stone hatchet. This glacial pace of early invention may be contrasted with the flood of technological devices that have inundated our culture in recent decades. The general principle marking this acceleration of cultural development has been stated by Hornell Hart. He indicated that the entire range of prehistory and history has been characterized by an accelerating rate at which human beings have been able to achieve their basic purposes, despite temporary and local setbacks.[32]

This general analysis suggests that the folk saying about necessity being the mother of invention must be seriously modified, if not discarded altogether. It is true that necessity *does* give a prod to invention. The evolution of the atomic bomb during World War II is a spectacular example of this process. But the Romans facing the barbarian hordes also would have given a great deal for this "absolute" weapon. Necessity was obviously there for the Roman legions, but not the culture base from which the new invention could be forged. The atomic and hydrogen bombs could never have been produced without the achievements in the physical sciences marking the early decades of the present century.

The popular conception of the individual inventor must also be revised. Lonely men puttering in attics do not, for the most part, create the inventions of the modern day. It is rather in the research laboratories of large corporations, scientific foundations, universities, and government bureaus that new ideas are currently evolved. The world has recently seen two impressive examples of this group process of invention—the production of the atomic bomb and the discovery of the Salk vaccine for infantile paralysis. In each case, one or more gifted scientists are associated in the popular mind with the major discovery. These men, however, would be the first to deny that they had done their work alone. The development of material invention today reflects the steady accumulation of thousands of able and trained laboratory scientists.[33]

We have been speaking as if technological innovation were the only form of invention. The combination of existing elements may also occur in the field of social relationships, institutions, and structures. These combinations are known as *social* inventions, and they range from a new divorce law to the United Nations. The "inventors" of such new ideas often evoke the most violent hostility, for they question the entrenched institutional patterns of their day. Woodrow Wilson "invented" the League of Nations and thereby challenged the sacred values of nationalism. Franklin D. Roosevelt "invented" the New Deal and thereby appeared to threaten certain economic values. A juvenile

[32] Hornell Hart, "Technological Acceleration and the Atomic Bomb," *American Sociological Review,* 11:277-293 (June, 1946).

[33] Alfred B. Stafford, "Is the Rate of Invention Declining?" *American Journal of Sociology,* 57:539-545 (May, 1952).

court judge "invented" companionate marriage and brought down the outraged wrath of the community upon his head.

The problems of the social inventor are often more complex than those of
the technological inventor. The social climate is very different for these two
forms of innovation. Inventors of novel technics in the manufacture of physical
products are rewarded with prestige and money. The reward of the social inventor is often something very different. Furthermore, controlled experiment
is difficult for the social inventor. Conclusions about the success or failure of a
new religion, family system, or form of government must be drawn from a mass
of uncontrolled and uncontrollable factors.

Material invention can, furthermore, be measured by objective means. People are, however, usually unable to agree upon the goals, values, and standards
relating to such social inventions as public housing, the city manager plan, and
contraception. The physical scientists, despite their subsequent reservations,
were initially able to agree on the technical problems to be solved in producing
the atomic bomb. The social inventors show only negligible agreement on the
type of international instrument (a social invention) for controlling nuclear
energy and utilizing it for peaceful purposes.

The present necessity for social invention is, if anything, even more pressing
than for technological invention. It has been said that men could continue to
live adequately for an indefinite period at the current stage of technological
invention, without a single innovation in this field. Many persons, on the other
hand, have expressed grave doubts as to man's ability to exist in ordered society
without important advances in social invention. The disparity in the level of
development between technological and social invention is indicated by
Hornell Hart in connection with the atomic bomb: "The supremely challenging fact is that the apparently sudden increase in the potential power of aggres-
sors is only a spectacularly dramatic expansion of technological developments
which have been slowly accelerating for hundreds of thousands of years, and
which now have a speed of increase which threatens to disorganize
civilization."[34]

The Nature of Diffusion

Diffusion is the process whereby a culture trait or pattern is spread from one
individual, group, or society to another. This process is carried out by a variety
of agents and agencies. Trade, warfare, prisoners, intermarriage, literature,
scholars, travelers, universities, newspapers, the radio, motion pictures, and
television have all spread traits and patterns within a society and from one
society to another.[35] More self-conscious attempts at diffusion have included
such diverse activities as the work of Christian missionaries to propagate the
faith and the efforts of communist agents to foment world revolution.

---

[34] Hart, *op. cit.*, p. 291.
[35] Cf. Sanford Winston, *Culture and Human Behavior* (New York: The Ronald Press, 1933), Chapter
6, "The Agents of Culture-Spread."

The earliest scientific attempts to study cultural diffusion were made by the cultural anthropologists. They initially suggested that diffusion occurs in much the same way as expanding concentric circles follow the dropping of a pebble in water. The implication was that culture diffuses in tidy circles, at a constant rate of speed, and in a homogeneous medium. According to this explanation, there should be one central point of origin from which the innovation spreads. The oldest traits would then have the widest distribution and the newest traits would be the most restricted.[36]

This explanation has a certain validity in preliterate societies, where the only means of communication is by word of mouth. Under modern technological conditions, however, the concept of concentric circles loses much of its relevance. An original dress design may be created in Paris and immediately leap the Atlantic Ocean to reach a dress shop just off Fifth Avenue in New York City. It may then vault the rest of the United States to take root in Hollywood. Furthermore, the Paris creation may not even spread to the Paris shop girls, much less to the peasant women of neighboring Normandy. Cultural diffusion may follow class patterns as well as geographical limitations.[37]

The process of diffusion is also related to the social milieu of the donor and the recipient society. The goals of the latter may or may not be in accord with the innovation. Purposes and motives are important considerations. Material culture ordinarily travels faster and with less opposition than nonmaterial culture. The Eskimo hunter can readily grasp the advantages of the steel blade over his slate knife, but he is very uncertain of the alleged advantages of Christianity over his own simple pantheon. The western nations likewise accepted the military advantages of the armored *Blitzkrieg* without embracing the philosophy and ethics of National Socialism.

Material traits, moreover, may be diffused without any transmission of the technics needed to produce them. The Plains Indians were as eager to accept the white man's rifle as they were incapable of producing this weapon. A material trait may also be used in a sense quite foreign to the original. The Indians of the Northwest Coast weave blankets in a design to imitate the label on a tomato can. Flattened oil containers are used for roofing by primitive peoples in the South Pacific. Commenting on this tendency of culture traits and patterns, Linton stated this general principle: "One of the most important factors in connection with the diffusion of cultural elements is that they transfer from one society to another almost exclusively in terms of their form. In other words, the borrowing society copies particular patterns of behavior as it apprehends them, usually without understanding their original culture context."[38]

The extent of diffusion and its impact upon society and culture are tremendous. In their naïve ethnocentrism, most people believe that the bulk of the

---

[36] George P. Murdock, "Clark Wissler, 1870-1947," *American Anthropologist*, 50:292-304 (April-June, 1948).

[37] Cf. E. C. McVoy, "Patterns of Diffusion in the United States," *American Sociological Review*, 5:219-227 (April, 1940).

[38] Ralph Linton, *The Tree of Culture* (New York: Alfred A. Knopf, Inc., 1955), p. 45.

cultural elements in their society (or at least the desirable ones) are wholly their own, and that they are beholden to no one for their techniques or their institutions. Like many folk beliefs, this one is largely false. No single society, even one as prolific as the United States, can innovate more than a fraction of its culture. Linton has estimated that possibly ten per cent of the culture traits used in modern America were invented by this society. The other ninety per cent were borrowed from other societies.[39]

A further consideration is important in the introduction of a new cultural element, whether the innovation comes from within the society (invention) or from without (diffusion). This is the derivative aspect of the innovation— the effects not directly related to its use, but rather "derived" from them. The derivative effects of an invention reflect the changes in the way of life of persons who use it, often without any realization of what is happening. In this sense, cultural change brings about social change. The cultural invention

---

[39] Ralph Linton, *The Study of Man* (New York: Appleton-Century-Crofts, Inc., 1936), p. 325.

Diffusion is the process whereby a culture pattern is spread from one society to another; a Peace Corps volunteer instructs two natives of Tanganyika (East Africa) in the operation of a tractor.

brings immediate behavior changes in the society. These changes produce still further changes that may continue as long as the culture exists.[40]

The derivative effects of an invention may be illustrated by the changes in American society resulting from the "invention" of the automobile. These changes were first apparent in the *economic institutions* directly related to the manufacture of automobiles, such as the steel, rubber, glass, and petroleum industries. The *governmental institutions* were affected in a variety of ways, ranging from the revenues from the sale of gasoline to the detection and control of crime. *Religion* has felt the impact of this invention in a number of ways, with the automobile often competing with the church for the time and energies of the people. The *family*, finally, has seen the automobile bring about new patterns of recreation, social control, and economic expenditure, not to mention sexual morality and adolescent discipline. The culture and the society of America are very different since the automobile came into common use.[41]

The integration of a new element into a culture is not a haphazard process, reflecting the personal whims of the leaders of the society. People will not discard the patterns of the past if the latter have proved satisfactory in reaching goals and satisfying needs. Likewise, they will not accept the new pattern unless it appears to fulfill their genetic or socially acquired drives more adequately than the old. The diffusion and integration of culture involve learning. This process is the work of individual human beings.[42]

We have examined some of the ways in which new elements of culture are first created and then integrated into a society. The substitution, addition, and modification of culture patterns change the web of relationships within which social interaction takes place. The social structure based upon the old norms is disturbed and a new equilibrium emerges. The general process of cultural diffusion has been summarized as: "the (1) *acceptance*, (2) over *time*, (3) of some specific *item*—an idea or practice, (4) by individuals, groups, or other *adopting units*, linked (5) to specific *channels* of communication, (6) to a *social structure*, and (7) to a given system of values, or *culture*." [43] As the agencies of mass communication increase in efficiency, diffusion plays an increasingly important role in social change.

Patterns of Social Change

Social change is so complex that it can be approached from a number of directions. One of these is through technology, which has become such a pervasive and spectacular cultural prime mover in modern society. Ogburn observes

[40] William F. Ogburn, "The Process of Adjustment to New Inventions," Chapter 2 in William F. Ogburn (ed.), *Technology and International Relations* (Chicago: University of Chicago Press, 1949), pp. 20-23.

[41] Cf. S. C. Gilfillan, "The Prediction of Inventions," in National Resources Committee, *Technological Trends and National Policy* (Washington, D.C.: 1937), pp. 15-23.

[42] John Gillin, "Parallel Cultures and the Inhibitions of Acculturation in a Guatemalan Community," *Social Forces*, 24:1-14 (October, 1945).

[43] Elihu Katz, Martin L. Levin, and Herbert Hamilton, "Traditions of Research on the Diffusion of Innovation," *American Sociological Review*, 28:237-252 (April, 1963), p. 240. (Their italics.)

that "Technology changes society by changing our environment to which we, in turn, adapt. This change is usually in the material environment, and the adjustment we make to the changes often modifies customs and social institutions."[44] Succinctly stated, this is the relationship between culture and social change. Technology is a cultural element, and this knowledge is part of the culture that is communicated from generation to generation.

As an aspect of culture, technology is theoretically subject to control by man. This control, however, appears to be decreasing as technology becomes more complex. The question has become one of where technology is leading *us*, rather than of where *we* are leading technology. In a sense, technology has become a force outside of the rational control of men in society—at least in any comprehensive sense. Technological research is geared more and more to turning the discoveries of science to industrial profit, rather than directly to meet human needs. The latter are often obscured by the planned obsolescence of technological products, ranging from automobiles to television sets. This obsolescence is partially the result of conscious design and partially the result of the growth of technology itself. The latter spawns more and more products by its own momentum.

The role of technology in social change has been the subject of considerable study. As we have said, there is no *single* cause of social change, nor is there a single and all-embracing theory of social change. Modifications in structure may arise from religious, political, or revolutionary changes, in which the role of technology is marginal. We are here merely presenting *one* pattern out of *several possible patterns* of change. With this reservation, we may indicate the process by which technology, which is a cultural instrument, gives rise to social change. In order of their occurrence, the typical stages in this pattern are as follows.

1. Technological innovations. An innovation is "any thought, behavior, or thing that is new because it is qualitatively different from existing forms." An invention is "a technological innovation, a new thing."[45] Technology is the application of pure science to the immediate, "practical" ends of human beings. When the average person thinks of the changes brought about by "science," he is usually thinking of technology and its manifold wonders.[46] Many recent major modifications in status and role have followed innovations on the technological level, from the cotton gin to the internal combustion engine. Technological development is a recognized part of modern industry, and thousands of trained men are working on new applications of pure science. Changes on this level occur every day, and their combined effects upon human behavior are literally impossible to calculate.

2. Economic organization. Economic organization ordinarily feels the first

---

[44] William F. Ogburn, "How Technology Changes Society," *Annals of the American Academy of Political and Social Science,* 249:81-88 (January, 1947), p. 81.

[45] Barnett, *op. cit.,* pp. 7-8.

[46] Barber, *op. cit.,* p. 95.

impact of change from advances in technology within the society or the introduction of new industrial techniques from without. Economic organization is
the pattern of social relationships existing for the production, distribution,
and consumption of goods and services.[47] Changes in economic organization
followed the technological innovations that gave rise to the Industrial Revolution. The base of living moved from the farm to the factory and from the
country to the city. The application of technology to economic organization
may also produce entirely new industries. The present century has seen the
rise of such mass industries as the automobile, steel, rubber, glass, and petroleum industries, with chemicals, aviation, and electronics comprising even
more recent industrial complexes. The application of technology has given
the United States the highest standard of living in the world.[48] In no other
nation has technological innovation been applied so directly and efficiently
as in this country.[49]

3. *Social institutions.* The organized patterns of relationships constituting
the family, church, school, and government are next to feel the impact of social
change. This is especially true of the *structure* of the institutions; it is less true
of the *concept* or underlying cluster of values, which changes more slowly.
Each individual plays a role in these institutions, and the influences are brought
to bear upon him from a number of sources. The structure of the family has
undergone many important changes in recent decades because of the gainful
employment of married women. With one in every three married women employed outside the home, the family will never be the same again. These and
other changes have largely been communicated through technological innovations in industry. In the future, the application of science to the cultural and
biological fields will doubtless still further alter the family.[50]

4. *Social values.* The values at the basis of the institution are the goals for
which men strive, the ends they seek. Monogamy is a social value at the heart
of the Christian family; freedom is the basis of our economic and political
institutions. Most of the fundamental values are grouped about the institutional patterns and form their spiritual basis. These ideological elements
change very slowly. They are deeply imbedded in the personality and remain
long after the conditions that gave rise to them have disappeared. Technolo-
gies change, economic institutions follow suit, and the other institutional structures undergo drastic modifications—but the values remain at the heart of the
living personality. Behavior is still defined by the values of an earlier day.
This situation, as we shall see later, gives rise to social problems.[51]

---

[47] Moore, *Social Change, op. cit.,* pp. 98-100.
[48] William F. Ogburn, "Technology and the Standard of Living in the United States," *American Journal of Sociology,* 60:380-386 (January, 1955).
[49] William F. Ogburn and Francis R. Allen, "Technological Development and Per Capita Income," *American Journal of Sociology,* 65:127-131 (September, 1959).
[50] Nimkoff, "Technology, Biology, and the Changing Family," *op. cit.*
[51] Francis E. Merrill, "The Study of Social Problems," *American Sociological Review,* 13:251-262 (June, 1948).

Social Change and Cultural Lag

The elements in a society do not change at the same rate of speed or with the same intensity and completeness. Airplanes and television sets are obsolete in a matter of months. The *structures* of the major institutions change more slowly. The *values* are so deeply incorporated in the personality that their rate of change is often imperceptible. This disparity in the rate of change between the different elements is responsible for many, although by no means all, of the difficulties of modern man.

This general situation is known as *cultural lag*. In his original statement of this hypothesis, William F. Ogburn observed: "The thesis is that the various parts of modern culture are not changing at the same rate . . . and that since there is a correlation and interdependence of parts, a rapid change in one part of our culture requires readjustments through other changes in the various correlated parts of culture." [52] These readjustments are often difficult, if not impossible, to make, because of a variety of factors ranging from ignorance to active resistance. In this sense, technological change is a Pandora's box, releasing all manner of unpredictable forces.[53]

In a later essay, Ogburn amplified the theory of cultural lag and presented its essential features in a series of steps: "(1) the identification of at least two variables; (2) the demonstration that these two variables are in adjustment; (3) the determination by dates that one variable has changed while the other has not changed or one has changed in greater degree than the other; (4) that when one variable has changed earlier or in greater degree than the other, there is a less satisfactory adjustment than existed before." [54] In the family, the church, the school, the government, and other institutions, one element changes while the other remains unchanged or changes more slowly.

Cultural lag is most readily apparent in a dynamic society at a particular time. We are today faced with examples of this disparity on every hand, both in our own society and (perhaps even more) in traditional societies that are currently changing under the impact of industrial technology and the mass media. People in rural communities cling to the values of a self-sufficient society, even when they are living in a mass society that they cannot understand, much less control.[55] People in the underdeveloped countries of the Middle East are suddenly catapulted into advanced political nationalism, although their family systems have not changed for a thousand years.[56]

In the long perspective of historical development, however, cultural lag

---

[52] William F. Ogburn, *Social Change* (New York: B. W. Huebsch, Inc., 1922), pp. 200-201. A revised edition has subsequently been published by the Viking Press, New York, 1950.

[53] "Social Implications of Technical Change," *International Social Science Bulletin,* Volume 4, Number 2 (Paris: UNESCO, 1952).

[54] William F. Ogburn, "Cultural Lag as Theory," *Sociology and Social Research,* 41:167-174 (January-February, 1957), p. 169.

[55] Arthur J. Vidich and Joseph Bensman, *Small Town in Mass Society* (Princeton: Princeton University Press, 1958).

[56] Daniel Lerner, *op. cit.*

becomes blurred. As Ogburn says, lags in the distant past are not usually visible "because they have been caught up." [57] Cultural disparities in Periclean Athens and Augustan Rome were very real to the Greeks and Romans, but they are much less so to us. The cultural problems of Renaissance man no longer seem so complex or difficult, as we look back from the vantage point of four centuries upon this "golden age" of human advancement. The society of the Industrial Revolution was plagued by wide differences between other cultural variables, as the introduction of textile machinery made child labor profitable in a time when there were no child-labor laws. In our preoccupation with our own problems, we have lost sight of the fact that other people had problems too.

It is not sufficient merely to say that the various elements of society change at a different rate. We must explore some of the factors giving rise to this condition, inasmuch as such knowledge is important to an understanding of social problems and social control. These factors arise largely, although not wholly, from the nature of personality, itself a partial product of the society and its culture.

1. Conservatism of the personality. In the process of socialization, each individual acquires the attitudes, values, goals, and norms of his own society. The agents of socialization include the family, age groups, religious leaders, teachers, friends, and, more recently, the mass media of newspaper, magazine, radio, television, and motion picture. Values are incorporated into the personality and become an integral part of it. Any change that threatens or appears to threaten these values becomes a threat to the personality itself. The Southerner will defend the racial values he has been taught. The religious person will react emotionally to any attempt to deny the revealed truths of his faith.

Innovations in society that involve family relationships, religious beliefs, or governmental credos encounter the emotional hostility of many persons. This hostility is often unconscious, for the person does not understand the true reasons for his reactions. He is convinced that his objections are rational and logical, when in reality they are based upon fear of the new. His own sense of security depends upon the maintenance of the values at the core of his personality. Change undermines these values and thereby causes *personal* anxiety. The dynamic modern world is productive of many situations that give rise to such anxiety.[58]

2. Attitudes toward different changes. A second reason for the disparity in the rate of change is the difference in attitude toward various aspects of this process. The "social climate of invention" in our society is such that technological changes are regarded as desirable, since they presumably make life easier, richer, and more satisfactory. The innovator in these fields is received with appreciation and his efforts crowned with financial reward. In technology and applied science, there is an atmosphere of anticipation and acceptance, and the

---

[57] William F. Ogburn, "Cultural Lag as Theory," *op. cit.,* p. 174.
[58] Talcott Parsons, "Certain Primary Sources and Patterns of Aggression in the Social Structure of the Western World," *Psychiatry,* 10:167-181 (May, 1947).

average American eagerly looks forward to the next model of his favorite automobile, television set, or electric refrigerator. In short, there is a long tradition of *expecting* change in the technological devices that allegedly enrich human life.[59]

The social climate has been traditionally receptive to innovations in technology and related fields. This climate may be changing, at least in terms of patent statistics. Using the number of patents as an index to trends in technology and material culture, the rate of invention in the United States appears to be declining for the first time since the inception of the patent system. Among the possible reasons for this trend are the declining importance of property (patent) rights, the increase in the income tax, the changed attitudes toward unrestricted competition, and the increased interest in personal and social security as opposed to risk. This trend may presage a future shift from technological to biological, medical, and even social invention.[60]

3. Action of vested interests. The differential rate of social change also reflects the deliberate action of vested interests in delaying certain innovations. A vested interest is an individual, group, or institution with a preferred position in things as they are. These persons or groups naturally resist any changes that threaten their position. Vested interests range from wealthy individuals through tax-free institutions to majority groups in a mixed society.[61] In an earlier day, the landed aristocracy and the privileged church were important vested interests. At the present time, large corporations are vested interests, whether monopolistic or not. In many cases, the corporation is in a strong position because of its control of a particular patent. A new and revolutionary device would undermine this position and hence may be put aside through what is known as "pre-emptive research." In such cases, large corporations undertake research in order to make certain that competitors do not develop a process, mechanism, or material that would make present practices obsolete.

4. Role of social institutions. As patterned forms of behavior, social institutions are highly resistant to change. Institutional behavior (e.g., family structure) is invested with strong social sanctions. Such behavior is more enduring than that with neither sanctions nor structures (e.g., dating behavior). Social institutions are rooted in society as it now exists, not as it may conceivably exist in the future. Institutions and the roles of their members depend, or seem to depend, upon maintaining the *status quo*, and any threat thereto involves both institutions and members alike. The latter are convinced, rightly or wrongly, that their best interests require the maintenance of a given institutional structure virtually without change. Accordingly, they *consciously* resist change with all their resources.

Far more important in this resistance to change, however, is the *unconscious* conservatism of the institution, its members, and its functionaries. These per-

---

[59] Barnett, *op. cit.*, p. 56.
[60] Stafford, *op. cit.*
[61] Cf. James W. Vander Zanden, "Accommodation to Undesired Change: The Case of the South," *The Journal of Negro Education*, 31:30-35 (Winter, 1962).

sons tend to reject institutional change—whether in the family, church, business organization, or government—as a direct threat to themselves. Each man holds part of the institutional culture in his personality, and this culture is invested with rightness because persons have learned it during their formative years. Christianity, monogamy, private enterprise, and democracy are social values deeply imbedded in the personality by the institutions of our society. By so presenting an established pattern of belief and behavior, backed by sanctions, institutions act as conservative forces.

Social Change in Underdeveloped Countries

We have hitherto been largely concerned with social change in advanced, industrialized, and technologically complex societies such as our own. The problems of such societies, as we shall see, reflect industrialization, urbanization, heterogeneity of population, and conflicting value patterns. But social change is also occurring in other areas, to which we refer (somewhat disdainfully) as "underdeveloped" countries. Changes in these societies are caused by such varied factors as Western technology, industrial methods, modern medicine, adequate sanitation, and mass communications. These elements, furthermore, are being introduced to societies whose culture and social structure have heretofore remained virtually unchanged for a thousand years. The marriage customs, family systems, sexual roles, class relationships, moral norms, cultural values, and personal aspirations of many underdeveloped peoples are virtually the same as they were at the time of the Crusades.

This confrontation of twentieth-century technology and twelfth-century social structure often produces an unprecedented cultural lag. As one sociologist remarks, we face "an increasingly interdependent world in a century of revolutionary change." [62] Such a revolutionary change is itself the heritage of what Moore calls the "modernization" of the rest of the world—that is, the "transformation of a traditional or pre-modern society into the types of technology and associated social organization that characterize the 'advanced,' economically prosperous, and relatively politically stable nations of the Western World." [63]. This modernization takes a variety of forms, the most spectacular of which is usually industrial and technological. In addition, however, changes often take place simultaneously in such diverse fields as bureaucracy (modern civil service), education, land reform (distribution of land to the peasants), and agricultural methods.[64] Any one of these major innovations, whether coming from within the society or introduced from without, would set in motion profound changes. When these innovations—and many more—all come at once, the result is often chaotic.

We shall consider the related questions of social change and social problems

---

[62] Leo F. Schnore, "Social Problems in the Underdeveloped Areas: An Ecological View," *Social Problems*, 8:182-201 (Winter, 1960-61), p. 182.

[63] Moore, *Social Change, op. cit.*, p. 89.

[64] *Ibid.*, pp. 90-93.

in Chapter 25, where the emphasis will be largely upon the problems of "advanced" societies, notably our own. In the United States, social change has long been apparent in many apsects of life, and the urban-industrial environment has brought widespread normlessness, deviation, and disorganization.[65] Among the problems of contemporary American society are juvenile delinquency, adult crime, alcoholism, mental illness, race prejudice, and family disorganization.[66] In contrast, many (but by no means all) of the problems of underdeveloped areas stem from stagnation, rather than change. Among these age-old problems are "illiteracy, extreme poverty, over-population, poor housing and sanitation, high rates of disease and death, and lack of recreational and cultural amenities. . . ." [67]

In their efforts to eliminate, or at least alleviate, the problems of underdeveloped countries, the Western nations have encountered a variety of difficulties, ranging from apathetic ignorance to outright hostility. A pervasive fallacy of these well-meaning Western efforts is the idea that the above problems are wholly (or at least largely) economic in origin, and that the underdeveloped countries merely require large and continued injections of Western technology and capital. The problems are more complicated, however, and social engineering calls for sociological, as well as economic, knowledge. In other words, *most of the problems of 'economic development' facing backward countries are non-economic in nature.*"[68] We may explore some of the implications of this statement.

In the first place, it should be remembered that the underdeveloped areas do not merely comprise a handful of obscure sections of the globe, where a few thousand savages subsist miserably in miasmic swamps. In terms of sheer numbers alone, the "underdeveloped" areas contain perhaps three-fifths of the world's population, or well over a billion people. Hundreds of millions of "underdeveloped" people live in societies whose continuity stretches back before the Christian era, and whose cultures were established for centuries when the ancestors of present-day Americans were eking out a savage and marginal existence in the dank forests of northern Europe. Hence we have the clash between an advanced technology and a venerable social structure that is currently convulsing many of the "underdeveloped" areas.

This combination of the old and the new means that social change takes different forms in the underdeveloped areas than in the Western World. Certain superficial similarities exist in the sense that some of the underdeveloped countries have recently become "democracies" with a fervent "nationalism" that is largely the product of the mass media of communication.[69] But most of

[65] Leo F. Schnore, "Social Problems in an Urban-Industrial Context," *Social Problems,* 9:228-240 (Winter, 1962).

[66] For a discussion of these and other problems of "advanced" societies, see Mabel A. Elliott and Francis E. Merrill, *Social Disorganization* (New York: Harper & Row, 1961), Fourth Edition.

[67] Marshall B. Clinard, "The Sociologist and Social Change in Underdeveloped Countries," *Social Problems,* 10:207-219 (Winter, 1963), p. 207.

[68] Leo F. Schnore, "Social Problems in the Underdeveloped Areas: An Ecological View," *op. cit.,* p. 198. (His italics.)

[69] Cf. Moore, *Social Change, op. cit.,* p. 94.

these alleged similarities are not very profound. The "democracy" of a Middle East sheikdom that still practices human slavery is hardly the same as that of Sweden. The "nationalism" of a people that still consults witch doctors has very little relationship to that of England. And when an illiterate peasant in a dusty market place listens on the radio to a colonel who has just overthrown the latest "government" of the "republic"—such an encounter leaves something to be desired in terms of the democratic process.

The sequences of social change that apply to the advanced countries, furthermore, do not occur in the same way in the underdeveloped countries. The norms, values, and structures that pave the way for technological innovation in the United States are virtually unknown in many parts of the world. In terms of social structure, the Middle East is not the Middle Atlantic States; Indonesia is not Indiana; and Ceylon is not California. The people of the United States, as we have indicated, are extremely receptive to technological changes that promise, however indirectly, to raise the standard of living and thereby presumably promote the good life. In other areas, however, religious and moral values are more important than material. This does *not* mean, of course, that the average inhabitant of a remote Indian village is oblivious to the sober delights of a full stomach, a whole cotton garment on his back, and a piece of land he can call his own. It *does* mean that this poverty-stricken peasant has other values (religious, caste, familial) that are equally, if not more, important to him than more mundane considerations.

The class structure of many underdeveloped countries also differs from that of the United States. In our own country, technological development and industrial expansion have been welcomed by all classes, the rich as well as the poor. In the underdeveloped countries, however, wealth still largely rests in the land, which has been tightly controlled for centuries by a small hereditary elite. These groups see no personal advantage in raising economic production in the country, let alone in increasing expenditures for schools, hospitals, and sanitation. Such expenditures, in their view, are unprofitable ventures whose only beneficiaries are a despised peasantry. This is a shortsighted point of view in terms of the interests of the ruling classes themselves, not to mention the peasantry. But hereditary ruling classes in feudal countries are notoriously lacking in foresight.[70]

The central problem of social change in the underdeveloped countries is one of cultural adaptation and integration. In Clinard's words, the basic task of purposive social change is to "discover how to integrate values of a technological and materialistic Western world with those of a theological, pre-scientific, and feudalistic society."[71] The average American would consider it self-evident that the average dweller in India's 550,000 villages would eagerly welcome the techniques of the West, from contraception to DDT. But it is not that simple. Many elements of Western culture conflict with value

---

[70] Leo F. Schnore, "Social Problems in the Underdeveloped Areas: An Ecological View," *op. cit.*, pp. 185-186.

[71] Marshall B. Clinard, *op. cit.*, p. 209.

systems that have been imbedded for centuries in the social structure. When change threatens, or appears to threaten, these value systems, the people reject the offending elements.

As a practical matter, therefore, "Any element of technology that is being considered for export to backward areas should be evaluated with respect to its potential bearing upon social structure." [72] As Moore has shown, this bearing may have wide implications. In the process of modernization of underdeveloped countries, the following aspects of social structure are affected sooner or later: kinship systems, family structures, patterns of mate selection, parent-child relationships, women's roles, informal social controls (norms), agencies of education, methods of communication, popular culture, leisure-time activities, interest·groups, voluntary associations, religious organizations, status relationships (class and caste), consumption patterns, and political and administrative structures.[73]

The impact of technology upon one aspect of social structure is vividly illustrated in certain typical reactions to the problem of family planning. Two sets of factors are operative here, one involving mortality (medicine and sanitation) and the other involving fertility (contraceptive techniques). The first factors reduce the death rate, often in spectacular fashion, whereas the second have only a conditional influence upon the birth rate. In practice, techniques influencing mortality are often accepted; those influencing fertility are usually rejected. The reason for this differential rate of acceptance is clear. Most people fear mortality and welcome fertility. Furthermore, different levels of social structure are involved. Public health measures, such as malaria control, can be introduced without changing the social structure. An Indian village will accept the spraying of swamps with DDT without either understanding what is happening or facing any immediate change in the social system. The death rate from malaria will, other things being equal, fall precipitantly. At the same time, fertility remains high and the birth rate stays at the same level. The result is a rapid increase in population, thereby intensifying the age-old problem of too many people and too little food.[74]

In contrast to many such health and sanitation measures, however, contraception directly interferes with the most intimate social unit—namely, the family. Family values involve several related considerations, which touch the very roots of the society. Among these are: (a) the importance of children, especially sons, for reasons of religion and/or family pride; (b) the perennially high infant mortality rate, which has traditionally compensated for a high birth rate; (c) the importance of fathering many children as a demonstration of male virility; (d) the equal importance of mothering many children as a measure of female fertility; (e) the lack of significant communication between husbands and wives on such intimate matters as contraception; and

---

[72] Leo F. Schnore, "Social Problems in the Underdeveloped Areas: An Ecological View," *op. cit.,* p. 185.
[73] Moore, *Social Change, op. cit.,* pp. 102-105.
[74] Schnore, "Social Problems in the Underdeveloped Areas: An Ecological View," *op. cit.,* p. 185.

(*f*) the role of children as tangible forms of social security for parents in sickness and old age.[75] In the face of this powerful combination of value judgments, family limitation lags behind a declining mortality. The result is social change, but hardly of the type recommended by the technical experts of the Ford Foundation.[76]

In this example of family planning in underdeveloped countries, we see that changes in structure ordinarily precede changes in personal relationships. Economic and class systems must therefore change before family values can be expected to follow. Industrialization and urbanization are structural changes that produce changes in other institutional arrangements. In an industrial and urban environment, children cease to be either economic assets or status symbols and parents become correspondingly enthusiastic toward the prospect of limiting their progeny. Members of the family play many roles in addition to those of parents. When the socioeconomic structure calls for the gainful employment of women, the family undergoes substantial modifications. These and many other structural changes have occurred in our own society during the past half century. Many of these same changes are now taking shape in the underdeveloped areas of the world.[77]

In this chapter, we have examined some of the aspects of social change. This is a dynamic concept that involves large-scale modifications of status and role over time. As Moore phrases it, "Alterations in the properties of social systems through time . . . constitute the focus of social dynamics." [78] So many diverse factors give rise to social change that it is impossible to isolate any single and all-embracing cause, despite valiant efforts to do so.[79] We have considered at length only one of several possible "causal" sequences—that arising from the introduction of technological innovations. Changes resulting from this process occur at a differential rate, and social values tend to lag behind other and related aspects of society and culture (cultural lag). We have, finally, glanced at social change as it is currently convulsing large "underdeveloped" areas of the world, which contain more than a billion people.

---

[75] Marshall B. Clinard, *op. cit.*, p. 208.

[76] Cf. Edward G. Stockwell, "Socio-Economic and Demographic Differences Among Underdeveloped Areas," *Rural Sociology*, 28:165-175 (June, 1963).

[77] Leo F. Schnore, "Social Problems in the Underdeveloped Areas: An Ecological View," *op. cit.*, pp. 189-190.

[78] Moore, *Social Change*, *op. cit.*, p. 23.

[79] Martindale, *op. cit.*, p. 60.

SELECTED BIBLIOGRAPHY

Allen, Francis R., *et al.*, *Technology and Social Change*. New York: Appleton-Century-Crofts, Inc., 1957. In this symposium, a number of sociologists who are interested in various aspects of technology and social change have contributed essays reflecting their particular specialties.

Barnett, H. G., *Innovation: The Basis of Cultural Change*. New York: McGraw-Hill Book Company, Inc., 1953. This is a definitive study of cultural (as distinguished from social) change. The author defines innovation as "any thought, behavior, or thing that is new because it is qualitatively different from existing forms." He then gives a perceptive and closely reasoned analysis of the role of innovation in cultural change.

Bertrand, Alvin L., "The Stress-Strain Element of Social Systems: A Micro Theory of Conflict and Change," *Social Forces*, 42:1-9 (October, 1963). In this article, the author makes certain theoretical suggestions toward "reconciling" the conflict and the structural-functional approaches to social change. His general thesis is that "stress-strain" elements in a social system give rise to conflict, deviation, and eventual change.

Bock, Kenneth E., "Evolution, Function, and Change," *American Sociological Review*, 28:229-237 (April, 1963). The author makes the salutary and down-to-earth suggestion that changes in society arise from specific happenings (events), and that these happenings cannot be deduced from the nature of the society itself. In other words, things *happen* and these happenings cause change.

Bogue, Donald J., "The Quantitative Study of Social Dynamics and Social Change," *American Journal of Sociology*, 57:565-568 (May, 1952). This article suggests that social change can be quantitatively studied in terms of changes in status that can be measured. Such changes include place of residence, employment, fertility, and marital, educational, and other forms of status. In this way, the study of social change is taken out of the realm of the general and into that of the specific and the empirical.

Clinard, Marshall B., "The Sociologist and Social Change in Underdeveloped Countries," *Social Problems*, 10:207-219 (Winter, 1963). This article comments on "the role of sociologists . . . in helping to deal with the social problems of Asia, Africa, and South America, those underdeveloped countries which loom in the foreground of today's news." These problems reflect, directly or indirectly, the social changes that have occurred in recent decades.

Gerth, Hans, and C. Wright Mills, *Character and Social Structure*. New York: Harcourt, Brace and World, 1953. Among the many topics treated in this significant analysis is social change. Chapter 13 is entitled "Social-Historical Change" and deals with representative modern theories.

Ginsberg, Morris, "Social Change," *British Journal of Sociology*, 9:205-229 (September, 1958). This long and reflective article examines social change in its broad philosophical and historical perspectives. The author defines social change as "a change in social structure, e.g., the size of a society, the composition or balance of its parts or the type of its organization."

Lerner, Daniel, *The Passing of Traditional Society*. Glencoe, Ill.: The Free Press, 1958. Social change in the Middle East is the subject of this important book. The author reports on an extensive grassroots study of the effects of mass communication upon the emerging nations of this troubled area. In many instances, these changes are marked by violence and social disorganization.

Lippitt, Ronald, *et al.*, *The Dynamics of Planned Change*. New York: Harcourt, Brace and World, 1958. As the title indicates, this book examines some of the theoretical and practical problems arising from deliberate efforts to bring about or direct social change.

Macklin, June, "Culture Change," in J. B. Gittler (ed.), *Review of Sociology: Analysis of a Decade*. New York: John Wiley & Sons, Inc., 1957. This is an annotated bibliography of the literature on cultural (as distinguished from social) change in the decade 1945-1955. The references to anthropological analyses are especially valuable, inasmuch as cultural anthropologists have given more attention in recent years to broad problems of change than have sociologists.

Martindale, Don, *Social Life and Cultural Change*. Princeton: D. Van Nostrand Company, Inc., 1962. This is an extremely important contribution to the study of social change in its broadest perspective. The author believes (*a*) that this study is the crux of all sociological theory, and (*b*) that any approach neglecting social change is fatally lacking as an explanation of society. Social change, he believes, is in final analysis caused by *individuals*—and especially by those individuals known as "intellectuals." The latter are, in his words, "primarily responsible for bringing these systems (i.e., communities and societies) into being, making them work, and justifying them."

Moore, Wilbert E., *Social Change*. Englewood Cliffs, New Jersey: Prentice-Hall, Inc., 1963. The author is one of the leading sociologists who has interested himself in the nature, causes, and effects of social change as a crucial element in the study of society. In the present short volume, Moore presents a tightly reasoned analysis of social change, including such considerations as the normality of change, its qualities, "small-scale" changes, factors giving rise to change, changes in underdeveloped countries (modernization), and social evolution.

Ogburn, William F., "How Technology Changes Society," Annals of the *American Academy of Political and Social Science*, 249:81-88 (January, 1947). In this article, the late William F. Ogburn continues his explorations of the relationships between technology and social change, in which subject he was the leading figure in American sociology. This is a clear statement of the ways in which technology changes the social environment to which, in turn, men must submit. In a later article written just before his death, Ogburn deals with the role of technological development in raising the standard of living of a given society. William F. Ogburn and Francis R. Allen, "Technological Development and Per Capita Income," *American Journal of Sociology*, 65:127-131 (September, 1959).

Parsons, Talcott, "Some Considerations on the Theory of Social Change," *Rural Sociology*, 26:219-239 (September, 1961). In this article, a leading social theorist addresses himself to the problem of social change. "Theoretical analysis of change," he reminds us, "should distinguish between processes which maintain the equilibrium of a system and structural change wherein a system moves from one state of equilibrium to another."

Schnore, Leo F., "Social Problems in an Urban-Industrial Context," *Social Problems*, 9:228-240 (Winter, 1962). In our own society and those with a similar urban-industrial orientation, social change has reflected this background. Many of the problems of underdeveloped countries, on the other hand, represent social change at another stage—that of rural, traditional societies suddenly emerging into an urban-industrial setting.

Theodorson, George A., "Acceptance of Industrialization and Its Attendant Consequences for the Social Patterns of Non-Western Societies," *American Sociological Review*, 18:477-484 (October, 1953). The scope of this article is indicated by its title. Many areas of the non-Western world are witnessing social change at an accelerated pace, following the introduction of Western technology, mass communications, and industrial methods.

22   *Collective Behavior*

The Nature of Collective Behavior

A changing society is marked by collective behavior. This is the very stuff of social change; the two are part and parcel of the same dynamic process. In its simplest terms, social change arises when large numbers of persons respond to new situations in new ways. Collective behavior is "the behavior of associated individuals under circumstances for which their own prior habits . . . do not adequately prepare them." [1] The cumu-

---

[1] Nelson N. Foote and Clyde W. Hart, "Public Opinion and Collective Behavior," Chapter 13 in Muzafer Sherif and M. O. Wilson (eds.), *Group Relations at the Crossroads* (New York: Harper & Row, 1953), p. 308.

lative effect of the new responses further weakens the traditional patterns and takes much of their authority. Collective behavior is both the cause and the effect of social change. Through collective behavior, new institutions are born, social reforms are instituted, and outworn social structures are overthrown.[2]

In collective behavior, social interaction is spontaneous and unorganized, and out of this interaction grow new forms of social organization. Pfautz states this relationship between collective behavior and social change as follows: "... the study of concrete instances of collective behavior provides an empirical basis for insights into the nature and course of social change and the development of organized human groups and institutions."[3] As these new structures emerge in the dynamic process of change, many old structures are disorganized —that is, the network of role-expectations binding the members together becomes weakened or broken. Hence collective behavior is not only a sign of social change but also "an index of social disorganization."[4]

The classical definition of collective behavior, like that of many basic sociological concepts, was given four decades ago by Park and Burgess. They spoke of collective behavior as "the behavior of individuals under the influence of an impulse that is common and collective, an impulse ... that is the result of social interaction."[5] Collective behavior departs from the customary forms and transcends group sanctions. Traditional patterns are abandoned, temporarily or permanently, for the new, the unexpected, the untried, and the unconventional. Collective behavior represents social structures in the process of "becoming," as old patterns are strained or broken by new and unstructured situations.[6] It is in this sense that Lang and Lang speak of collective behavior (or collective dynamics, as they prefer to call it) as "those patterns of social action that are spontaneous and unstructured inasmuch as they are not organized and are not reducible to social structure."[7]

Collective behavior is the behavior of a "collectivity." This group is characterized by "the spontaneous development of norms and organization which contradict or reinterpret the norms and organization of society."[8] When people come together under conditions of high emotion, the resulting interaction temporarily obliterates many traditional norms. The crowd is an example of a collectivity in this sense, as many norms are momentarily ignored or swept aside. The individuals respond in unexpected ways to the collective stimulus, and in so doing they generate new and spontaneous norms.

[2] Anselm L. Strauss, "Research in Collective Behavior: Neglect and Need," *American Sociological Review*, 12:352-354 (June, 1947).

[3] Harold W. Pfautz, "Near-Group Theory and Collective Behavior: A Critical Reformulation," *Social Problems*, 9:167-174 (Fall, 1961), pp. 168-169.

[4] *Ibid.*, p. 169.

[5] Robert E. Park and Ernest W. Burgess, *Introduction to the Science of Sociology* (Chicago: University of Chicago Press, 1924), p. 865.

[6] Leon Bramson, *The Political Context of Sociology* (Princeton: Princeton University Press, 1961), p. 62.

[7] Kurt Lang and Gladys Engel Lang, *Collective Dynamics* (New York: Thomas Y. Crowell Company, 1961), p. 4.

[8] Ralph H. Turner and Lewis M. Killian, *Collective Behavior* (Englewood Cliffs, N.J.: Prentice-Hall, Inc., 1957), p. 4.

Change occurs in the role behavior of the members of a collectivity, as many persons act as they never would in their ordinary roles.[9] The impulse that generates the interaction of the collectivity stimulates such emotions as fear, hatred, or intolerance.[10] Members of a lynching crowd ignore the group restraints controlling violence and murder. In many cases, as we shall see, they are motivated by deep and unconscious impulses toward violence that are ordinarily controlled by the norms of organized society.

Blumer further characterizes collective behavior in terms of its relationship to sociology. The latter is interested in the social structure and its constituent elements (customs, norms, institutions) as they are at any one time. Collective behavior, on the other hand, is concerned with these elements as they come into existence, with the ways in which norms, institutions, and customs come into being.[11] This dynamic process of instability, emergence, and change is characteristic of contemporary society. Many ties of the family and the local community, for instance, are weakened by urbanization, secularization, and mobility. As the traditional patterns are disturbed or broken, modern man is increasingly subject to collective behavior.

Man in the mass has become an important symbol of modern society, both in the totalitarian states and in democratic countries. Dictatorships come into being through social unrest, collective interaction, and revolutionary social movements. By their very nature, these governments are dedicated to the techniques and goals of collective behavior. The people are in transition from the old to the new and are not allowed to relax their efforts and settle down, much less return to the old ways. At the same time, the totalitarian countries have no monopoly of collective forms of action. Indeed, it has been forcefully stated that collective behavior and mass communication are as important to democratic societies as to totalitarian states. The agencies of mass communication, for example, are said to foster democratic values and encourage individual participation in the interaction of a democratic society.[12] We shall consider these and related aspects of collective behavior in Chapter 24.

The Individual and Collective Behavior

The individual engaging in collective behavior does not thereby cease to be a human being, bound by the sanctions of organized society. Only in certain respects and, ordinarily, for limited periods does he abandon these controls. Hence collective behavior remains *social* behavior, resulting from social interaction and subject to many of the uniformities of other social behavior. In many

---

[9] G. E. Swanson, "A Preliminary Laboratory Study of the Acting Crowd," *American Sociological Review*, 18:522-533 (October, 1953).

[10] James W. Vander Zanden, "The Klan Revival," *American Journal of Sociology*, 65:456-462 (March, 1960).

[11] Herbert Blumer, "The Field of Collective Behavior," Chapter 19 in Robert E. Park (ed.), *An Outline of the Principles of Sociology* (New York: Barnes & Noble, Inc., 1939).

[12] Joseph R. Gusfield, "Mass Society and Extremist Politics," *American Sociological Review*, 27:19-30 (February, 1962).

instances, indeed, the difference between "ordinary" behavior and collective behavior is impossible to draw. Therefore we shall not try to make a distinction that will be operative under all conditions, but shall deal with those aspects of behavior that are unmistakably collective. Among these are crowds, publics, and social movements.

Under conditions of collective behavior, some of the traditional group restraints are temporarily removed, and the individual is free to indulge the hatreds and aggressions that lie deep in his personality. Freud explained this behavior by stating that the individual has certain innate, violent, and sadistic urges that are constantly held in check by social control. In collective behavior, these controls are swept aside and the individual expresses his dark impulses. The conscious part of the personality, Freud continued, ordinarily controls these impulses and forces the person to conform to the group norms. Under the stress of collective excitement, these restraints are wholly or partially dissolved, and the members of the crowd are free to hate, destroy, and murder.[13]

The Freudian approach offers many insights into behavior. It is not sufficient in itself, however, to explain the reaction of the crowd, mob, or mass. Many such collective impulses can be traced only in a remote sense to the "innate" tendencies of the individual. Prejudice, for example, is a learned rather than an inborn mental pattern. The child is taught the attitudes of the prejudiced person, because these, or any other, attitudes are completely lacking at birth. The caste organization of society is an arbitrary one and the discriminatory attitudes that support it are just as arbitrary. Hence the concept of "inborn" racial attitudes is fictitious.[14]

It is true that the basic emotions of hatred and fear rest upon inborn characteristics, but they are modified by the culture before they are expressed in a particular form of behavior. It is, therefore, only part of the story to state that *inborn* impulses are released in collective behavior and find expression in antisocial behavior. The attitudes behind the action, the prejudices and preconceptions, and the symbolic representations of the outside world to which the group members respond—these are important constituents in the total pattern of collective behavior.

Collective behavior may thus be fully explained only in terms of itself—that is, as a particular form of *social interaction*. We must look to the social, rather than to the individual, factors in collective behavior. The individual has a sense of power when he is participating in a large group enterprise, whether crowd or dedicated political party. He interacts on a different basis in a collectivity than in a small and face-to-face group. He participates in a complex structure when he engages in collective behavior. The nature of the interaction, not the individual psychology of the participants, is the important factor.[15]

---

[13] Sigmund Freud, *Group Psychology and the Analysis of the Ego* (London: International Psychoanalytical Press, 1922).

[14] Cf. Kenneth B. Clark, "The Social Scientist as an Expert Witness in Civil Rights Litigation," *Social Problems*, 1:5-10 June, 1953).

[15] Herbert Blumer, "Collective Behavior," in J. B. Gittler (ed.), *Review of Sociology: Analysis of a Decade* (New York: John Wiley & Sons, Inc., 1957).

Collective behavior illustrates the tendency of human beings to respond to common symbols; in this segregationist rally, various symbols, both verbal and physical, are evoked by the speaker.

This interaction has various effects upon the actors. On the one hand, there is a negative or destructive effect, as the motivations they have learned in their institutional roles are weakened or collapse. On the positive side, the individuals are sensitized to the presence of others in the collective enterprise and are carried along with them to break the bonds of the traditional in the direction of the new. The latter may or may not be "desirable" from the point of view of prevailing social values. The point is that, whatever the value judgments, the behavior emerging from the interaction is new. In collective as in ordinary behavior, man is both a psychological being with internal emotions and a cultural being with institutional roles.[16]

The Symbolic Basis of Collective Behavior

Collective behavior and "ordinary" behavior alike arise from the unique characteristics of man as a symbol-using animal. The early literature on collective behavior contained many analogies to animal behavior, based upon the assumption that crowds are like flocks of sheep and mobs like packs of wolves. Certain superficial similarities *do* exit between the behavior of animals and that of a lynching mob. Stampeding cattle and panic-stricken human beings *are* doing somewhat the same things. But they are doing them for very different

---

[16] Hans Gerth and C. Wright Mills, *Character and Social Structure* (New York: Harcourt, Brace and World, 1953), pp. 436-437.

reasons. Man can stimulate himself through symbols, an ability that is not shared with animals.

In the process of self-stimulation, man takes the role of the other and reacts to this process.[17] He generates love, hate, fear, and other emotions in himself by responding to internal stimuli that do not depend upon any immediate external event. The member of a lynching mob reacts to the hatreds and fears of a society that has systematically hated and feared the Negro. He responds to the fictions, slogans, myths, and stereotypes that have become part of himself. Some of these elements are found in his conscious personality, whereas others remain largely unconscious. He may therefore not completely understand why he responds as he does to the situation in which he finds himself.

Collective behavior thus reflects the background of the members of the collectivity, who have learned to respond to common symbols. The symbol may be a flag, a cross, a shrine, or other physical object. More often, however, the symbol rests in the mind, either in the form of verbal clichés, catchwords, and slogans, or as half-formulated beliefs, prejudices, and presuppositions. Among these latter formulations are "white supremacy," Negro inferiority," "100 per cent American," "racial purity," "Aryan blood," and "holy war." Whatever the nature of the symbol, the important consideration is that human beings respond through an internalized conversation with themselves. In this way, they stimulate themselves.[18]

The interaction resulting in collective behavior may occur on different levels. The most obvious form arises when a crowd is intent upon something in the immediate vicinity and its members stimulate each other both physically and psychologically. The resulting "circular reaction" intensifies the emotions of the members who are moved to heights of heroism or depths of cruelty that they would never attain alone. The mere physical nearness of large numbers of aroused people has an electric effect. Each person stimulates his neighbor, is stimulated in turn, and in addition stimulates himself. Collective behavior is more than the sum total of the individual behavior constituting it.[19]

This element of autostimulation distinguishes the collective behavior of human beings from that of animals. The latter, to the best of our knowledge, respond to a simple and direct stimulus—a sudden noise, an ominous smell, a physical gesture, or the gnawing pangs of hunger. Human beings respond to a symbolic stimulus that may range in complexity from a simple stereotype to a social myth that explains the entire social order. Men are moved by racial stereotypes to engage in fleeting mob behavior. They may also be moved by the great myths of religion, nationality, and revolution to carry through prolonged social movements that ultimately change an entire society. These "pictures in our heads"[20] determine the uniquely human character of collective behavior.

---

[17] George Herbert Mead, *Mind, Self, and Society* (edited by Charles W. Morris) (Chicago: University of Chicago Press, 1934).

[18] Harold D. Lasswell, *et. al.*, *The Comparative Study of Symbols*, Hoover Institute Studies (Stanford: Stanford University Press, 1952).

[19] Blumer, "The Field of Collective Behavior," *op. cit.*, p. 224.

[20] Walter Lippmann, *Public Opinion* (New York: The Macmillan Company, 1922).

Collective behavior should also be considered in its cultural context, for the individual responds only to the symbols of his own culture. Persons reared in a culture or subculture based upon racial superiority, discrimination, and fear will tend to react in one way when faced by an alleged act of aggression by a Negro. Persons reared in a culture with no such elements react differently to the same stimulus. The cultural definitions of an American on matters of race differ widely from those of a Frenchman or an Italian. The physical facts of race are the same in all societies, but the symbolic interpretation is not. Collective behavior is subject to wide cultural variations.

The influence of symbols in collective behavior was documented by the "zoot-suit" riots in Los Angeles during World War II. Crowd activity was here directed against young people of Mexican descent, who were allegedly molesting American soldiers, their wives, and their girl friends. The "zooter" symbol (peg-leg trousers, draped jacket, long, slick hair) had formerly been applied to groups of adolescents regardless of ethnic affiliation. During the war, however, crowd symbols were directed against any out-group, which in this case was composed of young Mexican-Americans. The latter were the victims of violent crowd behavior, inspired and stimulated by the hostile symbol of the zoot-suit. Rioting crowds of native-born (or at least non-Mexican) background expressed their aggressions through this symbol of an alien ethnic group.[21]

The Role of Social Unrest

People act most of the time in accordance with behavior that has been patterned by past generations and sanctioned by such usage. When this situation obtains on a wide scale, the society is stable and its members are comparatively well organized. Most persons are occupying the statuses ascribed to them and are playing the corresponding roles in accepted fashion. The agreement among the members of the society on important concerns of group life is substantially complete, and a high degree of consensus prevails. Under such conditions, collective behavior is comparatively rare. During times of social unrest, however, collective behavior tends to flourish.

Collective behavior occurs on a large scale when many persons do not occupy their traditional statuses or play their prescribed roles. The connection between collective behavior and social unrest is close. Times of social unrest are also times of transition, when one set of structures is in the process of change and a new one is struggling to appear. New institutions, forms of belief and behavior, and patterns of social expectations are in various stages of development. These emergent patterns represent responses to new situations and the individual is often obliged to act in unaccustomed ways because the past offers no established solution. With many of the old norms gone, he must perforce

---

[21] Ralph H. Turner and Samuel J. Surace, "Zoot-Suiters and Mexicans: Symbols in Crowd Behavior," *American Journal of Sociology,* 62:14-20 (July, 1956).

improvise many of his actions. Much of this improvisation takes the form of collective behavior.

Social change may also bring about social unrest. In such periods, normal routines are impossible or unpleasant to follow and many persons suffer from a pervasive feeling of anxiety and restlessness. They engage in random behavior with no special purpose except to do *something*. The individual is receptive to new suggestions and welcomes innovations that promise a fuller or more exciting life. These innovations may be as inconsequential as a new fad in dress, speech, or entertainment. At the other extreme, social unrest may presage a broad social movement that changes the social structure and convulses a society for generations. On whatever level of complexity or intensity, social unrest increases receptivity toward change.[22]

Social instability also brings fear, insecurity, and frustration. Learned responses are no longer adequate and many persons cannot play the roles they have been taught. Societies in the throes of religious unrest, large-scale unemployment, or revolutionary upheaval illustrate this situation. When large numbers of men and women cannot play their roles because of political absolutism, mass unemployment, or continuous warfare, individual anxieties are intensified. New social myths may arise, as the man on the street gropes for some ideal that will give him a sense of emotional identification. "The significance of social unrest," remark Park and Burgess, "is that it represents at once a breaking up of the established routine and a preparation for new collective action." [23]

The decades since World War II have been marked by unrest and insecurity throughout the world. The great convulsion of the war, following immediately upon a world-wide depression, left the social structure of the Western world (victors as well as vanquished) shattered in many places and shaken in others. The climate of the Cold War has maintained some of the tensions and mass anxieties of World War II itself. Many traditional behavior patterns of a peaceful world have been severely strained by the ideological conflicts and outright fears of a world divided into armed camps. The decades of the 1950's and 1960's have seen men groping for new certainties to take the place of the old. These perplexities and insecurities have been immensely complicated, as we saw in Chapter 21, by the rapid rate of social change.[24]

In the United States, this mass insecurity was marked by fear of outside attack and pressure for conformity in thought. The anticipated aggression from the outside world was both physical and ideological. The force of World Communism made the free nations fearful of both military attack and internal subversion. The "invention" of the atomic bomb and subsequent developments in nuclear fission on both sides of the Iron Curtain gave the general public an understanding of the importance of the pure scientist. At the same time, it

---

[22] Lang and Lang, *op. cit.*, p. 124.
[23] Park and Burgess, *op. cit.*, p. 866.
[24] See Wilbert E. Moore, *Social Change* (Englewood Cliffs, New Jersey: Prentice-Hall, Inc., 1963), Chapter 1.

increased the traditional American suspicion of the intellectual. This fear was capitalized upon by demagogues, both in and out of political life, with the result that many of the traditional freedoms seemed for a time in jeopardy.[25]

This climate of opinion was apparent with respect to nonconformity of all kinds, religious as well as political. A study of the relationships between fear, conformity, and civil liberties found that intolerance was highest among those who perceived the Communist danger to be greatest. In the author's words, "There is a consistent relationship . . . between perception of the internal Communist danger and tolerance. Those who see the danger as greatest tend to be the most intolerant." [26] The implication is that, if the real or alleged threat of Communist subversion were to increase, the tolerance of nonconformity would probably decrease. Other variables are clearly present in the degree of tolerance or intolerance, but the perception of danger and, by implication, the fear of that danger, constitute an important element.

"Social unrest," remark Park and Burgess, "is first communicated, then takes form in crowd and mass movements, and finally crystallizes in institutions." [27] Unrest and disorder are succeeded by the popular excitement of a mass movement, from which eventually emerges a new institution, a new religion, or a new social myth. Collective behavior goes through a life cycle of unrest, popular action, and the establishment of new institutions. The latter gradually become encrusted with age and tradition, new inadequacies emerge, and the cycle begins again. This process has increased both in rapidity and complexity until entire peoples and continents are currently in the throes of social unrest.

Social Movements as Collective Behavior

"A social movement," suggest Turner and Killian, "is a collectivity acting with some continuity to promote a change or resist a change in the society or group of which it is a part." [28] In Blumer's words, social movements are "collective enterprises to establish a new order of life." [29] King defines a social movement as a "group venture extending beyond a local community or a single event and involving a systematic effort to inaugurate changes in thought, behavior, and social relationships." [30] Lang and Lang characterize a social movement as "large-scale, widespread, and continuing, elementary collective action in pursuit of an objective that affects and shapes the social order in some fundamental aspect." [31] Social movements are attempts, more or less consciously conceived, to change the mores, the social structure, the institutional

---

[25] Edward A. Shils, "Security and Science Sacrificed to Loyalty," *Bulletin of the Atomic Scientists,* 11:106-109 (April, 1955).

[26] Samuel A. Stouffer, *Communism, Conformity, and Civil Liberties* (New York: Doubleday & Company, 1955), p. 217.

[27] Park and Burgess, *op. cit.,* p. 874.

[28] Turner and Killian, *op. cit.,* p. 308.

[29] Blumer, "The Field of Collective Behavior," *op. cit.,* p. 255.

[30] C. Wendell King, *Social Movements in the United States* (New York: Random House, Inc., 1956), p. 27.

[31] Lang and Lang, *op. cit.,* p. 490.

patterns, and the statuses and roles of a given society. Social movements are therefore important agencies of social change.

Social movements are similar to the type of collectivity that Kornhauser calls "mass movements." He indicates that the latter have the following characteristics: "their objectives are remote and extreme; they favor activist modes of intervention in the social order; they mobilize uprooted and atomized sections of the population; they lack an internal structure of independent groups (such as regional or functional units with some freedom of action)." [32] Totalitarian movements are mass movements, but the reverse is not necessarily true. Some mass movements are totalitarian (the Communist party) and others are non-totalitarian (the Prohibition movement). The difference is largely between the ultimate goals. The totalitarian movement, by definition, tries to seize control of the entire society, whereas the nontotalitarian movement merely seeks to gain some limited end—such as national prohibition, votes for women, or civil rights for Negroes. [33]

The emphasis in social movements is primarily upon social change. This is true of most, but not all, such collectivities. Some social movements, indeed, are organized attempts to *resist* social change and hence are "reactionary" rather than "progressive" forces. After the Supreme Court decision of 1954 *outlawing* segregation in the public schools, various White Citizens' Councils arose in the South for the express purpose of *maintaining* segregation. Members of these organizations regarded the traditional system of educational segregation as desirable and any change as undesirable. In like manner, organizations that resist the incorporation of their country or nationality into another state or federation of states are acting against, rather than for, social change. [34]

Such reactionary social movements, however, are in the minority. Most movements involve the change, rather than the preservation, of a former way of life. In this sense, social movements are new institutions in the process of being born. When we say that contemporary society is dynamic, we mean (among other things) that it is marked by extensive and powerful social movements. This dynamism is itself the product of such factors as "increasing social contacts, extending communications, technological innovation, mobility, industrial encroachment, and the breaking down of traditional cultural forms. . . ." [35] Many social movements ultimately involve the overthrow of old institutional patterns and the substitution of the new. The modern world cannot be fully understood without a realization of the role of these collective enterprises. [36]

The twentieth century has seen more large social movements than any comparable period in history. Two world wars, revolutions in Russia and China, the rise and fall of Fascism in Italy and Germany, the international drive for power by the communist parties of the world, the development of the labor movement,

---

[32] William Kornhauser, *The Politics of Mass Society* (Glencoe, Ill.: The Free Press, 1959), p. 47.

[33] *Ibid.*

[34] James W. Vander Zanden, "Resistance and Social Movements," *Social Forces*, 37:312-315 (May, 1959).

[35] Blumer, "Collective Behavior," *op. cit.*, p. 145.

[36] Rudolf Heberle, *Social Movements* (New York: Appleton-Century-Crofts, Inc., 1951).

and the nationalist movements of colonial peoples in Europe, Asia, and Africa are all massive social movements. These enterprises involve more people than have previously experienced rapid social change at any one time. The sociologist has only recently begun to study these forms of collective behavior. In the future, he may contribute to a greater understanding of them.[37]

The United States has had more than its share of social movements. In the century since the Civil War, this country has spawned such varied social movements as the Knights of Labor, the Know Nothing movement, the Populist movement, the Ku Klux Klan, Technocracy, Prohibition, Women's Suffrage, Christian Science, the Townsend Plan, the Civil Rights movement, and the many reactionary and semifascist movements that flourished in the decade before World War II. The society of the United States is heterogeneous, with different racial, religious, and ethnic strains. This heterogeneity has been one of the glories of American democracy, but it has also provided a fertile soil for all manner of social movements. Cultural confusion, lack of integration, and individual discontent have been among the factors that have precipitated these movements in the New World.[38]

Social movements are not necessarily confined to a single nation, but may assume international and even world-wide ramifications. Internationalism has been a characteristic of many twentieth-century movements, in contrast to the nationalism that marked many, but by no means all, of the social movements of the nineteenth century. In terms of the numbers now under the Red banner, the most important contemporary social movement is unquestionably international communism. The complexities of this explosive movement are so great that they cannot be considered here. We merely wish to indicate that, both in extent and emotional impetus, this movement involves more human beings than any other such movement in history.

Social movements, as distinguished from other forms of collective behavior, are of comparatively long duration. The crowd and the mob have a short span of existence and vanish into their individual parts once their immediate objective has been realized or the excitement has worn off. The social movement requires a considerable period to accomplish its purposes, which often involve major changes in the society. These changes affect the behavior patterns of large numbers of persons, and these patterns cannot be changed overnight. Men and women have learned to play their roles in the present institutions of society. In order for them to oppose the established church, government, economic organization, or family system, basic changes in incentive are required.[39]

These latter changes are facilitated by what Blumer has felicitously called "cultural drifts." By this term, he refers to widespread shifts in attitudes concerning basic statuses and roles. Among contemporary cultural drifts are: ". . . the increased value of health, the belief in free education, the extension of the

---

[37] Barrington Moore, Jr., "Sociological Theory and Contemporary Politics," *American Journal of Sociology*, 61:107-115 (September, 1955).

[38] King, *op. cit.*, pp. 13 ff.

[39] Gerth and Mills, *op. cit.*, p. 455.

franchise, the emancipation of women, the increasing regard for children, and the increasing prestige of science." [40] In addition, there is a growing belief that the individual should seek happiness in this world, instead of placing all his reliance upon the next world. This growing secularism is one of the most important (albeit intangible) "cultural drifts" of our day. Many more tangible social movements derive their emotional acceptance from this basic change in social values.

The Personnel of Social Movements

Social movements are mass enterprises involving persons who have real or supposed grievances against the present institutional order. These grievances may be limited and may refer merely to individual structures (particular churches, schools, businesses, governments) that are distasteful, annoying, or actively stultifying to certain individuals or groups. Other grievances may be more general and may reflect a change in mass attitudes toward the entire institutional order. Most persons in a social movement fall somewhere between (a) those dissatisfied with their status in a single institution, and (b) those who are alienated from the existing society as a whole.

Social movements reflect *discontinuities* in society—that is, breaks in social interaction resulting from social change. A rapid rate of industrialization and urbanization interrupts the primary relationships that mark the rural community. These interruptions have been apparent in the United States, as this country has changed in three generations from a predominantly rural to an increasingly urban society. Similar interruptions have been even more marked in Asia and Africa, where industrialization has changed many societies from a primitive tribalism to urbanism in less than a single generation.[41] In this connection, it is not urbanism *as such* that gives rise to social movements, for many European societies have been urbanized for centuries. The disorganizing factor is, rather, *rapid* urbanization that dissolves primary relationships and leaves nothing in their place.

The result of such discontinuities is to produce large numbers of frustrated and alienated persons. They may be *physically* uprooted, as they leave the land for the city in search of jobs and adventure. They may be *morally* uprooted, as they lose contact with family, friends, and religion. Their world is atomized, fragmented, and disorganized,[42] and they are ready for a social movement that will give them a sense of belonging. In the United States, these movements have for the most part been of an *intermediary* character—that is, between the primary groups of the family and local community on the one hand and the secondary bureaucracy of the national government on the other. The Townsend Plan and Technocracy were examples of such intermediary movements. In

---

[40] Blumer, "Social Movements," *op. cit.*, p. 256.

[41] Daniel Lerner, *The Passing of Traditional Society* (Glencoe, Ill.: The Free Press, 1958).

[42] Ephraim Harold Mizruchi, "Social Structure and Anomie in a Small City," *American Sociological Review*, 25:645-654 (October, 1960).

other countries, social movements often take the form of totalitarian parties that seek to overthrow the entire institutional structure.[43]

Alienation of the population means that social movements are drawn from all strata of a mass society. Many institutions, ranging from labor unions to churches, lose their hold on their members, who are then open to the appeals of mass movements. It is a mistake to assume that the participants in social movements all belong to the same segment of society—whether industrial workers, peasants, or middle-class shopkeepers. The personnel of the Nazi movement, for example, included: "Princes without thrones . . . subsidized landlords, indebted farmers, virtually bankrupt industrialists, impoverished shopkeepers and artisans, doctors without patients, lawyers without clients, writers without readers, unemployed teachers, and unemployed manual and white-collar workers. . . ." [44] These individuals and groups were, each in their own way, alienated from the traditional institutions of the old Germany.

In terms of both numbers and enthusiasm of support, however, certain groups have been among the most vulnerable to social movements, especially those of the totalitarian variety. Kornhauser singles out "unattached intellectuals, marginal members of the middle class, [and] isolated industrial and farm workers" [45] as among the groups most susceptible to such appeals. By unattached intellectuals, he refers to persons with a university education who are not attached to any university, corporation, or professional institution. These men have no strong attachment to the existing order and are therefore eager to find their identity in a mass movement. Marginal middle-class persons include small businessmen, impoverished shopkeepers, and isolated farmers; many of these individuals lack a strong stake in the society. Industrial and farm workers who are isolated from society, both physically and functionally, also flock to new social movements. Such industries as mining, maritime work, and longshore employment contribute more than their share to mass movements. These groups are, to a greater or lesser degree, cut off physically as well as socially from society as a whole and tend to form isolated and undifferentiated masses.[46]

Social movements must also be considered within the existing framework of social stratification. A social movement is not a class, but many of the appeals of social movements are directed along existing class lines. A social class in this sense is a group of persons with roughly similar *attitudes* that have arisen in the course of common experience toward the basic institutional patterns.[47] A social movement is a dynamic mass organization with a goal or purpose. When a new movement can be integrated into a class-conscious group, much of the

---

[43] Kornhauser, *op. cit.*, p. 125.

[44] Hans H. Gerth, "The Nazi Party: Its Leadership and Composition," in Robert K. Merton, *et. al.* (eds.), *Reader in Bureaucracy* (Glencoe, Ill.: The Free Press, 1952), p. 105, cited by Kornhauser, *op. cit.*, p. 181.

[45] Kornhauser, *op. cit.*, p. 182.

[46] *Ibid.*, p. 215.

[47] Richard Centers, "Social Class, Occupation, and Imputed Belief," *American Journal of Sociology,* 58:543-555 (May, 1953).

preliminary work of recruitment has been done. The movement automatically takes over many of the slogans of class, and this identity can be transferred to the new cause.[48]

It has become customary in recent decades to associate the proletariat (industrial workers) exclusively with social movements and to ignore the role of other classes. The insecurities of modern life are strikingly pronounced for the industrial worker in many countries, but this should not obscure the fact that other classes are also susceptible to the appeals of social movements. In the United States, such a social movement as the Townsend Plan, which promised large old-age pensions, found its strength largely among impoverished members of the lower-middle class and retired farmers. The social movement (or "cultural drift") somewhat vaguely known as "right-wing extremism" or "the new American right," on the other hand, derives much of its financial support from wealthy, ultraconservative persons who fear the implications of the welfare state for their own fortunes. Many members of the rank-and-file of this movement, conversely, are drawn from disgruntled ethnic groups who fear the social and religious influence of communism.[49]

In Europe, social movements among the peasants have existed for centuries, and many changes have been inaugurated by dissatisfied elements of this class. Peasant revolts have periodically convulsed European countries, from the Middle Ages to the latest organized dissatisfaction of the wine-growers of southern France. In Germany, the alienated and impoverished middle class after World War I constituted a large segment of the early Nazi movement, at a time when organized industrial workers were resisting Hitler with all the means at their command.[50] The goals of social movements reflect those of the members—or those which the members are convinced are theirs. In the United States, most people are satisfied with the political and economic system as it presently exists. Hence people are often recruited for undemocratic social movements under the name of "democracy" and for movements promoting racial inequality under the name of "states' rights." [51]

Social movements also contribute to social mobility and the formation of new elites. The latter term refers to persons who occupy a superior status in society either by birth or achievement.[52] Many new achievements of status arise in connection with social movements. Men who spent their lives in the labor movement occupy important positions in the government of European countries. In the United States, the increasing importance of organized labor has brought many persons with a variety of talents to associate themselves with it. Lawyers, journalists, economists, and research workers have risen with the

---

[48] Kornhauser, *op. cit.*, Chapter 9 ,"Social Classes and Mass Movements."

[49] Daniel Bell (ed.), *The New American Right* (New York: Criterion Books, 1955), especially Seymour M. Lipset, "The Sources of the 'Radical Right'," Chapter 7.

[50] Frederick L. Schuman, *The Nazi Dictatorship* (New York: Alfred A. Knopf, Inc., 1935).

[51] Cf. James W. Vander Zanden, "Accommodation to Undesired Change: The Case of the South," *The Journal of Negro Education*, 31:30-35 (Winter, 1962).

[52] Harold D. Lasswell, *et. al.*, *The Comparative Study of Elites*, Hoover Institute Studies (Stanford: Stanford University Press, 1952).

labor movement to new statuses and in this sense constitute a new career elite.[53]

The most spectacular evolution of new elites occurs in connection with revolutionary movements. The rise in the social scale may be highly dramatic, for the new revolutionary elite is often recruited from persons who have spent years as political prisoners or penniless exiles. The elite that emerged from the Russian Revolution included many such persons: Lenin and Trotsky spent long periods in exile, and Stalin was a hunted fugitive within his own country. The Fascist movement in Italy and the Nazi movement in Germany similarly brought to the top new elite groups, largely recruited on the basis of traits (aggression, organized violence, sadism) that are not considered desirable in an ordered society. The concept of the elite is here used in a technical sense, namely, as constituting a new group moving into positions of dominant status. This concept does not imply moral approval of the actions of these groups, either before or after seizing power.

Ideological Aspects of Social Movements

Men who are associated with social movements over long periods tend to develop similar attitudes toward their status and role. Some of these attitudes grow up spontaneously, whereas others are deliberately inculcated by the educational agencies of the movement. Each member acquires many common viewpoints because of his participation in the activities of the movement. The inner world of the individual reflects his outer world, with its definitions, hopes, aspirations, and norms. The sum total of the elements in this intellectual world of a particular group, class, or movement is known as its ideology.[54]

The ideology of a social movement has been defined by Blumer as follows: ". . . first, a statement of the objective, purpose, and premises of the movement; second, a body of criticism and condemnation of the existing structure which the movement is attacking and seeking to change; third, a body of defense doctrine which serves as a justification of the movement and of its objectives; fourth, a body of belief dealing with policies, tactics, and practical operation of the movement; and, fifth, the myths of the movement."[55] The ideology includes such diverse intellectual elements as stereotypes, slogans, clichés, and myths.

The concept of ideology is itself an outgrowth of the social structure of western Europe and the classes and social movements that have characterized the Old World for centuries. Intellectual products are seen in terms of the status of the individual, as well as in terms of the content of his thought. Persons who hold opinions on economic and political issues are influenced, however subtly, by their status and role, and this unconscious bias must be considered in assess-

---

[53] Nelson N. Foote, "The Professionalization of Labor in Detroit," *American Journal of Sociology,* 58:371-380 (January, 1953).

[54] Karl Mannheim, *Ideology and Utopia* (translated by Louis Wirth and Edward A. Shils) (New York: Harcourt, Brace and World, 1936).

[55] Blumer, *op. cit.,* pp. 267-268.

ing the product of their thought. As stated by Mannheim: "Opinions, statements, propositions, and systems of ideas are not taken at their face value but are interpreted in the light of the life-situation of the one who expresses them . . . the specific character and life-situation of the subject influence his opinions, perceptions, and interpretations."[56]

The ideology is a complex intellectual melange, composed partly of rational conclusions and partly of emotions, dreams, and aspirations. One of these components is the *stereotype*, a term applied many years ago by Lippmann to the "pictures in our heads" by which we give meaning to outside reality. These shorthand classifications emerge from life experience, as the individual learns them in his cultural indoctrination. Many such classifications denote invidious comparisons. The Italian-American is called a "wop," the Irish-American a "mick," and the Negro a "nigger." These symbols carry fixed meanings to the person using them and simplify his reactions to the persons so designated. He is able to *categorize* these persons and thereby place them in statuses defined by the culture. When he sees a member of the categorized group (an individual Negro), he responds to the stereotype ("nigger") rather than to the other person as an individual.[57]

Members of a social movement have a set of stereotypes that determine their reactions to other persons and groups. These pictures involve at least three categories: (a) the members of the in-group, who participate in the movement and hence are on the "right" side; (b) the members of the out-group, who oppose the movement and hence are on the "wrong" side; (c) the members of the general public, who have no interest one way or another in the movement and hence are defined in a neutral way. When the social movement has revolutionary goals, these three groups are reduced to two. The general public is largely opposed to the revolution and hence becomes fused with the out-group.

This type of ideological thinking is as easy as it is emotionally satisfying. It is by no means confined to the personnel of social movements, but characterizes the thinking of persons on all social levels. The emotions generated by an active social movement, whether political, economic, or religious, tend to encourage such thinking. These persons are involved in a conflict situation, where it is easy to categorize the out-group in the simple and emotion-freighted terms of the stereotype. The in-group is loved, the out-group is hated, and that is all there is to it. When a person is once identified with a particular group, the stereotype does the rest and saves the trouble of further thinking. The stereotype has no scientific validity; its importance lies in the functions it performs for the persons using it. If large numbers of people act *as if* the stereotype were true, then it *is* true for them.

The most important ideological element in the social movement is the *myth*. The myth deals with the great cosmic concerns of human life—the relationship

---

[56] Mannheim, *op. cit.*, p. 50. See also Norman Birnbaum, "The Sociological Study of Ideology (1940-60): A Trend Report and Bibliography," *Current Sociology*, Vol. 9, London, 1962, published for UNESCO.

[57] Lippmann, *op. cit.*

of man to his fellows and to God, the beginning of the world, and its possible future. Every society rests upon a substructure of myth, which provides the beliefs that hold it together. The myth is at once an explanation, a justification, and a hope. It is an explanation of how things came to be, a justification of the way they are, and a hope for better times in the future. The function of the myth is to bring about obedience of the individual to the society and make sure that this obedience is willing. The myth makes men *want* to do what they *have* to do.[58]

The myth contains the basic values of the society and the social movement. There is a rough harmony between the elements of the myth and the institutions of family, church, and state, provided the society is in a state of organization. When the society becomes disorganized, the relationships between the institutions and the myth are inconsistent and strained. The majority of the people cease to support or tolerate the reigning myth, and a new myth may be ushered in by revolution. In the Western World, the two most prominent contemporary myths are democracy and communism. The latter is a militant social movement that is in world-wide conflict with the democratic myth. Communism can succeed in the Western World only by replacing the democratic myth.

The concept of the myth carries a popular meaning of something that is fictitious, nonexistent, or false. The term is not used here in this sense. The scientific truth or falsity of the myth is not at issue. The important consideration is the *belief* and the explanation of the universe that the myth offers. If people *believe* in the divine right of kings, they can readily accept a social structure based upon an absolute monarchy. If they *believe* in the feudal system, with its elaborate hierarchy of relationships, they can easily adjust themselves to such a way of life. The majority of people seldom question the myth; to them this is the way it has always been and always will be. In final analysis, the myth rests upon *faith*.

The social myth is the ideological foundation for social action. The prevailing myth is accepted as true by most members of every society, however much they may scoff at the myths of other societies and other times. The myth is phrased in such simple terms that everyone can understand it. It gives the member of the society (or of the emergent social movement) an explanation of his role in this world and sometimes in the next. When the majority believe in the myth, elaborate formal controls are unnecessary. When they begin to lose faith in the myth, all the police in the world cannot hold the social structure together.

Revolution as a Social Movement

The myth is a dynamic concept, in the sense that it changes with the basic forms of the social structure. The great myths of antiquity and the Middle Ages

---

[58] Francis Delaisi, *Political Myths and Economic Realities* (London: Noel Douglas, 1925).

(the polytheistic and feudal myths) seemed timeless and unchanging in their day, since nobody lived long enough to see these beliefs go through their life cycle. Social change occurs more rapidly today and the life cycle of the myth is correspondingly shorter. Living men have seen the rise, decline, and fall of entire myth structures (Fascism); this would have been impossible in an earlier day.[59] In a dynamic society, myths have a shorter life cycle than in past centuries when life was more stable.

Revolution is a social movement whereby a new myth violently replaces the old. In a revolution, the social movement that has been in conflict with the old order reaches fruition and a new elite comes to power. Revolution is a successful attempt to substitute one set of institutions for another and establish a new pattern of norms upon the ruins of the old. In Park's words, "A revolution is a mass movement which seeks to change the mores by destroying the existing social order." [60] Other social movements try to *reform* the reigning myth, but the revolutionary movement tries to *overthrow* it and substitute a new myth in its place.

Revolution is therefore an example of collective behavior par excellence. Many of the generalizations about revolution have been drawn from the French and Russian Revolutions, which were both violent and successful attempts to change the institutional pattern of a society by substituting one myth for another. Furthermore, both of these revolutions have a continuing importance for the modern world. The French Revolution expressed many of the ideological elements that were subsequently incorporated into the democratic myth. The Russian Revolution dramatized the myth of international Communism that is today challenging democracy for the allegiance of half of the world. Drawing largely from French and Russian sources, but with supplements from the English and American Revolutions, scholars have worked out a pattern of revolution that indicates the typical stages of this form of social movement.[61]

1. Preliminary unrest. The period immediately before a revolutionary movement is marked by widespread social unrest, wherein the old myth loses popular support and the new myth gains it. Large numbers of persons cannot play their accustomed roles and suffer corresponding anxiety and insecurity. Social mobility increases and men lose their former institutional statuses. Social tensions are generated, reflecting such frustrations as hunger, inability to own property, loss of human life, deprivation of personal freedom, and lack of equality of opportunity.[62] The existing status structure is inadequate for men of ability, who feel that they can never realize their potentialities unless a dras-

---

[59] See William L. Shirer, *The Rise and Fall of the Third Reich* (New York: Simon and Schuster, Inc., 1960).

[60] Park and Burgess, *op. cit.*, p. 934.

[61] Cf. L. P. Edwards, *The Natural History of Revolution* (Chicago: University of Chicago Press, 1927); Crane Brinton, *The Anatomy of Revolution* (rev. ed.) (Englewood Cliffs, N.J.: Prentice-Hall, Inc., 1952).

[62] Pitirim A. Sorokin, *The Sociology of Revolution* (Philadelphia: J. B. Lippincott Company, 1925).

tic change is made in the social system. This combination of factors weakens the allegiance of many able persons to the former myth.

2. *Defection of the intellectuals.* The intellectuals in the society support the ruling class and its reigning myth during the great epochs. Long before the actual outbreak of the revolution, however, the intellectuals begin to sense the weakness of the old myth and flock to the banners of the new. This change of allegiance is largely sincere, and many intellectuals lose their lives in the subsequent revolutionary conflicts. For some intellectuals, however, the action is motivated by self-seeking factors in leaving a clearly sinking ship. Whatever the motives, this period is marked by a flood of pamphlets, books, plays, brochures, and satires—all either critical of the old myth or openly favoring the new. Intellectuals—from Voltaire to Trotsky—have exerted great influence in the formative stages of revolutionary movements.

3. *Revolutionary outbreak.* The outbreak of the revolution often takes a symbolic form. That is, it is marked by some such symbolic gesture by the revolutionary crowds as the Boston Tea Party or the storming of the Bastille. The British tax on tea and the Bastille in Paris symbolized, each in its own fashion, the regime against which the accumulated popular resentment was directed. When the Bastille fell, the French people knew that the monarchy was no longer able to maintain order, for this was the prison in which the political prisoners were kept. Such deliberate and violent acts against the old order emphasize that power has slipped from the hands of the regime that formerly held it.

4. *Liberal interlude.* Immediately after the fall of the old government, the revolutionary movement is often taken over by liberals. These elements are opposed to the old myth and its institutional structure, but they are not completely committed to the radical changes implicit in the new myth. The liberals attempt to reform the traditional structures, without realizing that their efforts will please neither the conservatives supporting the old order nor the radicals demanding the new. The liberals wish to change the social structure in certain respects and at the same time avoid the excesses of the extremists. The liberals end by pleasing neither faction, however, and are eventually swept from power. They are supplanted either by the extremists of the Left (if the revolution is "successful") or by the counter-revolutionaries of the Right (if the revolution is "unsuccessful"). In the Russian Revolution, the liberal role was played by the Kerensky government. The rule of the liberals is inevitably short.

5. *Reign of terror.* As the revolution follows its relentless course, the liberals are succeeded by the radicals. The followers of Robespierre followed the liberals in France and the Bolsheviks followed the Kerensky government in Russia. This period is marked by the efforts of the old regime to regain its power, often through civil war. To combat these counter-revolutionary movements, the radicals embark upon a reign of terror, which is intended to frighten the wavering masses into submission and stamp out active support of the former government. The reign of terror is accompanied by propaganda empha-

sizing the fate of those who do not cooperate with the new order. As its name indicates, the purpose of the Terror is to terrify.

6. *Revolution established.* The final stage in the revolutionary cycle is the emergence of a new social structure based upon the new myth. The efforts of the revolutionary party have been successful and the chief supporters of the old order have been silenced, banished, assimilated, or liquidated. This period is often marked by an emotional letdown and a partial return to the old ways. The people are tired of strife and wish to relax their heroic efforts. All revolutionary movements have such periods of mass relapse, and wise leaders offer minor compromises that do not jeopardize the basic revolutionary tenets. After this temporary relaxation, the leaders urge their followers to go forward once more. The new way of life must be built upon the ruins of the old. The new myth must urge the people on to still greater achievements.

The triumph of the myth is marked by great collective excitement. The victorious party comes to power and the masses are filled with a new zeal. They have seemingly gained a great victory and the new myth promises much for themselves and their children. Carried along by the exaltation of the new democratic myth, the people of France threw back the professional armies of Europe and established the French Revolution as a working principle. In like fashion, the hastily mobilized Red Army in Russia fought off the armies sent against them by the old regime and the nations of western Europe. This period is one of mass idealism, when hope for the future is unlimited and men strive to carry the myth to less fortunate nations across the frontiers. Fired with enthusiasm, they feel that nothing can stop them.

We have outlined the typical stages in the revolutionary process, with emphasis upon the role of the myth. The presentation has been simplified, for collective behavior does not occur in such neat and articulated stages. Furthermore, vestiges of one myth remain long after the society has embraced another. Many of the ideas and practices of feudalism still linger on in western Europe. The myth of absolute monarchy has lost its hold on the majority of Europeans, but generations elapsed before it ceased to be a vital force. Social institutions retain the earlier myths long after these concepts have ceased to be primary motivating forces.

This chapter has stressed the role of collective behavior in social change. In collective behavior, former institutional systems lose some of their force and behavior begins to deviate from the old norms. Collective behavior is part of the process of social change, whereby many persons abandon old roles and assume new ones. The social movement is the most dramatic and far-reaching type of social change, especially when the movement involves the entire order of society. As we shall see in the following chapter, other forms of collective behavior likewise involve departures from the norm, but do not ordinarily bring with them the same permanent changes in social structure. Revolution has ushered in some of the most important changes of our day.

SELECTED BIBLIOGRAPHY

Blumer, Herbert, "The Field of Collective Behavior," Chapter 19, and "Social Movements," Chapter 22, in Robert E. Park (ed.), *An Outline of the Principles of Sociology.* New York: Barnes & Noble, Inc., 1939. In Chapter 19, the field of collective behavior is defined. In Chapter 22, social movements are viewed as "collective enterprises to establish a new order of life." The author is perhaps the leading theoretician in the field of collective behavior.

————, "Collective Behavior," in J. B. Gittler (ed.), *Review of Sociology: Analysis of a Decade.* New York: John Wiley & Sons, Inc., 1957. In this comparatively brief essay, Blumer surveys the developments in collective behavior in the decade 1945-1955 and provides an extensive bibliography of these studies.

Bramson, Leon, *The Political Context of Sociology.* Princeton: Princeton University Press, 1961. This book is a significant attempt "to grapple with the problem of the influence of social and political theories on the practice of sociology." The author is especially interested in problems of conservatism and change in relation to collective behavior in mass society.

Brinton, Crane, *The Anatomy of Revolution* (Revised Edition). Englewood Cliffs, N. J.: Prentice-Hall, Inc., 1952. The general sociological pattern of revolution is here presented as a form of social movement, with a wealth of concrete historical detail. This is a sociological study of *revolution* (as a type of collective behavior), rather than of *revolutions* (as different historical phenomena).

Davies, James C., "Toward a Theory of Revolution," *American Sociological Review,* 27:5-19 (February, 1962). The thesis of this article is that "Revolutions are most likely to occur when a prolonged period of objective economic and social development is followed by a short period of sharp reversal . . . The actual state of socioeconomic development is less significant than the expectation that past progress, now blocked, can and must continue in the future."

Foote, Nelson N., and Clyde W. Hart, "Public Opinion and Collective Behavior," Chapter 13 in Muzafer Sherif and M. O. Wilson (eds.), *Group Relations at the Crossroads.* New York: Harper & Row, 1953. As the title indicates, this essay deals with some of the psychological aspects of collective behavior, with particular emphasis upon public opinion.

Heberle, Rudolf, *Social Movements.* New York: Appleton-Century-Crofts, Inc., 1951. This is a significant contribution to the sociology of social movements, with especial reference to those recently convulsing the world. The author is a sociologist with a European background, which perhaps explains his historical sense—a trait so often lacking in American sociologists.

King, C. Wendell, *Social Movements in the United States.* New York: Random House, Inc., 1956. This is an excellent brief study of social movements and the settings in which they occur. Among the topics considered are: the relationships between the mass society and social movements; the goals of social movements; their life cycles; the internal and external factors determining their growth; and their relationships to social change.

Kornhauser, William, *The Politics of Mass Society.* Glencoe, Ill.: The Free Press, 1959. This is an important contribution to the theory of mass society, as well as the source, composition, and role of social movements within it. The author deals, both theoretically and empirically, with the totalitarian movements that weaken democratic society.

Lang, Kurt, and Gladys Engel Lang, *Collective Dynamics*. New York: Thomas Y. Crowell Company, 1961. This thoughtful and inclusive text deals with the subject-matter conventionally known as "Collective Behavior." The concept "dynamics" in the analysis emphasizes the elements of social and institutional *change*, as distinguished from those of "continuity and relative stability." This is an important synthesizing work in a field where comparatively little such work has been done in recent decades.

Smelser, Neil J., *Theory of Collective Behavior*. Glencoe, Ill.: The Free Press, 1963. As the title indicates, this book offers a comprehensive and inclusive theory of collective behavior. As such, it is an impressive contribution to the *sociological*, as distinguished from the *psychological*, approach to this important but elusive field. The analysis is on a high intellectual level and the book is intended for students (and professors) with an advanced degree of intellectual sophistication.

Turner, Ralph H., and Lewis M. Killian, *Collective Behavior*. Englewood Cliffs, New Jersey: Prentice-Hall, Inc., 1957. This is the first of several recent (see above) books that deal with collective behavior in a systematic fashion in a sociological frame of reference. The authors present a theoretical analysis of collective behavior and then give selections from a wide range of empirical literature to illustrate and explain various aspects of this behavior.

Vander Zanden, James W., "Resistance and Social Movements," *Social Forces*, 37:312-315 (May, 1959); also "The Klan Revival," *American Journal of Sociology*, 65:456-462 (March, 1960); also "Accommodation to Undesired Change: The Case of the South," *The Journal of Negro Education*, 31:30-35 (Winter, 1962). Social movements are usually viewed as agencies of social change, whereby a new way of life is brought into being. In these articles, social movements are seen as forces for reaction, whereby persons and groups attempt (by peaceful or violent means) to maintain a way of life that they consider satisfactory.

23 *Crowd and Public*

The Crowd as Collective Behavior

The crowd has been defined as "any chance collection of individuals ... when a condition of *rapport* has been established among the individuals who compose it." [1] The term, *rapport*, "implies the existence of a mutual responsiveness, such that every member of the group reacts immediately, spontaneously, and sympathetically to the sentiments and attitudes of every other member." [2] Physical nearness and *rapport* thus constitute the basic elements of the crowd. The mutual responsiveness of the members arises from their familiarity with the same symbols and their consequent tendency to react in some-

[1] Robert E. Park and Ernest W. Burgess, *Introduction to the Science of Sociology* (Chicago: University of Chicago Press, 1924), p. 893.
[2] *Ibid.*

529

what the same way to a common stimulus. For a group of persons to form a crowd, a similar cultural background is important. The symbols must be sufficiently familiar to make collective action possible.

The crowd is a typical, although transitory, form of collective behavior. A number of persons are gathered together under conditions that by their very nature represent departures from customary behavior. Attention is directed toward some stimulus that is sufficiently strong to cause them to change their ordinary conduct, however momentarily. The stimulus is usually of a symbolic character and evokes reactions that are more complex than meet the eye. Although animals may engage in crowdlike behavior, the only true collective behavior is that of human beings. The members of a crowd temporarily change their status and role and hence experience social change. This process is neither so extensive nor so permanent as that arising from social movements. But the essence of change is, nevertheless, present with crowd behavior.

Crowd behavior has also been described as "uniform behavior," in the sense that everybody acts the same way for the time being. This temporary uniformity is in contrast to the wide range of *individual* behavior that occurs when people are acting alone. Crowd interaction breaks down individual roles and personal differences and unites the members by appealing to a few simple emotions.[3] The symbols of crowd behavior are clear, simple and unambiguous. When members of a lynching mob focus their hatred upon the symbol of "nigger" or (conversely) of "nigger-lover," there is no doubt in anyone's mind what the appropriate attitudes should be. For the time being, the crowd members cease to act as individuals and become members of a uniform collectivity.[4]

The crowd has been further characterized as a collective expression of many of the unconscious forces in the personalities of its members. This does not mean that there is such a thing as a "collective mind" that is independent of the minds of the constituent individuals. It merely means that, in the collective excitement of the crowd, some of the traditional social barriers are temporarily down and the individuals act out their unconscious wishes, hatreds, and fears.[5] The crowd member is consciously aware of what he is doing, but his *interpretation* of his action is dominated by unconscious factors. This action seems to be demanded by the circumstances and hence appears eminently right and just.[6]

The direct expression of many emotions is held in check by the norms of organized society. Under the impetus of crowd excitement, these inhibitions are temporarily dissolved. In some cases, the members of the crowd may panic and trample others to death in their blind desire to escape from a burning building. In other cases, the collective behavior may manifest itself in resigna-

[3] Herbert Blumer, "Collective Behavior," in J. B. Gittler (ed.), *Review of Sociology: Analysis of a Decade* (New York: John Wiley & Sons, Inc., 1957), p. 131.

[4] Ralph H. Turner and Samuel J. Surace, "Zoot-Suiters and Mexicans: Symbols in Crowd Behavior," *American Journal of Sociology*, 62:14-20 (July, 1956).

[5] Hans Gerth and C. Wright Mills, *Character and Social Structure* (New York: Harcourt, Brace and World, 1953), pp. 436-437.

[6] Everett Dean Martin, *The Behavior of Crowds* (New York: Harper & Row, 1920), pp. 35-36.

tion, as people fail completely to react to what *might* be a signal for atomic attack.[7] In still other cases, crowd behavior may give the members a "collective defense against anxiety,"[8] as the physical presence of others makes each individual feel safer against the fear that grips him. Under such conditions, people believe the most absurd and fantastic rumors because they *want* to believe them. Such belief offers a bulwark against the anxieties of an uncertain and potentially dangerous world. Whether this danger takes the form of the Black Death or mass bombing, men derive comfort from close physical and emotional contact with their fellows.

In these and many other ways, the collective excitement of the crowd lowers the moral resistance and raises the emotions of its members. The latter interact with each other and thereby heighten the uniformity of their response. People who do not agree with the crowd leaders are usually reluctant to speak out, because they are afraid of the hostility of their neighbors. The opponents are further isolated by their own silence, for each believes that he is the only one who does not share the general attitudes. An unreal or specious atmosphere of agreement is thus generated, wherein *everyone* appears to agree wholeheartedly with the crowd actions. In human interaction, each person both *stimulates* and *inhibits* himself because of the presence of others and the supposed uniformity of their attitudes. The person who does not want, say, to overturn a nonstriker's automobile, throw rocks through the windows of a foreign consulate, or beat up the members of a rival gang usually remains silent.[9]

The crowd is more than the sum total of its members. Collective social interaction generates excitement that would be impossible for the same individuals when acting alone. The members of the crowd transcend themselves, as it were, and perform actions that are both more base and more heroic than they would as individuals. Persons in a crowd can inflict torture and even death upon another human being without any visible hesitation. Most of them would not do this if they were alone. Conversely, men in a crowd may abandon all thought of self and rush to save others, often complete strangers, from fire, shipwreck, or battle. These flights of selfless idealism likewise would seldom be performed without the emotion of the crowd.

We may summarize as follows the characteristics of the crowd as a form of collective behavior.[10]

1. *Number of people.* The crowd by definition involves a number of people in interaction. This number may range from several score in a crowded hall to several thousand in a public square. Despite the traditional lover's adage,

---

[7] Robert E. Forman, "Resignation as a Collective Behavior Response," *American Journal of Sociology,* 69:285-290 (November, 1963).

[8] Kurt Lang and Gladys Engel Lang, *Collective Dynamics* (New York: Thomas Y. Crowell Company, 1961), p. 122.

[9] W. Phillips Davison, "The Public Opinion Process," *Public Opinion Quarterly,* 22:91-106 (Spring, 1958), p. 101.

[10] The following is adapted from Lang and Lang, *op. cit.,* pp. 118-121.

three do not make a crowd, but three hundred do. The actual number is not so important, however, as the type of interaction between the members.

2. *Heightening of feeling.* The crowd arises when an (indeterminate) number of persons experience an event or a series of events that arouses their emotions to an unusual degree. As we shall see, these emotions can range from affectionate adulation (for a pope) to blind hatred (for an alleged murderer), with emotional variations in between. Crowd behavior is not rational.

3. *Sharing of mood.* The crowd begins to emerge when the heightened feelings are translated into a mood that is shared (temporarily) by all or a substantial majority of the members. This mood causes people to depart from the traditional norms of organized society and commit acts they would not ordinarily commit. At this stage, the members are aware of what they are doing, but they do not care.

4. *Redefinition of the situation.* The crowd shifts from mood to direct action as the redefinition of the situation becomes more apparent. A situation that would ordinarily be defined as against the mores (murder) suddenly becomes right and just, as a retribution for the enormous crimes and/or injustices allegedly perpetrated by the accused. The member of the acting crowd acts under cover of anonymity and identification with persons who temporarily think and feel the same as he does.

5. *Formation of the crowd.* The crowd is now ready for action or, as is sometimes the case, merely for the expression of its collective emotions. At this point, the individual members become a "collectivity" which, temporarily at least, is more than the sum of its components. To be sure, *individuals* continue to act and the crowd does not become a "thing," capable of independent action. But the mood encourages the individuals to abandon their conventional roles, and violate the norms of the society.[11]

The Leader and the Crowd

Collective behavior may or may not involve a leader. Some situations are so ephemeral that there is no time for such a relationship to develop, as a crowd gathers about a central stimulus, reacts collectively, and then disperses. In the shifting and anonymous life of the city, many such temporary situations arise and disappear so quickly that they can scarcely be dignified as collective behavior. At the opposite extreme is the social movement, which continues for months, years, and even generations and where a definite leadership pattern is mandatory. Between these extremes, there are many situations where a leader will emerge to meet the demands of the moment, direct the aroused energies of the crowd into the appropriate channels, and then vanish again into the anonymous mass of individuals.

Leadership is a form of social interaction wherein one person influences

---

[11] *Ibid.,* p. 121.

others to perform an effective social action.[12] Leadership is essentially a *relationship* between the leader and the led, rather than a unilateral action by the leader. Hence the "followers" are as important (or more so) as the "leader," for the latter often merely stimulates action by the collectivity. The leader acts as a catalytic agent, stimulating others to action. He becomes the center of influence, whether formally (an army officer) or informally (a leader of a street mob). The role of the leader is stated by Gouldner as follows: "By emitting some stimuli, he facilitates group action toward a goal or goals, whether the stimuli are verbal, written, or gestural. . . . Whether these stimuli pertain to goals or to means, cluster about executive or perceptive operations is a secondary consideration, *so long as they result in the structuring of group behavior.*"[13]

The principal role of the crowd leader is to evoke the group symbols and direct the resultant behavior into directions that seem desirable. The leader is intuitively in touch with the mass culture and calls out and manipulates the related symbols. The extent to which he does this deliberately varies between individuals. Some leaders act largely by intuition and believe implicitly in the symbols that they are manipulating. Others cynically exploit symbols in which they themselves do not believe. The most successful crowd leaders are probably those that combine the qualities of intuition and intelligence. They are emotionally in touch with the masses and at the same time understand the basic issues.

The leader directs behavior in opposition to, or at least in departure from, the conventional standards. Collective behavior is by definition outside the realm of the customary and hence represents activity in the form of becoming and change. Much of this behavior is controversial and evokes strong value judgments from those affected by it. Conservatives regard such manifestations as undesirable departures from the *status quo*, whereas liberals and radicals applaud many of the same activities. The first group refers to the crowd leader as a "demagogue," "crackpot," or "rabble-rouser"; the second group calls him a "statesman" or a "friend of the common man."

In evoking the emotionally freighted symbols of the crowd, the leader directs attitudes already present in the minds of the members. Among such patterns are the stereotypes of prejudice, the slogans of racial hatred, the clichés of religious orthodoxy, and the fears of political unorthodoxy. The most successful leader is usually, although not always, the person who has the same cultural background as the rank and file and hence participates in their experience and shares their emotions. The outstanding example of such leadership was Adolf Hitler, who shared the prejudices, hatreds, and aggressions of the German people during and after World War I. In mobilizing the armed aggression of the German nation, Hitler was in effect manipulating a huge

---

[12] Lang and Lang, *op. cit.*, pp. 232-235.
[13] Alvin W. Gouldner (ed.), *Studies in Leadership* (New York: Harper & Row, 1950), p. 16. Cited by Lang and Lang, *op. cit.*, p. 233. (His italics.)

crowd, which he periodically aroused through the radio and other machinery of mass communication. The people responded by following him into World War II.

The leader suggests to the crowd the action that many of the members inwardly desire but that does not immediately occur to them. The action may be an excess of religious frenzy, the storming of the Bastille, or a juvenile gang attack. Many of the culture patterns for this behavior are already inculcated, and the leader merely proposes actions that are a part of the fantasy life of the crowd members. At the same time, the violent acts of the crowd are usually held in check by other culture patterns. Prejudice against ethnic minorities (Negroes, Mexicans, Puerto Ricans) is already in the culture; at the same time, the norms ordinarily inhibit violence against these groups. The role of the leader is to manipulate the hostile symbols against the minority group so as to neutralize (temporarily) the cultural inhibitions.[14]

The Acting Crowd

The acting crowd is the most typical form of crowd behavior. In this type of crowd, action is directed against an outside object that has become the focus of aggression and, possibly, affection. As defined by Swanson, the acting crowd is "that form of crowd in which the behavior aims at manipulating the environment external to the selves of the members." [15] The crowd may be motivated by love for some person or symbolic object. Crowd behavior in the Middle Ages was evoked by the symbol of the Cross, and the social movements known as the Crusades were motivated by affection for this symbol, as well as by more mundane considerations. In our own day, Gandhi brought out crowd behavior marked by the purest adoration of hundreds of millions of persons. Other great political figures (Churchill, Eisenhower, Roosevelt, Kennedy) have likewise evoked widespread popular affection.

These exalted and altruistic motives, however, are less common in crowd behavior than fear, rage, and hatred, all of which may culminate in some form of aggression. In this respect, man is often, as the Latin adage has it, "a wolf to his fellows." Indeed, he can be more cruel than the wolves. The mass murder of six million innocent persons by the Nazis demonstrated, both in terms of the refinement and scope of the torture, that human beings are capable of infinite cruelties when spurred by crowd stimulation. Many of the impulses customarily held in check by social control are given free play, and the crowd members vent their repressions, frustrations, and hatreds upon defenseless individuals or groups.

The acting crowd is rigid and absolutistic in its thinking. The members are convinced that they are right and that they are acting in accordance with the best of all possible intentions. The opposition group is, by the same token,

---

[14] Ralph H. Turner and Samuel J. Surace, *op. cit.*, pp. 14-15.

[15] G. E. Swanson, "A Preliminary Laboratory Study of the Acting Crowd," *American Sociological Review*, 18:522-533 (October, 1953), p. 523.

utterly wrong. There can be no argument with the motives or beliefs of the crowd, and any one who questions them is a traitor. Whatever lingering doubts the members may have concerning the wisdom or justice of their cause are temporarily swept aside by the overwhelming rush of emotional participation. Crowd members substitute slogans for clear thinking, utter clichés instead of examining the issues, and treat all opposition as dangerous heresy to be stamped out without mercy.

Members of the acting crowd are likewise unable to laugh at themselves. They take themselves and their mission with extreme seriousness and cannot maintain a sense of humor. Like grim and humorless fanatics, they are sure they are right and that any undue levity is reprehensible. This absolutism makes impossible any effort by the members to view their activities in perspective or to take the role of the other toward themselves. The crowd symbols become ends in themselves, to be upheld without compromise or question. Ridicule, irony, or mockery are feared like the plague, for these sentiments question the absolute rightness of the crowd.

The "paranoia" of the crowd may take other forms. Just as the paranoid individual has delusions of grandeur and persecution, so the crowd is simultaneously obsessed by beliefs in its own importance and by fears of persecution. Anti-Semites are afraid that the nation in general and themselves in particular are menaced by a gigantic, and unspecified, Jewish plot. The racist is obsessed by conscious and unconscious fears of a Negro conspiracy to dominate the deep South and inflict unmentionable reprisals upon the "superior" race. Delusions of grandeur and persecution accompany each other naturally. The person who has delusions of grandeur can easily convince himself that he is being persecuted because of his manifestly superior qualities. These confused emotions may lead to blind and irrational hatred, when the crowd is confronted by members of the subject, and presumably inferior, group.

The acting crowd is also characterized by behavior known as "projection," whereby the members unconsciously "project" their own undesirable qualities upon the "enemy." In its simplest form, projection means that an individual who unconsciously wishes to injure another will accuse the other of wanting to do the same thing. The advocate of preventive war is sure that the enemy is planning to attack him. The religious bigot who accuses others of intolerance is projecting his own bigotry upon adherents of the other creed. These are some of the ways in which the crowd members unconsciously attempt to justify themselves and prove to their own satisfaction that they are right and everyone else is wrong.[16]

Members of the acting crowd are certain of their position, not because of rational or scientific proof but because of blind faith. This faith must be kept intact and any possible threat is viewed with suspicion. Hence the crowd hates and fears the renegade, the heretic, or the traitor, who has once believed and now believes no more. He has strayed from the fold and raises the fear

---

[16] Martin, *op. cit.*, pp. 97-98.

that others may do likewise. The totalitarian who repudiates the movement is anathema to his former comrades. The religious believer who rejects the faith is scorned by the faithful. The crowd will tolerate a believer who is weak or even wicked, as long as he continues to reaffirm his faith. Here the question is one of the weakness and fallibility of human beings. When the symbols of the crowd are repudiated, however, tolerance changes to hatred.[17]

The Expressive Crowd

All forms of crowd behavior do not result in action toward some outside object. In many cases, the activity of the crowd turns inward, and the members engage in action that liberates their tensions, uncertainties, or frustrations. This expressive activity becomes an end in itself, rather than the means to some external end. The expressive crowd, in other words, is one in which "the behavior seems directed at manipulating the self-images and norms of the participants." [18] When their emotions have been liberated, the crowd disperses and the members assume their individual roles. A basic difference between the acting and the expressive crowd is the nature of the goal. In the one the goal is externalized; in the other it is internalized.

The preliminaries of the expressive crowd are similar to those of the acting crowd. There is the same physical nearness, the same focusing of attention, the same milling about, and the same growing excitement. The differences reflect the motivations of the members and the overt expression that these motivations take. The acting crowd usually takes action against some outside object or person. The action of the expressive crowd—whether singing, dancing, shouting, or praying—is important in itself, and the conscious and unconscious desires are thereby satisfied. The same persons may be members of different types of crowds under different circumstances. The conditions directing the action are the deciding factor.[19]

In the expressive crowd, the emotions are less aggressive than in the acting crowd. Religious piety, patriotic fervor, or sheer animal spirits may cause the members of the expressive crowd to let themselves go and temporarily emancipate themselves from the boring confines of ordinary life. The football game and the religious revival offer, each in its own way, an opportunity for this emancipation. In the game, victory or defeat brings strong emotions to the fervent spectators. In the revival, the religious experience offers the opportunity to enjoy an emotional catharsis or purging, while acting in the name of religion. The behavior of the revival crowd may be unorthodox, but the religious sanctions provide an acceptable setting.

Contemporary society breeds expressive behavior. Urban life is marked daily

---

[17] Cf. Richard Crossman (ed.), *The God That Failed* (New York: Harper & Row, 1949). This is an account of the failure of belief in Communism by several leading intellectuals.

[18] Swanson, *op. cit.*, p. 523.

[19] Herbert Blumer, "Collective Behavior," in Robert E. Park (ed.), *An Outline of the Principles of Sociology* (New York: Barnes & Noble, Inc., 1939), pp. 238-239.

by minor frustrations. A changing world produces many forms of anxiety, from the economic insecurity arising from unemployment to the emotional insecurity reflecting the lack of affection in a competitive society.[20] The individual has a need for collective diversions of the kind afforded by crowd behavior. At the same time, however, our society has not admitted the importance of such activities. In primitive societies and in those of the Old World, the group permits many expressive crowd manifestations, ranging from orgiastic tribal dances to periodic *fiestas*. The ostensible reasons for the latter holidays are usually the worship of a Christian saint, but they also allow departures from ordinary behavior (for example, getting drunk) that provide a socially sanctioned release of tensions.[21]

The emotional effect of the expressive crowd is one of temporary loss of inhibitions. The daily affairs of the ordinary person, whether a New York office worker or a Tuscan peasant, are so routinized that they evoke much cumulative boredom. Routine is necessary to orderly social living, and without it life would be chaotic. But at the same time the individual longs for a change, and expressive crowd behavior provides it. Men and women are allowed to sing, dance, drink, shout, and otherwise act outside of normal channels, and in the process are collectively purged of emotional tensions. This catharsis is accompanied by a feeling of exhilaration and excitement. Gone are many forebodings and longings. In their place are relaxation and peace, at least for the moment.

Expressive crowd behavior is often associated with the supernatural. So complete is their emotional possession that the members of the crowd assume that some force stronger than themselves has taken a hand. The person cannot experience these emotional satisfactions by himself, no matter how hard he tries. The crowd relationship is necessary to complete participation. As Blumer remarks, "This organic satisfaction unquestionably yields a pleasure and exhilaration that makes the experience momentous. The fact that this mood has such complete and unobstructed control over the individual easily leads him to feel that he is possessed or pervaded by a kind of transcendental spirit." [22]

The behavior of the expressive crowd is ordinarily sanctioned, or at least tolerated, by the larger society. The crowd members have a feeling of assurance because everyone is doing the same thing at the same time. In extreme cases, expressive behavior represents such a drastic departure from the norm that individuals acting in a similar fashion at other times would be considered psychotic. Some of the behavior at religious revivals would be defined as insane if the individual were to act in the same way by himself. In the expressive crowd, however, the implied sanctions are reassuring. The individual can enjoy himself, rid himself temporarily of some of his inhibitions, and at the same time act in a socially approved manner.

---

[20] Talcott Parsons, "Certain Primary Sources and Patterns of Aggression in the Social Structure of the Western World," *Psychiatry*, 10:167-181 (May, 1947).

[21] Richard T. La Piere, *Collective Behavior* (New York: McGraw-Hill Book Company, Inc., 1938), Chapter 18, "Revelous Behavior."

[22] Blumer, "Collective Behavior," *op. cit.*, pp. 239-240.

The Public as Collective Behavior

Crowd behavior is marked by emotion. Public behavior is based, in theory at least, upon rational differences of opinion. Both forms represent departures from traditional patterns and the introduction of new ones. The crowd is moved by emotional considerations, whereas the public is brought together, intellectually, for purposes of discussion. A crowd involves numbers of people in close physical contact; a public ordinarily does not gather in one place, and its members rarely see each other as a group. The public is primarily interested in discussion rather than action, although the latter is not altogether ruled out. In short, "A *public* consists of all those divided on an issue, who, because they take an interest, are actively thinking and talking about it." [23]

Members of the crowd are united by a common purpose for the duration of the relationship. They have temporary unanimity, whether for saving their own souls or expressing their hatred for their fellows. The public has no such unanimity. Its very purpose, indeed, is to discuss a number of alternatives and from this process to derive some degree of consensus. The public is a discussion group and arises because men have differences of opinion about the same issue. The members of a public may be united by their interest in a particular matter, but they are still in the discussion stage as to what to do about it. The baseball public is intensely interested in the national pastime, but its members are vociferous in their differences of opinion concerning the merits of the particular teams.

There is a distinction between the concept of *the* public and that of *a* public. In the latter and more precise sense, *a* public is "a social area of communication that may be defined by any common, nonintimate, group-making interest or interests; on matters outside of such common interests, it need not achieve unanimity of sentiment or opinion. Thus, in many respects, a public is a social area of interaction." [24] In modern society, the individual belongs to a number of these "social areas of interaction." He may be a member of a business or professional public, a sports public, a literary public, and a political public.

Each of these groups enlists a segment of the individual's personality, and he is linked to the other members of the public through one or more of its principal interests. The twin concepts of interest and issue are central to the functioning of the public. The latter interacts by way of these common issues. As defined by Davison, indeed, a public is "a large collection of individuals (either assembled at some point or scattered throughout a wide area) who do not know each other personally but who react to an issue with the expectation that certain categories of others will display similar attitudes on the same issue." [25] These issues represent collective behavior and social change, because

---

[23] Lang and Lang, *op. cit.*, p. 371.

[24] Alfred M. Lee, "Public Opinion in Relation to Culture," *Psychiatry*, 8:49-61 (Feb., 1945), p. 53.

[25] W. Phillips Davison, *op. cit.*, p. 102.

they are outside of the customary norms and deal with matters not ordinarily covered by them.

The conventional definitions reflect the regular activities of the group, whereas the interests of the public are often more immediate, ephemeral, and transitory. The latter are matters on which the person may have an "opinion," presumably based upon rational thought. A difference of "opinion" is implied in the concept of public opinion, in contrast to the mores, which admit of no such differences. The mores are accepted or rejected, but they are rarely *discussed*. As soon as they are brought into the realm of discussion, indeed, they lose their moral form. Definitions invested with right and wrong are seldom debated, for this would open up the dangerous possibility that there might be two sides to a moral question. In an ordered society, such matters are taken for granted.

The public is characteristic of an increasingly secular society, in which numerous issues *are* open to discussion. In a sacred and stratified society, the primary group is the central unit and the definition of behavior rests in the mores.[26] A secular society is marked by more secondary associations, is held together by more rational interests, and on certain issues operates on a discussion level. Many of these discussion groups are dispersed in space and become, in effect, publics. The identification of the individual with these groups determines many of his attitudes.[27] In the development of western European society, public opinion slowly emerged along with secularism, capitalism, and the rising power of the middle class. Only in such a society can "free and public communication" be carried on regarding matters of concern to the society as a whole.[28]

Each public has its own "universe of discourse" or special language, by which the members converse through the medium of specialized journals, news letters, house organs, and bulletins. Farmers in general—and wheat growers, dairy farmers, and other agricultural groups in particular—use terms that are known largely to themselves. The baseball public speaks in a jargon that is almost unintelligible to the uninitiated. Scientific publics have a universe of discourse that is virtually another language. These publics agree on the meaning of the terms; otherwise they could not carry on the discussion that is the basis of their relationship.

This specialization of interest is characteristic of a changing society. In an earlier day, people lived in small towns where community interests were comparatively simple, and where everyone had an approximate idea of the basic issues. The environment was less specialized than that of the city man today. Here the proliferation of interest groups makes a knowledge of all fields manifestly impossible. In our own society, social change means changes in social

---

[26] Howard Becker, "Sacred and Secular Societies," *Social Forces,* 28:361-376 (May, 1950).

[27] Tamotsu Shibutani, "Reference Groups as Perspectives," *American Journal of Sociology,* 60:562-569 (May, 1955).

[28] Hans Spier, "Historical Development of Public Opinion," *American Journal of Sociology,* 55:376-388 (January, 1950).

role over a given period by a number of persons. Men change their residence, their occupation, their marital status, and their institutional connections.[29] This process results in a segmentalization and specialization of interest that was formerly unknown. The rise of many special publics in this sense reflects an increasingly dynamic and complex society.

The contemporary public is increasingly dependent upon mass communication. The telegraph, newspaper, radio, and television are some of the forms of mass communication that have made possible the rise of the modern public. We shall consider the role of mass communication in the following chapter, insofar as it plays a central part in the creation and maintenance of mass society. We merely indicate here that agencies of mass communication are central in the operation of a public, which by definition consists of persons at a distance from each other. In face-to-face communication, furthermore, the individual can take the role of the other and adjust his responses accordingly. In mass communication, the communicator cannot do this. He must deliver his message in such a way that it will be understood, but he cannot modify it in the process.[30]

---

[29] Donald J. Bogue, "The Quantitative Study of Social Dynamics and Social Change," *American Journal of Sociology,* 57:565-568 (May, 1952).

[30] Wilbur Schramm (ed.), *The Process and Effects of Mass Communication* (Urbana: University of Illinois Press, 1954), pp. 18-21.

The public is characteristic of an urban and secular society in which numerous issues are open to discussion; these New Yorkers inform themselves on some of these issues as they ride to work on the subway.

The Nature of Public Opinion

From such complex and varied interaction, public opinion emerges. This concept refers to "action or readiness for action with regard to a given issue on the part of members of a public who are reacting in the expectation that others in the public are similarly oriented toward the same issue." [31] The emergence of public opinion is a dynamic process, and public opinion is constantly changing. Public opinion is a new thing, formed by the interaction of many minds with information common to them all. As soon as the opinion is formed, it is subject to further change, as the old is weighed in the light of new facts. The more dynamic the society, the greater the degree of change in public opinion.

We must continue to bear in mind the distinction between *the* public and *a* public, to which we have previously referred. This distinction has been stated in terms of the "general" public and a "special" public. The "general" public refers to *all* the members of a particular society, who interact (however remotely) and who are expected to have an "opinion" about certain general issues. The "special" public refers to persons who interact about a single issue or group of issues and emerge with an opinion.

These two concepts are not, however, basically different. They both refer to large numbers of persons, usually spatially separated, who do not know each other personally, who interact in terms of certain issues, and who form opinions on these issues based on various forms of information. Up to this point, we have been using the term, public opinion, in the limited or "special" sense. For the rest of the discussion, unless otherwise specified, we shall be concerned with public opinion in the larger and more inclusive sense. The people of the United States are, in this latter sense, a vast public. They have opinions about such diverse issues as price supports for farm products, relations with the Soviet Union, and the relative merits of popular film stars. Whatever the size of the public, however, the central consideration is social interaction. Out of this interaction comes change.

The sociological nature of public opinion has been analyzed in terms of the following propositions:

1. Public opinion has its setting in a particular society and grows out of the continuous interaction between the members of that society.

2. The society is a functional organization of groups, institutions, and voluntary associations, whose activities combine to make up the collective life.

3. These functional groups respond to the decisions of certain key individuals of high group status.

4. These key individuals assess the demands brought to bear upon them by their own members and the members of other groups and then act accordingly.

5. Public opinion is the product of this process of social interaction. Public

---

[31] W. Phillips Davison, *op. cit.*, p. 93.

opinion thus "consists of the pattern of the diverse views and positions on the issue *that come to the individuals who have to act in response to the public opinion.*" [32]

In this view of public opinion, the status of the individual in the group is of central importance. All persons do not have the same influence in forming group policies, and the "opinions" of the unskilled laborer and those of the president of the corporation do not carry the same weight. Hence the conventional sampling process by which public opinion is gauged does not, in Blumer's judgment, adequately assess the role of the individual in the various organizations whose interaction produces public opinion. In the presidential elections, of course, any individual is presumably as important as any other, in the sense that each has one vote. But even here the question arises as to whether the individual queried will influence any other votes. On the majority of issues, the position of the individual in the social structure is important.[33] This conception of public opinion has been documented by Lazarsfeld and associates in studies of voting and other forms of behavior.[34] The key figure in influencing others to make up their minds is the "opinion leader," who operates through interpersonal relations in a small group. This person is not necessarily a leading member of the community and he may not be known outside of his immediate group setting. Nevertheless, he is one to whom others, consciously or unconsciously, look for guidance on a variety of matters about which they are either too ignorant or too indifferent to make up their own minds. If one wishes to influence public opinion on matters ranging from presidential candidates to movie-going, he must therefore reckon with the opinion leaders.[35]

The interaction process does not end here. As the opinion leader is transmitting the pertinent information to other members of the primary group, he is also adjusting to his listeners. He takes into account the persons with whom he is interacting and phrases his message so that it will be understandable to them. The opinion leader must, in short, continually take other people into consideration. He must accept the standards of the group, adjust to group pressures, and look to the group for support. The communications network of the small group is marked by mutual and reciprocal interaction. The opinion leader is influenced by others at the same time that he influences them.[36]

These influential persons differ among types of interest groups. In one study, Lazarsfeld and Katz took four types of opinion leadership—those involved in marketing, fashion, public affairs, and movie-going. Three major criteria for leadership were taken: (*a*) *life cycle* ("from girlhood, through

---

[32] Herbert Blumer, "Public Opinion and Public Opinion Polling," *American Sociological Review*, 13:542-549 (October, 1948), p. 545. (His italics.)

[33] *Ibid.*, p. 546.

[34] Paul F. Lazarsfeld, Bernard Berelson, and Hazel Gaudet, *The People's Choice* (New York: Columbia University Press, 1948).

[35] Elihu Katz and Paul F. Lazarsfeld, *Personal Influence* (Glencoe, Ill.: The Free Press, 1955), Chapter 9.

[36] Elihu Katz, "Communication Research and the Image of Society: Convergence of Two Traditions," *American Journal of Sociology*, 65:435-440 (March, 1960).

marriage, to motherhood, and older matronhood"); (*b*) *gregariousness* ("the individual's sphere of intimate, informal relationships beyond the immediate environs of the household"); and (*c*) *social status* ("differential access to the economic and social opportunities of society," as roughly measured by education and rent).[37]

The most important single characteristic of the opinion leader was gregariousness. This trait was measured by the number of persons with whom the leader was friendly and the number of organizations, clubs, discussion groups, and the like to which he or she belonged. Social status was surprisingly unimportant in three of the four fields (marketing, movie-going, and fashion), and only in public affairs did it play an important role. Opinion leaders arise on all social levels and influence others on a *horizontal* basis within the same social level, rather than on a *vertical* basis up and down the various levels of society. In summary, the picture ". . . is one of concentrations of opinion leaders who can be located in varying densities in each of the different life-cycle types, in almost equal densities on every status level, and generally among the more gregarious people in those groups." [38]

Public Opinion in a Democracy

Democratic government is based upon the following related assumptions: (*a*) that the great majority of citizens will act as a public on important common concerns; (*b*) that this majority will reach their decisions with reasonable intelligence and tolerance; and (*c*) that they will express these decisions through the periodic exercise of the franchise. If this process breaks down at any stage, the entire operation of democratic government is threatened.[39] Hence public opinion and its formation are of vital concern in these changing times. The day has passed when important problems could be left largely to custom and tradition. Policy must be made on the basis of opinions, rather than on the basis of the mores. Despite the manifest importance of public opinion, its actual operation leaves much to be desired in our society. This problem is a vast one and we can only suggest some of the variables in the functioning of public opinion.

The first variable in the operation of public opinion is ignorance. Many persons simply do not know enough pertinent facts to form an intelligent opinion on domestic and foreign policies. The various agencies of education have, for one reason or another, failed in their responsibilities. The press, radio, television, the school, and the family have not succeeded in furnishing the mass of people with enough factual material to make up their minds intelligently on complex issues. The importance of such factual information (and the lack of it) was dramatically demonstrated in a study of conformity and

---

[37] Katz and Lazarsfeld, *Personal Influence, op. cit.,* pp. 223 ff.

[38] *Ibid.,* p. 325.

[39] Bernard Berelson, "Democratic Theory and Public Opinion," *Public Opinion Quarterly,* 16:314-330 (Fall, 1952).

civil liberties conducted in the mid 1950's. The study indicated that much intolerance in American society resulted simply from false information. Many persons, for example, believed that those who do not conform to the majority opinion on religious, economic, and social questions are either hard-core communists or communist dupes. [40] Depending upon the circumstances, substantial segments of the population would therefore deny elementary civil rights to atheists, socialists, and free thinkers, presumably because these groups might be connected, in some unspecified way, with the menace of internal communist subversion. Some of these bigots, concluded the study, "may have warped personalities, but many of them are simply drawing conclusions from premises which are based on false information." [41]

In a somewhat more sophisticated analysis of the role of ignorance in public opinion, Breed and Ktsanes call attention to what they term "pluralistic ignorance" in limiting or distorting public knowledge of the facts. "Pluralistic ignorance" means that large numbers of people *think* that they and those around them understand the issues, when in reality they do not. This widespread ignorance has the effect, Breed and Ktsanes point out, of strengthening existing beliefs and hence slowing down social change in such controversial fields as desegregation in the South. When an individual makes up his mind on such an erroneous estimate of the opinions of others, a "conservative bias" often exists, which further limits the effective functioning of public opinion.[42]

Even when confronted with correct knowledge, however, people often fail to function in the manner envisaged by the Founding Fathers. Persons with strongly held attitudes show a surprising tenacity in holding to them, no matter what the facts may be. The religious bigot, the racist, and the fanatic of the far right or far left hold their attitudes because they perform a function for them. The poor white *needs* his prejudice to bolster his self-esteem, and he will take elaborate evasive action to maintain this prop. When confronted with information that questions such an emotionally satisfying attitude as prejudice, the racist will do everything in his power (both consciously and unconsciously) to defend himself against the facts. As Davison points out, such persons do this "in part by refusing to expose themselves to unwelcome communications, by forgetting them, by distorting them, or by finding counter-arguments." [43]

The great majority of white persons at all social levels have thus far been successful in insulating themselves against the scientific facts concerning the *inherent* equality of the races. We have considered this problem in Chapters 12 (Race) and 13 (Caste), and need not repeat our analysis here. In such controversial fields, people not only refuse to accept information that ques-

---

[40] Samuel A. Stouffer, *Communism, Conformity, and Civil Liberties* (New York: Doubleday & Company, 1955), Chapter 2.

[41] *Ibid.*, p. 236.

[42] Warren Breed and Thomas Ktsanes, "Pluralistic Ignorance in the Process of Opinion Formation," *Public Opinion Quarterly*, 25:382-392 (Fall, 1961).

[43] W. Phillips Davison, "Political Communication as an Instrument of Foreign Policy," *Public Opinion Quarterly*, 27:28-36 (Spring, 1963), p. 31.

tions their biases, but may actively seek information that seems to strengthen them. When an occasional social "scientist" writes a book that purports to document the alleged genetic inequality of the races, thousands of persons eagerly read (or read about) this "evidence." The overwhelming majority of reputable authorities in the biological and behavioral sciences categorically deny any "innate" inferiority of the Negro, but this fact has little or no impact upon the prejudiced person. In the process of opinion formation, people go out of their way to find "information" that strengthens their prejudices and provides a rationalization for believing what they have always believed.[44]

Further insight on the process of public opinion formation is offered in a report by Baur on a controversy over methods of flood control and water conservation in a community in eastern Kansas. The study dealt with the way in which public opinion is formed, whether by intellectual debate based on the facts or by more devious and complex processes of group interaction. On the above issues, at least, Baur concluded that people simply do not make up their minds on the basis of the facts. There was, he commented, "little evidence to support the conception of the public opinion process as a logical confrontation and persuasion by rival proponents in public debate. Instead," he continued, "the changes, though initiated by formal organizations and projected through mass media, were amplified and supplemented by informal sources of information and transformed into opinions through interpersonal communication, especially effective in primary relationships." [45]

Other aspects of the public-opinion process are illuminated by the increasingly subtle analyses of the behavioral scientists. Back and Gergen, for example, examine the relationships between an individual's sense of time and the opinions he holds. They postulate two polar types of "time-sense" or orientation toward the future—the "apocalyptic" and the "serial time" orientation. The former orientation reflects a tendency to believe in an ultimate single catastrophe like the end of the world or the outbreak of nuclear warfare. In the face of such a shattering event, the person holding such an orientation tends to be "pessimistic, uncompromising, cautious, and consistent." The person whose attitude is based on an orderly progression of events, both in his own life experience and the experience of mankind, tends, on the other hand, to be more optimistic and to welcome the possibility of change. Back and Gergen suggest that the "apocalyptic" orientation is essentially that of the child, who lives from one moment to the next and does not plan for an orderly future. The "serial time" orientation, on the other hand, is a more mature point of view. This is one that most well-adjusted persons adopt as they leave childhood behind and move into adult responsibility. Some persons, however, never put away childish things in this sense. They remain "apocalyp-

---

[44] *Ibid.*, p. 32.

[45] E. Jackson Baur, "Opinion Change in a Public Controversy," *Public Opinion Quarterly*, 26:212-226 (Summer, 1962).

tic" in their opinions and spend their lives pessimistically expecting the worst.[46]

The public opinion process in the individual is also a function of his social self. As we have seen, a person's conception of himself reflects his interpretation of the conceptions of significant others toward him. In a brilliant application of this insight, Rosenberg starts with the assumption that the way a person views himself will inevitably be related to the way he views the world. Persons with negative self-feelings and a low degree of self-esteem, he finds, have comparatively little interest in public affairs. Such persons pay little attention to national and international affairs as presented in the mass media. They hesistate to express an opinion and are content to leave such expressions to others.[47]

The basic reason for this lack of involvement, Rosenberg continues, is the insecurity of such persons and their fear of being laughed at. Those with low self-esteem feel personally *threatened* by discussions of public affairs and hesitate to engage in them because of fear of ridicule. Such situations potentially involve the "Bad-Me" as postulated by Sullivan, and hence carry with them a sense of anxiety.[48] To avoid this basic anxiety, insecure persons stay out of situations where they appear (or think they appear) ridiculous or inadequate in the eyes of others. Such persons also express doubt that they have anything significant to contribute to such a discussion. "After all," they seem to say, "who wants to hear what *I* think about international Communism, the hydrogen bomb, or medical care for the aged?" Large numbers of such insecure and inarticulate persons in the electorate clearly present a grave threat to the democratic process. In Rosenberg's words, ". . . if democracy provides a mechanism by which citizens can have their wills translated into political policy, then it becomes farcical to speak of democracy if it is broadly based upon an ignorant, uninterested, and uninfluential electorate." [49]

Education is another factor that should be considered in assessing the role of public opinion in a democracy. In his study of civil liberties, Stouffer found that young people were, on the whole, more tolerant than their elders. This difference was found to be chiefly a function of the rising level of education, as each age group completed more years of school than its predecessors. In 1950, the median years of school completed by all males over 25 years of age was 9.0; in 1962, this figure had risen to 11.1 years. For females over 25, the comparable figures were 9.6 and 11.6 years. In 1962, males from 25 to 29 years had a median number of school years completed of 12.5; those 30 to 39 years had 12.3; from 35 to 44 years, the figure was 12.2; from 45 to 54 years, 11.0; from 55 to 64 years, 8.9; and 65 years of age and over, 8.0 years. The median

[46] Kurt W. Back and Kenneth J. Gergen, "Apocalyptic and Serial Time Orientations and the Structure of Opinions," *Public Opinion Quarterly,* 27:427-442 (Fall, 1963).

[47] Morris Rosenberg, "Self-Esteem and Concern with Public Affairs," *Public Opinion Quarterly,* 26:201-211 (Summer, 1962).

[48] Harry Stack Sullivan, *The Interpersonal Theory of Psychiatry* (New York: W. W. Norton & Company, Inc., 1953), pp. 161-162.

[49] Rosenberg, *op. cit.,* p. 211.

figures for the different age groups among the female population over 25 years of age in 1962 showed the same general trend.[50]

In view of this increasing general level of education, the degree of tolerance in public opinion will probably rise, slowly but surely. As we have indicated, people make valiant efforts to escape the impact of new information that threatens their ingrained attitudes and causes basic anxiety. Despite this tendency, we may conclude this aspect of our discussion on an optimistic note. Education will not solve all of the problems of an enlightened public opinion in a democracy. But the evidence indicates that, more than any other single factor, education helps to maintain and advance the democratic process.[51]

Propaganda and Public Opinion

Members of the general public are seldom allowed to make up their minds on important issues without help from others. Public opinion is subject to manipulation by persons or institutions with ulterior ends. This process is known as *propaganda*. Propaganda is defined as "the more or less deliberately planned and systematic use of symbols, chiefly through suggestion and related psychological techniques, with a view first to altering and controlling opinions, ideas, and values, and ultimately to changing overt actions along predetermined lines." [52] This form of manipulation may take such overt forms as advertising, wherein the seller openly attempts to influence the prospective buyer. More often, however, the propaganda is covert, and the intended object is largely unaware of the designs upon him.

Propaganda is a manifestation of modern society, in which mobility and social change are increasingly common. Propaganda is one of the agencies that have taken over social control from the mores. In a traditional society, the alternatives of behavior are comparatively limited, and the individual usually acts either with or against the mores. In a dynamic society, the number of choices of behavior is greater. These choices may range in importance from a brand of cigarettes to a social system. Propaganda is one of the ways in which such choices are deliberately manipulated.

Propaganda works primarily through the emotions, many of which are the same as those of the crowd. Hatred, fear, prejudice, and intolerance are mobilized by the propagandist, who appeals to the sacred symbols and manipulates them to his own ends. The leader of the acting crowd finds it easier to appeal to the negative emotions of hatred and fear than to the positive emotions of love and cooperation. Similarly, the propagandist directs the emotions of his public by exploiting symbols against another group. The ends are of primary importance to the propagandist; he is interested in action, not abstract morality.

---

[50] Bureau of the Census, *Current Population Reports: Population Characteristics*, "Educational Attainment: March 1962," Series P-20, No. 121 (February 7, 1963), Table A.

[51] Stouffer, *op. cit.*, Chapter 4.

[52] Kimball Young, *Social Psychology* (New York: Appleton-Century-Crofts, Inc., 1944), pp. 394-395.

The propagandist capitalizes upon attitudes already present. Anti-Semitism, racism, isolationism, and reaction are some of the explosive emotional elements endemic in American society. When exploited through such symbols as racial purity, 100 per cent Americanism, and white supremacy, these themes furnish a fruitful basis for action. The propagandist does not here seek to change the basic attitudes of his audience; he merely directs these attitudes along his own lines. The formation of social attitudes is a gradual process and reflects experience all the way back to the parental family. Propaganda seeks to stimulate these attitudes, not to change them.

Like many allied forms of collective behavior and social change, propaganda thrives in times of social unrest and mass insecurity. The outbreak of World War II found the United States at the end of a decade of unprecedented economic insecurity. The impact of these social changes upon millions of Americans had been great, and the nation was still figuratively staggering from the Depression. World War II gave rise to different tensions and insecurities, despite the fact that the United States was victorious. When large numbers of persons are deprived, for whatever reason, of the comforting assurance of traditional behavior patterns, collective behavior flourishes. Propaganda plays an important part in this process.

Propaganda has a differential effect upon its listeners. Some persons accept it readily and others are almost totally impervious to such attempts. Propaganda is, generally speaking, easier when the individual is highly prejudiced, comparatively uneducated, and personally frustrated. Studies of propaganda indicate that low education, low intelligence, and high prejudice form a syndrome that is unusually receptive to propaganda.[53] Like other forms of collective behavior, public opinion and propaganda represent a change from the conventional order as governed by the mores. Groups most receptive to organized efforts to change the social structure are often those least adjusted to the existing structure.

Propaganda presents the issues in terms of black and white. Critical reflection is not encouraged and the individual is presented with predigested opinions. Given the basic attitudes, propaganda provides the cue that will set them off. The racist hardly needs to have his attitudes of superiority strengthened by propaganda. The anti-Semite has formed his attitudes long before propaganda begins to take effect. The authoritarian has his own mental set in favor of authoritarianism, and he will willingly listen to information that proves him right. At the same time, as we have seen, individuals will reject or ignore information that does not fit in with their attitudes and hence threatens their basic security. Despite the increase in the scope and skill of the mass media, therefore, the individual is far from being a helpless pawn in the hands of the propagandists. If their message agrees with his preconceptions, he will accept it. If not, he will reject it.[54]

---

[53] Cf. Theodor W. Adorno, *et al.*, *The Authoritarian Personality* (New York: Harper & Row, 1950).
[54] Davison, "Political Communication as an Instrument of Foreign Policy," *op. cit.*

Political parties make extensive use of propaganda to overcome the apathy of a large minority of voters, who have little interest in politics except at national elections.[55] These efforts do little to sway the opinions of the stalwart supporter of either major party, who ordinarily votes on the basis of deeply ingrained attitudes and sectional prejudices. For millions of "independent" voters, however, the appeals of the propaganda strategists seem to be important. Many such undecided persons can be induced to change their opinions from one presidential election to the next.[56] Millions of normally Democratic voters switched their party allegiance to vote for General Eisenhower in 1952 and 1956.

Propaganda operates in connection with a number of special publics, which attempt to manipulate the opinions of the general public. Among these special fields are religion, medical care, taxation, social welfare, farm subsidies, civil rights, labor, and various aspects of business enterprise.[57] In all forms of propaganda, whether involving the general public or special publics, the question of terminology is important. Efforts are usually termed "educational," rather than propagandistic, since the latter term violates the traditional desire of the American people to make up their own minds on important matters. As we have indicated, however, this desire is often more honored in the breach than in the observance, as many persons vote on the basis of their prejudices rather than the facts.

The total nature of modern war has made propaganda a vital weapon of both sides in the struggle (whether in a hot or a cold war) between democracy and the various forms of totalitarianism. In an earlier day, wars were fought with hand weapons by small numbers of mercenary troups. The increased technological and industrial complexity of war now involves entire nations and groups of nations.[58] Morale becomes an important concern, both on the home front and in the enemy nation(s). Every effort is made by the belligerents to enlist the enthusiastic support of their own people, as well as to undermine the morale of the actual or potential enemy. The war of ideas continues to be fought in the minds of men in all parts of the world. It is fought with the most advanced technological devices of mass communication, as well as some of the oldest political techniques known to organized society.

The Soviet Union has carried the propaganda war to heights never before reached, even during the brief and violent life of Nazi Germany. In the field of radio alone, the Soviet radio broadcasts over 2,000 hours of propaganda material *every week*, directed in dozens of languages and dialects to hundreds of nations and peoples throughout the world. The United States has entered this aspect of the Cold War through the United States Information Agency, which has more than 200 offices in almost 100 countries all over the world.

---

[55] Morris Rosenberg, "The Meaning of Politics in Mass Society," *Public Opinion Quarterly*, 15:5-15 (Spring, 1951).

[56] Paul F. Lazarsfeld, *et al., The People's Choice, op. cit.*

[57] Frank Lang, "The Role of Research in Public Relations," *Public Opinion Quarterly*, 15:54-64 (Spring, 1951).

[58] Raymond Aron, *The Century of Total War* (New York: Doubleday & Company, 1954).

The Voice of America is the radio branch of this agency.[59] The general themes of this information/propaganda program are as follows "(1) to unite the free nations of the world for peace, (2) to expose international Communism, and (3) to have our own peaceful intentions understood." [60] In addition to radio programs in many languages, the United States Information Agency provides books, magazines, and newspapers to local audiences; makes available speeches by American officials; offers films on America to foreign groups; and facilitates the appearance abroad of American artists, singers, and concert performers.

In the battle of propaganda, the victory does not always go to the democratic nations. Among the reasons for this situation are the following: (1) The Soviet Union has a number of tangible deeds to its credit, notably its undeniable progress in space. (2) The United States has suffered propaganda defeats in the eyes of the world (especially the majority that is nonwhite) by its denial of civil rights to Negroes and the violence that has accompanied their efforts to attain these rights. (3) The United States does not speak with a single voice, as does the Soviet Union, and hence the image of this country is often confused in the eyes of the world. This latter factor is, however, the glory of a free nation. The United States *should not* speak with one voice, no matter what transient propagandistic benefits might accrue from such a policy. A multiplicity of voices is the tradition of this country, and our greatness lies in the free expression of these differences of opinion.[61]

An astute student of public opinion has recently called attention to one way in which the propaganda of the United States might be more effective. Davison suggests that our propaganda places too much emphasis upon convincing *individuals* in other countries of the justice of our cause and the wisdom of our aims. As we have seen, however, individuals have a surprising tenacity in holding on to their attitudes in the face of factual information to the contrary. Hence we should, Davison believes, shift our emphasis from trying to convince masses of isolated individuals, and should rather direct our primary attention to *organizations* in foreign countries. These organizations include governments, political parties, labor unions, agricultural cooperatives, educational institutions, and business groups.[62]

Furthermore, Davison continues, we should attempt to provide *services*, whether in the form of information (technical or otherwise), for these functioning organizations, rather than try to change the attitudes of the individual citizens. Agricultural cooperatives that are given specific information on, say, chemical fertilizers, will be grateful for this assistance, and hence will regard the donor nation (i.e., the United States) as a valuable friend. "Social science research," concludes Davison, "thus suggests that the principal target of propaganda should not be a mass of individuals whose attitudes are to be

---

[59] Harry Schwartz, "K-Day in the Propaganda War," *New York Times Magazine* (September 18, 1960).
[60] Edward L. Bernays (ed.), "What Do We Say to the World?" *The Saturday Review*, 28:11-18 (September 17, 1955), p. 12.
[61] Leo Cherne, "The Loin Cloth or the Rajah?" *The Saturday Review*, 38:13-14 (September 17, 1955).
[62] Davison, "Political Communication as an Instrument of Foreign Policy," *op. cit.*, p. 35.

changed, but more a set of groups and organizations that are to be assisted. . . ." [63]

In this chapter we have considered the crowd and public as forms of collective behavior. This behavior is essentially "unstructured," in that it is a response for which previous experience has not prepared the individual. Institutional behavior, on the other hand, is "structured" behavior and encourages submission to routine. Collective behavior by its very nature breaks institutional routines and provides flexibility in society. In the crowd, the members work out new forms of behavior through their emotions. In the public, the emphasis is presumably upon discussion, although emotion is not entirely ruled out. In either case, the result is a new form of behavior that departs from previous patterns. This departure may or may not be permanent, but in any event the traditional order has been broken and the old ways have been changed.

---

[63] *Ibid.*

SELECTED BIBLIOGRAPHY

Baur, E. Jackson, "Opinion Change in a Public Controversy," *Public Opinion Quarterly*, 26:212-226 (Summer, 1962). In the author's words, "The results of this study of a local controversy suggest that public opinion is formed through subtle processes of changing kinds of knowledge, affectivity level, and relative silence of values and interests." The rational weighing of facts does not appear to be as important as the classical theorists of public opinion hoped it would be.

Berelson, Bernard, "The State of Communication Research," *Public Opinion Quarterly*, 23:1-6 (Spring, 1959). In this brief article, the author surveys recent trends in communication research and concludes that the dynamism has largely gone out of the field—as the giants of an earlier generation (Lasswell, Lazarsfeld, Lewin, *et al.*) have either died or transferred their interests to other areas.

Blumer, Herbert, "Public Opinion and Public Opinion Polling," *American Sociological Review*, 13:542-549 (October, 1948). The author critically examines the theory and practice of public opinion polling. He suggests that some method of discovering the role of the individual in the group (and hence his influence upon the opinions of others) should be substituted for the conventional sampling and enumeration process.

Breed, Warren, and Thomas Ktsanes, "Pluralistic Ignorance in the Process of Opinion Formation," *Public Opinion Quarterly*, 25:382-392 (Fall 1961). "Pluralistic ignorance" in public opinion formation means (approximately) that the blind lead the blind in making up their minds on such matters as desegregation in the Deep South.

Davison, W. Phillips, "The Public Opinion Process," *Public Opinion Quarterly*, 22:91-106 (Spring, 1958). This article analyzes the concepts of the public and public opinion in a framework of social interaction. Also "Political Communication as an Instrument of Foreign Policy," *Public Opinion Quarterly*, 27:28-36 (Spring, 1963). The author turns his attention to the fine art of propaganda in foreign relations, with particular emphasis upon the activities of the United States. He suggests that the most effective propaganda is exercised by contacting existing organizations in foreign countries, rather than by attempting to appeal directly to a disparate mass of individuals.

Katz, Elihu, "Communication Research and the Image of Society: Convergence of Two Traditions," *American Journal of Sociology*, 65:435-440 (March, 1960). This article further examines the hypothesis of the "two-step flow of communication" (see immediately below) and indicates some of the interpersonal processes intervening between the media and the individual.

Katz, Elihu, and Paul F. Lazarsfeld, *Personal Influence: The Part Played by People in the Flow of Mass Communications*. Glencoe, Ill.: The Free Press, 1955. This book reports on a study of mass communications and interpersonal relations in a middle-western city. The authors develop the hypothesis of the "two-step flow of communication," whereby ideas flow from the mass media to the opinion leaders and from them to the other members of the small "communications network" at the end of the line.

Lang, Kurt and Gladys Engel Lang, *Collective Dynamics*. New York: Thomas Y. Crowell Company, 1961. Chapter 5 (Crowd Behavior) and Chapter 13 (Public Opinion) of this thoughtful textbook are especially pertinent to the present discussion.

Lasswell, Harold D., "Propaganda and Mass Insecurity," *Psychiatry*, 13:283-299 (August, 1950). The emotional climate of the postwar world is such that propaganda is a flourishing activity by persons and agencies wishing to capitalize upon the prevailing mass insecurity.

Lee, Alfred M., "Public Opinion in Relation to Culture," *Psychiatry*, 8:49-61 (February, 1945). This article is an extensive and well-documented analysis of the nature of public opinion. The author is a well-known specialist in public opinion, both in its theoretical and practical aspects.

Rosenberg, Morris, "Self-Esteem and Concern with Public Affairs," *Public Opinion Quarterly*, 26:201-211 (Summer, 1962). In this sophisticated analysis, attitudes toward the self are seen as influencing attitudes toward public affairs. As the author puts it, "how a man sees himself will bear a relationship to how he sees the world."

Stouffer, Samuel A., *Communism, Conformity, and Civil Liberties*. New York: Doubleday & Company, 1955. This is an important and timely study of public opinion, with particular reference to the extent to which traditional civil liberties were eroded during the first half of the decade of the 1950's. In this sampling, most persons *said* that they were not overwhelmingly worried by the Communist menace and that personal considerations bulked larger in their minds. At the same time, the degree of intolerance of nonconformity suggests that these fears were deeper than people thought.

Turner, Ralph H., and Samuel J. Surace, "Zoot-Suiters and Mexicans: Symbols in Crowd Behavior," *American Journal of Sociology*, 62:14-20 (July, 1956). This article is a case study of hostile symbolism in crowd behavior—notably that involving "zoot-suit" riots in and around Los Angeles during World War II. Crowd behavior was here largely directed against Mexican-Americans, who were identified in the public mind with the negative and hostile symbol of the "zoot-suit."

2 4 *Mass Society*

The Nature of Mass Society

Mass society is a new form of social interaction, in which collective behavior plays an increasingly important role. In mass society, people interact in larger numbers, at longer distances, and in more complex organizations than ever before. Newspapers, mass circulation magazines, motion pictures, and (above all) radio and television are the channels for this new interaction. Large, bureaucratic structures of business, government, education, and politics provide the setting. In a traditional, agrarian, and primary society, people take each other into account in face-to-face fashion and in small groups. The family,

553

the neighborhood, the play group, and the rest of the local community groups provide the setting for such interaction. In mass society, much of this primary interaction remains, and many social patterns are unchanged. But technological and structural changes have modified other aspects of interaction almost beyond recognition.[1]

Mass society is a "mixed" society. Much interaction remains on the primary-group level, with people communicating as they have always done. Men and women do not live in a completely new world, nor are they pushed, prodded, and cajoled by mass communications to the exclusion of everything else. Some students of mass society, both here and abroad, have exaggerated the impact of the mass media. In so doing, they suggest that the nightmare of the totalitarian state is about to become a living reality for Americans, who have become so isolated, alienated, and fragmented that they cannot call their souls their own. In strict reality, however, the primary group continues to be the center of social interaction. In so doing, it assures a continuity of basic human experience that changes in mass communication have not seriously threatened.

At the same time, the mass media cannot be ignored. In many ways, our society *has* changed—whether for better or worse. In many aspects of behavior, from teen-age fashions to political attitudes, conformity has increased. Mass communication and rapid transportation (among other forces) have increased the centralization of political power and hastened the decline of municipal government. In business and government, the growth of bureaucracy has changed many of the ways in which people interact. The family and local community agencies have lost influence and national agencies have gained it. Powerful voluntary associations, whose interests range from social welfare to political action, have weakened many smaller and less sophisticated groups of an earlier Jeffersonian democracy. Regional differences in politics, religion, and racial attitudes are changing, even though some sections maintain a stubborn, rear-guard action against modifications in the norms.

These and other massive social changes are viewed in different terms, depending upon the attitudes of the observer.[2] Whether a person approves or disapproves, however, he cannot deny the reality of these innovations. In spite of everything the individual can (or cannot) do, society is becoming more "mass-like" in many respects. The attributes of mass society have engaged the attention of many behavioral scientists, whose motivations range from a desire to understand this brave new world to a wish to manipulate its citizens. The present chapter will bring together some of these recent findings, although the literature is so extensive that we can barely scratch the surface. In our examination of mass society, the conceptual framework is again that of social interaction.

Mass society is characterized by the following general conditions: (1) It

---

[1] Louis Wirth, "Consensus and Mass Communication," *American Sociological Review*, 13:1-15 (February, 1948). See also Joseph Bensman and Bernard Rosenberg, *Mass, Class, and Bureaucracy* (Englewood Cliffs, New Jersey: Prentice-Hall, Inc., 1963), especially Chapters 11-12.

[2] Cf. Daniel Bell, "America as a Mass Society: A Critique," Ch. 1 in Daniel Bell, *The End of Ideology* (Glencoe, Illinois: The Free Press, 1960).

involves large masses of persons, numbered in the scores or even hundreds of millions; (2) These persons are dispersed over wide areas, instead of being concentrated into compact local groups; (3) Mass society is strongly influenced by powerful bureaucratic organizations; (4) It is equalitarian in theory, if not in practice; (5) It is *heterogeneous* in religion, ethnic background, style of life, and access to power; (6) It is *homogeneous* insofar as its members respond to mass culture; (7) It is composed of anonymous individuals, who know their local groups but not other members of the mass society who are removed in space; (8) It follows that an entire mass society seldom forms an organized group, except in such rare instances as a war; (9) Its members are all in some degree alienated by lack of access to the primary-group contacts of a simpler society; (10) It is secular in that its members have less veneration for tradition than do older societies; (11) It has undergone a complex technological development, and an important part of its interaction occurs through mass communication.[3] In short, "mass societies are a creation of the modern age and are the product of the division of labor, of mass communication, and a more or less democratically achieved consensus."[4]

The above description applies to many societies in Europe, America, and Asia, irrespective of their form of government. Some critics maintain that mass society is so unstable that it is subject to extremist political movements, which may come from the Left or the Right—i.e., either communist or fascist.[5] This sombre hypothesis is not warranted by the facts. We shall shortly consider the political implications of mass society. Suffice it to indicate that modern totalitarian movements, with the possible exception of Nazi Germany, have arisen in such "unmass-like" societies as Russia, Italy, and Spain. Furthermore, such movements have *not* arisen in England or the United States, where many of the characteristics of mass society are most clearly apparent. Indeed, such aspects of mass society as mass communication, bureaucratic government, and equalitarian ideologies may *strengthen*, rather than *weaken*, democratic institutions. Acting through these agencies, people are brought into contact with others to realize a common purpose.[6]

In this latter view, as Shils cogently remarks, "The new society is a mass society precisely in the sense that the mass of the population has become incorporated *into society*."[7] The major institutions and their accompanying value patterns have extended their limits and incorporated a greater proportion of the population than ever before. As a result of this incorporation, continues Shils, "Most of the population (the 'mass') now stands in a closer relationship to the

---

[3] The above is adapted from Louis Wirth, *op. cit.*, pp. 2-3.

[4] *Ibid.*, p. 2.

[5] Among the scholars discussing this problem are: Hannah Arendt, *The Origins of Totalitarianism* (New York: Harcourt, Brace and World, 1954); Erich Fromm, *Escape from Freedom* (New York: Holt, Rinehart and Winston, 1941); William Kornhauser, *The Politics of Mass Society* (Glencoe, Illinois: The Free Press, 1959).

[6] Joseph R. Gusfield, "Mass Society and Extremist Politics," *American Sociological Review*, 27:19-30 (February, 1962).

[7] Edward A. Shils, "Mass Society and Its Culture," *Daedalus*, 89:283-314 (Spring, 1960), p. 288. (His italics.)

center than has been the case in either pre-modern societies or in the earlier phases of modern society." [8] More people are therefore "inside" the vital functioning of society and there are fewer such "outside" groups as the very poor and the completely illiterate. The area of interaction, in other words, is greater in the mass society than ever before. We shall further explore the implications of this extension in our discussion of mass communication.

Insight into the nature of the "mass," as distinguished from the broader concept of "mass society" is offered by Lang and Lang. They suggest that the mass may be viewed in dynamic terms—that is, in terms of the way it *acts* as a form of collective behavior. They indicate three general categories in this context.[9]

1. The unqualified mass. This is the aggregate of unqualified persons in contemporary society, whose lack of education, discernment, and creativity causes them to interfere with the activities of the culture-bearing elite. As stated by Selznick, "A mass society is one which does not permit elites to carry out their cultural functions; hence it results in the sovereignty of the unqualified." [10] In this view, the unqualified mass is composed of the great, inert body of the people, whose power is based upon sheer numbers and who act as a depressing cultural influence upon society as a whole. They are the millions who listen happily to rock-and-roll music on the radio, who sit enraptured before the television screen showing the latest western drama, and who read the sleazy adventures of the heroine in the true-confession magazines. They are, in short, the chief supporters of, and participants in, mass culture, which we shall consider later.

2. The alienated mass. This refers to the aggregate of alienated persons, who are uprooted, disenchanted, and disaffected because of drastic changes that have torn them loose from their former statuses in society.[11] The alienated mass in this sense was illustrated in Germany after World War I. Millions of discharged soldiers, impoverished middle-class persons, and small shopkeepers saw their roles threatened by inflation, big business, and organized labor. This alienated mass formed the basis of the Nazi party, which directed their combined frustrations against the existing Weimar Republic.[12] Rapid social change spawns alienated masses in any society and they often seek to overthrow the political system.

3. The aggregate mass. This is the mass as conceived by the mass communication industry and by large corporations that deliver their advertising message through these facilities. In this sense, the mass is viewed as a large number of individuals, spatially separated, unknown to each other, whose individual actions constitute an aggregate known as "mass behavior." We shall consider

---

[8] *Ibid.*

[9] The following is adapted from Kurt Lang and Gladys Engel Lang, *Collective Dynamics* (New York: Thomas Y. Crowell Company, 1961), pp. 337-347.

[10] Philip Selznick, "Institutional Vulnerability in Mass Society," *American Journal of Sociology,* 56:320-331 (January, 1951), p. 321.

[11] William Kornhauser, *op. cit.,* p. 125.

[12] Cf. Hans H. Gerth, "The Nazi Party: Its Leadership and Composition," in Robert K. Merton, *et al.* (eds.), *Reader in Bureaucracy* (Glencoe, Illinois: The Free Press, 1952).

the possible qualifications of this conception below. Millions of persons make individual decisions to listen to a particular television program, attend a certain movie, or buy a specific brand of tooth paste. Each such decision means little in itself, but taken together their sum total represents an important force. Each person is free to make his own choice, whether for President, popular song, or deodorant. In making these choices, he seeks to satisfy his own emotional needs, whether for amusement, security, or affection. As Robert E. Park used to say, such persons have a "like" purpose, but not a "common" purpose.

This concept of the aggregate mass is closely related to that earlier developed and expanded by Herbert Blumer, who views the "mass" as a spontaneous and transitory form of collective behavior. In this respect, Blumer describes the mass as follows: (1) *Differentiation*—The mass comes from all segments and classes of society; (2) *Anonymity*—Its members are anonymous in that they are unknown to each other; (3) *Lack of Interaction*—Physical separation means that, by definition, the members interact very little with each other; (4) *Lack of Organization*—It follows that the mass lacks permanent organization. Its members are temporarily united about a particular stimulus, but they do not constitute a formal group. Hence the mass lacks the permanent qualities of interaction of a "true" communal society. In Blumer's words, "the mass has no social organization, no body of custom and tradition, no established set of rules or rituals, no organized group of sentiments, no structure of status roles, and no established leadership." [13]

This is a valuable hypothesis for understanding such forms of collective behavior as mass movements, audience reactions, and similar forms of activity centered about a single stimulus. In the present context, however, we are considering mass society as a permanent, ongoing entity, indistinguishable in many respects from modern society. In mass society, people react in the group setting of ordinary society; the element of novelty is that they react through mass communication. As Freidson phrases it, the mass communication behavior of the individual *"has been absorbed into the social life of the local groups."* [14] To these local groups should be added the institutions, bureaucratic agencies, and voluntary associations that constitute the larger society. These influences combine to make up the setting of interaction in mass society.

The Process of Mass Communication

Modern society interacts to a considerable extent through mass communication. The movies, radio, television, and the press are the agents in the interaction process. Mass communication may be defined as any form of communication "produced at a single source which is capable of being transmitted to an infi-

---

[13] Herbert Blumer, "The Crowd, the Public, and the Mass," in Alfred M. Lee (ed.), *New Outline of the Principles of Society* (New York: Barnes and Noble, Inc., 1946), p. 186.

[14] Eliot Freidson, "Communications Research and the Concept of the Mass," *American Sociological Review*, 18:313-317 (June, 1953), p. 315. (His italics.)

nitely large audience." [15] In somewhat different terms, this means "the use of technology by professional specialists to disseminate large amounts of identical content to a physically dispersed mass." [16] Radio and television are mass communications in this literal sense, for they can transmit messages to large audiences with no change in technology. A broadcast or telecast can, in principle, be heard or seen by an audience limited only by the number of people with receiving sets. Newspapers and magazines need additional copies to reach larger audiences, and movies need more prints of the same film. In a real sense, however, the latter are also mass communications as defined. They enable social interaction to take place between a single source and millions of individuals.

Mass communication, like all human communication, involves three related elements: (1) the source, (2) the message, and (3) the destination. That is, *someone* says *something* to *somebody*. In its simplest form, communication means that one individual takes the role of the other and phrases his message in terms understandable to his listener. The latter understands the message if his cultural background is approximately similar to that of the communicator. Language is the basic factor in this process, although other culturally defined symbols and signs are also employed. We have examined the communication process in Chapter 2, and need not repeat our analysis here. We shall merely indicate the ways in which mass communication differs from ordinary communication of the face-to-face variety.[17]

1. The source. The source in mass communication is a "communication organization or an institutionalized person." An organization is a newspaper, radio station, television network, motion picture studio, or magazine publisher. An institutionalized person is a newspaper editor, television commentator, movie actor, or magazine writer. These persons are invested with the prestige of the organization and their words carry more weight than those of a "private" citizen.

2. The message. The message in mass communication is the product of the organization and its personnel. The newspaper has a team of reporters, editors, and rewrite men, who jointly prepare the message. The average radio or television station receives much of its news from one or two other large communication organizations known as press associations. The commentator may merely read the dispatches as they come over the wire, or he may write his own interpretation of the news. The magazine article is also a product of many people who gather, write, rewrite, print, and disseminate the news. The motion picture is the most "institutionalized" of all the mass media, for its message involves a

---

[15] Franklin Fearing, "Social Impact of the Mass Media of Communication," Chapter 8 in *Mass Media and Education*, Fifty-third Yearbook of the National Society for the Study of Education (Chicago: University of Chicago Press, 1954), p. 166.

[16] Kurt Lang and Gladys Engel Lang, *op. cit.*, p. 423.

[17] The following is freely adapted from Wilbur Schramm, "How Communication Works," in Wilbur Schramm (ed.), *The Process and Effects of Mass Communication* (Urbana: University of Illinois Press, 1954), Ch. 1, especially pp. 18-26.

bewildering number of writers, directors, producers, camera men, publicity men, and (finally) actors.

3. *The destination.* The destination of mass communication is the recipient of the message—that is, millions of persons reading the newspaper, listening to the radio, viewing television, or attending the movie. Although the destination is an individual human being, the interaction differs from face-to-face communication. The reader, listener, or viewer responds to the message, but he is unable to exert much reciprocal influence upon the source. In technical jargon, the "feedback" in this form of communication is minimal, for the listener cannot respond except by such roundabout devices as writing an angry letter to the editor. As we shall see, much of this responsive interaction occurs in a primary-group setting, with members of primary groups responding to the message and thus making small communications networks of their own.

Mass communication operates through the least common cultural denominator of the society. When two persons interact directly, they speak of many intimate and/or diverse subjects of interest only to themselves. When a third person enters the conversation, the character of the interaction changes, for the group must be enlarged to include the new addition. The triad, in other words, differs qualitatively from the dyad.[18] As the "group" increases in size to millions of radio listeners or television viewers, the message becomes progressively diluted until it deals only with subjects that are presumably understandable to everybody. The topics discussed and the ideas presented often become bland and uncontroversial. In this way, it is hoped that they will interest the largest possible number of people and antagonize the smallest.

This happy goal is, of course, never actually realized by any single program, but the producers never stop trying. Television programs on national networks are so expensive that they must appeal to an audience of scores of millions. In an ingenious effort to promote togetherness, television has "created" or exploited new situations in addition to the old ones of novelty, comedy, love, and violence. These "creations" include family "situational" dramas, detective serials emphasizing mayhem, and variety programs with a little something for everybody. In so doing the media often copy each other, and a successful "formula" on one network is followed by an attempt at duplication on the others. A highly rated quiz program will be followed by more quiz programs; a western melodrama will produce more westerns; and a whimsical commentator will beget other whimsical commentators.[19] None of these efforts appeals to *all* of the people *all* of the time. But the sponsors hope that they will appeal to *some* of the people *most* of the time.[20]

---

[18] This insight is attributed to Georg Simmel, "The Quantitative Determination of Group Divisions and of Certain Groups," in Kurt Wolff (ed.), *The Sociology of Georg Simmel* (Glencoe, Illinois: The Free Press, 1950), pp. 112-113. The comparison is made by Rolf B. Meyersohn, "Social Research in Television," in Bernard Rosenberg and David Manning White (eds.), *Mass Culture* (Glencoe, Illinois: The Free Press, 1957), p. 352.

[19] Kurt Lang and Gladys Engel Lang, *op. cit.*, pp. 441-442.

[20] Rolf B. Meyersohn, *op. cit.*, pp. 352-353.

The Functions of Mass Communication

Mass communication expresses the "generalized other" of mass society. Like the primitive storyteller, the communication organizations transmit the norms, values, and folkways of the society. In our analysis of the social self in Chapter 8, we examined the process whereby each person takes first the role of the other *person* and then that of the *generalized other* or organized culture patterns of the society.[21] The mass media express the generalized other in terms both understandable and acceptable to their listeners. The radio commentator who voices patriotic sentiments, the magazine writer who extols the virtues of capitalism, and the motion picture that depicts a wise and good-hearted priest, all express elements of the generalized other. The basic tenets of these general culture patterns are affirmed and reaffirmed many times a day before a total audience that includes the majority of persons over five years of age.[22]

This expression of the generalized other has the broad function of integrating society about the past as well as preparing its members for the future. This function is stated by Breed as follows: "By expressing, dramatizing, and repeating cultural patterns, both the traditional and the newly emerging, the media reinforce tradition and at the same time explain new roles. Members of the society," the author continues, "thus remain integrated within the sociocultural structure. As a form of adult socialization, the media are seen as guarantors that a body of common ultimate values remains visible as a continuing source of consensus, despite the inroads of change."[23] It is by performing this function, which Lang and Lang aptly term "psychic mobilization,"[24] that the mass media come into their own.

In thus expressing the generalized other, the mass media perform several other and related functions. The concept of "function" here refers to what the media actually *do*, whether or not these actions are desirable from the standpoint of social welfare. In a classic analysis, Lazarsfeld and Merton suggest the following functions of mass communication.[25]

1. Status-conferral. Mass communications confer status upon individuals, organizations, and issues merely by considering them worthy of presentation to a nationwide audience. The man whose picture is on the cover of *Time* gains status because of this fact alone. If he is important enough to receive this distinction, he must therefore be a truly distinguished man. This is arguing in a circle, but such inconsistency is beside the point. The man on the front cover has, in a pragmatic sense, *arrived* merely because millions of people have heard

---

[21] George Herbert Mead, *Mind, Self, and Society* (Chicago: University of Chicago Press, 1934), p. 162.

[22] W. Lloyd Warner, *American Life: Dream and Reality* (revised edition). (Chicago: University of Chicago Press, 1962), Chapter 10.

[23] Warren Breed, "Mass Communication and Socio-Cultural Integration," *Social Forces*, 37:109-116 (December, 1958), p. 110.

[24] Kurt Lang and Gladys Engel Lang, *op. cit.*, p. 435.

[25] Paul F. Lazarsfeld and Robert K. Merton, "Mass Communication, Popular Taste, and Organized Social Action," in Lyman Bryson (ed.), *The Communication of Ideas* (New York: Harper & Row, 1948), pp. 95-118.

his name, read his biography, and learned what he eats for breakfast. He is no longer an anonymous part of the mass; he has become *somebody*.

2. *Norm-enforcement.* Mass communications also express the generalized other when they expose conditions that violate the norms: a newspaper launches a crusade against commercialized vice, a news magazine exposes the deplorable conditions in state mental hospitals, a television commentator presents a graphic exposé of police graft. Each of these situations violates social norms, and the mass media contribute to public morality by exposing them. The violation may be widely known before the exposure, even though it is not publicly admitted. Many persons are content to condone the deviation (vice, cruelty, gambling, graft) as long as it is kept quiet. National magazines, television programs, and newspaper headlines may finally shame the public into action.

3. *Narcotizing dysfunction.* Mass communications may also exert a narcotizing (depressing) influence upon their audience. The reader, listener, or viewer learns about crime, vice, misery, and neglect, but he does nothing about them. He spends more time reacting and less time acting. Knowledge is substituted for action, as long as his conscience is clear. The public-spirited citizen has responded in his mind but not in the real world. The complexity of mass society means that many of its problems are remote, even though more people may be aware of them. The mass media may therefore act as a "social narcotic" to lull the well-meaning but apathetic individual to sleep.

In mass communication, the communicator talks to other individuals, but he cannot take their roles as individuals. He delivers his message in the hope that he will be understood, but he cannot modify his presentation in the process. In an attempt to produce an atmosphere of intimacy, he may act "as if" he were actually communicating with his audience by taking their roles and appropriately adjusting his performance. This effort is especially apparent in television where the speaker enters directly into millions of living rooms. This process has been called "parasocial interaction," which means that it appears to have some of the "feedback" of true interaction, but is still not the real thing. The television comedian, disk jockey, and commentator try to give the impression that they are taking their listeners into account *as individuals* and are reacting accordingly.[26]

Mass communication, in summary, gives unity and cohesion to mass society. Among the elements of the generalized other transmitted to millions of viewers, listeners, and readers are "the political and social symbols of a society, the images of its leaders, its angels and its demons, and the patterns of mythology. . . ."[27] Government, business, and education are among the institutions of mass society that depend upon mass communication. Through this machinery, the individual is caught up in the larger society and consensus is produced and maintained. As Wirth puts it, "It is upon these mass media . . . that to an ever-

---

[26] Donald Horton and R. Richard Wohl, "Mass Communication and Parasocial Interaction," *Psychiatry*, 19:215-224 (August, 1956).

[27] Franklin Fearing, *op. cit.*, pp. 166-167.

increasing degree the human race depends to hold it together. Mass communication is rapidly becoming, if it is not already, the main framework of the web of social life." [28]

The Areas of Mass Interaction

Members of mass society interact on two levels—the group and the mass. The first level consists of "organized groups, ranging from informally constituted intimate groups to highly formalized organizations, such as the modern corporation, the union, the church, and the state." The second level consists of "the detached masses that are held together, if at all, by the mass media of communication." [29] Early studies stressed the unorganized aspect of interaction, and emphasized the impact of the media upon the mass of anonymous and unrelated individuals.[30] Later studies stress individual participation in primary groups, as well as in the larger organizations of politics, business, and government. This latter approach views the individual in his group setting, whether the family and neighborhood or the more extended groups of national society.[31]

We shall be primarily concerned here with the group approach. From the sociological point of view, behavior cannot be fully understood without reference to group membership. Response to a political debate on television must be related both to the groups of family and friends and to the relationships of these primary groups to the larger political, economic, and religious structures. The man whose family, friends, and business associates consistently vote Republican will have a different reaction to such a debate than the man whose group relationships are solidly Democratic. Perceptions in mass communication take on added significance when viewed in sociological, rather than purely psychological, terms. Man in mass society does not cease to be a social animal.

The sociological theory of mass communication owes much to the concept of the "reference group." This is the group to which the individual "refers" his behavior and from which he derives many of his norms and values.[32] As Merton and Kitt phrase it, the concept of reference group "centers on the process through which men relate themselves to groups and refer their behavior to the values of these groups." [33] Whether consciously or not, man reviews his actions in terms of the standards of his reference groups. As he listens to the radio or looks at television, he may appear to be an isolated individual, acting

---

[28] Louis Wirth, *op. cit.*, p. 10. Cf. Joseph T. Klapper, "What We Know About the Effects of Mass Communication: The Brink of Hope," *Public Opinion Quarterly*, 21:453-471 (Winter, 1957-1958).

[29] Louis Wirth, *op. cit.*, p. 5.

[30] For an analysis of these studies, see John W. Riley, Jr., and Matilda White Riley, "Mass Communication and the Social System," Chap. 24 in Robert K. Merton, *et al.* (eds.), *Sociology Today* (New York: Basic Books, Inc., 1959), pp. 537-547.

[31] Eliot Freidson, *op. cit.*

[32] Tamotsu Shibutani, "Reference Groups as Perspectives," *American Journal of Sociology*, 60:562-569 (May, 1955).

[33] Robert K. Merton and Alice S. Kitt, "Contributions to the Theory of Reference Group Behavior," in Robert K. Merton and Paul F. Lazarsfeld (eds.), *Continuities in Social Research* (Glencoe, Illinois: The Free Press, 1950), pp. 41-42.

in an amorphous mass society. But in many respects he is acting in the light of his reference groups.

The group approach to mass communication has been further documented by a number of studies of behavior in the community setting. In these investigations, the primary group has, as it were, been "rediscovered." As we saw in Chapter 23, people acquire opinions from the mass media on matters ranging from voting to movie-going, but they acquire them *through* primary group relationships. Certain key individuals act as transmitters from the mass media to other group members. These persons are called "opinion leaders" and they play a central role in the communication process. Ideas flow *from* the radio, television, newspaper, and mass circulation magazine to the opinion leaders and *from them* to others in the group.[34]

In this pattern of interaction, the primary group comes back into the picture with a vengeance. Mass communication no longer appears as a vast and impersonal process, whereby faceless communicators in radio, television, and print send out symbolic stimuli to millions of equally anonymous individuals. The primary group emerges as a channel of social interaction and constitutes a small "communication network" of its own. The centers of these human networks are the opinion leaders, who read the papers, listen to the radio, study the magazines, and otherwise expose themselves to the mass media. They influence their own intimate groups and thereby stimulate others to action. This action ranges in importance from buying cosmetics to voting in presidential elections.[35]

The peer group is a special form of primary group, whose communication role has been exhaustively examined by Riesman. In *The Lonely Crowd*, he suggests the process by which new songs, styles, and symbols are introduced to the average teen-ager. [36] Radio-listening, television-viewing, and movie-going are seen as *group*, rather than *individual*, experiences for the average adolescent, who likes nothing better than to listen to his favorite disk jockey in the close company of his best friends.[37] "The peer group," says Riesman, "stands midway between the individual and the messages which flow from the mass media. The mass media are the wholesalers; the peer-groups, the retailers of the communications industry." [38]

This interaction is not completely one-sided, since there is some feedback from peer group to mass media. Peer groups approve of certain singers and request their local disk jockeys to play their records. This discriminating public may likewise disapprove of a singer and banish him or her to the Siberia of disapprobation. In a more positive vein, the peer group invents new styles of dress

---

[34] Elihu Katz and Paul F. Lazarsfeld, *Personal Influence* (Glencoe, Illinois: The Free Press, 1955), p. 32.

[35] *Ibid.*, Ch. 14. See also E. Jackson Baur, "Public Opinion and the Primary Group," *American Sociological Review*, 25:208-219 (April, 1960).

[36] David Riesman, *et al.*, *The Lonely Crowd* (abridged edition) (New Haven: Yale University Press, 1961).

[37] Matilda White Riley and Samuel H. Flowerman, "Group Relations as a Variable in Communications Research," *American Sociological Review*, 16:174-180 (April, 1951).

[38] David Riesman, *et al.*, *op. cit.*, p. 84.

or language, which quickly get back to the media. "The mass media," concludes Riesman, "play the chief role in thus reducing to impersonality and distributing over a wide area the personal styles developed by individuals and groups." [39]

The youthful nature of large segments of the mass public is, indeed, one of the novel aspects of this form of social interaction. For the first time in history, millions of adolescents have both abundant leisure and money in their pockets. These teen-agers consume the products of mass communication in great gulps and with little discrimination. Hence, in Shils' words, "An extraordinary quantity of popular music, mediocre . . . films, periodical literature, and forms of dance are produced for and consumed by youth. This is something unprecedented, and this is the heart of the revolution of mass culture." [40] These adolescents constitute a new "leisure class," whose principal occupation is the consumption of mass culture in the company of their peers.

Mass communication transmits facts and opinions about many issues to thousands of local groups in mass society.[41] These ideas were initially developed in small, face-to-face groups, then organized by communication specialists, and finally transmitted to the opinion leaders. Nor does the process end here. Local primary groups are also related to secondary groups in the larger society. The citizen exerts his influence by voting for a national political party in a presidential election. The customer buys an automobile on the advice of a friend and thereby contributes to the welfare of General Motors. The machine operator works with a small group in a factory and is an important, although anonymous, cog in a giant enterprise. The soldier is loyal to his group of army buddies and helps to win the war.[42]

Primary groups are therefore in constant interaction with secondary groups in mass society. Local political groups are aligned, formally and informally, with larger organizations. A second-generation Italian-American living in Detroit, of the Roman Catholic faith, working in the Ford assembly plant, associates with persons of similar backgrounds and tends to vote Democratic. A fourth-generation Swedish-American, of the Lutheran faith, living in a small town in Kansas and owning his own business, tends to identify with people who vote Republican. Each person interprets mass communications through local groups that are influenced by certain presuppositions, norms, and values. These groups, in turn, are meshed into the national structure of the major political parties.[43]

---

[39] *Ibid.*

[40] Edward A. Shils, "Mass Society and Its Culture," *op. cit.*, p. 299.

[41] Elihu Katz, "The Two-Step Flow of Communication: An Up-to-Date Report on an Hypothesis," *Public Opinion Quarterly*, 21:61-78 (Spring, 1957).

[42] Robin M. Williams, Jr. and M. Brewster Smith, "General Characteristics of Ground Combat," in Samuel A. Stouffer, *et al.* (eds.), *The American Soldier* (Princeton: Princeton University Press, 1949), Vol. II, p. 100, quoted by John W. Riley, Jr. and Matilda White Riley, "Mass Communication and the Social System," *op. cit.*, p. 555.

[43] This process was conclusively demonstrated in Paul F. Lazarsfeld, *et al*, *The People's Choice* (New York: Columbia University Press, 1948).

The Mass Culture in Mass Society

Culture is the product of society. Mass culture is the product of mass society.[44] The central theme of this book is social interaction and the emergence of culture therefrom. In theory, society and culture may be distinguished in time, and social interaction may be said to antedate culture. In practice, man has interacted in an existing cultural setting as long as we have known him. Each member of a society is indoctrinated with the culture that is already present in the personalities of his family, friends, and associates. Mass culture is transmitted by mass communication and the resulting interaction is something new. Radio, television, and motion pictures have formulated and disseminated many patterns of culture that are new in breadth of acceptance, if not in quality. Modern productivity has increased the amount of leisure of the average man. Mass culture has evolved to fill this void and give modern man something to do when he is not working or sleeping.[45]

Mass culture, therefore, is the culture common to mass society and disseminated by mass communication. Mass culture is a unifying force in an otherwise heterogeneous and confusing world.[46] *Life* magazine, for example, is "read" by rich and poor; white- and blue-collar workers; executives and clerks; suburbanites and tenement-dwellers; sixth-generation Americans from Back Bay and second-generation Americans from the Lower East Side of New York; families from Maine to Mississippi and from New York to California; the college-educated and the functionally illiterate who look at the pictures and cannot understand the text. This successful publication has something for everybody, from stunning reproductions of the Sistine Chapel to the latest style in charm bracelets from Hollywood High School. As a vehicle of mass culture, remarks Dwight Macdonald acidly, this magazine (and its competitors) "mixes and scrambles everything together, producing what might be called homogenized culture, after another American achievement, the homogenized process that distributes the globules of cream evenly throughout the milk instead of allowing them to float separately on top." [47]

Mass culture, as noted, embodies the least common denominator of intellectual content. Mass culture is perforce neither incomprehensible nor distasteful to the majority of persons who are expected to buy the products sponsored by the mass media. Mass culture includes such diverse elements as baseball, romantic love, and fascination with shiny new gadgets that (presumably) make life simpler, happier, and richer. When one goes to the movies, listens to the radio, watches television, and reads mass circulation magazines he

---

[44] Hannah Arendt, "Society and Culture," *Daedalus*, 89:278-287 (Spring, 1960).

[45] Ernest Van Den Haag, "Of Happiness and of Despair We Have No Measure," in Bernard Rosenberg and David Manning White (eds.), *op. cit.*, pp. 504-508.

[46] John W. Bennett and Melvin M. Tumin, *Social Life: Structure and Function* (New York: Alfred A. Knopf, Inc., 1948), p. 609.

[47] Dwight Macdonald, "A Theory of Mass Culture," in Bernard Rosenberg and David Manning White (eds.), *op. cit.*, p. 62.

is, more often than not, experiencing mass culture in its unadulterated form.[48]

Mass culture is often viewed in disparaging terms, as though it were a force actively degrading modern—and especially American—life. In their strictures against mass culture, some intellectuals paint an idyllic picture of the happy peasants of a bygone feudal era, dancing about the village maypole, singing folk songs, and engaging in other forms of wholesome, uplifting activity. These blissful (but fictitious) serfs are then contrasted with the (equally fictitious) brutalized proletarians of modern industrial slums, who allegedly spend their leisure drinking in squalid taverns or, more often, seeing vapid movies, listening to moronic soap operas, and viewing murderous detective dramas on television.

Both of these pictures are exaggerated. The life of the feudal peasant was, in general, "poor, nasty, brutish, and short." He spent his leisure, when he had any, either in exhausted apathy or in such elevating pursuits as drinking, bear-baiting, and cock-fighting. He had little to look forward to but hunger, disease, premature old age, and death. Compared with this unhappy lot, the average industrial worker in the advanced countries lives a life of undreamed-of luxury, comfort, and leisure. His taste in recreation is not, to be sure, very elevated. He prefers rock-and-roll to Bach, and the comics to the classics. But he is still infinitely better off than his remote ancestors, crouching in their drafty huts and wondering where their next meal was coming from. As Shils puts it, "mass culture is now less damaging to the lower classes than the dismal and harsh existence of earlier centuries had ever been." [49]

Such comparisons of the lot of the common man before and after mass culture are, however, beside the point of the present discussion. We are interested in the role of mass culture in mass society, which is, beyond any doubt, an important one.[50] Whether one approves of it or not, mass culture is the culture of "the masses." Hence it cannot be ignored in any realistic picture of social interaction in contemporary society. Furthermore, in all probability the level of mass culture will always be "low" as measured by the standards of an intellectual elite. Traditional or "high" culture was produced for a specialized public, whose tastes were refined by constant exposure to the best that had been thought and said in their day.[51] Mass culture, on the other hand, is "consumed" by the mass society and its limitations are those of the members of this society. As one sympathetic critic has pointed out, responsibility for the "mental laziness and deplorable taste" of mass man should be extended to

---

[48] See Leon Bramson, *The Political Context of Sociology* (Princeton, New Jersey: Princeton University Press, 1961), Ch. 6, "Mass Society, Mass Culture, and Totalitarianism."

[49] Edward A. Shils, "Daydreams and Nightmares: Reflections on the Criticism of Mass Culture," *The Sewanee Review*, 65:587-608 (October-December, 1957), p. 606.

[50] For a balanced discussion of mass culture, see Raymond A. Bauer and Alice H. Bauer, "America, Mass Society and Mass Media," *The Journal of Social Issues*, 16:1-88 (1960), especially pp. 39-56. See also Lewis A. Coser, "Comments on Bauer and Bauer," *op. cit.*, pp. 78-84.

[51] Leo Lowenthal, "Historical Perspectives of Popular Culture," in Bernard Rosenberg and David Manning White (eds.), *op. cit.*, pp. 46-57.

include the schools, the family, the church, and the other institutions of mass society, rather than attributed solely to the mass media.[52]

Traditional and mass culture are simply different. They appeal to different segments of the population. When we have said this, we have indicated that one is not necessarily "good" and the other "bad." The two cultures are products of different types of society. In many respects, mass culture has swallowed up traditional culture. Millions of the listeners to, viewers of, and participants in mass culture are barely literate; they can read a newspaper, but they do not understand all of it. Members of an earlier, elite audience were not only more highly cultivated, but they constituted virtually *the entire audience* for the novels, dramas, and paintings of their time. "In consequence," conclude Lazarsfeld and Merton, "the *average* level of esthetic standards and tastes of audiences has been depressed, although the tastes of some sectors of the population have undoubtedly been raised and the total number of people exposed to communication contents have been vastly increased." [53]

In mass society, millions of men, women, and children seek emotional security and psychic gratification, as well as "mere" diversion, from mass communications. The lower-middle-class housewife, for example, looks to the soap opera to reassure her of the importance of her role. She wants to know that she is important to society, her family, and herself as she carries on the humdrum activities of housekeeping and child rearing. The heroine of the radio and television soap opera is an upper-middle-class woman with whom her lower-class listeners can nevertheless identify. Her problems become their problems, her triumphs their triumphs, and her (temporary) defeats their (temporary) defeats. In this sense, the soap opera functions "very much like a folk tale, expressing the hopes and fears of the feminine audience and on the whole [contributing] to the integration of their lives into the world in which they live." [54]

Other emotional gratifications are evident among children who watch television. Part of this gratification, of course, is merely that of providing entertainment for children who are bored. But some children appear to have a greater need for such gratification than others. In an interesting study of television-viewing, it was found that "the children who are highly frustrated in their current home life (subject to many restrictions and not treated permissively or warmly)" spend more time watching television than those who experience no such frustration. This was notably apparent among children in upper-middle-class families who, at the time of this study at least, were discouraged by their parents from watching television on the ground that it was certainly a waste of time and possibly productive of more serious emotional

---

[52] Leo Rosten, "The Intellectual and the Mass Media," *Daedalus*, 89:333-346 (Spring, 1960), p. 334.

[53] Paul F. Lazarsfeld and Robert K. Merton, "Mass Communication, Popular Taste, and Organized Social Action," *op. cit.*, cited by Bernard Rosenberg and David Manning White, *op. cit.*, p. 467.

[54] W. Lloyd Warner and William E. Henry, "The Daytime Radio Serial: A Symbolic Analysis," *Genetic Psychology Monographs*, 37:3-71 (February, 1948), p. 7. For a more recent analysis of these themes, see W. Lloyd Warner, *American Life: Dream and Reality* (revised edition) (Chicago: University of Chicago Press, 1962), Ch. 10.

results. The implication is that the child uses television to gain certain surrogate (substitute) satisfactions which he thinks he is deprived of by his nonpermissive parents.[55]

The adolescent in mass society has still other problems. He is unsure of himself, as he stands midway between child and adult. He is alternately torn between the desire to maintain the cozy security of his parental family and the desire to cut the silver cord that binds him to this emotional sanctuary. He looks to the peer group for identification and acceptance, and in this setting participates in mass culture.[56] Of all the age groups in mass society, the adolescent is the most completely enveloped in mass culture. Boys and girls in their teens furnish the bulk of the audience for the movies and for the daytime (or at least after school) radio and television programs. In addition, they constitute the largest single group of readers of many of the mass-circulation magazines. They participate in these activities as group members, rather than as isolated individuals, and thereby gain a sense of belonging.[57]

The United States is perhaps the most characteristic example of mass society as we have defined it. This does not mean that Americans "invented" mass society or mass culture, as certain jaundiced critics (both domestic and foreign) have suggested. It merely means that the technological and industrial factors that give rise to mass society are more prominent in the United States than in any other country. No traditional social structure held back the swift development of industry and technology in this country, as in the nations of the Old World. The Anglo-Saxon culture that was initially installed in New England and that formed the basis of "American" culture has furthermore become so diluted that, in many sections of the country, it is all but unrecognizable. As American society has become more industrialized and urbanized, technological innovations of mass communication have developed. Traditional culture has thus been modified, if not changed altogether, by mass culture.

But this conformity still does not mean that the mass culture of the United States is different in *kind* from, say, that of England, Sweden, France, or Germany. The difference is rather one of *degree*. The changes that produce mass culture merely came to this country earlier and to an intensified degree because they met with less resistance. Nor is *democracy* responsible for mass culture. Totalitarian states, such as the Soviet Union and Nazi Germany, demonstrate even more virulent manifestations of mass culture than the United States. There is, in many ways, a greater "massness" in totalitarian states than in this country, where conformity is enforced by example instead of by the police. Nor, finally, is *capitalism* the necessary cause of mass culture—for the same combination of reasons.

We may well ask, therefore, what factor or combination of factors *is* re-

---

[55] Eleanor T. Maccoby, "Why Do Children Watch Television?", *Public Opinion Quarterly*, 18:239-244 (Fall, 1954), p. 244.

[56] Matilda White Riley and Samuel H. Flowerman, *op. cit.*

[57] David Riesman, *et al., The Lonely Crowd, op. cit.*, pp. 96-108. Cf. Matilda White Riley and John W. Riley, "A Sociological Approach to Communications Research," *Public Opinion Quarterly*, 15:444-460 (Fall, 1951).

sponsible for the mass culture that is sweeping the world? A suggestive hypothesis has been offered by Rosenberg. In his words, "modern technology is the necessary and sufficient cause of mass culture. Neither national character nor the economic arrangement nor the political system has any final bearing on this question. All that really matters is the most recent industrial revolution."[58] Hence disgruntled English aristocrats, caustic French intellectuals, and conservative Hindu Brahmins are equally wrong in attributing the (to them) degrading influence of Hollywood, Coca-Cola, and juvenile delinquency to the deliberate cultural imperialism of the United States. The mass patterns that are submerging ancient cultures throughout the world are not a diabolical Yankee legacy. The villain in the piece—if villain there be—is modern technology.[59]

The Politics of Mass Society

Mass society also has important implications for political behavior. This latter term is broadly defined to include behavior toward political and social institutions in general. Democracy and totalitarianism are forms of political behavior in this sense, which involves more than voting habits or attitudes toward the major political parties. The political institutions of the United States are dedicated to the proposition that all men are created free and equal and that they will behave accordingly. The political institutions of the Soviet Union and Nazi Germany are (and were) dedicated to very different propositions. Although Fascism and Communism differ in many ideological respects, they have in common such totalitarian practices as a one-party system, centralized control of the mass media, and a belief that the state is more important than the individuals that constitute it.[60]

There is a widespread assumption among social theorists that mass society leads to totalitarianism, or at least to an increasingly totalitarian form of society.[61] As we have indicated, this assumption is not justified either by the historical facts or by the nature of mass society. The Soviet Union emerged from a nation that was almost totally devoid of the technological or industrial qualities of mass society. The United States and Great Britain are mass societies, but they are far removed from totalitarianism in any meaningful sense of that term. Indeed, many of the qualities of mass society militate *against*, rather than *toward*, political extremism. We may examine these qualities in view of their importance to social and political behavior.

In a penetrating article addressed to this theme, Gusfield advanced the hypothesis that "Conditions of mass societies . . . provide support to democratic political norms through the consequences of mass communications, equali-

---

[58] Bernard Rosenberg, *op. cit.*, p. 12. Cf. Edward A. Shils, "Mass Society and Its Culture," *op. cit.*, pp. 289-290.

[59] See Daniel Lerner, *The Passing of Traditional Society* (Glencoe, Illinois: The Free Press, 1958).

[60] See Hannah Arendt, *The Origins of Totalitarianism, op. cit.*

[61] For example: José Ortega y Gasset, *The Revolt of the Masses* (New York: Pelican Books, 1950); Erich Fromm, *Escape from Freedom* (New York: Holt, Rinehart and Winston, 1941); Karl Mannheim, *Man and Society in an Age of Reconstruction* (New York: Harcourt, Brace and World, 1950).

tarianism, and bureaucratization. . . ." [62] Mass communications, he continued, integrate local community members into national organizations and thereby break down parochialism and the accompanying reluctance to accept the modern world. It is no accident that the sections of the United States most resistant to liberalizing social change are those in which participation in mass culture remains at a low level.[63] Many of the qualities of mass society that earlier critics believed destructive of democratic values appear, on closer examination, to preserve and extend them. Among these qualities are the following.[64]

1. *Attachment to national institutions.* In mass society, an increasing segment of social interaction occurs on the national, rather than the local, level. State and local governments have lost much of their former importance, as compared with the growing power of the federal government. Such vital functions as social welfare, education, and public construction increasingly look to the federal government for financial support because local governments lack the taxing power to deal adequately with them. This trend toward centralization dismays many persons who look back with nostalgia to the allegedly stalwart virtues of an earlier and decentralized society. The factors that have produced mass society, however, are the same ones that have produced centralization. Conditions of mass society attach the individual to national institutions.[65]

2. *Consensus on national problems.* In mass society, a growing consensus (agreement) tends to emerge on many national problems. This consensus, in turn, minimizes social conflict. When class lines are strictly drawn, when sectional interests are tenaciously held, and when religious values are maintained to the point of intolerance, the society by definition contains many potential sources of conflict. In a significant study of religion in the United States, Herberg calls attention to the increasing secularism, which brings all three major faiths closer together in important respects.[66] In somewhat the same fashion, conditions of mass society bring greater national agreement on other basic issues. This process is roundly damned by many critics who contend that the resulting consensus is merely another name for conformity. This allegation is largely true. But it is more desirable to have greater religious uniformity than to suffer a massacre of St. Bartholomew.

3. *Tolerance and liberalism.* Mass society is also heterogeneous and pluralistic, which means that it is composed of different religious, educational, ethnic, racial and class groups. Such a society is more cosmopolitan and tolerant than one composed of tightly knit groups, each with its cluster of ethnocentric prejudices. National political parties, for example, must appeal to varied interest groups, and national platforms are correspondingly more

---

[62] Joseph R. Gusfield, *op. cit.,* Abstract, p. 19.
[63] See Samuel A. Stouffer, *Communism, Conformity, and Civil Liberties* (New York: Doubleday & Company, 1955), Chapter 2.
[64] The following is adapted from Joseph R. Gusfield, *op. cit.,* especially pp. 27-30.
[65] See Alvin W. Gouldner, "Cosmopolitans and Locals," *Administrative Science Quarterly, 2:281-306* (December, 1957) and 2:444-480 (March, 1958), cited by Joseph R. Gusfield, *op. cit.* p. 28.
[66] Will Herberg, *Protestant-Catholic-Jew: An Essay in American Religious Sociology* (New York: Doubleday Anchor Books, 1960), Chapter 11.

liberal than are the norms of many local constituencies where bigotry flourishes unopposed. Artistic activity and educational practices are, moreover, freer from censorship and repression on the national than on many local levels. Civil liberties derive their staunchest support from such agencies of the national government as the Supreme Court and the Department of Justice, as contrasted with some state and local governments. Once again, the quality of "massness" leads to freedom, not tyranny.[67]

4. *Acceptance of social change.* Mass society, finally, is more open to social change than is traditional, local society. Mass communication brings mass culture to millions who would otherwise experience few, if any, new ideas on any subject whatever. Critics of mass society, as we have seen, are understandably disenchanted with certain aspects of mass culture. These critics maintain that the general welfare is not demonstrably enhanced by the shoddy contents of radio soap operas, television spectaculars, and true-confession magazines. At the same time, however, mass society exposes its citizens to information and points of view that bear some relationship to the modern world. To this argument, the same critics reply that this is precisely the feature of mass culture which they dislike most heartily; in other words, they would prefer not to live in a world that is becoming increasingly bland, conformist, and standardized. The fact remains that we must continue to live in a society in which many vestigial sources of conflict persist. Whatever its esthetic drawbacks, mass culture helps to minimize these potential conflicts.

Many of the liberating effects of mass society were empirically demonstrated by Tumin in an important study of the acceptance of desegregation in a southern county. He discovered that, on balance, those persons who were in the habit of using a variety of news media were more ready to accept desegregation in the public schools than those who were less contaminated by such exposure. Tumin has summarized his findings as follows: "Increases in exposure to mass media are associated with small but consistent and persistent increases in readiness for desegregation. These small differences become larger . . . when the extremes of low and high exposure to the mass media are compared in their readiness for desegregation." [68]

It should be noted that, in the above study, exposure to the mass media did *not* substantially change any basic attitudes toward the Negro, even among those persons most willing to endorse integration. The latter still regarded the Negro as inferior in accordance with the norms, values, and institutions of the community. But at the same time they were more aware of the legal, political, and economic implications of all-out resistance to desegregation and hence were more willing to consider this drastic change in the social structure. As suggested by Klapper in a more general context, the mass media do not pro-

---

[67] For an empirical analysis of certain aspects of this general theme, cf. Scott Greer and Peter Orleans, "The Mass Society and the Parapolitical Structure," *American Sociological Review,* 27:634-646 (October, 1962).

[68] Melvin M. Tumin, "Exposure to Mass Media and Readiness for Desegregation," *Public Opinion Quarterly,* 21:237-251 (Summer, 1959), p. 248.

duce changes in attitude *by themselves*, but instead function along with other influences to bring about such effects.[69] In the Tumin study, the media were strong enough to evoke a grudging acceptance of desegregation, but not to change the traditional image of the Negro.[70]

The combination of conditions that produced mass society has, on balance, raised the general cultural level. Some persons will hotly deny this statement, but it would appear to be true. The level of education is steadily rising, as more people complete more years of schooling. The general income level is likewise rising, and more families can participate in mass culture. The level of religious, racial, and ethnic tolerance also seems to be rising, although this trend is harder to demonstrate statistically. Stated somewhat differently, "The less educated, the lowest income levels, the least protected minorities, the most fundamentalist in religion are least oriented to the rhythm of modernity with which so much of mass influence is carried." [71] Mass communication works from the bottom, rather than the top, of the social structure. Mass culture is raising the cultural level of the lowest segments of society and hence, on balance, that of society as a whole.

Mass society is incontestably the "wave of the future." The elements of "massness" which many sensitive persons find so depressing will continue to increase, rather than decrease. As Bell remarks, "The mass society is the product of change—and is itself change. It is the bringing of the 'masses' into a society, from which they were once excluded."[72] Social interaction will increasingly take place either directly through the mass media or through groups that are themselves influenced by the media. Other conditions of massness will continue to influence society to a greater extent. As we have indicated in Chapter 17, bureaucracy is likewise here to stay in education, business, industry, and government, with its attendant bureaucratic implications for mass society. The equalitarian ideology of mass society will also wax, rather than wane, as educational opportunities are available to more people. Styles of living will become more standardized, as white-collar and blue-collar families eat the same foods, buy the same automobiles, smoke the same cigarettes, watch the same baseball games, and read the same magazines. In many respects, mass society is the new way of life.

---

[69] Joseph T. Klapper, *op. cit.*, p. 457.
[70] Melvin M. Tumin, *op. cit.*, p. 249.
[71] Joseph R. Gusfield, *op. cit.*, p. 30.
[72] Daniel Bell, *op. cit.*, p. 36.

SELECTED BIBLIOGRAPHY

Bauer, Raymond A., and Alice H. Bauer, "America, Mass Society and Mass Culture," *The Journal of Social Issues*, 16:1-88 (1960). This is a survey of the literature on mass society and culture, with particular reference to the United States. The authors present a balanced view of this controversial subject, and the student is referred to this brief but sound presentation.

Bensman, Joseph, and Bernard Rosenberg, *Mass, Class, and Bureaucracy.* Englewood Cliffs, New Jersey: Prentice-Hall, Inc., 1963. This is a literate and provocative discussion of mass society, with particular emphasis upon mass culture. In Chapters 11 and 12, the student will find an especially stimulating treatment of the sociology of the arts, both popular and serious.

Freidson, Eliot, "Communications Research and the Concept of the Mass," *American Sociological Review*, 18:313-317 (June, 1953). This brief article makes an important contribution to the theory of mass society by demonstrating that mass communication and its related behavior must be considered within the framework of the group.

Gusfield, Joseph R., "Mass Society and Extremist Politics," *American Sociological Review*, 27:19-30 (February, 1962). This article presents and documents the hypothesis that the organizations of mass society *strengthen* democratic institutions and *weaken* the forces that make for political extremism.

Lazarsfeld, Paul F., and Robert K. Merton, "Mass Communication, Popular Taste, and Organized Social Action," in Lyman Bryson (ed.), *The Communication of Ideas.* New York: Harper & Row, 1948. In this seminal article, two leading figures in mass communication research offer some stimulating hypotheses concerning the nature and functions of these organizations.

"Mass Culture and Mass Media," *Daedalus*, Vol. 89 (Spring, 1960). This issue contains 12 essays devoted to various aspects of mass society and mass culture. The authors take different positions along the spectrum from enthusiastic acceptance to outright rejection of mass society and all its works. The most substantial contribution in this symposium is that of Professor Shils (see below), whose position is, on balance, favorable to mass culture.

Riesman, David, *et al.*, *The Lonely Crowd* (abridged edition). New Haven: Yale University Press, 1961. Among the wealth of insights in this book are several suggestions concerning the relationships between the mass media and the adolescent peer group in an increasingly "other-directed" society.

Riley, John W., Jr., and Matilda White Riley, "Mass Communication and the Social System," in Robert K. Merton, *et al.* (eds.), *Sociology Todays.* New York: Basic Books, Inc., 1959. This article surveys the major contributions to the *sociological*, as distinguished from the *psychological*, approach to mass communication.

Rosenberg, Bernard, and David Manning White (eds.), *Mass Culture.* Glencoe, Illinois: The Free Press, 1957. This symposium contains a variety of articles on mass culture, many of them highly critical. This is perhaps the best single source of information on this broad and expanding field.

Shils, Edward A., "Daydreams and Nightmares: Reflections on the Criticism of Mass Culture," *The Sewanee Review*, 65:587-608 (October-December, 1957); and "Mass Society and its Culture," *Daedalus*, 89:283-314 (Spring, 1960). In these two articles, an eminent social theorist delivers some penetrating remarks on mass society and its culture. The author conclusively demolishes many of the strictures against these related phenomena as he pictures them as *inevitable*, if not universally *desirable*, manifestations of modern life.

Wirth, Louis, "Consensus and Mass Communication," *American Sociological Review*, 13:1-15 (February, 1948). This analysis of mass communication is in the great tradition of social theory. The author states that the maintenance of consensus is the most important single problem confronting the democratic world and indicates that mass communication plays a crucial role in this process.

25 *Social Problems*

The Nature of Social Problems

Social change is occurring at the most rapid rate the world has ever seen. Both the "advanced" and the "underdeveloped" countries are experiencing unprecedented changes in technological development, industrial organization, and social structure. Adjustment to these changes is made more difficult by their differential character—that is, by the fact that some elements change faster than others.[1] Social change is one of the central themes of this book. We have considered it in various contexts, sometimes in its impact upon personality,

---

[1] Wilbert E. Moore, *Social Change* (Englewood Cliffs, N.J.: Prentice-Hall, Inc., 1963), Chapter 1.

sometimes in connection with social structure, and sometimes in its institutional implications. We have also examined the relationships between social change and collective behavior and indicated that the two are closely related. Men acting collectively try to work out solutions to situations resulting from social change and for which their previous experience has not prepared them.[2]

Social problems are one result of the above efforts to adjust to new situations by behavior that lacks the sanctions of traditional norms. Social problems also reflect the disparity in rate of change between the elements of a society, notably that between behavior and the social values that define it. Social problems are therefore the heritage of a dynamic, democratic society, where change is rapid and attitudes favoring constructive action are strongly developed. In this sense, as Burgess points out, social problems perform an essentially "constructive" function in that they provide an incentive to adapt to social change in a creative fashion.[3] Temporarily, however, the institutions of an older social order (family and church) lose some of their former control over their members. Behavior then deviates from the institutional norms, and people act in ways they are not "supposed" to act.

We may define a social problem as a condition believed to threaten a social value and conceived to be capable of betterment by constructive social action. The elements of a social problem are: (a) the social situation, (b) the value judgment, and (c) the appropriate social action. A social problem thus arises when large numbers of persons engage in behavior believed both contrary and injurious to some value that the society considers important. The members of the society, furthermore, are in agreement that some form of group action can eliminate, or at least ameliorate, the undesirable situation. When these related conditions exist, we have a social problem.[4]

In her analysis of social problems, Bernard refers to these problem conditions as "stress situations." The latter may be divided into three related elements, namely: (a) the "stress-factor" that causes the threat; (b) the social value that is threatened or believed to be; and (c) the reactions by individuals or groups to the threat.[5] The "stress-situation" may be defined in humanitarian terms, as discrimination is practiced against human beings. It may also be defined in functional terms, as disobedience of the norms results in crime. These activities are detrimental to the functioning of the society, and most people are agreed that something should be done about them. In Bernard's words, "Social problems . . . are situations which for humanitarian, utilitarian,

---

[2] Nelson N. Foote and Clyde W. Hart, "Public Opinion and Collective Behavior," Chapter 13 in Muzafer Sherif and M. O. Wilson (eds.), *Group Relations at the Crossroads* (New York: Harper & Row, 1953).

[3] Ernest W. Burgess, "Social Problems and Social Processes," Chapter 20 in Arnold M. Rose (ed.), *Human Behavior and Social Processes* (Boston: Houghton Mifflin Company, 1962), p. 383.

[4] Francis E. Merrill, "The Study of Social Problems," *American Sociological Review*, 13:251-262 (June, 1948).

[5] Jessie Bernard, *Social Problems at Midcentury: Role, Status, and Stress* (New York: Holt, Rinehart & Winston, 1957), p. 70.

or dysfunctionality reasons are felt to demand positive, usually reformistic, action on the part of society." [6]

Social problems are in large part "correlates, concomitants, or consequences of urban-industrialism." [7] This means that the city—and particularly the large city—is directly or indirectly related to most of the behavior that our society defines as problematic. The sheer mass of people, buildings, institutions, and other structures means that change occurs at a differential rate in the large city and that the resulting situations present seemingly insurmountable difficulties for social adjustment. This relationship of the urban community to social problems applies (although in somewhat different ways) both to societies that are already fully "developed" in an urban industrial sense (United States) and to those that are presently in the process of such development (Indonesia). [8] The urban "way of life" [9] produces stresses, strains, dislocations, and disorganization that both violate the traditional norms and call for the most enlightened social action to cope with them.

Social problems arose historically in a society dominated by middle-class, humanitarian values, in which strong emphasis was laid upon the betterment of the underprivileged masses through cooperative social action. Many of these earlier problems reflected economic insufficiency and the technological inability of the industrial system to produce the basic physical necessities. In the underdeveloped countries today, problems of extreme poverty, undernourishment, inadequate housing, nonexistent sanitation, endemic disease, overpopulation, high infant mortality, and illiteracy are in many ways similar to those that faced the Western nations a century ago. [10] But in the latter countries, many of these problems are now at least ameliorated (poverty) or in process of eventual solution (illiteracy), thanks to the high state of the technological development and effective democratic action. [11] From federal unemployment relief to aid for mothers with dependent children, large-scale efforts toward social welfare have mitigated many basic socioeconomic problems in a way considered impossible a few decades ago. With the aid of technology and industry, the humanitarian middle classes have partially won their crusade against many ancient social problems. [12]

But many others remain. Modern society is still plagued by a variety of behavior that jeopardizes (or is believed to jeopardize) basic social values. Juvenile delinquency, adult crime, prostitution, alcoholism, mental deficiency, mental disease, divorce, desertion, unemployment, religious prejudice, and

---

[6] *Ibid.*, p. 174. Cf. also Alvin L. Bertrand, "The Stress-Strain Element of Social Systems: A Micro Theory of Conflict and Change," *Social Forces*, 42:1-9 (October, 1963).

[7] Leo F. Schnore, "Social Problems in an Urban-Industrial Context," *Social Problems*, 9:228-240 (Winter, 1962), p. 228.

[8] Leo F. Schnore, "Social Problems in the Underdeveloped Areas: An Ecological View," *Social Problems*, 8:182-201 (Winter, 1960-61).

[9] Louis Wirth, "Urbanism as a Way of Life," *American Journal of Sociology*, 44:1-26 (July, 1938).

[10] Marshall B. Clinard, "The Sociologist and Social Change in Underdeveloped Countries," *Social Problems*, 10:207-219 (Winter, 1963).

[11] William F. Ogburn, "Technology and the Standard of Living in the United States," *American Journal of Sociology*, 60:380-386 (January, 1955).

[12] Francis E. Merrill, "Social Character and Social Problems," *Social Problems*, 3:7-12 (July, 1955).

racial discrimination are some of the forms of behavior that still constitute major social problems. Problem behavior, furthermore, differs from one society to another and within a single society at different times. Witchcraft is no longer a social problem, but political unorthodoxy is. Religion has been supplanted by nationalism as an emotional determinant of social problems. In a dynamic society, behavior that is important for one generation may lose much of its importance for the next. Value judgments *do* change, although sometimes with glacial slowness.

A dynamic society also has a great deal of social disorganization. This is the process whereby group ties are weakened or broken.[13] Social problems and social disorganization are related but not synonymous. As we have seen, social problems arise when a given situation is judged to threaten a basic value and people believe that something can be done about it. Social disorganization, on the other hand, is a *process* of group dissolution. The decline of many traditional patterns binding the family together is an example of social disorganization. Many persons also regard this situation as a social problem. The resulting emancipation of women, on the other hand, is also viewed as a desirable change and hence not as a social problem at all. Social disorganization is an *objective* process, whereas social problems are at least partially *subjective*. In one sense, social problems exist in the minds of men.

Social problems involve *both* objective and subjective factors. The *objective* factors comprise actual human behavior, whether cases disposed of by the juvenile courts, crimes known to the police, persons unemployed and seeking employment, or marriages broken by divorce. The *subjective* factors are social values and normative definitions. The objective situation must be defined as such before it is a social problem.[14] Whether real or imaginary, the threat to social values is important if it is *believed* to be. Many social problems, such as the alleged "decline" of the family, are no less worrisome because they exist largely in the minds of large numbers of persons. Social problems, in short, are what people think they are.

Social Problems and Social Values

Social values play a central role in social problems. Social values are normative beliefs pertaining to the important relationships of a society. The institutional structures embody the values.[15] Democracy, Christianity, monogamy, and private enterprise are among the values at the heart of our society. Other related values include "life, health, property, privilege, freedom, security, status, 'face', honor, self-respect, opportunity, future prospects—all as related either to one's own self, to one's loved ones, or to one's group, or to all

---

[13] Mabel A. Elliott and Francis E. Merrill, *Social Disorganization* (New York: Harper & Row, 1961), Fourth Edition, Chapter 2.

[14] William I. Thomas, *The Unadjusted Girl* (Boston: Little, Brown and Company, 1923), pp. 42-43.

[15] Robert C. Angell, *Free Society and Moral Crisis* (Ann Arbor: University of Michigan Press, 1958), p. 85.

three . . . ." [16] These values are the very stuff of human life. Any threat, real or supposed, to these values involves serious consequences for individual and society alike.[17]

Social values grow out of social interaction and become part of the culture. They are transmitted from generation to generation through the agencies of socialization, such as the family, the church, and the school. Social values are a vital force for agreement, or disagreement, in any society. As stated by Angell, ". . . moral integration in any group is the degree to which there is a set of common ends and values toward which all the members are oriented and in terms of which the life of the group is organized." [18] The study of social problems emphasizes the crucial importance of social values. Human beings are evaluating animals, and this quality is particularly clear when we deal with social problems.[19]

Social values are based upon a way of life that is or was widely accepted and followed. By trial and error, each society works out its own value patterns, which are invested with overtones of social welfare. Permanent monogamous marriage was the way of life of the vast majority while the patterns of western European culture were being established. A normative belief in the indissolubility of marriage became a basic value of our society. The way of life of the family has undergone tremendous changes in recent decades, making divorce an increasingly "natural" response to the changed conditions. A value (permanent monogamy) that once reflected a virtually universal practice has encountered a new situation, and the resulting disparity is a social problem.

Social values are not completely fixed and immutable. Changes in structure occur on a large scale and eventually produce a change in value judgments. Social values do not have any existence independent of human beings, although they are independent of *any one* individual. In the family, many social values have changed since the turn of the century, as both the gainful employment and higher education of women have become widely accepted. The *practice* of divorce has increased to approximately 400,000 per year, and the *tolerance* of divorce has likewise increased. The value of permanent monogamy is still accepted in principle, even though more and more persons believe that their own marriage is an "exception" and hence should not be judged by the old value.

1. Social values cause social problems. Social values *cause"* social problems, in the sense that the problem would not exist without the value. Crime would

---

[16] Bernard, *op. cit.*, p. 75.

[17] William R. Catton, Jr., "Exploring Techniques for Measuring Human Values," *American Sociological Review*, 19:49-55 (February, 1954).

[18] Robert C. Angell, "The Moral Integration of American Cities," Special Supplement, *American Journal of Sociology*, 57:1-140 (July, 1951), p. 115.

[19] Alvin W. Gouldner, "Anti-Minotaur: The Myth of a Value-Free Society," *Social Problems*, 9:199-213 (Winter, 1962).

not exist without the values attached to person and property and the legal patterns that specify and clarify them.[20] Sexual promiscuity would not be a social problem without the Christian value that sexual relationships should be confined to marriage. Divorce would not be a social problem if marriage were not ideally defined as indissoluble. Racial discrimination is a social problem in a society based, in theory at least, upon human equality and the dignity of man.[21]

Social values cause social problems in another sense. Social institutions defend their own values and thereby threaten other institutions with other values. In this way, they cause still other social problems.[22] One of the most powerful values in contemporary society is connected with the nation. The individual is taught to identify himself so completely with his country that he will give his life in its support. At the same time, conflicts between national states lead to war and threaten the safety of all the nations concerned. In the defense of one value, modern man mobilizes forces that lead to the destruction of many other values, notably human life. The institutionalization of one value (nationalism) threatens a whole chain of other values, as modern war sets in motion or intensifies many of the pressing problems of our society.[23]

2. Social values may conflict. Social values may also differ as to whether or not a situation is actually a social problem. The same behavior may be judged differently by different groups, depending upon their value judgments. Situations are defined as problems by some groups and not by others. The employment of children in difficult and hazardous jobs is widely considered a social problem. The democratic value of an equal chance for education and personal development is threatened when children of 15 years of age work in factories. Other groups do not consider child labor a social problem, however, but think of it as an opportunity for children to earn money and acquire practical experience at an early age. Furthermore, certain religious groups regard any attempt to ameliorate this situation by constitutional amendment as an unwarranted interference with the rights of the family.

The most spectacular example of conflicting values in our society is racial discrimination. The democratic creed is embodied in the Declaration of Independence and the Bill of Rights, and asserts the equality of all men, regardless of race, creed, or national origin. Discrimination against the Negro is widely regarded as an infringement upon these values and hence as a social problem. The traditional institutional structure of the South is based upon the practice of discrimination on the grounds that the values of white supremacy and "race purity" would otherwise be endangered. Attitudes of discrimi-

---

[20] E. Adamson Hoebel, *The Law of Primitive Man* (Cambridge: Harvard University Press, 1954), p. 276.

[21] The definition of social problems in these terms is clearly associated with the late Richard C. Fuller. Cf. Richard C. Fuller and Richard R. Myers, "The Natural History of a Social Problem," *American Sociological Review*, 6:320-329 (June, 1941).

[22] Joseph S. Himes, "Value Analysis in the Theory of Social Problems," *Social Forces*, 33:259-262 (March, 1955).

[23] Francis E. Merrill, *Social Problems on the Home Front* (New York: Harper & Row, 1948).

nation are indoctrinated in the southern white child, and the practice is regarded at worst as a necessary evil and at best as a desirable way of life.

The impact of such practices upon the personality of the Negro has, until recently, been largely ignored. In terms of educational discrimination, these influences have been summarized as follows: "Statutes requiring racial segregation in education are based upon arbitrary and unreasonable classifications of human beings; result in state-imposed determinants of stigma, inferior status, and inferiority feelings which inhibit the Negro child's ability to profit from the available educational opportunities; and contribute to social instability and the creation of a social climate in which interracial violence is more likely to occur." [24] The social practices of the North are themselves by no means free of discrimination. But such activities are viewed as a social problem—that is, as an unfortunate departure from a value system, and not as desirable in themselves. Two sets of social values are thus incorporated in institutions and produce conflicts in the definition of the problem situation.[25]

3. Social values obstruct solutions. Social values may, finally, obstruct the solution of social problems, when the proposed solution infringes upon other values. In a simple society, values are more consistent than in our own. Value conflicts seldom arise in primitive and homogeneous societies as they do in complex and heterogeneous ones. In initiating action to eliminate threats to one value, other values may be endangered, either actually or in the minds of many persons. The relative strength of the competing values—or the strength of the groups supporting them—often determines what program of action is undertaken and what set of values is preserved.[26]

Social values obstruct social action in the case of illegitimacy, which is widely accepted as a social problem. More than 225,000 unmarried mothers give birth to illegitimate children every year in the United States. The plight of both mother and child is unfortunate, for society disapproves of the woman who transgresses the sexual codes and bears a child out of wedlock. Many programs for the amelioration of this particular problem, however, threaten other values and hence receive short shrift.

One such solution would involve sex education in the secondary schools; another would involve the legalized dissemination of information on, and techniques of, contraception. Either of these programs, however, would encounter such widespread opposition that they are not seriously considered as possible solutions to the problem of illegitimacy. The values threatened by such suggested actions are related to sexual relationships outside of marriage. Increased knowledge of sex or contraception is presumed to lead to greater sexual experimentation by young people. In the value judgments of many persons, therefore, the remedy would be worse than the problem.

---

[24] Kenneth B. Clark, "The Social Scientist as an Expert Witness in Civil Rights Litigation," *Social Problems*, 1:5-10 (June, 1953), p. 7.

[25] Gunnar Myrdal, *An American Dilemma* (Revised Edition) (New York: Harper & Row, 1963).

[26] Cf. David F. Aberle, "Shared Values in Complex Societies," *American Sociological Review*, 15:495-502 (August, 1950).

Social Problems and Social Action

Social problems depend, finally, on the assumption that the undesirable (stress) situation can be ameliorated or eliminated by appropriate social action. This action may in theory be taken by any responsible group, and many voluntary associations (National Association for the Advancement of Colored People) devote their activities to such amelioration. More often, however, the agencies of government have assumed this function, often virtually by default. The rise of democratic government has coincided with the decline in the power of the family and the church to carry through social action on a scale necessary to cope with many present-day problems. The alleviation of social problems is therefore increasingly conducted by people acting through the agencies of democratic government.

The theoretical foundation of social action has been examined by Weinberg, who bases his analysis upon what he calls "action systems." In his words, an action system "consists of the ideologies, institutionalized services, programs, and personnel which are required to meet or to solve given social problems." [27]

---

[27] S. Kirson Weinberg, "Social-Action Systems and Social Problems," Chapter 21 in Arnold M. Rose (ed.), *op. cit.*, p. 402.

The alleviation of social problems is increasingly conducted by people acting through the agencies of democratic government; group in New York City waits for unemployment insurance.

These social structures comprise: (a) the ideological commitment to employ human knowledge in the interests of social welfare; (b) the appropriate institutions, public and private, of the (urban) community; (c) the "accrued knowledge" of the varied types of behavior, ranging from alcoholism to poverty, that come within the purview of social problems; and (d) the preservation of individual freedom in the face of social planning by large organizations.[28]

In all static, feudal, primitive, and/or "underdeveloped" countries, as noted, many situations exist which persons in "advanced" countries would call social problems. Poverty, infant mortality, disease, starvation, undernourishment, and illiteracy are some of the characteristic features of "backward" societies.[29] But in many such societies, these conditions are not viewed as social problems because the people do not consider the conditions capable of improvement by group action. The situations are instead regarded either as indications of divine displeasure or as inherent in the nature of things. The most obvious way to deal with these situations is therefore to propitiate the supernatural powers.

Such underdeveloped societies are not indifferent to poverty, undernourishment, endemic disease, and the other situations which advanced industrial nations view as social problems. The prevailing explanation of these phenomena, and hence the ways of dealing with them, merely differ from our own. In the Western nations, increased scientific knowledge has emphasized the scientific remedies for many undesirable situations. In the less advanced countries (technologically), however, the level of commonsense, let alone scientific, knowledge of hygiene and related matters is abysmally low. Clinard cites a study of 25 villages in India where only ten per cent of the people knew that water could be purified by boiling, and almost half of the people thought that dysentery was caused by the heat. Some 3 per cent of the families had latrines and only a third of them used these facilities regularly. Men and women alike preferred to relieve themselves in the fields, the men being unwilling to walk the long distance back to the village and the women preferring to stroll about the fields and gossip with their friends.[30]

Under such conditions, many obvious social problems present virtually insurmountable obstacles to constructive social action. Furthermore, societies where religious and spiritual values predominate often do not really *want* to relieve their social problems if this means an infringement upon their basic values. In final analysis, religion is more important to them than a reduction in infant mortality. For those who look upon religion (broadly defined) as the basic answer to all human problems, a growing reliance upon science is itself a social problem. The secular values at the heart of social problems stress this world rather than the world to come. Such a growing preoccupation with worldly matters in turn questions many of the values of religion.[31]

---

[28] *Ibid.*
[29] Clinard, "The Sociologist and Social Change in Underdeveloped Countries," *op. cit.*
[30] Clinard, *op cit.*, p. 209.
[31] Harold W. Pfautz, "The Sociology of Secularization: Religious Groups," *American Journal of Sociology*, 61:121-128 (September, 1955).

In the amelioration of social problems, social action is more effective in some fields than others. For purposes of our discussion, we may consider problem behavior as either "public" or "private." Social action is, in general, more effective with the former than with the latter. "Social-action systems" (to use Weinberg's phrase) can be more readily mobilized in the "public" direction than in the "private." These two general types of behavior may be viewed as follows:[32]

1. *Public behavior*. Public behavior involves the economic status, physical health, mental condition, or social security of the individual in a democratic society. In this category are such problem conditions as unemployment, poverty, physical and mental illness, old-age insecurity, child labor, and inadequate housing. Many persons face some or all of these situations, largely without the aid of family and church. Public behavior therefore comes within the general purview of social welfare agencies, both public and private, whereby the individual or family is physically aided, economically supported, or psychologically rehabilitated. Social problems involving such behavior lend themselves to appropriate social action, in which organized group activity deals with the undesirable situation.

The modern democratic nation is increasingly dedicated to the principle that the resources of government should be applied to the alleviation or elimination of the most pressing forms of public behavior. The unemployment of the 1930's demonstrated conclusively that the unaided efforts of the individual or family are inadequate to cope with problems of this magnitude. The role of the federal government in these functions is now accepted, although disagreement still exists over the mechanics of administration. The family and the church can no longer adequately care for the individual in unemployment, sickness, and old age, and the national government has perforce assumed many of these functions.

Among the specific procedures established for such purposes are unemployment insurance, old age and survivors' insurance, pensions to the aged, grants to widows with dependent children, and workmen's compensation. The state and federal governments have assumed much of the care of the mentally deranged. The federal government has also taken an active role in providing low-cost housing to persons who could not otherwise afford it. The most ambitious program of the federal government is the assumption of responsibility for the regulation of the economic system so that mass unemployment will in the future be eliminated, or at least mitigated.

These broad trends are giving the citizens of the United States and other democratic societies a new attitude toward government. The early concept of democracy stressed the right to "life, liberty, and the pursuit of happiness" as the unalienable privilege of all free men. These rights are essentially those of freedom *from* the arbitrary restraints of autocratic governments. But they are not enough to cope with the massive problems of an urban-industrial society. The role of government is increasingly one of overcoming the major problem situations and thereby helping to equalize opportunities for self-development.

---

[32] Francis E. Merrill, *et al.*, *Social Problems* (New York: Alfred A. Knopf, Inc., 1950), Chapter 4.

This "revolution of rising expectations" recognizes these increasing responsibilities of government. Pursuant to this end, Weinberg points out that "the
contemporary urban community has . . . accepted social planning and corrective social changes which do not throttle individual liberties. It has accepted
higher taxes to defray the cost of government services and the application of
the immensely accruing knowledge of the social and psychological sciences for
dealing with social problems, especially those resulting from deviant behavior.
It has trained personnel for these purposes." [33]

This large-scale cultural drift is, however, contrary to many of the traditional
values of a pioneer society. Hence the situation in itself constitutes a social
problem to many persons. The former values reflect an agrarian and small-
town society, where the individual could rely on his own efforts, plus those of
his family and the church, to see him through the major vicissitudes of life.
These values came down virtually intact from an earlier day, even though the
world has changed in many respects. Hence many millions of persons live in a
mass society that they cannot control, but continue to cling tenaciously to the
values of a pioneer way of life. They cannot face the fact that the old order has
changed, giving place to the new.[34]

The trend toward the acceptance of social action has not come as the result
of the deliberate efforts of "alien bureaucrats" to dominate the private lives of
the citizens. Instead, it has come as the inevitable response to new social conditions. The social problems of the modern age—mass unemployment, economic
insecurity, chronic poverty, crippling disease, and prolonged illness—are so
complex that the knowledge and resources of the traditional institutions are
unable to cope with them. The social values in this country have strongly emphasized individual freedom to stand or fall in the competitive struggle, and
the movement toward increasing public responsibility for many social problems
has met with stubborn and widespread hostility. The central (internal) challenge of our day, indeed, is to retain this traditional freedom in certain realms
of private behavior while extending it to many phases of public behavior.

2. *Private behavior.* Private behavior involves sexual morality, marital relationships, and other aspects of personal conduct defined by the mores. Private
behavior does not readily lend itself to organized action, inasmuch as the relationships are more delicate and individual. Representative social problems in
this field are desertion, divorce, premarital sexual relations, homosexuality,
alcoholism, and suicide. The threatened values have grown out of the moral
judgments of the group, some of them with religious sanctions and others
without. The values defining these forms of behavior are firmly imbedded in
the personality structure and carry strong emotional overtones. Hence social
problems involving private behavior are both serious and complex.

Attempts are continually made to apply the power of the state to social

---

[33] Weinberg, *op. cit.*, p. 413.
[34] Arthur J. Vidich and Joseph Bensman, *Small Town in Mass Society* (Princeton: Princeton University
Press, 1958), pp. 313-314.

problems related to private behavior. These attempts are not ordinarily success-ful, since they endanger the democratic value of individual liberty. The attempt to legislate the national prohibition of alcoholic beverages following World War I was an example of such a misguided action. The strong public reaction against this invasion of individual freedom indicated the depth of the senti-ment against legislation in this general realm.

Other groups seek to divert the power of the state toward the solution of other problems of private behavior. Family disorganization is sometimes con-sidered capable of amelioration by such legal measures as tightening the divorce laws or even forbidding divorce altogether. A basic value in our society, however, is individual freedom to marry whomever one chooses and, by impli-cation, to divorce whenever one chooses. If the state were to intervene against divorce in this fashion, other and even more basic values would be endangered.

Some behavior has both public and private connotations. Sexual relations are usually considered as private behavior, and therefore as coming within the sole jurisdiction of the family and the church. Venereal disease was formerly viewed as a strictly private matter and without any public implications. As a result of this attitude, venereal disease was long a major health menace and little effective effort was made to eliminate it on a national scale. Only when the active efforts of the United States Public Health Service were combined with changing public opinion was social action applied to this problem. The majority have since accepted venereal disease as a public concern and hence as a matter for the ameliorative work of the state. The individual who transgresses the sexual mores is no longer expected, along with his wife and children, to submit to the crippling and perhaps fatal consequences of venereal disease.

Some observers have suggested that a fundamental change in social problems is taking place on the level of private behavior. This involves the increasing stress on conformity and the tendency to regard nonconformity as a social problem. There is considerable empirical evidence that many millions of Americans are strongly intolerant of any real or suspected deviations by their fellow citizens from the majority opinions on matters ranging from religious belief to political orthodoxy. In some instances, this intolerance is confined to mild expressions of disapproval. In others, it takes the form of a violent un-willingness to grant elementary civil liberties to the nonconformist.[35]

This trend, if it does exist, may be an expression of a basic shift in social values. The problem becomes one of lack of conformity *in general*, rather than deviation from any particular value. Problem behavior may be in process of change from individual acts (sexual irregularity, alcoholism, divorce) to the more general orientation of the personality. The basic "problem" of private behavior may be "failure" as a person, by which is meant inability or unwilling-ness to conform to the group. The *positive* actions of an earlier problem ori-entation may be replaced by the essentially *negative* condition of nonconformity

---

[35] Samuel A. Stouffer, *Communism, Conformity, and Civil Liberties* (New York: Doubleday & Company, 1955), Chapter 2.

in general. The sense of *guilt* of the person who formerly committed sexual lapses, drank too much, or became a criminal may be replaced by a feeling of *anxiety* at the possibility that he will not be able to conform.[36]

There may thus be a shift in the nature of future problem behavior. The middle class, whose values dominate our society in large part, may direct their attention less to "public" and more to "private" behavior, with particular emphasis upon conformity to the norm. The middle class may regard such traditional problems as poverty, unemployment, and old-age insecurity as largely "solved" in an economy of abundance. Its members may not be so much concerned with the plight of the underprivileged as with their own adjustment to a society that demands conformity as the price of success. Many of the social conditions that originally gave rise to "public" problems have changed, although these problems are by no means completely eliminated. In their place has arisen an emphasis upon conformity, adjustment to the group, and the minimization of individuality. The new (and unforgivable) problem behavior may be noncomformity.[37]

Personal problems may increasingly involve the conception of the self. As we have seen, the idea of the self is in large measure a reflection of the real or imputed appraisals of others. A whole range of interpersonal relations is directly or indirectly related to these self-conceptions. Dating, courtship, marriage, status, role, and ethnic and racial prejudice are among the situations that reflect the attitudes of others toward the self. A favorable self-attitude is an important social value, and situations that threaten such an attitude are in a real sense social problems. With the search for material security at least partially realized in the United States, the private problems of the future may be those of maintaining a satisfactory self-image.[38]

Social Problems and Social Structure

Social problems also have important implications for social structure. Social problems arise when large numbers of persons are not playing their expected roles.[39] This failure is usually not deliberate. In some cases, the individual understands his role but is unable to play it. In other cases, he does not even understand it. In still other cases, the same role involves conflicting expectations. The salesman is expected to be aggressive toward his prospective customers, at least to the extent of convincing them to buy his product. He is also expected to be kindly and sympathetic toward his fellow salesmen and his friends. The demands of his role conflict and he may suffer from insecurity and anxiety. In a heterogeneous society, behavior has become so complex that many of the old patterns do not apply and the person must improvise his role

---

[36] Merrill, *op. cit.*, "Social Character and Social Problems."

[37] Cf. Erich Fromm, *The Sane Society* (New York: Rinehart & Company, Inc., 1955), Chapter 2.

[38] Francis E. Merrill, "The Self and the Other: An Emerging Field of Social Problems," *Social Problems,* 4:200-207 (January, 1957).

[39] Roland L. Warren, "Social Disorganization and the Interrelationship of Cultural Roles," *American Sociological Review,* 14:83-87 (February, 1949).

as best he can. Furthermore, the social structure may be such that he is prevented from playing his expected role by circumstances outside his control. In a simpler and more static society, men and women are better able to fulfill their basic roles.

The major premise of the traditional marital role is its permanency. In an earlier day, people married for life and were separated only by death. Today, many people refuse, for reasons best known to themselves, to play this permanent role, and the result is a social problem. Another basic family role is that of breadwinner. In an agricultural society, the male is usually able to play this role, at least to the extent of being regularly employed. Millions of men in an industrial society have been periodically unable to carry out this central role because of mass unemployment. The resulting situation is another social problem.

The middle-class housewife is faced with a bewildering pattern of role obligations, a pattern that she is sometimes unable to perform either to her own or, perhaps more often, her husband's satisfaction. She is often expected to be gainfully employed and help with the family budget. At the same time, she is supposed to play the exacting roles of mother, housewife, hostess, entertainer, glamour girl, and companion. It is clearly impossible to play all these roles according to the expectations held by many husbands, who enter marriage with romantic dreams of ideal wives. This inability to play the many roles expected of the wife may lead to the frustration of both spouses. Many divorces result from such frustration of expectations. In this way, failure in role-playing gives rise to a social problem.

The complexities of life in an urban, secular society have likewise confused many of the definitions of sexual behavior that were clear in a rural, religious society. Many young people are honestly bewildered by their sexual roles, and this bewilderment often takes the form of experimentation—that is, working out their own roles. The situation is further complicated by the presence of *different* roles and value judgments among the various segments of the population. In the lower-class subculture, value judgments sanction, or at least condone, premarital sexual intercourse by the male. The lower the class status, the greater the incidence and frequency of sexual experience. This situation is viewed as a social problem by middle-class persons, whose norms place a positive value upon premarital chastity.[40]

Other social problems reflect other inconsistencies in the social structure. The boy who steals an automobile is obviously failing to observe the legal norms that define his role. The man who cannot stop drinking is likewise failing to play his expected role. The psychotic ("insane") person who unconsciously seeks a way out of his difficulties in systematic delusions of grandeur represents an even more striking role violation. His conception of his role is so foreign to that held by other persons that they are unable to put themselves

---

[40] Alfred C. Kinsey, *et al., Sexual Behavior in the Human Male* (Philadelphia: W. B. Saunders Company, 1948), p. 335.

in his place. He is cut off from significant communication with others and lives in a private world. He has, in short, failed to maintain a satisfactory adjustment to the expectations of his role.[41]

The major social roles carry strong emotional overtones because they are closely related to the value judgments of society. Husbands, wives, children, employees, managers, ministers, and presidents must play their roles as they are expected to do. The institutions of family, church, state, and business depend upon such a consistency of role-playing. Only by ordered activity can the institutions continue to function. Husbands who do not work, wives who do not bear children, spouses who do not stay married, and children who consistently disobey their parents all fail to perform their expected roles in the family institution.

In playing his role, the individual is an object to himself. He looks at himself through the eyes of others and passes judgment upon himself accordingly. He has been told from infancy what his roles are supposed to be and that his success or failure in life will largely depend upon his role performance.[42] The unemployed, the drifter,[43] the divorced, the delinquent, the criminal, the alcoholic, the neurotic, the psychotic, and those who fail generally to reach their desired goals[44] are problems to themselves as well as to society.[45] The self-judgment of the individual is based upon the (real or supposed) judgments of others toward him. In problem behavior, the reciprocal relationship between individual and group is once more strikingly apparent.

Social Problems and Social Control

We have examined the relationships between social change and social problems, with particular emphasis upon social action. We shall continue the discussion with a glance at social control as a prelude to democratic social action. Without some element of consensus and control, a society could never agree upon the *principle* of social action, much less its possible forms. The logic of this general approach is as follows:

1. Modern society is faced with a situation in which technology is changing more rapidly than the other elements.

2. Social behavior must adjust to these changes in technology and its related industrial and institutional aspects.

3. This adjustment tends to be imperfect because of the very nature of the constituent elements, with some forms of behavior more dynamic than others.

---

[41] Harrison G. Gough, "A Sociological Theory of Psychopathy," *American Journal of Sociology,* 53: 359-366 (March, 1948).

[42] A. R. Mangus, "Role Theory and Marriage Counseling," *Social Forces,* 35:200-209 (March, 1957).

[43] Warren Breed, "Occupational Mobility and Suicide Among White Males," *American Sociological Review,* 28:179-188 (April, 1963).

[44] Robert J. Kleiner and Seymour Parker, "Goal-Striving, Social Status, and Mental Disorder: A Research Review," *American Sociological Review,* 28:189-203 (April, 1963).

[45] Robert Dubin, "Deviant Behavior and Social Structure: Continuities in Social Theory," *American Sociological Review,* 24:147-164 (April, 1959).

4. Tensions arise because of the lack of adjustment between different elements of a rapidly changing society.[46]

5. Social problems reflect a disparity between behavior and the values that define it.

6. Social problems are likewise marked by tensions growing out of the widespread failure of persons to perform their roles as defined by the norms.[47]

7. In a democratic society, a social problem suggests action by the people working cooperatively, either through private or (more often) public associations.

8. Social action requires at least a minimum of social control, informally through the group and formally through the government.

9. "Social-action systems" mobilize existing knowledge, institutional structures, and trained personnel to alleviate or eliminate social problems.[48]

In its most general sense, social control is the process whereby the group makes use of its various resources to bring about conformity to its norms and values. In order to function effectively, the group must have at least a minimum of acceptance and conformity to its normative expectations. If such conformity is not present, the members will not follow the norms and hence cannot adequately take the behavior of the others into account. In this case, one of the principal aspects of social interaction is impaired or lost—namely, its *predictability*. In their group relationships, the members will be unable to count on the behavior of the others and hence will be uncertain of their own. Social control refers to the general process by which the group tries to avoid this possibility.

The resources to insure this conformity are many and varied. In essence, they involve the needs that the group fulfills for the members. In the primary group, these needs include a personal defense against the outside world, a friendly relationship within which to develop one's personality, and a medium for engaging in activities (love, friendship, admiration) that are pleasant in themselves.[49] In a more general sense, the needs that motivate a person to join groups include such matters as personal attraction, prestige, and task performance.[50] These needs can be met only through group activity, and the fulfillment of needs makes up the positive resources at the command of the group.

Through the medium of social control, the group stands ready to *withhold* these resources in varying degrees from the individual. In order to be a member in good standing, the latter must have a certain status and acceptance in the group. Without a minimum of these conditions, he cannot enjoy the benefits the group can bestow. The deviant violates the norms of the group and runs the

---

[46] Moore, *Social Change, op. cit.*, pp. 70ff.

[47] Bertrand, "The Stress-Strain Element of Social Systems: A Micro Theory of Conflict and Change," *op. cit.*

[48] Weinberg, "Social-Action Systems and Social Problems," *op. cit.*, p. 402.

[49] Robert E. L. Faris, "Development of the Small-Group Research Movement," Chapter 7 in Muzafer Sherif and M. O. Wilson (eds.), *Group Relations at the Crossroads* (New York: Harper & Brothers, 1953), pp. 178-180.

[50] Kurt W. Back, "Influence Through Social Communication," *Journal of Abnormal and Social Psychology*, 46:9-23 (January, 1951).

risk of losing some or all of these benefits.[51] The needs fulfilled by group inter-action are the most fundamental of all *social* needs—assuming that the biologi-cal needs are satisfied in other ways. Hence the group member usually guards his privileges jealously and attempts to hold on to them as fully as he can. By the threat, actual or implicit, of withdrawing its privileges, the group exercises social control over the individual.

Means by which the group tries to maintain its control may vary from ridi-cule to execution. The boys' gang tries to keep its members from deviating from the norms of toughness by ridiculing behavior that appears to be gentle, sensi-tive, or "feminine." If the behavior violates such a basic norm as gang loyalty, the reaction against the deviant may be more violent and aggressive. In the adult criminal gang, control may in extreme cases involve complete exclusion from the gang by murder. Group sanctions differ both in terms of the nature of the group and the circumstances under which the group interaction occurs.

Social control is an important function of institutional groups. Cultural values are vested in institutions and they control many of the satisfactions of the larger society. The family, the school, the church, and the state instruct their members with the normative expectations of their roles. These expecta-tions are incorporated into the personality by socialization, and the individual in effect controls himself. He tries to do what is expected of him by following the group norms as best he can. He has learned to value the rewards that the group can bestow upon him, and he is, ordinarily, anxious to retain his access to these rewards. This is essentially the process of *informal* social control, as the individual follows the learned patterns that lead to the goals of the group.

In its *formal* aspects, social control involves more deliberate coercive efforts by the group to insure conformity to the norms. In our own society, much of this control is vested in the various agencies of government, from the local community to the national state. As society becomes more complex, the burden of social control shifts from the informal to the formal agencies. The primary group still controls many important phases of behavior, whether through the family, the peer group, the neighborhood group, or the informal work group. But the institution of government is increasingly important in enforcing con-formity to the normative patterns of the modern world.[52]

Social control is ordinarily more effective in a primitive and comparatively static society than in a complex and dynamic society. Methods of meeting recur-rent situations and reaching group goals evolve over the generations and are known and accepted by everyone. Sons learn from fathers and daughters learn from mothers and older sisters the roles and behavior patterns expected of them. Novel situations seldom arise and the folkways and mores answer most of the questions of conduct. This does not mean that conformity to the norms is in any sense "automatic" in the primitive society or that the members follow

---

[51] Theodore M. Mills, "Equilibrium and the Processes of Deviance and Control," *American Sociological Review*, 24:671-679 (October, 1959).
[52] Cf. Richard T. La Piere, *A Theory of Social Control* (New York: McGraw-Hill Book Company, Inc., 1954).

the customary patterns without any deviation whatsoever. As Malinowski pointed out in his studies of the Trobriand Islands, primitive men are also individualistic in their reactions and often try to evade a norm if they believe they can do so without inviting group sanctions.[53]

The norms in primitive society are of different degrees of importance, and some of them are more consistently followed than others. Rules of etiquette are not as important as rules pertaining to such "sacred" matters as exogamy, magical ritual, and funerary ceremony. The degree of moral force regarding these and other practices varies widely, and both spontaneous and formalized means of evading the norms are always present.[54] Despite the fact that there is no "slavish" and "unthinking" obedience to social norms among primitive peoples, however, the degree of conformity is nevertheless greater than in a complex society.

In the changing, heterogeneous, and imperfectly integrated society of America, consensus does not come easily. The group must resort to formal methods of social control. The process of socialization is more contrived and deliberate than in primitive societies, and modern societies require their children to go through a formal educational experience in addition to that provided by the parental family. The educational machinery is reinforced by an elaborate system of group norms codified into law. This process is itself a self-conscious activity, conducted by many secondary agencies. In these and other ways, modern society directs more of its attention to reaching and maintaining some degree of working conformity to its basic norms.

Social planning is one aspect of this deliberate process. Planning demands a degree of *conscious* cooperation that is unnecessary in a society where consensus is more spontaneous. Such cooperation is not always forthcoming in our society, as the individual resents the invasion of his traditional freedom in the (to him) dubious interests of the society as a whole. This increase in formal control does not, however, *necessarily* mean a net loss of personal freedom. The pressures of modern society are such that the individual may lose many of his freedoms to the impersonal mechanisms of urban living, unless efforts are made by some larger agency to prevent this loss. One such agency is the local, state, or federal government, acting in the interests of the general welfare.

Structure and Change

We began this study of society and culture on a note of social change. We end it on the same note. We have sometimes referred to this process as the breakdown of primary-group controls and the substitution of secondary-group controls. We have referred to it in other contexts as a decline of the sacred way of life and the consequent rise of secularism. At still other times, we have spoken of the change from status to contract—that is, from an unthinking acceptance

---

[53] Bronislaw Malinowski, *Crime and Custom in Savage Society* (London: Routledge & Kegan Paul, Ltd., 1926), Chapter 10.
[54] *Ibid.*

of the traditional norms to a growing desire to better the place of the individual within the society. We have, finally, viewed the changing social scene as one in which an earlier folk society has given way to an urban way of life.

However we may designate this change in the nature of social interaction, it is clear that a major modification is taking place. The society of the future will be very different from that of the past. This does not mean, however, that all the lessons of the past can be disregarded in the brave new world of the thermonuclear age. Many of the basic elements of social interaction will continue very much as they have done. Despite growing urbanization, the primary group of the family will continue to play a central role in the structure of the society as well as in the personality of the individual. Most of the basic processes of social interaction will remain substantially unchanged, even though they will occur in a setting of mass society.

Social change is therefore important, but it is not the whole story. Society and culture can also be studied at a given moment in time. The groups, patterns, statuses, roles, castes, classes, and institutions of a going society can be viewed as parts of a functioning whole, each of which contributes to the activities of the society. The bulk of our discussion has been devoted to an analysis of society in this sense. Culture, personality, social structure, social institutions, and voluntary associations are all parts of this complex phenomenon. Society can be examined both at a particular point in time and as a moving equilibrium. Concentration upon the social structure leads to a static distortion of reality. Concentration upon change to the exclusion of structure leads to scientific chaos. *Both* stability and change are necessary for a complete understanding of society in interaction.

Structure and change are related in another sense. Social structure is a basic element making for stability, as men and women act in accordance with the expectations of their roles. In the course of events, each person learns to expect certain ordered responses from others in the roles each has been taught to play. This orderly character of interaction is especially apparent in the major social institutions, as people act out their learned responses in the setting of the family, church, school, government, and economy. These role patterns are incorporated into the personality of every member, and it is this structural element that gives much of the stability to a society.

At the same time, however, these elements are subject to stresses and strains arising from social change. As we have seen, such factors as technological innovation, new industrial processes, transportation, mass communication, and urbanization cause drastic modifications in the setting in which men play their traditional roles. The latter are less flexible than, say, technological elements, and hence the roles often do not adjust to the changes in society. Many institutional roles remain as anachronisms in a society that has otherwise changed almost beyond recognition. The idea that woman's role is always in the home is a case in point; the idea that any government is best that governs least is another; the idea that the family can protect its members against all the vicissitudes of life is a third. Formalism of roles is necessary to the ordered functioning of society. At the same time, this conservatism of the role structure may intensify the very instability it is assumed to prevent.[55]

Society is neither completely static nor completely dynamic. The very process of social interaction implies a certain element of change, inasmuch as two persons never take each other into account in precisely the same fashion twice. At the same time, the patterns of social interaction have a certain uniformity. Otherwise, behavior would be unpredictable and organized social relationships impossible. Society is not, therefore, a stable system that is occasionally disturbed by forces bringing about change. Neither is it an unpredictable mass of individuals, in which the groups and institutions lack any stability. Society should be viewed rather as a "balance among forces in interaction," [56] containing elements of *both* stability and change.

These elements differ in degree from one society to another. The dynamic forces in our own society have tipped the balance in the direction of change more heavily than in any other society. The contemporary social structure reflects changes set in motion by technological, industrial, and ideological forces that are so vast and impersonal that they defy human understanding. The increasing concentration of the population in urban and, especially, metropolitan centers; the rapid rate of horizontal mobility; the declining importance of the primary community; the growing secularization of group relationships; and the cumulative increase in the power of mass communication—these are among the causes and effects of social change.

Under these conditions, social problems are both inevitable and desirable. As Burgess puts it, "Social problems in their total impact upon society may . . . be regarded . . . as natural, inevitable, modifiable, and normal." [57] Modern society is marked by a perpetual state of tension—between an acceptance of change and an attempt to cope with its consequences. The ordered knowledge of sociology provides an understanding of the structure of society, as well as the changes occurring through social interaction. We have been concerned throughout this book with both of these elements—that is, with structure and change. The central theme is social interaction in a changing social order.

---

[55] See William J. Goode, "A Theory of Role Strain," *American Sociological Review*, 25:483-496 (August, 1960).

[56] Everett C. Hughes, "Foreword" to Georg Simmel, *Conflict* and *The Web of Group-Affiliations* (translated by Kurt H. Wolff and Reinhard Bendix) (Glencoe, Ill.: The Free Press, 1955), p. 9.

[57] Burgess, "Social Problems and Social Processes," *op. cit.*, p. 399.

SELECTED BIBLIOGRAPHY

Bernard, Jessie, *Social Problems at Midcentury: Role, Status, and Stress.* New York: Holt, Rinehart & Winston, 1957. This is an important addition to the literature of social problems. The author approaches social problems in terms of stress situations, involving three elements: "(1) the stress-factor, which threatens, (2) the value, which is being threatened, and (3) the re-actions, individual and collective, to the threat."

Burgess, Ernest W., "Values and Sociological Research," *Social Problems,* 2:16-20 (July, 1954). In this article, a leading authority on social problems explores some of the relationships between social values and behavior.

————, "Social Problems and Social Processes," Chapter 20 in Arnold M. Rose (ed.), *Human Behavior and Social Processes.* Boston: Houghton Mifflin Company, 1962. This is one of the most important contributions to the theory of social problems that has appeared in recent decades. Burgess surveys the various conceptions of social problems: (*a*) as aggregates of individual organic pathology, (*b*) as social pathology, (*c*) as social and personal disorganization, (*d*) as conflicts of values, and (*e*) as process. He then gives an analysis of social problems as "social process."

Clinard, Marshall B., "The Sociologist and Social Change in Underdeveloped Countries," *Social Problems,* 10:207-219 (Winter, 1963). On the basis of his extensive empirical experience as a sociological consultant and research scholar in underdeveloped countries, the author indicates some of the difficulties encountered in attempting to bring constructive social action to bear on certain age-old social problems.

Dubin, Robert, "Deviant Behavior and Social Structure: Continuities in Social Theory," *American Sociological Review,* 24:147-164 (April, 1959). This article is a complete theoretical exposition of the concept of deviant behavior. As such, it is closely related to the theory of social problems, since much (although not all) deviant behavior is also problem behavior. Many deviants are a threat to social values and hence represent a problem to themselves as well as to society.

Elliott, Mabel A., and Francis E. Merrill, *Social Disorganization* (Fourth Edition). New York: Harper & Row, 1961. Social disorganization is the process whereby the relationships binding persons together in groups are impaired or broken. In this book, specific problem situations involving the individual, family, community, nation, and the world are examined in the conceptual framework of social disorganization.

Fox, Byron, "American Social Problems in a World Setting," *Social Problems,* 6:99-107 (Fall, 1958). This article advances the proposition that American social problems can no longer be viewed purely as domestic situations, but that many have worldwide implications. Among these broad problems are the race problem, the health problem, unemployment, and juvenile delinquency.

Gouldner, Alvin W., "Anti-Minotaur: The Myth of a Value-Free Society," *Social Problems,* 9:199-213 (Winter, 1962). This presidential address to the Society for the Study of Social Problems demolishes the myth of a value-free sociology and with it the dogma that "Thou shalt not commit a value judgment."

Kolb, William L., "The Impingement of Moral Values on Sociology," *Social Problems,* 2:66-70 (October, 1954). The author examines the relationships between values and research and indicates that values provide a moral framework within which, as human beings, social scientists may establish a science of society.

Merrill, Francis E., "The Study of Social Problems," *American Sociological Review,* 13:251-262 (June, 1948). In this article, the elements of a social problem are analyzed in terms of: (*a*) the situation, (*b*) the value, and (*c*) the action. In subsequent articles, "Social Character and Social Problems," *Social Problems,* 3:7-12 (July, 1955); and "The Self and the Other: An

Emerging Field of Social Problems," *Social Problems,* 4:200-207 (January, 1957), other aspects of social problems are considered in the same theoretical framework. The field may be in process of change from problems of "public" to those of increasingly "private" (or interpersonal) behavior.

Mills, C. Wright, *The Sociological Imagination.* New York: Oxford University Press, 1959. In this rousing manifesto, the late Professor Mills called upon his fellow sociologists to inculcate the "sociological imagination" into their students so that the latter may understand and, ultimately, come to grips with the major social problems of our day.

Schnore, Leo F., "Social Problems in the Underdeveloped Areas: An Ecological View," *Social Problems,* 8:182-201 (Winter, 1960-61); also "Social Problems in an Urban-Industrial Context," *Social Problems,* 9:228-240 (Winter, 1962). These two articles, whose titles are self-explanatory, represent some of the work of a keen and insightful student of social problems. The author combines the theoretical with the empirical, and the student is urged to read these two essays to see sociological writing on social problems in a broad context.

Social Problems. Published quarterly by the Society for the Study of Social Problems. This journal, as the title indicates, is devoted to the scientific study of social problems. It contains articles on the theory of social problems, as well as reports on research in the various fields included under this theoretical framework.

Stouffer, Samuel A., *Communism, Conformity, and Civil Liberties.* New York: Doubleday & Company, 1955. In this revealing account of the state of civil liberties in the decade of the Cold War, the widespread intolerance of nonconformity emerges as an important fact. This study offers strong, although indirect, evidence that the field of social problems may (as noted) be shifting from "public" behavior to "private" behavior involving personal nonconformity. The "problem" person may, in the future, be the nonconformist.

Weinberg, S. Kirson, "Social-Action Systems and Social Problems," Chapter 21 in Arnold M. Rose (ed.), *Human Behavior and Social Processes.* Boston: Houghton Mifflin Company, 1962. Traditional social theory in the field of social problems has been largely devoted to *understanding* the nature and causes of such stress situations. In this article, the author gives a full-length analysis of the theory of social *action* to meet or solve social problems. This essay is therefore a much-needed contribution to the literature.

Illustrations

Name Index

Name Index

Subject Index

Subject Index